C000048694

THE SUBLIME CONTINUUM AND
ITS EXPLANATORY COMMENTARY
with
THE SUBLIME CONTINUUM
SUPERCOMMENTARY

Treasury of the Buddhist Sciences series

Editor-in-Chief: Robert A.F. Thurman, Jey Tsong Khapa Professor Emeritus of Indo-Tibetan Buddhist Studies, Columbia University

Executive Editor: Thomas F. Yarnall, Columbia University

Series Committee: Daniel Aitken, David Kittelstrom, Tim McNeill, Robert A.F. Thurman, Christian K. Wedemeyer, Thomas F. Yarnall

Editorial Board: Ryuichi Abé, Jay Garfield, David Gray, Laura Harrington, Thubten Jinpa, Joseph Loizzo, Gary Tubb, Vesna Wallace, Christian Wedemeyer, Chun-fang Yu

The *Treasury of the Buddhist Sciences* series is copublished by the American Institute of Buddhist Studies and Wisdom Publications in association with the Columbia University Center for Buddhist Studies and Tibet House US.

The American Institute of Buddhist Studies (AIBS) established the *Treasury of the Buddhist Sciences* series to provide authoritative translations, studies, and editions of the texts of the Tibetan Tengyur (*bstan 'gyur*) and its associated literature. The Tibetan Tengyur is a vast collection of over 4,000 classical Indian Buddhist scientific treatises (*śāstra*) written in Sanskrit by over 700 authors from the first millennium CE, now preserved mainly in systematic 7th–12th century Tibetan translation. Its topics span all of India's "outer" arts and sciences, including linguistics, medicine, astronomy, socio-political theory, ethics, art, and so on, as well as all of her "inner" arts and sciences such as philosophy, psychology ("mind science"), meditation, and yoga.

Volumes in this series are numbered with catalogue numbers corresponding to both the "Comparative" (*dpe bsdur ma*) Kangyur and Tengyur ("CK" and "CT," respectively) and Derge (Tōhoku number) recensions of the Tibetan Tripiṭaka.

The *Supercommentary* within the present work is included within the *Complete Works of Jey Tsong Khapa and Sons* collection, a subset of the *Treasury of the Buddhist Sciences* series. Comprised of the collected works of Tsong Khapa (1357–1419) and his spiritual sons, Gyaltsap Darma Rinchen (1364–1432) and Khedrup Gelek Pelsang (1385–1438), the numerous works in this set of Tibetan treatises and supercommentaries are based on the thousands of works in the Kangyur and Tengyur, the Tibetan Buddhist canon.

THE DALAI LAMA

Message

The foremost scholars of the holy land of India were based for many centuries at Nālandā Monastic University. Their deep and vast study and practice explored the creative potential of the human mind with the aim of eliminating suffering and making life truly joyful and worthwhile. They composed numerous excellent and meaningful texts. I regularly recollect the kindness of these immaculate scholars and aspire to follow them with unflinching faith. At the present time, when there is great emphasis on scientific and technological progress, it is extremely important that those of us who follow the Buddha should rely on a sound understanding of his teaching, for which the great works of the renowned Nālandā scholars provide an indispensable basis.

In their outward conduct the great scholars of Nālandā observed ethical discipline that followed the Pāli tradition, in their internal practice they emphasized the awakening mind of *bodhichitta*, enlightened altruism, and in secret they practised tantra. The Buddhist culture that flourished in Tibet can rightly be seen to derive from the pure tradition of Nālandā, which comprises the most complete presentation of the Buddhist teachings. As for me personally, I consider myself a practitioner of the Nālandā tradition of wisdom. Masters of Nālandā such as Nāgārjuna, Āryadeva, Āryāsaṅga, Dharmakīrti, Candrakīrti, and Śāntideva wrote the sūtras that we Tibetan Buddhists study and practice. They are all my gurus. When I read their books and reflect upon their names, I feel a connection with them.

The works of these Nālandā masters are presently preserved in the collection of their writings that in Tibetan translation we call the Tengyur (*bstan 'gyur*). It took teams of Indian masters and great Tibetan translators over four centuries to accomplish the historic task of translating them into

Tibetan. Most of these books were later lost in their Sanskrit originals, and relatively few were translated into Chinese. Therefore, the Tengyur is truly one of Tibet's most precious treasures, a mine of understanding that we have preserved in Tibet for the benefit of the whole world.

Keeping all this in mind I am very happy to encourage a long-term project of the American Institute of Buddhist Studies, originally established by the late Venerable Mongolian Geshe Wangyal and now at the Columbia University Center for Buddhist Studies, and Tibet House US, to translate the Tengyur into English and other modern languages, and to publish the many works in a collection called *The Treasury of the Buddhist Sciences*. When I recently visited Columbia University, I joked that it would take those currently working at the Institute at least three "reincarnations" to complete the task; it surely will require the intelligent and creative efforts of generations of translators from every tradition of Tibetan Buddhism, in the spirit of the scholars of Nālandā, although we may hope that using computers may help complete the work more quickly. As it grows, the *Treasury* series will serve as an invaluable reference library of the Buddhist Sciences and Arts. This collection of literature has been of immeasurable benefit to us Tibetans over the centuries, so we are very happy to share it with all the people of the world. As someone who has been personally inspired by the works it contains, I firmly believe that the methods for cultivating wisdom and compassion originally developed in India and described in these books preserved in Tibetan translation will be of great benefit to many scholars, philosophers, and scientists, as well as ordinary people.

I wish the American Institute of Buddhist Studies at the Columbia Center for Buddhist Studies and Tibet House US every success and pray that this ambitious and far-reaching project to create *The Treasury of the Buddhist Sciences* will be accomplished according to plan. I also request others, who may be interested, to extend whatever assistance they can, financial or otherwise, to help ensure the success of this historic project.

May 15, 2007

THE SUBLIME CONTINUUM AND ITS EXPLANATORY COMMENTARY

(*Mahāyānottaratantraśāstravyākhyā*)
by Maitreyanātha and Āryāsaṅga

with

THE SUBLIME CONTINUUM SUPERCOMMENTARY

(*theg pa chen po rgyud bla ma'i ṭīkka*)
by Gyaltsap Darma Rinchen
Revised Edition

Introduction and Translation by
Bo Jiang

TREASURY OF THE BUDDHIST SCIENCES SERIES
TENGYUR TRANSLATION INITIATIVE
CT 3256–57 (TŌH. 4024–4025)

COMPLETE WORKS OF JEY TSONG KHAPA AND SONS COLLECTION
(TŌH. 5434)

COPUBLISHED BY
THE AMERICAN INSTITUTE OF BUDDHIST STUDIES AND WISDOM PUBLICATIONS
IN ASSOCIATION WITH THE COLUMBIA UNIVERSITY CENTER
FOR BUDDHIST STUDIES AND TIBET HOUSE US

Treasury of the Buddhist Sciences series
Tengyur Translation Initiative
Complete Works of Jey Tsong Khapa and Sons collection
A refereed series published by:

American Institute of Buddhist Studies   Wisdom Publications
Columbia University   132 Perry Street
80 Claremont Avenue, Room 303   New York, NY 10014
New York, NY 10027   www.wisdomexperience.org
www.aibs.columbia.edu

In association with Columbia University's Center for Buddhist Studies
and Tibet House US.
Distributed by Wisdom Publications.

Copyright © 2017, 2023 by Bo Jiang. All rights reserved. Second edition.

No part of this book may be reproduced in any form or by any means, electronic or mechan-
ical, including photography, recording, or by any information storage and retrieval system or
technologies now known or later developed, without permission in writing from the publisher.

Library of Congress Cataloging-in-Publication Data for the previous edition is as follows:
Names: Asaṅga, author. | Bo Jiang, 1967– translator. | Asaṅga.
    Mahāyānottaratantraśāstravyākhyā. English. | Asaṅga.
Mahāyānottaratantraśāstravyākhyā. Chinese. | Rgyal-tshab
    Dar-ma-rin-chen, 1364–1432. Theg pa chen po rgyud bla ma'i tikka. English.
    | Rgyal-tshab Dar-ma-rin-chen, 1364–1432. Theg pa chen po rgyud bla ma'i tikka. Chinese.
Title: The sublime continuum and its explanatory commentary
    (Mahayanottaratantrasastravyakhya; Theg pa chen po rgyud bla ma'i bstan
    bcos dang de'i rnam par bshad pa) / By Maitreyanatha and Noble Asaṅga. And
    The Sublime Continuum Super-Commentary (Theg pa chen po rgyud bla ma'i
    tikka) / By Gyaltsap Darma Rinchen.
Description: New York: American Institute of Buddhist Studies, Columbia
    University, 2016. | Series: Treasury of the Buddhist sciences series |
    "Introduction and translation by Bo Jiang." | Includes bibliographical
    references and index. | In English and Chinese; includes translations from
    Sanskrit and Tibetan.
Identifiers: LCCN 2016018802 | ISBN 9781935011255 (alk. paper)
Subjects: LCSH: Yogācāra (Buddhism)—Early works to 1800.
Classification: LCC BQ7490 .A8612 2016 | DDC 294.3/92—dc23
LC record available at https://lccn.loc.gov/2016018802

ISBN 978-1-949163-24-7 (hardcover)   ebook ISBN 978-1-949163-30-8
27 26 25 24 23   1 2 3 4 5

Cover and interior design by Gopa & Ted2. Cover typeset by Tony Lulek.
Set in Diacritical Garamond Pro 11/14.

Printed on acid-free paper and meets the guidelines for permanence and durability
of the Production Guidelines for Book Longevity of the Council on Library Resources.

Printed in the United States of America

Contents

Appendix

Selected Bibliographies

Indexes

Editor's/Series Editor's Preface

USUALLY THE PROFESSOR teaches the student and the student learns from the professor. Maybe Bo "Marty" Jiang learned a little from me, but I definitely learned a great deal from him. His doctoral dissertation project was to study Lama Tsong Khapa and Sons' interpretation of the "buddha-nature" issue ("nature" here—a Western convention probably from the Chinese *hsing*—can also be translated as "element," "essence," "embryo," and even "womb" [Sanskrit *garbha*]).

In the context of my own studies of Buddhist Centrist (*mādhyamika*) philosophy I had learned to view "buddha-nature" as a doctrine promulgated by the Buddha to comfort those who are addicted to "soul-theories." As a skillful teacher, or therapist, the Buddha understood that such persons needed help to approach the voidness or emptiness that the Buddha discovered to be the ultimate (absolute or supreme) reality of all things, recognizing that people often misunderstand and fear such an ultimate, due to their tendency to confuse voidness with nothingness, and the fixated idea that "realization of the ultimate" is just a spiritualist euphemism for self-annihilation.

This teaching of "buddha-nature" was thus offered, I thought, along with the idealistic (*vijñānavāda* or *cittamātra*) school of thought, which from the Centrist viewpoint is also a kind of reassuring—"interpretable" not "definitive"—teaching that helps aspiring bodhisattvas scientifically and contemplatively dissolve the apparent solidity of the physical world while feeling confident in the reality of it in its more subtle mental nature. I had also noted that the Centrist's own view is that the "buddha-nature" is really just emptiness itself, in that—on the ultimate level—beings are primordially indivisible from the buddhas in their reality body (*dharma-kāya*). And I had pretty much left it at that, not going into it further or more deeply.

Working with Marty on *The Sublime Continuum* of Maitreyanātha, its *Commentary* by Āryāsaṅga, and its *Supercommentary* by Tsong Khapa's heart-son Gyaltsap Rinpoche, I gained a whole new perspective, even a touch of insight into the much more beautiful reality explored in these works. Again, I had heard that the Tibetans in general consider Maitreya's *Sublime Continuum* to be a Centrist work, not an idealist one, as the great Indian and Tibetan philosopher-practitioners were often not locked up within a particular rigid ideology, but were true dialecticist (or dialogical [*prāsaṅgika*]) pedagogues, who attuned their theories to the level of resilience (or even neural receptivity) of their students or fellow seekers.

I knew this was somewhat controversial, in that there were some Tibetan philosopher-yogis who considered the idealist school the highest school, and had come up with what they presented as an innovative synthesis of idealism with Centrist relativism. This was called the "great Centrism" (*dbu ma chen po*), and it was connected with a teaching called "other-emptiness" (*gzhan stong*), which stepped back from or stepped beyond the rigorously logical nondualism of mainstream Indian and Tibetan Centrism wherein ultimate emptiness is understood as empty of itself, and hence something like the mere negation that is nothing other than the inconceivable relativity of the world (and not an absolute nothingness like a blank space) within which relative things appear with an illusory quality.

However, if the absolute emptiness is misconceived as an "other," "alternative," reality separate from the relative, a space empty of the relative that is "other" than it, the "realization" of that "other" becomes a destruction of the relative, an ultimate isolation of the realizer from the relative world of other beings, and it is like the dualistic relative-vs.-absolute view of the individual vehicle[1] philosophers, such as the Theravādins, etc.

But the Tibetan "other-emptiness" philosophers are not formal individual vehicle dualists. They are universal vehicle bodhisattva way practitioners, so they added to their view of a substantial absolute the possession of excellent qualities, which is the kind of theological assertion that asserts the relativity of the absolute, out of enthusiasm and faith, making a kind of hyperbolic fact out of a divine absolute, as in the various theisms of the

---

1. *Hīnayāna, theg dman.* To avoid the pejorative in the Sanskrit and Tibetan words, I translate this as the "individual vehicle," by which a person seeks their own individual nirvana, as contrasted with the "universal vehicle" (*mahāyāna, theg chen*), by which a person seeks nirvana for all. After all, a universal vehicle must take care of all individuals.

world, or in the absolute "other-power" (*zettai tariki*) forms of East Asian Buddhisms, such as the Pure Land schools (which doubtless started with now unknown Indian Amitābha-in-Sukhāvatī paradise cults, religiously beautiful movements). They therefore presented a path to sudden enlightenment, evolutionarily super-swift pathways, since just by "realizing emptiness," conceived as losing oneself in an infinite space-like experience, all the relative qualities of buddhahood would automatically adhere to one, and the relative buddha bodies of beatitude and emanation would emerge from the pregnant absolute and become one's relative buddha vehicle. This assertion becomes highly attractive to impatient bodhisattvas, since it seems to obviate the need for the inconceivably arduous evolutionary path of relative self-transcendences through generosity, ethical actions, and patient forbearances that mainstream universal vehicle Buddhism insists is the essential causality making possible the inconceivable relative excellences of buddhahood. This attribution of excellent relative qualities in the supreme absolute then was claimed by these other-emptiness philosophers as the real secret offering of the Buddhist tantras, enabling the acceleration of the evolutionary causality of billions of lives into a single life, etc.

So the tantric secret for them becomes a different reality-teaching that the Buddha is supposed to have withheld from his non-esoteric disciples, which makes the Buddha into the kind of teacher who held the highest teaching hidden behind his back in what he himself called "the closed fist of a [bad] teacher" (*ācāryamuṣṭi*). Finding this not in character for a perfect buddha, we return to rigorous reasoning in the ordinary causation plane of relative reality, and rather consider the tantric super-swift way to be high-tech compression of the billion-lifetime path into one or three or seven or sixteen lifetimes of relative self-transcendences, highly dangerous but possible for a select group of bodhisattva disciples, taught freely to all, but usable only by those at a certain level of ability.

In the approach of the present works of Maitreyanātha, Asaṅga, and Gyaltsap, *The Sublime Continuum* is persuasively revealed to be a dialogical Centrist text, not an idealist one, addressing the deep issue of the seemingly contradictory relationship between the buddhas' experience of beings as blissfully, indivisibly, inseparable from themselves in their inconceivable truth body ultimate level and the suffering beings' experience of themselves as suffering and alienated and separated not only from buddhas, but from all other beings and things. This issue is addressed therein without using the cloak of inconceivability to hide the incoherence of the assertion that an uncaused, uncreated, quiescent absolute can cause relative phenomena such as buddha excellences. Instead, it takes radical nonduality taught by such teaching as the voidness of voidness, emptiness of emptiness, to affirm that the evolutionary causality of the billion lifetimes of self-transcending evolution can be compressed on a subtle dream-like causal plane into a relatively short period, due to the power of universal compassion drawing on the immense demand of beings' suffering to fuel a subnuclear fusion energy of immense power to miniaturize vast lengths of time into microseconds. So the inconceivable artfulness (skill-in-means) of buddhas is here seen not as involving a withholding of access to reality from disciples, but rather as giving each one artful access to aspects of reality that they are capable of using. And it brings the buddha-nature teaching and tantric revelation back into complete harmony with Nāgārjuna's famous use of "voidness the womb of compassion" (*śūnyatā-karuṇā-garbham*), which itself is drawn from Shākyamuni's unexcelled yoga tantric revelations (the phrase is especially prominent in the *Kālachakra Tantra*).

The most important scholar-practitioner of this other-emptiness theory happened also to be an expert in the Kālachakra Tantra practices, and it is likely that he got his theory from Kālachakra terminology, which refers to outer Kālachakra, inner Kālachakra, and "Other" or "Alternative" Kālachakra. In this case, the Other Kālachakra refers to the mandalic, purified, or perfected universe of the Kālachakra, the compassion-infused relative world as a time-machine that is the ideal evolutionary hothouse for beings aspiring to buddhahood. This amazing art of world reshaping is marvelous, even miraculous (meaning supernormal), but it is not "absolute," just as the buddha-lands, Sukhāvatī, Abhirati, etc., are not absolute, but are the beautiful relative, the optimal evolution-assisting relative. They have to be relative in order to be relevant to beings' experience. No one could enter them if they were absolute. Absolute emptiness is like nirvana, no one can enter it because it is uncreated, primordial. One can only realize one has always been there, or has always not not been there—or "here" has always really been "there." Words do fail to capture this kind of thing, which is no excuse for using words utterly meaninglessly, as they are always relatively meaningful or meaningless.

So Maitreya, Asaṅga, and Gyaltsap encourage the bodhisattvic practitioner and the bodhisattva admirer by showing how the buddhahood reality is as close to us in all our sufferings as our own jugular vein, to borrow a phrase from Islam. And they provide this demonstration in a way that gives us an intellectual and experiential hold on this "cataphatic emptiness," as our author, Marty Jiang, entitled his dissertation on this work.

Coming back to my purpose in this preface, our author did the translation of the key part of Gyaltsap's great work from Tibetan simultaneously into Chinese and into English. His main focus since graduating as a scholar and teacher has been in Chinese; indeed, he translated and published the present work in several Chinese versions (i.e., in both Taiwanese and mainland characters) some time ago. In doing so, in my humble estimation, he has performed a great service to the East Asian understanding and scholarship about this text and this issue, since the Tibetan scholarship on Maitreya and Asaṅga is in some ways light years ahead of the modern understanding, and also has a lot to offer the classical East Asian understanding, as the Tibetan curriculum is much closer to the Indian curriculum whence these works originated.

In completing the work in English, however, Dr. Jiang did need quite a bit of editorial help, as he has not been currently working that much in English. So if there are things in the English version we have finally worked out that are problematic for anyone, then we the editors must take the blame.

I strongly wish to thank Dr. Jiang for bringing to light these wonderful works, translating the words of the three authors from Sanskrit and Tibetan into three languages—traditional Buddhist Chinese, mainland simplified Chinese, and English—and opening the door for us to learn this wonderful teaching of "cataphatic emptiness," helping us to feel the closeness we all enjoy, either consciously or subliminally, with the truth body (*dharmakāya*) of all buddhas.

As always, I would also like to thank the many generous patrons of our *Treasury of the Buddhist Sciences* series, emphasizing in the case of this work in particular, The Robert N. Ho Foundation and its generous, patient, and persistent officers and staff. I would like also to mention the scholarly help received indirectly from Dr. Karl Brunnhölzl, whose excellent study, *When the Clouds Part*, on *The Sublime Continuum*, its *Commentary*, and associated works by great Tibetan scholars of the Kagyu tradition, came out while completing the present work. In regard to the editorial process, I gratefully acknowledge the initial philological help received from Dr. Paul Hackett, the ongoing technical help from Dr. Jensine Andresen, and as ever the careful and persistent editing and preparation of the publication by our executive editor, Dr. Thomas Yarnall. I take responsibility for any remaining errors.

Robert A.F. Thurman (Ari Genyen Tenzin Choetrak)
Jey Tsong Khapa Professor of Indo-Tibetan Buddhist Studies,
Columbia University
Director, Columbia Center for Buddhist Studies
President, American Institute of Buddhist Studies
President, Tibet House US

Ganden Dechen Ling
Woodstock, New York
March 12, 2017 CE,
Buddha Miracle Festival Full Moon
Tibetan Royal Year 2144, Year of the Fire Bird

Note on Occasion of This Revised Edition

ON BEHALF OF US COPUBLISHERS, I am delighted we are issuing this second edition, which has enabled us to honor this great work by polishing and improving it a bit more. I am also thankful that I have had the chance to read it again with the excuse of further editing, because I so much enjoy the insights afforded by these remarkable texts (as much as I have been able to understand them) by the future buddha Maitreyanātha, the great compassion pioneer Āryāsaṅga, the Tibetan Renaissance man Gyaltsap Darma Rinchen, and the Tibetan to Chinese scholar and translator Dr. Bo Jiang, heir to the late, great Ven. Fa Tsun. Each time you read through a great text such as this you see new things, and you can begin to infer that what you think you know now may come to more than you thought upon further review.

The idea that there are countless perfectly wise and loving and capable beings in this universe—so called "buddhas," fully awakened and enlightened beings—who experience themselves as completely one with us, and that their experience may be deeper and more true than our own experience of ourselves as separate individuals in an infinite, mostly alien universe, is at first disconcerting, but also at moments warmly consoling and reassuring. Reading this work strongly strengthens that warmth and sense of realistic trust, while offering the opportunity to meet the challenge of exploring with reason and heart whether our habitual feeling of being lost in space is accurate, or whether the buddha's experience of our indivisible interfusion might actually be more real, sensible, and thus ultimately commonsensical.

I offer my thanks again to all mentioned above in the first preface, and add my thanks for this updated, copublished revised edition to Wisdom Publications' Dr. Daniel Aitken and his team, especially the kind and meticulous Ben Gleason and his colleagues.

Robert A.F. Thurman (Ari Genyen Tenzin Choetrak)
Jey Tsong Khapa Professor Emeritus of Indo-Tibetan Buddhist Studies
Treasury of the Buddhist Sciences Editor-in-Chief
May 10, 2022

Author's Preface and Acknowledgments

THE CENTRAL THEMES of this study and translation were developed and produced during a Tibetan text reading class from September 2003 to May 2004 at Columbia University under the direction of Professor Robert A.F. Thurman. I thank the late Gene Smith at the Tibetan Buddhist Resource Center for providing me with the Tibetan texts for this project. I also thank Acharya Dr. Lobsang Jamspal and Dr. Paul Hackett for their philological suggestions, and my Columbia Department of Religion colleagues, Drs. Christopher Kelley, David Kittay, Michelle Sorensen, and Wen-Ling Jane, for their edifying discussions. I thank the Fulbright-Hays Doctoral Dissertation Research Abroad Program of the U.S. Department of Education for supporting my year-long research in China from 2005 to 2006, and The Robert N. Ho Foundation and the American Institute of Buddhist Studies for continuing that support for three years while I completed the translations. I am indebted to Dr. Klaus-Dieter Mathes and Dr. Kazuo Kano for providing me with their latest researches on the subject. Particular mention should be made of my friends Alexander and Emily Ma for their encouragement and ongoing support. I thank Annie Bien for her insightful editorial comments, and also Drs. Marina Illich, David Mellins, and Annabella Pitkin. Most of all I would like to thank Professor Robert A.F. Thurman for his tutelage and inspiration. Without his constant support, I would not have been able to finish the two versions of this translation in Chinese and this version in English. Finally, I must express my deepest gratitude to my parents, Liang-nian Jiang and Sun-di Wang; to my sister, Jane Jiang, whose understanding and unfailing support have made it possible; and to my beloved wife, Grace.

Abbreviations, Sigla, and Typographical Conventions

THROUGHOUT THIS VOLUME transliteration of Tibetan terms is done in accordance with the system devised by Turrell Wylie; see "A Standard System of Tibetan Transcription," *Harvard Journal of Asiatic Studies* 22 (1959): 261–67. Tibetan proper names are represented phonetically. Wylie transliterations of these names appear in the appendix below.

The full Tibetan and Sanskrit titles of texts are to be found in the bibliographies, which are arranged alphabetically according to author.

For referencing Chinese sources, both Chinese characters and romanization are used. I have followed the pinyin romanization system because it is increasingly used in both scholarly and popular literature.

[TL ###A]   A three-digit number (followed by "A" or "B") enclosed in square brackets is a reference to the folio number and side of the Tashi Lhunpo edition of Gyaltsap's text.

[...]   Material added by translator or editor

«###»   Numbers in angle brackets create points of connection between topics in Asaṅga's explanatory *Commentary* and the corresponding sections of Gyaltsap's *Supercommentary*.

#.#.#.#.# ...   Throughout the translation of the *Supercommentary*, light gray numbered outline entries have been inserted from Gyaltsap's general outline (*sa bcad*).

ACIP   Asian Classics Input Project

AIBS   American Institute of Buddhist Studies (at Columbia University)

CCBS   Columbia Center for Buddhist Studies (in the Department of Religion at Columbia University)

CT	"Comparative" (*dpe bsdur ma*) edition of the Tibetan Tengyur
D###	Folio number and side (A or B) of the Derge edition of the Tibetan canon
H###	Folio number and side (A or B) of the Lhasa edition of the Tibetan canon
MSA	*Mahāyānasūtrālaṁkāra*
PD	Pedurma (*dpe bsdur ma*) edition of the Tibetan Tengyur
*saṁskṛta	Sanskrit terms prefaced with an asterisk represent reconstructions from Tibetan
T. or Taishō	Taishō edition of the Chinese Buddhist canon
Tōh.	Tōhoku catalogue of the Derge edition of the Tibetan canon

Typographical Conventions

WE HAVE STRIVED generally to present Tibetan and Sanskrit names and terms in a phonetic form to facilitate pronunciation. For most Sanskrit terms this has meant that—while we generally have kept conventional diacritics for direct citations—when used as English words or names we have added an *h* to convey certain sounds (so *ś*, *ṣ*, and *c* are rendered as *sh*, *ṣh*, and *ch* respectively, the conventional Sanskrit transliteration *ch* rendered as *chh*). Tibetan phonetical renderings have not yet been standardized, so we write them as they sound in Lhasa dialect, for want of a generally agreed-upon system. For Sanskrit terms that have entered the English lexicon (such as "nirvana"), we use no diacritical marks. In more technical contexts (notes, bibliographies, appendixes, and so on) we use standard diacritical conventions for Sanskrit, and Wylie transliterations for Tibetan.

Part One

INTRODUCTION

Introduction to *The Sublime Continuum,*
Its Commentary, and Its Supercommentary

1. Introduction to *The Sublime Continuum* and Its *Commentary*

The Sublime Continuum appeared in India around the fourth century CE, a time when tathāgata essence theory-related sutras seem to have been popular. Hence, this text can be viewed as an authoritative treatise that adopts a systematic approach to the content and purpose of these sutras. Regarding the authorship of the work, we have the account of the Tibetan tradition,[2] which maintains that it was first taught by the celestial bodhisattva Maitreya in the Tushita heaven, then brought down to earth by Asaṅga, who authored a commentary on the root text. This root treatise and four other works (*Analysis of Phenomena and Reality, Analysis of the Middle and Extremes, Ornament of the Universal Vehicle Sutras,* and *Ornament of Clear Realization*) are collectively referred to as the "Five Books of Maitreya." In general, both Maitreya and Asaṅga are viewed as the founders of the Experientialist (*yogācāra*) school represented by some of these texts.[3] Whoever the actual author was, it is clear from analysis of the works as a whole that they must have been well versed in the philosophy of the Experientialist school.

In terms of the writing style and formal elements of all the works, there are numerous similarities. In addition to *The Sublime Continuum* (subtitled *Analysis of the Precious Spiritual Potential*), two more of the five are styled

---

2. The Chinese tradition has a slightly different list, including the *Yogācārabhūmi,* a lost *Yogavibhāga,* and a *Vajracchedikā Sutra* commentary, along with the *Mahāyānasūtrālaṁkāra* and the *Madhyāntavibhāga.*

3. In the Chinese tradition however, the founding of the school is attributed to Sthiramati. Although Sanskrit *yogācāra* is generally equated with the *vijñānavāda* (consciousness-theory) or *cittamātra* (mind-only) school, in the Sanskrit and Tibetan traditions it is more broadly used, even referring to some Centrist (*mādhyamika*) works, such as Āryadeva's *Experientialist Four Hundred* (*yogācāra-catuḥśataka*). Also, the majority of scholars in the Tibetan tradition considers the Maitreyanātha-Asaṅga team as having produced two Centrist works, the *Ornament of Clear Realization* and the present *Sublime Continuum,* in addition to the other three Experientialist works.

as "analytical" (*vibhāga*) commentaries. In *The Sublime Continuum*, as well, the author follows a scheme of six topics—nature (*svabhāva*), cause (*hetu*), fruition (*phala*), actions (*karma*), endowment (*yoga*), and engagement (*vṛtti*)—in his presentations of the tathāgata essence theory and of enlightenment (*bodhi*). This is a strategy similar to the one seen in the narrative systems of both Maitreya's *Ornament of the Universal Vehicle Sutras* and Asaṅga's *Mahāyāna Abhidharma Compendium*.

Regarding theories of buddha bodies (*buddhakāya*), *The Sublime Continuum* adopts a threefold buddha-body theory that includes a twofold truth body—a feature that appears to be exclusive to the Experientialist school—whereas Nāgārjuna seems to assert a twofold buddha-body theory, consisting of a truth body (*dharmakāya*) and a material body (*rūpakāya*). In contrast, the *Ornament of the Universal Vehicle Sutras* and Asaṅga's *Universal Vehicle Compendium* advocate a threefold buddha-body theory: nature body (*svabhāvikakāya*), beatific body (*saṃbhogakāya*), and emanation body (*nirmāṇakāya*). *The Sublime Continuum* presents a twofold model of the truth body: instructional and realizational. In addition, *The Sublime Continuum* accepts the concept of the "thorough transformation of the basis" (*āśrayaparāvṛtti*) and a theory of two spiritual potentials—ideas generally exclusive to the Experientialist school and seen in texts that pre-date *The Sublime Continuum*.

The Sublime Continuum nonetheless argues against the idea of three final vehicles as found in sutras such as the *Elucidation of the Intention Sutra*, and instead advocates the single vehicle (*ekayāna*) doctrine espoused in the *Lotus Sutra*. With regard to passages found in the *Ornament of the Universal Vehicle Sutras* that disparage the idea of spiritual potentials, *The Sublime Continuum* presents its reasons against such a view:

[The *Ornament of the Light of Wisdom Sutra*] states as follows:[4]

---

4. PD70 (phi), pp. 1033.20–1034.3; D100, f. 285b.6–7. See translation below, p. 92. While having nearly completed this present book, Karl Brunnhölzl published his own excellent study of the *Uttaratantra*, etc., accompanied by a different Tibetan commentarial tradition. In going through it, we noticed his references to the Derge (D) edition of the Kangyur. After verifying the accuracy of several of these references, we decided to add his D folio references to our PD folio references, as many scholars may not have access to the PD edition we consulted.

After this, the intuitive wisdom light rays of the Tathāgata sun disc fall upon the bodies of even those people who are confirmed in error, thus benefiting them and producing a proper cause of their future [liberation], thus causing their virtuous qualities to increase.

And Asaṅga's *Sublime Continuum Commentary* continues:

As for the statement that "the wrong-desiring ones[5] have no chance for nirvana forever," it is so declared because feeling enmity toward the universal vehicle teaching is the cause of being a wrong-desiring one. With the intention that this ["forever" really] means "for a certain period of time," it is so stated in order to avert such enmity.

None could be impure forever because of the existence of a naturally pure potential.

In addition, *The Sublime Continuum* gives a new meaning to the Experientialist concepts of "thorough transformation of the basis" (*āśrayaparāvṛtti*) and "spiritual potential" (*gotra*). As part of its theory of universal vehicle praxis, the Experientialist school regards salvation as the purification and transformation of the tainted "knowledge basis"—in other words, it regards salvation to be the so-called transformation of the eightfold consciousness into the four wisdoms. However, although *The Sublime Continuum* talks about "transformation of the basis" from the same viewpoint of praxis, it explains it in a different way: "the element . . . is termed the 'tathāgata essence' when unreleased from the sheath of addictions; however, it is in the nature of transformation when it is purified." Indeed, Asaṅga would appear to be the first to introduce a theory of a twofold spiritual potential—natural (*prakṛtistha*) and cultivated or developmental (*samudānīta*). In the *Bodhisattva Stages,* he states:[6]

What is spiritual potential? [Answer:] In sum here are two kinds: one is called "natural," the other "developmental." "Natural"

---

5. *log sred can.* This would be appear to be a term similar to "the desire-doomed" (*icchantika, 'dod chen po*).

6. *Bodhisattvabhūmi,* PD73 (wi), p. 527.7–15.

refers to the special quality associated with a bodhisattva's six sense-media (*āyatana*), and is naturally inherited from the series of beginningless lifetimes. "Developmental" refers to that which is attained by means of previous cultivation of virtuous roots. The spiritual potential refers to these both. Moreover, this spiritual potential is also called "seed," "element," and "nature." Furthermore, this spiritual potential is called "subtle," when it has not yet reached its cultivated level, and "coarse" when it reaches its cultivated level, since it is associated with fruition at that time.

According to this theory, developmental spiritual potential is the fruition of the cultivation of natural spiritual potential. Therefore, natural spiritual potential is the spiritual gene with a compounded nature (1.151). The theory further evolves in the *Ornament of the Universal Vehicle Sutras*. Apparently, the author of *The Sublime Continuum* accepts this form of the spiritual potential theory but takes natural spiritual potential as the cause for attainment of the nature buddha body. Both natural spiritual potential and the nature body are viewed as uncompounded.

In short, in spite of the fact that the author of *The Sublime Continuum* is Experientialist, as he usually or deeply teaches by deploying Experientialist thought, when elucidating the purpose of tathāgata essence-related sutras he does not introduce at the same time the Experientialist ontology and its soteriologically defined spiritual potential theory.

The Titles of the Texts

The author of *The Sublime Continuum* and its *Commentary* did have a close relationship with the Experientialist school. The author uses the term "precious spiritual potential" (*ratnagotra*) to cover all of the tathāgata essence theory. This reflects the tendency of Experientialist scholars, who have attached great importance to the spiritual potential concept. In *The Sublime Continuum* and its *Commentary*, the term "element" (*dhātu*) refers to the tathāgata essence in a consistent manner. This indicates that "spiritual potential" and "element" can be used interchangeably, as seen in the *Bodhisattva Stages* and the *Ornament of the Universal Vehicle Sutras*.

The term "sublime continuum" (*uttaratantra*) appears only once, in verse 160 of the first chapter. From the context, it is clear that the text itself takes this term to refer to the corpus of tathāgata essence-related sutras. The Sanskrit word *uttara* has multiple connotations (later, superior, etc.). Thus, this corpus could have been called *uttara* (later) in reference to its appearance in India "later" than the "earlier" universal vehicle sutras such as the *Transcendent Wisdom Sutras*. However, the Indian and Tibetan translator teams chose a different equivalent to *uttara* when translating the title of the work, opting for "sublime" or "superlative" (*bla ma*) rather than "later" (*phyi ma*); so it is this "sublime" reading that we follow here.

In terms of content, *The Sublime Continuum* seems to maintain this distinction between so-called earlier and later universal vehicle sutras. Nonetheless, while there are statements in the text such as "so has it been arranged previously, and again in *The Sublime Continuum*" (I.160ab), such a distinction does not indicate a doctrinal discrepancy between the early and later universal vehicle sutras, but rather—as Asaṅga's commentary indicates—the word "again" (*punar*) is taken to mean "furthermore," "in addition," etc., and is not to be taken as a contrastive connective. This suggests that the mass of later universal vehicle sutras on tathāgata essence is considered a doctrinal supplement—not a corrective—to the early universal vehicle sutras such as the *Transcendent Wisdom Sutra*.

In the *Elucidation of the Intention Sutra* category of the "sutras of the third turning of the Dharma wheel," the avowed purpose is to correct five faults and to cultivate five virtues of interpretation. Among these five faults, not understanding the meaning of reality (*bhūta*) refers to the habitual thought of the unreal addictions as being real, and disparaging the excellence of reality refers to not considering the excellence of reality to be existent. As to the meaning of "reality," *The Sublime Continuum* clearly states that it is identical to the so-called "thatness of all things, the pure universal excellences," as taught in the *Transcendent Wisdom Sutra*. *The Sublime Continuum* says:[7]

> It should be understood that [engagements with] the tathāgata element have been taught to bodhisattvas in the *Transcendent Wisdom Sutras*, etc., with reference to the nonconceptual intuitive wisdom. There are three different kinds of engagement with the general characteristic of the pure reality of all things—as

7. PD70 (phi), p. 1036.15–21. See translation below, p. 95.

taught [in the sutra]—those of alienated individuals who do not perceive reality, of noble ones who see reality, and of tathāgatas who have attained the ultimate purity in seeing reality.

According to the *Transcendent Wisdom Sutra*, thatness is identical to the intrinsic emptiness of all things. Therefore, the opposite of reality is intrinsic existence. Moreover, *The Sublime Continuum* puts forth that intrinsic existence, since it is the opposite of reality, does not exist, while the unerring, true ultimate reality does exist:[8]

> Furthermore, one should understand that no matter how much one investigates realistically, one can not see any sign or object whatsoever. When one does not see any causal sign or object, one sees truly. Thus, by means of such equanimity, a tathāgata attains completely perfect buddhahood in total equality.
>
> Thus, since no object can be perceived as a result of its non-[intrinsic] existence, and since the ultimate reality can be perceived for its existence as real as it is, it is neither negated nor established. [Thus, the Tathāgata] has realized the equality of all things by his intuitive wisdom of equanimity. And this [wisdom of equanimity] should be recognized as the antidote for all kinds of obscurations such as experiencing only [either] a realization of nonexistence [or a situation] wherein if any one thing is produced, another is definitely lost.

Therefore, more specifically, not understanding the meaning of reality refers to habitually thinking of the addictions as being intrinsically existent; and disparaging the excellence of reality refers to considering the excellence of intrinsic realitylessness as existent even on a conventional level. Thus, here "intuitive wisdom" refers to the wisdom that perceives ultimate reality, while "wisdom" refers to the wisdom that perceives conventional reality. This presentation is perfectly compatible with the mādhyamika theory of the two truths. From this we can understand that the existence and nonexistence that are taught in *The Sublime Continuum* are the two aspects of the same reality. *The Sublime Continuum*, therefore, does not argue that the

8. See translation below, p. 66.

tathāgata essence theory, which puts emphasis on existence, is ontologically superior to the philosophy of emptiness, which places emphasis on nonexistence; indeed, the author of *The Sublime Continuum* argues that one needs to study the *Transcendent Wisdom Sutra* in order to master the nonfabricating intuitive wisdom—a necessity for the attainment of buddhahood:[9]

> As for the details of the paths of insight and meditation where nonconceptual intuitive wisdom serves as the cause of attaining the truth body, they should be understood following the *Transcendent Wisdom Sutra*.

In addition, the praxis of great love and so on does not contradict the philosophy of emptiness as taught in the *Transcendent Wisdom Sutra*. Rather, for intelligent bodhisattvas, the proper understanding of emptiness is conducive to the development of loving compassion and the spirit of universal enlightenment, just as Nāgārjuna stated in his *Precious Garland of Advice to the King*. The purpose of tathāgata essence theory, therefore, is to assist universal vehicle Buddhists, who have understood the philosophy of emptiness as taught in the *Transcendent Wisdom Sutra*, in cultivating loving compassion, the spirit of universal enlightenment, to complement their wisdom and thereby achieve buddhahood quickly. Hence, the mass of tathāgata essence sutras are supposed to enhance the philosophy of emptiness of the *Transcendent Wisdom Sutra* in the praxis dimension, being called "sublime" (*uttara*), meaning "superior," in this sense.

The Sublime Continuum explains this dual meaning of "sublime" by citing the preface chapter of the *Questions of King Dhāraṇīshvara Sutra*:[10]

> O noble child, take for example a skillful jeweler who knows well how to cleanse a gem. Having picked out a precious jewel that has been thoroughly tainted from the mine, and having soaked it in a strong solution of sal-ammoniac, he then polishes it by rubbing it with a very refined ox-hair cloth. But his efforts in just this way are not yet finished. After that, having soaked the jewel in strong, fermented fruit juice, he polishes it with a cloth of wool.

9. See translation below, p. 66.

10. PD70 (phi), pp. 992.15–993.14. See translation below, p. 57 ff.

But his efforts in just this way are still not yet finished. After that, having soaked it in a great medicine essence, he polishes it with fine cotton cloth. Being thus completely purified, when it is free of all impurities, it is called "precious sapphire."

O noble child, just so a tathāgata, knowing the scope of the sentient beings who are not purified, by means of disturbing descriptions of impermanence, suffering, selflessness, and impurity, makes those sentient beings who delight in the life cycle [instead] become averse to it, and so causes them to enter into the noble Dharma code of discipline.

With just these [acts], a tathāgata does not cease in his efforts. After that, he causes them to realize the way of the Tathāgata, by means of the instructions on emptiness, signlessness, and wishlessness. With just these [acts], a tathāgata does not cease in his efforts. Next, he installs those sentient beings in the buddha realm by means of the teaching of irreversibility and the teaching of the total purification of the three sectors [of actions]. When they have entered and have realized the reality of a tathāgata, they are called "the unsurpassed worthies for offerings."

Here, "codes of discipline" refers to the lower philosophical and practice systems, while the teachings on emptiness, signlessness, and wishlessness refers to the "prior continuum" (*pūrvatantra*), i.e., the *Transcendent Wisdom Sutra*, and so on. The teachings of the wheel of irreversibility and the total purification of the triple sector (*trimaṇḍalapariśuddhi*) refers to the "later continuum," i.e., tathāgata essence, and so on.[11] The purification of the triple sector can be seen as a methodical application of emptiness philosophy in specific universal vehicle praxis such as generosity. Again, these teachings are not a doctrinal critique of the emptiness theory. "[Causing] sentient beings with various dispositions to engage with the sphere of a tathāgata" is clearly related to the "single vehicle" (*ekayāna*) doctrine. Consequently, the three stages theory taught in the *Questions of King Dhāraṇīshvara Sutra* is different from the "three turnings of the wheel of Dharma" theory.

11. This may have its source from the *Great Drum Sutra* (*Mahābherīhāraka-sūtra*).

In the extended title of the work, the term *ratnagotra* refers to the spiritual potential of the Three Jewels, and in particular, to the content of the texts of the so-called later universal vehicle sutras, i.e., the *Tathāgata Essence Sutra*. The word *vibhāga*—according to *Analysis of the Middle and Extremes*—has a dual meaning: to distinguish and to clarify. *The Sublime Continuum* thus distinguishes each of the seven subjects that constitute the theory of the spiritual potential of the Three Jewels. It also clarifies the purpose of this theory.

The Content of the Texts

The Sublime Continuum consists of five chapters. The first four explain the seven vajra subjects, or topics: Buddha, Dharma, Saṅgha, element, enlightenment, excellences, and enlightened activities. The first chapter consists of the first four subjects, while the subsequent three chapters cover the three subjects of enlightenment, excellences, and enlightened activities. Among these seven, Buddha, Dharma, and Saṅgha are together called the Three Jewels, while the final four are referred to collectively as the spiritual potential (*gotra*). According to *The Sublime Continuum*, the spiritual potential is in reality the cause and conditions (*kāraṇa*) of the Three Jewels. Specifically, the element is the cause, while enlightenment, excellences, and enlightened activities are the conditions. The Three Jewels are, of course, the effect of the causal element.

The Sublime Continuum explains the spiritual potential for attainment of the Three Jewels as having four characteristics that become the cause and conditions of the Three Jewels:[12]

> In that regard, we should understand that the first of these four topics is the cause of the production of the Three Jewels, depending on its purification, because it is the seed of the transcendent excellences and the focus of an individual's proper mentation, by which that [tainted reality] is purified. Thus, one single topic is the cause. How do the other three [topics] serve as conditions? These should be understood to be the conditions for the production of the Three Jewels in the way that the production of

12. See translation below, p. 79.

the Three Jewels depends on the purification of that [tainted ultimate reality element], and this purification is based upon the messages from others. This is because a tathāgata, having realized the unsurpassed perfect enlightenment, performs the thirty-two activities of a tathāgata with those qualities of a buddha such as the ten powers, and so on. Thus, these three serve as conditions.

Roughly speaking, the suchness reality mingled with the taints (*samalatathatā*), which is possessed by living beings, is the seed of transcendence, and when it is purified, it becomes the inner cause for the Three Jewels achieved in the future. Nevertheless, the proper mentation (*yoniśomanasikāra*) that purifies that suchness is actually the real seed, since suchness itself is uncompounded. A tathāgata, who possesses a purified essence, acts with enlightened activities by means of the excellences, such as the ten powers and so on. For example, the act of giving teachings embodies enlightened activity. Only by means of teaching others does it become possible for ordinary beings to develop the proper mentation to purify their own contaminated essence. Hence, the other three are the conducive conditions for the Three Jewels to be achieved by sentient beings in the future. This specific use of the terminology of seed, cause, condition, and element appears to be a unique feature exclusive to the Experientialist school in the way they are identified as the spiritual potential.

In conclusion, *The Sublime Continuum*'s structure and content can be arranged as in the table on page 13.

It should be noted that although the last three are the conducive conditions for actualizing such a goal, they are not qualities possessed by those who are not yet buddhas. Rather, they are the conditions provided by others who are buddhas already, and are just as necessary as the element to help a sentient being become a buddha. Therefore, these three factors collectively constitute an important dimension of tathāgata essence or the spiritual potential/gene of the Three Jewels.

Roughly speaking, in *The Sublime Continuum*, the precious spiritual potential, the element, and the tathāgata essence are synonymous. More specifically, however, the "element" and the "tathāgata essence" have narrow and broad senses. In their narrow sense, both terms refer to reality mingled with the taints of the precious spiritual potential, while in their broad sense, the two terms are identical to the concept of the precious

CHAPTERS	VERSES	VAJRA TOPICS	SCHEMA
I. Tathāgata Essence	1–3	(Prelude)	
	4–8	Buddha	Fruition
	9–12	Dharma	
	13–22	Saṅgha	
	23–167	Element	Cause
II. Enlightenment	1–73	Enlightenment	Condition
III. Excellences	1–39	Excellences	
IV. Enlightened Activities	1–98	Enlightened Activities	
V. Benefits	1–28	(Benefits)	

spiritual potential itself. This indicates that reality mingled with the taints, which is the foundation of the attainment of buddhahood, is the kernel of the tathāgata essence theory. In contrast to this, the terms "spiritual potential of a tathāgata" and "spiritual potential of a buddha" exclusively refer to the twofold spiritual potentials: "natural" (*prakṛtistha*) and "cultivated/developmental" (*samudānīta*).

The author of *The Sublime Continuum* asserts that the tathāgata essence as taught in the *Tathāgata Essence Sutra* has three meanings, or aspects: the truth body of a tathāgata that can diffuse itself in permeating all sentient beings (*tathāgata-dharmakāya-parispharaṇārtha*), meaning that all beings are receptive to a tathāgata's liberative activities; the reality of the nondifferentiation of a tathāgata and a suchness-permeated sentient being (*tathāgata-tathatāvyatireka-artha*), since the suchness reality mingled with taints exists within all sentient beings; and the naturally existing spiritual potential that is fit for transforming into the truth body, as well as the developmental spiritual potential that is fit for transforming into the material body, exist within all sentient beings (*tathāgata-gotra-sambhavārtha*).

The *Tathāgata Essence Sutra* explains the tathāgata essence with the device of nine similes. *The Sublime Continuum* elucidates by further dividing each into two, giving nine showing what obscures and nine showing what is obscured. What obscures are the obscurations such as the instinctual predisposition for attachment, and so on. What is obscured is the tathāgata essence, or the element. This shows the tainted status of sentient beings' suchness, the foundation of the attainment of buddhahood. Furthermore, according to *The Sublime Continuum,* the nine meanings of the nine similes showing the obscured can be condensed into the three aspects of the tathāgata essence. The correlation between the nine similes for the obscured and the three aspects of the tathāgata essence can be illustrated as follows:

Similes	Obscured Element	Tathāgata Essence
1. Buddha's image	Dharma in the form of realization	Diffusion of the truth body
2. Honey	Teaching expounding the ultimate reality	
3. Grain	Teaching expounding conventional reality	
4. Gold	Reality	Reality
5. Treasure	Naturally existing spiritual potential	Spiritual potential
6. *Nyagrodha* tree	Developmental spiritual potential	
7. Precious image	Truth body	
8. Ruler	Beatific body	
9. Precious statue	Material body	

Here it is worth noting that in spite of the fact that in the similes, the relation between what obscures and the obscured (for instance, bee and honey) is definite, the relation between the things represented by these similes (the instinctual predisposition for hatred and the instructional truth body, for example) is not definite. In other words, the instinct for hatred is not the only factor that obscures the instructional truth body, nor is the instructional truth body necessarily obscured by the instinct of hatred alone, since sentient beings' tathāgata essence is enclosed by countless millions of addictions. In addition, a tathāgata's realizational truth body, which is obscured by addictions for beings, is not yet possessed by them, because it has a nature that is free of taints and hence is only possessed by a buddha.

It seems that the author of *The Sublime Continuum* made a systematic arrangement of the doctrine of the tathāgata essence sutras that were prevalent at the time, in order to elucidate their purpose. Moreover, he enhanced the impact of the tathāgata essence theory by connecting it to the Experientialist theory of jewel spiritual potential. Nevertheless, it also seems clear that he upheld the meaning of the tathāgata essence revealed in the mass of tathāgata essence sutras as distinct from the Experientialist interpretation of the tathāgata essence. For instance, both Maitreya's *Ornament of the Universal Vehicle Sutras* and Asaṅga's *Universal Vehicle Compendium* teach the tathāgata essence from the perspective of all things' being undifferentiated, or in terms of a universal general nature; thereby they assert that all things have tathāgata essence. This diminishes the key role of the tathāgata essence in the universal vehicle soteriology, wherein it serves as the cause of enlightenment and the foundation of practices leading to it. They use the tathāgata essence as a purely ontological concept. The Experientialist school takes such a stance in order to ameliorate the discrepancy between the sutras' tathāgata essence theory and their three final vehicles theory. The author of *The Sublime Continuum*, however, has endeavored to maintain the role of the tathāgata essence in the universal vehicle soteriology, while associating it, but not equating it, with the Experientialist school's own theory of jewel spiritual potential.

Finally, it is worth noting that despite the fact that the tathāgata essence theory played an important role in Chinese Buddhist history, few Chinese scholars showed interest in this important text. In contrast, the Tibetan Buddhist traditions paid significant attention to *The Sublime Continuum* and its *Commentary* from the period of its first translation into Tibetan. Beginning with Ngog Loden Sherab in the eleventh century, notable scholars from all the major traditions in Tibet—Kadam, Nyingma, Sakya, Kagyu, Jonang, and Geluk—wrote commentaries on the text. As a result of the sometimes significant differences between their interpretations of the tathāgata essence theory, these commentaries contain a lot of information about the doctrinal debates among the different traditions—a fact that will prove indispensable in the study of the history of Tibetan Buddhist thought.

2. Introduction to Gyaltsap's *Supercommentary*

The Author

Gyaltsap Darma Rinchen was born at Rinang in the Nyangtö area of Tsang in 1364. At a young age, he took novice ordination at Nenying Monastery[13] from Khenchen Rinchen Gyaltsen and Draktokpa Shönnu Tsultrim and received the name Darma Rinchen. He went on to receive a variety of exoteric and esoteric teachings from several great masters. Especially under the Sakya scholar Rendawa Shönnu Lodrö (1349–1412), Gyaltsap studied both exoteric texts—on topics such as transcendent wisdom, epistemology and logic, the monastic disciplines, abhidharma, and Centrist philosophy—and esoteric texts, such as the *Guhyasamāja Tantra*. Along with Tsong Khapa Losang Drakpa (1357–1419), Gyaltsap became one of the seven closest disciples of Rendawa and earned the title "the best in serious debate."

Following his studies with Rendawa, Gyaltsap went on a monastic debate tour of Buddhist learning centers, including Sakya, Sangpu and Tsetang, where he distinguished himself by debating on ten different philosophical texts. He thus became famous as a scholar, and after debating with many Sakya scholars received the formal title Kachupa (*bka' bcu pa*; literally "[a master of] ten texts")—the first such entitlement in Tibetan intellectual history.

At the age of twenty-five (1388), Gyaltsap took the vows of a fully ordained monk in Tsang from Kungapal, Rendawa, and others, then continued his debate tour in central Tibet. Having defeated two Sakya masters—Rongtön Shakya Gyaltsen (1367–1449) and Khenchen Yakpa—Gyaltsap decided to challenge the famed Tsong Khapa. Several of Gyaltsap's biographies mention this fated meeting, which took place at Nyeltö Radrong, where Tsong Khapa was teaching. But the account in the

13. Sometimes spelled *gnas rnying*.

Reservoir of Excellences (yon tan chu gter) gives the most detail, relating the encounter as follows:[14]

> Intending to provoke Tsong Khapa into debate, Gyaltsap Rinpoche acted with pride and entered the monastery without removing his hat [in the customary way]. Master Tsong Khapa noticed him but continued to teach, while stepping down from the teacher's throne. The precious teacher [Gyaltsap] proudly strode up [and seated himself on] the master's throne, still wearing his hat. However, as he listened, Gyaltsap heard eloquent speech that he had never heard before from any other scholar, and the mountain of his arrogance began to collapse. First he removed his hat, then he got down from the throne and seated himself among the disciples. The desire to challenge Tsong Khapa had left him completely; instead he became his student. [In retrospect] it was said that Gyaltsap's act of mounting the throne was an auspicious indication that later he would be the throne holder [of Ganden (*dga' ldan*) Monastery].

Tsong Khapa gave Gyaltsap many essential teachings, explaining the most difficult points of sutras and treatises with stainless reasoning. This filled Gyaltsap with such faith and devotion that he requested permission to seek out no other teachers but to remain with Tsong Khapa for the rest of his life. His request was granted and he became the foremost disciple of Tsong Khapa,[15] serving him for twelve years.

As a result of his excellence in monastic discipline and intellectual prowess, even during Tsong Khapa's lifetime, many of the master's students also studied with Gyaltsap. When Tsong Khapa was establishing Ganden Monastery, Gyaltsap, along with Dulzin Drakpa Gyaltsen (1374–1434), assumed personal responsibility and participated in building the monastery. The

---

14. Dragyap Losang Tenpa, *Rgyal tshab kyi rnam thar yon tan chu gter*, as cited in Gyalwang Trinlay Namgyal, *'Jam mgon chos kyi rgyal po tsong kha pa chen po'i rnam thar thub bstan mdzes pa'i rgyan gcig ngo mtshar nor bu'i phreng ba* (Xining: Mtsho sngon mi rigs par khang, 1981), 248–49.

15. For a discussion of later, revisionist accounts of the early history of the Geluk lineage that would attempt to undermine Gyaltsap's status, see Elijah Ary, *Authorized Lives: Biography and the Early Formation of Geluk Identity* (Boston: Wisdom, 2015).

main construction was completed in 1410. Before Tsong Khapa passed away, he gave his paṇḍita's hat and cloak to Gyaltsap as a sign that Gyaltsap was his successor. When Tsong Khapa died in 1419, Gyaltsap became the second holder of the Ganden throne at the age of fifty-six, by unanimous request from Tsong Khapa's students, and he has been known as Gyaltsap (lit. regent) since then. He held the position for thirteen years, extensively engaging in teaching, debate, and writing. Following Tsong Khapa, Gyaltsap emphasized the importance of monastic vows and rules to preserve the Buddhist tradition, in addition to giving extensive discourses on philosophy and tantric practice. As a much loved and highly respected teacher, Gyaltsap was considered by his followers to be the same as Tsong Khapa himself and one of the founding fathers of the Gelukpa order.

Gyaltsap visited Nenying Monastery for the last time at the age of sixty-eight (in 1431). The same year, he retired and installed Khedrup Gelek Palsangpo (1358–1438), Tsong Khapa's other close disciple, as the next holder of the Ganden throne. Gyaltsap lived for one more year, primarily in meditation. He died in 1432 at the age of sixty-nine.

Gyaltsap's chief disciples proved skilled and vigorous in continuing the widely recognized Tsong Khapa tradition of teaching and practice. To name a few: Tashi Palden (1379–1449), who founded Drepung Monastery near Lhasa in 1416; Dulzin Drakpa Gyaltsen (1374–1434), who founded Tsunmotsal Monastery; Gendundrup (1391–1474), retroactively the First Dalai Lama, who founded Tashi Lhunpo Monastery in Tsang in 1447; Gungru Gyaltsen Sangpo (1383–1450), the third abbot of Sera Monastery; and Kyektön Kachupa Lodrö Denpa (1402–1478), who became the eighth abbot of Ganden in 1473.

Gyaltsap received the complete transmission and explanation of Tsong Khapa's teachings on both exoteric and esoteric subjects. He listened to, memorized, and wrote down numerous discourses. Some of his writings are lecture notes and mnemonic notes, many of which are included in Tsong Khapa's collected works. Gyaltsap's independent works—including *The Sublime Continuum Supercommentary* (translated here)—are primarily based on the teachings he received from Rendawa and Tsong Khapa, especially the latter. All these works were written while he was the abbot of Ganden (ca. 1419–1431), and a number of his writings are considered indispensable for study. For instance, the oral tradition maintains the proverb: it is impossible to debate on Dharmakīrti's *Commentary on Validating*

Cognition if you have not memorized (Gyaltsap's) *Illuminator of the Path to Liberation* (*thar lam gsal byed*); it is impossible to debate on Maitreya's *Ornament of Clear Realization* if you have not memorized (Tsong Khapa's) *Golden Rosary of Eloquence* (*legs bshad gser phreng*).

Historical Background

The year Gyaltsap was born was also the year Butön Rinchendrup (1290–1364) and Tai Situ Jangchup Gyaltsen (1302–1364) died. Both Butön and Jangchup Gyaltsen were important in the establishment of the Gelukpa school. Tsong Khapa received much intellectual heritage, especially the esoteric teachings, from Butön's Shalu tradition, whereas Jangchup Gyaltsen created social-political conditions favorable for this newcomer into the Tibetan religious scene. The hundred-year period of Sakyapa hegemony over Tibet ended in 1349 with the military victory of Jangchup Gyaltsen, who founded the Pagmo Drupa (*phag mo gru pa*) religio-political establishment that would last for the next hundred years. Jangchup Gyaltsen was well aware that widespread corruption among high-ranking officers, laxity of monastic discipline, and political conflicts in the name of religion were the main causes of the collapse of Sakyapa rule. Correspondingly, in the *Last Testament Annals* (*bka' chems deb ther*), Jangchup Gyaltsen issued decrees for the new government, placing great emphasis on the personal integrity of lay officials, on harmonious relationships between different orders, including Sakya, Tshalpa, Taglung, Drigung, Kadam, etc., and on monastic discipline and the education of monks. In fact, as a devoted monk, Jangchup Gyaltsen set an example to others in terms of keeping the vows of celibacy and abstinence. He was concerned that his tradition lacked exegetical education because of its strong orientation toward meditation; therefore, he founded Tsetang College in 1351 as a complement to his Densatil meditation center.

The Pagmo Drupa religio-political establishment reached the height of its power and splendor during the reign of Wang Drakpa Gyaltsen (1374–1432), who became the fifth Pagdru Regent in 1385 and was well versed in both religious and political affairs. During his reign, he undertook a series of administrative reforms and also endeavored to maintain the ancient traditions of Tibetan culture. The relationship between his government and the Chinese Ming government was cordial, and he supported all the monastic

institutions without sectarian bias, laying great stress on monastic education. He donated lavishly to Pagdru centers like Densatil and Tsetang and
sponsored summer retreats conducted by monastic institutions that held
the precept lineage coming down from Kashmiri Paṇchen Shākya Shrī (ca.
1127–1225). Wang Drakpa Gyaltsen greatly respected many famous masters from different backgrounds from whom he received many teachings,
including Tsong Khapa, Chenga Kunpangpa, Tsungmey Rinchen Shönnu
(b. 1333), the Fifth Karmapa Lama, Deshin Shekpa (1384–1415), and others.
Because of his outstanding political achievements in creating a period of
peace and prosperity, Wang Drakpa Gyaltsen was remembered by the
Tibetan people with the honorific title His Eminence, the Great Dharma
King (*gong ma chos rgyal chen po*).

When Tsong Khapa instituted the Great Prayer Festival in 1409, Wang
Drakpa Gyaltsen supported it with substantial resources. He was also the
chief benefactor to the Ganden Monastery project launched in the same
year. In just forty years after Ganden Monastery was established, three other
important Gelukpa centers in central Tibet and Tsang were built by Tsong
Khapa's disciples: Jamyang Chöjey Tashi Palden (1379–1449) founded
Drepung Monastery in 1416; Jamchen Chöjey Shākya Yeshe (1354–1435)
founded Sera Monastery in 1419; and Gendundrup (1391–1474), the First
Dalai Lama, founded Tashi Lhunpo Monastery in 1447. All these projects
were sponsored by local Pagdru governors. The tax revenues from a number of estates were donated to these monastic centers and were sources of
a stable income. Tsong Khapa's disciples came from different regions of
Tibet: U, Tsang, Ngari, Kham, and Amdo. When they returned to their
hometowns, they built many monasteries dedicated to Tsong Khapa and
his teachings.

It seems clear that the Pagmo Drupa religio-political establishment
played a significant role in the rapid expansion of the Gelukpa order and
was exceptional in its influence on the history of Tibetan Buddhism. Very
little detailed research has been done regarding the early history of the
Gelukpa school and its close relationship to the Pagdru authorities. Suffice
it to say that the Pagdru government was sympathetic to Tsong Khapa
not only because of his personal charisma but also because it served their
own interests in reform. Indeed, there are three reasons Wang Drakpa
Gyaltsen might have been sympathetic to Tsong Khapa's endeavors. First,
Wang Drakpa Gyaltsen and his government could easily have found the

situation created by the rise of Tsong Khapa's itinerant group congenial to advancing Tai Situ Jangchup Gyaltsen's policy on monastic discipline, since strict adherence to the pure monastic life was a well-known trademark of Tsong Khapa's lineage. Second, it seems clear that the Pagdru authorities—including Chenga Sönam Drakpa (1359–1408), the fourth Pagdru regent, and Wang Drakpa Gyaltsen himself—were attracted to Tsong Khapa's intellectual achievements and effective teaching, and so would have considered him useful in their aspiration to build a monastic educational system. Third, during that period, Tsong Khapa's followers were purely religious in nature without political aspirations, thus posing no threat to the Pagdru government.

The Text

The Sublime Continuum Supercommentary is one of Gyaltsap's most important works, studied in the Geluk monastic universities usually within the curriculum of transcendent wisdom studies. Historically, the works of Tsong Khapa, Gyaltsap, and Khedrup from the early fifteenth century served to some extent as the Gelukpa charter literature, representing the advent of the latest tradition of interpretation and practice in the world of Tibetan Buddhism. Given the historical conditions under which *The Sublime Continuum Supercommentary* was written, it played an important role in the founding of the Gelukpa curriculum.

The central philosophical view realized and taught by Tsong Khapa was that of the dialecticist Centrist school (*prāsaṅgika-mādhyamika, dbu ma thal 'gyur pa*), which served as the cornerstone for his far-reaching interpretation of Buddhist thought. Tibetan Buddhism's emerging traditions took the Centrist (*mādhyamika*) view as foundational from the eighth century, with the declaration by King Trisong Detsen that all Buddhists in Tibet should follow Nāgārjuna's teachings. In the early transmission period, under the influence of the Indian masters Shāntarakṣhita and Kamalashīla, the dogmaticist Centrist view (*svātantrika-mādhyamika; dbu ma rang rgyud pa*) prevailed. But from the eleventh century onward, in the later transmission period, Tibetan scholars began to show more interest in the dialecticist Centrist works by Chandrakīrti, as soon as these were available in their language. However, Tsong Khapa considered the mainstream views of dialecticist Centrism as still having certain problems in his time. Some scholars asserted that the true meaning of Centrism is that things neither exist nor do not exist, while others believe that a real Centrist should not advance any sort of assertion at all. According to Tsong Khapa, these views fall into indeterminism or even nihilism, because they all make the mistake of overly negating things that are not supposed to be negated. Therefore, in Tsong Khapa's view, these theories tend to deny everything, including the teaching on evolutionary ethical action (karmic evolution), which is the foundation of Buddhist ethics, and the teaching on the two truths, which is the foundation of universal vehicle practice.

It was also during Tsong Khapa's lifetime that a new philosophical stance began to gain in popularity: the so-called other-emptiness (*gzhan stong*) view, discovered by Dolpopa Sherab Gyaltsen (1292–1361). The view of "other-emptiness," as Dolpopa asserted it, is that the theory of emptiness negates conventional things, which therefore are themselves empty, so "self-empty," whereas emptiness itself, as the ultimate foundation, is only empty of those other, conventional things, hence "other-empty." This implies that the ultimate reality is permanent, stable, and unchangeable, and is the realm of an intuitive wisdom that all along has lain within the fundamental consciousness. It also asserts that this ultimate reality is the Three Jewels as the ultimate noumenon, being pervasive in the universe. Further, it is the tathāgata essence possessed by all beings, which eternally possesses all transcendent excellences of a buddha.

Having critiqued the nihilistic views mentioned above, Tsong Khapa also strongly opposed this view as absolutist, or eternalist, in fact no different from classical Hindu absolutist views. In Tsong Khapa's view, all the Indian Buddhist schools are in agreement that any permanent thing (*nityadharma, rtag chos*) is a negative thing, the opposite of a concrete entity (*bhāva, dngos po*). If the ultimate, or the tathāgata essence, were a concrete entity and also permanent, it would be unknown to all Buddhist philosophical schools, and in fact would amount to a concrete absolute of such Indian outsiders as the Vedāntins. Thus, Tsong Khapa considered the "other-emptiness" theory to be a kind of absolutism that was the very opposite of the Buddhist theory of relativistic origination (*pratītyasamutpāda, rten 'brel*).

In his works, Tsong Khapa strongly critiques these popular ideas in both nihilistic and absolutistic directions, with a clearly genius's talent for Buddhist exegesis. By means of intricate, subtle analysis, Tsong Khapa explains Chandrakīrti's Centrist view in an innovative, systematic way that achieved mainstream success in all the Tibetan Buddhist orders, with the exception of a few vociferous individual objectors arising in subsequent decades. As a result of his critique of all sides, his theory—especially his radical nondualism—was regarded by some as a dangerous heresy, which threatened the mainstream Centrist philosophy of Tibetan Buddhism.

How to evaluate the tathāgata essence doctrine was a major concern facing Tsong Khapa when he elucidated his Centrist theory. On the one hand, because it was an undeniably integral part of universal vehicle Buddhist thought, Tsong Khapa had to underscore the important position of the tathāgata essence teaching and explain its relation to the dialecticist Centrist view. On the other hand, since the tathāgata essence sutras and Asaṅga's commentary were among the most important canonical sources for Dolpopa's other-emptiness interpretations, Tsong Khapa had to make his own interpretation of the tathāgata essence theory in connection with the *Transcendent Wisdom* and *Elucidation of the Intention* sutras in order to prove that Dolpopa's absolutist interpretations could not withstand critical analysis. Nevertheless, Tsong Khapa does not discuss the tathāgata essence issue in his own works, except on a few occasions in his *Illumination of the Intent: Commentary on the Introduction to the Central Way* (*dBu ma la 'jug pa'i rnam bshad dgongs pa rab gsal*) and his *Essence of True Eloquence Treatise on the Analysis of Interpretable and Definitive Meanings* (*Drang nges legs bshad snying po*). Thus, he trusted Gyaltsap to be the one to articulate the extraction of the exquisite tathāgata essence theory from the absolutist, other-emptiness interpretation of the *The Sublime Continuum of the Universal Vehicle, Analysis of the Precious Spiritual Potential* literature and its sources. According to the epilogue to Gyaltsap's *Supercommentary*, the work is based on the teachings he received from his two main mentors, Rendawa and Tsong Khapa, with Tsong Khapa in particular to be seen as the co-author of the work.

In his *Ocean of Definitive Meaning* (*Ri chos nges don rgya mtsho*), master Dolpopa, although writing before Tsong Khapa was born, can be understood as presenting—by means of overall view and detailed interpretation of every point in *The Sublime Continuum* text—the philosophical opposition (*purvapakṣa*) of Tsong Khapa-Gyaltsap's unique understanding of Asaṅga's *Commentary* and the tathāgata essence theory. Therefore, the *Supercommentary* should be read in light of its dialogue with the other-emptiness theory, as it elucidates the inner intention of Maitreyanātha and

Asaṅga in revealing the *Tathāgata Essence Sutra* discourses as the Buddha's love and compassion-enhancing complement to the profound discourses of the *Transcendent Wisdom Sutra*.

The strength of Tsong Khapa and Gyaltsap's critique may be appreciated if one evaluates the ethical impact of the kind of absolutism they discern in the other-emptiness theory. If absolute emptiness stands aloof from self-empty relative things and can be entered in a final blissfulness apart from the beings caught in the sufferings of the cycles of ordinary life, then the bodhisattva's motivation to deploy intense compassion to create her buddha land to alleviate those beings is clearly undercut, since beings' suffering is reduced, as by brahmanical Vedānta, to the status of sheer illusion. On the other hand, if absolute emptiness *is* nothing but the relativity of all things of the life cycle and the realm of nirvanic liberation, indeed of emptiness itself, then while beings' suffering may be *illusory*, it is not a *total* illusion; it is real enough to be taken seriously and never tolerated, and the resolutely non-dual bodhisattva and tathāgata must find their bliss as the energy of their unceasing compassionate activities for the sake of all beings.

Gyaltsap's work was written in Nenying Monastery and is one of his later works. He wrote it upon the request of Gungru Gyaltsen Sangpo (1383–1450), the third abbot of Sera Monastery. According to biographical sources, Gungru Gyaltsen Sangpo himself held a philosophical view not approved by Tsong Khapa and Gyaltsap. Therefore, it is quite possible that Gyaltsap's later undertaking was meant to eliminate the doctrinal divergence among early tathāgata essence followers and to consolidate the foundation of Tsong Khapa's Ganden movement and its Geluk order of Tibetan Buddhism.

The Philosophical View

According to Tsong Khapa and Gyaltsap, the five treatises of Maitreya and the works of Asaṅga should not simply be classified as Experientialist just because their authors are considered to belong to the Experientialist school. Maitreya and Asaṅga—both in their unequivocally Experientialist works as well as in *The Sublime Continuum* and its *Commentary*—do write on a number of the same topics, such as the "Three Jewels" and "spiritual potential." Furthermore, Gyaltsap acknowledges that *The Sublime Continuum* can be interpreted either as Experientialist, dogmaticist Centrist, or dialecticist Centrist in terms of its philosophical viewpoint (with Gyaltsap himself clearly preferring a dialecticist Centrist reading). However, a peculiarity of the dialecticist Centrist school is that it asserts that every other Buddhist philosophical school should be validated as useful and even preferable for certain practitioners at certain phases of their philosophical and realizational development. Thus, it is not the case that the best Buddhist philosophers dogmatically uphold in each of their writings an unchanging view that can be formulated into one strict school with a single fixed theory. Even the Buddha himself taught different things to different disciples in different contexts.

As to the doctrinal position of Maitreya and Asaṅga's *Commentary*, prior to Tsong Khapa, Tibetan scholars had diverse opinions. Ngog Lotsawa believed its view is dogmaticist Centrist. According to Maja Jangchup Tsöndru (d. 1185), its view is dialecticist Centrist. To Butön Rinchendrup, it is either Experientialist or Centrist. To Rendawa, it is idealist. To Dolpopa Sherab Gyaltsen, it is "other-emptiness." Gö Lotsawa Shönnu Pel (1392–1481), on the other hand, uses Maitreya's tathāgata essence theory to explain the Mahāmudrā doctrine of the Kagyu school.

In his *Supercommentary*, Gyaltsap follows Tsong Khapa's position and claims that Asaṅga's philosophical view is the same as Nāgārjuna's, because the principal ideas that Maitreya's root text and Asaṅga's *Commentary* promote are those of the ultimate single vehicle and subtle emptiness. According to Tsong Khapa's dialecticist Centrism, "subtle emptiness" refers to subtle subjective selflessness, which means that the person is ultimately truthless, and subtle objective selflessness, which means that things such as matter, and so on, are truthless. These two kinds of selflessness differ in terms of their basis of negation, not in terms of their negatee, i.e., truth status. Hence, in terms of both being ultimate reality, there is no difference between coarse and subtle levels of selflessness. Tsong Khapa's dialecticist Centrist theory also asserts that the truth-habit is an addictive obscuration (*kleśāvaraṇa*), which is the root of cyclic life and hence ought to be eliminated for both individual vehicle and universal vehicle Buddhists to achieve salvation; whereas the tendency of the truth-habit itself is an objective obscuration (*jñeyāvaraṇa*), which is the final obscuration to buddhahood and is only removed by universal vehicle Buddhists. Gyaltsap believes that these thoughts can be found in Maitreya's root text and Asaṅga's *Commentary*.

When he explains Asaṅga's commentary's statement in chapter II (« 47 »), Gyaltsap says:[16]

All kinds of taints in connection with the life cycle, i.e., the childish ones' addictions, evolutionary actions, and births, are caused by the ignorance of the sole element, the suchness reality mingled with taints, which is the lack of intrinsic reality status of persons and aggregates, not truly knowing them as they are. This implies that we have to understand the element of the lack of intrinsic reality status in order to liberate ourselves from the life cycle, since it states that the life cycle is caused by the lack of understanding it. This clearly teaches that the lack of intrinsic reality status of persons and aggregates is the reality-limit, or thatness, as well as the tathāgata essence mingled with taints. It implies that grasping at truth status is the root of the life cycle and of tainted ignorance since it states that the ignorance of that [lack of intrinsic reality status] is the root of the life cycle. [TL 041A] There is no doubt as to whether the saints of the disciple vehicle and the hermit buddha vehicle have been liberated from the life cycle because there is no doubt as to whether one shall cut down the root of the life cycle in order to be liberated from it. It should be known that the liberation from the life cycle depends on the realization of truthlessness, and disciples and hermit buddhas also have experientially realized the two kinds of selflessness, since the root of the life cycle is not eradicated like thornbushes but is eradicated by means of the negation of habitual misperception by rational reasoning. This point is well established by [Asaṅga's] *Commentary* and is repeated later. As to the personal self-habit, the habit of [holding to] an individual substantial self alone does not qualify as its complete definition. Just as the grasping at the truth status of the aggregates is the grasping at the true establishment of phenomena, likewise the grasping at personal truth status is accepted as the grasping at a self of persons.

16. See translation below, p. 267.

Gyaltsap explains that "ignorance of the sole element" is the truth-habit, which is the misknowledge with respect to intrinsic realitylessness or selflessness. According to dialecticist Centrism, this truth-habit is the addictive obscuration that is the root of cyclic life and must be eliminated, even for individual vehicle Buddhists to achieve salvation. In Asaṅga's *Commentary*, there are a number of expressions of this idea in the same vein. For instance:[17]

The word "impure" refers to ordinary beings because of their addictive obscurations. The phrase "somewhat tainted" refers to disciples and hermit buddhas because of their objective obscurations. The phrase "addicted" refers to bodhisattvas because of their retaining of one or both [obscurations].

As to the assertion that there is no difference between coarse and subtle levels, Asaṅga's commentary states that "here, noumenally omniscient [intuition] should be understood as the realization of the reality-limit of the selflessness of everything, so-called 'things' and 'persons.'" Gyaltsap explains:[18]

Here, noumenally omniscient realization, [as shown by the word "liberation,]" should be understood as the experiential realization of the reality-limit of the selflessness or lack of intrinsic reality status of all beings, of just the so-called "things" including aggregates, etc., and "persons." This reality-limit is the ultimate knowable, ultimate reality, or reality as it is.

This clearly shows that the perfect understanding of subjective selflessness depends on the understanding of subjective truthlessness, since it states that subjective and objective selflessness is the limit of reality, knowable as it is.

In addition, Gyaltsap asserts that the account given in Asaṅga's *Commentary* is fully compatible with Nāgārjuna's dialecticist Centrist philosophy.

---

17. See translation below, p. 62.
18. See translation below, p. 271.

Again, Asaṅga elucidates the meaning of the *Transcendent Wisdom Sutra* by saying that:[19]

> It is said that the reality-limit is ever empty
> Of compounded things, and hence,
> Addictions, evolutionary actions,
> And effects are like clouds, etc. //I.158//

> Addictions are likened to the clouds,
> Evolution is like the experience in dreams,
> And the aggregates, effects of addictions and actions,
> Are likened to the illusions made by magic. //I.159//

Gyaltsap explains that the tathāgata essence as the suchness or the pure nature of mind is free from compounded things such as suffering and origin, which are incidental taints without the power to penetrate the nature of mind. Hence, he continues:[20]

> [T]he mere emptiness of suffering and its origin stated in this [final wheel] is taught within the context of the teaching on the emptiness of the reality of all things. The foremost addiction is the truth-habit, the conviction of the truth of things. This [truth-habit] is [merely] incidental, unable to penetrate the nature of the mind. This refers to the fact that nothing can be established in the mind as that which is apprehended by this [truth-habit], since no other techniques than the negation of the supposed object of the truth-habit can be used to establish the emptiness of the intrinsic reality of all things. If the addictions are proved to be incidental, then karmic evolution and development, which are produced by the addictions, are incidental as well.

Therefore, Gyaltsap asserts that it makes sense in the context of Asaṅga's *Commentary* that incidental taint is understood, according to Chandrakīrti's

---

19. See translation below, p. 141.
20. See translation below, p. 478.

system, as the truth-habit, which is the addictive, not the objective obscuration, as suggested in the dogmaticist Centrist system.

In brief, although Maitreya's root text and Asaṅga's *Commentary* do not present clear explanations of selflessness, different Buddhist philosophical schools have different arrangements of soteriology, such as the meditative object on the path, the negatee on the path, etc. Gyaltsap uses these philosophical devices to elucidate that the philosophical standpoint of *The Sublime Continuum* and Asaṅga's *Commentary* ought to be dialecticist Centrist.

The Tathāgata Essence Teaching

In his *Supercommentary*, Gyaltsap follows Tsong Khapa's thought and asserts that the way of deciding whether a sutra is of definitive meaning or interpretable meaning has two canonical sources: the *Teaching of Akshayamati Sutra* and the *Elucidation of the Intention Sutra*. Nāgārjuna's Centrist system follows the former, thereby viewing the *Elucidation of the Intention* as interpretable. Asaṅga's idealist system follows the latter, thus taking the *Elucidation of the Intention* as definitive in meaning.

From the standpoint of dialecticist Centrism, Gyaltsap asserts that the mass of tathāgata essence sutras such as the *Tathāgata Essence Sutra* is definitive meaning teaching, since these sutras advocate the insight that all things are intrinsically empty:[21]

> [The Buddha] explicated extensively with emphasis in the extensive, middling, and brief *Transcendent Wisdom Sutras* that all things, from matter up to omniscience, are devoid of intrinsic reality and are therefore free from all the extremes of reification. Similarly, in this *Tathāgata Essence Sutra*, which belongs to the final [Dharma] wheel, [the Buddha] explicated emphatically that the minds of sentient beings are naturally pure, as they are void of intrinsic existence and the obscuring taints are incidental in this regard. In this treatise, which is an accurate commentary on the intention of the *Tathāgata Essence Sutra*, the way of proving that taints are incidental is explicated with reference to the

21. See translation below, p. 313.

fact that addictions and conceptuality are isolated from intrinsic existence, as Asaṅga states that "addictions are terminated primordially." Just as this establishment of taints as incidental is declared in the *Transcendent Wisdom Sutra*, the reason proving that the mind is truthless[22] is also similar in meaning to what is taught in that sutra. Hence, we can know that the *Tathāgata Essence Sutra*, as an ultimate definitive meaning sutra, just like the *Transcendent Wisdom Sutra*.

In addition, the ideas presented in the tathāgata essence sutras contradict the standpoints of the *Elucidation of the Intention Sutra*. First:[23]

> In the *Elucidation of the Intention Sutra*, the bodhisattva Paramārthasamudgata asks the Buddha which sutras are interpretable in meaning and which sutras are definitive in meaning, because in some sutras the Bhagavān proclaims without distinction the intrinsic identifiability of all things, which are included in the three realities, whereas in other sutras he proclaims that all things without distinction do not have intrinsically identifiable status. The Buddha replies, with specific discrimination, that the imagined [reality] is not established by intrinsic identity, whereas the conventional and perfect [realities] are established by intrinsic identity. Paramārthasamudgata then reports to the Buddha his understanding that the first two types [of sutras mentioned in his own question] are interpretable in meaning, whereas the discriminating [sutras mentioned in the Buddha's answer] are definitive in meaning. Thus, the *Tathāgata Essence Sutra* is not involved in being an example of the definitive meaning sutras according to the *Elucidation of the Intention Sutra*, defined by the Teacher in his answer that I just quoted.

Second:[24]

But [in fact these two are not the same:] while the former states

---

22. *bden stong.*
23. See translation below, p. 238.
24. See translation below, p. 238.

that the imaginatively constructed reality is devoid of intrinsic identity and that the relative and perfect realities are established with intrinsic identity, the latter teaches that all things are devoid of intrinsic reality, thus naturally pure, and taints are [only] incidental. There are other similar [mistaken] assertions, including the assertion that the *Elucidation of the Intention Sutra*, which teaches the three final vehicles, and the *Tathāgata Essence Sutra* along with its commentary, *The Sublime Continuum*, which [latter two, in fact] promulgate the ultimate single vehicle, are in mutual agreement.

With respect to the idealist theory that can be divined in *The Sublime Continuum*, Asaṅga's *Commentary* maintains a critical stance. Further, *The Sublime Continuum* and Asaṅga's *Commentary* never talk about the fundamental consciousness (*ālayavijñāna*), which has great importance for the idealist theory.

Meanwhile, Gyaltsap points out that for Dolpopa, the form of tathāgata essence theory presented in the *Visit to Laṅka Sutra* is interpretable in meaning because Buddha himself declares that the real meaning behind this kind of theory is emptiness; its purpose is to help those outsiders who are afraid of the Buddhist idea of selflessness to gradually give up their egocentrism. The tathāgata essence sutras, and so on, are clearly not examples of this form of tathāgata essence theory. The purpose of the tathāgata essence theory presented in these sutras is to correct the five faults and to cultivate the five virtues. Therefore, it is entirely different in character from the form presented in the *Visit to Laṅka Sutra*.

The Tathāgata Essence Teaching as Belonging to the Third of the Three Stages of the Questions of King Dhāraṇīshvara Sutra

In his *Supercommentary*, Gyaltsap proposes that this three stages theory aims at the establishment of the ultimate single vehicle and presents a procedure by which a tathāgata can guide one single Buddhist to the achievement of buddhahood, and it is totally different from the three Dharma wheel theory presented in *Elucidation of the Intention Sutra*, which, as mentioned above, targets three different kinds of people who have different philosophical inclinations.

Gyaltsap explains the first stage of this three stages theory to be the preliminary to the universal vehicle, i.e., the teachings on the determination for freedom from the life cycle and the coarse form of selflessness; and he explains the second stage to be the teaching on the subtle form of selflessness. These two stages are indispensable for both individual vehicle and universal vehicle practitioners. By that explanation, Gyaltsap endeavors to show that individual vehicle Buddhists are also required to realize the subtle form of selflessness in order to achieve liberation, as mentioned above. The third stage is exclusively for a universal vehicle practitioner. Gyaltsap points out that this procedure is followed by those intelligent Buddhists who first understand the philosophy of emptiness and then cultivate the spirit of enlightenment, which is the doorway to the universal vehicle. He says:[25]

> [A]s taught in Master Shāntarakṣhita's *Ornament of the Central Way*, there are two types of stages: the stage of engaging in the path for the intelligent ones and the stage of engaging in the path for the dull ones. Here too, *The Sublime Continuum of the Universal Vehicle* directly demonstrates the stages of engaging in the path for the intelligent ones among those who possess specific potential for the universal vehicle as its intended chief disciples, and indirectly causes the other [types of stages] to be understood. What the treatise has proved is that the intelligent ones who also possess specific potential for the universal vehicle first try to convince themselves with validating cognition of the necessity and the possibility of attaining perfect buddhahood for the benefit of all sentient beings; and that they then make the commitment to conceive the actual spirit of enlightenment. Making the commitment without valid reasons is the way of the dull ones. Furthermore, while the recognition of the necessity of attaining buddhahood for the benefit of sentient beings comes from the mastery of the method of producing the genuine great compassion and high resolve,[26] the recognition of the possibility of attaining buddhahood comes from the realization of emptiness and related ideas. In light of this significance, we should know

25. See translation below, p. 236.
26. *adhyāśaya, lhag bsam.*

that for the intelligent ones it is necessary to realize emptiness before producing the desire for liberation. As for the dull ones, we can understand that they try to conceive the supreme spirit of enlightenment first, and then go on to master emptiness as taught in the third stage. We should also know that the emptiness taught in the third stage is distinguished by its connection with liberative art, thus being secondary [in terms of importance in this stage].

Gyaltsap's explanation also shows that—despite the fact that the tathāgata essence teaching that belongs to the third stage is not different from the transcendent wisdom thought, which belongs to the second stage in terms of philosophical viewpoint—the tathāgata essence teaching puts more emphasis on the universal vehicle liberative art of compassion, high resolve, and the spirit of enlightenment, etc. In short, according to Gyaltsap, the third stage is more advanced in terms of enhanced soteriology rather than a correction to the philosophical view of the second stage.

Empty and Nonempty Tathāgata Essences as Referring Respectively to the Empty Reality of Addictions and the Intrinsic Realitylessness of Addictions

With respect to the famous dual concept "empty tathāgata essence" and "nonempty tathāgata essence" as taught in the *Shrīmālādevī Lion's Roar Sutra*, Asaṅga's *Commentary* elucidates this as the dual characteristic of tathāgata essence as emptiness—its empty character eliminates the reification extreme, which mistakenly reifies something nonexistent as existent, and its nonempty character eliminates the nihilistic extreme, which mistakenly repudiates something existent as nonexistent. The real emptiness must have both characteristics. In his commentary, Gyaltsap further explains:[27]

From this element, intrinsically real addictions are absolutely nothing previously present to be newly removed. The element is primordially empty of grasping at the truth status of incidental [taints], which have a character of being separable from it by the

27. See translation below, p. 466.

cultivated affinity for antidotes. This teaches the objective condition of the twofold truth; that is, it is possible to separate the addictions by the habitual affinity for antidotes, while the addictions have never partaken of intrinsic reality from the beginning.

The emptiness of grasping at the truth status of the addictions is absolutely nothing original to be newly added upon this element. The element is not empty from the beginning of the emptiness of grasping at the truth status of the addictions, the object [of the wisdom of emptiness] that makes possible the production of the unsurpassed buddha excellences such as the powers, etc., of character indivisible from it. This teaches that the ultimate truth, the object of the wisdom that directly realizes selflessness, which is the cause of producing the buddha excellences such as the powers, etc., exists from the very beginning.

In brief, the intrinsic reality of addictions does not exist, so it is empty; the intrinsic realitylessness of addictions does exist, so it is nonempty, since on the daily conventional level, if we assert that something does not exist, at the same time we have to agree that this fact that something does not exist is true or nonempty. Hence, it is clear that Gyaltsap's statement that "the ultimate reality is primordially existent" means that the ultimate reality exists conventionally but does not exist intrinsically.

Dolpopa's view of other-emptiness has a different interpretation of this dual concept. He takes empty tathāgata essence as self-emptiness of conventional things, which means a conventional thing such as a vase is empty of itself; in other words, he thinks that a self-emptiness advocate considers that the vase does not exist at all, just like rabbit horns. He himself considers that emptiness is the absolute—the nonempty tathāgata essence—which is utterly empty of anything other than it, such as conventional things. He therefore considers the absolute to be absolutely absolute. Regarding this view, Gyaltsap asserts that for a Buddhist it will lead to the worst form of reification (*samāropa, sgro 'dogs*) and nihilism (*apavāda, skur 'debs*). As to nihilism, he comments that:[28]

Asserting the inability of any conventional thing whatsoever to

---

28. See translation below, p. 231.

be suitable as something to be apprehended, and that [for example,] a vase's being empty of being a vase is the meaning of "self-emptiness," is ultimately a nihilistic view—a repudiation of all conventional things.

According to Dolpopa's view of other-emptiness, all beings are already endowed with all transcendent excellences, which are eternal, firm, and immutable. Gyaltsap asserts that this is a form of reification; in the traditional Buddhist view, transcendent excellences are compounded things, which are instantaneous and changeable, in contrast to permanent things. Gyaltsap points out that in Indian Buddhist thought there is no such idea that something can be both a compounded thing and a permanent thing. He says:[29]

> Viewing [the ultimate truth] as a permanent entity, like blue or yellow, not depending on the negation of the negatee, amounts to the [notion] of permanence [as conceived] only by the ones outside this tradition.

Furthermore, tathāgata essence is explained as self-arisen intuition (*rang byung ye shes*) in the Dzogchen system of Tibetan Buddhism; as ordinary primordial mind (*tha mal gyi gnyug ma'i shes pa*) in the Mahāmudrā system; and as the unity of clarity and emptiness (*snang stong zung 'jug*) in the Lamdre (*lam 'bras*) system. In short, these systems assert that tathāgata essence qua ultimate reality cannot be simply a negative thing—emptiness—but it has to be possessed of intuition, mind, awareness to be nonempty tathāgata essence. Otherwise, one would fall to the extreme that holds nonexistence, since the real ultimate reality is free from the four extremes as taught in Nāgārjuna's *Root Verses on Centrism*. Therefore, Gyaltsap asserts that this view is a misunderstanding of the meaning of Nāgārjuna's *Root Verses [on Centrism]*, and a rejection of the basic principle of dual negation:[30]

> According to the root text translation, the text explains the lack of intrinsic status of non-existence, existence, and both existence

---

29. See translation below, p. 305.

30. See translation below, p. 258.

and non-existence. As for [the attempt to] explain the [proof of the] freedom from the four extremes—elaborating the lack of ultimate existence, the lack of ultimate non-existence, etc.—as easily obviated, since it is refuted by the direct contradiction that relies on mutual exclusivity; that [attempt] is just useless babbling. You may argue, "No problem, since we in our system do not assert either truth-status or truth-voidness." Well then, how do you negate asserting both of them? You may answer, "Asserting the common base of both is contradicted because they are negated [by the rule that] when you determine truth-voidness [of something], its truth-status is also excluded." Since it is necessary that truth-voidness be determined by negating through the exclusion of truth-status, then if you do not assert either one of the pair of the direct contradiction, [TL 036A] that itself is very self-contradictory! You may say, "Well those reasonings do not harm us, because we do not make any kind of assertion at all!" If you do not assert even ethics you are going to have only suffering, but maybe that is not obvious [to you]!

Again, Gyaltsap believes that in Buddhist thought, mind and so on are compounded things but not permanent things; the assertion that mind or validating cognition (*pramāṇa, tshad ma*) is a permanent thing is the non-Buddhist view of Indian Shaivism; therefore, mind and so on cannot be treated as a side of ultimate reality. He says:[31]

> In regard to the statement of [Dharmakīrti's] *Commentary on Validating Cognition*, "validating cognition is not permanent," it would be catastrophic to say that the text [merely] refutes [the position that] conventional validating cognition is permanent, for the outsider Shaivist accepts Shiva as the validating cognition of a permanent entity.

In its self-defense, the other-emptiness system claims that the permanence of the ultimate excellences is not the kind that is the opposite of impermanence; it is neither a thing nor permanent, and is totally beyond

31. See translation below, p. 317.

human intelligence. In Gyaltsap's view, those who hold the view of a thing's being neither existent nor nonexistent reject the basic principle of binary negation and are totally against the normal way of thinking about how language functions. According to Gyaltsap, this view inevitably leads to the nihilistic repudiation that claims that no assertion can be upheld. He puts forth his critique as follows:[32]

> Someone claims that the meaning of self-emptiness is similar to the assertion above. [According to this philosophical position,] no identification of anything can be made in the slightest, and hence, no distinction between being correct and incorrect can be drawn in the slightest. This position renders earnest determinations of ethical choice [undertaking-and-abandoning][33] quite useless. In such a system, the arrangement of all conventional things cannot be established by validating cognition.

The Tathāgata Essence As Not Identical to the Tathāgata

Asaṅga's commentary clearly states that "since the tathāgata element ... is the cause of attainment of the three bodies, the word 'element' is here used in the sense of 'cause.'"[34] Nevertheless, many Tibetan Buddhist scholars tend to view the tathāgata essence as the inner buddha within living beings, who already have all the excellences of buddhahood. They believe that these excellences will reveal themselves naturally when the addictions that conceal the tathāgata essence are eliminated. In Gyaltsap's view, this kind of thought is unacceptable because it is very similar to the tathāgata essence theory as taught in the *Visit to Laṅka Sutra*, and is proved neither by sutra authority nor reasoning. First, the *Visit to Laṅka Sutra* itself declares that this theory is interpretable in meaning. Second, it is rationally untenable that one person at the same time has a living being's addictions and a buddha's excellences, since addiction and excellence are in complete opposition. Gyaltsap states:[35]

32. See translation below, p. 472.
33. *heyopādeya, blang dor.*
34. See translation below, p. 453.
35. See translation below, p. 230.

Asserting that the twofold purity—i.e., the natural purity and the purity isolated from all incidental taints—exists primordially in the continuum of a sentient being, while asserting a presentation of the purifying agents, contradicts the elimination [of taints] and contradicts the actual basis of the relationship between the mental continuum of a sentient being being free from incidental taints and not being free, respectively. [These are just] the words of a confusion maker[36] who would assert such a common locus of a direct contradiction relying on a mutually exclusive contradiction.

However, some scholars also tend to use the literal meanings of the tathāgata essence sutras to find canonical support for their views. With respect to this stance, Gyaltsap shows the absurdity in a sequence of reasons that accrues to one who is only interested in a literal reading of sutras; for example, the *Buddha Garland Sutra* states that "the continuum of each sentient being is akin to the immeasurable intuitive wisdom of a tathāgata," etc. Regarding this, Gyaltsap first puts forth some questions:[37]

Reply: Let us closely examine this assertion that the truth body endowed with the twofold purity exists within the continuum of a sentient being. Do you mean that the intrinsic purity of a sentient being's mind is isolated from all incidental taints? Or do you mean that the truth body endowed with the twofold purity exists within the continuum of a sentient being as the same nature of their mind? Do you assert that [the truth body] exists in an entirely different way? Or in an inseparable way? Because you accept [the ultimate truth] as a phenomenon, do you think of it as a permanent entity? Or impermanent?

Gyaltsap then responds to a series of possible positions regarding these questions. If one responded by asserting that a living being's mind is naturally pure, Gyaltsap would reject this with the following statement:

36. *aślīla, mun sprul.*
37. See translation below, p. 303ff. for the following series of questions and answers.

In the case of the first position, any sentient being would be inevitably a buddha, yet he or she never recognizes that he or she is a buddha! If you insist that there is no fault in such an assertion, then you would be forced to make such a speech, repudiating the Buddha as a foolish, idiotic, and ignorant person, not even knowing whether he himself was a buddha or a sentient being.

If one responded by asserting that a buddha's truth body that is possessed by a sentient being and the mind of a sentient being are of the same nature, Gyaltsap would reject this with the following statement:

In the case of the second position, by taking that truth body endowed with the twofold purity that exists within the continuum of a sentient being as the basis of differentiation, is it or is it not obscured by the incidental taints in the continuum of a sentient being? If the former were the case, then it would be in contradiction to the [notion] of the truth body endowed with the twofold purity. If the latter were the case, then the continuum of a sentient being and the twofold purity would be the same in nature. This would refute your own position that the continuum of a sentient being is thoroughly tainted by taints. Furthermore, if the truth body endowed with the twofold purity existed within the continuum of a sentient being as the [mind's] reality, what else would be more incorrect than saying that [the continuum of a sentient being] is both mingled with taints and free from incidental taints in its objective condition? There is no other way that would stand up to the examination above.

If one responded by asserting that a buddha's truth body that is possessed by a sentient being and the mind of a sentient being are *not* of the same nature, Gyaltsap would reject this with the following statement:

In the case of the third position, it would be totally incorrect to assert that a sentient being and a buddha are mingled together, because two opposite simultaneous things are not able to have a relation of relativity.

If one responded by asserting that a buddha's truth body that is possessed by a sentient being has nothing to do with the mind of a sentient being, Gyaltsap would reject this with the following statement:

> In the case of the fourth position, the assertion that the truth body endowed with the twofold purity primordially and intrinsically dwells within the continuum of a sentient being in an inseparable manner would contradict all reasonings.

The same, (*Buddha Garland Sutra*) also states that "hence, a tathāgata, having seen the ultimate realm, the state of all the sentient beings, with his unobstructed intuitive wisdom, resolves to be a teacher." Based on this statement, Gyaltsap explains:[38]

> This expression clearly shows that the reality that exists within all sentient beings is designated as the intuitive wisdom of the Tathāgata, as reality is the object of the equipoise wisdom of the Tathāgata and the Tathāgata's intuitive wisdom is produced by directly realizing the ultimate, and meditating on it to completion.

In Gyaltsap's view, here "tathāgata intuition" cannot be taken as the intuition itself. Instead it refers to the object of a tathāgata's intuition, which is the ultimate reality. In the same vein, the Buddha states that "all these tathāgatas [within sentient beings' addiction] are just like me without any difference." Here "tathāgata" means the tathāgata noumenon, as indicated by the sutra itself. It is worth noting that according to Tsong Khapa's hermeneutics, some statements have to be understood as having a "specific qualification" (*khyad par sbyar ba*) in order to properly understand their meaning. For example, the *Transcendent Wisdom Heart Sutra* states that there is no matter, no feeling, no thought, etc. If such statements were taken literally, then one would draw the conclusion that this sutra rejects the existence of any possible thing. Hence, Tsong Khapa explains that statements like these need to be interpreted as having an understood "specific qualification"—in this case, "ultimately"—in order to properly convey their meaning.

38. See translation below, p. 306.

That is to say, teachings such as "there is no matter" in a sutra such as the *Transcendent Wisdom Heart Sutra*, where the qualifications "in the ultimate" and "in truth" are not explicitly applied, are not fit to be accepted literally as taught, and thus are interpretable, requiring further interpretation by supplying the qualifications "in the ultimate," etc., since "eye" and "ear," etc., are only nonexistent ultimately and are not nonexistent conventionally. However, this analysis also means that the sutras such as the *Transcendent Wisdom Hundred Thousand*, which apply such qualifications as "in the ultimate sense" to their negatees, are established as literally definitive in meaning; thus, the statement that some sutras of the second Dharma wheel are interpretable in meaning does not apply to all (the sutras) of the second wheel.

Again, some scholars often cite one of the similes in the *Tathāgata Essence Sutra*—that of treasure underneath the ground in the house of a poor family—in order to show that a living being already has all buddha excellences without knowing it. Starting from the meaning of "treasure," Gyaltsap explains that no such implication can be found in the sutra:[39]

> This passage does not demonstrate that a buddha endowed with the twofold purity exists within the continuums of sentient beings, since it states literally that the tathāgata essence is a treasure from which the powers, etc., will come about. It does not state that the tathāgata essence is the excellences such as the powers, etc., in and of themselves, since earlier the sutra states:
>
>> Within afflicted beings possessing all addictions there exists the reality of the Tathāgata that is immovable and is not affected by any state of existence. Perceiving this, the Buddha proclaims: "They are all like me!"
>
>> Intending sentient beings' possession of reality as the mind's nature, which is not different from the reality of the Tathāgata and is never penetrated by the taints, the Buddha proclaims: "They are all like me!"

39. See translation below, p. 473.

Gyaltsap then comes to the conclusion that:[40]

> If this meaning of the word as stated in the sutra were unacceptable, since in this sutra the Buddha also states "perceiving all living beings' tathāgata essence," you have to accept sentient beings themselves as tathāgata essence. In order to avoid the misunderstanding that there exists within the continuum of a sentient being a buddha's truth body endowed with the twofold purity, the sutra clearly states the existence of the reality, not the truth body endowed with the twofold purity as fabricated in someone's system.

The Tathāgata Essence: Foundation of Universal Vehicle Soteriology

Gyaltsap talks about the seven subjects, the Buddha, and so on, which are called the seven vajra topics. In his *Supercommentary*, Gyaltsap explains the seven vajra topics in two dimensions: ultimate and conventional. Here both the terms "ultimate" and "conventional" have meanings that differ from their regular meanings used in connection with ontology. In the context of the element, "ultimate" here refers to the inner realizations of buddhas or bodhisattvas, and "conventional" refers to the outer embodiment of these realizations.

According to *The Sublime Continuum*, a causal relation, that is, a progression of thought, exists among the seven subjects. Specifically, Buddha, Dharma, and Saṅgha are the fruition; the element is the cause; and enlightenment, the excellences, and the activities are the conditions. Gyaltsap gives a detailed exposition on this relation based on Maitreya's verse I.3. First, he explains that Buddha, Dharma, and Saṅgha are the spiritual goal or fruition for a universal vehicle Buddhist to achieve:[41]

> From the perfect complete Buddha [who is enlightened] with regard to all things comes the turning of the wheel of Dharma for noble beings. The gathering of numerous noble assemblies

40. See translation below, p. 474.

41. See translation below, p. 242.

of disciples, the supreme Saṅgha Jewel, comes in turn from the turning of the wheel of Dharma. The turning of the wheel of Dharma after attaining perfect buddhahood is the object[42] of the spirit of enlightenment in the universal vehicle produced in the continuums of the intended disciples of *The Sublime Continuum*, while the arising of numerous noble assemblies dependent on that wheel is the objective of the conception of the spirit of enlightenment.

Because of the holy assemblies, the tathāgata essence occurs. It means that, in order to attain the ultimate Three Jewels, the [causal] Three Jewels are the immediate causes, and then to gather the noble assemblies as the fruition of the turning of the wheel of Dharma, we wish to purify the tathāgata essence of the taints. Thus, there arises the tathāgata essence that is purified from taints to a certain degree.[43] How long will this tathāgata essence last? It will last until its attainment of the "element of a buddha's intuitive wisdom,"[44] freed from all taints. Throughout this duration, the suchness reality mingled with taints, the receptivity[45] of the continuums of sentient beings for the entrance of the Buddha's enlightened activities, and the spiritual potential are called the "tathāgata essence." After the attainment of a buddha's intuitive wisdom, this designation no longer exists.

And the purification of the inner cause can only be successful when the outer conditions provided by enlightened ones' enlightenment, excellences, and activities are met:[46]

The attainment of a buddha's intuitive wisdom, which is free of all taints after the purification of the element, is called "supreme

42. *ālambana, dmigs pa.*

43. *ci rigs pa.*

44. *jñāna-dhātv-āpti-niṣṭhaḥ.* Owing to the ambiguity in Ngog-lo's translation (*snying po ye shes khams thob mtha'*), Rong-ston takes *garbho jñāna* as a compound, referring to a buddha's intuitive wisdom. See *Legs bshad*, 59. This seems not to be the correct rendition as suggested by the Sanskrit edition.

45. *'jug rung.*

46. See translation below, p. 243.

enlightenment." The excellences dependent on that enlightenment, including the powers, confidences, and distinctive excellences of a buddha, are indicated as the distinctive features
of enlightenment. And the enlightened activities dependent
on the excellences, which benefit all sentient beings in both
simultaneous and ceaseless ways, are indicated as the distinctive
features of the excellences.

Here the enlightened activities are mainly the giving of teachings, which
theoretically is never absent, since buddhas continuously engage in teaching
activity that springs from their compassion. In short, the sutra statement
that all living beings are endowed with the tathāgata essence is based on
the fact that a living being's mind is always free from intrinsic reality and
the buddha activity is always present. Since all beings do not lack such a
foundation, by means of practice we all can eliminate our own addictions
and achieve the final goal of buddhahood. This is the gist of Gyaltsap's
commentary.

In summary, by means of a thorough exegetical analysis rooted in the
texts themselves, Gyaltsap points out that the concept of tathāgata essence
has a dual meaning in both the ontological-philosophical sense and the
soteriological sense; and he emphasizes the latter. Gyaltsap clearly opposes
the idea that there is a distinctive view of the tathāgata essence that is independent of the universal vehicle philosophical schools, either Maitreya's
Experientialism or Nāgārjuna's Centrism. This is in marked contrast with
other theories of the tathāgata essence developed in Tibetan Buddhism.

In the Gelukpa monastic curriculum many of the topics raised by Asaṅga
reference Gyaltsap's works. These topics include the Dharma wheels, the
Three Jewels, the spiritual potential, the ultimate single vehicle, whether
the life cycle has an end or not, whether all beings ultimately become buddhas or not, a buddha's ten powers, the truth body, and so on.

After Gyaltsap, Gelukpa scholars who wrote commentaries on Asaṅga's
Commentary include Panchen Sönam Drakpa (1478–1554), Choney
Drakpa Shedrup (1675–1749), Mugey Samten Gyatso (1914–1993), and so
on. Once the *Ornament of Clear Realization* (Maitreya), the *Commentary
on Validating Cognition* (Dharmakīrti), the *Introduction to the Central Way*
(Chandrakīrti), the *Discipline Sutra* (Guṇaprabha), and the *Treasury of*

Abhidharma (Vasubandhu) were established as the core curriculum texts in the Gelukpa monastic university education system, Gyaltsap's commentary was rarely taught as a solo text, but it was often referenced during the study of the *Ornament of Clear Realization* and the *Introduction to the Central Way.*

Part Two

TRANSLATIONS

*Maitreyanātha's Sublime Continuum
and
Noble Asaṅga's Commentary*

CHAPTER I
The Tathāgata Essence

I bow down to all buddhas and bodhisattvas!

«1» The body of the whole treatise is condensed
Into these seven vajra topics:
The Buddha, the Dharma, and the Saṅgha, the element,
The enlightenment, the excellences, and last,
The enlightened activities of a buddha. //I.1//

The vajra-like topics, that is, the topics to be understood, are vajra topics, because they are the topics [of the teachings].

«2» Because these [topics] are difficult to realize by means of only the knowledge that comes from learning and critical thinking, they should be known as vajra-like topics, whose inexpressible nature is to be realized by one's experientially discerning [intuitive wisdom]. The letters that express these topics are called "sites," because they are the means of teaching the path that leads to the attainment of that [realization], so are its sites. Hence, since the [topics] are hard to realize and [the letters serve as their] sites, one should understand that the topics and the letters [expressing them] are the vajras and the sites, [respectively].

«3» Now, what are these topics, and what are the letters?

The seven topics that are to be understood are as follows: the topic of the Buddha, the topic of the Dharma, the topic of the Saṅgha, the topic of the element, the topic of the enlightenment, the topic of the excellences, and the topic of the enlightened activities. They are called "topics." The letters, with which the seven topics to be understood are taught and elucidated, are called "letters."

«4» The details of the teaching of the vajra topics should be understood in accordance with the sutras:[47]

«5» O Ānanda, the Tathāgata cannot be shown, for he cannot be seen with the eyes. O Ānanda, the Dharma cannot be expressed, for it cannot be heard with the ears. O Ānanda, the Saṅgha is not created, for it cannot be served by body or mind.

Thus, [the first] three vajra topics should be understood by following the [above cited] *Chapter on Firm High Resolve Sutra.*
    «6» [Likewise, the *Sutra Teaching the Absence of Increase and Decrease (in the Realm of Beings)* reads:][48]

O Shāriputra, this topic is an object for a tathāgata. It belongs to a tathāgata's sphere of experience. O Shāriputra, since even temporarily this topic can be neither known, seen, nor discerned correctly by all the disciples and hermit buddhas by means of their own wisdom, what need is there to mention childish, alienated individuals? It is realized by means of faith in the Tathāgata, and not otherwise. O Shāriputra, ultimate reality is to be realized by means of faith. O Shāriputra, this so-called ultimate reality is a term for the element[49] of sentient beings. O Shāriputra, the so-called element of sentient beings is a term for the tathāgata essence. O Shāriputra, the so-called tathāgata essence is a term for the truth body.

[Thus,] the fourth vajra topic should be understood by following the *Sutra Teaching the Absence of Increase and Decrease [in the Realm of Beings].*

---

47. PD70 (phi), p. 988.9–12. H225, fol. 280a.4–6. D224, f. 172b.2–3.

48. The Tibetan identifies the source of the quote as the *'grib pa med pa dang 'phel ba med pa nyid bstan pa*, Skt., *Anūnatvā-pūrṇatva-nirdeśa-parivarta*. This text does not appear to be extant in Tibetan translation (although Nanjio indicated that it was); however, there is an apparent translation of this sutra found in the Chinese canon (佛說不增不減經; T.668), translated by Bodhiruci in 525 CE (6th year of Cheng Kuang [正光], Yüan Wei dynasty [元魏]): PD70 (phi), pp. 988.14–989.2; T.668, 467a.

49. *dhātu, khams.*

«7» [Another sutra passage reads:]⁵⁰

> O Bhagavān, the so-called unsurpassed perfect complete enlightenment is a term for the "realm of nirvana." O Bhagavān, the so-called realm of nirvana is a term for the "truth body of a tathāgata."

Here, the fifth vajra topic should be understood by following the *Shrīmālādevī Lion's Roar Sutra*.

«8» [Again, a sutra passage reads:]⁵¹

> O Shāriputra, the truth body taught by the Tathāgata is like this: it has the excellence of the intuitive wisdom that never loses its endowment with qualities indivisible from the qualities of tathāgatas more numerous than the grains of sand of the Ganges river.

Thus, the sixth vajra topic should be understood by following the *Sutra Teaching the Absence of Increase and Decrease [in the Realm of Beings]*.

«9» [Another sutra passage reads:]⁵²

> O Mañjushrī, a tathāgata does not conceptualize, nor does he engage in discrimination. However, [a tathāgata] effortlessly engages in all natural activities, without conceptualizing and without engaging in discriminations.

Thus, the seventh vajra topic should be understood by following the *Sutra Showing the Entry into the Realm of the Inconceivable Excellences and Wisdom of the Tathāgatas*.

Thus, to summarize, one should understand these seven vajra topics to be the body of the whole of this treatise, since they serve to collect the meanings that give access to the teaching.

---

50. PD70 (phi), p. 989.4–7. H92 fol. 440a.4–7. D92, f. 269a.1–2.
51. PD70 (phi), p. 989.8–12. T.668, 467a.
52. PD70 (phi), p. 989.13–17. H186 fol. 187b.4–5.

«10» Regarding these [seven topics]:[53]

Connected in proper order by their defining characteristics,
The [first] three of these topics should be known
From the introductory chapter of the *[Questions of] King
    Dhāraṇīshvara Sutra,*
And the [remaining] four from [the chapters on] the excel-
lences of the intelligent [bodhisattvas] and the Victors.
//I.2//

«11» From among these seven vajra topics, connected in proper order by
their own defining characteristics, the [first] three topics should be known
from the introductory chapter of the *Questions of King Dhāraṇīshvara
Sutra,* and the remaining four that follow, from the chapters on the excellences of bodhisattvas and tathāgatas.
 «12» In that [same sutra, it states]:[54]

The Bhagavān became manifestly and perfectly enlightened in
the equality of all things, beautifully turned the Dharma wheel,
and commanded a limitless host of disciples who are extremely
calm.

One should understand these three sutra phrases, respectively, as presenting
the sequential arising of the Three Jewels. The remaining four topics should
be known as the statement of the causes that correspond to the arising of
the Three Jewels.
 «13» Now, since when one arrives on the eighth bodhisattva stage, one
comes to attain sovereignty over all things, the sutra says:[55]

Having gone to the supreme essence of enlightenment, [the
Bhagavān] became directly and perfectly enlightened in the
equality of all things.

53. PD70 (phi), pp. 989.20–990.2.
54. PD70 (phi), p. 990.6–9. D147, f. 142a.4–5.
55. PD70 (phi), p. 990.14–15. D147, f. 142a.6.

«14» Since on the ninth bodhisattva stage one becomes the unexcelled exponent of the teaching, knowing full well the thought patterns of all sentient beings, having reached the transcendence of supreme spiritual faculties and become expert in the destruction of the chain of addictive evolutionary instincts in all sentient beings, the sutra says:[56]

> The manifest perfect Buddha beautifully turned the wheel of the Dharma.

«15» Since on the tenth bodhisattva stage, immediately after obtaining consecration as the unsurpassed Dharma regent of the Tathāgata, one will attain the effortless and uninterrupted activities of a buddha, thus it states:[57]

> [Having] beautifully turned the Dharma wheel, [the Bhagavān] commands a numberless host of disciples who are extremely calm.

The meaning of "numberless disciples who are extremely calm" is further taught by this text. Immediately after that sentence, [there is the sutra statement] from:[58]

> [The Buddha was dwelling] together with a great assembly of mendicants...

up to:

> ... together with an inconceivable number of hosts of bodhisattvas.

Regarding the statement "being endowed with such excellences," since [these disciples] were perfectly calm—[and destined] either for

---

56. PD70 (phi), p. 990.20–21. D147, f. 142b.2.
57. PD70 (phi), p. 991.3–5. D147, f. 143a.1.
58. PD70 (phi), p. 991.5–7. D147, f. 143a.2–4.

the enlightenment of a disciple or for the enlightenment of a buddha, respectively—[they are said to be] endowed with such excellences.

«16» And then, immediately after [the section of] the teaching on the praises of excellences of disciples and bodhisattvas, one should understand [the section of] the accomplishment of a magnificent hall adorned with precious jewels, created by the inconceivable royal samādhi of the Buddha, the gathering of the Tathāgata's retinue, the accomplishment of various celestial offerings, and the showering of rain from the cloud of praises as the orderly presentation of the distinctive excellences of the Buddha Jewel.

«17» And then, by the splendid array of the Dharma throne and the light, and by widely proclaiming the name of this formulation of teachings and its excellences, one should understand [this section] as the orderly presentation of the distinctive excellences of the Dharma Jewel.

«18» And then, one should understand [the section of] teaching on the power of each of the objects of engagement of the samādhis of bodhisattvas, and various praises of their excellences, as the orderly presentation of the distinctive excellences of the Saṅgha Jewel.

«19» And then, by being consecrated by the light rays of the Buddha, the unsurpassed principal child of the Dharma King becomes endowed with fearlessness and supreme eloquence and teaches the praise of the ultimate impeccable excellences of the Tathāgata. [This section of the sutra] actually states the substance of the discourse concerning the supreme Dharma of the universal vehicle and teaches the attainment of the supreme sovereignty of the Dharma as the fruition of [those] led to realize it. In light of this, [this section] is regarded as the orderly presentation of the distinct unsurpassed excellences of the Three Jewels and indicates the ending of the introductory section.

«20» Then, after the introductory section of the sutra, the teaching on the sixty types of thorough purification of the excellences that [constitute] its thorough purity serves to elucidate the buddha element. This is because only if the object that is to be thoroughly purified is endowed with excellences will its thorough purification be feasible.

«21» In the light of this, the *Sutra on the Ten Stages* uses the simile of the process of purifying gold. In this *[King Dhāraṇīshvara] Sutra* too, after the teaching on a tathāgata's enlightened activities, the simile of unpurified sapphire is used:[59]

---

59. PD70 (phi), pp. 992.15–993.14. D147, ff. 215b.1–7; 159a.6–167b.1.

O noble child, take for example a skillful jeweler who knows well how to cleanse a gem. Having picked out a precious jewel that has been thoroughly tainted from the mine, and having soaked it in a strong solution of sal-ammoniac, he then polishes it by rubbing it with a very refined ox-hair cloth. But his efforts in just this way are not yet finished. After that, having soaked the jewel in strong, fermented fruit juice, he polishes it with a cloth of wool. But his efforts in just this way are still not yet finished. After that, having soaked it in a great medicine essence, he polishes it with fine cotton cloth. Being thus completely purified, when it is free of all impurities, it is called "precious sapphire."

O noble child, just so, a tathāgata, knowing the scope of the sentient beings who are not purified, by means of disturbing descriptions of impermanence, suffering, selflessness, and impurity, makes those sentient beings who delight in the life cycle [instead] become averse to it, and so causes them to enter into the noble Dharma code of discipline.

With just these [acts], a tathāgata does not cease in his efforts. After that, he causes them to realize the way of the Tathāgata, by means of the instructions on emptiness, signlessness, and wishlessness. With just these [acts], a tathāgata does not cease in his efforts. Next, he installs those sentient beings of various dispositions in the buddha realm by means of the teaching of irreversibility and the teaching of the total purification of the three sectors [of actions]. When they have entered and have realized the reality of a tathāgata, they are called "the unsurpassed worthies for offerings."

«22» Intending this tathāgata element, which is the totally pure potential, [the Buddha] declares [in a certain sutra]:[60]

Just as in the gravelly sand,
The pure gold cannot be seen,

60. PD70 (phi), p. 992.16–17. See Brunnhölzl, n. 1144 for various similar verses in a few sutras.

But does become visible when purified,
Such is the Tathāgata in this world.

«23» Now, which are the sixty purifications with excellence in purifying the buddha element? They are: the four types of bodhisattva ornaments; the eight types of bodhisattva illuminations; the sixteen types of a bodhisattva's great compassion; and the thirty-two types of bodhisattva activities.

«24» Immediately after this statement, [the *King Dhāraṇīshvara Sutra*] elucidates a buddha's enlightenment by teaching the sixteen types of great compassion. Next, the sutra elucidates a buddha's excellences by describing the ten powers, four fearlessnesses, and eighteen special qualities of a buddha. And next, the sutra elucidates a buddha's thirty-two enlightened activities by describing the unsurpassed activities of a tathāgata.

«25» Thus, these seven vajra topics should be understood—according to the sutra—extensively, from the perspective of the teachings on their defining characteristics.

If you ask, "What is the connection between these?"

From the Buddha comes the Dharma;
From the Dharma in turn comes the noble assembly;
From the assembly comes the [tathāgata] essence,
Which ends by attaining the intuition element.
Attaining that intuitive wisdom is supreme enlightenment,
Endowed with the excellences that benefit all beings. //I.3//

This concludes the explanation of the coherence of the treatise.

[THE BUDDHA JEWEL]

«26» Now the meaning of the verses should be explained.

Those sentient beings who were educated by the Tathāgata take refuge in the Tathāgata, and take refuge in the Dharma and Saṅgha by means of the pure faith that is causally concordant with reality.

«27» Thus, since that is the very first of [the Three Jewels], one verse is composed concerning the Buddha Jewel:

I bow to Him who attained buddhahood,
Peaceful, without beginning, middle, or end,
Who from His realization taught the path,
Fearless and firm, to awaken the unenlightened,
Who raises the supreme sword of wisdom
And wields the thunderbolt of compassion
To cut through all the weeds of suffering
And smash the great barrier of perplexity
Buried deep in the jungle of various views. //I.4//

What is shown by this [verse]?

Uncreated and spontaneously established,
Not realized by depending on others,
Endowed with intuition, compassion, and power,
Only buddhahood gives the two kinds of benefit. //I.5//

«28» This [verse] briefly explains buddhahood, which is endowed with
eight excellences. What are the eight excellences? They are: (1) being uncreated; (2) being spontaneous; (3) not realized by relying on others; (4) intuitive wisdom; (5) compassion; (6) power; (7) fulfillment of self-benefit; and
(8) fulfillment of bringing benefit to others.

It is uncreated because its nature
Is without beginning, middle, or end.
It is said to be spontaneous,
Possessing the peace of the body of truth. //I.6//

It is not realized by relying on others,
Since it must be realized by oneself alone.
It is wisdom, since it realized these three.
It is love because it shows the path. //I.7//

It is power, since with wisdom and compassion
It banishes suffering and addictions.
The first three fulfill self-benefit;
The last three are altruistic. //I.8//

«29» The word "uncreated" should be understood as the opposite of the created, which is to be understood as what is born, endures, and is destroyed. Free of these things, buddhahood should be seen as uncreated, being free of beginning, middle, and end, distinguished as the truth body.

«30» It is "spontaneous" since all elaborations and conceptualizations have been eradicated.

«31» It is "not realized by the influence of others" because it is realized by means of the self-arisen intuitive wisdom. Here the word "realized" (*udaya*) means "clear realization," not referring to "production." Thus, though it is uncreated, being the tathāgata reality, and of the characteristic of nonengagement, all buddhas' activities spontaneously proceed until the end of cyclic life, without obstacle or interruption. Not having heard from others about such an absolutely wonderful, inconceivable goal, buddhas themselves, without a mentor, became perfectly awakened in their inexpressible nature by means of their self-arisen intuitive wisdom.

«32» [Buddhas] should be understood as being endowed with the unsurpassed intuitive wisdom and compassion since they cause the others, who are totally blind to such realization, to realize it, and show the path to its realization. This path is fearless because it is transcendent; it is transcendent because it is irreversible.

«33» The way both the intuitive wisdom and the compassion of the Tathāgata are capable of destroying the roots of others' suffering and addiction are shown by the similes of sword and thunderbolt, respectively. Of these, the root of suffering, in brief, is any kind of name and matter (*nāmarūpa*) produced in cyclic life. The root of addiction is any view or doubt based on a conviction about the futile aggregates (*satkāya*). Here, the suffering involved in name and matter should be regarded as weed-like because of its character of production. The simile of a sword shows the power of the Tathāgata's intuitive wisdom and compassion, since both cut that [root]. The delusion included in view and doubt, which is to be removed on the path of insight, is difficult to understand and hardly to be realized by mundane knowledge. Therefore it is akin to a wall surrounded by dense jungle. It should be known that [the power of] the Tathāgata's intuitive wisdom and compassion is illustrated by the simile of a thunderbolt because both destroy that [root].

«34» Thus, the six excellences of the Tathāgata aforementioned should be understood by this very order and with detailed statements according to the *Ornament of the Light of Wisdom Engaging the Sphere of All Buddhas Sutra*. In that sutra, [the Buddha says]:[61]

> O Mañjushrī, this [saying] "without production and destruction" is a designation for the Tathāgata, the Saint, the Perfectly Enlightened One.

This statement shows that the Tathāgata is of uncreated nature. And immediately after this, [the sutra] gives nine similes with respect to this point, starting with the simile of the reflection of Indra on the surface of a stainless sapphire floor:[62]

> «35» Likewise, O Mañjushrī, the Tathāgata, the Saint, the Perfectly Enlightened One neither moves nor intends any proliferation. He does not make notions, does not use concepts, has no notions, no concepts, no intentions, and no mentation. He is cool. He has neither birth nor cessation. He cannot be seen, or heard, or smelled, or tasted, or touched, and has no sign, no consciousness, and is not to be recognized.

Such is the statement on the term "peace." This shows that the Tathāgata is spontaneous since, in his own activities, all imagination and conceptualization have ceased to exist.

«36» After this, i.e., after the statement of [nine] similes, the remaining sutra shows that the gate to the perfect enlightenment in the thatness of all things is not something realized by other conditions.

«37» And after the statements on a tathāgata's sixteen kinds of enlightenment, [the Buddha says]:[63]

> O Mañjushrī, once manifestly perfectly enlightened about all things having such a nature, the Tathāgata sees the element in

---

61. PD70 (phi), p. 997.6–8. D100, f. 280a.2–4.

62. PD70 (phi), p. 997.12–20. D100, f. 280a.4–6.

63. Adopting this more sensible translation from the Tibetan. PD70 (phi), p. 998.5–10 (with an error in editing, omitting a *ma* in *dri ma dang {ma} bral ba*). See Brunnhölzl, 340n1167, referring to D100, f. 298a.6–7. Also the further phrase in the D. version "as pure, taintless, and unaddicted" added to the second mention of "all beings," is not in this quote.

all sentient beings as impure, not untainted, and addicted, and he then unleashes the Tathāgata's great compassion for all beings known as "skillful love."

This expresses the Tathāgata's possession of intuitive wisdom and compassion. There, shown in an orderly manner, the phrase "all things having such a nature" means being free of intrinsic reality. The phrase "once manifestly perfectly enlightened" means knowing truly and exactly with the buddha nonconceptual intuitive wisdom. The phrase "all sentient beings" means those who belong to the three types: impure [ordinary beings], somewhat tainted [saints], and addicted [bodhisattvas]. The word "element" means the buddha essence, which is not different from the nature of [the Buddha] himself. The phrase "sees" means perceives all kinds through the buddha eye for which nothing is obscure. The word "impure" refers to ordinary beings because of their addictive obscurations. The phrase "somewhat tainted" refers to disciples and hermit buddhas because of their [remaining] objective obscurations. The phrase "addicted" refers to bodhisattvas because of their retaining one or both [obscurations]. The word "skillful love" is used for the reason that [a buddha purifies] disciples by means of various techniques. The phrase "unleashes the great compassion for all beings" means that a buddha realizes that his enlightenment is equally present in all beings and so is moved to [help them] realize their own true [buddha] nature.

Then, having developed the unsurpassed intuitive wisdom and compassion, [a buddha] acts constantly to make the unparalleled Dharma wheel enter into [the disciples' continuums]. It should be known that this [activity] shows the power of both [intuitive wisdom and compassion] to bring benefit to other beings.

≪38≫ Here, of these six excellences of a tathāgata, in the order of the list, the endowment of the first three excellences, uncreated, etc., is the fulfillment of self-benefit, and endowment of the remaining three, intuitive wisdom, etc., is the fulfillment of others' interests. Or else, the word "intuitive wisdom" shows the fulfillment of self-benefit since it is the excellence of [a buddha's] own enlightenment, the absolutely eternal, peaceful place. The words "compassion" and "power" show the fulfillment of benefit to others because it is the excellence of constantly making the unsurpassed Dharma wheel enter [into the continuums of disciples].

[THE DHARMA JEWEL]

≪39≫ Now, from the Buddha Jewel there originates the Dharma Jewel. Therefore, immediately after [the explanation of the Buddha Jewel], there is one verse concerning the Dharma Jewel:[64]

> Not something, not nothing, not both, nor other [than those],
> Inconceivable, unverbalizable—inwardly realized peace,
> Shining with light rays of stainless intuition,
>   Conquering lust, hate, and delusion toward all objects—
> I bow down to that holy Dharma sun! //I.9//

What is shown by this verse?

> The Dharma has the nature of two [of the four] truths,
> Which are, respectively, the cause of nonattachment and nonattachment itself,
> [The former] with its purity, illumination, and medicinal force,
> [The latter] inconceivable, nondual, and nonconceptual.
>   //I.10//

≪40≫ This [verse] briefly explains the Dharma Jewel as having eight excellences. What are the eight excellences? Namely: (1) inconceivability; (2) nonduality; (3) nonconceptuality; (4) purity; (5) illumination; (6) medicinality; (7) nonattachment; and (8) the cause of nonattachment.

> Nonattachment itself is included
> In both [noble] truths, of cessation and path.
> It should be known that each of these
> Has three excellences, respectively. //I.11//

≪41≫ The truth of cessation is shown, in order, by the first three of the six excellences, i.e., inconceivability, nonduality, and nonconceptuality— and thus one should understand that nonattachment is included there. The truth of the path is shown by the remaining three excellences, i.e., purity,

---

64. PD70 (phi), p. 1000.

illumination, and medicine; and so one should understand that the cause of nonattachment is included there. That which is nonattachment is the truth of cessation and that which causes nonattachment is the truth of the path. Including the two together, the Dharma is said to be "the nonattachment characterized by these two truths concerned with purification."

> Not being a conceptual object, being inexpressible,
> To be known by noble ones, Dharma is inconceivable.
> It is peaceful, nondual, and nonconceptual—
> With its three [excellences,] purity, etc., it is like the sun.
> //I.12//

«42» In short, the truth of cessation should be known to be inconceivable for three reasons. If you ask, "What are these three?" It is not an object of conceptions of the four possibilities—nonexistence, existence, both existence and nonexistence, neither existence nor nonexistence; it cannot be expressed by any sound, language, expression, referent, symbol, convention, or verbalization; and it is realized by the individual introspective wisdom of noble ones.

«43» If you ask, "How should the truth of cessation be known as nondual and nonconceptual?" The Bhagavān declares as follows [in the *Sutra Teaching the Absence of Increase and Decrease (in the Realm of Beings)*]:[65]

> O Shāriputra, this "cessation" is the truth body; with its quality of nonduality, it is nonconceptual reality.

«44» Here "duality" refers to evolutionary actions and the addictions. "Conceptual" refers to inappropriate mental engagement, the cause that originates evolutionary actions and addictions. This teaches that, since there is a natural cessation that is individually experienced, the definite nonorigination of suffering by way of non-engagement with conceptuality and duality is the truth of the cessation of suffering, and [does] not [teach] that the truth of cessation of suffering is the destruction of something. This is explained in detail in the *[Ornament of the Light of Wisdom] Sutra*:[66]

65. PD70 (phi), p. 1001.10–11; T.668, 467b.
66. PD70 (phi), pp. 1001.18–1002.3; D100, ff. 297a.7–297b.2.

O Mañjushrī, this unborn and unceased [reality] is not engaged as mind, mentality, and consciousness. What is not engaged as mind, mentality, and consciousness is free of any conceptuality conceiving any sort of inappropriate mental engagement. Applying oneself with appropriate mental engagement never causes the arising of ignorance. The nonarising of ignorance means the nonarising of the twelve links of cyclic life. It is the unborn, etc.

Also stated in the *[Shrīmālādevī Lion's Roar] Sutra*:[67]

O Bhagavān, the destruction of something is not the cessation of suffering. O Bhagavān, the "cessation of suffering" indicates the Tathāgata's truth body, which is beginningless in time, uncreated, unproduced, unarisen, unexhausted, free of exhaustion, permanent, stable, peace, undestroyed, naturally totally pure, liberated from the sheath of all addictions, indivisible, and endowed with the inconceivable excellences of a buddha, which are far beyond the sands of the Ganges in number. O Bhagavān, this very truth body of the Tathāgata, when not yet released from the sheath of addictions, is called the "buddha essence."[68]

Full details of how to arrange the truth of cessation of suffering should be understood according to these sutras.

« 45 » The causes of the attainment of the truth body of a tathāgata under the name "cessation of suffering" are the path of insight and the path of meditation based on nonconceptual intuitive wisdom. It should be understood that [nonconceptual intuitive wisdom] is like the sun as a result of three correspondences. [Namely], it corresponds to the sun's (1) purity, since it is free from all taints of addictions; (2) illumination of forms, since it illuminates all aspects of knowable objects; and (3) remedy for darkness, since it is the remedy to all obstructions of perceiving thatness.

---

67. PD70 (phi), p. 1002.4–13; D92, f. 272a.

68. *tathāgata-garbha. Garbha* literally means "womb," which causes one to wonder why the euphemistic translation of Tib. *snying po*, "essence." What would the centuries of discussion on non-Sanskrit Buddhist languages be like if it were about whether or not beings all have the "buddha-womb?" A womb is something pertaining only to female mammals, not males.

«46» "Obstruction" means the instinctual and activated production of attachment, hatred, and delusion, which is preceded by the mental orientation toward causal objects that are unreal things. The childish ones develop attachment from the causal instinct for unreal phenomena—which lack intrinsic reality—because of things' desirable looks; develop hatred, because of their detestable looks; and develop delusion, because of their obscure looks. The cause of attachment, hatred, and ignorance is the inappropriate mental engagement from observing unreal things. Hence, the childish ones whose minds are occupied by inappropriate mental engagement will activate attachment, hatred, or ignorance.

«47» On these bases, the karmic evolution that is produced by attachment associated with body, speech, and mind will develop, and also that produced by hatred and ignorance. Karmic evolution will inevitably be connected with birth. Hence, immature beings who have instinctually latent sign-habits[69] engage with objects and originate inappropriate mentation, which originates addictions. Their origination of addictions originates karmic evolutionary actions which in turn originate birth. For these immature beings, all these forms of total addictiveness of addictions, evolutionary actions, and birth function from their not knowing realistically the sole element. Furthermore, one should understand that no matter how much one investigates realistically, one can not see any sign or object whatsoever. When one does not see any causal sign or object, one sees truly. Thus, by means of such equanimity, a tathāgata attains completely perfect buddhahood in total equality.

«48» Thus, since no object can be perceived as a result of its non-[intrinsic] existence, and since the ultimate reality can be perceived for its existence as real as it is, it neither is negated nor established. [Thus, the Tathāgata] has realized the equality of all things by his intuitive wisdom of equanimity. And this [wisdom of equanimity] should be recognized as the antidote for all kinds of obscurations such as experiencing only [either] a realization of nonexistence [or a situation] wherein if any one thing is produced, another is definitely lost.

«49» As for the details of the paths of insight and meditation where nonconceptual intuitive wisdom serves as the cause of attaining the truth body, they should be understood following the *Transcendent Wisdom Sutra*.

69. *mtshan mar 'dzin pa.*

[THE SAṄGHA JEWEL]

«50» Now, from the universal vehicle Dharma Jewel, there originates the Saṅgha Jewel of nonregressing bodhisattvas. Therefore, immediately after [the explanation of the Dharma Jewel], there is one verse concerning the Saṅgha Jewel:[70]

> I bow down to those who command the wisdom vision
> That sees the infinity and purity of sentient beings,
> And sees the insubstantiality of the addictions
> With the natural clear-light of that mind—
> Whose unobscured intelligence truly realizes
> All migrant beings as selfless and at last at peace—
> Thus sees them permeated by the perfect Buddha. //I.13//

«51» What is shown by this verse?

> The intelligent Saṅgha that never regresses
> Possesses unsurpassed excellences
> As a result of their purity of inner intuitive wisdom vision
> Of [both] ultimate and phenomenal realities. //I.14//

«52» This [verse] briefly explains that the Saṅgha Jewel of nonregressing bodhisattvas possesses unsurpassed excellences as a result of their purity of transcendent intuitive insight with its two causes, [insights] that see the ultimate reality of things and [also] their phenomenal reality.

> They have omniscient [intuition] that sees things just as they are,
> Because they realize the peaceful reality of beings
> —Their absolute purity of nature—
> And that all addictions have been primordially ended. //I.15//

«53» Here, omniscient [intuitive wisdom] that sees things just as they are should be understood as the realization of the final reality of the selflessness of all beings—"things" and "persons"—as it is. In brief, the realization of the

---

70. PD70 (phi), p. 1004.16–20.

nondestruction of persons and things as a result of their nature of eternal, primordial peace is produced by two causes: the insight into the natural clear-light of the mind, and the insight into the primordial exhaustion and cessation of addictions.

«54» Here, these two facts, "natural clear-light of the mind" and "primordial exhaustion and cessation of addictions," are extremely difficult to realize supremely, in terms of their connection with the untainted element, as a result of the rule that with virtuous minds and nonvirtuous minds, when one mind functions, the second mind cannot continue. Thus, [the sutra states]:[71]

> O Bhagavān, in the moment of the virtuous mind, the addictions cannot cause addiction. In the moment of the nonvirtuous mind, that mind is not addicted by the addictions. O Bhagavān, the addictions do not touch that mind, that mind is not present in addictiveness. O Bhagavān, the mind that is free of such contact is only addicted when darkly confused. O Bhagavān, there are such things as derivative addictions, but no mind has such derivative addictions. Nevertheless, O Bhagavān, such indeed being the case, the meaning of the naturally pure mind being derivatively addicted is hard to realize.

Noumenally omniscient [intuitive wisdom], in the context of its being hard to understand, should be known in detail according to the sutra.

«55» [The root text states:][72]

> The mind that realizes all knowables
> Experiences the reality of omniscience
> As present [also] in all sentient beings—
> Being existence itself in all variety. //I.16//

«56» Here, with regard to "existence in all variety," one should know—by means of transcendent intuitive wisdom—of the actual existence of the tathāgata essence in all sentient beings, even those who dwell in the animal

---

71. The *Shrīmālādevī* again, PD70 (phi), p. 1005.15–1006.4; D92, f. 275a.5–7.
72. PD70 (phi), p. 1006.6–8.

realms. That bodhisattva insight, moreover, arises from the first bodhisattva stage, because such is realized as the meaning of the all-pervading reality realm.[73]

«57» [The root text states:]

> Such realization is the insight
> Of one's own individual wisdom.
> It is pure because in the stainless element
> There is no attachment and no hindrance. //I.17//

«58» The realization of the transcendent path by the noumenally omniscient [intuitive wisdom] that perceives things just as they are, and by the phenomenally omniscient [intuitive wisdom], is accepted as the insight of transcendent intuitive wisdom of noble beings, which are individually introspective and are not ordinary. It is called "pure" in comparison to its opposite and the experience of partial intuitive wisdom—in brief, as a result of two causes. Which ones? It is because of nonattachment and nonhindrance. Here, it is free from attachment since omniscient [intuitive wisdom] that perceives things just as they are has as its object the natural purity of sentient beings' [buddha-]element, and it is free from hindrance since phenomenally omniscient [intuitive wisdom] has as its object the limitless objects of knowledge.

«59» [The root text states:]

> The nonregressing noble beings
> Are a refuge for all beings
> Because of their unsurpassed buddha intuition—
> Since their intuition's experience is pure. //I.18//

«60» Thus, irreversible bodhisattvas are a refuge for all beings, since the wisdom insight of those bodhisattvas who abide on the stage of irreversibility is close to that of the unsurpassed tathāgata; or they [actually] possess such [insight]. It should be known that they are unsurpassed in comparison to the [other] bodhisattva excellences such as ethics, etc.

«61» There is no mention of the Saṅgha Jewel of disciples, immediately after the saṅgha of bodhisattvas, since the former is not [as] worthy

---

73. *dharmadhātu*; *chos kyi dbyings*.

of worship. Having known the difference between [such] expert bodhisattvas and the disciples, one should never abandon the crescent-moon-like bodhisattvas who will complete the extensive stores of merit and intuitive wisdom—illuminating countless beings with the light of the atmosphere of wisdom and compassion, while entering the path in accordance with attainment of the full moon of the unsurpassed tathāgata—and never bow down instead to starlike disciples who have perfected partial intuitive wisdom, [merely] self-illuminating, since their altruistic spirit is not pure. Owing to their excellence of the authentic reliance, even bodhisattvas who have just first cultivated the altruistic spirit surpass holy disciples who have perfected their pure uncontaminmated ethics, but lack compassion and do not cause others to improve, not to mention other bodhisattvas who have excellences such as the ten powers, etc. Why? As it is said:[74]

> Developing himself by ethical acts for his own sake,
> Lacking love for beings whose ethics are false,
> So pure with his treasure of self-serving ethics—
> Though noble, I do not call him pure in ethics.

> One is ethical who has engaged in ethical acts,
> Having supremely conceived compassion for others,
> And taken care of others like earth, water, fire, and wind—
> And the others are but their mirror reflections.

« 62 » Now, for what purpose and for the sake of whom did the Bhagavān make the arrangement of the three refuges?

> The refuges are established by the Bhagavān as three,
> By means of their aspects of teacher, teaching, and learners,
> In relation to the three vehicles and
> To the three kinds of convictions. //I.19//

The purpose of teaching the Teacher's excellences by the statement "who is supreme among all two-footed beings" is to establish the Buddha as the refuge for persons of the bodhisattva vehicle who seek buddhahood, and

---

74. The source of these verses is not identified. PD70 (phi), p. 1008.7–12.

[also] for those who have conviction about offering excellent service to the Buddha. The purpose of teaching the excellences of the Teacher's teaching by the statement "who is the supreme being among all who are free from attachment" is to establish the Dharma as the refuge for persons of the hermit buddha vehicle who strive to realize the profound teaching of relativistic origination for themselves, and [also] for those who have conviction about offering excellent service to the Dharma. The purpose of teaching the excellences of the learners of the Teacher's teaching by the statement "who is supreme among all entourages" is to establish the Saṅgha as the refuge for persons of the disciple vehicle who try to realize by following others' verbal [teaching], and [also] for those who have conviction about offering excellent service to the Saṅgha.

«63» Thus, in brief, these statements were taught by the Bhagavān to make the arrangement of the differentiation of the three refuges in terms of six kinds of people for three kinds of purposes. This [arrangement] is made in the conventional reality in order to make sentient beings gradually enter [different] vehicles.

«64» [The root text states:]

> Neither the Dharma nor the noble Saṅgha
> Constitutes a supreme refuge that will last forever:
> Because they are to be abandoned, are deceptive,
> Are [ultimately] nonexistent, and they experience fear. //I.20//

«65» The Dharma has two aspects: the Dharma as teaching and the Dharma as realization. The Dharma as teaching is the expressions in the sutras, etc. It is included in the collection of names, terms, and letters and is called "ferry-like," since [it will be abandoned] when the ultimate path is realized.

«66» The Dharma as realization has two divisions: causal and fruitional, which are the truth of the path and the truth of cessation, and are called "that by which one realizes" and "that which is realized," respectively. Here one shall realize that the path has the characteristic of creation. Anything that is recognized as having the characteristic of creation is false, of deceptive character. Anything deceptive is untrue. Anything untrue is impermanent. Anything impermanent is not a refuge. The cessation that is realized by means of such a path is distinguished from others by the mere nothingness of addiction and suffering by the way of the disciples, just like the extinction of a lamp. Nothingness is not suitable as a refuge.

«67» This so-called "saṅgha" is a designation for the community settled on the three vehicles. They take refuge in the Tathāgata out of constant fear, seek freedom, still have something to learn and to do, and are [merely] approaching the unsurpassed perfect enlightenment. How do they fear? The saints who have abandoned rebirths live in constant fear of all synthetic activity as something unbearable, just like facing enemies who raise swords, since they have not yet abandoned karmic evolutionary instincts. Therefore, they have not attained the ultimate delightful freedom. An [ultimate] refuge does not seek refuge. The saints still feel fear, just as sentient beings without protection seek freedom from fear. Thus, they take refuge in the Tathāgata out of fear. Anyone who takes refuge out of such fear must seek freedom from fear. Therefore, [the saints] still have things to learn and to do with respect to the abandonment of the basis of fear. And they are [only] approaching the unsurpassed perfect enlightenment since they still need to learn and work on attaining the status of the Supreme Bull, who is fearless. Thus, [the Saṅgha] is a partial refuge, not an ultimate one.

«68» This declares that these two kinds of refuge are not refuges in an ultimate sense.

> Only the ultimate-reality Buddha
> Is a refuge for beings,
> Because that Sage is the truth body,
> Which is the ultimate goal of the Saṅgha. //I.21//

This states that, in this world without protection and refuge, only the Tathāgata, the Saint, the Perfectly Enlightened One, is the unexhausted refuge equal to all future realities, the eternal refuge, everlasting refuge, unchangeable refuge, and ultimate refuge, since, as aforementioned, the Sage is distinguished from others by being "without production and without destruction," possessing the truth body that is free from attachment and has the nature of the two pure realities, and since the entourage of the three vehicles sets the attainment of the ultimate pure truth body as the ultimate goal. This eternal, immutable, peaceful, firm refuge should be known in detail by following the *Shrīmālādevī Lion's Roar Sutra*.

«69» [The root text states:]

[They are] "jewels," since they rarely appear,
Stainless and powerful,
The ornaments of the world,
Supreme and changeless. //I.22//

«70» In short, by their sixfold features common with jewels, these Three Jewels named "Buddha, Dharma, and Saṅgha" are said to be similar to jewels. That is to say, (1) by means of the common feature of rarity since those people who have not cultivated the root of virtue over many eons cannot get any chance to meet them; (2) by means of the common feature of purity since they are free from all kinds of taint; (3) by means of the common feature of power since they are endowed with inconceivable excellences such as six superknowledges, etc; (4) by means of the common feature of being the ornament of the world since they are the cause of virtuous thought developed by all beings; (5) by means of the common feature of being superior to artificial jewels since they are transcendent; and (6) by means of the common feature of being unchangeable by praise, criticism, etc., because of their uncreated nature.

«71» Immediately after the teachings on the Three Jewels, there is one verse with reference to the circumstances of the production of the Three Jewels, the source of common and transcendent purities.

«72» [The root text states:]

The reality mingled with taints, and [the reality] free of taints,
The stainless excellences of a buddha, and a victor's enlightened activities;
[These four are] the objects of those who perceive the ultimate,
From which arise the Three virtuous Jewels. //I.23//

«73» What is elucidated by this verse?

The spiritual potential of these Three Jewels
Is the object of the All-Seeing Ones,
And is inconceivable in four ways,
For four reasons, respectively. //I.24//

«74» Here, the "reality mingled with taints" is the element, which is termed the "buddha essence" when not yet released from the sheath of addictions. The "[reality] free of taints" is of the nature of the transformation of that reality at the stage of a buddha, which is termed "the truth body of a tathāgata." "Stainless excellences of a buddha" refers to the transcendent excellences of a buddha, including the ten powers, and so on, existing within the truth body of a tathāgata in the nature of the transformation. "A victor's enlightened activities" refers to the unsurpassed activities of these buddha excellences, the ten powers, etc., which constantly give prophetic messages to bodhisattvas without disappearance, without interruption, unceasingly. Furthermore, these four facts are inconceivable for four reasons, respectively; thus, they are called "objects of those who perceive the ultimate."

«75» Then, how are these four facts to be understood?

Because [reality is] pure, yet mingled with addictions,
[The truth body is both] free of addictions and pure,
[The excellences are] the indivisible good qualities,
And [the enlightened activities are] spontaneous and without
    conceptual thoughts. //I.25//

«76» Here, the reality with taints is simultaneously mingled with [both] purity and addiction; this is an inconceivable fact, because this is not the object even for hermit buddhas who believe in the pattern of the profound teaching.

«77» Thus, [the Buddha declares in the *Shrīmālādevī Lion's Roar Sutra*:][75]

O Devī, these two things are quite difficult to understand. It is difficult to understand that the mind is intrinsically pure. It is also difficult to understand that this very mind has derivative addictions. O Devī, only you, or bodhisattvas endowed with great excellences, can understand these two things. O Devī, for others, the disciples and hermit buddhas, these two things are to be understood only by means of their faith in the Tathāgata.

75. This identification of the sutra source is lacking in the Tibetan translation. PD70 (phi), p. 1013.15–21; D92, f. 275b2–4 (Brunnhölzl, p. 1075, n. 1217).

«78» Here, it is an inconceivable idea that the [ultimate] reality free of taints never originally consisted of addiction involving taints yet needs to be purified.

«79» Thus, [the Buddha declares in the *King Dhāraṇīshvara Sutra*:][76]

> The mind is naturally clear-light transparency. This is known just as it is directly [by noble beings]. Thus, the Buddha achieved unsurpassed perfect enlightenment by the intuitive wisdom endowed with the singular momentariness [that incorporates all time].

«80» Here, the stainless excellences of a buddha are always found even in the stage of ordinary individuals who are totally mentally addicted, although, because they are free of any distinction between earlier and later, this utterly undifferentiated reality abides; and this is inconceivable.

«81» Thus, [the Buddha declares in the *Buddha Garland Sutra*:][77]

> There is no one among the mass of sentient beings in whom the whole intuition of the Tathāgata does not penetrate. Nevertheless, the intuitive wisdom of the Tathāgata does not manifest because of the concept-habit. When free from this concept-habit, the intuition of the omniscient, original wisdom, arises, [still] with obscuration.

> O victor child, suppose there were a canvas with a big painting equal to the billion-world galactic universe. And on this big canvas, the whole billion-world galactic universe would be painted completely. The vast surrounding horizon would be painted in the exact size of the vast surrounding horizon. The great earth would be painted in the exact size of the great earth. The two-thousand-world universe would be painted in its exact size. [Likewise,] the one-thousand-world universe, the four

76. PD70 (phi), p. 1014.2–5; D147, f. 210b.6–7. Cf. Chinese translation, "知心性淨。是故唱言如來一念得阿耨多羅三藐三菩提。" 大方等大集經, T.13.397.20b21.

77. The *Tathāgatotpattisaṁbhavaparivarta* according to Chinese. PD70 (phi), pp. 1014.8–1017.1; D44, phal po che, ga, ff. 116b4–117b.6.

continents, the great ocean, the southern Jambu continent, the eastern Videha continent, the [western] Godānīya continent, the northern Kuru continent, Mount Sumeru, the mansions of celestial beings living on earth, of celestial beings living in the desire realm, and of celestial beings living in the [pure] material realm; all of these would be painted in their exact sizes. Hence, this big canvas would have the same width and length as the billion-world galactic universe.

This very big canvas would then be placed within one subatomic particle. Just as this big canvas was placed within one subatomic particle, in each of all the other subatomic particles there would be a big canvas of the same size to be placed. Suppose there should be born one person, sagacious, shrewd, clever, and intelligent, knowing how to recognize that [big canvas]. And his eyes were divine eyes that were perfectly pure and clear-light transparent. With these divine eyes he would perceive [and wonder]: "Why does this big canvas of such a great nature dwell in such a small subatomic particle! It is of no use to anybody!" So he would think: "Aha! I shall break this subatomic particle with the force of my thunderbolt of great effort and make this great canvas useful for the beings." Then, producing the force of great effort, he would break this subatomic particle with a tiny thunderbolt vajra and would make that great canvas useful for all the beings. Not only for one subatomic particle, he would also do the same for all the other subatomic particles.

Similarly, buddha child, the immeasurable intuitive wisdom of a tathāgata, the wisdom of caring for all sentient beings, thoroughly penetrates the continuums of sentient beings. And the continuum of each sentient being is akin to the immeasurable intuitive wisdom of a tathāgata. Fettered by the concept-habit, however, the naive ones are unaware of a tathāgata's wisdom; they neither know it well nor do they directly experience it.

Hence, a tathāgata, having seen the ultimate realm, the state of all the sentient beings, with his unobstructed intuitive wisdom, resolves to be a teacher [and declares:] "Alas! These sentient beings are not properly aware of the intuitive wisdom of a tathāgata, though it permeates them. I shall free these sentient beings, no matter how fettered they have been made by concepts, by means of the teaching of the holy path. In this way, they will loosen the big knot tied around [their] intuitive wisdom by producing the strength of their very own holy intuitive wisdom; and [they] will personally realize the intuitive wisdom of a tathāgata, obtaining equality with a tathāgata's intuitive wisdom."

[Accordingly], he teaches those beings the path of a tathāgata, thereby removing all the fetters made by conceptual constructs. And when all the fetters made by concepts are eliminated, this immeasurable intuitive wisdom of a tathāgata then becomes useful to all sentient beings.

≪ 82 ≫ Here, the enlightened activities of the Victor simultaneously reach all [the disciples], at any time, spontaneously, without effort, without conceptual thought, [yet act] according to the intentions [of the disciples], according to [the conditions of] the disciples, with none left out, correspondingly; this is the inconceivable fact.

Thus, [the Buddha declares in the *King Dhāraṇīshvara Sutra*:][78]

In order to introduce[79] sentient beings to the activities of a tathāgata, though the activities [of a tathāgata] are immeasurable, [sentient beings] are taught briefly with a concise number [of activities]. However, O noble child, the true activities of a tathāgata are inconceivable, immeasurable, unknown to all the world, inexpressible by words, difficult to attain by others. They are present in all buddha fields, equal to all buddhas, beyond any effort and exertion. They [are] free of conceptual thought, being vast as space, and free of differentiation as being the activity of the ultimate element.

---

78. PD70 (phi), pp. 1017.5–1018.4; D147, ff. 215b.7–216a.3. This includes the subsequent quotes below.

79. *avatāraṇa, gzud pa* (D147), *gzhug pa* (as cited in D4025 *Commentary*).

Then, after showing the simile of a pure sapphire jewel, [the Buddha] teaches in detail:

> Noble child, you should know the activities of a tathāgata by means of alternate ramifications as follows: inconceivable, equally pervasive,[80] without blemish whatsoever, pervading past, present, and future, and keeping the continuation of the Three Jewels from being cut off. The body of a buddha, in which these inconceivable activities of a tathāgata are present, never casts off its sky-like nature, and shows itself in all buddha fields. The speech [of a buddha] never casts off its inexpressible reality, and teaches sentient beings the Dharma with the proper language skill. And the mind [of a buddha] is free from all objects of the mind, yet is perfectly aware of the activities and intentions of the minds of all sentient beings.

[The root text states:]

> The object to be realized, the realization,
> Its components, and the [activities] that cause the realization;
> [of these four;] respectively,
> One topic is the cause of purification,
> [The remaining] three are the conditions. //I.26//

«83» Of these four topics of import, the first topic, [the buddha element], should be regarded as the "object to be realized" because all objects of knowledge are included in it. The realization of it is the second topic, "enlightenment," as this is the realization. The components of enlightenment is the third topic, the "enlightenment components," as these are the excellences of the Buddha. The fourth topic is the "[activities] that cause the realization" because those components of enlightenment cause other people to realize. Hence, in terms of this, we should know that these four topics, being the factors of cause and conditions, are presented as the spiritual potential of the Three Jewels.

---

80. *samatānugata, kun tu rjes su song ba* (D147); *mnyam pa nyid rjes su thob pa* (as cited in D4025 *Commentary*).

«84» In that regard, we should understand that the first of these four topics is the cause of the production of the Three Jewels, depending on its purification, because it is the seed of the transcendent excellences and the focus of an individual's proper mentation by which that [tainted reality] is purified. Thus, one single topic is the cause. How do the other three [topics] serve as conditions? These should be understood to be the conditions for the production of the Three Jewels in the way that the production of the Three Jewels depends on the purification of that [tainted ultimate reality element], and this purification is based upon the messages from others. This is because a tathāgata, having realized the unsurpassed perfect enlightenment, performs the thirty-two activities of a tathāgata with those qualities of a buddha such as the ten powers, and so on. Thus, these three serve as conditions.

Henceforth, the remaining text should be known as a detailed teaching of the analysis of these four topics in stages.

«85» Here, in terms of the reality mingled with taints, [the Buddha] states that all sentient beings are endowed with the buddha essence.

«86» By which meaning does [the Buddha state thus]?[81]

> The buddhas' wisdom permeates the hosts of beings;
> That stainless reality is nondual;
> The spiritual potential for buddhahood is designated after
>   fruition,
> Therefore, it is said: all beings possess tathāgata essence. //I.27//

«87» In short, by three kinds of factors, the Bhagavān states that all sentient beings always possess the buddha essence.

> All sentient beings always possess the buddha essence
> By virtue of the diffusion of the buddhas' bodies,
> The indivisible reality, and
> The existence of the spiritual potential. //I.28//

---

81. The following verse as found in Ngog's Tibetan translation is inserted between the first two sentences of the following prose. Gyaltsap, in his commentary, skips over this seemingly redundant verse without exposition, while other Tibetan authors comment upon it, raising the question of its authenticity.

These [three] factors that [include] all ramifications of that [statement] are taught in all sutras without making any distinctions.[82] With reference to these [three], I shall now explain as follows: (1) the truth body of a tathāgata spreads into all sentient beings; (2) the indivisible reality of a tathāgata; and (3) the existence of the spiritual potential [in every sentient being].

«88» These three factors will be taught [in detail] below according to the *Tathāgata Essence Sutra*.

> The nature, the causes, the fruition, actions, possession, and
>   engagement,
> As well as the states and all-pervasiveness,
> Unchangeable eternity and indivisible excellences:
> These should be known as the intended meaning of the ultimate
>   element. //I.29//

«89» In summary, as for the intention of the ten points: this [verse] should be known as the arrangement of [the element,] the tathāgata essence, which is the object of the ultimate wisdom of reality. What are the ten points? They are: (1) nature [of the element]; (2) causes [of its purification]; (3) fruition [of its purification]; (4) actions [of the element]; (5) possession [of the element]; (6) engagement [of the element in general]; (7) states [of its engagement]; (8) all-pervasiveness; (9) unchangeability [of the element by means of states]; and (10) its indivisible excellences.

«90» In that regard, here is the first verse concerning the points of "nature" and "causes."

> [Tathāgata essence] is ever untainted in terms of its nature,
> Like a jewel, space, and pure water;
> It emerges by means of faith in the Dharma,
> Higher wisdom, concentration, and compassion. //I.30//

«91» What is taught here by the first half of this verse?

---

82. Cf. Takasaki's treatment of this vague sentence: "Prior to it, however, there is [another] meaning by which this meaning in all its aspects is indicated in the sutra with no variance anywhere." *A Study on the Ratnagotravibhāga*, 198. My translation is made according to my reading of Gö Lotsawa's commentary. See Mathes, *'Gos Lo-tsā-ba Gzhon-nu-dpal's Commentary*, 253. Again, Gyaltsap does not comment on it in his *Supercommentary*.

Because of the characteristics of their natures
Being powerful, immutable, and moist,
These are analogous to the qualities of a jewel,
Space, and water. //I.31//

«92» Concerning these aforementioned three [factors],[83] the similarity of the tathāgata essence's excellences to those of the pure wish-fulfilling jewel, space, and water, respectively, should be recognized with reference to their particular and common characteristics. Now, in that regard, the truth body of a tathāgata should be known to be analogous to a wish-fulfilling jewel, with reference to its particular characteristic in terms of its nature of being able to fulfill wishes, etc. Its reality should be known to be analogous to space, with reference to its particular characteristic in terms of its nature being immutable. The potential of a tathāgata should be known to be analogous to water, with reference to its particular characteristic in terms of being moist with compassion toward sentient beings. And in this regard, with reference to their all being naturally ever untainted by addictions and naturally pure as the common characteristic, those [three things] should be known to be analogous to a wish-fulfilling jewel, space, and water.

«93» Now, what is demonstrated by the second half of this verse?

Enmity toward the Dharma, belief in a self,
Fear of the sufferings in cyclic life, and
Indifference to the welfare of sentient beings;
Are the four kinds of obscuration ... //I.32//

... of the desire-doomed[84] ones, outsiders,
Disciples, and hermit buddhas, respectively.
Strong faith, etc., are
The four causes of purification. //I.33//

«94» In brief, there are three kinds of sentient beings among the multitude: (1) those who lust for worldly existence; (2) those who lust for freedom from it; (3) those who wish neither of them.

83. See verse I.28, above.
84. *icchantika, 'dod chen po.*

«95» In regard to the kind who lust for worldly existence, they should be known as twofold: (a) those who feel enmity toward the path to liberation, and so do not have the spiritual potential for nirvana, only wishing for cyclic life and not for nirvana; and (b) those who are Buddhists but have certainly fallen into that way. Some of these are hostile to the teachings of the universal vehicle. With reference to them, the Bhagavān states as follows:[85]

> I am not their teacher; they are not my disciples. O Shāriputra, I speak of them as possessing a great darkness, going from darkness to ever greater darkness.

«96» As to the kind who aspire for liberation from worldly existence, it is also twofold: (a) those who have engaged with but are lacking in liberative art; and (b) those who have engaged with liberative art. Those who have engaged with but are lacking in liberative art are further divided into three types: (i) various outsider groups, outsiders of this Dharma such as the Chārvākas,[86] the Parivrājakas, and the Jains, etc.; and (ii–iii) those who are Buddhists but whose conduct is in conformity with the outsiders, taking a negative view of [the Buddha's teaching]. Then, who are those people? They are (ii) those who lack faith regarding the ultimate truth and believe in a personal self. With reference to these, the Bhagavān states:[87]

> One who lacks confidence in emptiness is not different from a fundamentalist.

And they are also (iii) those who feel overly proud and hold a wrong view of emptiness. Here the door of liberation [asserted by these people] also is held with a wrong view of emptiness. With reference to these, [the Buddha] states [in the *Questions of Kāshyapa Sutra*] as follows:[88]

---

85. PD70 (phi), p. 1021.17–20; Brunnhölzl identifies as Taishō 668, 467c, the *Anūnatvā-pūrṇatva-nirdeśa-parivarta Sutra*, following Takasaki. This quote is so far unidentified in a Tibetan translation.

86. According to Chinese translation, it refers to the Sāṁkhya school.

87. PD70 (phi), p. 1022.5–6.

88. PD70 (phi), p. 1022.10–11; D87, f. 132b.1–2.

Kāshyapa, the wrong conviction of a personal self as great as Mount Sumeru is far less bad than the wrong view of emptiness on the part of those afflicted with intellectual arrogance.

«97» Those who have engaged with liberative art are further divided into two types: (i) those who have engaged in final determination, conforming to the disciple vehicle; and (ii) those conforming to the hermit buddha vehicle.

«98» As to the kind who wish for neither, these are the people who are extremely sharp in intelligence, standing firmly upon the universal vehicle. They have no desire for cyclic life as the desire-doomed do, nor are they engaged with but lacking in liberative art like the outsiders, nor do they have realization with liberative art like disciples and hermit buddhas; but they have entered the path to obtain the equality of cyclic life with nirvana. They are intent upon unlocated nirvana and act in an addiction-free cyclic life. The root is perfectly pure, as being grounded in firm compassion and high resolve.

«99» Here, those desire-doomed people who have desire for worldly existence and those Buddhists who have certainly fallen into the same way are called the group of people who are definitely mistaken. Those people who aspire for liberation from worldly existence but are lacking in liberative art are called the unsettled group of people. Those people who aspire for liberation from worldly existence with liberative art and those who wish for neither and have entered the path to obtain equality are called the group of people who have settled in reality.

«100» Aside from those people who stand firmly in the universal vehicle and have realized that there are no obscurations, the other four kinds of people—namely, the desire-doomed, the fundamentalists, the disciples, and the hermit buddhas—cannot understand the tathāgata element or perceive it directly as a result of their four obscurations.

«101» What then are the four obscurations? These are: (1) enmity toward the universal vehicle teaching—the obscuration of the desire-doomed— and its antidote is the meditation on faith in the bodhisattvas' teachings of the universal vehicle; (2) the belief in a self—the obscuration of outsiders— and its antidote is the meditation on the bodhisattvas' wisdom transcendence; (3) knowing cyclic life as dreadful and fearing its sufferings—the obscuration of those associated with the disciple vehicle—and its antidote is the bodhisattvas' space-treasure concentration, etc.; and (4) aversion and indifference to the welfare of sentient beings—the obscuration of those associated with the hermit buddha vehicle—and its antidote is the meditation on the great compassion by bodhisattvas.

«102» These are the four types of obscurations of the four kinds of sentient beings. By meditating on the four kinds of antidotes to these obscurations such as faith, etc., bodhisattvas will obtain the ultimate purity of the truth body, the unsurpassed goal.

«103» Sustained by these four causes for achieving the four purities, they become Dharma King children in the Tathāgata's family. How so?

«104» It is said:

Whosoever has the seed, faith in the universal vehicle,
The mother, wisdom that creates the Buddha qualities,
The blissful womb of meditation, and the nurse, compassion—
They are children born to follow the Sage. //I.34//

«105» Here, a verse focused on the meanings of "fruition" and "action":

Fruition consists of the transcendences
Of purity, self, bliss, and permanence.
The actions are suffering, disgust,
Ambition to gain peace, and prayer. //I.35//

«106» Here, what is taught by the former half of this verse?

The fruition of these [causes] is, in brief,
Distinguished by the antidotes
That remedy the four kinds of delusion
About the truth body. //I.36//

«107» In brief, the fruition of these four qualities, faith, etc., explained to be the causes of purification of the tathāgata element, are the four transcendent excellences of the truth body, and the antidotes are the opposites of the four delusions, respectively. [In general,] there are notions of permanence, bliss, self, and purity regarding impermanence, suffering, selflessness, and impurity of things such as matter, etc., respectively. Such notions are called the "four delusions." The opposite of these notions should be known as the four nondelusions. Which four? They are the notions of impermanence, suffering, selflessness, and impurity regarding impermanent, etc., things such as matter, etc. Such notions are called the "four anti-delusions." However, these very [anti-delusion notions] are accepted here as delusions with reference to the truth body of a tathāgata, whose defining characteristics are permanence, etc. The antidotes to these delusions are established as the four transcendent excellences of the truth body of a tathāgata, the transcendences of permanence, bliss, self, and purity.

≪108≫ Furthermore, this passage of the treatise should be understood in detail according to the sutra. [In the *Shrīmālādevī Lion's Roar Sutra*, Shrīmālā states:][89]

O Bhagavān, sentient beings have mistaken notions regarding their experience of the five compulsive aggregates; they have a notion of permanence about the impermanent, a notion of bliss about suffering, a notion of self about the selfless, and a notion of purity about the impure. O Bhagavān, even all the disciples and hermit buddhas have a confusion about the truth body of the Tathāgata, which is the object of the omniscient intuitive wisdom and was never previously seen by their wisdom of emptiness. O Bhagavān, those sentient beings who have the notions of permanence, bliss, self, and purity are children born of the heart of the Buddha. O Bhagavān, those sentient beings will not become confused. O Bhagavān, those sentient beings will see correctly.

For what reason? O Bhagavān, this is because the actual truth body of the Tathāgata is the transcendence of permanence, the transcendence of bliss, the transcendence of self, and the transcendence of purity. O Bhagavān, those people who see the truth body of the Tathāgata in this way truly see. Those who see truly are the heart children of the Buddha.

89. PD70 (phi), pp. 1025.13–1026.9; D92, ff. 273b.3–274a.1.

«109» The order of the four transcendent excellences of the truth body of the Tathāgata should be known in reverse of that of the causes. Here:

(1) Since it counters taking delight in the impure cyclic life by the desire-doomed who feel enmity toward the universal vehicle teaching, the purity transcendence should be understood to be the fruition obtained by the bodhisattvas' meditation on faith in the universal vehicle teaching.

(2) Since it counters taking delight in the outsider fundamentalists' self-habit regarding the five compulsive aggregates, which are selfless, the self transcendence should be understood to be the fruition obtained by means of meditation on the transcendence of wisdom. Indeed, all the outsider fundamentalists assert that things such as matter, sound, etc., have a self as their nature, but [in reality] they do not. And things asserted in this way are deceptive in terms of their characteristic of seeming to be a self yet always being selfless. [On the contrary], by wisdom that knows reality exactly, the Tathāgata has obtained the transcendence of supreme selflessness. And the selflessness truly experienced by the Tathāgata is not deceptive as a result of some characteristic of [seeming to be, yet] not being self; hence the Tathāgata always accepts [his selflessness] as self. Selflessness itself is taken as the self. As [a sutra states:] "One abides by way of nonabiding."

(3) Since it counters taking delight in the cessation of the suffering of cyclic life by those associated with the disciple vehicle who fear the suffering of cyclic life, the transcendence of the supreme bliss [that remains] concerned with all matters, mundane and transcendent, should be understood to be the fruition obtained by the meditation on the space-treasure concentration, etc.

(4) Since it counters the taking of delight in the tranquil abode by those associated with the hermit buddha vehicle who are indifferent to the welfare of sentient beings, the transcendence of permanence with respect to the perfectly pure accomplishment of the aims of sentient beings, which works without interruption for as long as cyclic life exists, should be understood to be

the fruition obtained by the bodhisattvas' meditation on the great compassion.

«110» Thus, the attainment of four kinds of transcendent excellences regarding the purity, self, bliss, and permanence of the truth body of a tathāgata are, respectively, the fruitions of the bodhisattvas' meditations on faith, wisdom, concentration, and great compassion. As a result of these four [causes], the Tathāgata is acclaimed as the ultimate reality element, the infinite realm of space, and reaching to the end of time. Indeed, the Tathāgata is the one who has become the ultimate element because he has obtained the utterly pure ultimate element by the meditation on faith in the universal vehicle teaching. He is the one who has become infinite space because he has realized the space-like ultimate selflessness of sentient beings and their environments by the meditation on the transcendence of wisdom. He has become the supreme fortunate one of the Dharma, pervading all and teaching all, because of his meditative concentration of the space treasury, etc. He is the one who will reach the end of time, because he is endowed with endless compassion toward all sentient beings by the meditation on the great compassion.

«111» As for the attainment of the four kinds of transcendent excellences of the truth body of a tathāgata, there are four impediments for disciple saints and hermit buddhas, who are staying in the uncontaminated element, as well as for bodhisattvas who have obtained powers, [impediments] having defining characteristics of (1) condition, (2) cause, (3) origination, and (4) destruction. Here (1) condition is defined as the ground of the instinct for ignorance,[90] just as ignorance is the ground for creations. (2) Cause is defined as uncontaminated evolutionary action conditioned by the ground of the instinct for ignorance as well as creations. (3) Origination is defined as the accomplishment of the threefold mind-made body,[91] conditioned by the ground of the ignorance instinct and caused by uncontaminated evolutionary actions, just as the accomplishment of the threefold worldly existence is conditioned by the four kinds of compulsive function and caused by contaminated evolutionary action. (4) Destruction is defined

---

90. *avidyā-vāsa-bhūmi, ma rig pa'i bag chags kyi sa.*
91. *manomayātmabhāva-kāya, yid kyi rang bzhin gyi lus.*

as inconceivably transformative death, conditioned by the accomplishment of the threefold mind-made body, just as old age and death are conditioned by birth.

≪112≫ Saint disciples, hermit buddhas, and bodhisattvas who have obtained powers will not obtain the supreme ultimate purity transcendence, insofar as they have not extirpated the ground of the ignorance instinct, which is the foundation of all addictions, and thereby are not utterly free from the taint of the bad smell of addictions. They will not obtain the uncreated self transcendence insofar as they follow a habitual pattern of subtle identity-elaboration[92] depending on the ground of the ignorance instinct. They will not obtain the supreme bliss transcendence as the extinction of the origination of the mind-made aggregates, insofar as these aggregates have originated depending on the ground of the ignorance instinct and uncontaminated evolutionary action, which are motivated by the habit of subtle identity-elaboration conditioned by the ground of the ignorance instinct. And they will not obtain the immutable eternity transcendence, insofar as they have not overcome the inconceivably transformative death as long as they have not actualized the buddha essence by stopping all taints of addiction, evolution, and birth. Here the ignorance instinct is similar to the taint of addictions. The creations of uncontaminated evolutionary action are similar to the taints of evolutionary action. The accomplishment of the threefold mind-made body and inconceivably transformative death-migration are similar to the taint of birth.

≪113≫ Again, this passage of the treatise is to be understood in detail according to the sutra. [In the *Shrīmālādevī Lion's Roar Sutra*, Shrīmālā states:][93]

> O Bhagavān, conditioned by grasping and caused by contaminated karmic evolution, there is the origination of the threefold worldly existence; likewise, O Bhagavān, conditioned by the ground of the ignorance instinct and caused by uncontaminated karmic evolution, there is the origination of the threefold mind-natured body of disciple saints, hermit buddhas, and bodhisattvas who have attained powers. O Bhagavān, for the origination

---

92. *sūkṣma-nimitta-prapañca, mtshan ma'i spros pa spyod pa phra mo.*
93. PD70 (phi), p. 1030.2–9; D92, ff. 265b.7–266a.2.

of the threefold mind-made body in these three stages and for the accomplishment of uncontaminated karmic evolution, the ground of the ignorance instinct is the condition.

«114» Thus, in these three mind-made bodies of saints, hermit buddhas, and bodhisattvas, there are no transcendences of purity, self, bliss, and permanence. Seeing this, [the *Shrīmālādevī Lion's Roar Sutra*] states:[94]

> Only the truth body of a tathāgata has the transcendence of purity, the transcendence of self, the transcendence of bliss, and the transcendence of permanence.

[The root text states:]

> It is purity, because it is naturally pure,
> And because the instincts are abandoned.
> It is the supreme self, because the elaborations
> Of both self and selflessness are eradicated. //I.37//

> It is bliss, because the mind-made aggregate
> And its causes have been abolished.
> It is permanence, by virtue of the realization
> Of the equality of cyclic life and nirvana. //I.38//

«115» In brief, the purity transcendence of a tathāgata's truth body should be known for two reasons: (1) because it is naturally pure as its common characteristic; and (2) because it is pure by the abandonment of taints as its special characteristic. The supreme self transcendence, too, should be understood for two reasons: (1) because it is free from self-reification by rejecting the outsiders' extremism; and (2) because it is free from selflessness-reification by rejecting the extremism of the disciples. The bliss transcendence is to be known likewise for two reasons: (1) because of the

---

94. PD70 (phi), p. 1030.13–16; D92, f. 273b.7. In the PD version, there is no indication that this is another quote from the sutra.

destruction of taking rebirth by the evolutionary instincts, on account of
the elimination of all kinds of sources of suffering; and (2) because of the
actualized cessation of the mind-made bodies on account of the actualization of all kinds of cessation of suffering. And the permanence transcendence is to be known for two reasons: (1) because one does not fall to the
nihilistic extreme of minimizing cyclic life to the extent of impermanence;
(2) nor does one fall to the eternalistic extreme of exaggerating nirvana to
the extent of permanence.

«116» As [the *Shrīmālādevī Lion's Roar Sutra*] states:[95]

> If someone perceives the created as impermanent, Bhagavān,
> that becomes a nihilistic view, thus becoming an unrealistic view.
> If someone perceives nirvana as permanent, O Bhagavān, that
> becomes an eternalistic view, thus becoming an unrealistic view.
> It is said by way of the ultimate element, that ultimately cyclic
> life itself is nirvana, because [the Tathāgata] has actualized the
> unlocated nirvana without constructing such duality.

«117» This passage shows that the unlocated place, which is neither close
to nor remote from all sentient beings, is obtained by two causes. Which
two? The bodhisattvas do not get close to all sentient beings, because all
evolutionary instincts for attachment have been eliminated by their wisdom. Likewise, bodhisattvas do not feel remote from them, because they
will never abandon those beings owing to their great compassion. These
[two] are the liberative arts for the attainment of the perfect enlightenment
of which nonlocation is the nature. Indeed, bodhisattvas have eliminated
all evolutionary instincts for attachment by wisdom for their own sake,
thereby being deeply intent upon nirvana and not staying in cyclic life as do
those who do not have spiritual potential for nirvana. Owing to their great
compassion, they never abandon suffering sentient beings and so act for the
sake of others, remaining in cyclic life and not staying in nirvana as do those
who aspire only for peace.

«118» Thus these two qualities are the root of the unsurpassed enlightenment, [as the treatise states:]

95. PD70 (phi), p. 1031.11–16; D92, f. 273a.6–7.

Having completely severed self-cherishing by wisdom,
By their other-cherishing, loving ones do not gain peace;
Thus relying on wisdom and love as arts for awakening,
Noble ones dwell in neither cyclic life nor nirvana. //I.39//

«119» Now, with reference to the aforementioned meaning of "action,"
what is demonstrated by the latter half of that verse (I.35)?

If the tathāgata element did not exist,
Aversion to suffering would not arise.
Desire, aspiration, and prayer for nirvana
Would also not arise. //I.40//

«120» So the [*Shrīmālādevī Lion's Roar*] *Sutra* states:[96]

O Bhagavān, if there were no tathāgata essence, then there would
arise neither aversion to suffering nor desire for nirvana, nor the
wish, aspiration, or prayer for it.

Here in brief, the tathāgata element—the pure spiritual potential—of even
those people who are confirmed in their errors causes two kinds of action.
It develops aversion to cyclic life on the basis of perceiving the faults of suffering, and it calls forth wishing, desire, aspiration, and prayer for nirvana
on the basis of perceiving the virtues of its bliss. Here "wishing" means
manifested desire. "Desire" means longing for the attainment of the desired
aim. "Aspiration" means searching for the means to obtain the desired aim.
And "prayer" means causing the will by thinking of the desired aim.
    «121» [The root text states:]

Seeing cyclic life as having the fault of suffering
And nirvana as having the excellence of bliss
Occurs for those who have the potential;
And not for those without the potential. //I.41//

---

96. PD70 (phi), p. 1032.17–20; D92, f. 274b.5.

Because they have the spiritual potential, the people who have positive qualities perceive cyclic life as having the fault of suffering and nirvana as having the excellence of bliss; they do not do so for no cause and no condition.

«122» For what reason? If such insight could happen without the potential, without a cause or a condition, without ending negative actions, it would also happen for beings who are wrong-desiring ones, who have no spiritual potential for nirvana. But [such insight] does not happen for beings who have no faith in any one of the three [vehicles], who lack the spiritual potential to become free of incidental stains by implementing the four wheels [of practice] by relying on superior persons, etc.

[The *Ornament of the Light of Wisdom Sutra*] states as follows:[97]

> After this, the intuitive wisdom light rays of the Tathāgata sun disc fall upon the bodies of even those people who are confirmed in error, thus benefiting them and producing a proper cause of their future [liberation], thus causing their virtuous qualities to increase.

«123» As for the statement that "the wrong-desiring ones[98] have no chance for nirvana forever," it is so declared because feeling enmity toward the universal vehicle teaching is the cause of being a wrong-desiring one. With the intention that this ["forever" really] means "for a certain period of time," it is so stated in order to avert such enmity.

«124» None could be impure forever because of the existence of a naturally pure potential. Intending the existence of potential purity in all beings without discrimination, the Bhagavān therefore declares:

> Being beginningless yet having its end,
> It is naturally pure and has the property of permanence;
> It is unseen since it is covered by a beginningless sheath,
> Just like a golden thing concealed [in mud].

«125» Here is a verse about the meaning of "possession."

---

97. PD70 (phi), pp. 1033.20–1034.3; D100, f. 285b.6–7.

98. *log sred can.* This would be appear to be a term similar to "the desire-doomed" (*icchantika, 'dod chen po*).

Like a great ocean, an inexhaustible store
Of immeasurable jewels of excellence, and
Like a lamp, because its nature
Possesses inseparable excellences. //I.42//

«126» Here, what is shown by the former half of this verse?

Because it consists of the truth body,
The Victor's intuitive wisdom and compassion,
The element is shown to be similar to an ocean
By being an ocean bed, jewels, and water. //I.43//

«127» On account of the three meanings, which are, respectively, analogous to three aspects of a great ocean the meaning of "possession" should be understood in terms of the tathāgata element possessing [the excellences of] the cause.

Then, what are the three meanings? They are (1) the cause for purifying the truth body; (2) the cause for obtaining a buddha's intuitive wisdom; and (3) the cause for receiving the Tathāgata's great compassion. Here one should know that (1) the cause for purifying the truth body is the meditation on faith in the universal vehicle; (2) the cause for obtaining a buddha's intuitive wisdom is the meditation on wisdom and concentration; and (3) the cause for receiving the Tathāgata's great compassion is the meditation on great compassion of bodhisattvas. Here, the meditation on faith in the universal vehicle is analogous to an ocean bed since it holds immeasurable and inexhaustible jewels of wisdom and concentration as well as the water of compassion. The meditation on wisdom and concentration is analogous to a jewel because it is free of conceptual thought and endowed with inconceivable powerful excellences. The meditation on the great compassion of bodhisattvas is analogous to water because it has the one taste of supreme moist nature [permeating] all beings. This conjunction of [the element] with that [causal fourfold excellence] in terms of these three causes of the three things is called "possession."

«128» Now, what is shown by the latter half of the verse?

In the stainless state, since the superknowledges,
Intuitive wisdom, and stainlessness itself

Are inseparable from the reality of thatness,
They resemble the light, heat, and color of a lamp. //I.44//

On account of the three meanings that are, respectively, analogous to three aspects of a lamp, the meaning of "possession" should be understood in terms of the tathāgata element possessing [the excellences of] the fruition. Then, what are the three meanings? They are (1) superknowledges; (2) the intuitive wisdom of the cessation of contaminations; and (3) the cessation of contamination [itself]. Here, the five superknowledges are analogous to the light because they have the characteristic of engaging in the elimination of darkness that is discordant with the experiential knowledge of whatever object. The intuitive wisdom of the cessation of contaminations is analogous to heat because of its characteristic of engaging in consuming the fuel of karmic evolution and addictions without remainder. The transformed cessation of contamination is analogous to color because of its characteristic of being stainless, pure, and clear-light transparency. Here, it is stainless because it has eliminated addictive obscuration. It is pure because it has eliminated objective obscuration. It is clear-light because it is not in its nature to be these two incidental[99] [obscurations]. Thus, these seven things, which consist of five superknowledges, intuitive wisdom, and the cessation, in the continuums of those people who have nothing further to learn are inseparable from one another in the stainless ultimate element, not being differentiated but identical to the ultimate element. This is called "possession."

«129» And with reference to its meaning, the simile of a lamp is to be understood in detail according to the *Sutra [Teaching the Absence of Increase and Decrease (in the Realm of Beings)]*:[100]

Shāriputra, just as a lamp is indivisible and inseparable from its light, heat, and color, a precious stone is also indivisible and inseparable from its light, color, and shape. Likewise, Shāriputra, the truth body taught by the Tathāgata is indivisible from the

99. *āgantuka, glo bur ba.*

100. PD70 (phi), p. 1036.15–21; Taishō 668, 467a. This sutra seems not to have been translated into Tibetan, existing only in full in the Taishō Tripitaka.

qualities of the Tathāgata, which are far beyond the sands of the Ganges in number, and is inseparable from the excellences of the intuitive wisdom.

«130» Here, there is a verse focused on the meaning of "engagement."

Since it engages with reality differently
In alienated beings, noble ones, and perfect buddhas,
The seer of reality teaches that
The victor essence is in sentient beings. //I.45//

«131» What is shown by this verse?

Alienated individuals live in error,
The seers of the truth are the opposite.
Tathāgatas are error-free and correct,
Free from elaboration itself. //I.46//

«132» It should be understood that [engagements with] the tathāgata element have been taught to bodhisattvas in the *Transcendent Wisdom Sutras*, etc., with reference to the nonconceptual intuitive wisdom. There are three different kinds of engagement with the general characteristic of the pure reality of all things—as taught [in the sutra]—those of alienated individuals who do not perceive reality, of noble ones who do see reality, and of tathāgatas who have attained the ultimate purity in seeing reality. In other words, they are erroneous, correct, and absolutely correct without elaboration, respectively. Here, "erroneous" refers to alienated people on account of their erroneous notions, thoughts, and views. "Correct" refers to nobles because they, being the opposite of alienated people, have eliminated error. And "absolutely correct without elaboration" refers to perfect buddhas because they have destroyed addictive obscuration and its evolutionary instincts as well as objective obscuration.

«133» Four other meanings taught hereafter should be understood to be the ramifications of the meaning of engagement. Here is one verse with reference to the meaning of "states":

Impure, [both partially] impure and pure, and
Perfectly pure are, respectively,
Called an alienated being,
A bodhisattva, and a tathāgata. //I.47//

«134» What is shown by this verse?

The element, subsumed under these six,
The meanings of nature, etc,
Is, in accordance with its three states,
Demonstrated by three names. //I.48//

The stainless element, taught by the Bhagavān in detail in numerous ways, is here subsumed under six meanings, namely: nature, causes, fruition, actions, possession, and engagement. This element is also to be known as being taught by means of the teaching of three names in accordance with its three states, respectively. That is to say, (1) it is called the "element of sentient beings" in the impure state; (2) it is called "bodhisattva" in the [both] pure and impure state; and (3) it is called "tathāgata" in the perfectly pure state.

«135» As the Bhagavān states [in the *Sutra Teaching the Absence of Increase and Decrease (in the Realm of Beings)*]:[101]

O Shāriputra, this, the truth body itself, when it is [in beings and so] covered with limitless sheaths of addictions, being carried by the current of cyclic life and circling between death and birth in the course of beginningless and endless cyclic life, is called the "element of sentient beings."

This same truth body itself, O Shāriputra, when it has felt aversion to the sufferings in the current of cyclic life and become free of attachment to all the objects of desire, ventures forth into the practices for the sake of enlightenment by means of the ten transcendences; and after mastery of all of the eighty-four thousand heaps of Dharma, is called "bodhisattva."

101. PD70 (phi), pp. 1038.13–1039.7; T.668, p. 467b.

Furthermore, O Shāriputra, when this very truth body itself, having been released from all the sheaths of addictions, having gone beyond all the sufferings, having been freed of all addictive taints, has become pure, perfectly pure, and supremely pure, ascends to the stage to be looked upon by all sentient beings, obtains the power of a person who is unsurpassed in all knowable objects, and, unobscured in nature, obtains the unimpeded power of mastery over all things. Then [this truth body] is called "the Tathāgata, the Saint, the Perfectly Accomplished Buddha."

≪136≫ Here is a verse referring to the meaning of the "all-pervasiveness" of the tathāgata element in those three states.

Just as space—free of conceptual thought—
Is naturally all-pervading, so too
The nature of the mind—the stainless element—
Is likewise all-pervasive. //I.49//

≪137≫ What is shown by this verse?

Its general characteristic pervades
Faults, excellences, and the ultimate,
As space does the inferior,
Mediocre, and supreme aspects of forms. //I.50//

≪138≫ The nature of the mind of an alienated being, a noble one, and a perfect buddha, being free of conceptual thought, is the general characteristic [of the element]. Therefore, it is all-pervading, all-engaging, equal, without difference in these three states of having faults, excellences, and the ultimate pure excellences, just as space pervades all the vessels of clay, copper, and gold.

≪139≫ For this reason, immediately after the teaching on the states, the Buddha declares [in the *Sutra Teaching the Absence of Increase and Decrease (in the Realm of Beings)*]:[102]

102. PD70 (phi), pp. 1039.20–1040.3; T.668, p. 467b.

Therefore, Shāriputra, the element of sentient beings and the truth body are not different from each other. The element of sentient beings is nothing but the truth body, and the truth body is nothing but the element of sentient beings. These two are non-dual in fact but different merely in words.

«140» Moreover, the tathāgata element, being all-pervading in these three states, is unchangeable either by addictions or by purification. There are fourteen verses with reference to this subject. The gist of these verses is to be understood by the following verse:

> Though possessing incidental faults,
> Because it has excellences by nature,
> It is the immutable reality,
> The same after as it was before. //I.51//

«141» In the impure state as well as in the [both] pure and impure state, which are shown by the [following] twelve verses and by the [next] one verse, respectively, [the tathāgata element] is endowed with incidental [faults] of fundamental and minor addictions. [On the other hand], it is endowed by nature with the buddha excellences in the perfectly pure state, which are indivisible, inseparable [from the truth body], inconceivable, and far greater in number than the sands of the Ganges, as demonstrated by the fourteenth verse. Therefore it is demonstrated that the tathāgata element is eternally unchangeable like space throughout different times.

«142» What are the twelve verses with reference to the unchangeable characteristic in the impure state?

> As space is all-pervading and,
> Because subtle, is completely unaffected,
> So, that state,[103] present in all beings,
> Is completely unaffected. //I.52//

> Just as all worlds
> Arise and disintegrate in space,

---

103. *sthita, gnas.*

So in the uncreated element
All sense media arise and disintegrate. //I.53//

Just as space has never before
Been burnt by fires,
So this is not burnt by the fires of
Death, sickness, and aging. //I.54//

Earth is sustained by water,
Water by wind, and wind by space;
Space, however, is not sustained
By wind, water, or earth. //I.55//

Likewise, aggregates, elements, and sense media
Are based upon evolution and addictions.
Evolution and addictions are always based
Upon an incorrect mental process. //I.56//

This incorrect mental process is grounded
Upon the purity of the mind,
Yet the mind's nature is not grounded
Upon any of all the things. //I.57//

The aggregates, elements, and media
Should be recognized as like the earth.
The evolution and addictions of sentient beings
Should be known as akin to water. //I.58//

Incorrect mental processes seem
To be similar to the wind;
With no basis and no location,
Their nature is like space. //I.59//

Incorrect mentation stays
In the nature of the mind.
Incorrect mentation manifests
Karmic evolution and addictions. //I.60//

From the water of evolution and addictions
The aggregates, elements, and media emerge,
Arising and disintegrating,
Just as [water] rises and subsides. //I.61//

The nature of the mind is like space:
It has no causes or conditions,
Neither these in aggregation,
Nor arising, enduring, or decaying. //I.62//

The nature of the mind is clear-light,
Just as immutable as space.
It never becomes addicted by incidental taints,
Attachment, etc., arising from wrong mentation. //I.63//

«143» How is this tathāgata essence in the impure state shown to be immutable in nature by this simile of space? It is said:

This [element] cannot be made [impure],
By the water, etc., of evolution and addictions.
The fires of death, sickness, and aging,
Though unbearable, cannot consume it. //I.64//

«144» The arising of the world that consists of aggregates, elements, and sense media is based upon the water of evolution and addictions, which is in turn produced by a wind-circle of improper mentation. This evolution, however, does not cause the spatial formation of the nature of the mind. In the same way, in order to destroy the world that consists of the aggregates, elements, and sense media founded on the wind-like improper mentation and water-like evolution and addictions, a group of fires arise that are death, sickness, and aging. It should be known, however, that even by this arising of the fires of death, etc., this [nature] cannot be destroyed. Thus, in the impure state, though all the taints of karmic evolution, addictions, and birth arise and disintegrate like world environments, the uncreated tathāgata essence, like space, is without arising and cessation. Therefore, it is shown to be an absolutely immutable reality.

≪145≫ This space simile that refers to the door of the truth-illumination coming from the natural purity is to be understood in detail according to the *[Questions of Gaganagañja] Sutra*:[104]

> Great seer, it is like this: addictions are the dark; purity is luminosity. Addictions are weak; transcendent analysis is powerful. Addictions are incidental; the natural purity is radical. Addictions are the imagined; the nature is free of imagination. For example, great seer, this great earth is supported by water. Water is supported by wind, and wind is supported by space. But space, in turn, is not supported by anything. Thus, among these four elements, space is more powerful than any of the three elements of earth, water, and wind. It is also firm and immovable. It has no decrease and no increase. It is not created and does not cease. It is supported by its own nature. [However], the three elements are endowed with creation and disintegration, being unstable. These are perceived as changeable, but space is not [changeable] in the slightest. Likewise, the aggregates, elements, and sense media have their support in karmic evolution and addiction. Evolution and addiction have their support in incorrect mentation and the latter, in turn, has its support in the natural purity. Therefore, it is said: the mind is naturally clear-light, but it is tainted by incidental addictions. . . .

≪146≫ Here, all these things: incorrect mentation, karmic evolution, addictions, aggregates, elements, and sense media are created by the conglomeration of causes and conditions. When these causes and conditions are absent, they will cease. [On the contrary], the nature has no cause and no condition. Consequently, it has no conglomeration. It is not created and does not cease. Here, the nature is akin to space, incorrect mentation to wind, evolution and addiction to water, and the aggregates, elements, and sense media to earth. Therefore, it is said that all things are completely devoid of any root. Their root is essence-free, their root is unlocated, their root is purity, and their root is rootlessness.

104. PD70 (phi), pp. 1042.17–1043.14; D148, ff. 320b.6–321a.7.

«147» Nature in the impure state has been explained as analogous to space on account of its immutable characteristic; incorrect mentation, evolution, and addictions as analogous to wind and water, respectively, on account of their characteristic of cause; and the aggregates, elements, and sense media, which are produced [from the former two], as analogous to the earth element, on account of their characteristic of fruition.

«148» Fires of death, sickness, and aging, which cause the disintegration [of the former three], have not yet been explained as being like the fire element on account of their characteristic of headaches. So I will explain.

The three fires—the fire at the end of the world,
The fire of hell, and the ordinary fire—
These are to be known, respectively, as analogies
For the three fires of death, sickness, and aging. //I.65//

«149» Death, sickness, and aging being analogous to the [three mentioned] fires should be known for three reasons, respectively: (1) because [death] causes the six sense media to be unowned by the person; (2) [sickness] causes various kinds of sufferings to be experienced; and (3) [aging] causes the compounded to decay. Even by these fires, the tathāgata element in the impure state cannot be changed at all.

«150» With reference to this point, it is stated in the *[Shrīmālādevī Lion's Roar] Sutra:*[105]

O Bhagavān, this so-called death and this so-called birth are merely mundane, conventional terms. O Bhagavān, this so-called death causes the senses to cease, and this so-called birth causes the senses to be obtained. O Bhagavān, the tathāgata essence, however, is never born, never ages, never dies, and is never born [again]. Why? Because, O Bhagavān, the tathāgata essence, beyond the sphere marked as created, is eternal, stable, peaceful, and everlasting.

---

105. PD70 (phi), pp. 1044.20–1045.6; D92, f. 274b.3–6.

«151» Here is a verse on immutability in the pure and the impure states:

Delivered from birth, death, sickness, and aging,
They have realized its nature correctly.
Free from the ruin of birth, etc., by that cause,
The intelligent rely on it [anyway],
To develop compassion for migrant beings. //I.66//

«152» What is shown by this verse?

The noble ones have completely eliminated
The suffering of death, sickness, and aging.
It does not (apply) to them because their lives
Are not under the power of evolution and addictions. //I.67//

«153» In the impure state, the substantial cause of the fires of death, sickness, and aging is the fuel-like birth based upon improper mentation, karmic evolution, and addictions. In [both] the pure and impure states, however, for bodhisattvas who have obtained the mind-made body there are no such fires to be experienced, because they have no [ordinary] appearance whatsoever.

«154» [The root text states:]

Since they see the stainless reality,
They have passed beyond birth, etc.;
Yet the compassionate-natured still display
Birth, death, aging, and sickness. //I.68//

Indeed, because of their all-engagement as a result of their virtuous roots, bodhisattvas properly engage with the three realms out of compassion on the basis of their power to voluntarily control their births. They may display the appearance of birth, aging, sickness, and death. But for them, there are in reality no such things as birth, etc., since, of course, they have correctly seen that the element in reality is without birth and without origination.

«155» One should understand this occasion of those bodhisattvas in detail, according to the *[Questions of Sāgaramati] Sutra*, as follows:[106]

> What are the addictions associated with the virtuous roots that serve as the cause of cyclic life for those [bodhisattvas]? They are namely: nonsatisfaction in searching for the store of merit; taking voluntary rebirth in worldly existence; an earnest wish to meet with buddhas; tirelessness in working for the perfect development of sentient beings; making efforts toward the thorough apprehension of the holy Dharma; working to fulfill all kinds of needs of sentient beings; a non-aloofness from passionate thought for the Dharma; a nonabandonment of thorough engagement with the transcendences. O Sāgaramati, these are addictions associated with the virtuous roots by which bodhisattvas join themselves [to cyclic life], but they are never affected by the faults of addictions. . . .

«156» [The sutra continues:]

> [Then, Sāgaramati asked:] Why then, O Bhagavān, are the virtuous roots called "addictions"?

> [The Bhagavān answered:] O Sāgaramati, it is in the sense that bodhisattvas join themselves to the three realms by these addictions of such a nature, for the three realms are originated from addictions.

> Here, the bodhisattvas join themselves to the three realms out of their own volition, by their skill in liberative art, and by their cultivation of the power of virtuous roots. Thus, these are called "addictions associated with virtuous roots," inasmuch as these cause bodhisattvas to join themselves to the three realms, but not because of [their being actual] addictions of the mind.

> O Sāgaramati, suppose there was an only son of some merchant or householder. Suppose he was beloved, handsome, cherished,

---

106. PD70 (phi), pp. 1046.6–1048.10; D152, ff. 85b.5–86b.4. This includes the quotes below.

and attractive. Suppose this boy, being a child, fell into a filthy pit while playing. The mother and relatives of this boy saw him fall into the filthy pit. Upon seeing this they cried, were distressed, and screamed. They could not, however, take the boy out by entering the pit. Then the boy's father came to that place and saw his only son fallen into the filthy pit. Upon seeing this and impelled by the fervent wish to pull out his only son, he jumped quickly into the filthy pit without any feeling of disgust, and took out his only son.

O Sāgaramati, this analogy is made in order to make clear a special meaning. What meaning is suggested by this analogy? O Sāgaramati, "filthy pit" is a synonym for the three realms. "Only son" is a synonym for sentient beings, for bodhisattvas have a notion of the only child toward all sentient beings. "Mother and relatives" is a synonym for those people who belong to the disciple vehicle and hermit buddha vehicle since they, having seen sentient beings fallen into cyclic life, are distressed and cry out, but have no ability to rescue them. "Great merchant or householder" is a synonym for bodhisattvas, who are pure, untainted, of untainted mind, have directly realized the uncreated Dharma, but still take rebirth in the three realms of their own volition for the sake of sentient beings' development.

O Sāgaramati, such is the great compassion of bodhisattvas that, being thoroughly free from all rebirths, they still take rebirths in worldly existence. Empowered by wisdom and skill in liberative arts, they are never harmed by taints; and, in order to liberate sentient beings from all the bondage of addictions, they teach the Dharma.

«157» By means of this sutra passage, the [both] pure and impure state is shown in a sense that powerful bodhisattvas take rebirth of their own volition for the sake of others, by the power of their virtuous roots and their compassion, but at the same time, as a result of the power of their skill in liberative art and their wisdom, they are not tainted.

«158» Here, when bodhisattvas have obtained the accurate realization of the tathāgata element as being unproduced and unoriginated, they immediately attain that reality. This point should be understood according to the [same] sutra as follows:[107]

> O Sāgaramati, realize that things are of no real essence and there is no creator, no owner, no sentient being, no life, no person, and no self. Indeed, these things are established according to the [bodhisattva's] wish. Thus do not think or imagine, Sāgaramati, that bodhisattvas who believe this immutable reality would ever cultivate the feeling of hostility toward anything. They are endowed with the pure intuitive perception that there is nothing that causes benefit or harm. Thus, they know correctly the reality of things, and thus they will never cast off the armor of great compassion.

> Sāgaramati, suppose there were an invaluable sapphire gem, well purified, well cleaned, and stainless. Suppose it were left in mud and remained there for a thousand years. Then, this stone was taken from the mud and cleaned by washing and purification. Even being cleaned well, however, it never abandoned its nature of a jewel, pure and stainless. In the same way, Sāgaramati, bodhisattvas know the mind of sentient beings as being naturally clear-light. But they also perceive that the same mind is tainted by incidental addictions.

> Then, bodhisattvas think as follows: "These addictions would never penetrate the naturally clear-light mind of sentient beings. Being incidental, these addictions are the product of incorrect imaginations. We can teach these sentient beings the Dharma in order to purify their addictions." Thus, they will never let their minds become discouraged. Instead, they will cultivate the spirit of engaging with sentient beings many times. Again they will think as follows: "These addictions have no power and strength. They are powerless, weak, and have no real support at all. These

107. PD70 (phi), pp. 1048.18–1050.14; D152, f. 85a.2–85b.5.

addictions are [produced] by incorrect imaginations. We will never feel angry with addictions if we investigate them with correct and proper mentation. We will never connect ourselves with addictions, so we will investigate them in detail. We would do better not to connect with addictions. It is not good to connect with addictions. If we connected ourselves with addictions, how could we teach the Dharma to sentient beings who are bound by the bondages of addictions in order to eliminate these bondages of addictions? In any case, we will never connect ourselves with addictions, and then we will teach the Dharma to sentient beings in order to eliminate their bondages of addictions. On the other hand, we will connect ourselves with those addictions associated with virtuous roots that cause cyclic life in order to develop sentient beings."

«159» Here, the expression "cyclic life" is accepted as the threefold mind-made body, which is the reflection of the three realms within the uncontaminated element. It is cyclic life because it is created with uncontaminated virtuous roots. At the same time, it is nirvana because it is uncreated by contaminated karmic evolutionary actions and addictions. With regard to this point, the *[Shrīmālādevī Lion's Roar]* Sutra states:[108]

Therefore, O Bhagavān, there is cyclic life, created as well as uncreated. There is nirvana, created as well as uncreated.

Being endowed with overall engagement arisen from the mind that is a mixture of created and uncreated, this occasion is called the "[both] pure and impure state." «160» This state is chiefly established for the confrontation[109] bodhisattva stage, because [in this stage] bodhisattvas—proceeding to the attainment of the knowledge of the cessation of taints[110] by means of their meditations on the unobscured transcendent wisdom and great compassion—still do not actualize that attainment in order to protect all sentient beings.

---

108. PD70 (phi), p. 1050.19–21; D92, f. 271b.2–3.

109. *abhimukhī, mngon du gyur pa.*

110. *āsravakṣayajñāna, zag pa zad pa'i mngon par shes pa.*

«161» Concerning this knowledge of the cessation of contamination, there is the simile of a man [who has just arrived in a city], in the *[Questions of Ratnachūḍā] Sutra.*[111]

> Thus, O noble child,[112] bodhisattvas cause the five superknowledges to be cultivated by means of practices on the basis of great effort, great exertion, and high resolve. Having the mind purified by concentration and superknowledges, they confront the cessation of contamination. Having the mind purified by intuitive wisdom from the cessation of contamination and by means of the cultivation of the spirit of great compassion in order to protect all sentient beings, they are confronted by the cessation of contamination again when they have produced unobscured wisdom on the sixth stage.

Thus, bodhisattvas who are at the confrontation bodhisattva stage obtain the power to actualize the cessation of taints, so their state is explained as "pure." Bodhisattvas having such natures wish to protect wandering sentient beings with their great compassion, proclaiming: "I shall lead others to this correct realization." While familiarizing themselves with the techniques for the bliss of peace, bodhisattvas do not taste it. When looking at sentient beings who are confronting cyclic life, bodhisattvas confront nirvana by contrast. In order to perfect the accessories of enlightenment, they return from their places of meditation and voluntarily take rebirths in the desire realm. Wishing to work for the sake of sentient beings as quickly as possible, they have obtained the power to manifest all kinds of bodies of ordinary people, and to take various rebirths [even] in the form of animals. From this point their state is explained as "impure."

«162» There follows another meaning of the verse [66]:

> Those blinded by ignorance see a victor child
> Who has realized this immutable reality,

111. PD70 (phi), p. 1051.8–16; D91, f. 242a.5–7.

112. I agree with Takasaki that the word *kulaputra* is probably an excess because the simile is missing and the following passage is best seen as a paraphrase of the *Ratnachūḍā Sutra*. But it is also possible, as Takasaki has pointed out, that the Sanskrit original and Tibetan redaction have a lacuna here. *A Study on the Ratnagotravibhāga*, 251.

As though they were born, and so on—
This is really wonderful!//I.69//

Having attained the sphere of noble beings,
They show themselves in the sphere of ordinary beings;
Thus the art and compassion of these friends of beings
Are truly excellent. //I.70//

Though they have transcended all worlds,
They are not separate from the world.
They act within the world for the world,
Without being affected by worldly taints. //I.71//

Just as a lotus born of water
Is not corrupted by water,
Similarly, though they are born in the world,
They are never corrupted by worldly things. //I.72//

In order to accomplish their activities,
Their intelligence is always burning like fire.
At the same time, they are always immersed
In the equipoise of peace. //I.73//

Because of the power of [their previous prayers]
And their freedom from all conceptual thoughts,
They do not make any effort
In order to develop sentient beings. //I.74//

They know precisely whichever art is needed
To educate disciples, and whichever teaching,
Physical form, conduct, and behavior
Will be the most appropriate. //I.75//

In this way, those of unimpeded intelligence
Properly engage themselves in helping beings
As limitless in number as the sky,
Continually and spontaneously. //I.76//

During their meditative post-attainment state,
Bodhisattvas become equal to the Tathāgata
As a result of the way they act properly in the worlds
To liberate sentient beings. //I.77//

There is, however, as great a difference
Between a bodhisattva and a buddha
As between the atom and the earth,
And a bull's hoof-print puddle and the ocean. //I.78//

«163» Of these ten verses, taken in order, [the first] nine verses refer to
[the "purity" of noble bodhisattvas] in comparison with the total addictive taint below the joyous bodhisattva stage, and the tenth verse refers to
[the "impurity"] in comparison with the supreme purity above the Dharma
cloud stage. In brief, this explains the purity and impurity of the four kinds
of bodhisattva in the ten bodhisattva stages. The four kinds of bodhisattva
are as follows: (1) bodhisattvas who have conceived the spirit for the first
time; (2) bodhisattvas who have engaged in activities; (3) bodhisattvas who
have reached the stage of nonregression; and (4) bodhisattvas who are only
one birth away from enlightenment.

«164» Here, the first and second verses demonstrate the characteristics of pure excellences of bodhisattvas in the first, the joyous, stage who
have conceived the [enlightenment] spirit for the first time, because these
bodhisattvas have perceived the transcendent reality that they had never
perceived before, since time without beginning. The third and fourth
verses demonstrate the characteristics of the pure excellences of the bodhisattvas in the immaculate stage up to the far-reaching stage, who have
engaged in activities, because these bodhisattvas perform unblemished
activities. The fifth verse demonstrates the characteristics of pure excellences of bodhisattvas in the immovable stage, who have reached the
stage of nonregression, because these bodhisattvas constantly remain in
the meditation pertaining to the attainment of the great enlightenment.
The sixth, seventh and eighth verses demonstrate the characteristics of
pure excellences of bodhisattvas in the Dharma cloud stage who are one
birth away from enlightenment, because these bodhisattvas have perfected
all the techniques for benefiting themselves and others and because this
is their last birth prior to the attainment of the stage of a buddha, the

supreme unsurpassed perfect enlightenment. The ninth and tenth verses demonstrate the equality as well as the difference between bodhisattvas who have achieved perfection and a buddha in terms of the excellences of benefiting themselves and others.

«165» Here is a verse concerning the immutability in the absolute pure state.

> Its nature is immutable, because it is endowed with inexhaustible
>   excellences.
> It is the refuge of beings, because it has no limit in the future.
> It is always nondual, because it is nonconceptual.
> It is also of indestructible character, because its nature is not
>   altered. //I.79//

«166» What is taught by this verse?

> It has no birth, no death,
> No sickness, no aging.
> Because it is permanent,
> Enduring, peaceful, and immutable. //I.80//

> It has no birth even with a mind-made body,
> Because it is permanent.
> Inconceivable, it has no death,
> Because it is enduring. //I.81//

> It is unharmed by the sickness of the subtle evolutionary
>   instincts,
> Because it is peace.
> It has no aging conditioned by uncontaminated [evolution],
> Because it is immutable. //I.82//

«167» While remaining on the buddha stage that is absolutely stainless, pure, and naturally clear-light, this tathāgata element has no birth even in the form of a mind-made body, in regard to its beginning, because it is eternal. It has no death even in the manner of inconceivable transformation, in regard to its end, because it is enduring. It is unharmed by the disease of the ignorance instinct producing ground, in regard to both its beginning and its end, because it is peace. It has no aging, free of things by means of the development of the fruition of uncontaminated karmic evolution, and thus is unaffected, because it is immutable.

«168» [The root text states:]

> The meaning of permanent, etc.,
> With respect to the uncompounded element
> Is to be known, respectively,
> By each pair of terms. //I.83//

«169» The distinction of each pair of terms shows the statement and exposition of the meaning of each term—permanence, enduringness, peace, and immutability, respectively—and should be understood according to the *Sutra [Teaching the Absence of Increase and Decrease (in the Realm of Beings)]* as the uncreated element. As it is said [in summary]:[113]

> It is changeless in nature, having inexhaustible qualities,
> Its refuge for migrants endures for the infinite future,
> It is always nondual, so inconceivable,
> Indestructible, its nature uncreated.

What does this teach? [From the sutra:][114]

> This immutable truth body, Shāriputra, is permanent, because it is of an inexhaustible nature. This refuge truth body, Shāriputra, is enduring, because it exists as far as the reality-limit. This nondual truth body, Shāriputra, is peace, because it is of nonconceptual nature. This indestructible truth body, Shāriputra, is immutable, because it has the characteristic of being unaltered.

---

113. This verse is not found in the Chinese version and the current Sanskrit redaction. According to Takasaki, this verse in Ngog Lotsawa's translation is an interpolation (*A Study on the Ratnagotravibhāga*, 258). In fact, no Tibetan translator would interpolate a verse that he did not find in the Sanskrit from which he was working. It is more likely that this verse was in the Sanskrit text Ngog used for his translation. Tibetan PD70 (phi), p. 1054.12–14.

114. Taishō 668, 467a–b.

«170» Here is a verse concerning the meaning of "indivisible [excellences]" in connection with this pure state of the tathāgata essence that has reached the ultimate meaning of being absolutely pure:

> It is the truth body. It is the Tathāgata.
> It is the noble truth. It is nirvana.
> Like the sun and its rays, excellences are indivisible.
> Therefore, there is no nirvana apart from buddhahood. //I.84//

«171» Here, what is demonstrated by the former half of this verse?

> It should be recognized, in brief,
> There are four synonyms, the truth body, etc.,
> Because the meaning of this stainless element
> Is classified into four aspects. //I.85//

In short, the tathāgata essence as the stainless element has four synonyms in accordance with these four meanings.

«172» Then, what are the four meanings?

> It is indivisible from the buddha qualities,
> Is the attainment of the potential as it is.
> It is reality, neither false nor deceptive,
> And natural peace from time primordial. //I.86//

«173» With reference to [the first meaning that is the tathāgata essence, it is] indivisible from the buddha qualities. The following statement from the *[Shrīmālādevī Lion's Roar] Sutra* states:[115]

> O Bhagavān, the tathāgata essence is not devoid of the buddha excellences that are indivisible, inseparable, and inconceivable, far greater in number than the sands of the Ganges.

---

115. PD70 (phi), pp. 1056.15–1057.6; D92, ff. 272a.7–272b.1.

In terms of [the second meaning that] its spiritual potential has obtained the nature of inconceivability, a sutra states as follows:[116]

This [spiritual potential], naturally acquired from its beginning-less continuum, is like the distinctiveness of the six sense media.

In terms of [the third meaning of] being neither false nor deceptive, the sutra states as follows:[117]

Here, the ultimate truth is nirvana that is in fact not deceptive. For what reason? Because this spiritual potential is eternal, naturally being at peace.

In terms of [the fourth meaning that] it is always peace, the *[Ornament of the Light of Wisdom] Sutra* states as follows:[118]

Being primordially in total nirvana itself, the Tathāgata, the Saint, the Perfectly Enlightened One is neither created nor ceased.

«174» For these four meanings, there are four synonyms, namely: (1) truth body; (2) tathāgata; (3) ultimate truth; and (4) nirvana, respectively. For what reason? A sutra states as follows:[119]

O Shāriputra, the so-called tathāgata essence is a synonym for the truth body.

[The *Shrīmālādevī Lion's Roar Sutra* states:][120]

116. PD70 (phi), p. 1056.19–20. Unidentified; possibly from the *Sutra on the Six Sense Media*.

117. PD70 (phi), pp. 1056.21–1057.3; resembles a passage from the *Shrīmālādevī Lion's Roar Sutra* (D92, ff. 272b.7–273a.1).

118. PD70 (phi), p. 1057.4–6; D100, f. 283a.3.

119. PD70 (phi), p. 1056.19–20. This passage in found in both the *Ornament of the Light of Wisdom Sutra* and the *Sutra Teaching the Absence of Increase and Decrease (in the Realm of Beings)* (Taishō 668, 476a).

120. PD70 (phi), pp. 1056.21–1057.6; D92, f. 269a.2–3; 272a.2–5; 269a.1–2.

O Bhagavān, the Tathāgata and the truth body are not different from each other. O Bhagavān, the truth body is nothing but the Tathāgata.

And:

The so-called cessation of suffering, O Bhagavān, indicates the truth body of the Tathāgata who is endowed with such excellences.

And:

The so-called ultimate element of nirvana, O Bhagavān, is a synonym for the truth body of the Tathāgata.

«175» Now, what is demonstrated by the latter half of the verse?

Being the perfect enlightenment regarding all kinds [of things],
And being the elimination of taints along with instincts,
The Buddha and nirvana
Are nondual in the ultimate sense. //I.87//

For what reason? These four synonyms for the uncontaminated element converge into the single meaning of the tathāgata element. Therefore, these four are identical in meaning, and hence, in terms of the Dharma of nonduality, "the Buddha" and "nirvana" should be viewed as "indivisible" or "inseparable"; that is to say, they are "nondual." The former is so called because of his perfect enlightenment regarding all kinds of things, and the latter is so called because of its elimination of taints along with their evolutionary instincts, which takes place simultaneously with the perfect enlightenment in the stainless element.

«176» It is said:[121]

Liberation is of a nature
Indivisible from the excellences,
Immeasurable, inconceivable, and stainless;
This liberation is the Tathāgata.

121. PD70 (phi), p. 1058.6–8. This is generally considered to be a verse from the *Commentary*.

«177» This point is made clear in the *[Shrīmālādevī Lion's Roar] Sutra* in connection with the nirvana of the saints and the hermit buddhas:[122]

O Bhagavān, this "nirvana" is an art used by tathāgatas.

This sutra passage demonstrates that this [nirvana of saints and hermit buddhas] is an art used by a perfectly enlightened one who is the supreme lord of Dharma in order to prevent regression, just as an illusory city in the forest is created for exhausted travelers after their long journey.

«178» [On the other hand,] the *[Shrīmālādevī Lion's Roar] Sutra* states as follows:[123]

O Bhagavān, the Tathāgatas, Saints, the Perfectly Enlightened Ones are endowed with the immeasurable, inconceivable, and ultimate pure excellences because of their attainment of nirvana.

«179» This sutra passage demonstrates that, having attained nirvana, which is characterized as being indivisible from the accomplishment of four kinds of excellence, the perfectly enlightened ones are identified with this nirvana. Therefore, as both a buddha and nirvana are endowed with an inseparable excellence, no one can attain nirvana without becoming a buddha.

«180» The buddhas are endowed with all excellences because the "emptiness endowed with every supreme aspect"[124] has been established within the stainless element. This point is to be known by means of our verses based on the simile of the painters [in the *Questions of Ratnachūḍā Sutra*]:

Compare this to painters
Specialized in different parts.
So whichever part one knows,
The others cannot understand. //I.88//

---

122. PD70 (phi), p. 1058.10–11; D92, f. 264a.5.
123. PD70 (phi), p. 1058.14–17; D92, f. 264a.5–264b.2.
124. *sarvākāravaropetaśūnyatā, rnam pa thams cad kyi mchog dang ldan pa'i stong pa nyid.*

Their ruling king gives them
A canvas, with the following order:
"You all must paint
My portrait on this!"//I.89//

Having received the command,
They start their work of painting.
However, one of them engaged in this work
Leaves for a foreign land. //I.90//

Because of his absence,
Having gone to another land,
This portrait, all parts, remains unfinished.
This is the simile. //I.91//

These painters are
Generosity, ethics, tolerance, and so on.
Emptiness endowed with every supreme aspect
Is said to be the portrait. //I.92//

≪181≫ Here, even each of these [excellences], such as generosity, etc., should be known as being "immeasurable," since it is differentiated into limitless varieties in the sphere of the Buddha. It is "inconceivable" on account of its number and power. It is "supremely pure" because of the removal of its resistant instincts, such as that of stinginess, etc.

≪182≫ By the means of concentration on emptiness endowed with every supreme aspect, the [tolerance of] the uncreated reality is attained. Because of this attainment, [bodhisattvas] at the eighth immovable stage accomplish all excellences of buddhas in the stainless element on the basis of their nonconceptual, faultless, uninterrupted, and spontaneously engaging knowledge of the path. By innumerable ocean-like means of concentration and incantation, [bodhisattvas] at the positive intelligence ninth stage accomplish immeasurable excellences on the basis of their knowledge of holding the immeasurable excellences of a buddha. [Bodhisattvas] at the Dharma cloud tenth stage accomplish inconceivable excellences on the basis of their knowledge of the revelation of the secret of all buddhas. Immediately after [this stage], the supreme pure excellences are accomplished on the basis of the knowledge that liberates from addictive obscuration along with its evolutionary instincts and from objective obscuration because of the attainment of buddhahood.

«183» As disciple saints and hermit buddhas cannot perceive these four foundations of the intuitive wisdoms in these stages, they are said to be far from the element of nirvana that is characterized as indivisible from the accomplishment of the [aforementioned] four kinds of excellence.

«184» [The root text states:]

Wisdom, intuitive wisdom, and liberation
Are clear, clear-light, and pure,
And are indivisible, thereby being like the light,
The rays, and the sun itself. //I.93//

«185» Wisdom, intuitive wisdom, and liberation are the illustrations of the element of nirvana that is characterized as being indivisible from the accomplishment of the four kinds of excellence. They are demonstrated to be analogous to the sun in four aspects, namely, by three [particular] aspects and by one [in general].

Here, (1) the transcendent nonconceptual wisdom in the continuum of a buddha is analogous to light because it dispels darkness [that hides] the ultimate reality of knowable objects; (2) the omniscient intuitive wisdom that is obtained subsequently is analogous to the luminosity of the net of rays because it permeates all aspects of objects of knowledge in their entirety; (3) the natural liberation that is the basis of the above two is analogous to the purity of the sun because it is absolutely free from taints and is clear-light transparency; (4) as these three are indivisible from the ultimate element in terms of their entities, they are analogous to the light, etc., because of their indivisibility [from the sun].

«186» [The root text states:]

Therefore, until buddhahood is attained,
There is no attainment of nirvana,
Just as the sun cannot be seen
Without its light and rays. //I.94//

«187» This element that is endowed with virtuous excellences as its own nature since beginningless time is the reality that is indivisible from the excellences of buddhas. Therefore, until the attainment of the state of a tathāgata who possesses unobscured intuitive realization, it is unfeasible to actualize the realization of nirvana that is characterized as the liberation from all obscurations, just as the sun cannot be seen without perceiving its light and rays. Therefore, the *[Shrīmālādevī Lion's Roar] Sutra* states as follows:[125]

> O Bhagavān, the realization of nirvana does not exist among the inferior and superior things. O Bhagavān, the realization of nirvana is equal to wisdom. O Bhagavān, nirvana is equal to intuitive wisdom, equal to liberation, and equal to the intuitive perception of liberation. Therefore, O Bhagavān, it is said that the element of nirvana is of one taste, of equal taste; that is to say, [it is of one] taste with knowledge and liberation.

≪188≫ [The root text states:]

> In this way, the tathāgata essence has been
> Explained by means of the arrangement of ten aspects;
> The fact that it exists within the husk of addictions
> Is known by the following similes. //I.95//

Thus, with reference to the existence[126] of the reality that is eternal in that it is analogous to the ultimate limit of the future, the arrangement of this tathāgata essence has been hitherto explained by ten meanings.

≪189≫ With reference to the covering of addictions—which is essentially unconnected [to the tathāgata essence] although coexisting since beginningless time—and the naturally pure reality—which likewise exists since beginningless time, are essentially connected [to the tathāgata essence]: they should be understood, by nine similes according to the *[Tathāgata Essence] Sutra*, that the tathāgata essence is concealed by limitless addictions.

≪190≫ What are the nine similes?

> Like a buddha within a faded lotus, honey amid bees,
> Kernels within their husks, gold within filth,

---

125. PD70 (phi), pp. 1061.17–1062.2; D92, f. 267a.2–4.
126. *saṁvidyamānatā, rig par bya ba nyid.*

Treasure beneath the floor, and sprouts, etc., grown from a
   small fruit,
A buddha's image in tattered rags, and //I.96//

Like a king in a poor woman's womb,
A precious statue existing within a clay [mold];
Similarly, this element exists in all sentient beings,
Obscured by the taints of incidental addictions. //I.97//

The taints are analogous to the lotus, the bees, the husks, filth,
   the floor, the fruit,
The tattered rags, the woman severely afflicted by burning misery,
   and clay.
The Buddha, honey, grain, gold, treasure, a *nyagrodha* tree, a
   precious image,
The supreme ruler of the world, and a precious statue are akin
   to this supreme, stainless element. //I.98//

«191» The addictions are like the petal sheath of the faded lotus, and the
tathāgata element is akin to a buddha.

Suppose a buddha, shining with a thousand signs,
Were abiding within a faded lotus.
When perceived by a man with the pure divine eye,
It would be extracted from the lotus's petal sheath. //I.99//

Likewise, the Sugata sees with his buddha eye
His own reality even in those who are in the Avīchi hells.
Unobscured, staying with compassion till the future limit,
He liberates us from obscurations. //I.100//

Just as someone with the divine eye sees the Tathāgata
Within the closed lotus flower and cuts away the petals,
So the Tathāgata sees the perfectly enlightened essence
Covered with the sheath of taints, attachment, hatred, etc.,
And destroys such obscurations by means of compassion.
   //I.101//

«192» The addictions are like honeybees, and the tathāgata essence is akin to the honey.

> Suppose a clever person, having seen
> Honey surrounded by a swarm of bees,
> And endeavoring to get it, with certain techniques,
> Would completely separate the swarm of bees from it; //I.102//

> Similarly, the Great Sage, with his omniscient eye,
> Perceives this honey-like essence of the mind,
> And brings about the complete and perfect
> Elimination of the bee-like obscurations. //I.103//

> Just as a man who endeavors to get honey surrounded by myriad
>   bees
> Disperses them all and makes use of the honey as he planned,
> The uncontaminated wisdom within sentient beings is like the
>   honey, the taints are like bees,
> And the Buddha, skillful Victor over bee-like obscurations, is
>   like that man. //I.104//

«193» The addictions are like the outer husk, and the tathāgata element is akin to the inner kernel.

> The kernel of grain is covered by the husk,
> And cannot be consumed by any person;
> Those seeking food, and so on,
> Must remove it from the husk. //I.105//

> Similarly, the tathāgata [essence] in sentient beings
> Is mixed with the taints of addictions.
> And as long as it is not freed from them,
> It cannot perform the buddha activities in the three realms. //I.106//

> Just as the kernels of grain, like rice, wheat, barley, etc., as long
>   as they have not been fully threshed

And still have beards, cannot be enjoyed as a delicious food for
humans,
So the king of Dharma, present in sentient beings, having his
body unreleased from the husk of addictions,
Will not grant the taste of Dharma joy to beings afflicted by the
hunger of addictions. //I.107//

«194» The addictions are like a place rotting with filth, and the tathāgata
element is akin to the gold.

Suppose, while a person was walking in a hurry, their gold
Fell into a place rotting with filth.
This gold, being of indestructible nature,
Would remain there as it was for many centuries. //I.108//

Then a god with the pure divine eye, seeing it there,
Would tell a man: "Here is a piece of gold,
Cleanse this supreme precious thing,
And fashion it into something valuable."//I.109//

Similarly, the Sage sees the excellences of sentient beings
Drowned in filth-like addictions,
And pours the rain of holy Dharma over all beings
In order to purify that mire of addictions. //I.110//

Just as a god, perceiving the gold fallen into a place rotting with
filth,
Showed to the people with great insistence that most beautiful
of things, so that it could be completely cleansed;
So, seeing that the precious perfect buddhahood within all
beings has fallen into addiction's great mire,
The Victor teaches them the Dharma in order to purify it.
//I.111//

«195» The addictions are like a [covering] ground, and the tathāgata element is akin to a treasure of jewels.

Suppose there was an inexhaustible treasure
Beneath the floor within a poor man's house.
This man does not know of it. Also, the treasure
Cannot say to him, "Here I am!" //I.112//

Similarly, though in the mind there is a treasure of jewels,
The stainless reality, neither established nor negated;
Without recognizing it, these sentient beings
Constantly experience the sufferings of their poverty in various
ways. //I.113//

Just as a treasure of jewels in the house of a poor man would
not say to him,
"I, the treasure of jewels, am here!," nor would the man know it
to be there;
Just so, all beings, who have the treasure of Dharma in the
house of their mind, are like the poor man;
In order to enable those beings to obtain this treasure, the Sage
skillfully takes rebirth. //I.114//

«196» The addictions are like a fruit-skin sheath, and the tathāgata element
is akin to a sprout contained within a seed.

The imperishable quality [able to produce] a sprout is
contained
Within a seed of the fruit of a mango tree and the like.
When in the presence of plowed soil, water, and so on,
The sprout will gradually grow into the reality of a kingly tree.
//I.115//

Likewise, enclosed in the fruit skin of misknowledge, etc.,
Of sentient beings, is the pure ultimate element.[127]
And so, by depending on this and that virtue,
It gradually transforms into the nature of a king of sages. //I.116//

---

127. *śubha-dharma-dhātu, chos khams dge ba* (as cited in D4025 *Commentary*).

Just as a tree grows from within the skin of a banana or mango
　　fruit,
Conditioned by water, sunshine, air, soil, time, and space;
So the seed and the sprout of perfect buddhahood, contained
　　within the fruit skin of addictions of sentient beings,
When conditioned by this and that virtue, will emerge and
　　develop as the Dharma. //I.117//

«197» The addictions are like the tattered rags, and the tathāgata element
is akin to a precious image.

Suppose a buddha image made of precious jewels,
Wrapped in tattered, smelly rags and fallen on a road,
Was seen by a god. In order to retrieve it,
He would point out this matter to the travelers. //I.118//

Likewise, the one who has an unobstructed eye
Sees, even in animals, the tathāgata nature
Wrapped in the various forms of addictions,
And so deploys his arts in order to deliver it. //I.119//

Just as a god with a divine eye, seeing a buddha image wrapped
　　in smelly rags and
Fallen on a road, would point it out to people in order to
　　retrieve it;
So the Victor, seeing even in animals the element fallen on the
　　road of cyclic life,
Wrapped in tattered rags of addiction, teaches the Dharma in
　　order to deliver it. //I.120//

«198» The addictions are like a pregnant woman, and the tathāgata element is akin to a chakravartin contained in the embryonic elements.

Suppose an ugly woman, unprotected
And staying in a shelter for the homeless,
Bore a glorious king inside her womb,
Yet did not realize that a ruler existed within her belly. //I.121//

Birth in cyclic life is like a shelter for the homeless,
Impure sentient beings are like the pregnant woman,
And the stainless element is like that within the womb;
Having it, one is protected. //I.122//

Just as an ugly woman, dressed in dirty clothes,
Is feeling the greatest suffering in a homeless shelter, even though
    the ruler is inside her womb,
Living beings believe themselves unprotected, even though the
    protector resides within,
And never find peace by the power of addictions, so remaining
    in the state of suffering. //I.123//

«199» The addictions are like a clay mold, and the tathāgata element is akin
to a golden image.

Suppose that inside [a mold] there was a complete, peaceful
    statue of melted gold,
But outside was something of the nature of clay.
By seeing and knowing of it, a person
Would remove the outer covering to expose the gold inside. //I.124//

Likewise, the one who has attained supreme enlightenment,
Clearly seeing that the nature [of the mind] is luminosity
And that the taints are incidental,
Purifies sentient beings, like jewel mines, from their obscura-
    tions. //I.125//

Just as an expert removes the clay, knowing a peaceful statue
Made of pure, shining gold is enclosed within,
So the omniscient knows the peaceful mind, which is like pure
    gold,
And removes its obscurations by teaching the Dharma, like
    chipping away the clay. //I.126//

«200» The summarized meaning of the similes is as follows:

Within a lotus, amid bees,
Inside a husk, filth, and ground,
Within a fruit skin, within tattered rags,
In the womb of a woman, and inside clay //I.127//

Is that like a buddha, the honey,
The grain, the gold, a treasure,
A tree, a precious image,
A chakravartin, and a golden image. //I.128//

Likewise, it is said that the stainless nature
Of the mind is beginningless, and is not bound
By the covering of sentient beings' addictions,
Which are beginningless as well. //I.129//

«201» In brief, these similes given in the *Tathāgata Essence Sutra* demonstrate the fact that, for all sentient beings, the defiling factors on their beginningless minds are incidental, whereas the pure excellences are simultaneous with and inseparable from the mind without beginning. Therefore, the sutra states as follows:[128]

Living beings are totally tainted because of the taints on the mind; they are pure because their mind is pure by nature.

«202» Here, which of the nine similes, the lotus sheath, etc., have been demonstrated? Which are the taints on the mind?

Attachment, hatred, and ignorance,
Their intense outbursts, and evolutionary instincts,
The eliminations of the paths of insight and meditation,
And [those related to] the impure and pure stages: //I.130//

These nine taints are demonstrated well
By the similes of the lotus sheath, etc.

128. PD70 (phi), pp. 1067.20–1068.1. *Saṁyuttanikāya* III. 151.22–23, 151.31–32, 152.8–9.

The coverings of secondary taints
Have limitless millions of divisions. //I.131//

«203» In brief, these nine kinds of addictions are incidental in connection to the tathāgata element that is pure by nature, just as the lotus sheath, etc., [is incidental] to a buddha image, etc. What are the nine addictions? They are, namely: (1) the addiction characterized as the latent state of attachment; (2) the addiction characterized as the latent state of hatred; (3) the addiction characterized as the latent state of ignorance; (4) the addiction characterized as the intense outburst of attachment, hatred, and ignorance; (5) the addiction included in the ground of evolutionary instincts for ignorance; (6) the addiction to be eliminated by [the path of] insight; (7) the addiction to be eliminated by [the path of] meditation; (8) the addiction related to the impure stages; and (9) the addiction related to the pure stages.

«204» In regard to this, (1–3) the addictions existing in the continuums of those worldly people who are freed from attachment and that, as the cause of synthetic activity that accumulates immovable karmic evolution, give rise to the material and the immaterial worlds, are to be destroyed by transcendent intuitive wisdom. They are called the addictions characterized as the latent state of attachment, hatred, and ignorance. (4) Those [addictions] existing in the continuums of those sentient beings who indulge in attachment, etc., and that, being the cause of synthetic activity that accumulates karmically evolutionary merit and demerit, give rise only to the desire world and are to be destroyed by the wisdom of the meditation on impurity, etc. They are called the addictions characterized by the intense outburst of attachment, hatred, and ignorance. (5) Those [addictions] existing in the continuums of saints, being the cause that produces the uncontaminated karmic evolution, give rise to the pure mind-made bodies and are to be destroyed by the tathāgata's intuitive wisdom of enlightenment. These are called the addictions included in the ground of evolutionary instincts for ignorance. There are two kinds of person who enter higher education [on the path]: ordinary people and nobles. Here, (6) those [addictions] existing in the continuums of ordinary people being educated on the path, and that are to be destroyed by the wisdom obtained by means of the first insight into transcendent reality, are called the addictions to be eliminated by [the path of] insight. (7) Those [addictions] existing in the continuums of nobles being educated on the path, and that are to be destroyed by the wisdom of the meditation on transcendent reality, perceiving it as it is, are called the addictions to be eliminated by [the path of] meditation. (8) Those [addictions] existing in the continuums of bodhisattvas who have not reached the ultimate perfection and that are, in contradiction to the wisdom obtained on the [first] seven stages, to be destroyed by the wisdom of the meditation of the three stages, the eighth stage, etc., are called the addictions related to the impure stages. (9) Those [addictions] existing in the continuums of bodhisattvas who have reached the ultimate perfection, and, in contradiction to the wisdom obtained by means of the meditation of the [last] three stages beginning with the eighth, are to be destroyed by the wisdom of the "vajra-like" concentration and are called the addictions related to the pure stages.

≪205≫ [The root text states:]

These nine addictions, attachment and so on,
In short, are, respectively, demonstrated well
By the nine similes of
The lotus sheath, and so on. //I.132//

And, if taken in detail, these addictions can be differentiated into 84,000 types, and hence are as infinite as the tathāgata's intuitive wisdom. On this point, *The Tathāgata Essence Sutra* states that the tathāgata essence is covered by the sheath of addictions with limitless divisions.

≪206≫ [The root text states:]

By these taints, the naïve,
Saints, persons being educated, and the wise,
Are respectively contaminated by
Four, one, two, and two. //I.133//

≪207≫ The Bhagavān states [in *The Tathāgata Essence Sutra*] that all sentient beings are endowed with the tathāgata essence. Here, "all sentient beings," in brief, refers to the four types of beings. They are: (1) ordinary people; (2) saints; (3) persons being educated [on the path]; and (4) bodhisattvas. These are tainted by four, one, two, and again by two kinds [of addictions], respectively, in connection with [the obscurations to] the uncontaminated element.

«208» Furthermore, how should the respective similarity between nine addictions, attachment, etc., and the lotus sheath, etc., be understood? How should the buddha essence be understood to be analogous to a buddha image, etc.?

Just as a lotus, grown from the mire,
Delights the mind when first appearing,
But later that delight disappears,
So is attachment's joy. //I.134//

Just as a swarm of bees
Sting when irritated,
Likewise, when hatred arises,
It brings suffering to the heart. //I.135//

Just as the kernel of rice and so on
Are obscured by the external husk,
Likewise, the perception of the meaning of the essence
Is obscured by the covering of ignorance. //I.136//

Just as filth is something unpleasant,
Those having attachment
Engage in passion—in this way,
Intense outbursts are similar to filth. //I.137//

Suppose that wealth is obscured.
Not knowing it, that treasure cannot be obtained;
Likewise, that self-arising [intuitive wisdom] in sentient beings
    is obscured
By the earth of evolutionary instincts for ignorance. //I.138//

Just as the sprout and such gradually grow
And split the skin of the seed,
Likewise, the perception of reality overcomes those
[Addictions] eliminated by [the path of] insight. //I.139//

Having connected with the holy path,
Those who have overcome the essence of the futile views,
[Addictions] eliminated by the wisdom of the path of
    meditation,
Are demonstrated to be similar to the tattered rags. //I.140//

The taints related to the seven [bodhisattva] stages
Are similar to the impurities of the womb.
Release from that womb is like the
Nonconceptual intuitive wisdom, well matured. //I.141//

The taints related to the three [higher] stages
Are known as being like stains of mud,
The [addictive] objects to be destroyed by
The Bhagavān's vajra-like concentration. //I.142//

«209» [Thus, the root text states:]

Thus the nine taints, attachment, and so on,
Are analogous to the lotus and the other.
Because the element is included within the threefold nature,
It is like the similes of a buddha [image] and so on. //I.143//

«210» The analogy between the tathāgata essence, being the cause for purifying the mind,[129] and a buddha image, etc., should be understood with
reference to the threefold nature [of the tathāgata essence].
    «211» What is the threefold nature?

The natures of this [essence] are the truth body,
Reality, and also spiritual potentials.
They are known by three,
One, and five similes. //I.144//

---

129. *cittavyavadābahetu*. Ngog's translation reads *sems kyi rnam par byang ba'i khams* ("the
pure element of the mind").

«212» This element, being of the nature of the truth body, is understood by the [first] three similes: the buddha image, the honey, and the kernel [of grain]. Its being of the nature of reality is understood by one simile: the gold. Its being of the nature of the spiritual potentials from which the Buddha's three bodies are produced is understood by [the remaining] five similes: the treasure, the tree, the precious image, the chakravartin, and the golden statue.

«213» Here, how is the truth body understood?

> The truth body is known by two aspects:
> The ultimate element, which is perfectly stainless;
> And its natural outflow, the profound teaching
> And that taught in diverse ways. //I.145//

«214» The Buddha's truth body should be understood by two aspects: (1) the perfect stainless ultimate element is the object experienced directly by the nonconceptual [intuitive wisdom]. Moreover, this is known with reference to the Dharma realized by the Tathāgata's individual introspective wisdom; (2) natural outflow (*nisyanda, rgyu mthun pa*) of the perfect stainless ultimate element as the cause for its attainment, from which comes forth the teaching for other beings according to their educational needs. Moreover, this is known with reference to the Dharma to be taught. The teaching is further divided into two, according to the means of arranging either subtle or extensive Dharma: (a) the teaching expounding the ultimate reality, the way of profound Dharma, in the sutra collection for bodhisattvas; and (b) the aphorisms, the discourses in prose and verse mingled, prophecy, verses, the special utterances, the narration, etc., expounding the conventional reality, a variety of things.

«215» [The root text states:]

> Because it is transcendent, there is
> No conceivable analogy with it in the world.
> Thus, the Tathāgata and the element
> Are demonstrated as being similar. //I.146//

> The subtle, profound teaching
> Is like the one taste of honey,
> While the teaching on various aspects
> Are known as like the kernel of various grains. //I.147//

«216» Thus, the statement that "sentient beings are endowed with the tathāgata essence" is made with these three similes: a buddha image, the honey, and the kernel, with reference to the meaning that, with no exception, the Tathāgata's truth body is all-pervading in sentient beings. Indeed, among sentient beings, there is no one who remains outside of the Tathāgata's truth body, just as no material can exist outside of space.

«217» As [Maitreya's *Ornament of the Universal Vehicle Sutras*] states:[130]

Just as space is always all-pervading,
Similarly, this is accepted as being all-pervading.
Just as space is always permeating the material objects,
Similarly, this permeates all sentient beings.

«218» [The root text states:]

Being unchangeable by nature,
Virtuous, and pure,
Reality is therefore said
To be like the forms of gold. //I.148//

«219» Being associated with limitless addictions and sufferings notwithstanding, because it is naturally clear-light, the mind does not show any change. Therefore, it is called "reality" in the sense that it is unchangeable like excellent gold. Furthermore, without difference in nature, all sentient beings, even those who have the causes of definite wrongdoing, will join the rank of "the Tathāgata" whenever they have purified all incidental addictions. Thus, the statement that "sentient beings are endowed with the tathāgata essence" is made by this simile of gold, in reference to the meaning that reality is indivisible.

«220» Having in view the nature of the mind, the pure and nondual reality, the Bhagavān states [in the *Ornament of the Light of Wisdom Sutra*] the following:[131]

130. PD70 (phi), p. 1073.6–9. MSA, ch. 9, v. 15.
131. PD70 (phi), p. 1074.1–5; D100, f. 297a.5–6.

O Mañjushrī, the Tathāgata knows full well his own substantial basis, and hence, he protects. By means of his own purity, he has understood the purity of sentient beings. His own purity and the purity of the sentient beings are nondual; they cannot be divided into two.

«221» It is also stated in [Maitreya's *Ornament of the Universal Vehicle Sutras*] as follows:[132]

Though being undifferentiated among all,
The reality, after purification,
Is tathāgatahood; therefore, all sentient beings
Are endowed with the tathāgata essence.

«222» [The root text states:]

Like a treasure and a fruit tree,
The spiritual potential is known to be twofold:
That by nature existent without beginning, and
That of supreme development. //I.149//

By this twofold potential, a buddha's
Three bodies are considered to be attained:
The first body by the former;
The other two by the latter. //I.150//

The beautiful natural body is
Known to be like a precious statue,
Not created by nature,
As well as the precious treasure of excellences. //I.151//

Owing to possession of the kingdom of the great Dharma,
The perfect beatific [body] is analogous to the chakravartin.
Because it has the nature of a reflective image,
The incarnational [body] is like a golden statue. //I.152//

132. PD70 (phi), p. 1074.6–8; MSA, ch. 9, v. 37.

《223》 Thus, the tathāgata element is demonstrated to be the essence of all sentient beings by these five similes: a treasure, a tree, a precious image, a chakravartin, and a golden statue, with reference to the fact that there exist the spiritual potentials that produce a buddha's three bodies. Indeed, buddhahood is distinguished by a buddha's three bodies. Therefore, since the tathāgata element is the cause of the attainment [of these three bodies], the word "element" is used here in the sense of "cause." So it is said [in *The Tathāgata Essence Sutra*]:[133]

> There exists in each sentient being the essence, the established tathāgata element. But these sentient beings do not know about it.

《224》 The Buddha states [in the *Abhidharma Universal Vehicle Sutra*] as follows:[134]

> The element that exists without beginning
> Is the foundation of all things.
> Because of its existence, there is cyclic life,
> And the attainment of nirvana.

《225》 Here, how is it that it "exists without beginning"? It has been taught and ascertained by the Buddha, with reference to the tathāgata essence, that "a beginning-limit is not to be perceived."

《226》 As to the "element," it is stated [in the *Shrīmālādevī Lion's Roar Sutra*] as follows:[135]

> Bhagavān, this tathāgata essence is the essence of transcendent qualities, and the essence of naturally pure qualities.

---

133. PD70 (phi), p. 1075.1–3; D258, f. 253b.5–6.

134. PD70 (phi), p. 1075.4–6. This text seems to be nonexistent in the Tibetan and Chinese canons. Brunnhölzl (988n41, 995n140) kindly identifies a number of other texts that quote it as a sutra taught by the Buddha.

135. PD70 (phi), p. 1075.12–18; D92, f. 275a.3–4.

«227» As to the statement "the foundation of all things," this sutra states as follows:[136]

> Therefore, Bhagavān, the tathāgata essence is the foundation, basis, and support of the uncompounded things, which are connected, not dissociated, and inseparable. [At the same time], Bhagavān, this tathāgata essence is also the foundation, basis, and support of the compounded things, which are unconnected, dissociated, and separable.

«228» As to the statement "because of its existence, there [is] cyclic life," the [same] sutra states as follows:[137]

> Owing to the existence of the tathāgata essence, Bhagavān, this [essence] is designated as "cyclic life."

«229» As to the statement "and the attainment of nirvana," the [same] sutra states as follows:[138]

> Bhagavān, if there were no tathāgata essence, there would be neither aversion toward suffering nor desire, longing, and prayer toward nirvana.

«230» Furthermore, this tathāgata essence, which is as vast as the truth body, has the characteristic of being indivisible from the Tathāgata, and is of the nature of the definitive potential, existing the whole time among all [sentient beings] without distinction. This fact should be perceived on the valid evidence of reality.

«231» The Buddha states [in *The Tathāgata Essence Sutra*] as follows:[139]

136. PD70 (phi), p. 1075.12–18; D92, f. 274b.2–4.

137. PD70 (phi), p. 1075.18–20; D92, f. 274a.6–7.

138. PD70 (phi), pp. 1075.21–1076.3; D92, f. 274b.5.

139. PD70 (phi), p. 1076.7–10; D258, f. 248b.6.

O son of good family, this is the reality of things. Whether the Tathāgata appears in the world or not, these sentient beings are always endowed with the tathāgata essence.

«232» [The reasoning of] the reality here refers to the reasoning (*yukti*), syllogism (*yoga*), or the liberative art (*upāya*) that realizes that things would reasonably become such and not otherwise. In all cases, as for the mind's proper understanding and realistic understanding, one should not conceive of it as the realization or as the reasoning of reality itself. This [reality] is not accessible to conceptual thought. It is accessible only to extreme faith.

«233» [The root text states:]

Self-arisen ones' ultimate reality
Can be understood only by faith,
[Just as] the radiating sun
Cannot be seen by the blind. //I.153//

«234» In brief, there are four kinds of individuals who are classified as being blind to the tathāgata essence. What are these four? They are: (1) ordinary people; (2) disciples; (3) hermit buddhas; and (4) bodhisattvas who have just entered the vehicle.

«235» As it is stated [in the *Shrīmālādevī Lion's Roar Sutra*]:[140]

Bhagavān, for those who have fallen into the futile view, for those attached to misconceptions, for those whose mind has deviated from emptiness, the tathāgata essence is not their object of experience.

«236» Here "those who have fallen into the futile view" refers to (1) ordinary people. Indeed, they cannot believe in an uncontaminated element that stops the futile view, because of their habitual adherence to egoism and possessiveness by accepting a personal self and property in connection with contaminated things such as the aggregates, etc. Being so, how could

140. PD70 (phi), pp. 1076.21–1077.3; D92, f. 275a.2–3.

they be expected to recognize the tathāgata essence that is the object of the omniscient [Buddha]? This is impossible.

«237» [Next,] "those who have an affinity for misconceptions" refers to (2) disciples and (3) hermit buddhas. Why? This is because, although the tathāgata essence should be meditated upon as being eternal, they indulge in the meditation on the notion of impermanence instead of meditating upon the notion of eternity. Likewise, although the tathāgata essence should be meditated upon as being blissful, they indulge in the meditation on the notion of suffering instead of meditating upon the notion of bliss. Although the tathāgata essence should be meditated upon as being self, they nevertheless indulge in the meditation on the notion of selflessness instead of meditating upon the notion of self. And, though the tathāgata essence should be meditated upon as being pure, they indulge in the meditation on the notion of impurity instead of meditating upon the notion of purity. Thus, this enumeration explains that this element, which is characterized as the supreme eternity, the supreme bliss, the supreme self, and the supreme purity, is also not the object experienced by any disciple or hermit buddha because they indulge in the path that is in direct contradiction to the attainment of the truth body.

«238» As to this fact that [the element] is not the object experienced by those who indulge in misconceptions about the notions of impermanence, suffering, selflessness, and impurity, the Bhagavān has explicated in detail in the *Great [Total] Nirvana Sutra* with the example of a jewel in the pond, as follows:[141]

> O mendicants, suppose that in the hot season, people put on their swimsuits and were playing in the water with various ornaments and enjoyments. Suppose then that someone lost a valuable vaiḍūrya jewel in the water. Thus, in order to retrieve this vaiḍūrya jewel, all the people, leaving aside their ornaments, would dive into the water. They would mistake pebbles or gravel in the pond for the real jewel and take them out, thinking: "I have got the jewel!" Looking at them on the bank of the pond, they would notice: "It is not the jewel at all!" Meanwhile, the water of that pond would seem to shine by the power of that

141. PD70 (phi), pp. 1078.9–1079.9; D120, ff. 33a.4–33b.2.

jewel. Such perception would make them realize its quality and proclaim: "How wonderful!" Then a skillful and intelligent person would get the real jewel out.

Likewise, mendicants, you who are ignorant of the ultimate reality of things meditate with all perceptual habits, maintaining that all things are impermanent, that all things are suffering, that all things are selfless, and all things are impure, and meditate repeatedly and increasingly. But all these attempts are useless. Therefore, mendicants, you should become skillful, not taking those like the pebbles or gravel in the pond. Mendicants, these things upon which you meditate with all perceptual habits, maintaining that all things are impermanent, that all things are suffering, that all things are selfless, and all things are impure, and upon which you meditate repeatedly and increasingly, are [actually] eternal, blissful, pure,[142] and endowed with self.

These [perceptual habits] should be understood in detail, according to the sutra, as misconceptions with regard to the arrangement of the ultimate reality of things.

«239» [Lastly,] "those whose minds have deviated from emptiness" refers to (4) bodhisattvas who have just entered the vehicle, deprived of [the understanding of] the tathāgata essence with regard to emptiness. They are the people who either accept emptiness as the door to liberation because it destroys phenomena, thinking that nirvana means annihilation and destruction of any current existence, or who have the apprehension of emptiness as an entity that is different from matter, etc., which is what we should realize, and upon which we should meditate.

«240» How then is this tathāgata essence expressed with regard to emptiness? [The root text states:]

From this there is nothing whatever to be removed
And absolutely nothing to be added;
Reality should be perceived correctly,
And correct perception comes into liberation. //I.154//

---

142. The PD text here has *sdug bsngal*, reporting it from various Tibetan recensions, but it is obviously wrong, and *sdug pa* (or *gtsang pa*) is required.

The element is empty of the incidental [taints],
Which have a character separable from it.
It is not empty of the unsurpassed qualities
Of character indivisible from it. //I.155//

«241» What is demonstrated by this statement? There is no cause of taint whatsoever that is to be removed from this naturally pure tathāgata element, since it is by nature devoid of incidental taints. Also, there is no cause of purification in the slightest that is to be added to it, since its nature is the reality indivisible from the pure excellences.

«242» Therefore, it is said [in the *Shrīmālādevī Lion's Roar Sutra*]:[143]

The tathāgata essence is empty of the whole sheath of addictions that can be differentiated and separated [from the essence]. It is not empty of the buddha excellences, which are undifferentiable, inseparable, inconceivable, and far more numerous than the grains of sand in the Ganges.

Thus, the [fact] that something does not exist is correctly observed as "emptiness of something." The [fact] that something remains is correctly known as really existing. These two verses demonstrate the exact definition of "emptiness" because [they teach about it] as being free from the two extremes of reification and repudiation.

«243» Those whose minds have deviated from emptiness and are distracted, neither doing meditation nor concentrating upon it, are called for this reason "those whose minds have deviated from emptiness." Indeed, lacking intuitive wisdom of ultimate emptiness, no one would be able to realize and obtain the pure reality free of conceptual thought. Intending this point, the Buddha states [in the *Shrīmālādevī Lion's Roar Sutra*]:[144]

The intuitive wisdom of the tathāgata essence is nothing but the buddhas' intuitive wisdom of emptiness. This tathāgata essence has never been perceived, never been realized by disciples and hermit buddhas.

143. PD70 (phi), p. 1080.8–12; D92, f. 272a.7–272b.1.
144. PD70 (phi), p. 1081.1–4; D92, f. 272a.5–6.

«244» This tathāgata essence, as the essence of the ultimate element, is said to be the object not experienced by those who have fallen into the futile view, since the ultimate element is an antidote to such a view. The tathāgata essence, as the truth body, the essence of transcendent qualities, is said to be the object not experienced by those who indulge in misconceptions, since the truth body is demonstrated as being an antidote to worldly things, such as impermanence, etc. The tathāgata essence as the truth body, the essence of the perfectly pure excellences, is said to be the object not experienced by those whose mind has mentally deviated from emptiness, since the transcendent truth body, from which the pure excellences are indivisible, is by nature empty of incidental taints, which are separable.

«245» Being the realization of [the element] with reference to the unique intuitive wisdom that is undifferentiated from the ultimate element, this perception of the natural purity of the transcendent truth body is here accepted as the slight observation of the tathāgata essence by bodhisattvas who are abiding in the ten stages; as it is said:[145]

> Those with biased intelligence, even if noble and pure in vision,
> Cannot clearly behold You—who are like the sun—through
>   gaps in the clouds,
> Those with infinite intelligence fully behold You, O Bhagavān,
>   as a body of reality,
> Since [their intelligence] pervades everything knowable,
>   infinite like space.

«246» [Question:] If this tathāgata essence is thus so difficult to recognize, inasmuch as it is not always the object even for the supreme noble ones who are abiding in the stage characterized as being ultimately free of attachment, then what is the use of this teaching to the naïve?

«247» [Reply:] There are two verses summarizing the purpose of this teaching: the first is a doubt, and the second is the response.

> Since it has been taught in this and that [sutra]
> That all objects of knowledge are ever empty—like clouds,
>   dreams, and illusions—

145. PD70 (phi), pp. 1081.20–1082.2; canonical source not identified.

Why has the Buddha declared here again
The presence of the tathāgata essence in sentient beings? //I.156//

Being disheartened, [having] contempt for inferior beings,
Apprehending the unreal, repudiating reality,
[Having] excessive attachment to oneself:
It is taught to those with these five faults,
For the purpose of dispelling them. //I.157//

«248» The meaning of these two verses should be known in summary by the following ten verses:

It is said that the reality-limit is ever empty
Of compounded things, and hence,
Addictions, evolutionary actions,
And effects are like clouds, etc. //I.158//

Addictions are likened to the clouds,
Evolution is like the experience in dreams,
And the aggregates, effects of addictions and actions,
Are likened to the illusions made by magic. //I.159//

So has it been established previously,
And again, in this *Sublime Continuum*,
In order to dispel these five faults,
The presence of the tathāgata essence has been taught. //I.160//

Indeed, not learning this,
Some of them, being disheartened,
Caused by the fault of self-contempt,
Will never conceive the spirit of enlightenment. //I.161//

Someone has cultivated this spirit
By means of pride, thinking: "I am better!"
They insistently promote the notion that
Those who have not conceived this spirit are inferior. //I.162//

Correct understanding will never arise
In those who think in this way.
Thus, since they are grasping the unreal,
They will not recognize the reality. //I.163//

These faults of sentient beings are not real,
As they are elaborations and incidental.
In reality, these faults do not have a self,
While the excellences are pure by nature. //I.164//

If one apprehends the unreal faults
And repudiates the real excellences,
One will not obtain the love with which the wise
See the equality between oneself and others. //I.165//

On the contrary, by means of learning this teaching,
There arises enthusiasm, respect for the Teacher,
Wisdom, primal intuition, and great love.
Because of the production of these five qualities, //I.166//

Faults will be absent and equality will be perceived.
Being devoid of faults and endowed with excellences,
Seeing the equality between oneself and sentient beings,
One will swiftly attain buddhahood. //I.167//

This completes the exposition of the first chapter concerning the tathāgata essence in *The Sublime Continuum of the Universal Vehicle, Analysis of the Precious Spiritual Potential*, in the context of an exposition of reality that is mingled with taints.

Chapter II
Enlightenment

«249» Now the suchness free of taints should be explained.

Here, what is suchness free of taints? It is what is established as the place of transformation, as a result of the uncontaminated element of the buddha bhagavāns' being free of all kinds of taints. Further, in summary, it should be understood in terms of eight kinds of meanings.

«250» What are the eight meanings?

> With its purity, attainment, cessation,
> One's own aims and others' aims, reliance,
> Profundity, vastness, and the great being,
> Duration, and suchness. //II.1//

This verse talks about the following eight meanings: those of actuality, cause, fruition, action, endowment, engagement, permanence, and inconceivability.

«251» Here, it should be known that the element is designated as the tathāgata essence when it has not yet been released from the sheath of addictions, and as the actuality of transformation when purified. Why? The [Shrīmālādevī Lion's Roar] Sutra states:[146]

> O Bhagavān, if one has no doubt about the tathāgata essence trapped within the sheath of a hundred trillion addictions, one will have no doubt about the Tathāgata's truth body, which is free from the sheath of addictions.

---

146. PD70 (phi), p. 1084.8–11; D92, f. 271a.4–5.

The two intuitive wisdoms refer to the transcendent intuitive wisdom of nonconceptual meditative equipoise and the common intuitive wisdom of subsequent attainment equipoise. The causes for transformation, which are the transcendent intuitive wisdom and the common intuitive wisdom, are expressed under the name "attainment" since these are capable of attainment.

The fruition is the two kinds of freedom from addictive obscuration and objective obscuration, bringing about self-benefit and benefit for others, respectively.

The endowment refers to the basis of the twofold benefit.

The engagement refers to the three [buddha] bodies distinguished by the features of being profound, vast, and great in being, the duration of their engagement, and the feature of inconceivability.

«252» The summary verse is as follows:

> By nature, cause, fruition,
> Function, endowment, engagement,
> Permanence, and inconceivability,
> The stage of buddhahood is presented. //II.2//

«253» Here buddhahood and the means to attain it are taught by the verse with respect to the meanings of actuality and cause.

> [Enlightenment, of which the Buddha] said, "It is naturally
>   clear-light," is akin to the sun and space.
> It is free from the taints of the incidental dense clouds of addic-
>   tive and objective obscurations.
> Buddhahood is permanent, eternal, and immutable, possessing
>   all the buddha excellences.
> It is attained by relying on the nonconceptual intuitive wisdom
>   and the discriminating wisdom. //II.3//

«254» The meaning of this verse, in brief, should be understood by the following four verses:

> Buddhahood is indivisible,
> Yet discerned by its feature of purity;

Its nature is twofold, with its abandonment
And its intuitive wisdom, like space and sun. //II.4//

Natural luminosity is not created,
Yet it is indivisible from material things,
Endowed with all buddha excellences,
[Countless] as particles in the Ganges riverbed. //II.5//

Lacking any intrinsic reality status,
Pervasive, yet totally incidental,
The addictive and objective obscurations
Are pronounced to be like clouds. //II.6//

The cause of freedom from the two obscurations
Is both the intuitive wisdoms,
The nonconceptual intuition and its aftermath wisdom;
The two are claimed to be wisdom intuitions. //II.7//

The purity is the actuality of the transformation. Here this purity in brief
is of two kinds: natural purity and taintless purity. The natural purity is
[primordially] released, but has not yet been [experientially] freed, since
the natural luminosity of the mind has not been separated from incidental
taints. The taintless purity is free by means of a separation like that of particles [being separated] in water, since the natural transparency of the mind
is [primordially] separated from all incidental taints.

«255» Here, the verse regarding the meaning of the fruitional taintless
purity is as follows:

Like a lake gradually filled with lotuses in clean water,
Like the full moon released from the mouth of Rāhu,
Like the sun released from a cloud mass of addictions,
The same [essence] shines with light rays,
Since endowed with taintless excellences. //II.8//

The victor state is like the bull of sages, honey, essence,
Gold, a jewel treasure, a fruit tree,
A taintless jewel body of the Sugata,
An emperor, and a golden form. //II.9//

«256» The meaning of these two verses, in brief, should be understood by the following eight verses:

In sum, the purity from incidental addictions
Such as attachment, and so on,
Is just like the lake, etc.,
Proclaimed as the fruit of nonconceptual intuition. //II.10//

The definite attainment of the buddha body,
Endowed with supremacy of all kinds,
Is taught to be the fruition
Of the post-attainment wisdom. //II.11//

Having abandoned the taint of attachment,
One pours the water of meditation
Upon the lotus of disciples,
And thus is like the lake of clear water. //II.12//

Released from the Rāhu demon of hatred,
One pervades all beings with one's light
Of universal love and compassion,
And thus is like the clear full moon. //II.13//

Released from the cloud mass of ignorance
And dispelling beings' darkness
By means of the light of intuitive wisdom—
Buddhahood is like the taintless sun. //II.14//

Since [buddhahood] is endowed with unsurpassed excellences,
Since it bestows the taste of the holy Dharma,
And since it is free from the husk [of the obscurations],
It is like the Sugata, the honey, and the essence. //II.15//

Since it is pure, since poverty
Is eliminated with excellent substances,
And since it causes the fruit of liberation to ripen,
It is like the gold, the treasure, and the tree. //II.16//

Since it is endowed with the jewel of the truth body,
Since it is the supreme lord among two-footed beings,
Since it has precious forms,
It is like the bejeweled, the emperor, and the gold. //II.17//

«257» The transcendent nonconceptual intuition and its post-attainment intuitive wisdom are the causes of the transformation called the "fruition of freedom." Their functions are said to be the fulfillment of the two interests of self and others.

Here, how is the fulfillment of the two interests achieved? The fulfillment of self-interest refers to the attainment of the truth body without obscurations, as a result of the liberation from the addictive obscurations along with their instincts and from the objective obscurations. Based on that [self-interest fulfillment], the fulfillment of others' interests refers to the effortless engagement of [both] the display of the two [material] bodies and the mastery of the teaching, as long as the world may last.

«258» Here are three verses regarding the meaning of "action":

Freedom from contamination and the all-pervasive [excellences]
    have the feature of indestructibility
Since their state is firm, peaceful, permanent, and immutable.
The six senses of the pure space-like tathāgata purity
Serve as the cause of experiencing the sense objects. //II.18//

[Although] it serves as the cause for [his] forms and resources
    to be seen,
For [his] wonderful speech to be heard,
For [his] Sugata fragrance of [his] pure ethics to be smelled,
For the ambrosia of great noble beings' Dharma to be tasted,
    //II.19//

For the bliss of meditative equipoise to be enjoyed,
And for the meaning of the natural profundity to be realized,
When thought through subtly, he gives the ultimate bliss—
The Tathāgata is like space, free from all causality. //II.20//

«259» The meanings of these three verses should be understood, in sum, by the eight verses as follows:

In short, [the two bodies] are to be understood
As the actions of the two intuitive wisdoms:
The perfection of the liberated body
And the purification of the truth body. //II.21//

Liberation and truth bodies are to be known
As being of two kinds and of one kind,
Since they are all-pervasive and uncontaminated,
And since their place is the uncreated. //II.22//

[The truth body] is uncontaminated
Since addictions and instincts have been eliminated.
The intuitive wisdoms are claimed to be all-pervasive,
Since they have no hindrances and no obstacles. //II.23//

[The truth body] is uncreated
Since its nature is ultimately indestructible.
Indestructibility is explained
By four aspects, such as stability, etc. //II.24//

The four kinds of destruction should be known
As the opposite of stability, etc.,
[The truth body] should be known as
Stable, peaceful, permanent, and immutable, //II.25//

Since it is free from decay, change,
Interruption, and inconceivable death,
Uncontaminated intuitive wisdom is the ground,
Since it is the basis for all goodness. //II.26//

Just as space, while not being a cause,
Is the cause that makes it possible that
Forms, sounds, scents, tastes, textures,
And mental objects can be seen, heard, etc., //II.27//

Likewise, the unobscured two bodies, [the uncreated],
Their work is the cause that creates
The uncontaminated excellences,
The aim of the teaching!//II.28//

«260» [The *Ornament of the Light of Wisdom Sutra*] states that "the Buddha has the characteristic of space." This is stated in terms of the Tathāgata's distinctive ultimate characteristic. For what reason? If the Tathāgata were seen [merely] by his thirty-two marks of a great person, then a chakravartin would be a tathāgata as well.

Here the verse with respect to the meaning of endowment with the ultimate excellence states as follows:

Buddhahood is inconceivable, permanent, stable, at peace, and
    immutable.
It is peaceful, pervasive, without thought, and unattached like
    space.
It is free from obscuration, without rough texture.
It cannot be seen or apprehended. It is virtuous and free from
    taints. //II.29//

«261» The meaning of this verse is to be understood in sum by the following eight verses:

The benefits for self and others
Are demonstrated by the liberated truth body.
It, being the basis of this twofold benefit,
Is endowed with the excellences such as inconceivability, etc.
    //II.30//

Being the object of the omniscient intuitive wisdom,
Buddhahood is not an object for the three types of insight.
Thus even those with a wisdom body must recognize
That it is inconceivable. //II.31//

Being subtle, it is not an object for study;
Being ultimate, it cannot be reflected upon.

Since its reality is so profound, it is not an object
For any mundane meditation, etc. //II.32//

Why? Like the blind with regard to forms,
The childish have never experienced its vision.
Even the noble ones see it as a baby would [glimpse]
The sun from within the house where it is born. //II.33//

Since it is free from birth, it is permanent.
Since it is without cessation, it is stable.
Since these two are not present, it is at peace.
It is immutable, for reality ever exists. //II.34//

It is very peaceful, as a result of the truth of cessation.
Since it realizes everything, it is all-pervasive.
Since it is unlocated, it is concept-free.
Since it banishes addictions, it is unattached. //II.35//

Since all objective obscurations are purified,
It is unobstructed in every way.
Since it is fit for nonduality,
It is free from any harsh experience. //II.36//

Since it is without form, it is invisible.
Since it is free from signs, it cannot be apprehended.
Since it has the natural purity of virtue
And it abandons taints, it is taintless. //II.37//

«262» This tathāgatahood is akin to space, with its uncreated quality yet functioning indivisibly as long as cyclic life remains, bringing about help and benefit to sentient beings by distinctive purification with inconceivable great arts, compassion, and wisdom. It should be known that the causes of such [activities] are the nature [body], the beatific [body], and the emanation [body]. These three taintless [bodies] uninterruptedly, constantly, and spontaneously engage [in such activities], since they are endowed with distinctive features.

«263» Here are four verses concerning the analysis of the buddha body with respect to the meaning of engagement:

Without beginning, middle, and end, indivisible,
Nondual, free from three [obscurations], taintless,
    nonconceptual,
The realization of the nature of the reality element
Is experienced by the yogi in meditative equipoise. //II.38//

The taintless tathāgata element is endowed with [five] excellences,
Unfathomable, beyond the sand grains in the river Ganges,
Inconceivable, and peerless,
All faults abandoned, along with their instincts. //II.39//

With bodies shot through with the various lights of the holy
    Dharma,
With its enthusiasm to accomplish the task of beings'
    liberation,
Its activities are akin to the activities of a royal wish-fulfilling
    jewel;
[It appears as] a variety of things, yet is not of the nature of
    them. //II.40//

[The emanation body] causes worldly beings to enter the path
    toward peace;
It fully matures them, and grants them prophecies.
These material bodies remain forever in this [world],
Like the realm of matter within the realm of space. //II.41//

«264» The meanings of these four verses should be understood by the following twenty verses:

The omniscience of those self-arisen ones
Is given the name of "buddhahood."
It is also called "supreme nirvana," "the inconceivable,"
"Saint," and "the introspective [intuitive wisdom]." //II.42//

When these are analyzed, they can be engaged
As the three bodies, the nature [truth body], etc.,
And with their properties, which are the excellences
Of profoundness, vastness, and greatness of person. //II.43//

Of these, the natural reality body
Of the buddhas is to be known
As endowed with five characteristics
And, in brief, five excellences. //II.44//

It is uncreated and totally indivisible.
The two extremes are completely abandoned.
It is definitively freed from the three obscurations
Of addiction, cognition, as well as trance [fixation]. //II.45//

It is stainless and not conceptualized,
Being the object of the yogis
And the ultimate reality element,
Being naturally pure, clear-light transparency. //II.46//

The beatific body truly has
Excellences of being unfathomable,
Countless, inconceivable,
Unequaled, and ultimately pure. //II.47//

Since it is vast, not to be numbered,
Not an object of thought, and unique,
And since the evolutionary instincts are eliminated,
It is in the same order of unfathomable, and so on. //II.48//

It perfectly enjoys the various aspects of Dharma
As its nature, as well as the appearance of Dharma.
Corresponding to the pure cause of its compassion,
The benefit of sentient beings is uninterrupted. //II.49//

Totally without any calculation, spontaneously,
It completely fulfills all wishes exactly as desired,

With magic powers, like a wish-fulfilling gem.
It therefore fully abides in beatific bliss. //II.50//

Uninterrupted expression, display, and action
Without strenuous effort,
Showing that it is not of the nature of these,
The varieties and the five [excellences] are explained here.
//II.51//

Just as, as a result of various colors,
A jewel appears as [those colors] but in reality is not,
So, as a result of the various circumstances of sentient beings,
The pervasive Bhagavān appears in ways that he is not. //II.52//

By means of great compassion, knowing the world,
Having seen all worlds,
Not stirring from the truth body,
Using varieties of emanations, [the Bhagavān appears]. //II.53//

Being born into the excellent birth,
Descending from the Tuṣhita heaven,
Entering the womb and taking birth,
Becoming skilled in the sciences and crafts, //II.54//

Delighting in the company of royal consorts,
Practicing the austerities of renunciation,
Proceeding to the foot of the bodhi tree,
Overcoming the hosts of demons, //II.55//

Complete enlightenment, [turning] the wheel of Dharma,
All these activities, and passing beyond sorrow,
Are displayed in thoroughly impure worlds
As long as cyclic life remains. //II.56//

Declaring "impermanence," "suffering," "selflessness," and
    "peace,"
[The buddhas] display the skill of encouraging beings

To develop weariness with the three realms of existence
And to enter fully into the nirvana realm. //II.57//

Those who had perfectly followed the path of peace
Believed that they had attained a state of nirvana.
[But,] with the *White Lotus Sutra* and others,
The Bhagavān explained the reality of things. //II.58//

Thus he caused them to give up their former belief,
Educating them with art and intuitive wisdom,
And so caused them to mature to the [path of] the universal
    vehicle,
Then granted them their prophecy of great enlightenment.
    //II.59//

Since [these bodies] constitute depth, various powers,
And supreme guidance attuned to the aims of alienated
    persons,
They should be known in accordance with this number,
As being profound, vast, and majestic personalities. //II.60//

Here, the first is the truth body,
And the latter are the material bodies.
As matter abides in space,
The latter abide in the first. //II.61//

«265» Here is a verse concerning these three bodies' permanent performance of benefiting beings and bringing about happiness:

Since causes are infinite and beings are inexhaustible,
Since [tathāgatas] have love, magic, intuitive wisdom, and
    perfections,
Mastering the Dharma and vanquishing the devil of death,
And since they are [intrinsically] unreal, the world saviors are
    permanent. //II.62//

«266» Its condensed meaning should be known by the six verses as follows:

Having offered bodies, lives, and enjoyments,
They uphold the holy Dharma.
In order to benefit all sentient beings
They fulfill their vow as anciently undertaken. //II.63//

Buddhahood is both cleansed and purified,
With full engagement of compassion.
Showing the mobility of magic powers,
[Buddhas] stay and act forever by these means. //II.64//

With intuitive wisdom, they are freed from the habit
Fixed on the duality of cyclic life and nirvana.
They always possess the perfect bliss
Of samādhi, beyond imagination. //II.65//

While acting in the world,
They are untainted by worldly things.
Free from dying, they have attained peace.
No devil of death roams therein. //II.66//

The Sage, being of uncreated nature,
Has been primordially at peace.
For all those who are bereft of refuge
He is worthy of being the eternal refuge, etc. //II.67//

The first seven reasons show
The permanence of the material bodies,
While the latter three clarify
Why the truth body is eternal. //II.68//

«267» It should be understood that the manifestly attained transformational place of the tathāgatas is inconceivable. The verse concerning the meaning of inconceivability is as follows:

It is not an object of speech and is incorporated in the ultimate.
It is not a field for thought, beyond any example,
Unsurpassed, not contained by existence and peace.
Even the noble ones cannot conceive the victors' sphere.
  //II.69//

«268» This summary meaning should be understood by the following four verses:

It is inconceivable since it cannot be verbally expressed.
It is inexpressible since it consists of the ultimate.
It is ultimate since it cannot be conceptually constructed.
It is not conceptually constructed since it is inscrutable.
  //II.70//

It is inscrutable since it is unsurpassed.
It is unsurpassed since it is not included in anything.
It is excluded since it does not dwell [on any extreme].
This is because there is no concept of excellence or fault.
  //II.71//

For the [first] five reasons, the truth body is subtle,
And thus beyond the reach of conceptual thought.
For the sixth, the material bodies are inconceivable,
[Showing various forms,] they are not [intrinsically] real.
  //II.72//

Since with unexcelled wisdom, great compassion, etc.,
All excellences are finally perfected, the Victor is inconceivable.
Thus, this final way of the Self-Arisen Ones
Is unknown even by great seers who have attained power.
  //II.73//

The second chapter, "Enlightenment," of *The Sublime Continuum of the Universal Vehicle, Analysis of the Precious Spiritual Potential* is completed. The taintless reality has been explained.

Chapter III
Excellences

«269» Now I should discuss those stainless excellences based on that enlightenment, which are no different in their natures that are like the lights, colors, and shapes of wish-granting jewels. Therefore, in accord with that, a verse on the buddha excellences is presented as follows:

> The ultimate body benefiting self and others,
> And relying on it, the conventional bodies themselves,
> As they are fruitions of freedom and development,
> They are [endowed with] sixty-four kinds of excellences.
> //III.1//

«270» What does this teach?

> The place of one's own good fortune
> Is the ultimate reality body;
> The symbolic body of the seers
> Is the place of others' successes. //III.2//

> The first body is endowed with excellences of freedom,
> Which are the powers, and so on;
> The second has the excellences of development,
> Which are the signs of a majestic person. //III.3//

«271» The following passages discuss the powers, and so on, and how to understand these. The summary verse states:

> Power is like a vajra [to shatter] the ignorance obscuration,
> Confidence makes one like a lion amid one's entourage.

The distinctive qualities of a tathāgata are like space,
And the two kinds of the Sage's teaching are like a water-moon.
//III.4//

«272» The powers possessed [by the two bodies] refer to the following:

Knowing right from wrong,
Knowing the consequences of actions,
Knowing inclinations, types, and capacities,
Knowing all paths that lead everywhere, //III.5//

Knowing meditations, and so on,
Knowing tainted and pure [states],
Knowing former lives, divine sight, and peace—
These are the ten kinds of power. //III.6//

«273» The term "vajra-like" means:

[Knowing] right from wrong, the consequences, the various
  types, the capacities of beings,
Their inclinations, both tainted and pure, and remembering
  former lives,
Divine sight, ending contaminations, piercing the armor of
  ignorance, destroying the hard walls,
And felling the trees—such powers are like a vajra. //III.7//

«274» The attainment of the four confidences refers to the following:

Perfectly enlightened in all things,
Putting an end to obscurations,
Teaching the path, and teaching cessation
Are the four kinds of confidence. //III.8//

Knowing and causing others to know all objects of knowledge,
  having abandoned and causing abandonment
Of all things that are to be abandoned, having relied on what is
  to be relied upon,

Having attained and causing attainment of the unsurpassed and
   stainless to be attained, they teach the truth
About the benefits to self and others. Thus the great sages are
   unhindered anywhere. //III.9//

«275» The term "lion-like" means:

Just as the lord of beasts is ever confident, to the far ends of the
   jungle,
Roaming undaunted among the other animals,
Among the hosts, the Lord of Sages is a lion as well,
Dwelling at ease, endowed with independence and firm
   strength. //III.10//

«276» The possession of the eighteen special qualities of the Buddha refers
to the following:

Making no errors and never frivolous,
The Teacher never fails to remember,
Nor does his concentration falter,
And he does not hold with various notions. //III.11//

He is never indifferent, without analysis.
His will, energy, mindfulness,
Wisdom, and liberation never fail,
Nor does his vision of liberated intuition. //III.12//

All actions are preceded by wisdom,
Which is unobscured as to time.
Thus, these eighteen qualities and more
Are distinctive for the Teacher. //III.13//

Errors, frivolity, forgetfulness, mental agitation,
Diverse notions, and indifferent equanimity—the Sage does
   not have any of these.
His will, energy, and mindfulness, his pure and unstained wisdom, his constant liberation,

And his intuitive insight of liberation seeing all knowable
    objects do not fail. //III.14//

His three activities are preceded and controlled by wisdom.
He manifests his vast knowledge, always unhindered in its
    vision of the three times.
With such insight, he confidently turns the great wheel of
    Dharma for beings.
Only buddhas are endowed with universal compassion; it is
    what all buddhas will attain. //III.15//

«277» The term "space-like" means:

The nature of things, such as hardness, etc., is not the character-
    istic of space;
The characteristics of space, such as being non-obstructive, etc.,
    are not features of matter.
Earth, water, fire, wind, and space, being equal, have something
    in common in the world.
The distinctive [buddha] qualities and worldly beings have
    nothing in common, not even as much as a single atom.
    //III.16//

«278» The physical endowment of the thirty-two signs of the majestic
person refers to the following:

His feet are well set and he has wheel signs
On the palms [of his hands and feet].
His arches are broad
And his ankle bones do not protrude.
He has long fingers and toes
That are webbed. //III.17//

His skin is soft and smooth and remains youthful.
His body has seven round curves.
His calves are like an antelope's.
His penis is retracted in a sheath like an elephant's. //III.18//

His torso is like a lion's and
There is no hollow between his clavicles.
His shoulders are round and even.
His hands and arms are round, soft, and even. //III.19//

His arms are long and his stainless body
Is endowed with an aureole of light.
His neck, unblemished, resembles a conch.
He has a lion's cheeks. //III.20//

His forty teeth are equal [in number in both jaws],
Without gaps, even, pure, and very white. //III.21//

His tongue is long and slender.
He has a limitless, keen sense of taste.
He has an original voice like a kalavinka [bird]'s
And the melody of Brahmā. //III.22//

His beautiful eyes are like blue lotuses,
With lashes like a cow's.
A white hair-tuft between his eyebrows
Embellishes his face,
And his head has a turban-shaped crown protrusion.
His clean, firm skin is golden-hued like that of a supreme being.
    //III.23//

His bodily hairs are fine and soft,
Each of them curls to the right and stands straight up.
His stainless hair resembles [in color] a blue gem.
His body has the proportions of a banyan tree. //III.24//

The Great Sage, who is all-good and beyond any example,
Has a thick trunk endowed with Narāyana's strength.
The Teacher described the inconceivable thirty-two signs
As those of a lord of humans. //III.25//

The term "like a reflection of the moon in water" means:

Just as in autumn the form of the moon is seen
In the cloudless sky and in the deep blue water of a lake,
The body of the pervasive Lord is seen by victor heirs
In the mandala of the perfect Buddha. //III.26//

Therefore, in total the Tathāgata has sixty-four kinds of [excellences]: the
ten powers, the four confidences, the eighteen special qualities, and the
thirty-two signs of a majestic person.
    «279» [The root text states:]

These sixty-four excellences
Each along with its cause
Should be known in their order
To follow the *Questions of Ratnadārikā [Sutra]*. //III.27//

Therefore, the sixty-four excellences of the Tathāgata described in such
order should be understood according to *Questions of Ratnadārikā*.
    «280» The similes of the vajra, the lion, space, and the water-moon are
taught respectively for these excellences. Their summary should be understood by the following ten verses:

Being indestructible and never weakened,
Incomparable, and unmoving, they are taught
By the similes of the vajra, the lion,
Space, and the water-moon. //III.28//

Of the powers, six powers, three, and one,
In this order, have totally dispelled
[The obscurations of] cognition and meditation,
Along with that of the evolutionary instincts. //III.29//

Resembling armor, a wall, and a tree,
They were pierced, shattered, and felled.
Being heavy, essential, steadfast, and unbreakable,
The powers of the Great Sage are similar to a vajra. //III.30//

Why do they have weight? Because they are the essence.
Why the essence? Because they are steadfast.

Why steadfast? Because they are immutable.
Being immutable, they are like a vajra. //III.31//

Since he is not intimidated, is independent,
Stable, and endowed with power,
The Sage is like a lion. The lion [of humans]
Does not have fear in any entourage. //III.32//

Knowing everything directly,
He always remains fearless of anyone,
No matter who they are,
Seeing that even pure beings are not his equal. //III.33//

He is not dependent.
His mind is stable since it is one-pointed regarding all things.
He is endowed with power, having fully transcended
Ignorance- and instinct-driven evolutionary action. //III.34//

The consciousness of naïves, of disciples,
Of biased practitioners, of those who have insight,
And of hermit buddhas, getting ever subtler,
There are five similes. //III.35//

Sustaining the lives of all worldly beings, [the first four]
Are likened to earth, water, fire, and wind.
Transcending the features of the worldly and of those
Beings beyond the world, they are similar to space. //III.36//

So the truth body manifests
As these thirty-two excellences,
Indivisible like a precious gem
With its light, radiance, and shape. //III.37//

Granting satisfaction whenever it is seen,
This excellence depends on the "thirty-two [signs],"
Connecting the emanation and beatific [bodies]
With the perfect enjoyment of [the reality of] Dharma.
   //III.38//

Those far from and close to purity [see them]
In the world and the mandala of the Victor,
Like the form of the moon in water and sky—
Thus, these are beheld in two ways. //III.39//

The third chapter, "Excellences," of *The Sublime Continuum of the Universal Vehicle, Analysis of the Precious Spiritual Potential* is completed.

CHAPTER IV
Enlightened Activities

«281» Now I should proclaim the activities of the Victor, which are the activities of those [excellences]. In sum, [buddhas] engage in these [activities] in two ways: effortlessly and continuously. Therefore, here is a verse regarding the effortlessness and continuity of the Buddha's activities as follows:

> The Pervasive Lord always effortlessly engages
> In going to the places and eras of the disciples,
> [Adapting to] their abilities, the means of educating them,
> And [devising] the duties that suit their abilities. //IV.1//

> Buddhahood, an intuitive wisdom ocean filled with a mass of
> supreme jewel excellences, possessing the sunlight of merit
> and wisdom,
> Surely produces all vehicles, pervasive as the magnificent vast-
> ness of space without limit or center,
> And bestows stainless excellences, seeing all beings as equal
> without distinction,
> While the wind of the buddha compassion scatters the cloud
> nets of addictive and objective [obscurations]. //IV.2//

«282» The summary meaning of these two features should be understood by the following two and eight verses, respectively:

> For whom? By whom to be tamed? How?
> By what practice? By which education? Where? When?
> Since such conceptual plans are not produced,
> The Sage always [acts] spontaneously. //IV.3//

The temperaments of the disciples,
Which of the many means for each,
Which education at what place and time:
[He] acts accordingly. //IV.4//

Since, concerning the definitive cause, its basis,
Its fruition, those sustaining their obscurations,
And the conditions for cutting away those [obscurations],
There is no thought, [buddha] activities are continuous without
    interruption. //IV.5//

The ten stages definitely bring about [enlightenment].
The two stores provide its cause.
Great enlightenment is the fruition of these;
Enlightenment is sustained in beings. //IV.6//

These are obscured by the endless addictions,
The secondary addictions, and the evolutionary instincts.
A buddha's great compassion is the condition
That, at all times, destroys those [obscurations]. //IV.7//

These six points, being similar
To an ocean, the sun, space,
A treasure, clouds, and wind,
Are to be understood accordingly. //IV.8//

Holding intuitive wisdom's water and excellences
Like gems, the stages are like an ocean.
Nourishing all sentient beings,
The two stores are like the sun. //IV.9//

Being vast and without any middle or end,
Enlightenment is like the realm of space.
The element of beings, which is the reality
Of the enlightened ones, is like a treasure. //IV.10//

Incidental, pervasive, and nonexistent,
Their addictions are like a host of clouds.

Always ready to dispel these [addictions],
Endless compassion is similar to wind. //IV.11//

Since [even] renunciation happens depending on others,
And they see the equality of themselves and beings,
And their activities will never be completed,
Their activities will not cease till the end of cyclic life.
    //IV.12//

«283» The Buddha is called "the one distinguished by no creation and
no destruction." Here, why does the Buddha, having such an uncreated and
indestructible nature, spontaneously and continuously engage in activities
without any discriminating thought until the end of cyclic life? In order to
stop any doubts and worries about a buddha's magnificent nature and to
help us to develop faith in the inconceivable sphere of a buddha, similes are
used to demonstrate such a magnificent nature.

«284» [The root text states:]

A tathāgata is like an indra,
To a drum [in heaven], clouds,
To a brahmā, the sun, a precious gem,
To an echo, space, and the earth. //IV.13//

The detailed exposition of the analysis of this verse, which seems like one
from a sutra, should be understood from the remaining verses, in respective
order [of the similes].

«285» The [simile] of the appearance of an indra [god-king] is as follows:

If the surface of the floor changed into stainless sapphire,
Because of its purity one would see in it
The [form] of the lord of all the [Meruvian] gods,[147]
With his following of many goddesses. //IV.14//

---

147. One is tempted to say "Olympian gods" here, since Indra is the king of those gods of
the 33 Heaven, which is atop the axial Mount Meru (or Sumeru) in the ancient cosmology.
Also, given the universal vehicle Buddhist multiversal cosmology, there are "indras" and
"brahmās" in other universes, being cosmic roles rather than singular individuals as in this
world, just as there are buddhas in other universes.

One would see his beautiful palace, the All-Victorious,
And other divine abodes,
The various palaces of the [33] gods,
And manifold celestial items. //IV.15//

Once the assembly of men and women
Who inhabit the surface of the earth
Saw this appearance,
Each would say: //IV.16//

"Before a long time passes, may I too
Become like the lord of gods!"
And to achieve this feat they would adopt
Virtue and would remain within it. //IV.17//

"This is just an appearance." There would not be
Any such understanding. Still their virtuous activities
Would lead them to be reborn in a celestial existence
After they departed from the surface of the earth. //IV.18//

Such an appearance is free from conscious intention
And does not involve the slightest movement at all,
And yet it accomplishes great benefit on the earth. //IV.19//

Those endowed with untainted faith and so on,
Having cultivated the excellences of faith, etc.,
Will perceive in their own minds the Buddha's appearance,
Which is endowed with the [auspicious] signs and marks.
    //IV.20//

They will see the Buddha
While he is walking and standing,
While he is sitting or sleeping.
They will see him in many forms of conduct. //IV.21//

They will see him giving a teaching leading to peace,
As well as silently resting in meditative trance

Or displaying various kinds of miracles;
Endowed with great splendor and magnificence,
[The Buddha] will be seen by all sentient beings. //IV.22//

Once having seen that, they too will wish
To practice in order to attain buddhahood.
Pursuing its causes in a genuine way,
They will attain the state they long for. //IV.23//

These appearances are totally free from thought,
And do not involve the slightest movement.
Nevertheless, they are accompanied by
Great benefit in the world. //IV.24//

"This is the appearance of my own mind."
Ordinary beings do not have such insight.
Yet, the sight of that form
Will become meaningful for these beings. //IV.25//

Relying on gradually beholding this form,
All those who follow this vehicle
Will see their own truth body within,
By means of the eye of intuitive wisdom. //IV.26//

If the earth was rid of bad places and turned into an even surface of sapphire,
That was flawless, radiant, and beautiful, having a gem's qualities and unstained luster,
Various divine abodes and the form of gods and their lord
would shine forth within it because of its purity.
Then, as the earth gradually lost these properties, they would be
invisible again and appear no more. //IV.27//

Yet, for their attainment, the men and women would keep
vows,
Pure conduct, practice of generosity, and so on, scattering flowers, and so on, with solemn vows.

Likewise, to make the Sage appear in their minds, which are
    similar to pure sapphire,
The victor child, with sheer delight, would conceive the spirit
    [of enlightenment]. //IV.28//

Just as, reflected by the pure sapphire ground,
The physical appearance of the lord of gods is seen,
Likewise, the form of the Sage is reflected
In the purified ground of sentient beings' minds. //IV.29//

Whether these reflections will rise or set in beings
Depends on their own minds being polluted or unpolluted.
Like the reflection [of an indra] appearing in the worlds,
They are not viewed as "created" or "extinct." //IV.30//

«286» The [explanation of the simile of the] heavenly drum is as follows:

By the power of the gods' former virtues,
The Dharma drum [arises] among them.
Involving no effort, origin, or thought,
No matter and no intention at all, //IV.31//

The drum resounds again and again
With "impermanent" and "suffering,"
"Selflessness" and "peace,"
Admonishing all the careless gods. //IV.32//

Likewise, though free from effort and so on,
The buddha speech of the Pervasive Lord
Permeates sentient beings without exception,
Teaching the Dharma to those of good fortune. //IV.33//

Just as the sound of the drum arises among the gods from their
    own [prior] activities,
The Dharma spoken by the Sage arises in the world from the
    [prior] activities of beings.

Just as the sound [of the drum] accomplishes peace without
   effort, origin, matter, or intention,
Likewise the Dharma causes accomplishment of peace without
   effort or any other such thing. //IV.34//

The sound of the drum in the heavenly city acts as the cause,
   yielding the gift of fearlessness and granting them victory
Over the host of the antigods, when these, driven by their
   addictions, make war upon them, and it suspends the playing
   of the gods.
Likewise, arising in the worlds, as the cause of meditative stability, formless trance, and so on, [the Dharma] expresses the
   way
Of the unsurpassed path, which will overcome all addictions
   and sufferings and thus lead all beings to peace. //IV.35//

«287» Why is the drum used as the simile but not other instruments in
heaven? Only these attractive sounds [of the Dharma drum] arise in their
ears as a result of [their] previous activities.

   The voice of a tathāgata has the four qualities different from those [instru-
ments]. What four? Being impartial, beneficial, delightful, and motivating
liberation. The Dharma drum illustrates "being impartial" since it exhorts
careless gods and does so in time. It illustrates "being beneficial" since it protects gods from the harm and fear caused by the antigods, etc., and makes
them maintain caution. It illustrates "being delightful" since it is free from
delight in improper desires and accomplishes the delight and bliss of the
Dharma. It illustrates "motivating liberation" since it resounds the voices
of "impermanence, suffering, emptiness, and selflessness" and pacifies all
mishaps and harm.

   «288» In brief, the mandala of the buddha voice is by far superior because
it has the common feature of these four aspects of the Dharma drum. Thus
the verse regarding the mandala of the buddha voice goes as follows:

Pervasive, beneficial, bestowing delight,
And endowed with the threefold miracle,
The Sage's voice is by far superior
To the instruments in heaven. //IV.36//

«289» These four features by which [the buddha speech] is explained, in short, should be understood by the following four verses:

> The mighty sound of the drum in heaven
> Does not reach the ears of those dwelling on earth,
> Whereas the drumming sound of the buddha [speech]
> Even reaches the underground worlds in cyclic life. //IV.37//

> Millions of instruments resound in heaven
> To set the fire of attachment ablaze and to increase it.
> The unique voice of the Lord of Compassion
> Resounds to quench all the fires of suffering. //IV.38//

> The sweet beguiling sound of the heavenly instruments
> Causes an increase of distraction among the gods,
> Whereas the speech of the Lord of Compassion
> Exhorts to reflection and commits the mind to meditation.
> //IV.39//

> Any cause of happiness for earthly beings and gods
> In all the worlds without exception,
> Briefly spoken, fully depends upon this voice
> That pervades all the worlds, not forsaking one. //IV.40//

«290» The miracle of body refers to the bodies that pervade all worlds in ten directions by the power of miracle. The miracle of mind refers to the mind that knows different states of the mind, seeing even the unconsciousness of beings. The miracle of speech refers to the speech that teaches the path to liberation.

«291» Such an unimpeded mandala of the buddha speech continues without interruption just like space. It cannot be perceived [by naïve people] in all times and in all aspects. This is not the fault of the mandala of the buddha speech itself.

A verse regarding this fault is as follows:

> Without hearing, one cannot experience subtle sound, and all
> [such sounds] do not reach even the ears of gods.

Likewise, as the object of apprehension of the very finest intui-
tive wisdom,
The subtle Dharma only reaches the ear
Of someone whose mind is free from addictions. //IV.41//

«292» The [simile] called cloud-like is [explained] as follows:

The monsoon clouds in summertime
Continuously and without any effort
Pour down vast torrents of water,
Causing the best possible crops on earth. //IV.42//

Just so, from the cloud of compassion
The rain of the Victor's holy Dharma
Pours down its waters without any scheming,
Causing a harvest of virtue for beings. //IV.43//

Just as the wind-born clouds cause rain to fall
When worldly beings follow the path of virtue,
From the buddha cloud stirred by compassion's wind,
The holy Dharma rains to nurture the virtue of beings. //IV.44//

By means of intuitive wisdom and great compassion with
regard to existence
It abides in the midst of space, unaffected by change and
nonchange.
Holding the essence of the untainted waters of memory spells
and samādhis,
The cloud of the Lord of Sages is the cause of the harvest of virtue.
//IV.45//

«293» The difference caused by various vessels:

Water that is cool, delicious, soft, and light when it falls from
the clouds
On earth acquires a great many tastes by touching salty and
other soils.

When the waters of the holy eightfold path rain from the heart
of the vast cloud of love,
They will also acquire many kinds of tastes from the different
soils of beings' continuums. //IV.46//

«294» The engagement without bias:

Those devoted to the universal vehicle,
Those who are neutral, and those with animosity
Are three groups [of beings] who are similar
To humans, peacocks, and hunger beings. //IV.47//

At the end of spring, when there are no clouds, human beings
and peacocks that rarely fly [are unhappy or neutral,
respectively].
When rain is falling in summertime, the hunger beings suffer.
Similarly, the arising and nonarising of the Dharma rain from
the mass of compassion clouds
Also [lead to opposite reactions] in worldly beings who long
for the Dharma or are hostile to it, respectively. //IV.48//

When releasing a deluge of heavy drops or hurling down hailstones and thunderbolts,
A cloud does not heed any being, even those who have sought
shelter in the hills.
Likewise, the cloud of wisdom and love does not heed whether
or not its vast and subtle art and reason drops
Will purify the addictions or the evolutionary instinct for
clinging to the view of self. //IV.49//

«295» Extinguishing of the fire of suffering:

In this cycle of beginningless birth and death, five paths are
open for sentient beings to tread.
Just as no sweet scent is found in excrement, no happiness will
be found among the five kinds of beings.
Their suffering resembles the continuous pain arising from fire

and weapons, or [from a wound] being touched by salt, and
so on.
The great rain of holy Dharma pours down in cascades from the
cloud of compassion, soothing and appeasing this pain.
//IV.50//

Realizing that "[Even] gods have the suffering of death and
transmigration, and humans [the suffering] of desperate
seeking,"
Those endowed with discriminative wisdom have no desire for
even the highest [states] of kings and gods.
With their intuitive wisdom, they faithfully follow the holy
words of the Tathāgata,
Their insight makes them see: "This is suffering! This is its
cause! And this is cessation of suffering!" //IV.51//

In the case of illness, one needs to diagnose it, remove its cause,
Attain the happy state [of health], and rely on suitable
medicine;
Similarly, one needs to recognize suffering, remove its cause,
Come in touch with its cessation, and rely on the suitable path.
//IV.52//

≪296≫ The [simile] of Brahmā is as follows:

Just like the way Brahmā,
Without departing from his abode,
Effortlessly shows his appearance
In all the residences of the gods, //IV.53//

Without moving from the truth body,
The Sage effortlessly demonstrates
Illusory appearances in every realm
To beings who have the karmic fortune. //IV.54//

When Brahmā, never departing from his place, has manifested in
the desire realm, he is seen by the gods.

This vision inspires them to abandon their delight in [sensuous]
objects.
Similarly, without moving from the truth body, the Tathāgata is
seen in the worlds
By beings with karmic fortune. This vision inspires them to dispel all their taints. //IV.55//

Just as by his own former votive prayers
And the power of the virtue of the gods,
Brahmā appears without deliberate effort,
So does the self-arisen emanation body. //IV.56//

«297» As for being invisible:

He moves from [Tuṣhita] and enters the womb, is born, and
goes to his father's palace.
He enjoys amusements, then seeks solitude, undergoes
[extreme] austerity, and defeats all devils.
He finds great enlightenment and shows the path to the citadel
of peace.
The Sage, though having displayed [such activities], is invisible
to those without karmic fortune. //IV.57//

«298» The [simile] of the sun is explained as follows:

When the sun blazes down, lotuses, etc., open,
While simultaneously kumuda flowers close.
To the benefit and fault of water-born flowers' opening and
closing
The sun does not give a thought, just like that ultimate Noble
One. //IV.58//

«299» There are two kinds of sentient beings: disciples and nondisciples.
Here the similes of lotus and vessel of pure water refer to disciples:

As the sun shining its own light
Simultaneously and without thought

Makes lotus flowers open their petals
And ripens other [crops], //IV.59//

So the sun of the Tathāgata manifests,
Shedding its rays of the holy Dharma
On the lotus-like beings to be educated,
Without harboring any notion or scheme. //IV.60//

By the truth body and the material bodies,
The sun of omniscience rises in the sky,
Which is the very essence of enlightenment,
To shed light beams of wisdom on beings. //IV.61//

In all disciples, as in water vessels,
The sun of the Tathāgata simultaneously
Is mirrored in countless reflections
Owing to the purity [of these beings]. //IV.62//

«300» Although buddhas do not have any scheme, they reveal themselves and teach the three kinds of being. As for being "sun-like," its meaning is:

[From] within the space of the truth body,
Which continuously pervades everything,
The buddha sun shines on the disciples
[Like] on mountains, as merited by each. //IV.63//

Just as the rising sun with thousands of far-reaching beams
Illuminates all the worlds, gradually shining its light
On the highest mountains, then the medium-sized, and the
    small,
The buddha sun gradually shines on the host of beings.
    //IV.64//

«301» The mandala of light is superior:

The sun does not penetrate to the depth of space in every field,
    nor can it show

The meaning of the knowable [to those] confined to the darkness of unknowing.
Appearing in clarity using an abundance of light emitting various colors,
Those of compassionate nature show the meaning of the knowable to beings. //IV.65//

When the Buddha goes to the city, people without eyes become sighted.
Freed from all meaningless things, they see the meaningful and experience [happiness].
When blinded by delusion, they fall into the sea of existence and are wrapped in the darkness of views,
The light of the buddha sun illumines their vision and they see the very points they never saw before. //IV.66//

«302» Being "wish-fulfilling jewel-like" is as follows:

A wish-fulfilling jewel, though free from notions,
Grants all those who dwell in the field of activity
Each of their desires simultaneously,
Doing so in the most perfect manner. //IV.67//

Likewise, beings of different ways of thinking,
When they rely on the wish-fulfilling Buddha,
Will hear various kinds of teachings,
Though he generates no thoughts of these. //IV.68//

As a precious jewel, which is free from thought, fully bestows
The desired riches on others, doing so without any effort,
The Sage always stays for others' sake, as merited by each,
And as long as existence lasts, doing so without any effort.
    //IV.69//

«303» It is rare for a buddha to appear:

The good jewel lying underground or in the ocean
Is very hard to find for beings who want it.

Likewise, one should understand that beings held in the grip of
  the addictions
And whose evolutionary gifts are poor will hardly see the
  Tathāgata in their minds. //IV.70//

«304» Being "echo-like" is as follows:

Just as the sound of an echo arises
As a result of the perception of others,
Without thought or purposeful labor
And abiding neither without nor within, //IV.71//

So the speech of the Tathāgata arises
As a result of the perception of others,
Without thought or purposeful labor
And abiding neither without nor within. //IV.72//

«305» Being "space-like" is as follows:

Space is nothing at all and does not appear.
It is neither an object [of the senses] nor a support.
It is totally beyond being a path for the eye.
It has no form and is not to be demonstrated. //IV.73//

Nevertheless, it is seen as being high and low,
But it is not at all like that.
Likewise, all are seen as the Buddha,
But he is not at all like that. //IV.74//

«306» Being "earth-like" is as follows:

Everything that grows from the earth
Will increase and become firm and vast
On the support of
Its thought-free soil. //IV.75//

Likewise, relying on the Buddha,
Who, like the earth, is free from thought,

Every root of virtue of sentient beings
Without exception will flourish and grow. //IV.76//

«307» The summary of those similes:

It is not obvious that one could act
Without exerting deliberate effort.
Therefore nine similes are taught,
To cut the doubts of the disciples. //IV.77//

The place where these nine similes
Are explained in great detail
Is the sutra that, by its very name,
Teaches their necessity and purpose. //IV.78//

Adorned with the far-reaching light
Of wisdom arisen from hearing it,
Those of insight will quickly enter
The fields of experience of a buddha. //IV.79//

This point is made clear
In the nine examples
Of Indra's reflection in sapphire and so on.
Their concise meaning, when apprehended precisely, //IV.80//

Is to illustrate the display [of body] and speech, and the all-
    pervasiveness [of mind],
Illusory emanation, the radiation of wisdom,
The secrecies of body, speech, and mind,
And the fact that compassion itself is attained. //IV.81//

All streams of effort being fully pacified
And the mind being free from all thought
Are similar to Indra's reflection appearing
Within stainless sapphire, etc. //IV.82//

Pacification of effort [is the proposition],
Mind free from thought is its reason.

To establish the meaning of such a nature,
The similes of Indra's form, etc., are given. //IV.83//

Here the meaning of the chapter is as follows:
The nine aspects of physical display, and so on,
[Show] that the Teacher has no birth and death,
And yet perfectly manifests without any effort. //IV.84//

«308» Here are four summary verses of similes regarding this point:

Something that, like Indra, the drum, clouds, Brahmā,
The sun, the precious king of wish-granting jewels, an echo,
    space,
And the earth, effortlessly and as long as existence may last
Fulfills others' benefit, yogis should understand. //IV.85//

[Bodies] being displayed are like the lord of gods appearing [in]
    the jewel.
Explanation well bestowed resembles the drum of the gods.
With cloud hosts of intuitive wisdom and great compassion,
    the Pervasive Lord
Permeates the limitless number of beings up to the peak of exis-
    tence. //IV.86//

Like Brahmā, not stirring from his uncontaminated place,
He displays manifold illusory appearances.
Like the sun, intuitive wisdom radiates its brilliance.
The Buddha mind resembles a pure and precious wish-fulfilling
    jewel. //IV.87//

Buddha speech has no letters, like an echo resounding from a
    cliff.
Like space, his body is pervasive, formless, and permanent.
Like the earth, a buddha is the soil, upholding without
    exception
And in any way, all medicinal herbs of the stainless qualities of
    beings. //IV.88//

«309» Furthermore, how do these similes illustrate that buddhas are permanent without arising and ceasing but appear to be so, as well as that buddha activities are effortlessly performed for all beings without interruption?

> The cause for the Buddha to be seen in the mind
> Is the purity of this ground,
> Similar to pure sapphire,
> [Achieved] by a firm sense of irreversible faith. //IV.89//

> Since virtue arises and ceases,
> The buddha form arises and ceases.
> Like Indra, the Sage who is the truth body
> Is free from arising and ceasing. //IV.90//

> Effortlessly, like [Indra], he manifests his activities,
> Displaying [physical forms], etc.,
> From the birthless and deathless truth body
> For as long as cyclic life may last. //IV.91//

> Here are the summary meanings of the similes,
> Explained in this order so that each latter one
> Eliminates any meaning in the former one
> That [touches on] any dissimilarity. //IV.92//

> A buddha is like a reflection, and yet dissimilar,
> Since a reflection is not endowed with his melody.
> He is like the drum of the gods, and yet dissimilar,
> Since the drum does not ever bring benefit. //IV.93//

> He is similar to a vast cloud, and yet dissimilar,
> Since a cloud does not eliminate worthless seeds.
> He is like the mighty Brahmā, and yet dissimilar,
> Since Brahmā does not cause ultimate maturity. //IV.94//

> He is like the orb of the sun, and yet dissimilar,
> Since the sun does not always overcome darkness.
> He is like a wish-granting jewel, and yet dissimilar,
> Since the jewel's appearance is not so rarely found. //IV.95//

He is similar to an echo, and yet dissimilar,
Since an echo arises from causes and conditions.
He is similar to space, and yet dissimilar,
Since space is not a ground of pure virtue. //IV.96//

Being the lasting basis for every goodness,
The best possible for all without exception
For worldly beings and those beyond the world,
[His activity] is similar to the mandala of earth, //IV.97//

Because, based upon the enlightenment of all buddhas,
The path beyond the world will arise, as will
The path of virtuous activities, mental stability, and
The immeasurable and formless contemplations. //IV.98//

The exposition of the meaning of the verses within the fourth chapter, "Enlightened Activities," of *The Sublime Continuum of the Universal Vehicle, Analysis of the Precious Spiritual Potential* has been completed.

CHAPTER V
Benefit

«310» There are six verses regarding the benefit of having faith in these four places, as follows:

Buddha element, buddha enlightenment,
Buddha excellences, and buddha activities
Are inconceivable, even for purified beings.
They are the field of experience of their Teacher. //V.1//

Those of insight, who have devotion to this buddha domain,
Will become vessels for the host of all buddha excellences,
While those truly delighting in these inconceivable qualities
Will exceed in merit all sentient beings. //V.2//

Someone striving for enlightenment may turn to the Dharma
    kings, offering golden fields adorned with jewels,
In [number] equal to the atoms in the buddhaverses, and may
    continue doing so every day.
Another may just hear a word of this, and upon hearing it
    become filled with devotion.
He will attain merit far greater and more manifold than the
    virtue sprung from that practice of generosity. //V.3//

An intelligent person wishing for enlightenment may by body,
    speech, and mind
Guard flawless moral conduct and do so effortlessly, even over
    the course of many eons.
Another may just hear a word of this, and upon hearing it
    become filled with devotion.

He will attain merit far greater and more manifold than the
virtue sprung from that practice of ethics. //V.4//

Some here may finally achieve the divine meditative stabilities
and Brahmā's abode, thus quenching all addictions' fire
Within the three realms of existence, and may cultivate these as
a means to reach unchanging and perfect enlightenment.
Another may just hear a word of this, and upon hearing it
become filled with devotion.
He will attain merit far greater and more manifold than the
virtue sprung from that practice of meditation. //V.5//

Generosity only yields wealth,
Discipline leads to the higher states of existence, and medita-
tion removes addiction.
Wisdom abandons all addictive and objective [obscurations].
It is therefore supreme, and its cause is studying these. //V.6//

«311» The meaning of these verses is further explained in the nine verses,
as follows:

The presence [of the element], its result,
Its excellences, and the achievement of benefit
Are the objects of understanding of a buddha.
When toward these four, as explained above, //V.7//

The intelligent one is filled with devotion
To their presence, ability, and excellences,
He will be quickly endowed with the fortune
By which one attains the state of a tathāgata. //V.8//

Those who realize that "this inconceivable object is present,
And someone like me can attain it;
Its attainment will hold such excellences and endowment"
Will aspire to it, filled with faith. //V.9//

Thus becoming vessels of all excellences,
Such as longing, diligence, mindfulness,

Meditative stability, intuitive wisdom, and so on,
They will have the spirit of enlightenment ever-present in them.
   //V.10//

That being ever-present in them,
The victor children will not fall back.
The transcendence of merit will be refined
Until it is transformed into total purity. //V.11//

Once these five transcendences of merit
Are not considered by way of the three sectors,
They will become perfect and fully pure,
As their opposite forces are abandoned. //V.12//

The merit of generosity arises from giving,
That of ethics arises from moral conduct.
The two aspects of patience and meditative stability
Stem from meditation, and diligence accompanies all.
   //V.13//

Whatever concepts there are within the three spheres
Are viewed as objective obscurations.
Whatever is the impulse of greed, and so on,
Is to be regarded as the addictive obscuration. //V.14//

Since apart from intuitive wisdom
There is no other cause of their removal,
This intuitive wisdom is supreme.
Its foundation being learning, such study is supreme. //V.15//

Based on the trustworthy words of the Buddha and on
   reasoning,
I have explained this for the sole purpose
Of purifying myself and supporting all those
Whose understanding has the best of virtue and wisdom.
   //V.16//

«312» Here are verses regarding the content, as follows:

As someone with eyes sees by relying on a lamp,
Or on lightning, a jewel, the sun, or the moon,
This has been truly explained by relying on the Sage,
The brilliant Dharma, and confidence about the great benefit.
//V.17//

Whatever speech is meaningful and well connected with the
    Dharma,
Removes all addictions of the three realms,
And shows the benefit of peace
Is the Sage's speech, while any different speech is other. //V.18//

«313» Here is a verse regarding the speaker, as follows:

Whatever someone has explained with undistracted mind,
Exclusively in the light of the Victor's teaching
And conducive to the path of attaining liberation,
One should place on one's head as the words of the Sage.
//V.19//

«314» Here is a verse regarding self-protection, as follows:

There is no one in this world more skilled in Dharma than the
    Victor.
No other has such omniscient intuitive wisdom, knowing
    everything without exception and knowing supreme reality
    as the way it is.
Thus one should not distort the sutras presented by the Sage
    himself,
Since this would destroy the Sage's manner and furthermore
    cause harm to the holy Dharma. //V.20//

Those blinded by addictions and ignorance
Revile the noble ones and despise the teachings they have
    spoken.

Since all this stems from a fixated view, [one's] mind should not
be joined with such a polluted vision.
Clean cloth is totally transformed by dye, but cloth soaked with
oil never is. //V.21//

«315» Here is a verse regarding the cause of degeneration, as follows:

As a result of a feeble intellect, lack of striving for virtue, reliance on false pride,
A nature obscured by being bereft of the pure Dharma, taking
the interpretable for the definitive meaning, craving for
profit,
Being under the sway of [wrong] views, relying on those who
disapprove and staying away from those who uphold the
teachings,
And as a result of inferior devotion, the teachings of the saints
are abandoned. //V.22//

«316» Here are verses concerning the effect of degeneration, as follows:

As they should be deeply afraid of abandoning the profound
Dharma,
Wise persons must not be as afraid of fire, vicious poisonous
snakes, murderers, and lightning;
For fire, snakes, enemies, and thunderbolts only separate us
from this life,
But cannot send us to the utterly fearful hells of direst pain.
//V.23//

Even someone who has repeatedly relied on evil friends and
thus heeded harmful intentions toward a buddha,
Who has committed one of the most heinous acts—killing
his father, mother, or a saint, or breaking up the Saṅgha
community—
Will be quickly freed from the [results], once truly realizing
reality.

But where would freedom be for someone whose mind is hostile to the Dharma? //V.24//

Having properly explained the seven topics and the places of
   the Jewels, the pure element,
Flawless enlightenment, excellences, and activities, may any virtue I have harvested from this [exposition]
Lead all beings to see the Seer Amitāyus, who is endowed with
   infinite light.
Upon seeing, may their stainless Dharma eye open and may
   they reach the great enlightenment. //V.25//

«317» The summary meaning of these ten verses should be understood by the following three verses:

On what basis, for what reason, and in what way
[This has been composed], what it explains
And what the causally concordant [effect] is about
Have been taught by means of four verses. //V.26//

Two verses [show] the means to purify oneself
And one [shows] the cause of loss.
Therefore, by means of two further verses
The fruit [of the loss] is explained. //V.27//

[Being born] in the mandala of a buddha's retinue,
Attaining tolerance, and [then] enlightenment:
The two aspects of the fruit of giving the teaching
Are explained by the last in a summary way. //V.28//

   This is the fifth chapter, "Benefit" of *The Sublime Continuum of the Universal Vehicle, Analysis of the Precious Spiritual Potential.* The exposition of the verses belonging to the body of the treatise is completed.
   «318» [As his dedication, Asaṅga states:]

By the inconceivable merit I have gained by this explanation
Of the holy Dharma Jewel of the universal vehicle,

May all beings become stainless vessels
For the holy Dharma Jewel of the universal vehicle!

The *Commentary* of the holy savior Maitreya's *The Sublime Continuum of the Universal Vehicle, Analysis of the Precious Spiritual Potential*, composed by master Asaṅga, is completed. It was translated from Sanskrit into Tibetan by the great Paṇḍita Sadjana, who was the grandson of the Brahmin Ratnavajra, a great scholar of the Glorious Incomparable City in the land of Kashmir, and by the Tibetan translator, the Shākya monk, [Ngog] Loden Sherab, in this Incomparable [Shrīnagar] City.

*Gyaltsap's Supercommentary on
Maitreyanātha's Sublime Continuum and
Noble Asaṅga's Commentary*

INTRODUCTION
[Opening Stanzas]

I bow down to the venerable teachers,
Whose flawless reason made the precious lamp
Of Shākyamuni's sutras shine like the gold
That has been [tested] by melting, cutting, and rubbing.

I bow my head to the feet of that excellent virtuous friend,
The supreme commentator on the intention of the sutras,
Who, having uprooted all faults by the power of his
    intelligence,
Perfected the excellent qualities of realization and
    abandonment,
Illuminated the three realms with the light of his fame,
And with his glorious compassion
Looked upon all beings as if each were his child.

I bow to the victor son, Ajita (Maitreya), anointed regent
By the Lord of Sages, superb guide of gods and humans,
And to the victor son, Mañjughoṣha,
Singular embodiment of the wisdom of all victors. [TL 002A]

The one renowned in these three realms as Asaṅga—
Foretold by the Victor as the perfect elucidator of the intention
Of the sutras of interpretable and definitive meaning—
While clarifying the words and meanings
Of the supreme sutras, carefully analyzed them.

And yet, some vulgar people,
Delighting in their own clever fabrications,
Incapable of distinguishing our own from others' theories,
Call the outsider systems "the intention of the Sage."
They have corrupted the system of this great champion.

It is difficult to realize well the intention behind the sutras;
The fault of wrongly explaining the holy Dharma is severe.
When it is so very difficult even to find good spiritual friends,
The discerning should always be conscientious!

As the ambrosial taste of the marvelous holy Dharma,
When enjoyed, bestows the deathless state,
So the cherished meaning of the discourses
Of the middle and final Dharma wheels
Should be explained according to the holy master's teachings.

[Asaṅga and the Five Treatises of Maitreya]

Now then, since a life that has liberty and opportunity is very difficult to find, and yet when found can be greatly meaningful, in this lifetime we should do something better than following the worldly systems of our ancestors. Instead of striving to gain profit and status in this life—which are like chaff in the wind—we should lay a sound foundation for achieving the temporary and ultimate aims of future lives. [TL 002B] Having come to know that our behavior is no better than that of animals, we should earnestly strive to make the best use of the essence of our liberty and opportunity.

Thus, as the embodiment of validating cognition, [the Buddha] established the spiritual paths and their fruitions that—following the system that has been settled upon in reference to the great collection of sutras and reasonings—noble beings throughout the three times have traveled, are traveling, and will travel, for they came to comprehend the meaning of these [teachings]. Consequently, [we too] should proceed to practice in the appropriate manner by means of the three precious educations, realizing that there is no other finer way to please the victors.

Furthermore, recall that the master Noble Asaṅga had previously performed outstanding enlightened activities in the presence of many victors
and created extensive roots of virtue. Even then, [in that life,] under the care
and protection of buddhas and bodhisattvas, his genius was superior. He
fulfilled his vow to take responsibility for Buddha Shākyamuni's teachings,
it having also been foretold that he would perfectly explain the intention
of the interpretable and definitive sutras. He realized that future disciples
are similar to passengers losing their way when they view the ocean-like
universal vehicle sutras, seeing that it is hard to understand the connection
between early and later expressions [in the sutras], let alone the extremely
profound meanings. He also knew that all the secret meanings of the
Tathāgata remained obscure even to him. Thus, thinking, "I can achieve
my desired aim if I propitiate the holy regent [Maitreya], [TL 003A] who has
unobstructed insight into all the secrets of the Sage's speech!"—he went to
meditate and came to behold Maitreya directly. By the miraculous power
of the Bhagavān [Maitreya], Asaṅga arrived in the Tuṣhita heaven, where
he received teachings and fully understood the intentions of all sutras. For
the purpose of helping future disciples in our Jambudvīpa world, Asaṅga
showered us with gifts of the holy Dharma, and in particular, the five great
treatises of Maitreya: the two *Ornaments* [the *Ornament of the Universal
Vehicle Sutras* and the *Ornament of Clear Realization*], the two *Analyses*
[the *Analysis of the Middle and Extremes* and the *Analysis of Phenomena and
Reality*], and *The Sublime Continuum of the Universal Vehicle*.

It is said that there are, in general, two ways to discriminate between the
interpretable meaning and the definitive meaning of the sutras taught by
the Bhagavān. One method is spoken of in sutras such as the *Teaching of
Akṣhayamati Sutra* and the *King of Samādhis Sutra*, while the other one is
found in the *Elucidation of the Intention Sutra*. The first system teaches that
those sutras that teach that all things are empty of any intrinsic identity
status[148] are definitive in meaning, and those sutras that teach about "persons," "aggregates," etc., by means of various words and expressions are interpretable in meaning. The latter system of the *Elucidation of the Intention*,
however, teaches that although the imagined [nature][149] is not established

---

148. *svalakṣaṇasiddha, rang gi mtshan nyid gyis grub pa.*
149. *parikalpita-svabhava, kun brtags gyi rang bzhin.*

by its intrinsic identity, the relative[150] and perfect[151] [natures] do have their own intrinsic identity. Thus, [according to this latter system,] a sutra that unequivocally teaches all things as not established in terms of their own identities, or that unequivocally teaches all things as established in terms of their own character, is said to be interpretable in meaning; and a sutra that clearly differentiates between [some things] being established in terms of their own identity and [other things] being not established in terms of their own identity is said to be definitive in meaning.

Following the former [group of sutras, i.e., the *Teaching of Akshayamati Sutra* and the *King of Samādhis Sutra*], the savior [TL 003B] Nāgārjuna pioneered the way, as a champion [of the Centrist system], to differentiate the interpretable meaning from the definitive meaning, and thereby prove without effort that the latter sutra [the *Elucidation of the Intention Sutra*] is interpretable in meaning; Asaṅga, the holy master, mainly pioneered the way, as a champion of the information-only (*vijñaptimātra*) [system], [to differentiate interpretable and definitive meaning teachings] according to the criterion of distinction laid down in the *Elucidation of the Intention*, by following the two *Analyses* and the *Ornament of the Universal Vehicle Sutras*. In addition, he explained the intention of the mass of individual vehicle sutras.

The treatise, *Analysis of Phenomena and Reality*, teaches that phenomena—truly established relative realities, which dualistically appear as subject and object—are the basis for the establishment of cyclic life, and that reality (*dharmatā*)—the emptiness of a substantial difference between subject and object—is the foundation of the attainment of liberation by means of meditation, having taken that as an object. Having taken the true establishment of dualistic appearances as the basis, the treatise *Analysis of the Middle and Extremes* differentiates it into three realities with different natures, and presents an arrangement of the basis, path, and fruition for both the common and uncommon vehicles. Then, the *Ornament of the Universal Vehicle Sutras*—without refuting the truth status of dualistic appearances—picks up at this point with the methods for activating the spiritual potential for the universal vehicle, and proceeds to extensively spell out the procedure by which a bodhisattva proceeds to higher and higher

---

150. *paratantra, gzhan dbang.*
151. *parinispanna, yongs grub.*

realizations, as well as the means of caring for other disciples. These three texts do not provide a clear articulation [TL 004A] of an ultimate reality that is the emptiness of intrinsic identity status, but rather teach merely a kind of ultimate that accords with the inclination of disciples.

Having followed these treatises, the Master (Asaṅga) pioneered the way as a champion of the information-only [theory] in his five-section, two-summary *Stages* text (*Yogācārabhūmi*), conforming with the *Elucidation of the Intention Sutra*'s way of differentiating between the interpretable and the definitive. In his *Disciple Stages*, he mentions that a certain individual vehicle sutra teaches the manner in which a rhinoceros-like[152] hermit buddha and someone who has the specific potential for the universal vehicle, having accumulated a collection (of merit) on the path of accumulation for a hundred eons and three incalculable eons, respectively, can then progress in one session[153] up to the "heat" level of the path of preparation, and even beyond. Despite the fact that the *Ornament of Clear Realization* reiterates the ultimate view of emptiness, its overriding concern is to clearly indicate the hidden meanings of the extensive, middling, and concise *[Transcendent Wisdom] Sutras*: the definitive nature[154] of the stages of clear realizations by the three kinds of beings with spiritual potentials,[155] their definite enumeration, and their definitive sequence.

As for *The Sublime Continuum of the Universal Vehicle*, it should be taught at a later time to those who have become spiritually mature by means of familiarizing themselves with the information-only system. It can be taught at once, however, to supremely intelligent persons who have a spiritual potential for the universal vehicle, since it clearly shows that there is no difference between the *Tathāgata Essence Sutra* and the extensive, middling, and brief *[Transcendent Wisdom] Sutras* in terms of [the presentation of] an ultimate truth that is free of all conceptual elaborations—that is, [in terms of] the emptiness of the truth [status][156] of all phenomena, which are the observed objects of the path and must be definitely realized in order to attain even the enlightenment of a disciple or the enlightenment of a hermit

---

152. *khaḍgaviṣāṇakalpa, bse ru lta bu.*
153. *ekāsana, stan gcig.*
154. *bhāva, ngo bo.*
155. **gotraka, rigs can.*
156. **satya[siddha]śūnya, bden par [grub pas] stongs pa.*

buddha. Hence, the main teaching expressed in this treatise [TL 004B] is what the Master (Asaṅga) clarifies in conformity with [Maitreya's] intention.

In reference to the knowledge of paths[157] in the *Transcendent Wisdom Sutra [in Eighteen Thousand Lines]*, there is the statement:[158]

> Those who have entered [the state of] complete faultlessness lack the ability to cultivate the mind of unsurpassed, perfect, full enlightenment. Why? It is because they have severed their connection to the continuum of the life cycle.

When explaining this passage, the son of victors, Haribhadra, in his *Great Commentary*[159] mentions that the master Noble Nāgārjuna is an advocate of the "single vehicle" theory,[160] and the master Asaṅga is an advocate of the "multiple vehicles" theory.[161] However, the difference between these two masters' ways of explanation is intentional [in their respective contexts] because Asaṅga pioneered the way as a champion by demonstrating that there are three final vehicles, for the sake of helping those who have a specific potential for the information-only [system]; but the master himself should not be thought of as an advocate [only] of the information[-only] system. This would severely contradict the fact that in his commentary on this treatise, he establishes that there is one final vehicle and extensively elucidates the subtle emptiness. We should therefore not think of this master as one who pioneered a champion's way different from that which Nāgārjuna pioneered, for he was in reality a follower of Nāgārjuna.

---

157. *mārgajñana, lam shes.* The second of the "eight topics" in transcendent wisdom studies in the Tibetan monastic university curriculum.

158. H12: vol. 30, fol. 365a.3–5.

159. *Clear Meaning,* D3791, vol. 85, fol. 76a.4–5.

160. *ekayāna, theg pa gcig.*

161. *theg pa sna tshogs su smra ba.*

[Overview and Explanation]

There are four parts to the explanation of *The Sublime Continuum of the Universal Vehicle Treatise* and its *Commentary*: the meaning of the title, the translator's homage, the meaning of the text itself, and the meaning of its conclusion.

1. The Meaning of the Title

1.1. The Translation of the Title

The [meaning of the] title of this treatise in Sanskrit is as follows: *mahā* is "great," *yāna* is "vehicle," *anuttara* or *uttara* [TL 005A] is "unsurpassed," *tantra* is "continuum," and *śāstra* is "treatise."

1.2. The Explanation of the Title

The word "vehicle" refers to both the traveling causal vehicle and the traveled fruitional vehicle. That vehicle is called "great," since it is endowed with the seven greatnesses, such as "great apprehension" in terms of the apprehension of the extensive textual literature. "Continuum" means continuation,[162] which refers to the sutras that teach how to purify a tainted consciousness. Since "unsurpassed" [also] has the meaning of "later" (i.e., the later Dharma wheel), it denotes the later classics of the universal vehicle. A "treatise," which comments on the intention of those [sutras], has an etymological explanation of *śāstra* as follows: *śās* means "to correct," and *tra* means "to protect." Hence, in brief, [a *śāstra* is a work that] corrects the addictions, the [student's] enemy, and protects [the student] from the dangers of a lower rebirth and the dangers of worldly existence.

2. Translator's Homage

In order to accomplish a variety of immediate and ultimate desired aims, the translator adds his homage [at the beginning of his translation], in this case: "I bow down to all buddhas and bodhisattvas!" From the perspective

---

162. *anubaddha, rgyun chags pa.*

of teaching the stages of the path, since this homage is a teaching on taking refuge, [readers] should remember just this meaning on all occasions, such as lectures, etc.

3. The Meaning of the Text ... 3.1. Actual Explanation ... 1.1. Textual Body ... 1.1. The Nature of the Textual Body ... 1.1. General Meaning ... 1.1. Identifying the Seven Vajra-Like Topics

[TL 005B] Each topic should be understood in terms of two aspects: ultimate and relative.

(1) The ultimate Buddha is the truth body,[163] of which perfect elimination[164] and perfect intuitive wisdom[165] are its marvelous defining characteristics; the relative aspect is the material body of a buddha.

(2) The ultimate Dharma is both true cessations and true paths[166] in the mental continuum of a universal vehicle practitioner (bodhisattva); the relative one is the sutra literature.

(3) The ultimate Saṅgha is knowledge[167] and liberation[168] in the mental continuum of a noble[169] universal vehicle bodhisattva; the relative one is the assembly of noble universal vehicle bodhisattvas.

(4) The ultimate element[170] is the ultimate truth of suchness,[171] mingled with the obscurations, which is the emptiness of the intrinsic reality status[172] of the mental continuum of a sentient being; the relative one is the ability possessed by a sentient being's mind to produce transcendent qualities.

163. *dharmakāya, chos kyi sku.*

164. *pratikṣepa, spang ba.*

165. *jñāna, ye shes.*

166. *marga-satya, lam gyi bden pa.* Here "path" is being used in its technical sense in the context of the four noble truths as a type of consciousness—specifically, one that leads to liberation from saṁsāra.

167. *vidyā, rig pa.*

168. *vimukta, rnam par grol ba.*

169. *ārya, 'phags pa.* That is, a disciple, hermit buddha, or bodhisattva who has directly realized ultimate truth and attained the path of insight.

170. *dhātu, khams.*

171. *tathatā, de bzhin nyid.*

172. *svabhāvasiddhaśūnya, rang bzhin gyis grub pas stong pa.*

(5) The ultimate enlightenment is the truth body; the relative one is the material bodies—as explained [in *The Sublime Continuum* (III.2ab)]:

> The place of fulfillment of one's own self
> Is the ultimate reality body ...

... and so on. If you ask, "How is this distinct from [being] a buddha?" although both are similar to the Jewel that is the Buddha, it is merely a difference of positing one as arising within one's own continuum and the other as having been established in the continuums of others.

(6) The ultimate excellences are the thirty-two excellences of freedom,[173] including the [ten] powers, etc.;[174] the relative ones are the thirty-two excellences of development [of karmic evolution into the material body of a buddha].[175]

(7) The ultimate enlightened activities are the all-accomplishing intuitive wisdom;[176] the relative ones are the sutra literature.

3.1.1.1.1.2. Ascertaining the Number [of Vajra-Like Topics]

More than seven [vajra-like topics] are not needed; while it is not possible to cover [the meaning of the text] with less than that, this is because the causal coherence [that is, the causal progression of the topics] in this treatise is completed by just this number of topics.

[TL 006A] With regard to this [text], the great master translator [Ngog Lotsawa][177] composed two modes of exposition: one from the perspective of the wheel of unlocated nirvana and the other from the perspective of the wheel of jewels. Although the former mode of exposition follows the literal meaning of the verse showing the sequence later in the text, I think that explaining the primary meaning of the treatise according to the latter mode of exposition is the correct way.

---

173. *bral ba'i yon tan.*

174. The remaining excellences are the four fearlessnesses and the eighteen unique qualities.

175. *rnam smin yon tan.* The thirty-two major marks of the material body of a buddha.

176. *kṛtyānuṣṭhānajñāna, bya ba sgrub pa'i ye shes.*

177. An appellation for Ngog Loden Sherab.

The final Three Jewels are the fruition of one's objective, for it is certain that only they constitute the marvelous perfection of the two aims. I will explain the reasoning [for this] later. It is also certain that there are two aspects of the cause of the accomplishment of the fruitional Three Jewels: the substantial cause and contributing conditions. The first aspect is the element, which is the suchness reality mingled with taints, for if the element were not naturally pure, then since it would be untenable for incidental taints[178] to be removed, there would be no enlightenment. Hence, [anything whatsoever that by its absence serves as] a reason for something to not arise has been designated as a "substantial cause,"[179] even though it is neither a product nor a producer of it. [Likewise,] the spiritual potential that has come about as a result of one's attainments is also a productive cause.[180] The second aspect is the cooperative conditions, which are the enlightenment, the excellences, and the enlightened activities that have been accomplished by other beings. They are no more than external conditions in the sense that other beings—having become perfectly and completely enlightened by the turning of the wheel of Dharma—are what make the thorough purification of one's own taints possible.

Furthermore, having taken reality mingled with taints as the principal subject to be settled once and for all, it is presented in terms of the coarse cause-and-effect [relations that] serve to purify that. Hence, [this treatise] is restricted to teaching merely [TL 006B] the causes and their effects, and is not an exhaustive treatment of the divisions of their various instances. The inner conditions, such as proper mental engagement,[181] etc., are what are to be realized in reliance upon the teachings on how to purify the element, and hence should be understood as included in [the teachings on] the element.

Moreover, the arising of the final Three Jewels within one's own continuum comes from meditation on the correct view. This view comes about, in turn, from having relied upon the two causes and the two conditions. The two causes are one's own constituents and proper mental engagement. The two conditions are the three factors comprising the enlightenment, etc., of previous tathāgatas, and the pronouncements of others. The pronounce-

---

178. *āgantukamala, glo bur gyi dri ma.*
179. *upādāna-hetu, nyer len gyi rgyu.*
180. *bskyed pa'i rgyu.*
181. *yoniśo-manasikāra, tshul bzhin yid la byed pa.*

ments of others should also be understood as included within [the category of] "enlightened activities."

3.1.1.1.1.3. Dispelling Doubts

If someone thinks, "It [seems] it is sufficient to teach solely about the Buddha Jewel as the fruit to be attained. Why then is it necessary to teach about the Three Jewels?" then we reply, "There is no fault [in teaching about all Three Jewels]."

In order to care for beings endowed with [one of] the three types of spiritual potential, [the teaching about the Three Jewels] demonstrates different names for fruitional refuges with respect to [such] different types [of people]: the person who has the spiritual potential for the universal vehicle aspires to become a perfect buddha as their object of fruitional refuge; the person who has the specific potential for the hermit buddha vehicle aspires to the extinction of the suffering of the life cycle by means of realizing relativistic origination as their object of fruitional refuge; and the person who has specific potential for the disciple vehicle, in his [or her] last worldly lifetime, aspires to the extinction of suffering by means of relying on the words of others. Hence, for the sake of caring for [these beings], the Three Jewels are presented as the fruitional refuges.

If someone says, "If [this text] explains that the Three Jewels are the fruits of the three types of beings with spiritual potential, [TL 007A] then it is not a distinctively universal vehicle treatise, for it would then necessarily teach only that enlightenment, not also that of the disciple vehicle and of the hermit buddha vehicle," then we reply, "There is no fault [in this]."

The final Three Jewels that are taught in this [treatise] are subsumed by the ultimate refuge, the sole, unique Buddha [Jewel]. As for the Three Jewels as the immediate causes of its attainment, on the eighth stage it is designated as the Buddha Jewel, on the ninth stage as the Dharma Jewel, and on the tenth stage as the Saṅgha Jewel. The remote cause [of its attainment] is—on the seventh stage and below—the Saṅgha Jewel. When considered as the objects of causal refuge, the Three Jewels that are taught here are the refuges for the individual vehicle. Yet, [this treatise] does not explicitly teach the enlightenment of disciples and hermit buddhas in terms of being objects of fruitional refuge. Hence, there is no fault. In this way, [disciples of those two vehicles] are progressively led into the universal vehicle by way of teaching [those enlightenments as] merely the similarly named "Dharma" and "Saṅgha" [respectively]. In summation, the Jewels explicitly taught here are [taught] from the perspective of the first stage onward, and since the Jewels of the first stage up to the tenth stage are given from the perspective of accomplishing [the attainment of] the final Three Jewels, there is no fault that [this treatise] is necessarily something common to all vehicles. I shall explain this point later.

CHAPTER I
The Tathāgata Essence

3.1.1.1.2. Meaning of the Branches ... 2.1. The Root Text ... 1.1. Identifying the Essential [Meaning]

«1» The body of the whole treatise is condensed
Into these seven vajra topics:
The Buddha, the Dharma, and the Saṅgha, the element,
The enlightenment, the excellences, and, last, the enlightened
  activities of the Buddha. //I.1//

The Buddha, who is composed of the three bodies, the Dharma, which is composed of [the truths of] cessation and path, [TL 007B] and the Saṅgha, which is the assembly of noble universal vehicle bodhisattvas—these three sites—designate the temporary and final fruits to be attained. The remaining four topics are treated in terms of causes and conditions: the element, i.e., tathāgata essence, which includes reality mingled with taints and the ability to develop transcendent excellences that exist within the minds of beings; the enlightenment, which is comprised of abandonment and the wisdom that perfects one's transformation; the excellences of freedom and development that depend on that [enlightenment]; and, the last of the seven topics, the enlightened activities of a perfect, complete buddha. Alternatively, the Three Jewels can be presented from the perspective of what they accomplish for others; and the last three—enlightenment, [excellences, and enlightened activities]—from the perspective of what they give rise to in one's own continuum. Furthermore, if one relies on the explanation of that part of the latter sequence, then [this presentation] is somewhat applicable. In either case, the element is presented solely as a causal factor. Therefore, taking this as the final fruit produced is just the senseless babbling of someone who does not know how to explain the treatise. I shall explain this later. As for this, and what remains, that leads to a discussion of the sevenfold enumeration.

3.1.1.1.2.1.2. Teaching the Enumeration as Seven

The object of discussion of this treatise—the whole body of explanations that follows—is condensed into seven topics that are to be understood, and hence the body of the whole treatise is condensed into topics to be understood, that is, these seven vajra-like topics. Furthermore, the meaning of the sutra quotations associated with the seven topics given here, in the *Questions of King Dhāraṇīshvara* and other sutras, [TL 008A] also follow this collection into these seven.

3.1.1.1.2.2. The Commentary . . . 2.1. Detailed Exposition . . . 1.1. The Reasons for Explaining "Vajra-Like" and "Sites" . . . 1.1. Teaching

The seven topics that are to be realized by the individual introspective wisdom[182] of noble beings are vajra-like, and the words that indicate them are the sites. Because they are the places where [the seven topics] can be understood, elucidated, and taught, they are called "vajra sites."

3.1.1.1.2.2.1.1.2. Explanation

The seven topics that are to be understood should be known to be "vajra-like," because they have a nature that is not expressible in a perfect way, that is, since realizing them by means of language and conceptual thought [is imperfect],[183] and because they are what is to be known by means of the individual discriminating [wisdom] of noble beings. Not only is this the ultimate truth, but also it is the wisdom that directly realizes it. Having been distinguished[184] in terms of ultimate truth, since all seven vajra-like topics are to be directly realized, they are "inexpressible." As for the "individually discriminating [wisdom]," this refers not only to a noble being's meditative equipoise comprehending the ultimate [truth] but also to the

---

182. *pratisaṁvid, so so rang gis rig pa.*
183. *sgra rtog gis rtogs tshul.*
184. *viśiṣṭatā, khyad par du byas.*

post-attainment wisdom as a [type of] individually discriminating [wisdom]. [It is important to recognize that] an intrinsically identifiable thing's not being an object of verbal expression[185] and the ultimate truth's lack of expressibility in words[186] are not similar. This is because being an object of verbal expression simply does not apply to the nature of a intrinsically identifiable thing [since it does not exist,] whereas [TL 008B] one [can] perfect the method of understanding [of ultimate truth] by using [conventional] dualistic appearances. Hence, even though reality[187] can be expressed correctly using words and concepts, and mentally contemplated in this manner, it is an object that is impossible to be realized in that manner by a noble being's meditative equipoise, although it is not impossible for ultimate truth to serve somewhat as the object of words and concepts. This is because if you were to assert that ultimate truth is not an object of knowledge, then it would follow that you would be deprecating the very meaning of [its being] the mode of existence [of all things],[188] and as a result any assertion of engaging in practices of purification would be meaningless. Thus, since this is a terrible theory, you should discard it.

«2» As for the proof of the former reason, it logically follows because [the topics] are difficult to penetrate in a complete way by means of the knowledge that arises from studious listening and critical thinking [about them]. [Now, Asaṅga] having intended that one should be able to understand [from this] the difficulty of penetrating [the nature of reality] by means of [wisdom] arisen from a worldy meditation, he did not explicitly elaborate [on this]. Nonetheless, when one has understood ultimate truth by means of these three forms of knowledge, [one] has still not transcended dualistic perceptions, for only when one has perfected the manner of realization is it a realization like water poured into water. It follows that the letters that express these seven topics are called vajra-like sites, because they serve as the support for those meanings since those meanings must first be understood by means of the wisdom that has arisen by means of studious learning, which is then the basis for the attainment and actualization of that objective. It follows that this is the case because [there is a basis for

185. *rang mtshan sgra'i brjod bya ma yin pa.*
186. *don dam bden pa sgras brjod du med pa.*
187. *dharmatā, chos nyid.*
188. *gnas lugs kyi don.*

attainment and actualization] only when those letters reveal, as expressible topics, the paths that conform to the attainment of that status, which is the realization of those seven topics.

Previously, someone—having resolved the contradiction between the explanation here that these meanings are expressible and the explanation above that [ultimate truth] is inexpressible—explained that although the ultimate truth is inexpressible in words, the paths of direct realization are verbally expressible. However, [TL 009A] I disagree, because it is not possible to find any distinction whatsoever, in terms of expressibility or inexpressibility, between the ultimate truth and the intuitive wisdom that realizes it. Consequently, the treatise that teaches the seven topics conveys the meaning [of the words] that serve as the foundation of the seven topics, and hence, having relied upon the wisdom that comes from studious learning and critical thinking about what was initially expressed in the treatise about these meanings, we develop transcendent paths. Hence, that is the meaning of also taking those paths as expressible objects.

3.1.1.1.2.2.1.1.3. Summary

One should realize that the seven topics and the letters that express them are the "vajra-like" and the "sites" [respectively], because, as in the aforementioned explanations, [the vajra] means hard to penetrate in a complete way by means of the knowledge that comes from studious learning and critical thinking, and [the letters] mean the support of the elucidation of those points as the subjects.

3.1.1.1.2.2.1.2. Identifying the Basis of the Etymology . . . 2.1. Question

«3» Now, if you ask, "What are the topics? And what are the letters?"

3.1.1.1.2.2.1.2.2. Answer

This was previously explained in the passage from "the seven topics that are to be understood as 'topics,'" up to "they are called 'meanings.'" The "letters"—which really means collections of words and phrases—by which the seven topics that are to be understood [1] are taught as the subject and [2] are elucidated as the object of an intuitive wisdom consciousness, are called "letters." The word "letter" here does not exclusively refer to the letter that is a part of the letter-word-phrase hierarchy, but rather to the treatise that teaches the seven topics.

3.1.1.1.2.2.1.3. Associating the Hard-to-Realize Meanings with the Sutràs . . . 3.1. Taking up [the Topic]

«4» [As for the topic,] the [text] states "teaching of the vajra topics."

3.1.1.1.2.2.1.3.2. The Actual Connection with Sutras . . . 2.1. Connection with Sutras on the Three Jewels

[TL 009B] [The statement from the *Chapter on Firm High Resolve Sutra* is:]¹⁸⁹

«5» O Ānanda, the ultimate Tathāgata, who is empty of being established in terms of any intrinsic identity and is free from any incidental taints, cannot be shown to the eye consciousness, and cannot be seen with the eyes. In addition to that, he cannot be understood by conventional knowledge.

O Ānanda, the ultimate Dharma cannot be expressed fully in a manner comprehended by means of terms and concepts; it cannot be heard with the ears.

O Ānanda, the ultimate Saṅgha is uncreated, that is, empty of intrinsic identity. Here, "ultimate" means in the ultimate reality. It cannot be served by making prostrations with the body, or by making offerings to it, [or] by means of directly perceiving it with the mind.

It is well known in the world that the Buddha is the object worth seeing, the Dharma is the object worth listening to, and the Saṅgha is the field

189. This quote as given in Asaṅga's *Commentary* (above, p. 52) is much shorter but with the same meaning. This version is definitely mixed by Gyaltsap with qualifiers, and is thus a commentarial paraphrase, though written by the scribe as a direct quote. This seems to be the pattern of many *Commentary* quotes cited in the *Supercommentary*.

[of merit] worth serving. When these three are expounded individually— from the perspective of reification and repudiation, as objects grasped as if truly existent that are to be cut off—they are all similar in the sense that ultimately they cannot be seen, etc. From the perspective of teaching the ultimate manner of existence of the Three Jewels, even the conventional [Three Jewels] are something to be discarded. As it says in the *[Transcendent Wisdom] Sutra [in Eighteen Thousand Lines]*, "(all noble beings) are distinguished in terms of the uncreated,"[190] that is, noble beings are designated in terms of their direct realizations of the uncreated ultimate truth. In addition to that, the universal vehicle's Three Jewels and the individual vehicle's [TL 010A] Saṅgha and Dharma Jewels—in terms of completing [the path] by means of vast or limited methods, respectively—must be definitely designated in the same way. In his commentary, Asaṅga teaches that disciples and hermit buddhas do have the realization of subtle selflessness. I will explain this later.

3.1.1.1.2.2.1.3.2.2. Connection with Sutras on the Remaining Four Sites . . .
2.1. The Element and Its Connection with Sutras . . . 1.1. Teaching That the Element Is Always an Object Solely for the Tathāgata

«6» [The *Sutra Teaching the Absence of Increase and Decrease (in the Realm of Beings)* states:]

> O Shāriputra, this topic of suchness mingled with the taints is an object for the Tathāgata. If there existed elaborations of true [existence], they would be suitable as something to be objectified, but the Tathāgata always remains in meditative equipoise by way of not seeing any elaborations of true [existence] whatsoever, and by the disappearance, as well, of all elaborations of

---

190. *gzhan yang rgyun du zhugs pa'i 'bras bu ni 'dus ma byas kyis rab tu phye ba'o zhes bya bar dmigs pa'i tshul gyis gnas par mi bya'o//de bzhin du lan gcig phyir 'ong ba'i 'bras bu dang/phyir mi 'ong ba'i 'bras bu dang/dgra bcom pa nyid dang/rang sangs rgyas ni 'dus ma byas kyis rab tu phye ba'o zhes bya bar dmigs pa'i tshul gyis gnas par mi bya'o//rnam pa thams cad mkhyen pa nyid kyi bar du 'dus ma byas kyis rab tu phye ba'o zhes bya bar dmigs pa'i tshul gyis gnas par mi bya'o/*. From: *Transcendent Wisdom Sutra in Eighteen Thousand Lines* (H12, vol. 30, fol. 373a.3–373a.6). Similar, though not exact, quotations also occur in the *Transcendent Wisdom in One Hundred Thousand Lines* (H9, vol. 24, fol. 196b.1–196b.2), the *Transcendent Wisdom in Twenty-Five Thousand Lines* (H10, vol. 28, fol. 190b.2–190b.3), and others.

dualistic appearances. The clear explanation of just this point is [the import of] the statement, "it belongs to the Tathāgata's sphere of experience."

3.1.1.1.2.2.1.3.2.2.1.2. Not Being an Object Determined by Others[191]

[The sutra continues, with] "O Shāriputra!" [to state that] since a final, single vehicle is established [for disciples and hermit buddhas], in the future it will be realized by means of their own wisdom, or even if [, before then,] not realized by means of their own wisdom, it will be contingent on their stage of realization by means of faith. Being contingent on the stage of these two types of beings who lack realization [either by means of their own wisdom or by faith], "even temporarily" is said. Since all the disciples and hermit buddhas are cut off from the ability to perfectly meditate on the selflessness of phenomena—as bodhisattvas in the universal vehicle do—and this topic can be neither known, seen, nor discerned correctly, on the three stages—the preliminaries, the main body, and the conclusion of meditation—by means of their own wisdom consciousnesses, or on the three stages of studious learning, critical reflecting, and meditating, respectively, then what need is there to speak about childish, ordinary individuals?

Objection: Someone says, [TL 010B] "It is unacceptable to connect these, respectively, to the three paths of application, insight, and meditation, because it says, 'If [this] cannot be seen by all the disciples and hermit buddhas,[192] what need is there to speak about childish, ordinary individuals?'" Someone also says, "It is unacceptable as well for you to explain this as the wisdom arisen from studious learning, for that is the wisdom that relies upon sutras, and therefore it cannot be one's own wisdom consciousness."

Reply: It is clear that you do not understand the meaning of the phrase "one's own wisdom consciousness." Although noble disciples and hermit buddhas also directly see the ultimate reality, they do not master it thoroughly by means of a limitless mass of reasonings that cut off conceptual elaborations with regard to the ultimate reality, as taught in [Nāgārjuna's] *Root Verses on Centrism*. Unlike followers of the universal vehicle with sharp

---

191. The text appears to be corrupt here, reading: *gzhan gyi gtan du ba'i yul ma yin*. We follow a contextually preferred reading: *gzhan gyi gtan 'du 'bab pa'i yul ma yin*.

192. The text appears to be corrupt here, reading: *so so skyes bos blta mi nus na.* . . .

intellects, they are unable to realize the ultimate truth by way of the ever-increasing force of their own wisdom consciousness; this is the meaning of "unable" in the statement "unable to see by means of their own wisdom consciousness," etc. Moreover, if you wonder whether or not disciples and hermit buddhas are able to realize the ultimate reality at all, then [as the sutra states,]

> [That] is realized with a wisdom consciousness from the perspective of a follower of faith with respect to the Tathāgata, and not otherwise. O Shāriputra, the ultimate reality is to be realized by means of faith by disciples and hermit buddhas.

Although they realize the selflessness of things, if they must rely upon universal vehicle practitioners to do so, then they are said to be of dull intelligence. The assertion that disciples and hermit buddhas do not realize the selflessness of phenomena, and that they realize the Tathāgata to be the personification of validating cognition merely by means of [the faith of] conviction, does not withstand close examination. If the ultimate truth were not realized by means of an act of validating cognition, then it would contradict that realization by means of faith. If the ultimate were realized by validating cognition, then in general, [TL 011A] we would not need to explain emptiness as the object of mere faith. We can understand that in this treatise and its commentary, it is proved that there exists one final vehicle, and also that there are noble disciples and hermit buddhas who are able to realize the [objective] selflessness of things.

3.1.1.1.2.2.1.3.2.2.1.3. Identifying the Nature of the Ultimate

[The sutra continues by saying] "O Shāriputra! That this so-called unique nature of suchness, being the ultimate mingled with taints—at the time when it remains impure as a result of even the slightest taint—is a term for the element[193] of sentient beings. O Shāriputra! The so-called element of sentient beings—at the time when taints have been abandoned to whatever degree but still slightly remain—is a term for tathāgata essence. O

---

193. *dhātu, khams.*

Shāriputra, the so-called tathāgata essence—at the time when it has been completely isolated from the taints—is a term for the truth body."

Thus it is "[the fourth] vajra [topic]."

This unique nature of suchness, in the context of its association with taints, is referred to as the "element of sentient beings" and as the "tathāgata essence"; however, when it is isolated from all taints, it is the "truth body."

Objection: Someone says that it follows that the unique nature of suchness is the tathāgata essence, because it is the tathāgata essence in the context of its association with taints.

Reply: [We respond], if you assert this, then it also follows that the unique nature of suchness is a buddha's truth body, because it is a buddha's truth body in the context of its isolation from taints. Such objections are just from one who does not know reasoning.

As for the word "term," it means [these terms are] terminologically synonymous, but not equivalent in meaning. For example, "possessing [a trunk like] a hand"[194] is a term for "elephant," but "possessing a hand" is not necessarily exclusive to an elephant. Similarly, the former two terms—the "element of sentient beings" and the "tathāgata essence"—are mutually inclusive in meaning, but the former two ("element of sentient beings" and "tathāgata essence") do not necessarily include the latter ("truth body"), [TL on B] because the treatise and all commentaries teach that the prior two exist on a causal level and do so exclusively within the continuum of a sentient being, and there is not even the slightest mention that the enlightenment isolated from all taints is taught to be the "tathāgata essence." As for the three sentences of the sutra passage, as to whether they teach that the tathāgata essence itself, when it is completely purified of the taints, gets to gain the name of the truth body, is made very clear [not to be the case],[195] where it states "Impure, [both partially] impure and pure, and . . . ," and so on. The assertion that a perfectly complete buddha exists primordially within the continuum of a sentient being is nothing more than a mere difference in name from the Shaivite fundamentalist claim of a permanent, self-arisen omniscience.

Objection: Someone also says, "All environments are primordially perfect as an immeasurable celestial mansion and all sentient beings are

194. *hasti, lag ldan.*
195. Later in Maitreya's text (I.47).

[likewise primordially perfect] vajradharas; this is the holy teaching of the great perfection."[196]

Reply: [We respond that] this assertion is well known to be no more than nominally different from the Shaivite claim of a self-arisen omniscience—but one that is impermanent, being produced from a previous similar type since beginningless time—and hence is simply following the meaning asserted by the Mīmāṁsakas. Consequently, one should not fixate on words.

3.1.1.1.2.2.1.3.2.2.2. The Other Three [Topics]—Enlightenment, etc.—and Their Connection with Sutras

«7» [As for the element, it is stated in the *Shrīmālādevī Lion's Roar Sutra*:]

> O Bhagavān, the so-called unsurpassed perfect complete enlightenment, which is naturally pure and also pure by the extinguishment of all incidental taints, is a term for the realm[197] of nirvana. If one asks, "Do disciples and hermit buddhas have a nirvana that is free of incidental taints as well?" O Bhagavān, the so-called realm of nirvana, having the twofold purity, is a term for the truth body of the Tathāgata.

Thus it is "[the fifth] vajra [site]."

«8» As for the sutra quote that pertains to the excellences, [a statement from the *Sutra Teaching the Absence of Increase and Decrease (in the Realm of Beings)* reads:] [TL 012A]

> O Shāriputra, the excellences of the truth body taught by the Tathāgata are like this: [the truth body] is endowed with the excellences of the Tathāgatas' qualities, such as powers and so forth, more numerous than the particles of sand of the Ganges River, and have qualities—the excellences of freedom and evolutionary development—that are undifferentiated from the

196. This quote appears verbatim in a number of Mahāyoga works by late Sakya authors, but none cites its source.

197. *dhātu, dbyings.*

perspective of being similar in terms of type, like the lights and colors of [different] jewels, but not similar in terms of their specific manifestations.

To explain this, the Buddha states in the same text:

> It is endowed with the excellences of wisdom that are indivisible from the other [tathāgatas' wisdoms], even though these excellences individually exist.

Thus it is "[the sixth] vajra [site]."

«9» As for the sutra that connects to the enlightened activities, [there is this statement from the *Sutra Showing the Entry into the Realm of the Inconceivable Excellences and Wisdom of the Tathāgatas*]:

> O Mañjushrī, the Tathāgata, by pacifying all striving and exertion, does not entertain concepts such as that "the three [components of an action]—the action itself, the receiver, and the agent—[at the time] of benefiting others, are actually there," nor does he engage in discriminations, finely distinguishing [those three things,] thinking, "this is so." However, without forgoing activity when a disciple is due to be educated, the Tathāgata— acting for the benefit of all sentient beings and doing so without reservation—effortlessly engages in just such natural activities, and does so without entertaining concepts that such things are there, and without engaging in discriminations.

Thus it is "[the seventh] vajra [topic]." These last three meanings are extensively explained below.

3.1.1.1.2.2.2. Summary

Having been summarized in the manner of the above explanation, these seven vajra topics should be known as the entire body of the extensive explanation of this treatise, which elucidates the intentions of these, and the sutra sources that are cited above and below. If you ask, "How does this summary come to embody [the treatise]?" [TL 012B] The teachings are the elucidation of its intention and its sutra sources, and their introduction is an introduction to the reasons for engaging in the composition of the treatise. Since they are the object of the summarization of that meaning into seven aspects, and since it has the nature of what is summarized, it is the body [of the text].

The actual presentation of the body [of the text] is [specified by] this first verse. However, I think there is no contradiction in including within that [specification] the [next] two [verses] on the connections to sutras and the definite stages of understanding.[198]

3.1.1.2. The Teachings, Just As They Are, in Sutra

3.1.1.2.1. The Root Text

《10》 If you wonder whether this treatise, which is comprised of seven topics, is an independent work or follows others, then [you should know that] it is free from the fault of being the author's own fabrication, for these seven vajra-like sites, are taught (I.2) [by the Buddha] in the *Questions of King Dhāraṇīshvara Sutra*. How are they taught? By teaching the distinctive nature of each one, such as the Buddha, etc., the sutra teaches each one's own defining characteristics. It also teaches that [these seven sites] are connected in proper order by their defining characteristics, as taught in the treatise. Which words of the sutra teach which site? [TL 013A] The [first] three of these sites, the fruitional Three Jewels, should be known as being taught in the introductory chapter. The last [remaining] four topics are taught in the chapters teaching the sixty qualities of the intelligent bodhisattva's purification of the element, which is the topic of the element, and the teaching on the eighty qualities of the Victor, the perfectly complete Buddha, which are the three topics of enlightenment, etc.

3.1.1.2.2. The Commentary . . . 2.1. How the Fruitional Three Jewels Are Taught . . . 1.1. Explaining Just the Meaning of the Words

《11》 From among these seven sites, the uncommon nature of each topic is connected in proper order, as taught before, by their defining characteristics; the first three topics should be known from the introductory chapter

198. Verses I.2 and I.3, respectively.

citing the *Questions of King Dhāraṇīshvara Sutra*, and the remaining four from the chapters[199] on those teachings of the qualities of bodhisattvas and of tathāgatas.

3.1.1.2.2.1.2. The Connection with Sutra . . . 2.1. The Way of Establishing the Identity of Each in Connection with Sutra . . . 1.1. Brief Statement

«12» The Buddha states in that same sutra:[200]

> The Bhagavān directly, by means of perfect experience, became enlightened in the equality of all things without exception, [having realized] the freedom from all elaborations of truth status [in things], from having observed all things, [all] objects of observation. He beautifully turned the wheel of Dharma for those disciples who had the spiritual potential, having taken to heart the methods for extinguishing all obscurations. [Thus] he commanded a limitless host of disciples who became extremely calm.

These three root sentences also teach the final, fruitional Three Jewels. Following these in the proper order—as three pure [bodhisattva] stages and the immediate causes[201] of the attainment [TL 013B] [of the fruitional Three Jewels]—in the context of abiding on the eighth stage, it is designated as the Buddha Jewel; in the context of abiding on the ninth stage, it is designated as the Dharma Jewel; and in the context of abiding on the tenth stage, it is designated as the Saṅgha Jewel. Hence, this should also be known as the presentation of establishing the Three Jewels in stages. It is unacceptable to explain that these three root sentences teach the immediate causes alone, since it is in contradiction to the explanation that [these three root sentences] are a teaching of the distinctive nature of the Three Jewels, and because it would be absurd to teach the Buddha Jewel solely in a causal context.

---

199. *nirdeśa-bheda*. Ngog's translation omits *nirdeśa*, but Gyaltsap clearly uses *dbye ba bstan pa nas* here, which may indicate that he checked a Sanskrit original or an alternate translation when he was working on the *rgyud bla ma'i ṭikka*.

200. Once again, Gyaltsap's quote of this key passage is accurate, but adds qualifications and glosses, which he no doubt did verbally, and the scribe included them in the quotation.

201. *nye rgyu*.

3.1.1.2.2.1.2.1.2. Subsequently Identifying Causality

The remaining four sites, the element, etc., should be known as the statement of substantial causes and cooperative conditions that are concordant with the occurrence of the fruitional Three Jewels. This is only a supplementary presentation and will be taught below in the proper context.

3.1.1.2.2.1.2.1.3. Detailed Exposition ... 3.1. The Way of Establishing Three Stages of Purification That Are Immediate Causes as Three Jewels in Stages

≪13≫ Now, that [the Bhagavān], once gone to the supreme bodhi tree, the seat of enlightenment, the goal to be attained, has perfectly awakened experientially as to the equality of all things.

Since, when one abides on the eighth bodhisattva stage, one attains the ten sovereignties, such attainment of the sovereignty over all things, such as the nonconceptual wisdom, is presented as the reason for the occasion of attaining the Three Jewels.

≪14≫ In the future, oneself—[becoming] a perfect complete buddha [TL 014A]—will attain the supreme Dharma Jewel, [hence] it is stated that one "beautifully turns the wheel of the Dharma" that establishes the desired goals of one's own four kinds of noble children. Hence, when one abides on the ninth bodhisattva stage, one attains the four perfect intellectual insights;[202] one becomes the unsurpassed exponent of the Buddhadharma; one knows well the variety of thought patterns of all sentient beings who have different spiritual potentials and inspirations; one has the transcendence of the supreme spiritual faculties[203] such as faith, etc., because there is no difference in spiritual faculties between sharp, middle, and dull among those who have attained the ninth stage; and one becomes an expert in the destruction of the chain of addictive evolutionary instincts,[204] which are the different kinds of objective obscurations in all sentient beings.

≪15≫ Since at the time when one attains the tenth bodhisattva stage, immediately after obtaining consecration as the unsurpassed Dharma

202. *catvārimpratisaṁvid, so sor yang dag pa rig pa bzhi.*
203. *indriya-paramapāramitā, dbang mchos gi pha tol tu phyin pa.*
204. *kleśa-vāsanā, nyon mongs pa'i bag chags.*

regent of the Tathāgata, one attains the effortless and uninterrupted activities of a buddha, which will be expounded below. Thus, it states:

> [Having beautifully turned the wheel of Dharma,] one commands a limitless host of disciples who have become extremely calm.

The meaning of "effortless and uninterrupted activities" will be explained below.

3.1.1.2.2.1.2.1.3.2. The Explanation in Detail of the Saṅgha Jewel

The meaning of "a limitless host of disciples who have become extremely calm" is further taught by that text. Immediately after that sentence, there is the sutra statement, from:[205]

> [The Buddha was dwelling] together with a great assembly of mendicants...

up to:

> ... together with an inconceivable number of assemblies of bodhisattvas.

[TL 014B] The explanation of the phrase "extremely calm," in particular, is as follows: since the assemblies of mendicants and of bodhisattvas were extremely calm, insofar as they had the ability and were well suited to act to accomplish the enlightenment of disciples and the enlightenment of buddhas, respectively, they dwelt together as those endowed with such excellences.

This [statement] explains in particular the significance of "having command of a limitless host of disciples who have become extremely calm,"

---

205. It seems that the long quotes Gyaltsap provides in the next pages come from the *King Dhāraṇīshvara Sutra*, but there is a puzzle: he is quoting much longer passages than did Asaṅga in his *Commentary* on the *Sublime Continuum*. This also should be understood, as mentioned before (note 189), as commentarial paraphrase merged into the quotation by the scribe.

where the word "having" should be understood as also indicating their ultimate fruition.

3.1.1.2.2.1.2.2. Sutra Reference to the Excellences . . . 2.1. The Connection to the Sutra of the Excellences of the Magnificent

≪16≫ And then, immediately after [the section on the] teaching of the praises of the excellences of disciples and bodhisattvas, [the next section of the sutra] teaches the excellences of the Buddha:[206]

> Then, the Bhagavān taught a formulation of teachings[207] called the "door of unobscured renunciation through engagement in a bodhisattva's activities." At that time, sixteen years after he had attained perfect enlightenment, the Bhagavān knew that divinely pure conduct had prevailed. He also saw and knew [the presence of] a huge assembly of bodhisattvas. . . . He decided to teach the set of teachings called the "door of unobscured renunciation through engagement in a bodhisattva's activities." Then, the Bhagavān entranced himself in the tathāgata samādhi that is called "the true display of the miraculous emanations of the sphere of buddhas." Immediately after that samādhi, by the power of the Buddha, there appeared in the space between the desire realm and the pure material realm a mandala hall for the assembly, [TL 015A] a buddha abode manifested from the Tathāgata's root of virtue, purified by the inspirations of the bodhisattvas, illuminating worlds in the ten directions, satisfying the measureless wishes of sentient beings, and outshining all the palaces of the gods. . . . It had a white sapphire foundation, rose gold walls, and a variety of jewels as its porticos, vestibules, platforms, ledges, and upper stories, and was decorated with dangling pearl garlands, upstanding parasols, flags, victory banners, and divine tassels. The praise of [its magnificence] was unfathomable and endless. Its size was equal to the billion world universe. The hall was anointed with [paste of] "snake-heart" sandalwood, [emit-

206. H148, 156a.3–156b.3.
207. *dharma-paryāya, chos kyi rnam grangs.*

ting] its fragrance in timely waves. It was filled with the scent of the essence of the supreme eaglewood, decorated with nāga flowers and precious flowers, covered with flower petals, and beautified with precious trees and space ornaments. Every display of beautiful ornaments in the worlds of the ten directions appeared in that hall. A hundred thousand million billion lion thrones also appeared. On the grounds of the four continents [of this world], there were four thousand precious ladders with various ornaments mounting to that hall. This applied to all the four continents [of the billion world systems of the universe].

In brief, this is the creation of a magnificent hall adorned with precious jewels that was conditioned by the inconceivable royal samādhi of the Buddha.

[TL 015B] The same sutra continues, from:[208]

> Then, the Bhagavān, in accordance with his intention and his knowledge, arose from that samādhi and immediately caused the worlds to quake in six ways and emit intense lights. Then the Bhagavān, surrounded by bodhisattvas and led in front by the disciples, with praises offered by celestial beings, the nāgas, etc., . . .

up to:[209]

> . . . the Bhagavān disappeared from Vulture Peak and proceeded into the hall.

> The six classes of the deities of the desire realm heavens showered celestial flowers, incense, clothing, precious clouds, ornaments, and flower garlands in turn, and praised him in verse. They all followed the Buddha as servants and arrived at that precious hall and sat down. This applied to all four continents [in the billion world systems of the universe].

---

208. H148, 158a.2–4.

209. Gyaltsap appears to be paraphrasing the following long passage. H148, fol. 158b.1 ff.

And then the Bhagavān entranced himself in the samādhi called the "the unobstructed liberation buddha play."[210] Immediately after his entrancement, lights streamed forth from all the Bhagavān's pores, each pore filled with as many lights as the number of the sand grains in the Ganges River, illuminating the ten directions and thereby cutting off the streams of suffering in the lower rebirths and pacifying the addictions of all sentient beings. All beings attained the mind of mutual love. Those lights produced many verses and caused them to be heard in all buddha-lands, encouraging bodhisattvas, [TL 016A] benefiting all sentient beings, and destroying the pride of all devils. The lights went back and dissolved into the top of the head of the Tathāgata. Then, ten bodhisattvas, surrounded by retinues of countless bodhisattvas, came from ten directions, showering offering rains of various celestial precious substances. Having made myriad circumambulations, they praised the Buddha in verse and sat down.

[Together with these paragraphs on] the gathering of the Tathāgata's retinue, the production of various celestial offerings, and the shower of rain from the cloud of praises, [this section] should be known as the orderly arrangement of the distinctive excellences of the Buddha Jewel.

«17» [The following section] demonstrates the excellences of the Dharma. The sutra continues:

And then, knowing the great assembly of the retinue, the Bhagavān radiated from the tuft of hair between his eyebrows the light called "demonstrating the power of bodhisattvas."[211] That light circumambulated the entire retinue seven times, and then disappeared into the heads of the bodhisattvas. Touched by the light, the Bodhisattva Kusumashrīgarbha Sarvadharmeshvara[212] was entranced in the bodhisattva samādhi called "the array of orna-

---

210. *sgrib pa med pa'i rnam par thar pa la sangs rgyas rnam par rol ba.*

211. *byang chub sems dpa'i stobs nye bar ston pa.*

212. *me tog dpal gyi snying po chos thams cad la dbang bsgyur ba* ("Essence of the Glorious Flower Controlling All").

ments."²¹³ Immediately after his entrancement, a lion throne of a
tathāgata appeared at the center of that precious hall of a height
of a hundred thousand million billion tāla trees, decorated with
all kinds of precious substances. A variety of fabrics were spread
out upon it, and it was overspread by a beautiful canopy . . .

—from that point, [TL 016B] up to:

. . . Bodhisattva Kusumashrīgarbha²¹⁴ magically created such a
tathāgata lion throne called "eons of endless praises."²¹⁵ Then,
arising from his samādhi, the bodhisattva joined his palms
together, and having praised the Bhagavān with verses, sat on
the lion throne.

In brief, [these paragraphs teach] the splendid array of the Dharma
throne and the light.
The sutra continues:

And then, having attained the unobstructed definite freedom,
the Bhagavān first proclaimed the name of this set of the teachings as "the door of unobstructed definite freedom by means of
engagement in bodhisattva activities." Then, widely proclaiming
its excellences, such as the apprehension of the arrayed paths of
the bodhisattvas, the accomplishment of all profound excellences of the Buddha, the ten powers, the four confidences, and
their source of intuitive wisdom, . . . the Bhagavān sat on the lion
throne.

[This section] should be known as the orderly presentation of the distinct excellences of the Dharma Jewel.
«18» [The following section] teaches the excellences of the Saṅgha,
from:

213. *rgyan bkod pa.*
214. *me tog dpal gyi snying po* ("Essence of the Glorious Flower").
215. *bskal par mtha' yas* (as cited in D4025 *Commentary*); *bskul par mtha' yas* (D147).

And then, by the power of the Buddha, the bodhisattva Rat-navamsha[216] was entranced in the samādhi called the "array of ornaments." From his samādhi, the bodhisattva blessed the entire retinue with the ornaments of the Buddha . . .

up to:

. . . The Bhagavān gave the prophecy that [the devils] would be freed from their demonic behavior by the power of their requests for him to turn the wheel of the Dharma.

In brief, [TL 017A] [these paragraphs teach] the power of each of the ranges[217] of the samādhis of the bodhisattva.

The same text continues, from:

And then, included within that entourage and sitting there, was a bodhisattva named Dhāraṇīshvararāja,[218] who made a request in these words: "O Bhagavān, this sphere of a buddha is blessed by the Tathāgata, and its teachings are inconceivable . . .

up to:

. . . O Bhagavān, whatsoever noble son or noble daughter who, with an earnest intention, has produced or will produce the spirit of enlightenment, after a long time, they will come to have just such excellences."

Along with teaching various praises of the bodhisattva's excellences, [this section] should be known as the orderly arrangement of the distinct excellences of the Saṅgha Jewel.

3.1.1.2.2.1.2.2.2. Profound Excellences

«19» [The sutra statement that teaches] the excellences of the Buddha is as follows:

216. *rin chen srog shing* ("Precious Mainstay").
217. *avacara, spyod yul.*
218. *gzungs kyi dbang phyug rgyal po* ("Powerful King of Mnemonic Spells").

And then, the Bhagavān beheld that great assembly of bodhisattvas. "Marvelous!" he thought, "these bodhisattvas are aspiring for
the Dharma, capable of upholding the treasury of the Tathāgata's
Dharma!" By being consecrated by the light ray of the Buddha,
the bodhisattva Dhāraṇīshvararāja, with his accomplished fearlessness with respect to all secrets of the Tathāgata and supreme
unimpeded eloquence, became the unsurpassed principal child
of the Dharma King.

Consequently, the bodhisattva Dhāraṇīshvararāja taught the
praise of the ultimate impeccable excellences of the Tathāgata
with the following verses:

Illuminating [TL 017B] and brilliant in all ways,
You, O Supreme King of Beings,
Teach the ultimate[219] with your omniscient eye,
Being adept in the self-existing reality of things
And endowed with inconceivable excellences.

You, O Leader of Humans, emanate light rays;
Just your face radiates [them] and energizes the light;
By being so directed, and caused to circle a hundred times
Around our bodies, [the rays] dissolve into [our] heads.

Once touched by the light rays of the Guide of Humanity,
Whosoever recalls their own prior attainments,
And as when seeing a flash of bright insight, holds [it],[220]
Comes to be distinguished in a thousand ways.

Even more, the courage and limitless wisdom
Of the buddhas enters into one's own body.
Though the great power of buddhas is hard to approach,
Those of feeble strength cannot be satisfied by me.

---

219. *don rnams* (D147).
220. The text reads *gzungs* (*dhāraṇi*), but appears to be a mistake for *gzung*.

Moreover, for the Buddha to benefit all transmigrants,
One needs to ask a question of the Buddha.

Each one needs to pray for the wisdom consecration,
The arising of a guide for this transient world,
The sphere of activity of a perfect bodhisattva,
And the projection of his appearance and renunciation.

—from that point, up to:

Please tell us: how does the Bhagavān know and engage?
And how did you practice for a long period of time?
When were you ready to be the potent king of Dharma?
What are the spheres of activity of the guides?

This and what follows [in the sutra] proclaim the excellences of the Buddha.

[Then, this section of the sutra teaches] the excellences of the Dharma, as follows:

And then, the bodhisattva Dhāraṇīshvararāja entreated [the Buddha] thus: "O Bhagavān, the sphere of a tathāgata is inconceivable. . . ."

[This section of the sutra] actually states the substance of the discourse concerning the supreme Dharma of the universal vehicle.

[TL 018A] As for the excellences of the Saṅgha, the sutra teaches the attainment of the supreme sovereignty of the Dharma—the fruit to be attained by the Saṅgha Jewel [comprised of] those realized beings who were led to realize the supreme teachings of the universal vehicle. "The sovereignty of all things" means the attainment of sovereignty over all teachings. As it is taught in the sutra:

O Bhagavān, these bodhisattvas by whatsoever means, having destroyed the demons and hostile forces, and being without any doubt [in this regard]. . . .

In light of this, [this section] is regarded as the orderly arrangement of the distinct unsurpassed excellences of the Three Jewels and indicates the ending of the introductory section.[221]

3.1.1.2.2.2. Summary [How the Last Four Topics Are Taught] ... 2.1. The Sutra Statements Regarding the Element ... 1.1. The Element Is Indicated by Sixty Purifying Factors

«20» Then, as for the section on the excellences of the Three Jewels, after the introductory section of the sutra in which Dhāraṇīshvararāja asks his question, there is [a presentation of] the sixty types of excellences that bring about its thorough purity—being reality mingled with taints. Since it is also the agent of purification of the element, by teaching the thorough purification of the sixty types of excellences, it subsumes the conventional tathāgata element and serves to clearly teach the suchness reality mingled with taints.

3.1.1.2.2.2.1.2. Its Proof ... 2.1. Proof of Reasoning

[TL 018B] If someone asks, "While [the sutra] does teach the sixty types of excellences, how do [you] establish that it teaches the element? There is not the slightest contradiction in saying that although something teaches the sixty excellences, it does not establish the existence of the element."

[We respond, there is no such contradiction, because] the teaching of the sixty agents that purify the element establishes that the element to be purified exists. That is, because only if the object that is to be thoroughly purified of all taints—being the mind in the continuum of a sentient being, or suchness reality mingled with taints, [itself] being the ultimate truth or the emptiness of any intrinsic reality—is endowed with the excellences

---

221. Not as found in available Tibetan and Chinese translations. The section of the profound excellences of the Three Jewels is included in the second chapter (*bam po gnyis*, 大方等大集經陀羅尼自在王菩薩品第二) or the fourth chapter (大哀經莊嚴法本品第四) of these translations. Therefore it is reasonable to speculate that Asaṅga's *Commentary* takes the fourth topic, the element, as the core subject of the *Questions of King Dhāraṇīshvara Sutra*, thereby treating the first three topics as its introduction but not a real textual chapter—particularly since the sutra itself often uses "chapter" (*le'u*) to express the idea of some other sort of conceptual division, as in: *sgrib pa med pa'i sgo'i le'u'i chos kyi rnam grang.*

of the ability to have the intuitive wisdom of a buddha born [within that continuum] and the ability to be purified of taints, [respectively,] then even though a method of bringing about the thorough purification of that object of purification were feasible, if there were no object of purification, then [positing the existence of] an agent of purification would not be feasible [either].

Asserting that the twofold purity—i.e., the natural purity and the purity isolated from all incidental taints—exists primordially in the continuum of a sentient being, while asserting a presentation of the purifying agents, contradicts the elimination [of taints] and contradicts the actual basis of the relationship between the mental continuum of a sentient being being free from incidental taints and not being free, respectively. [These are just] the words of a confusion maker[222] who would assert such a common locus of a direct contradiction relying on a mutually exclusive contradiction.

If they reply, "The final essential nature[223] of a sentient being is free from taints, although it is accompanied by incidental taints," then this is clearly just a testimony to their ignorance of logical reasoning. When you say that anything whatsoever that accords with the manner of apprehending something by grasping at it with the conception of truth status and the addictions of attachment, etc., does not abide within the final actuality of the mind, that is reasonable; but there is a flaw in your statement that "the essential nature[224] is free from taints." This is because it entails that the nature of a sentient being's mind is perfectly and completely enlightened because that is the nature of a mind that is naturally pure [TL 019A] and is free of all incidental taints—and you have accepted the latter part of this reason.

If someone else says, "Having asserted that ultimate truth is a permanent entity,[225] its being empty of all conventionalities is its profound other-emptiness,"[226] then again we reply, [these are] merely the words of a confusion maker. As for the meaning of "other-emptiness," does other-emptiness mean that ultimate truth is empty of being conventional truth? Or does it mean that ultimate truth is empty of existing conventionally? If

222. *aślīla, mun sprul.*
223. *chos nyid kyi ngo bo.*
224. *ngo bo.*
225. *rtag dngos.*
226. *gzhan stong.*

it is like the latter, then it contradicts your assertion that the ultimate truth exists in such as way as to pervade all [things, both] inanimate [environments] and animate [beings]. You need to think about how ultimate truth existing as a pervader of all objects of knowledge and ultimate truth being empty of existing conventionally could not be anything but contradictory! And if it is like the former, then it seems that your disciples who are worthy of the teaching of the other-emptiness are actually quite intelligent, because having entertained the doubt "Is the ultimate truth, as a permanent entity, a conventional reality?" [they are clearly] disciples who need to dispel this sort of doubt!

If you say, "This is the meaning of the conventional reality not abiding in the final reality of the ultimate reality," then does that mean that the conventional things such as a vase, woolen cloth, etc., are not established as permanent entities? Or does it mean that they are not truly established? Or does it mean that these things are not ultimate truths?

If it is like the first, then it follows that disciples such as Sautrāntika [Realists] also would fully understand the meaning of other-emptiness, because of correctly realizing, by means of validating cognition, that a vase, woolen cloth, and so on, are impermanent. If you accept that, then it seems that any disciple who understands that would be a "great Centrist" (*dbu ma chen po pa*). If it is like the second, [TL 019B] then if the emptiness of the truth status of conventional things—such as a vase, woolen cloth, etc.—is the "self-emptiness" of [those] conventional things, then how would it not be a mistake for anyone to say something else, like "[other-emptiness] is being empty of something other than that?" Asserting the inability of any conventional thing whatsoever to be suitable as something to be apprehended, and that [for example,] a vase's being empty of being a vase is the meaning of "self-emptiness," is ultimately a view of nihilism—a repudiation of all conventional things. Finally, if it is like the third, then since conventional things not being ultimate realities is also asserted by proponents of Experientialism, then it would follow that they as well would be "great Centrists," who understand the final meaning of the actuality [of things].

If you respond, "Ultimate reality is an object to be understood by means of meditation, and does not exist as an object in even the slightest way that can be investigated by means of studious learning and reasoned contemplation," then although it is an object to be directly realized by means of meditating on ultimate truth, the last part [of your statement] is just desperate rambling, because if you look at it, saying, "It is just like this!" to a disciple who needs to be taught the ultimate truth, it is really just your inability to teach. Since these are the mistaken concepts of the deluded, and although doubtful points are few, nevertheless, it seems that numerous people who have amassed very little stores of merit have become involved in this, so from time to time I will explain its refutation.

3.1.1.2.2.2.1.2.2. Sutra References . . . 2.1. The Teaching on What Is Said in the *Sutra on the Ten Stages*

«21» The mind of a sentient being and its actuality, its suchness reality mingled with taints, was previously unpurified of the taints, but can be purified in stages [TL 020A] by the power of corrective antidotes[227] in meditative equipoise. In light of this, the *Sutra on the Ten Stages* uses the analogy between the process of purifying gold and the way of purifying the taints to be removed on the path of insight[228] and on the path of meditation.[229]

3.1.1.2.2.2.1.2.2.2. Its Connection with the *King Dhāraṇīshvara Sutra* . . . 2.1. The Segué

In this *King Dhāraṇīshvara Sutra*, after the teaching on the enlightened activities of the Tathāgata, the analogy of unpurified sapphire mixed with stone, dirt, etc., is also used.

3.1.1.2.2.2.1.2.2.2.2. Explanation of the Analogy

[The analogy proceeds as follows:]

> O noble child, take for example a skillful jeweler who knows well how to cleanse a gem. Having picked out a precious jewel that has been thoroughly tainted from the mine, and having soaked it in a strong solution of sal-ammoniac, he then polishes it by rubbing it with a very refined ox-hair cloth. But his efforts in just this

227. *pratipakṣa, gnyen po.*
228. *dṛṣṭiheya, mthong spangs.*
229. *bhāvanāheya, sgoms spangs.*

way are not yet finished. After that, having soaked the jewel in strong, fermented fruit juice, he polishes it with kambala wool. But his efforts in just this way are still not yet finished. After that, having soaked it in a great medicine essence, he polishes it with fine cotton cloth. Being thus completely purified, when it is free of all impurities, it is called "precious sapphire."

3.1.1.2.2.2.1.2.2.2.3. The Connection to the Meaning

[The sutra continues:]

> O noble child, just so a tathāgata, knowing the scope of the sentient beings who are not purified, by means of disturbing descriptions of impermanence, suffering, selflessness, and impurity, makes those sentient beings who delight in the life cycle develop disgust, and so causes them to enter into the noble Dharma codes of discipline.

> With these many acts, a tathāgata does not cease in his efforts. After that, he causes them to realize the way of the Tathāgata, by means of the instructions on emptiness, signlessness, and wishlessness. Even with these many acts, a tathāgata does not cease in his efforts. Next, he installs those sentient beings in the buddha realm by means of the teaching of irreversibility and the teaching of the total purification of the three sectors [of actions]. And he causes those sentient beings with various dispositions to engage with the sphere of a tathāgata. When they have entered and have realized the reality of a tathāgata, they are called "the unsurpassed worthies for offerings."

Analogous to the three stages of purification, just so the Tathāgata, knowing the scope of sentient beings who are not purified of the impurities, [TL 020B] enacts the three stages of guiding disciples. First, those beings of slight spiritual capacity, having [been led to] contemplate impermanence and death in this life in which one cannot long remain, and the faults of bad transmigrations, [are led to] properly generate the aspiration to seek a higher rebirth in a future life. To disciples, hermit buddhas, and anyone who possesses the spiritual capacity for the universal vehicle, first having taught them (1) the special teaching of the truth of suffering, impermanence as moment-to-moment creation and cessation; (2) suffering as created by addictions and actions; (3) selflessness of persons as the negation of a self-sufficient, substantial person;[230] and (4) impurity as falling into the filthy pit of the life cycle, by means of disturbing descriptions of the life cycle being like entering a pit of fire, [he] makes those sentient beings who, having seen it as pleasant and delight in and crave the life cycle, generate disgust with the life cycle. Hence, [he] causes them to enter into the practice of the three types of precious educations, the path that is to be practiced in common by all those who either comprehend or do not comprehend the subtle selflessness of persons and things, the noble Dharma discipline, the antidote to the life cycle.

The selflessness that is taught here is coarse [selflessness], and the comprehension of that is the path that ripens the continuum of those who are being guided onto the path of a noble person of either the universal or the individual vehicle. As for the subtle selflessness of person and thing, being the object of observation in the path that directly severs the root of mundane existence, that will be taught in the context of the last two stages. [Āryadeva's *Experientialist*] *Four Hundred* also describes this first stage as the path that ripens the continuum. As the *[Experientialist] Four Hundred* states:[231]

> First prevent the nonmeritorious,
> Next refute [ideas of a coarse] self,
> Later eliminate views of all kinds. [TL 021A]
> Whoever knows of this is wise.

The first line of [this verse] shows the path of the lower level of beings, which prevents [them from falling into] the lower realms. The connotations of the next two lines are comparable to the latter two stages taught in this sutra.

[The sutra continues:]

---

230. *rang rkya thub pa'i gang zag.*
231. VIII.15. D3846, 9b.5–6.

With these many acts, the Tathāgata does not cease in his efforts. After that, he causes them to realize the ultimate truth of their actuality, which is the actuality of the Tathāgata, by means of the instructions in wishlessness, signlessness, and emptiness, which is the emptiness of intrinsic reality status,[232] in accordance with the three stages of essence, cause, and fruit, and the three objects that are to be observed, practiced, and obtained by those of all three kinds of spiritual potential.

By this [passage], [the Bhagavān] teaches the person's emptiness of intrinsic reality status and the subtle selflessness that is the emptiness of the intrinsic reality of the aggregates. Without realizing this, disciples and hermit buddhas will not attain even the fruit of a saint's liberation.

Now I shall explain how this treatise demonstrates that disciples and hermit buddhas have the realization of the two types of subtle emptiness. They do, because this treatise teaches the first two stages as guidance on how to attain the realization of individual vehicle sainthood and above, and then teaches the third stage as well, thereby establishing the ultimate single vehicle.

Someone asserts that it is not fitting to discuss whether the noble beings of the disciple vehicle and the hermit buddha vehicle have the realization of personal selflessness. Consequently, he loudly debates whether they have the realization of the selflessness of things. But he should be convinced of the fact that, if one lacks the realization of the person's emptiness of intrinsic identifiability, the personal self [TL 021B] cannot be completely negated, so then it is impossible for a person who has realized that not to realize the realitylessness of the aggregates. Thus, the differentiation between emptiness being coarse and subtle is made in connection with the negation ground,[233] persons, and aggregates, which [negation refers to as] either

---

232. The phrase "which is the emptiness of intrinsic reality status" is the usual qualification of all Tibetan Centrist schools and the *Transcendent Wisdom Sutra in One Hundred Thousand Lines* that no doubt Gyaltsap injected into the quote he remembered or read, and the scribe merged with the direct quote. From here on, we will not comment on this, unless the qualification is controversial.

233. *dgag gzhi.*

their substantial existence[234] or their designative existence,[235] instead of being made in connection with the [subtle] object of negation,[236] which is the intrinsic identifiability of the [subject or the] object, which cannot be logically differentiated as having coarse and subtle types.

Objection: In the case of this teaching system concerning the universal vehicle person, it would be incorrect to have a third stage in this system after the teachings of the two types of selflessness, because the profound meaning of reality should be taught in a timely way after the complete teaching of liberative art.[237] In the case of this system concerning the stages of spiritual development in the continuum, it would also be incorrect to do so, because the transcendence of wisdom occurs after the attainment of the first five transcendences, and the discourse on the purification of the three sectors [of an act] of the third stage is the one that also teaches the subtle selflessness. Therefore, the second stage concerns the three doors of liberation, which negate the coarse negatee.

Reply: Such doubt is quite reasonable. But you should know the following: as taught in Master Shāntarakṣhita's *Ornament of the Central Way*, there are two types of stages: the stage of engaging in the path for the intelligent ones and the stage of engaging in the path for the dull ones. Here too, *The Sublime Continuum of the Universal Vehicle* directly demonstrates the stages of engaging in the path for the intelligent ones among those who possess specific potential for the universal vehicle as its intended chief disciples, and indirectly causes the other [types of stages] to be understood. What the treatise has proved is that the intelligent ones who also possess the potential for the universal vehicle first try to convince themselves with validating cognition of [TL 022A] the necessity and the possibility of attaining perfect buddhahood for the benefit of all sentient beings; and that they then make the commitment to conceive the actual spirit of enlightenment. Making the commitment without valid reasons is the way of the dull ones. Furthermore, while the recognition of the necessity of attaining buddhahood for the benefit of sentient beings comes from the mastery of the method of producing

234. *rdzas yod.*
235. *btags yod.*
236. *dgag bya.*
237. *upāya, thabs.*

the genuine great compassion and high resolve,[238] the recognition of the possibility of attaining buddhahood comes from the realization of emptiness and related ideas. In light of this significance, we should know that for the intelligent ones it is necessary to realize emptiness before producing the desire for liberation. As for the dull ones, we can understand that they try to conceive the supreme spirit of enlightenment first, and then go on to master emptiness as taught in the third stage. We should also know that the emptiness taught in the third stage is distinguished by its connection with liberative art, thus being secondary [in terms of importance in this stage].

[The sutra continues:]

> Even with these many acts, the Tathāgata does not cease to make efforts in guiding disciples. Next, he installs those sentient beings in the buddha realm, which is the emptiness realized under the sway of liberative art, by means of the teaching of irreversibility, defusing the situation of producing the selfish thought that indifferently abandons other beings and aspires for private liberation alone, and by means of the teaching of purification of the grasping at the true establishment of the three sectors [of acts, that is, agent, action, and recipient] conjoined with liberative arts. And he causes those sentient beings, [TL 022B] having various dispositions such as different psychological makeups (*khams*), genealogies, and different aspirations (*mos pa*) for three types of enlightenment—[those on] the disciple vehicle, the hermit buddha vehicle, and the universal vehicle—to engage with the object of the Tathāgata, the realization of emptiness associated with complete liberative art. When they have entered into the universal vehicle and have realized the reality of the Tathāgata, they are called the "unsurpassed worthies for offerings."

The phrase "various dispositions" indicates the three kinds of spiritual potential. The first two stages guide the disciples who have specific potential for the disciple vehicle or the hermit buddha vehicle to their respective enlightenment, and then the third stage guides them to the universal vehicle.

238. *adhyāśaya, lhag bsam.*

The assertion that the stages taught here are identical to the three wheels [of Dharma] taught in the *Elucidation of the Intention Sutra*, and that the *Tathāgata Essence Sutra* is an example[239] of the third wheel taught in the *Elucidation of the Intention*, is an audacious claim based on very little understanding. In the *Elucidation of the Intention*, the bodhisattva Paramārthasamudgata asks the Buddha which sutras are interpretable in meaning and which sutras are definitive in meaning, because in some sutras the Bhagavān proclaims without distinction the intrinsic identifiability of all things, which are included in the three realities, whereas in other sutras he proclaims that all things without distinction do not have intrinsically identifiable status. The Buddha replies, with specific discrimination, that the imagined [reality] is not established by intrinsic identity, whereas the relative and perfect [realities] are established by intrinsic identity. [TL 023A] Paramārthasamudgata then reports to the Buddha his understanding that the first two types [of sutras mentioned in his own question] are interpretable in meaning, whereas the discriminating [sutras mentioned in the Buddha's answer] are definitive in meaning. Thus, the *Tathāgata Essence Sutra* is not involved in being an example of the definitive meaning sutras according to the *Elucidation of the Intention*, defined by the Teacher in his answer that I just quoted.

Likewise, someone asserts that there is no difference between the *Elucidation of the Intention Sutra* and the *Tathāgata Essence Sutra* in their being definitive meaning sutras. But [in fact these two are not the same:] while the former states that the imaginatively constructed reality is devoid of intrinsic identity and that the relative and perfect realities are established with intrinsic identity, the latter teaches that all things are devoid of intrinsic reality, thus naturally pure, and taints are [only] incidental. There are other similar [mistaken] assertions, including the assertion that the *Elucidation of the Intention*, which teaches the three final vehicles, and the *Tathāgata Essence Sutra* along with its commentary, *The Sublime Continuum*, which [latter two, in fact] promulgate the ultimate single vehicle, are in mutual agreement. Someone asserts that both the *Tathāgata Essence Sutra* and the *Elucidation of the Intention* teach the ultimate truth as being a permanent entity, with its meaning being elucidated in *The Sublime Continuum* and its *Commentary*. Someone claims that the nonconceptual intuitive wisdoms

239. *mtshan gzhi.*

of the paths of insight and meditation, which are contained in the Dharma Jewel taught in *The Sublime Continuum*, should be recognized as [the same as] what is taught in the *Transcendent Wisdom Sutra*, and that sutra just teaches the self-emptiness of the conventional but not the other-emptiness of the ultimate. All these assertions are tales told by persons whose minds are not at ease![240]

[TL 023B] The teaching of the three stages here is also the demonstration of the guidance for one person [on how to make progress] in the stages for the sake of establishing the ultimate single vehicle. So it stands in contrast to the statement of the *Elucidation of the Intention* that the three wheels in stages are meant for different persons. Someone asserts that the *Transcendent Wisdom Sutra* is an example of the third wheel as taught in the *Elucidation of the Intention*. This should be known as something deviant from the intention of the sutras, [coming from] not examining in detail the way the *Elucidation of the Intention* teaches and the way the *Transcendent Wisdom Sutra* teaches.

3.1.1.2.2.2.1.2.2.3. To the Other Sutra

«22» Intending that this naturally pure tathāgata element is the pure spiritual potential[241] possessed by sentient beings for the origination of the Buddha's intuitive wisdom, [the Buddha] declares in another sutra that just as pure gold is not visible when it is obscured by rocky sands but becomes visible after purification, so, in this world, the naturally pure reality of the Tathāgata is not directly perceived when it is obscured by conceptual thought that grasps at truth status [in things] but is directly perceived when the seeds of conceptual thought that grasps at truth status are eliminated. When this happens, the freedom from all taints is called the truth body of the perfect complete buddha.

This declares that the natural purity, the reality of the perfect complete buddha, exists in sentient beings without distinction, but to explain this as saying that the truth body with its twofold purity exists within the continuums of sentient beings [TL 024A] is clearly to close one's eyes to the connection between simile and meaning made by this sutra. If the freedom from abandoning all incidental taints existed in the continuums

240. *sems rnal du mi gnas pa'i gtam.*
241. *viśuddhagotra, yongs su dag pa'i rigs.*

of all sentient beings, there would not be even the slightest unfavorable condition obscuring the naturally pure element of sentient beings, [and it could easily] be directly perceived. How could that fit properly with this simile and its meaning? You must think!

Objection: Although the truth body with the twofold purity exists within the continuums of sentient beings, it cannot be perceived by sentient beings because of the incidental taints.

Reply: If the incidental taints existed within the continuums of sentient beings, which continuums would have the freedom from those taints? It is not correct to say [that freedom] is in one's own continuum; otherwise, that freedom would have already existed in one's own continuum from beginningless time in the life cycle, wherein there would never have been the slightest taint to be eliminated.

Objection: I meant that taints of another person's continuum do not exist on one's own continuum.

Reply: Then it would follow that the attainment of the truth of cessation would not depend on the direct realization of the meaning of reality. Instead, one is claiming that it is as if there is no vase in a place where there could never be a vase! That is quite ridiculous!

3.1.1.2.2.2.1.3. Statement of Purifying Factors

«23» Now, which are the sixty purifications by the excellence that purify the tathāgata element? They are: the four types of bodhisattva ornaments that enhance the performance of the bodhisattva deeds that are their three educations in ethics, concentration, and wisdom, and their [mastery of] mnemonic commands;[242] [TL 024B] the eight types of bodhisattva illuminations: those of mindfulness, intelligence, realization, teachings, consciousness, truth, superknowledge, and attainment, which brightly illuminate the doors of the Dharma reality, as they are free from delusion's darkness by the light of the holy Dharma; the sixteen types of a bodhisattva's great compassion, the will for the following sixteen types of sentient beings to be free from suffering: those holding various unrealistic views, those with four distorted convictions, those with egotism and possessiveness, those with five types of obscurations, those with attachment to sense objects, those

242. *dhāraṇī, gzungs.*

with seven types of deluded pride, those who have lost the noble paths, those who are powerless, those possessed by hatred, those who commit evil actions, those lacking holy wisdom, those lacking realization of profound relativity, those lacking the elimination of evolutionary instincts for mistaken views, those lacking freedom from the burden of suffering, those acting in deceitful and arrogant ways, and those having regressed from a higher rebirth and liberation; and the thirty-two types of a bodhisattva's activities, as follows: [helping sentient beings to] awaken from the sleep of folly; correct inferior aspirations to magnificent ones; correct intentions from nonvirtuous to virtuous; correct lifestyles from impure to pure; correct views from unrealistic to realistic; correct mental engagement from inappropriate to appropriate; correct adherence from perverse teachings to correct teachings; correct the factors of the six transcendences from unfavorable to favorable; correct liberative arts from unskillful to skillful; change mental addictions to nonaddictions; change the object [of the truth status habit] to the nonobject; correct being undisciplined to being disciplined; rectify being unresponsive to being responsive and kindly; correct having fallen into the four streams [of craving, etc.] to being liberated; correct discomfort with the Buddha's discourse [TL 025A] to being comfortable; correct being obsessed to not being obsessed; correct the lack of the noble wealth to the possession of such wealth; correct illness to wellness; correct the lack of the wisdom light to having that light; correct not knowing the [reality of the] three realms to knowing it; rectify engagement in the path from the left to the right; correct attachment to body and life to nonattachment; correct the lack of refuge in the Three Jewels to not cutting off the spiritual potential of the Three Jewels; rectify the loss of the Dharma to adherence to the Dharma; correct losing the six remembrances to not losing them; correct being obscured by addictions to not being obscured by addictions; and correct practices from nonvirtuous to virtuous.

3.1.1.2.2.2.2. The Sutra Statements Concerning Enlightenment, Excellences, and Enlightened Activities

«24» As for enlightenment, immediately after the statement about the element in the context of the teaching of the sixty purifications, [the *King Dhāraṇīshvara Sutra*] elucidates the Buddha's enlightenment, which is both naturally pure and free from all incidental taints, by teaching the sixteen types of great compassion.

If you ask, "What are these sixteen types of compassion?" They are engagement in sixteen types of the great compassion of great enlightenment, based on the observation of sentient beings who have not attained the sixteen properties of the great enlightenment and do not understand the meaning of the reality of the great enlightenment. The sixteen properties of the great compassion of the Victors' great enlightenment are as follows: no root and location; tranquil and peaceful; naturally clear-light; free of acceptance and rejection; no signs and objects; equal presence in the three times; bodyless and uncreated; no differentiations and places; not in the range of body or mind; neither an object nor a basis; void; [TL 025B] space-like; appropriate in placement; entering forms by entering the formless; free of pollutions and free of compulsions; and pure, stainless, and free of addictions.

Next to this statement on enlightenment, the sutra elucidates a buddha's excellences by demonstrating the ten powers, four confidences, and eighteen distinctive excellences of a buddha, which will be expounded later.

And after the statement on a buddha's excellences, the sutra elucidates thirty-two of a buddha's enlightened activities by demonstrating the unsurpassed enlightened activities of a tathāgata: the enlightened activities of the ten powers, which are the ten unmistaken teachings conforming to the occurrence of the ten powers; the enlightened activities of the four confidences, which are the four teachings on fear; and eighteen distinctive excellences' enlightened activities, which are the eighteen fruitional teachings.

3.1.1.2.3. Précis

«25» Thus, these seven vajra topics, just expounded, should be understood in detail according to the *Questions of King Dhāraṇīshvara Sutra*, from the perspective of the teachings on the uncommon nature of their defining characteristics. [TL 026A]

3.1.1.3. Verifying Their Order

If you ask, "What is the connection between these seven meanings to be realized?"

From the perfect complete Buddha [who is enlightened] with regard to all things comes the turning of the wheel of Dharma for noble beings. The gathering of numerous noble assemblies of disciples, the supreme Saṅgha Jewel, comes in turn from the turning of the wheel of Dharma. The turning of the wheel of Dharma after attaining perfect buddhahood is the object[243] of the spirit of enlightenment in the universal vehicle produced in the continuums of the intended disciples of *The Sublime Continuum*, while the arising of numerous noble assemblies relying on that wheel is the objective of the conception of the spirit of enlightenment.

Because of the holy assemblies, the tathāgata essence occurs. This means that, in order to attain the ultimate Three Jewels, the [causal] Three Jewels are the immediate causes, and then to gather the noble assemblies as the fruition of the turning of the wheel of Dharma, we wish to purify the tathāgata essence of the taints. Thus, there arises the tathāgata essence that is purified from taints to a certain degree.[244] How long will this tathāgata essence last? It will last until its attainment of the "element of a buddha's intuitive wisdom,"[245] freed from all taints. Throughout this duration, the suchness reality mingled with taints, [TL 026B] the receptivity[246] of the continuums of sentient beings for the entrance of a buddha's enlightened activities, and the spiritual potential are called the "tathāgata essence." After the attainment of a buddha's intuitive wisdom, this designation no longer exists. Some dull-minded ones assert that the meaning of the tathāgata essence as taught in the *Tathāgata Essence Sutra* remains relevant even in the state of ultimate fruition. We can understand that this treatise obliquely takes a stand against such an assertion in light of [the analysis of this verse].

According to the aforementioned alternative way of exposition, the Three Jewels appear in the world as the objects of the causal refuge.[247] Because of the Three Jewels, the purification of our elements takes place, and from the purification comes the attainment of the enlightenment, etc. Although this way of exposition is somewhat fit for this verse indicating a sequential order,

243. *ālambana, dmigs pa.*

244. *ci rigs pa.*

245. *jñāna-dhātv-āpti-niṣṭhaḥ.* Owing to the ambiguity in Ngog-lo's translation (*snying po ye shes khams thob mtha'*), Rong-ston takes *garbho jñāna* as a compound, referring to a buddha's intuitive wisdom. See *Legs bshad*, 59. This seems not to be the correct rendition as suggested by the Sanskrit edition.

246. *'jug rung.*

247. *rgyu'i skyabs 'gro.*

the gist of this treatise is very clear in taking the enlightenment, etc., as conducive conditions for purifying the element from taints. The attainment of a buddha's intuitive wisdom, which is free of all taints after the purification of the element, is called "supreme enlightenment." The excellences dependent on that enlightenment, including the powers, confidences, and distinctive excellences of a buddha, are indicated as the distinctive features of enlightenment. And the enlightened activities dependent on the excellences, which benefit all sentient beings in both simultaneous and ceaseless ways, are indicated as the distinctive features of the excellences.

Thus end the expositions of the coherence and preface of the treatise. [TL 027A] The "coherence" mentioned here is not identical to the one in the question above; the latter relates to the question of sequentiality, while the former is the final summary of [the first] three verses.

3.1.2.1.1. Determining the Seven Meanings to Be Realized . . . 1.1. Detailed Exposition of Fruitional Three Jewels . . . 1.1. The Main Meaning . . . 1.1. General Prelude

«26» Now the meaning of those verses establishing the body [of the treatise] should be explained in detail in terms of its components. Of these, the Three Jewels should be explained.

Those sentient beings who were led and educated by the three magic powers[248] of the Tathāgata take refuge in the Tathāgata. By means of the force of having gone for refuge to the Buddha, they also take refuge in the Dharma and Saṅgha because going for refuge to the other two Jewels is the causally concordant[249] fruit of purity of faith in the suchness reality— that is, in the truth body of the Buddha.

3.1.2.1.1.1.2. Exposition of Each Meaning . . . 2.1. Exposition of the Buddha Jewel . . . 1.1. Prelude

«27» Thus, according to the order of taking refuge, [TL 027B] since that is the very first of [the Three Jewels], there is one verse with regard to the Buddha Jewel:

248. *cho 'phrul gsum.*
249. *niṣyanda, rgyu mthun pa.*

3.1.2.1.1.1.2.1.2. Statement

There are eight excellences, divided according to self-benefit and benefit to others. However, these should be understood as two kinds of excellent qualities: the uncreated and the created.

3.1.2.1.1.1.2.1.2.1. Natural Purity

The first has two parts: natural purity and incidental purity. This is a teaching that accords with the stages of the first [part].

I bow down to the Buddha, himself, who is the sole incomparable one in the three realms. What kinds of excellent qualities are possessed by the Buddha? These are natural purity, which is without intrinsic reality status in the beginning, middle, and end, and thereby the ultimate truth free from all extremes of elaboration.

3.1.2.1.1.1.2.1.2.2. Incidental Purity

The antidotes have pacified all the incidental stains, and in reliance upon that, he has attained the utter pacification of all effort at engaging in enlightened activities.

As for the intuitive wisdom that is the realization, just as they are, of the excellent qualities in the category of created [things], if there existed any elaborations of truth status for the Buddha in his own enlightenment, then [it] would be suitable as something to be objectified; however, not even the slightest elaboration of truth status is seen. And having relied upon ultimate truth, it is a process of understanding like water pouring into water, in which all dualistic perceptions pass away. As for the intuitive wisdom that knows the varieties of things, that is being enlightened in terms of directly perceiving these three aspects, it is just so.

If you ask, "Having awakened, what does he do?" With regard to loving compassion, in order that those sentient beings with no realization of objects of knowledge—both as they are and their varieties of appearance— will attain realization, he acts to teach the path to disciples. With regard to the uniqueness of the path, [TL 028A] because of its transcendent aim, it is fearless, and because of its nonregression, it is the permanent path— and that is what he teaches. As for the statement that irreversibility is the meaning of "permanent," the assertion that it is actually permanent is just senseless babble. As for the uniqueness of his power, the Buddha has the power of wielding the supreme sword of wisdom and compassion that cuts down all sprouts of suffering, including those in the name-and-form of the twelve links of relativistic origination, and has the power of holding the supreme vajra of wisdom and compassion that annihilates the wall of the addictive doubts surrounded by the dense, dark forest of various views. The addictive doubts are the ones exclusively included in the category of conceptual notions.

3.1.2.1.1.1.2.1.3. Exposition . . . 3.1. Question

What is shown by this verse?

3.1.2.1.1.1.2.1.3.2. Answer

This has two parts: the root text and the commentary.

3.1.2.1.1.1.2.1.3.2.1. The Root Text

The excellences of the Buddha Jewel are contained in two categories: the truth body, which is for one's own benefit, and the material body, which is for the benefit of others.

The first [the truth body] has two factors: the element and knowledge. In the first, natural purity is the uncreated, that is, the ultimate truth. Incidental purity is what is spontaneously established along with the thorough pacification of all striving and effort. Knowledge, the intuitive wisdom of the knowledge of things just as they are, is not realized by the influence of others, but as a result of one's own discriminating knowledge.

The second, the material body that is the benefit for others, refers to the intuitive wisdom of knowledge of the varieties of things, compassion, and the power of both wisdom and compassion. Only the Buddha Jewel itself has the body endowed with these two kinds of benefit.

3.1.2.1.1.1.2.1.3.2.2. The Commentary

«28» This verse briefly explains buddhahood, which is endowed with eight excellences. What are the eight excellences? [TL 028B] They are: (1) the uncreated natural purity, included in the truth body; (2) spontaneity of helping others, having eradicated all striving and effort. The reason spontaneity is mentioned in the context of incidental purity is as follows: the subtle adverse condition preventing spontaneous, effortless engagement to benefit others is the uncontaminated karmic action in the twelve links of relativistic origination with respect to the objective obscuration category. It is a synthetic motivation for bodily and verbal actions with subtle effort. When it is at peace, the elimination is perfect and the engagement of benefiting others is spontaneous and effortless; (3) realization of reality, which is not realized under the influence of others' words; (4) intuitive wisdom that knows the varieties of things, which realizes these three and is included in the material bodies; (5) great compassion; (6) the power of both wisdom and compassion; and in general there are two excellences: (7) fulfillment of self-benefit; and (8) fulfillment of bringing benefit to others. This [verse] only gives enumeration. Its details will be explicated below.

3.1.2.1.1.1.2.1.4. Application of Exposition to Statement . . .
4.1. The Root Text

The natural purity aspect of the truth body is said to be uncreated because its nature is without beginning, middle, or end in connection with production, abiding, and disintegration. [Buddhahood] is said to be spontaneous in benefiting others because it is endowed with the distinction of a truth body that is the utter pacification of all striving and effort. It is not realized by the influence of others' words and conceptual thought since its realization is due to individual introspective concentration. [TL 029A] It is endowed with an intuitive wisdom that knows the varieties of things since it has realized these three things, i.e., natural purity, incidental purity, and intuitive wisdom that knows things just as they are.

One may wonder whether or not this intuitive wisdom that knows the varieties of things would become intuitive wisdom that knows things just as they are since it perceives the ultimate truth. Answer: Although a buddha's intuitive wisdom that knows the varieties of things also perceives reality, here it is not so posited on the differential[250] of intuitive wisdom that knows things just as they are alone, but on the fact that a buddha sees the ultimate truth, a transcendent knowable, which permeates all sentient

250. *ldog pa.*

beings. Despite the fact that the true cessation within a buddha is an ultimate truth, it is also distinguished from others by its association with an
intuitive wisdom that knows the varieties of things and can be called so.
[Buddhahood] is compassion because it shows the ones with no realization of those inconceivable objects the path to realize them. It is perfect
power since its intuitive wisdom and compassion eliminate delusion and
the resulting miseries of others. The first three demonstrate the marvelous
[accomplishment of] one's own objectives, while the last three demonstrate
the marvelous [accomplishment of] others' objectives.

3.1.2.1.1.1.2.1.4.2. The Commentary . . . 2.1. Each Explanation . . . 1.1.
The Main Meaning . . . 1.1. Natural Purity

«29» The word "uncreated" should be understood as the opposite of
"created." [TL 029B] Understanding creation in the beginning, duration in
the middle, and disintegration at the end [is the point of] calling it "created." Because of the absence of these three [characteristics], i.e., creation,
duration, and disintegration, buddhahood—as subsumed by ultimate
truth—should be perceived as being beginningless, middle-less, and endless, represented as the uncreated truth body, the reality-limit.[251] The statement "represented as the uncreated truth body," according to the translation
of the root text, should be understood as the uniqueness of [its excellent
qualities of] elimination. [Buddhas] spontaneously engage in benefiting
others since buddhas are distinguished from others by their perception of
the truth body, the reality-limit, with the peace of effortlessness. According
to the translation of [Asaṅga's] *Commentary*, this statement refers to the
ultimate truth to be perceived, because all noble beings are so called as a
result of their clear realization of the uncreated, as a sutra states, "all noble
beings are distinguished from others by the uncreated," and buddhas are
distinguished from others by their eternal concentration on it.

3.1.2.1.1.1.2.1.4.2.1.1.1.2. Incidental Purity

«30» It is "spontaneous" in benefiting others since all efforts, subject-
object reifications, and conceptual thoughts along with evolutionary

---

251. *bhūtakoṭi, yang dag pa'i mtha'.*

instincts²⁵² have ceased to exist. Although "spontaneity" is included in the body of benefit to others, its cause, the perfection of elimination, is the main content here.

3.1.2.1.1.1.2.1.4.2.1.1.1.3. Noumenal Intuitive Wisdom

«31» The ultimate truth is "not realized by the influence of others' words and conceptual thought" because it is realized by means of the self-arisen intuitive wisdom by way of the disappearance of dualistic vision. [TL 030A] The word *udaya* has connotations of both "clear realization" and "production." Here it means "clear realization," not referring to "production." Therefore, it should be read as "not realized by others" instead of "not produced by others."

3.1.2.1.1.1.2.1.4.2.1.1.1.4. No Contradiction between Effortlessness and the Engagement in Enlightened Activities

[Question:] If no efforts were made to teach the Dharma, how is it possible [for buddhas] to engage in all kinds of activities?

[Answer:] Thus, though the truth body is uncreated as being a tathāgata in eternal concentration on thatness and is of the characteristic of non-engagement without the slightest effort and motivation to teach, all the enlightened activities of buddhas spontaneously proceed for all beings until the end of cyclic life, without regression by obstacle and interruption. This is due to the votive prayer and the perfection of the compassion of buddhas.

Someone asserts that the material body only exists in other disciples' vision. This contradicts many sutra statements and reasoning lines. If so, even the truth body that is included in a buddha's own continuum would be impossible to posit. Hence, all efforts in accumulation of merit would be pointless.

3.1.2.1.1.1.2.1.4.2.1.1.2. Explaining the Material Body as Benefit to Others
. . . 1.2.1. Explaining Phenomenally Omniscient Intuitive Wisdom

In demonstrating the previous three [excellences] as objects of intuitive wisdom, the explanation of the first two as objects is [as follows]. [TL 030B]

252. *bag chags.*

Not having heard from other mentors about such an absolutely wonderful, magnificent, profound, and inconceivable object, the buddhas themselves, without a mentor, were perfectly awakened to the inexpressible nature of ultimate reality by means of their self-arisen intuitive wisdom that knows things just as they are. It should be known that buddhas are endowed with the unsurpassed intuitive wisdom since they perceive the three things.

3.1.2.1.1.1.2.1.4.2.1.1.2.2. Explaining Compassion

«32» [Buddhas] should be understood as being endowed with the unsurpassed intuitive wisdom and compassion since they cause other disciples, who are ignorant of buddhas' realization of the three things as if blind from birth, to realize those three things and show the path to their realization. As to the uniqueness of the path mentioned here, it is a fearless path because it is a transcendent path above the first stage—as stated elsewhere, "who have attained the stages are free from the five fears"; its transcendence is because of its nonregression in terms of nondestruction of the spirit of enlightenment and the extinction of the seeds of imaginative grasping at truth status.

Someone in the past, who had a habitual affinity for the outsiders' view, asserted that the word "eternality" used everywhere in the root text and its commentary inevitably refers to a permanent entity. If it were true, then read how the root text explains the words "showing the path to eternity"!

3.1.2.1.1.1.2.1.4.2.1.1.2.3. Showing the Power of Intuitive Wisdom and Compassion . . . 3.1. The Simile for the Power

«33» The way both the intuitive wisdom and the compassion of the Tathāgata are capable of destroying the roots of suffering and the delusions of others is shown by the similes of sword and vajra, respectively. [TL 031A] Here, it shows that [a buddha] is endowed with the power of destroying the deluded cause and result alone, in order to educate those who have the spiritual potential for the disciple vehicle, who temporarily seek the mere elimination of addictive obscuration; since those who are determined to be in the disciple vehicle lineage accept the Buddha who has utterly eliminated addictive obscuration as their root teacher as well as the object of causal refuge, and they temporarily do not seek a teacher with total elimination of objective obscuration as the refuge. [Buddhahood] endowed with the power of destroying what is to be eliminated to such an extent should not be taught as a fruitional refuge, because those who are determined to have the spiritual potential for the universal vehicle seek the total elimination of objective obscuration as their goal, whereas those who are temporarily determined to be in the disciple vehicle lineage do not seek to achieve buddhahood as their goal. The treatise shows this much of the excellences of elimination in order to let us know that [this Buddha Jewel] is the causal refuge for disciples and hermit buddhas. With respect to those who have the spiritual potential of the universal vehicle, [the Buddha Jewel is said] to be endowed with the excellences of elimination mentioned above. [The Buddha's] intuitive wisdom and compassion serve as the conducive condition[253] for Dharma teachings that are capable of destroying suffering and delusion in a disciple, but not as a direct antidote.

3.1.2.1.1.1.2.1.4.2.1.1.2.3.2. Recognition of What Is to Be Eliminated

Of these, the root of suffering, in brief, is any kind of name-and-form first produced by the condition of consciousness in the life cycle. [TL 031B] As mentioned in [Nāgārjuna's] *Letter to a Friend*, "this birth is suffering": birth in connection with the next worldly existence is the root of all [sufferings], from the six sense media [link] to the old age and death [link of relativistic origination]. The root of delusions consists of extreme views, false views, holding wrong moral disciplines and conduct as supreme, unrealistic views, and doubt, which are eliminated by the path of insight and are based on the futile views of the aggregates, which are views of any thing or property as having intrinsically identifiable status. It should be understood that [membership in] the Saṅgha Jewel is posited [for a person only] after their attainment of the path of insight, since he or she will keep faith in their own refuge as a result of total elimination of doubt tending toward refuge when the path of insight is attained, and will not be enticed by outsiders' doctrines other than the Buddha's teaching. The deluded doubt tending toward the four noble truths, the Three Jewels, etc., is also eliminated by the path of insight. Based on this specification, it should be understood [that the Saṅgha Jewel is posited after the attainment of the path of insight].

253. *bdag po'i rkyen.*

Although the futile view and extreme view are also the ones eliminated by the path of meditation of all three spiritual lineages, here only the ones eliminated by the path of insight are mentioned. This shows that [the Buddha Jewel] is endowed with the power of destroying the three kinds of bondage[254] that are the main obstacles to reaching liberation. Hence, by implication [from this explanation], we should know that [the Buddha Jewel] is also endowed with the power of destroying the delusions that are eliminated by the path of meditation.

3.1.2.1.1.1.2.1.4.2.1.1.2.3.3. Explaining the Correspondence between Simile and Meaning

Here, the suffering included in name-and-form, which has consciousness as its condition, should be regarded as sprout-like because of its character of production of the result from two sets of the twelve links of relativistic origination: projecting causality and activating causality.[255] [TL 032A] Name-and-form is produced first, followed by the six sense media up to old age and death. The simile of the sword shows the power of a tathāgata's intuitive wisdom and compassion since both cut that [sprout].

The characteristics of delusion included in view and doubt, which is to be removed on the path of insight, are difficult to realize by mundane knowledge and hard to be destroyed and penetrated by it. Therefore it is akin to a wall surrounded by a dense forest. It should be known that the power of a tathāgata's intuitive wisdom and compassion is illustrated by the simile of the vajra thunderbolt because both destroy that [root] in the sense that, [out of intuitive wisdom and compassion,] buddhas teach the Dharma, destroying what is to be eliminated within a disciple's continuum by means of practice.

3.1.2.1.1.1.2.1.4.2.1.2. Application to Sutra Reference ... 2.1. General Statement

«34» Thus, the [six] excellences of a tathāgata aforementioned, i.e., nature, elimination, intuitive wisdom that knows things just as they are, intuitive wisdom that knows the varieties of things, compassion, and power,

---

254. *kun sbyor.*
255. *'phen byed kyi rgyu 'bras* and *'grub byed kyi rgyu 'bras.*

should be understood by this very order and with detailed statements according to the *Ornament of the Light of Wisdom Engaging the Sphere of All Buddhas Sutra*. In that sutra:

3.1.2.1.1.1.2.1.4.2.1.2.2. Explanations of Each Excellence ... 2.1. Evidence for Self-Benefit's Truth Body ... 1.1. Evidence for Natural Purity

[Mañjushrī asks the Buddha:]

O Bhagavān, [I have heard a term] called "no birth and no cessation." [TL 032B] For whom is it used as a designation? The Buddha replies: O Mañjushrī, this [term] "no birth and no cessation with respect to the Tathāgata's reality body, which is included in ultimate reality" is a designation for the Tathāgata, the Saint, the Perfectly Enlightened Buddha.

This statement teaches that, among many bodies of the Tathāgata, the reality body is of uncreated nature.

3.1.2.1.1.1.2.1.4.2.1.2.2.1.2. Evidence for Incidental Purity

«35» And immediately after this, the sutra gives nine similes, elaborated in the activities chapter, with respect to this point, i.e., spontaneity in bringing benefit to others without any effort, starting with the simile of a reflection of an indra on the surface of a stainless sapphire floor, expressing [the notions] of "no movement" up to "not to be known." [The sutra continues:]²⁵⁶ "Likewise, O Mañjushrī, the Tathāgata, the Saint, the Perfectly Enlightened One, ..." [explaining that he] is free from any exertions within his three bodies. He neither moves his body motivated by effort, nor intends anything in his mind by imaginative thought, nor speaks motivated by imaginative thoughts. He is free of mistaken habits, free of imaginings about the reality of objects, without imaginative constructs of any sort of specifics. He does not reify the objects in the three periods of time, is free of reifications about the reality of the past, [TL 033A] without reification of

---

256. The extent of Gyaltsap's mixing of phrases of the sutra with explanatory comments is such that this entire passage (to the end of this paragraph) is not rendered as a direct quote, except for the initial address to Mañjushrī and the reciting of the Buddha's names.

any sort of specifics, without intentions of imagining the present, without mentation about the future. He has broken the causality with respect to suffering and its cause. He is cool, without the heat of karmic evolution and delusion. He has neither suffering of birth at the start nor of cessation at the end. He cannot be understood by other conventional cognitions or by the five sense cognitions; he cannot be seen, heard, smelled, tasted, or touched. He cannot be measured by means of the line of reasoning made by unconscious alienated people. Signless, he is free from any truth identity, not to be recognized as a real subjectivity free of intrinsic reality, nor to be recognized as any real objectivity free of intrinsic reality.

Such is the statement on the term "peace" of effortlessness. This shows that the Tathāgata is spontaneous, since, in his own activities, all imagination and reification in connection with effort or exertion have ceased to exist.

3.1.2.1.1.1.2.1.4.2.1.2.2.1.3. Evidence for Noumenally Omniscient Exalted Wisdom

«36» After this, i.e., after the statement of the [nine] similes, the remaining sutra passage shows that the thatness of all things is something realized not by other conditions, but by means of individually introspective concentration. In what way is thatness realized? It is [realized] by means of concentration on the gate to the perfect enlightenment as long as the life cycle exists, [TL 033B] as the place of the experience of all objects of knowledge.

3.1.2.1.1.1.2.1.4.2.1.2.2.2. Evidence of the Material Body as the Benefit for Others ... 2.1. Evidence for Phenomenally Omniscient Exalted Wisdom ... 1.1. The Sutra Reference

«37» And after the statements on the Tathāgata's sixteen kinds of enlightenment just mentioned, [the Buddha says]:

> O Mañjushrī, when enlightened about all things with such a nature of the emptiness of intrinsic identifiability, the Tathā-gata's phenomenally omniscient intuitive wisdom has seen the element, the tathāgata essence that exists in all sentient beings with no distinction, as impure, not free from taint, with faults,

and thereby he engages in the Tathāgata's great compassion named "energetic initiative"[257] for all beings in order to purify their taints.

The word "energetic initiative" is a name for [a buddha's] great compassion. It also appears as "play"[258] in another text.

3.1.2.1.1.1.2.1.4.2.1.2.2.2.1.2. Explaining Its Meaning

By this, a tathāgata's possession of intuitive wisdom and compassion is expressed. There, shown in an orderly manner, the phrase "all things with such a nature" means "[a nature] without intrinsic reality of any things." The phrase "being enlightened" means "having known truly and exactly with a buddha's nonconceptual intuitive wisdom in the equipoised concentration." The phrase "in sentient beings" means "in those who possess [one of] the three definitive types: those who are definite about one of the three spiritual potentials, those who are indefinite about a superior lineage or both, and those whose spiritual potential has been severed as a result of wrongdoing." I shall explain later that there is no ultimate severing of a spiritual potential—that is, one who is incapable of enlightenment. [TL 034A]

The word "element" means the tainted tathāgata essence, which exists in all beings with no distinction and is not different from the nature of the Buddha himself. The phrase "has seen" means "has perceived all kinds, i.e., all beings who have [tathāgata essence] with no distinction, by means of intuitive wisdom that knows the varieties of things, the Buddha's eye for which nothing is obscure." As to the explanation of tainted thatness, different people have different taints. The word "impure" refers to [the thatness] of ordinary people, because their addictive obscuration is active and the seeds of grasping at truth status, addiction, etc., have not been eliminated in the slightest. The phrase "not free from taints" refers to the thatness of disciples and hermit buddhas because addictive obscurations have been eliminated by the saints but objective obscurations have not yet been eliminated. The phrase "with faults" refers to the thatness of bodhisattvas because they retain one or both obscurations. [Bodhisattvas] below the eighth stage have

257. *rnam par brtson pa.*
258. *rnam par brtse ba.*

the faults of both obscurations and [bodhisattvas] above that stage have only objective obscurations. The word "love" is so called because thereby [the Buddha] purifies obscurations in disciples with his various arts. The phrase "has engaged for all beings" means that the Buddha has become enlightened for [the purpose of] purifying the taints of all beings equally, and for the attainment of his buddhahood [TL 034B] with the intention to lead [them] to attain the realization of his own reality.

3.1.2.1.1.1.2.1.4.2.1.2.2.2.2. Evidence for Compassion

The root text and [Asaṅga's] *Commentary* explain compassion in connection [with the excellences of intuitive wisdom that knows the varieties of things], or more specifically, by the statement that "he has engaged in the Tathāgata's great compassion named 'love' for all beings."[259]

3.1.2.1.1.1.2.1.4.2.1.2.2.2.3. Evidence for Power

Then, having developed the unsurpassed intuitive wisdom and compassion, [a buddha] acts constantly in this world to make the unparalleled Dharma wheel enter into disciples' continuums by means of the twelve enlightened activities. It should be known that this [activity] shows the power of both [intuitive wisdom and compassion] to bring benefit to other beings. If there were no great compassion, a buddha would have entered into the sphere of peace immediately after the attainment of nirvana and would not have turned the Dharma wheel.

3.1.2.1.1.1.2.1.4.2.2. Conclusive Statement . . . 2.1. Division of Six Excellences into Bodies of Two Benefits

«38» Here [of these six excellences of a tathāgata, in the order of the list, the endowment of the first three excellences, uncreated, etc., is the fulfillment of self-benefit, and the endowment of the remaining three, intuitive wisdom, etc., is the fulfillment of benefit to others.][260]

---

259. This is another instance of our expanding Gyaltsap's abbreviated reference to Asaṅga's passage above.

260. Here again we insert Asaṅga's full passage, this one in brackets, to help the reader, since

3.1.2.1.1.1.2.1.4.2.2.2. Analysis of the Latter Three Excellences

Or else, the word "intuitive wisdom" shows the fulfillment of self-benefit first since it is the excellent qualities of [a buddha's] own enlightenment, the absolutely eternal, i.e., no regression of elimination and realization—the effortless place. The words "compassion" and "power" show the fulfillment of the benefit to others because it is the excellence of constantly making the unsurpassed Dharma wheel enter into the continuums of disciples in the three spiritual lineages. As for the analysis of the two benefits, Buddha's intuitive wisdoms that are not perceivable by disciples belong to his self-benefit, [TL 035A] and the two material bodies that are perceivable by disciples belong to the benefit to others. This division is based on the act of bringing benefit to others with respect to the disciples' perception. Compassion and power are arranged as the benefit to others as perceived by disciples, thereby making Dharma teaching possible. Phenomenally omniscient intuitive wisdom is included in the benefit to others as the cause of compassionate engagement. It is so posited inasmuch as [this intuitive wisdom] sees that all beings have the tainted thatness with no distinction. As for intuitive wisdom that knows things just as they are, it is posited with respect to the decline of dualistic perception, not with respect to omniscient [intuitive wisdom] that perceives phenomena.

3.1.2.1.1.1.2.2. Exposition of the Dharma Jewel . . . 2.1. Prelude

«39» Now, from the Buddha Jewel, there originates the Dharma Jewel. Therefore, immediately after [the explanation of the Buddha Jewel], there is one verse concerning the Dharma Jewel. In terms of the ultimate attainment, this statement means that the Dharma Jewel, the ultimate cessation and path, originates from the Buddha Jewel. It does not indicate a temporal sequence. In terms of time, this means that cessation and path within disciples' continuums originate from the Dharma wheel turned by the Buddha. It should be known that both meanings are shown here.

Gyaltsap simply says, "Here, . . ." (*de la zhes so*).

3.1.2.1.1.1.2.2.2. Explaining the Meaning . . . 2.1. Statement

"I bow down to the sun of the Dharma since all noble beings depend on it." There is no mistake in explaining the sun of the Dharma as the truth of the path alone. What kinds of excellent qualities are possessed [by the Dharma]? [TL 035B] These are included in the truth of cessation and path. First, I shall explain the natural purity and the incidental purity of the truth of cessation.

The natural purity is realized neither by the self, nor by the consciousness with dualistic perception, nor by others. It is realized by the way of the decline of dualistic perception. First, [dualistic perception refers to the perception of] intrinsic reality status in connection with existence, nonexistence, both existence and nonexistence, and something other than existence and nonexistence, which are unexaminable, beyond the four extremes of reification. This is explicated according to the translation of [Asaṅga's] *Commentary*. Only the first three negations [of those four extremes] are mentioned in the translation of the root text, so it is not as clear as the translation of [Asaṅga's] *Commentary*.

According to the root text translation, the text explains the lack of intrinsically real status of nonexistence, existence, and both existence and nonexistence. As for [the attempt to] explain the [proof of the] freedom from the four extremes—elaborating the lack of ultimate existence, the lack of ultimate nonexistence, etc.—as easily obviated, since it is refuted by the direct contradiction that relies on mutual exclusivity, that [attempt] is just useless babbling. You may argue, "No problem, since we in our system do not assert either truth-status or truth-voidness." Well then, how do you negate asserting both of them? You may answer, "Asserting the common base of both is contradicted because they are negated [by the rule that] when you determine truth-voidness [of something], its truth-status is also excluded." Since it is necessary that truth-voidness be determined by negating through the exclusion of truth-status, then if you do not assert either one of the pair[261] of

---

261. The TL woodblock text itself reads *gyil gyal*, which could be a word for "something senseless," but more likely is a typo for *gyi ya gyal* ("one of a pair"), which makes more sense here.

the direct contradiction, [TL 036A] that itself is very self-contradictory! You may say, "Well those reasonings do not harm us, because we do not make any kind of assertion at all!" If you do not assert even ethics you are going to have only suffering, but maybe that is not obvious [to you]![262]

The assertion that the root text teaches the information-only system does not accord with either the root text or [Asaṅga's] *Commentary*, as I shall explain later.

Second, [the natural purity] is not realized by means of reliance on others: it is beyond the expression of sounds, various dialects, and verbal definitions, which are unable to perfectly realize [the natural purity].

Third, [the natural purity] is realized by individual introspective intuitive wisdom of noble beings in the process of the decline of dualistic perception in the equipoised concentration. These statements explain the natural purity with respect to its nature and realizing subjectivity.

Next, I shall explain the incidental purity, which has two parts: the rootlessness and the foundationlessness. The root of suffering refers to karmic evolution and addictions, such as attachment; the foundation of suffering refers to the seeds of imaginative and unconscious improper mentation, the habitual insistence on the truth status [of everything]. The cessation with respect to incidental purity is peace attained by destroying [the seeds] with all kinds of antidotes.

As for the truth of the path, there are three factors: purity, clarity, and antidote. First, the wisdom experientially realizing selflessness is free from the taints of all kinds of seeds of obscuration. Second, it is brilliant with the light of intuitive wisdom that experientially realizes thatness. It should be known that the postattainment intuitive wisdom in connection with the meditative nonconceptual intuitive wisdom also belongs to the truth of the path. [TL 036B] Third, the sun of the Dharma completely destroys the attachment to objects, such as form, imagining them to be intrinsically attractive, as well as hatred, imagining objects to be nonattractive and turning away from them, and the mental cataract of ignorance. This statement directly

---

262. At the end of a certain number of passages, Gyaltsap engages in this kind of somewhat brusque debate with his unnamed adversary. We sometimes tone down such debate battles as detracting from the main point of his more positive interpretations.

shows the path and the cessation of the universal vehicle. The verbal expression "Dharma Jewel" here is identical to the one sought by hermit buddhas in their continuums insofar as the name, and this should be understood by the explanation above.

3.1.2.1.1.1.2.2.2.2. Explanation . . . 2.1. Question

What is shown by this verse?

3.1.2.1.1.1.2.2.2.2. Answer . . . 2.1. The Root Text

The truth of cessation is inconceivable from the viewpoint of the four extremes; it is nondual with karmic evolution and addiction; it has no foundation as the concept of grasping at truth status. [The truth of the path] is pure, brilliant, and the antidote. The four truths are divided into two categories: impure and pure. The Dharma has the characteristics of the two pure truths, i.e., the truth of cessation in the nature of freedom from attachment and the truth of the path, which causes liberation from addiction.

3.1.2.1.1.1.2.2.2.2.2. [Asanga's] Commentary

≪40≫ This [verse] briefly explains the Dharma Jewel as having eight excellences in two categories. What are the eight excellences? They are: (1) inconceivability; (2) nonduality; (3) nonconceptuality, which should be understood by now; (4) purity, which refers to the nature of path, not mixed with obscuration; (5) illumination, which refers to noumenally omniscient knowledge and phenomenally omniscient knowledge; (6) medicinality, which refers to healing power; (7) nonattachment; and (8) the cause of nonattachment. [TL 037A]

3.1.2.1.1.1.2.2.2.3. Application of Explanation to the Statement . . . 3.1. General Explanation . . . 1.1. The Root Text

Nonattachment is included in both truths: cessation, which is in the nature of the objective, and path, which is in the nature of the actions. It should be known that each of these has three excellences respectively, as aforementioned in the two categories.

3.1.2.1.1.1.2.2.2.3.1.2. [Asaṅga's] Commentary

« 41 » The truth of cessation is shown by the first three of these six excellences: inconceivability from the viewpoint of the four extremes; nonduality with respect to karmic evolution and addictions; and nonconceptuality, not grasping at truth status. Therefore, these [three excellences] make known that nonattachment as objective constitutes [the truth of cessation]. The truth of the path is shown by the remaining three excellences, i.e., purity without taint, the illumination of thatness, and the medicine for the opposing resistance. Thus, it should be known that the cause of nonattachment is included therein. That which is nonattachment is the truth of cessation, and that which causes nonattachment is the truth of the path. The Dharma is nonattachment and [also] has the characteristics of these two pure truths together. This shows that nonattachment is the Dharma Jewel.

3.1.2.1.1.1.2.2.2.3.2. Explanation for Each Excellence . . . 2.1. The Root Text

[The truth of cessation] is not a conceptual object in connection with the four extremes, it cannot be perfectly expressed by language and concept, and it is known by each noble one by means of inwardly concentrated discernment; therefore, the Dharma is inconceivable.

By means of just this pacification of evolutionary actions and addictions, there is nonduality, freedom from truth-habituated thoughts, and the presence of purity, clarity, and healing power, etc., like the sun. [TL 037B]

3.1.2.1.1.1.2.2.2.3.2.2. [Asaṅga's] Commentary . . . 2.1. Explanation of the Truth of Cessation . . . 1.1. Explanation of Natural Purity . . . 1.1. General Statement

« 42 » In short, the truth of cessation should be known to be inconceivable for three reasons.

3.1.2.1.1.1.2.2.2.3.2.2.1.1.2. Explanation of Each Point

If you ask, "What are these three?" Since (1) it is not experientially realized by one's own language and conception since it is not an object of conception of the four categories, i.e., nonexistence, existence, both existence and nonexistence, and neither existence nor nonexistence, in light of the fact that the intrinsic reality of existence cannot be found; (2) it is not experientially realized by means of reliance on others' language and conception since it cannot be expressed by any comprehensible sound, local language, mental expression, speech object, or definition, for example, the truth of cessation is defined as cessation of suffering, verbal designation, and verbalization by name, thus it cannot be perfectly realized by these means; and (3) it is realized in the way of the decline of dualistic perception by the noble one's individual introspective intuitive wisdom.

3.1.2.1.1.1.2.2.2.3.2.2.1.2. Explanation of Incidental Purity ... 2.1. Recognizing Incidental Taint to Be in Cessation ... 1.1. Question

«43» If you ask, "How should the truth of cessation be known as nondual and nonconceptual?"

3.1.2.1.1.1.2.2.2.3.2.2.1.2.1.2. Answer ... 2.1. Sutra Reference

The Bhagavān states as follows:

O Shāriputra, this "cessation" is the truth body; with its quality of nonduality, it is nonconceptual reality. [TL 038A]

3.1.2.1.1.1.2.2.2.3.2.2.1.2.1.2.2. Explanation of the Sutra Statement

«44» Here, "duality" refers to evolutionary actions and the addictions, such as greedy attachment. "Conceptual" refers to the mental attachment to the truth status of the person and its aggregates. "Inappropriate mental engagement" is the cause that originates evolutionary actions and mental addictions.

3.1.2.1.1.1.2.2.2.3.2.2.1.2.2. Detailed Explanation of the Nature of the Truth of Cessation ... 2.1. Recognizing Its Nature ... 1.1. Intrinsic Realitylessness Being Natural Cessation

Because of knowing precisely, by means of the noble one's meditative concentration in natural exhaustion and the emptiness of intrinsic identity, that those addictions and concepts are naturally ceased, then in dependence upon that, because of the absence of engagement in conceptual activity and those two—actions and addictions—since there is finally no arising of suffering, such a one has the freedom of abandoning the [evolutionary] seeds, and this is called "the truth of cessation." As for the addictions and concepts being empty of intrinsic reality, natural cessation is the ultimate truth, while the attainment of the cessation that is the freedom from incidental taints is contingent upon the direct realization of that.

3.1.2.1.1.1.2.2.2.3.2.2.2.1.2. Truth of Cessation That Is Free from Taint Shown by Freedom from Taint, Not Destruction of Existence

The Bhagavān does not teach that the destruction of previously produced suffering and origination is the truth of the cessation of suffering. The reason that the Bhagavān does not teach so is that created things' disintegrating after their production is the natural law of relativistic origination; thus [their destruction] requires no meditation on the path. Otherwise all beings would have been liberated without any effort. [TL 038B] Intelligent ones should carefully make the distinction between the truth of cessation and the destruction of existence.

3.1.2.1.1.1.2.2.2.3.2.2.2.2. Sutra Reference ... 2.1. Sutra Reference for the Former Point in Order to Recognize the Reverse Procedure of Cyclic Life

The detail is explained in the *Shrīmālādevī Lion's Roar Sutra*:

O Mañjushrī, this so-called unproduced and undestroyed ultimate truth is not apprehended by mind, mentality, and consciousness with dualistic perception.

"Mind" is so called because it is a collection of various virtuous and nonvirtuous evolutionary instincts. "Mentality" is so called because [mind] is the thing that relies. "Consciousness" is so called because [mind] is the thing to be relied upon. Although there is a different way of interpretation by the ones who assert the existence of a fundamental consciousness other than the six consciousnesses, this treatise does not follow such a system. I shall explain this later.

In that which is not apprehended by mind, mentality, and consciousness, there is not the slightest conception by means of improper mental engagement with respect to the grasping at truth status. There is no dualistic perception involved in the mind perceiving reality, not to mention the grasping at truth status. One who strives with rational meditation realizing the lack of any intrinsic reality status never allows tainted ignorance, the grasping at truth status, to arise. Nonarising of ignorance means the nonarising of the twelve links of the life cycle, starting from ignorance up to aging and death. [TL 039A] It is called the nonproduction of the next rebirth in the life cycle, etc.

3.1.2.1.1.1.2.2.2.3.2.2.2.2.2. The Sutra Reference for the Latter Meaning Teaching the Existence of the Tathāgata Essence, Suchness Reality Mingled with Taints

Also stated in the sutra:

> O Bhagavān, the destruction of something is not the cessation of suffering, because of the reason aforementioned. The "cessation of suffering" that exhausts all taints indicates the Tathāgata's truth body, which, from beginningless time, lacks intrinsic reality status, thereby being not created by other conditions; not produced by self; nonarisen by means of depending on both; free from exhaustion by others; free from exhaustion by self; permanent, since it is unproduced; stable, since it is non-aging; peace, since it is not sick; undestroyed, since it is deathless; naturally pure; liberated from the sheath of all addictions, since the antidotes have been perfectly applied; and endowed with all indivisible, inconceivable excellences of the Buddha, which are far beyond the sands of the Ganges in number and are attained by the remedies. O Bhagavān, this truth body of the Tathāgata, free of any intrinsic reality status, when not yet released from the sheath of addictions, is called the tathāgata essence, the suchness reality mingled with taints.

Full details of how to arrange the truth of cessation of suffering should be understood according to the sutras. This shows that reality free from intrinsic reality status is the truth body when it is purified from taints, and remains as the tathāgata essence as long as it is mingled with taints. It would not fit the meaning of these sutras if the tathāgata essence were accepted as a suchness reality [primordially] purified of taints, as someone does. [TL 039B] The suchness reality mingled with taints can only exist within the continuums of sentient beings, while the suchness reality purified of taints can only exist within a buddha's continuum. It reveals one's stupidity if one asserts that reality exists simultaneously with taints and without taints, or that what exists within a sentient being also exists within a buddha, and vice versa.

3.1.2.1.1.1.2.2.2.3.2.2.2. Explanation of the Truth of the Path . . .
2.1. Summary Statement

《45》 The causes of the attainment of the truth body of a tathāgata under the name "cessation of suffering" are the path of insight and the path of meditation based on nonconceptual intuitive wisdom. If sentient beings already possessed in their continuums the truth body with the two kinds of purity, it would not be rational to teach the cause of attaining the path of insight and the path of meditation, since [the truth body] would have already been accomplished since beginningless time with no need to depend on causes.

3.1.2.1.1.1.2.2.2.3.2.2.2.2. Detailed Explanation . . . 2.1. Being Akin to the Sun

It should be known that [nonconceptual intuitive wisdom] is akin to the sun in three aspects: [namely], it is akin (1) to the purity of the sun, since the intuitive wisdom that experientially realizes selflessness is free from all taints of addiction; (2) to the sun's illumination of forms, since the truth of the path illuminates all aspects of all objects of knowledge just as they are and in their varieties; and (3) to the sun as the antidote to darkness, since the intuitive wisdom that experientially realizes selflessness is the antidote to the two kinds of obscurations of realizing thatness. Someone takes grasping at truth status as the objective obscuration mentioned in the treatise. [TL 040A] This is incorrect since, were it so, it would completely contradict the statements below regarding the intention of the tathāgata essence teaching.

3.1.2.1.1.1.2.2.3.2.2.2.2.2. Recognizing What Is to Be Eliminated . . .
2.1. Showing the Process of Cyclic Life . . . 1.1. Summary Statement

«46» "Obscuration of liberation" means the production of attachment, hatred, and ignorance by their activation and evolutionary instincts or seeds, which are preceded by the mentation of grasping at truth status in the causal object [of attachment, etc.] that is the truth held by grasping at truth status on the basis of unreal phenomena, i.e., person and aggregates as the objective object. The way the three poisons are produced is as follows: the childish ones develop attachment from the karmic instincts for unreal things that lack intrinsic reality because of their desirable looks, hatred because of their detestable looks, and ignorance because of their obscure looks. [In sum,] the karmic evolutionary instincts are the cause of improper mental functions that reify things [as being intrinsically real].

3.1.2.1.1.1.2.2.3.2.2.2.2.2.1.2. Detailed Explanation

«47» The cause of attachment, hatred, and ignorance is the grasping at truth status and its seeds, or the improper mental functions observing the unreal things such as person and aggregates, and imagining them as attractive, etc. Those whose minds are occupied by the improper mental engagement will activate attachment, hatred, or ignorance. [TL 040B] On these bases, the virtuous, non-virtuous, and immovable karmic evolutionary actions that are produced by attachment and associated with body, speech, and mind will originate, as well as those produced by hatred and ignorance. Karmic evolution will be invariably connected with birth.

3.1.2.1.1.1.2.2.3.2.2.2.2.2.1.3. Précis

Hence, in the manner just explained above, the childish ones have attachment for the signs of truth status as well as evolutionary instincts for grasping at truth status. Their origination of improper mentation observing these things results in the origination of addiction; origination of addiction results in the origination of karmic evolution; origination of evolution results in the origination of birth.

3.1.2.1.1.1.2.2.2.3.2.2.2.2.2.2. Recognizing the Main Cause of Cyclic Life

What is the main cause of the life cycle? All kinds of taints in connection with the life cycle, i.e., the childish ones' addictions, evolutionary actions, and births, are caused by the ignorance of the sole element, the suchness reality mingled with taints, which is the lack of intrinsic reality status of persons and aggregates, not truly knowing them as they are. This implies that we have to understand the element of the lack of intrinsic reality status in order to liberate ourselves from the life cycle, since it states that the life cycle is due to our lack of understanding of it. This clearly teaches that the lack of intrinsic reality status of persons and aggregates is the reality-limit, or thatness, as well as the tathāgata essence mingled with taints. It implies that grasping at truth status is the root of the life cycle and of tainted ignorance since it states that the ignorance of that [lack of intrinsic reality status] is the root of the life cycle. [TL 041A] There is no doubt as to whether the saints of the disciple vehicle and the hermit buddha vehicle have been liberated from the life cycle because there is no doubt as to whether one shall cut down the root of the life cycle in order to be liberated from it. It should be known that the liberation from the life cycle depends on the realization of truthlessness, and disciples and hermit buddhas also have experientially realized the two kinds of selflessness, since the root of the life cycle is not eradicated like thornbushes, but is eradicated by means of the negation of habitual misperception by rational reasoning. This point is well established by [Asaṅga's] *Commentary* and is repeated later. As to the personal self-habit, the habit of [holding to] an individual substantial self alone is not qualified as its complete definition. Just as the grasping at the truth status of the aggregates is the grasping at the true establishment of phenomena, likewise the grasping at personal truth status is accepted as the grasping at a self of persons. This point will be explained in the section on the Saṅgha Jewel.

3.1.2.1.1.1.2.2.2.3.2.2.2.2.2.3. Recognizing Its Antidote . . .
3.1. Initial Realization of Truthlessness Free from Reification

Furthermore, while investigating ultimate truth, the truth status of persons and aggregates, no cause of grasping by any means at truth status or at any objects that are persons and aggregates can be found as having truth status in the slightest. It should be understood in this way by the reasoning of "not being identical or separate."

3.1.2.1.1.1.2.2.2.3.2.2.2.2.2.3.2. How Conception Becomes Realization

When no cause of grasping at truth status or object can be experienced as having truth status, [TL 041B] i.e., when no dualistic reification can be experienced, one truly knows ultimate truth. Therefore, the Tathāgata has become enlightened about the equanimity of all things included in persons and things by means of [the intuitive wisdom of] their equality in their lack of intrinsic reality status.

3.1.2.1.1.1.2.2.2.3.2.2.2.2.2.3.3. Teaching the Intuitive Wisdom of Reality with Neither Negation Nor Establishment as Antidote to Obscuration

« 48 » Thus, because no object with truth status can be experienced in objects of knowledge as the cause of the nonexistence of what is held by the truth-status-habit, and because the ultimate truth can be experienced in its existence as real, as it is: neither is truth status negated nor is truthlessness established. [Thus, the Tathāgata] has become enlightened in the equality of all things, i.e., the truth body, by his intuitive wisdom of equanimity. How? If this experiential intuitive wisdom of lack of intrinsic reality status is produced, the opposite side that is to be abandoned will be deserted forever and the nonexistence of intrinsic reality will be realized. It should be known that this intuitive wisdom is the antidote to all kinds of obscurations to experiencing reality. It also applies to the meaning of no negation and no establishment, below.

3.1.2.1.1.1.2.2.2.3.2.2.2.3. The Sutra Reference

« 49 » The cause of attaining the truth body is the path of insight and meditation, which should be understood in detail according to the *Transcendent Wisdom Sutra*.

This shows that the ultimate truth with no negation and no affirmation, and the cause of attaining the truth body that is the paths of insight and meditation experientially realizing reality should be understood in detail according to the *Transcendent Wisdom Sutra*.

Someone apparently explains the Buddha's word as really expounding the soul theory of the outsiders, by stating that the [TL 042A] *Transcendent Wisdom Sutra* in extensive, medium, and short lengths only teaches the self-emptiness of conventional [realities], but not of the ultimate truth. Furthermore, this someone asserts, the latter is taught by the final turning of the Dharma wheel, and its unmistaken intention is explained by *The Sublime Continuum* and [Asaṅga's] *Commentary*. Someone who makes such statements lacks the fortune to read these passages in [Asaṅga's] *Commentary*. Furthermore, it is indeed insane for them to assert that the *Elucidation of the Intention Sutra* is completely definitive in meaning, and its intention is explained by *The Sublime Continuum* and its [Asaṅga's] *Commentary*. This is because that sutra literally teaches that disciples who seek peace for themselves cannot attain buddhahood, and that there are three vehicles in the ultimate sense, while this treatise repeatedly establishes the ultimate single vehicle [theory] by following the *White Lotus Sutra*. Thus, it should be known that someone's assertion that this *[Sublime Continuum] Treatise* shows no other system than the information-only system departs from what is meant by the text itself.

3.1.2.1.1.1.2.3. Exposition of the Saṅgha Jewel . . . 3.1. Prelude

«50» Now, from the Mahayana universal vehicle Dharma Jewel originates the Saṅgha Jewel of nonregressing bodhisattvas. Therefore, immediately after [the explanation of the Dharma Jewel], there is one verse concerning the Saṅgha Jewel.

"Nonregressing bodhisattvas" refers to those on the first stage who will not regress to the situation in which one has to take rebirth by means of addiction and karmic evolution and will never again cultivate the thought of self-benefit. [TL 042B] They will not regress from [seeking] the perfect enlightenment not only by means of the way of action but also by means of the way of thinking.

3.1.2.1.1.1.2.3.2. Actual Meaning . . . 2.1. Statement

The eightfold excellent qualities [of the Saṅgha] are listed as follows: (1) noumenally omniscient knowledge; (2) phenomenally omniscient knowledge; (3) inner realization; (4) liberation from the obscuration of attachment; (5) liberation from the obscuration of hindrance; (6) liberation from the obscuration of inferiority; (7) knowledge; and (8) liberation. The last two are considered as the summary, having two kinds in total.

(1) Noumenally omniscient knowledge, the first excellent quality, is further divided into two aspects: nature and cause. The first is connected to the statement, "I bow down to these who possess such excellences." Here, "excellences" is the realization of the limit of selflessness of all things that includes persons and aggregates, in light of the fact that all things are instantaneously changing as well as free of intrinsic reality, or the ultimate truth of truthlessness, as it is. The cause of the insight of truth that the mind lacks intrinsic reality is the fact that the nature of the mind is luminosity, as well as the insight that the taint does not have any actuality of intrinsic reality. Literally, it seems that the former ["the nature of the mind is luminosity"] is the cause of the latter ["the taint is viewed to be without actual intrinsic reality"]. However, the latter refers to the realization that the taint is incidental, since the proofs are actually different.

(2) Phenomenally omniscient knowledge refers to the insight of the all-pervading presence of perfect complete buddhahood, which is the suchness reality or the lack of intrinsic reality status in each and every sentient being.

(3) It should be known that inner realization is nothing more than the two knowledges just mentioned.

The following three excellences, (4) to (6), are indicated by the line "those whose mind is no longer obscured." It would be no contradiction to take "liberation from the obscuration of inferiority" as the next excellence. [TL 043A] I bow down to those whose intuitive insight has as its object sentient beings' freedom from intrinsic reality, and that countless beings all possess such [freedom of] intrinsic reality. This praise of those who possess the two kinds of intuitive wisdom distinguished from others by abandonment indicates that [the Saṅgha] possesses the ultimate excellence, or liberation from the obscuration of inferiority.

These excellences are included in two kinds of excellences: knowledge and liberation. In short, knowledge has two kinds: noumenally omniscient knowledge and phenomenally omniscient knowledge. Inner realization, liberation from attachment, and liberation from hindrance are those which are distinguished by intuitive wisdoms.

3.1.2.1.1.1.2.3.2.2. Explanation ... 2.1. Question

≪51≫ What is shown by this verse?

3.1.2.1.1.1.2.3.2.2.2. Answer ... 2.1. The Root Text

The intelligent holy Saṅgha that never regresses possesses unsurpassed excellences as a result of the purity of intuitive insight: noumenal omniscience, phenomenal omniscience, and the inner realization of the two insights. This purity is also shown as the possession of excellence of liberation.

3.1.2.1.1.1.2.3.2.2.2.2. [Asaṅga's] Commentary

≪52≫ This [verse] briefly explains that the Saṅgha Jewel of nonregressing bodhisattvas possesses unsurpassed excellences as a result of their purity of transcendent intuitive insight by the two causes: omniscient [intuitive wisdom] that perceives things accurately, and phenomenally omniscient [intuitive wisdom]. It also shows that these two intuitive wisdoms are superior to others. [TL 043B]

3.1.2.1.1.1.2.3.2.3. Application of Explanation to the Statement ... 3.1. Excellences of Noumenally Omniscient Knowledge and Phenomenally Omniscient Knowledge ... 1.1. Noumenally Omniscient Knowledge ... 1.1. The Root Text

They perceive things just as they are, because of directly realizing that phenomena are empty of intrinsic reality, that is, the peaceful reality of beings, their absolute purity of nature, and that all the addictions have been primordially exhausted.

3.1.2.1.1.1.2.3.2.3.1.1.2. [Asaṅga's] Commentary ... 2.1. The Nature of Noumenally Omniscient Knowledge

≪53≫ Here, noumenally omniscient realization, [as shown by the word "liberation,"] should be understood as the experiential realization of the reality-limit of the selflessness or lack of intrinsic reality status of all beings, of exactly the so-called things including aggregates, etc., and persons. This reality limit is the ultimate knowable, ultimate truth, or reality as it is.

It clearly shows that the perfect understanding of subjective selflessness depends on the understanding of subjective truthlessness since it states that subjective and objective selflessnesses are the limit of reality, knowable as it is. It is quite clear that this exposition is completely identical to the savior Nāgārjuna's intention as revealed by the master Chandrakīrti.

3.1.2.1.1.2.3.2.3.1.1.2.2. Its Cause

In brief, the realization by the universal vehicle noble beings of the afore-mentioned nondestruction of lack of intrinsic reality status of persons and things, or the primordial emptiness of intrinsic reality, as a result of their nature of eternal primordial peace, is produced by two causes. Which two? They are the insight into the natural clear-light of the mind [TL 044A] and the insight into the primordial exhaustion and cessation of intrinsic reality, or lack of intrinsic reality status, of addictions.

The natural clear-light of the mind means that in ultimate [reality] the mind is not tainted by addictions. It also means that the mind does not have anything corresponding with the cognitive darkness of the perceptual habit of grasping at the truth status of persons and aggregates. Otherwise the mind would be truly established and the taints would not be purified. "Incidentality" means that in ultimate [reality] the addictions do not exist. This treatise explains it in this way. It explicitly states that the selflessness of persons and the selflessness of things are knowable precisely. Therefore [the view that] repudiates the truthlessness of created things [as if it were] emptiness [mistaken as] a nihilistic view, as an inert emptiness,[263] or a partial emptiness, and that claims that this treatise talks about an other-emptiness endowed with all kinds of excellences—some sort of true [abso-lute] entity—is an unrealistic view. This view deviates from the intention of the root text and [Asaṅga's] *Commentary,* so it should be discarded far away like so much spittle. The meaning of "emptiness endowed with all kinds of excellences" is not like that, as will be explained below.

263. *bem stong.*

3.1.2.1.1.1.2.3.2.3.1.1.2.3. Its Proof . . . 3.1. Difficulty of Realizing the
Untainted Element

«54» Here, these two facts, "natural transparency of the mind" and
"the derivative addiction of that mind," are supremely, extremely hard to
understand in terms of their connection with the untainted element, i.e.,
the ultimate [reality]. The reason is that, in the case of virtuous minds and
nonvirtuous minds, when the mind is made virtuous and is distorted by
addiction, [TL 044B] the later developed mind is the result and the developing addiction is the cause; and when both developed and developing
[mind] lack instrinsic reality status, it is hard to establish the cause and
effect functions. And as one doubts whether the two could be simultaneous
if they did have intrinsic reality status, the cause and effect functions would
be invalid, as when one functions, the other would lack connection, then
such a pattern is hard to understand.

In essence, one must accept causality, since otherwise there is a danger
of becoming nihilistic. But if one does not know how to present [causality
in the context of] voidness of intrinsic reality and does not negate all the
objective orientations of sign habits, when, having taken up the system of
the negation of objective orientations bearing signs[264] that hold on to intrinsic reality status in things, one asserts intrinsic reality emptiness as one's own
interpretation without having a place in one's system for causality, then,
ultimate and conventional realities would appear to one as the [discrete]
feet of a spider. Therefore, knowing how to fully present in one's interpretation ultimate reality, i.e., emptiness of intrinsic reality, and conventional
reality, i.e., causality, as established in a complementary way by validating
reasoning, is the ultimately hardest point to realize. If one does not realize
it, even if one claims that one can present the two realities properly, it will
not go beyond [being one or another of] the sixteen kinds of unrealistic
views described in the *Ornament of Clear Realization*.

I shall explain this point from time to time afterward. For a detailed
exposition, please refer to the two extensive commentaries on [Nāgārjuna's]
Wisdom: Root Verses on Centrism and [Chandrakīrti's] *Introduction to the
Central Way*, as well as a separate commentary, the *Essence of True Eloquence*, differentiating the interpretable and definitive meanings of the

264. *mtshan 'dzin.*

interpretable and definitive meaning sutras, and the chapters determining [the practice of] transcendent insight in the extensive and short treatises on the great beings' *Stages of the Path to Enlightenment*[265]—all by my precious mentor, the Omniscient [Tsong Khapa] Losang Drakpa, who was in reality the emanation of all enlightened activities of the buddhas of the three times, who explained the intention of the three baskets and the four classes of tantra without error, [TL 045A] and who promoted the holy Dharma in an ordinary form, as empowered by his compassion and vows.

3.1.2.1.1.1.2.3.2.3.1.1.2.3.2. Sutra Reference

Thus, as the *Shrīmālādevī Lion's Roar Sutra* states, [to the effect that,] "O Bhagavān!"[266] consider the virtuous mind; its addictions will not, intrinsically or derivatively addict it—it cannot be distorted by addictions—because it is momentary.

This sutra statement explains that a virtuous mind is not tainted by addictions with respect to its intrinsic reality since it is just for an instant. If what is negated is not qualified, then the mind would be not tainted at all; so it should be qualified as "in the ultimate sense." If the mind were not tainted at all, it would be in contradiction with the statement below against such a thesis. Thus, a valid reason is established in saying, "a nonvirtuous mind is not tainted by addictions with respect to its intrinsic reality, since it is just for an instant." If its logical pervasion were reversed, the validating reason that proves it harmful would run as follows: if what is tainted and what is tainting had intrinsic reality, these two would contact each other simultaneously. However, such does not happen. The sutra states:

O Bhagavān, the addictions do not touch the mind, the mind is not touched by the addictions. [TL 045B] O Bhagavān, the mind that is not in contact with the addictions is tainted only according to the darkness that is objectified by the truth habit.

265. The *Ocean of Reason* (*Rigs pa'i rgya mtsho*), the *Illumination of the Intent of the Central Way* (*dbU ma dgongs pa rab gsal*), the *Essence of True Eloquence* (*Drang nges legs bshad snying po*), and the two versions of the *Stages of the Path to Enlightenment* (*Lam rim che chung*), respectively, constitute Tsong Khapa's main opus on the realistic view.

266. Here the only part of the quote actually cited is the "O Bhagavān!" The rest is paraphrase couched in logical reasoning diction. This pattern continues with the rest of the quote.

This statement is identical to the reasoning that analyzes "contact" in [Nāgārjuna's] *Wisdom: Root Verses on Centrism*. It is invalid to assert that the mind is not tainted by addictions at all, as the sutra states:

O Bhagavān, there are taints and there are the minds tainted by addictions. Nevertheless, O Bhagavān, it is difficult to understand the meaning of the mind of natural purity being tainted.

Noumenally omniscient [intuitive wisdom]—with reference to being hard to understand—should be understood in detail according to the sutra.

3.1.2.1.1.1.2.3.2.3.1.2. Phenomenally Omniscient Knowledge . . .
2.1. The Root Text

«55» By means of the awareness that realizes, by means of direct experience, the final object of knowledge just as it is, the emptiness of reality that is the reality of omniscience, because of directly seeing that it exists in all sentient beings, is experiencing existence in all its varieties. The perfect, complete Buddha, by seeing things just as they are, sees the varieties of things, and that experience of the varieties of things is seeing things just as they are. As for noble bodhisattvas, however, since they are not like that, it is explained that they do so [only] having relied upon perceiving things just as they are in meditative concentration.

3.1.2.1.1.1.2.3.2.3.1.2.2. [Asaṅga's] Commentary

«56» Here, having explained the experience of existence in all its varieties by a buddha, a noble bodhisattva, having relied upon the realization in meditative concentration on the final suchness of all things that are objects of knowledge, [TL 046A] realizes by means of transcendent intuitive wisdom the very existence of a tathāgata essence, i.e., suchness reality mingled with taints, in all sentient beings, even those who dwell in the animal realms. Although these bodhisattvas experientially realize this reality of all beings, they do not realize all beings themselves, just as unenlightened noble beings who have not yet realized the twenty-one categories of untainted intuitive wisdom realize the reality of these intuitive wisdoms. This accords with the Discipline texts that state that a noble disciple who has directly seen the

Buddha's truth body would desire to go and see the Buddha's material body as well.[267] That insight of the bodhisattva is produced starting from the first bodhisattva stage since it first realizes the meaning of the all-pervading element-of-things,[268] which is a reality of all knowables not realized before. The first instant of the first stage is included in the path of insight that consists of sixteen instants of intuitive wisdom and patience. However, it should be known that part of the first stage is also included in the path of meditation since it will take many eons to complete the first stage. The realization of the meaning of the all-pervading ultimate element is applicable to the entire first stage.

3.1.2.1.1.1.2.3.2.3.2. Excellences of Individual Retrospective Wisdom, Liberation from the Obscuration of Attachment, and Liberation from the Obscuration of Hindrance . . . 2.1. The Root Text . . . 1.1. Individual Retrospective Wisdom

«57» Such realization is the noble beings' insight by means of their own wisdom, realizing all objects of knowledge just as they are and in their varieties. [TL 046B]

3.1.2.1.1.1.2.3.2.3.2.1.2. Liberation from the Obscuration of Attachment and Liberation from the Obscuration of Hindrance

The obscuration of attachment and the obscuration of hindrance are completely purified because the element without the taint of intrinsic reality is free from the attachment of grasping at truth status and hindrance to [knowing of] all objects of knowledge.

3.1.2.1.1.1.2.3.2.3.2.2. [Asaṅga's] Commentary . . . 2.1. Individual Retrospective Wisdom

«58» The realization of the transcendent path by the omniscient [intuitive wisdom] that perceives things just as they are and the phenomenally

---

267. This would appear to be a paraphrase of the statement in the *Vinaya-vibhaṅga*: gzugs kyi sku'i sgo nas ma mthong bas de'i slad du bcom ldan 'das kyi gzugs kyi sku blta bar 'tshal na mchi bar ci gnang/ (H3, vol. 5, fol. 376b.6–376b.7).

268. *dharmadhātu; chos kyi dbyings.*

omniscient [intuitive wisdom that sees what they are] is accepted as the insight of the transcendent intuitive wisdom of the noble beings, which are individually introspective and are not common.

3.1.2.1.1.1.2.3.2.3.2.2.2. Liberation from the Obscuration of Attachment and Liberation from the Obscuration of Hindrance

It is called "completely pure" in comparison to the opposite, which is the nonrealization of emptiness, and the seeing of partial intuitive wisdom, which does not engage in all objects of knowledge, in brief, because of two causes. Which ones? It is because of nonattachment and nonhindrance. Here it is free from the attachment to the truth-status-habit, since insight into the varieties of things has the object of the natural purity of the sentient beings' element; and it is free from hindrance, since omniscient [intuitive wisdom] that perceives things has the object of limitless objects of knowledge. [TL 047A]

3.1.2.1.1.1.2.3.2.3.3. Excellence of Liberation from Inferiority . . .
3.1. The Root Text

«59» The irreversible noble bodhisattvas are a refuge for all beings because of their closeness to the unsurpassed intuitive wisdom of a buddha, since their insights of the intuitive wisdom that knows things just as they are, the intuitive wisdom that knows the varieties of things, and their inner intuitive wisdom are pure. Therefore, these bodhisattvas have been liberated from the obscuration of inferiority. Furthermore, the excellences discussed here belong to bodhisattvas of the eighth stage and above, who have attained excellences superior to those of the seventh stage and below, thereby being freed from the obscuration of inferiority. According to [Asaṅga's] *Commentary*, these excellences refer to the pure insights of the intuitive wisdom possessed by bodhisattvas of the pure stages that know things just as they are, and their intuitive wisdom that knows the varieties of things. Holy irreversible bodhisattvas of the pure stages are a refuge for sentient beings since their insights are close to the unsurpassed Buddha's intuitive wisdom.

3.1.2.1.1.1.2.3.2.3.3.2. [Asaṅga's] Commentary

«60» Thus, irreversible bodhisattvas of the eighth stage and above are a refuge for all beings, since the insight of intuitive wisdom of those bodhisattvas who abide in the stage of irreversibility is either close to the intuitive wisdom that knows things just as they are and [to] the intuitive wisdom that knows the varieties of things of an unsurpassed tathāgata, or they may [actually] possess such intuitive wisdoms. Regarding the bodhisattva excellences such as ethics, etc., it should be known that they are unsurpassed when compared to the bodhisattvas of the seventh stage and below.

The eighth stage and above are called "the stages of irreversibility" since bodhisattvas who have attained these stages will never get a chance to produce selfish mentation because of their complete abandonment of addictive obscuration. This should not be taken as the same as the system explained in other treatises that the two obscurations are abandoned simultaneously and sainthood and buddhahood are attained simultaneously. Moreover, these statements explain that the transcendent wisdom of insight into the realities of things that [also] perceives [the variety of] phenomena is superior to the transcendence of ethics, etc.

3.1.2.1.1.1.2.3.3. The Reason the Disciples' Saṅgha Jewel Is Not Mentioned Here . . . 3.1. Summary Statement

«61» Here there is no explicit mention of the Saṅgha Jewel of the disciples immediately after the Saṅgha of the bodhisattvas, [TL 047B] since the former is not the goal for bodhisattvas to achieve in their continuums, and thus is not worthy of worship. If no negative word is used, this would refer to bodhisattvas. The *Questions of Ugra Sutra* states that a bodhisattva should worship disciples. However, there is no contradiction between these statements because bodhisattvas should pay equal respect to all beings though they do not take [sainthood] as their goal to be achieved.

3.1.2.1.1.1.2.3.3.2. Detailed Exposition . . . 2.1. The Difference between the Disciple Saṅgha and the Bodhisattva Saṅgha

Having known the difference between the wise bodhisattvas, who have the skill in arts to attain buddhahood, and the disciples, one shall never abandon the crescent-moon-like bodhisattvas, who are the cause of perfect enlightenment, and never instead bow down to the starlike disciples, who are not pure in terms of their spirit of altruism. Here, according to another edition, no negative word is used. In that case, this should refer to bodhisattvas.

The distinctions of a bodhisattva are those with respect to basis, nature, act, and fruition. First, [a bodhisattva] will complete the gradual path to enlightenment based on conventional and ultimate realities, as well as the extensive collection of merit and wisdom included in the profound and magnificent gradual path to enlightenment. These constitute the cause for the perfection of great enlightenment.

Second, [a bodhisattva] is endowed with the mandala of wisdom that realizes the meaning of emptiness and compassion, the votive wish that every being should be free from suffering.

[TL 048A] Third, [a bodhisattva] illuminates countless beings, eliminating their darkness of ignorance.

Fourth, [a bodhisattva] has entered into the path that accords with attainment of the full moon of the unsurpassed tathāgata.

[In contrast,] the starlike disciples' realization and abandonment are inferior since they have partial abandonment and have perfected partial intuitive wisdom. Their activities are also inferior because they do not have an aspiration to free sentient beings from their suffering, and are only self-illuminating with the cessation of suffering and its origination.

3.1.2.1.1.2.3.3.2.2. The Reason This Differentiation Is Valid

Owing to the excellence of the realistic reliance on bodhisattvas' pure high resolve, even bodhisattvas who have just first conceived the spirit in the conventional form surpass noble disciples, not to mention other bodhisattvas who have excellences such as the ten powers, etc. "The ten powers" here refers to the power of life, the power of mind, the power of wealth, the power of action, the power of birth, the power of magic, the power of conviction, the power of aspiration, [the power of motivation,] and the power of intuitive wisdom. Alternatively, "bodhisattvas who have just first conceived the spirit" can be interpreted as referring to those who cultivated the spirit in ultimate form, i.e., the bodhisattvas on the first stage.

Someone asserts that, in that case, it would be in contradiction with the thesis that noble disciples directly realize the selflessness of objects.

Answer: There is no such fault. The excellence of joy with which the bodhisattvas on the first stage surpass disciples and hermit buddhas is the spirit of enlightenment in conventional form. Even disciple saints are included, [TL 048B] since they do have the compassion for all beings like a mother who cannot bear to see her only child fallen into a pit of filth and wishes them be free from suffering. Nevertheless, they lack the compassion of taking the responsibility for doing so. Therefore, such noble saint disciples, who have perfected their pure ethics without taints but do not cause others to improve, are also surpassed.

3.1.2.1.1.1.2.3.3.2.3. Sutra Reference

The reason disciples who are concerned about self-benefit are inferior is explained as follows:

Why? Because it is stated that if noble disciples benefit and improve themselves by ethics for the cessation of their own suffering, their attainment is inferior. They are bereft of the aforementioned compassion for those who have broken vows, so their act is inferior. The third line is easy to understand. According to the statement:

> I do not call the noble disciples pure in their ethics, since they only seek their own liberation and do not cut off such [inferior] motivation.

[In contrast,] bodhisattvas are extolled for their distinctive motivation that is the supreme compassion for others, for their distinctive application that maintains pure ethics based on the prevention of selfish thought, and for their distinctive actions that are the bodhisattvas' nourishment for all beings, [supporting them just like] earth, water, fire, and wind; compared to those, the other disciples who maintain ethics [for themselves alone] are like mirror reflections.

3.1.2.1.1.2. Exposition of the Meaning of the Three Jewels . . . 2.1. General Meaning . . . 1.1. The Features of the Object of Refuge

[TL 049A] The positioning of the refuge here delineates the intention of the Buddha's word concerning the refuge; it is not only based on the meaning of the Three Jewels discussed above. The refuge has two aspects: causal and fruitional. As to the former, those who have the spiritual potential for the universal vehicle take the Three Jewels as the goal to be attained. Those who have the spiritual potential for the hermit buddha vehicle and disciple vehicle take the Dharma Jewel and the Saṅgha Jewel as the goals to be attained, respectively. Although disciples also take the Dharma Jewel as the goal, here [the Three Jewels] are specified [to be the goals] for three kinds of practitioners. As to the latter, all three kinds of practitioners who have the spiritual potential take refuge in the Three Jewels. They all regard the path revealer who has accomplished the Three Jewels in a separate continuum as the teacher, the path that was revealed by him as the path to liberation, and the holy Saṅgha that practices that path as the assistant. But they take one of the Three Jewels as the goal to be attained.

3.1.2.1.1.2.1.2. Means of Taking Refuge

Mentally one should regard the Three Jewels as the refuge and protection that will liberate him or her from the intense fear of suffering and obscuration. Orally one should admit so as well. [TL 049B] The fruitional refuge is a kind of refuge that takes one of the Three Jewels as the goal to be attained. The causal refuge is a kind of refuge that regards other persons who have become the protection from fears [for the one who is taking refuge]. As mentioned before, one who is taking causal refuge does not necessarily take all Three Jewels as the fruitional refuge. But for someone who is taking fruitional refuge, all Three Jewels must be taken as the causal refuge. Therefore, all three kinds of practitioners who have spiritual potential take both forms of refuge: causal and fruitional.

3.1.2.1.1.2.1.2. Proofs

Likewise, the *Questions of Ugra Sutra* states as follows:[269]

> O Householder, how does a bodhisattva take refuge in the Buddha? O Householder, a lay bodhisattva should think in this way: "I shall achieve a buddha's body, adorned by the thirty-two

---

269. H63, ff. 5a.7–6a.7. Unusually, Gyaltsap here expands the *Commentary*'s use of sutra quotes by quoting copiously from one not quoted by Asaṅga.

characteristics of a majestic person, and then make effort in cultivating virtuous roots for the attainment of the thirty-two marks
of a majestic person." O Householder! A lay bodhisattva should
take refuge in the Buddha in this manner.

O Householder, a lay bodhisattva should maintain mindfulness like this: "I shall respect and worship the Dharma, request
the Dharma, desire the Dharma, take delight in and believe in
the Dharma, concentrate on the Dharma, protect the Dharma,
promote the Dharma, become a Dharma friend, engage in
Dharma activities, be empowered by the Dharma, be satisfied
by the Dharma, be endowed with the Dharma might, [TL 050A]
be endowed with the tools of the generosity of the Dharma, and
perform the Dharma duty, thereby attaining perfect enlightenment due to the possession of the Dharma. And I shall equally
treat celestial beings, human, and non-celestial beings with the
generosity of the Dharma." O Householder, a lay bodhisattva
should take refuge in the Dharma in this manner.

O Householder, how does a bodhisattva take refuge in the
Saṅgha? O Householder, a lay bodhisattva who takes refuge
in the Saṅgha should maintain a mindfulness like this: "I shall
respectfully welcome a mendicant who is either a stream winner,
or a once returner, or a non-returner, or a saint, or a naive person, or a disciple vehicle person, or a hermit buddha vehicle person, or a universal vehicle person, and listen to his advice, keep
his harmony, and serve that practitioner who is making realistic
effort, thereby attaining unsurpassed perfect enlightenment. I
shall teach the Dharma in order to help beings accomplish the
excellences of the disciples and hermit buddhas." Respect them!
Do not hate them! A lay bodhisattva should take refuge in the
Saṅgha in this manner.

Such respect for the disciples, etc., [TL 050B] is taught in terms of gathering
respectful disciples as a part of the fruitional refuge upon the attainment of
buddhahood.

All Three Jewels are the refuge with respect to the causal refuge. The same
sutra states:

O Householder, a lay bodhisattva takes refuge in the Buddha when endowed with four things. Which four? Not forsaking the spirit of enlightenment, not breaking their commitment, not forsaking great compassion, and not following other vehicles. A lay bodhisattva takes refuge in the Buddha when endowed with these four things.

O Householder, a lay bodhisattva takes refuge in the Dharma when endowed with four things. Which four? Receiving the Dharma by relying upon and serving a Dharma teacher, properly analyzing the meaning of the Dharma, giving lectures to others based on their own study and understanding, and dedicating to the unsurpassed enlightenment the virtuous roots cultivated by means of the generosity of the Dharma. A lay bodhisattva takes refuge in the Dharma when endowed with these four things.

O Householder, a lay bodhisattva takes refuge in the Saṅgha when endowed with four things. Which four? Making faultless disciples conceive the spirit of enlightenment, collecting disciples by means of either the generosity of wealth or the generosity of Dharma, relying upon the bodhisattva Saṅgha of nonregression but not the disciple Saṅgha, and not seeking the liberation of the disciples.

Furthermore, the sutra states that one recalls the Buddha while seeing an image of a tathāgata, [TL 051A] recalls the Dharma while hearing the Dharma, and recalls the spirit of enlightenment while seeing the disciple Saṅgha. Moreover, one practices generosity out of the votive prayer that one will become close to the Buddha, and does so in order to guard the Dharma, and dedicates such generosity to attain unsurpassed perfect enlightenment. These three things in turn are taking refuge in the Three Jewels, respectively.

Therefore, any outsider refuge is not a realistic protection, since [in those traditions] certain distinguished persons [still] in the life cycle are labeled as liberated and sought as refuge. As an insider, one seeks liberation with the motivation driven by the determination to attain freedom and with the distaste for the pervasive suffering of creation. The ethics with such a motivation is the one that sets the practitioner free. It should be known that the outsiders have deviated from the Dharma. Anyone who studies and contemplates this treatise must first observe whether or not he or she can take refuge sincerely. If one perfectly knows this meaning of refuge, one will understand that all sutras and treatises are part of the object of refuge. Someone who lacks such practice declares that he will only practice a little of the refuge. This sort of humble statement is pretentious and foolish, lacking any understanding!

3.1.2.1.1.2.2. The Ramifications . . . 2.1. The Arrangement of Superficial Refuge . . . 1.1. Question

«62» [TL 051B] Now, for what intended purpose and for the sake of which disciples did the Bhagavān make the arrangement of the three refuges? This arrangement of the three refuges was made with respect to six kinds of people. It is not just about ultimate refuge. The main delineation here is about conventional refuge in order to guide disciples step by step into the three vehicles.

3.1.2.1.1.2.2.1.2. Answer . . . 2.1. The Root Text

The first line [of this verse] states the function [of refuge]. The next three lines state the specific disciples. Those who have the spiritual potential for the universal vehicle take all Three Jewels as the fruitional refuge. However, the Dharma Jewel and the Saṅgha Jewel are included within the Buddha Jewel since the latter is endowed with ultimate Dharma and [ultimate] entourages. Therefore, the Three Jewels are specified as the fruitional refuges for the three kinds of people that have spiritual potential. [Particularly,] those who have the potential for the universal vehicle take the Teacher, the Buddha, as the goal to be attained. Those who have the potential for the hermit buddha vehicle seek complete elimination of suffering by means of the teaching of realization, the holy Dharma Jewel, which is the teaching of the profound relativistic origination, and take it as the goal to be attained. Those who have the potential for the disciple vehicle seek sainthood by means of listening to others' oral teaching, and take the learners, the saints, as the goal to be attained. The refuges are arranged by the Bhagavān in three fruitional forms in relation to the practitioners of the three vehicles. [TL 052A]

The refuges are arranged in three causal forms in order to make us realize that the accomplished Three Jewels included in teacher, teaching, learner saints, and noble bodhisattvas are the causal refuge for the practitioners of the three vehicles. In addition, these are arranged in this way in relation to three kinds of conviction of those who have not yet entered into the path. They have different convictions in worshiping the Three Jewels, etc.

In short, the refuges are arranged in three fruitional forms with respect to the goals to be attained by three kinds of people who have spiritual potential. The accomplished Three Jewels are arranged as the causal refuge for all three kinds of people who have potential. The accomplished Three Jewels are arranged as specific causal refuges for those who have not yet entered the path, since they have different convictions in worshiping the Three Jewels, etc.

3.1.2.1.1.2.2.1.2.2. [Asaṅga's] Commentary

The purpose of teaching the Teacher's excellences and making it understood by the statement [TL 052B] "who is the supreme person among all who have two feet" is to arrange the Buddha Jewel as the refuge for persons of the bodhisattva vehicle who seek buddhahood as the goal to be attained, for three kinds of people who have spiritual potential and have conviction about offering excellent service to the Buddha (as the causal refuge), and for those who have not yet entered the path but have conviction about offering excellent service, such as offerings, etc., to the Buddha. It is valid [to arrange Buddha as a refuge] since this uses the common agreement in the world as the proof. Among all beings that have two feet, the Buddha is the most distinguished, since he is called "refuge." It is also based on many other lines of reasoning that prove the Buddha to be a refuge. It is done so in order to prove that our Teacher is superior to the other [teachers].

The purpose of teaching the excellences of the Teacher's teaching and making it understood by the statement "who is the supreme person among all who are free from attachment" is to arrange the Dharma Jewel as the refuge to persons of the hermit buddha vehicle who strive to realize the profound teaching of relativistic origination with respect to the process and counter-process of the life cycle as well as the limit of reification-free relativistic origination, thereby eliminating suffering and making this the goal to be attained, and to both who have conviction about offering excellent service to the Dharma. It is valid to arrange the excellences of abandonment that is free from the seeds to be abandoned and is endowed with the quality of nonregression as a refuge, since it is done to make it understood that the worldly nonattachment that can regress is not the Dharma Jewel.

The purpose of teaching the excellences of saints, learners of the Teacher's teaching, and making it understood by the statement "who is the supreme person among all entourages" is to arrange the Saṅgha Jewel as the refuge for persons of the disciple vehicle [TL 053A] who try to realize sainthood as the goal to be attained by following others' verbal [teaching], to three kinds of people who have the spiritual potential and take the accomplished Saṅgha Jewel as the causal refuge, and to those who have not yet entered the path but have conviction about offering excellent service, such as service to the Saṅgha, as a field of merit, regarding them as an assistant in practicing paths, etc. A person is established as a Saṅgha Jewel when he or she has become a holy being, since such a one has eliminated any doubts as to the authenticity of the refuge and is endowed with immutable faith. On the other side, childish ones cannot be so established, since it is possible for them to be converted to believe in other teachers. The Saṅgha consists of at least four persons, rather than a single person. Thus it is called "entourage."

This [passage] is an exposition of the arrangement of refuge in general, so it also talks about the noble persons of the individual vehicle. A certain wicked teacher asserts that noble disciples and saints are not worthy of being noble beings and saints. To this we respond: This would be like saying that the Buddha, our Teacher, could not make those disciples who made realistic effort in meditation attain authentic liberation by first turning the Dharma wheel of the four noble truths in Vārāṇasī. This is a serious wrong view that repudiates the Teacher and his teachings. This sin will be graver than killing many tens of thousands of sentient beings. Anyone who wishes good for oneself must be extremely cautious about this! [TL 053B]

3.1.2.1.1.2.2.1.2.3. Précis

«63» Thus, in brief, these statements were taught by the Bhagavān to make the arrangement of the differentiation of the three refuges in terms of six kinds of people for three kinds of purposes. This [arrangement] is given on a conventional basis, which is the arrangement of the conventional refuge, in order to make sentient beings gradually enter into [different] vehicles from the disciple vehicle up to the universal vehicle.

The meanings of the conventional refuge and ultimate refuge are as follows: those who are definite in disciple lineage or hermit buddha lineage regard the sainthood of the individual vehicle as the only goal to be attained. They do not desire a higher practice and do not think it is a necessity. A refuge that is not the ultimate in practice but is thought to be by some disciples is a conventional refuge, similar to the conventional reality that actually does not have truth status but is thought to have such. A refuge that is the real ultimate in practice is an ultimate refuge. The arrangement of conventional refuge is made in order to guide those of the disciple lineage who are determined to attain the fruition of sainthood. It is quite clear that [Asaṅga's] *Commentary* proves that there is only the one ultimate vehicle.

3.1.2.1.1.2.2.2. The Arrangement of Ultimate Refuge . . . 2.1. Establishing That Refuges Other Than Buddha Are Not the Ultimate Refuge . . . 1.1. The Root Text [TL 054A]

«64» The Dharma consists of two kinds: verbal and realizational. The teaching that is based on words, terms, and letters is not the ultimate refuge to be attained since it will be abandoned as [merely] a means to attain fruition, when the ultimate fruition, the perfect realization of ultimate reality, is attained, just like a ferry [that will be left behind when one has crossed a river]. This means that the teaching is not one's ultimate refuge. It does not mean that language is no longer useful upon the attainment of buddhahood.

The intuitive wisdom that realizes the emptiness of truth status and freedom from all reification in the mental continuum of a noble bodhisattva is not the ultimate refuge, since it is deceptive in terms of its appearance of taintlessness to the mind of a noble bodhisattva, while in reality the taints have not yet been purified. Someone asserts that the emptiness of truth status means deception, thereby accepting that anything created is not the ultimate refuge. Therefore, he also does not accept that the truth of the path within the Buddha's mental continuum as well as the two kinds of physical [buddha] body are the ultimate refuge. Someone claims that the two kinds of material body of the Buddha are not even the real Buddha. This statement cannot be differentiated from an outsider fundamentalist's [TL 054B] assertion that the Sage has not rectified his faults, since he speaks and has a mind and hands, etc. The Great Champions made a great effort

in proclaiming various validating reasons that prove that the excellent emanation of the Buddha is the Buddha who has rectified all his faults and is
endowed with all excellences. The person who made such a [contrary] statement pretended that he is a master of Buddhism, which would really make
a jackal king into a chief who will destroy the teaching, since he repudiates
[the excellent emanation of the Buddha] as being the Buddha. Anyone who
wants to be Buddhist should discard this as specious reasoning! Therefore,
it should be known that this also applies to the assertion that the physical
buddha bodies appear only in the disciples' vision and are nothing to be
included in the Buddha's own continuum, as well as the assertion that no
intuitive wisdom is included in the Buddha's own experience.

If the truth of the path within the mental continuum of a noble bodhisattva is not the ultimate refuge, it can be understood by the same token
that, for noble bodhisattvas, the truth of the path according to the disciple vehicle, etc., is not the ultimate refuge. The nirvana-without-remainder
within the mental continuum of a disciple saint, the total pacification of
suffering and its origination, is not the ultimate refuge, since their mere
cessation of addiction and suffering is a kind of cessation with [still a more
subtle] remainder. Therefore, it should be known by implication that they
still experience the fear of objective obscuration. [TL 055A] [Asaṅga's] *Commentary* gives a detailed explanation on this point. Saints of the disciple
and hermit buddha vehicles are not the ultimate refuge since their objective
obscurations still remain. Although it can be established only on the basis
of the reason just above, it is stated separately in order to prove the ultimate
one-vehicle [theory], since saints of the disciple and hermit buddha vehicles
do seek liberation from objective obscurations when they experience the
fear of them.

The two types of Dharma as well as the noble beings other than the Buddha are not the ultimate, unsurpassed refuge. There is no doubt [allayed by]
saying that the teaching is not [such a refuge], but it is done in order to make
the analysis complete.

3.1.2.1.1.2.2.2.1.2. [Asaṅga's] Commentary . . . 2.1. Showing That Teaching Is
Not the Ultimate Refuge

«65» The Dharma has two kinds: the Dharma as teaching and the
Dharma as realization. The Dharma as teaching is the expression of the

sutras, etc. This shows that the verbal teaching included within the Buddha's continuum is the ultimate truth. However, it is not so for the teaching that appears to the perception of hearing consciousness and mental consciousness included within disciples' continuums, as well as the Buddha's word consisting of the twelve branches that are distinguished from others by the disciples' continuums. It is included in the collection of name, term, and letter and is called "ferry-like" since [it will be abandoned] when the ultimate path is realized. One does not need to rely upon the crutch of words that are nevertheless necessary for the attainment of fruition, when the realization of the ultimate reality, which is the object of the path, has been perfected, as it is said that "all teachings are ferry-like for the one who knows the meaning." [TL 055B]

3.1.2.1.1.2.2.2.1.2.2. Showing That Realization[al Dharma] Is Not the Ultimate Refuge

«66» The Dharma as realization has two types: causal and fruitional, which are the truth of the path and the truth of cessation, and are called "that which realizes" and "that which is realized," respectively. This states the excellences of the realization of the truth of cessation, not the nature of the object to be realized. Here, one realizes that the path that realizes emptiness in the mental continuum of a noble bodhisattva has the characteristic of a created thing. This is a general statement. The meaning of deceptiveness and the way of impermanence are to be explained afterward. There is no doubt that anything created is necessarily not an ultimate refuge. As just mentioned, anything that is realized as the path having the characteristic of a creation is superficial, and not in accord with [ultimate] truth, hence is deceptive, as mentioned in the root text. Anything deceptive is unfit to be the refuge that is the ultimate for practice. Anything unfit to be the refuge that is the ultimate for practice is impermanent since it was cultivated before in the continuum and then does not exist in the ultimate for practice. Anything impermanent is not the ultimate refuge. Someone asserts that permanence is pervasive in all created things. This contradicts, and shows that he does not understand, the meaning of the root text statement below.

The cessation that is realized by means of such a path is distinguished from others by the mere annihilation of addictions and sufferings by way of the disciple vehicle, just like the extinction of a lamp. [TL 056A] This kind of nirvana-without-remainder, in which the perception that observes the mass of beings has declined and only the bliss of peace is experienced in meditative trance, is not the ultimate refuge. This should be determined, since an annihilation coming from the freedom from addiction and suffering is not worthy to be the ultimate or final refuge. It is indeed a refuge, but not the ultimate refuge.

As for the way of the disciples, someone claims that nirvana being like the extinction of a lamp is not accepted as [Asaṅga's] personal intention, since [Asaṅga's] *Commentary* says so in order to refute the disciples' wrong idea that such nirvana is the ultimate refuge, despite the fact that the root text proves this point. Answer: This is not true. As it says in [Haribhadra's] *Clear Meaning*, "since [he] intended a presentation of the three methods [of proof], they are condensed [into such]." Hence, the disciple vehicle arranged by the disciple schools does not accord with reality. It is not necessary to explain the example of a lamp's extinction as the extinction of the physical-mental continuum; instead [it should be explained] as the extinction of suffering produced by addiction and the decline of the perception that observes all beings, while becoming completely entranced in meditative equipoise in the untainted sphere. [TL 056B] Hence, the arrangement of the disciple school's nirvana-without-remainder as a conventional refuge, not the ultimate refuge, is made for those disciples who are not determined in that lineage and are changeable in their [goal of] enlightenment, as well as those who [once] were determined in that lineage, have relaxed from the suffering of the life cycle owing to the attainment of a nirvana-without-remainder, and are awakened and guided into the universal vehicle by the exhortation of the lights radiated by the buddhas. Thus, [Asaṅga] must accept the arrangement of the disciples' nirvana-without-remainder by the way of the disciple vehicle, which is proved by validating reason. As to the statement below that no nirvana will be attained before buddhahood, it refers to the nirvana that is free from all miseries in connection with the twelve links of relativistic origination, including [miseries arising from] both the category of addictive obscurations as well as the category of objective obscurations. Therefore, it is not correct to think that there is no real nirvana attained among disciples.

Some Experientialists who accept the three final vehicles assert that in the context of the disciples' nirvana-without-remainder there is no [subtle intuitive wisdom] corresponding to the [full] intuition that realizes selflessness.

Someone who does not understand the meaning of the root text and [Asaṅga's] *Commentary* does not accept the nirvana-without-remainder of the disciples as the ultimate refuge, without having a good reason. [TL 057A] He does not know that the word "mere" in [Asaṅga's] *Commentary* shows that the disciples have not yet overcome the fear of the objective obscurations; instead he takes the annihilation [nirvana], the extinction of the physical-mental continuum, as the reason. It is clear that he does not understand the meaning of this treatise.

« 67 » The Saṅgha assembly of nobles is not the ultimate refuge. This so-called Saṅgha here is a designation for the entourages of noble beings of the individual vehicle and noble bodhisattvas concerned with all three vehicles. They take refuge in the Tathāgata out of constant fear of obscurations, seek freedom from the fear, still have something to learn about the means to overcome the fear and something to be done in terms of the path, and are approaching the unsurpassed perfect enlightenment.

A detailed exposition regarding why they are approaching enlightenment has four parts: (1) having fear; (2) taking refuge; (3) seeking freedom; and (4) being in need of learning.

First, how do they fear? The saints who have abandoned rebirths live in constant fear of all tainted creational activity because of the unbearable objective obscuration that is untainted ignorance, just like facing enemies who raise swords, since they have not yet abandoned the evolutionary instincts of addiction. Therefore, they have not attained the ultimate blissful freedom.

Second, an ultimate refuge does not seek refuge. The saints still feel fear, just as sentient beings in the hells without protection [feel fear], and so seek freedom from fears. [TL 057B] Thus, they take refuge in the perfect Tathāgata out of fear of objective obscurations.

Third, anyone who takes refuge out of such fear must seek freedom from fear in order to overcome the fear of the objective obscurations in their continuums. Therefore, [the saints] still have things to learn and to do with respect to the abandonment of the basis of the fear, the subtle evolutionary instincts [that cause] the assumption of bad states.[270]

270. *gnas ngan len.*

Fourth, they are approaching the unsurpassed perfect enlightenment since they still need to learn and work on the attainment of the state of the Bull [of sages], who has no fear of either of the two kinds of obscuration. Those who are in favor of the Experientialist school assert that this treatise advocates only the three vehicles in the ultimate sense. Except for such people, no one doubts whether or not it proves the ultimate one vehicle. Someone claims that [the ultimate one vehicle] is taught for those whose enlightenment is changeable. Answer: If that were true, then the *White Lotus Sutra* would also be a sutra that advocates the three vehicles in the ultimate sense. But it is not true. Thus, the just-mentioned Saṅgha is a partial refuge as a cause of the ultimate refuge, not the ultimate one. In conclusion, this [passage] states that these two kinds of refuge are not a refuge in the ultimate sense. [TL 058A] Someone claims that it proves that [these two kinds of refuge] are not the ultimate truth body. But such a thesis cannot be established since it lacks a subject needing to be known.

3.1.2.1.1.2.2.2.1.2. Establishing That Only Buddha Is the Ultimate Refuge ... 2.1. The Root Text

Ultimately, only the Buddha is a refuge for beings because the Muni is endowed with the truth body that is free from all kinds of fear. The Buddha has attained fearlessness, not like someone who has fallen down relying upon other fallen ones. This shows the reason the Buddha is worthy of being the ultimate refuge. [Buddhahood] is the ultimate attainment of the Saṅgha of noble beings of the three vehicles who are in the final existence on the tenth stage and below. This shows the reason the Buddha is able to protect, since it states that the Muni Buddha Bhagavān is the causal refuge for them as well as that buddhahood is the fruitional refuge. Not only has the Muni Buddha Bhagavān overcome all fears, but he also protects all beings who still have fears with unbiased compassion, not for reward, reputation, etc. Therefore, the Buddha is the ultimate refuge.

3.1.2.1.1.2.2.2.1.2.2. [Asaṅga's] Commentary

«68» This states that, in this world of sentient beings without protection and refuge, only the Tathāgata, the Saint, the Perfectly Enlightened One is the unending refuge until the end of the life cycle benefiting beings, equal to the future reality-limit, the eternal refuge since the Buddha is deathless, everlasting refuge since there is no interruption, immutable refuge since the Buddha will not grow old, ultimate refuge since the Buddha is not deceptive. As aforementioned, the Muni is distinguished from others by the realization of "no production and no destruction," the limit of reality, possessing the truth body that frees from attachment and is free from attachment [TL 058B] and has the characteristic of two pure truths, as well as since the Saṅgha of the three vehicles sets the attainment of the ultimate pure truth body as the ultimate goal. This eternal, immutable, peaceful, firm refuge that is the only one should be known in detail by following the *Shrīmālādevī Lion's Roar Sutra.*

3.1.2.1.1.3. Exposition of the Word "Jewel" ... 3.1. The Root Text

«69» [The Sanskrit word] *ratna* means precious. Its contextual etymology would be "rare" and "supreme" when the word is expanded. [These are] jewels since they are endowed with six similar features. These are precious like jewels since they rarely appear. These do not have the problem that desired goals cannot be accomplished since they are free from stains of opposite force. These are endowed with great excellences since they are powerful. These are of great benefit since they are the ornament of the world. These are unique since they are supreme among all that are endowed with excellences. These are called "jewels" since they are changeless in bestowing fruitions whether given praise or criticism.

3.1.2.1.1.3.2. [Asaṅga's] Commentary

«70» In short, by the sixfold common feature with jewels, these Three Jewels named "Buddha, Dharma, and Saṅgha" are said to be similar to jewels. That is to say:

1. By means of jewels' common feature of rarity, [TL 059A] since those people who have not cultivated the root of virtue in many eons cannot get any chance to meet the Three Jewels. This shows that we should take refuge in them with great effort since they are supreme among all precious things, extremely rare.

2. By means of their common feature of purity, since they are free in all respects from taints of deceptiveness and inability to grant refuge. The

Three Jewels are similar to the wish-fulfilling jewels that are purified from taints of dust, etc. This shows that the Three Jewels do not have the fault of inability to offer protection, and that the Three Jewels are a worthy refuge, while worldly deities are not reasonably functional as refuges.

3. By means of their common feature of power, since they are endowed with inconceivable excellences such as six superknowledges, etc. The Three Jewels are similar to the wish-fulfilling jewels that can bestow necessities such as food, clothing, etc. This shows that the Three Jewels are endowed with the excellences of being refuges and providing protection.

4. By means of their common feature of being the ornament of the world, since they are the cause of virtuous thought, which seeks higher rebirth and ultimate excellences, developed by all beings. The Three Jewels are similar to wish-fulfilling jewels that bestow all desires in the world. This shows the benefit and the purpose of taking refuge in the Three Jewels.

5. By means of their common feature of being superior to artificial jewels, since they are transcendent. The Three Jewels are similar to wish-fulfilling jewels that are superior to artificial jewels. This shows that the Three Jewels are the unsurpassed, supreme refuge, unlike worldly deities, who are only apparent refuges.

6. By means of their feature in common with wish-granting gems of not being liable to change because of praise or contempt, etc., [TL 059B] because they are manifested by experiential realization of ultimate reality with its nature of not being created by cause and condition, thus [they] are not giving refuge because of praise or contempt, etc.

Completely described above is the fruition that consists of the Three Jewels to be found.

3.1.2.1.2. Arrangement of Cause and Conditions of Attaining Fruitional Three Jewels . . . 2.1. General Arrangement . . . 1.1. General Prelude

«71» Immediately after the teachings of the fruitional Three Jewels, there is one verse with reference to the cause and conditions of the production of the Three Jewels, which are the source of all common good things and transcendent purities.

3.1.2.1.2.1.2. The Implications of Inconceivability . . . 2.1. Statement

«72» I shall explain the cause and conditions comprised of the Victor's deeds from which arise the virtuous Three Jewels to be attained. "Virtuous" means excellent. Reality mingled with taints is the substantial cause.[271] And the enlightenment that is free from taints, the stainless excellences of the Buddha, and that Victor's enlightened activities are the cooperating conditions.[272] Whose objects are these? These four in their complete forms without remaining are the objects of buddhas, who perceive the ultimate.

3.1.2.1.2.1.2.2. Explanation . . . 2.1. Question

«73» What is elucidated by this verse? [TL 060A]

3.1.2.1.2.1.2.2.2. Answer . . . 2.1. Being Inconceivable, Shown to be the Sphere of Buddhas Alone . . . 1.1. The Root Text

The spiritual potential of these fruitional Three Jewels, namely, the complete cause and conditions [for the Three Jewels] without remaining, is the direct object of the omniscient buddhas. As it is inconceivable in fourfold for others to directly [behold them,] for four reasons, respectively, which I will explain later, it is the direct sphere of buddhas alone.

The former verse first describes one cause and three conditions and then shows whose objects these are; the latter further shows the reason.

3.1.2.1.2.1.2.2.2.1.2. The Commentary

«74» Here, the "reality mingled with taints" is the element, the naturally pure ultimate truth, which is termed the "tathāgata essence" when unreleased from the sheath of addictions. As to [reality] having two sorts of purities, there is not the slightest indication in the *Tathāgata Essence Sutra* along with its commentary, *The Sublime Continuum*, that the formal name[273] the "tathāgata essence" has such a connotation. Therefore, it is

---

271. *upādāna, nye bar len pa'i gnas.*
272. *sahakārikāraṇa, lhan cig byed pa'i rkyen.*
273. *dngos ming.*

merely out of someone's own whim to take the truth body as the essence. This is not taken as the system of this treatise and its explanation. To prove the essence to be the truth body that is free from taints by using other sutras is regarded as a sign of ignorance of reasonings. [TL 060B]

The "suchness free from taints" is a reality in which all taints have come to an end; therefore, it is in the nature of the transformation of that reality in the stage of the Buddha, which is termed "truth body of the Tathāgata."

Objection: "Your claim is completely contradictory, because you accept reality mingled with taints as the one [thing] free from taints."

Reply: "Nonsense! You did not examine it well with reasoning. What I said is that reality mingled with taints, when completely transformed, is called the "truth body." If not, then sentient beings themselves would inevitably be buddhas, if they are presumed to be buddhas whose taints no longer exist. Therefore, reality mingled with taints is accepted as the tathāgata essence and reality free from taints is accepted as the truth body. Consequently, we must not accept the essence as the truth body! Likewise, there is not the slightest contradiction in accepting reality mingled with taints as the truth body when all taints have come to an end. If reality mingled with taints could never be free from all taints, sentient beings would never become buddhas. You must also accept that white woolen serge would never be transformed into a red color. This is due to your not properly knowing how to present collections and continuities,[274] and finally amounts to accepting the outsiders' view of a permanent, real [entity].

"Taintless excellences of the Buddha" refers to the transcendent qualities of the Buddha, the excellences of freedom, including the ten powers and so on, and the evolved excellences, existing within or depending [TL 061A] upon this truth body of the Tathāgata, in the nature of the transformation of the mind mingled with taints into the pure mind. "The Victor's enlightened activities" refers to the thirty-two unsurpassed enlightened activities of these excellences of the Buddha, ten powers, etc., which, for example, constantly give prophetic messages to bodhisattvas, spontaneously acting without disappearance, firmly flowing without interruption, and unceasingly engaging. Furthermore, these four topics are inconceivable for four reasons, respectively; thus, they are called the "object of omniscience."

274. *tshogs rgyun legs par 'jog mi shes shing.*

3.1.2.1.2.1.2.2.2.2.2. Proof of Inconceivability . . . 2.1. Question

«75» Then, for which four reasons?

3.1.2.1.2.1.2.2.2.2.2.2. Answer . . . 2.1. The Root Text

Because reality mixed with taints is the intrinsic purity of the minds of sentient beings, it is naturally pure, and yet mixed with addictions. That these two [incompatible] things share a common ground is something inconceivable and difficult to understand. Because reality free from taints is originally free from addictions and also is pure and free from incidental taints, this is difficult to understand. Because the excellences are free from taints and yet are inseparable from the continuums of addicted ordinary individuals in the context of the nature of reality, this is difficult to understand. Because the enlightened activities are spontaneous and there are no conceptual thoughts about doing the activities, this fact is inconceivable and difficult to understand. [TL 061B]

3.1.2.1.2.1.2.2.2.2.2.2. The Commentary . . . 2.1. Difficulty of Understanding Reality Mingled with Taints . . . 1.1. The Main Meaning

«76» Here, reality mingled with taints, which is the emptiness of intrinsic reality of the minds of sentient beings, is simultaneously of intrinsic purity and addiction where the minds of sentient beings are contaminated; this is an inconceivable place in the sense that the two realities are difficult to understand. If the mind is contaminated by the addictions, then we must accept the relativity of the contaminated and contaminating. Such being the case, it would be extremely difficult to establish emptiness of intrinsic reality. But we must accept the following two concepts that share a common ground: all things are devoid of intrinsic identifiability even as small as a single atom, and all functionality is valid. This is similar to the difficulty of understanding the emptiness of intrinsic reality of the minds of sentient beings and to the difficulty of understanding reality mingled with taints. Furthermore, [this is an inconceivable place] because this object is not even realized by the wisdom of hermit buddhas themselves who believe that the way of the profound Dharma is emptiness free from reification. The claim that [hermit buddhas] could not understand it [even] a little is contradictory to the meaning of the reference.

3.1.2.1.2.1.2.2.2.2.2.1.2. Sutra Reference

«77» [To paraphrase the Buddha's statement in the *Shrīmālādevī Lion's Roar Sutra*:][275]

Thus, "O Devī, these two things are quite difficult to understand. What two things? It is difficult to understand" by validating cognition "that the mind is naturally pure, devoid of any intrinsic identity" even as small as single atom. "It is also difficult to understand that this same mind has derivative addictions," which alone is not difficult to understand, but its compatibility in [seeming] dichotomy with the former is difficult to understand. The difficulty of understanding the former, [TL 062A] knowing how to represent it as proved by validating cognition, is similar to the difficulty of understanding a compatible dichotomy. In knowing how to present properly the status of the emptiness of intrinsic reality as verified by validating cognition, there is no way not to accept the conventional as verified by validating cognition. Not knowing this will amount to mere presumption of the negation of truth status and prevent the person from entering into the company of experts in the two realities. Therefore, one should be expert in these two things: there is no such thing, even as small as a single atom, that is the functional basis of the sign-habit,[276] and [yet] all functionality must be accepted. "O Devī, you and bodhisattvas endowed with great excellences alone can understand these two things. O Devī, for the others, disciples and hermit buddhas, these two things," which can be accepted as the integration of the two realities, "are to be directly understood only by means of following their faith in the Tathāgata."

---

275. This quote is again paraphrased (see above, notes 189, 205, 256, etc.). To give an idea of the level of paraphrase here, in this instance I have put quote marks over the actual words from the sutra.

276. *mtshan 'dzin.*

3.1.2.1.2.1.2.2.2.1.2.2.2. Difficulty of Understanding Reality Free from Taints ... 2.1. The Main Meaning

«78» Here, reality free from taints does not originally have addictions from taints, yet is purified from incidental taints afterward; this compatible dichotomy is an inconceivable place, difficult to understand.

The intellect having the aspect of virtuously aspiring for the apprehension of reality is in the nature of beings, whereas the addictions such as attachment are inappropriate and unable to apprehend reality. We can understand a similar situation by examining each habit pattern[277] of other addictions. When the mind is tainted by the addictions, the addictions can apprehend the mind, and the "principal" mind consciousness and its "retinue," mental functions of addictions, [TL 062B] become the same entity.

Objection: If the addictions did not apprehend reality, then this would be in contradiction to [the fact that reality is] mingled with taints.

Reply: The mind is tainted by the addictions. If [the addictions] were not obscurations to [seeing] the emptiness of intrinsic reality of the mind, it would be reasonable for us to perceive [reality] directly. Just because our minds are obscured by the fault of these taints and are unable to perceive [reality], this reality is called "being mingled with taints."

Objection: In that case, reality free from taints would be inevitably mingled with taints, because if there were no obscuring taints, ordinary individuals would directly see; but the minds of ordinary individuals are obscured by these taints, thereby they do not see.

Reply: Ordinary individuals do not see the reality of the Buddha because of obscuration within their minds. That fact cannot prove the excellences of the Buddha are mingled with taints. [On the other hand,] it is valid to state that the reality of their continuums is mingled with taints when the minds of sentient beings are obscured by taints, as the minds of sentient beings and their reality are the same entities. Furthermore, although there is not the slightest habit pattern of taints infiltrated into the reality of a sentient being's mind, we shall not interpret "originally not tainted by erroneous engagement" as reality existing in the minds of sentient beings [already] free from taints.

277. *'dzin stangs.*

3.1.2.1.2.1.2.2.2.2.2.2.2. Sutra Reference

«79» Thus, [the Buddha states in the *King Dhāraṇīshvara Sutra*:]

The mind is naturally clear-light transparency. This is known as it is directly by noble beings. [TL 063A] Thus, once having contemplated that, the Buddha achieved the unsurpassed perfect enlightenment by the intuitive wisdom endowed with the singular momentariness [that incorporates all time].

The former half of this quote is the proof of [reality free from taints] as originally not having addictions, and the latter half is the proof of the purification of incidental taints afterward.

3.1.2.1.2.1.2.2.2.2.2.2.3. Difficulty of Understanding Excellences Free from Taints . . . 3.1. Thesis

«80» Here, the stainless excellences of the Buddha are just the absence of stains, and hence are always found even in the stage of ordinary individuals who are totally afflicted, although from the perspective of their own experience, because they exist without any distinction between earlier and later [times], this utterly undifferentiated reality abides [within them], and this is inconceivable. That is because it is difficult to understand that there is no distinction between reality that is isolated from all taints and reality mingled with taints in the context of nature, unlike [for example, differentiating between the colors] blue and yellow.

3.1.2.1.2.1.2.2.2.2.2.3.2. Proof

«81» Thus, [to paraphrase the Buddha's statement in the *Buddha Garland Sutra*:]

There is no one among the mass of sentient beings in whom producing all the intuitive wisdom of the Tathāgata regarding the emptiness of intrinsic reality, the reality of all things, does not penetrate. Nevertheless, the intuitive wisdom of the Tathāgata, the truth body, does not manifest in the continuums of ordinary individuals because they are bound by the grasping at the concept[278] of the truth status of the person and aggregates. When free from this concept-habit, the intuitive wisdom of omniscience, which is self-arising, makes its appearance unobstructedly. [TL 063B]

This statement shows that all sentient beings without discrimination have the possibility of producing all excellences of the Buddha in their continuums, as well as the so-called emptiness of intrinsic reality, which is established as the reality of the Buddha when purified from all taints and is also established as the reality of sentient beings when mingled with taints. But sentient beings cannot directly see emptiness because of the obscuration of their grasping at truth status; otherwise, the intuitive wisdom of the Tathāgata would arise. This is difficult to understand, similar to the difficulty of understanding the twofold truth above.

3.1.2.1.2.1.2.2.2.2.2.3.3. Sutra Reference . . . 3.1. The Metaphor

The metaphor for the factor to be obscured is [given in the *Buddha Garland Sutra*] as follows:[279]

O victor children, suppose there were a canvas with a big painting equal to the billion-world galactic universe. And on this big canvas, the whole billion-world galactic universe would be painted completely. The vast surrounding horizon would be painted in the exact size of the vast surrounding horizon. The great earth would be painted in the exact size of the great earth. The two-thousand-world universe would be painted in its exact size. [Likewise,] the one-thousand-world universe, the four continents, the great ocean, the southern Jambu continent, the eastern Videha continent, the [western] Godānīya continent, the northern Kuru continent, Mount Sumeru, the mansions of celestial beings living on earth, of celestial beings living in the

278. *'du shes kyi 'dzin pa*.

279. This and all of the subsequent quotes within this subsection are from the same passage in the *Buddha Garland Sutra*.

desire-world, and of celestial beings living in the material-world; all of these would be painted in their exact sizes. Hence, this big canvas would have the same width and length as the billion-world galactic universe.

The metaphor for the obscuring factor is:

This very big canvas would then be placed within one subatomic particle. Just as this big canvas was placed within one subatomic particle, in each of all the other subatomic particles there would be a big canvas of the same size to be placed.

The metaphor for the spiritual teacher who removes the obscuring factor is:

Suppose there should be born one person, sagacious, shrewd, clever, and intelligent, knowing how to recognize that [big canvas]. And his eyes were divine eyes that were perfectly pure and clear-light transparent. With these divine eyes he would perceive [and wonder]: "Why does this big canvas of such a great nature dwell in such a small subatomic particle! It is of no use to anybody!"

"Sagacious" and so on are the metaphors for the knowledge of things as they are, the knowledge of things as they are found, the clear sense faculties, the wisdom endowed with mindfulness, and the analytical skills.

The metaphor for the teacher's resolve to care for disciples is:

So he would think: "Aha! I shall break this subatomic particle with the force of my thunderbolt of great effort and make this great canvas useful for the beings." [TL 064A]

The metaphor for his engaging in the deed is:

Then, producing the force of great effort, he would break this subatomic particle with a tiny thunderbolt vajra and would make that great canvas useful for all the beings. Not only for one sub-

atomic particle, he would also do the same for all the other subatomic particles.

3.1.2.1.2.1.2.2.2.2.2.2.3.3.2. The Implications

The topic of the metaphor for the factor to be obscured is as follows:[280]

> Similarly, buddha child, the profound intuitive wisdom, the
> immeasurable extensive intuitive wisdom of a tathāgata, and
> the intuitive wisdom of caring for all sentient beings are possible
> to be produced in the continuums of sentient beings, and reality,
> which is the object of meditation producing the intuitive wis-
> dom of a buddha and is established as a buddha when it has been
> purified from taints, thoroughly penetrates the continuum of
> each sentient being. And the continuum of each sentient being
> is akin to the immeasurable intuitive wisdom of a tathāgata.

I shall slightly elaborate on the points of these metaphors. The metaphor of the inconceivable big canvas with the size equal to the billion-world
galactic universe was used [by the Buddha] for the purpose of stopping the
erroneous conceptual thought of a certain future disciple who would accept
that a buddha, who has perfected all the excellences of elimination and
realization, primordially exists within the continuum of a sentient being.
Otherwise, there is no need [for the Buddha] to use the metaphor that does
not exist among objects of knowledge.

Objection: "That has not been proved to be an erroneous conceptual
thought."

Reply: "Let us closely examine this assertion that the truth body endowed
with the twofold purity exists within the continuum of a sentient being. Do
you mean that the intrinsic purity of a sentient being's mind is isolated from
all incidental taints? Or do you mean that the truth body endowed with
the twofold purity exists within the continuum of a sentient being as of the
same nature as their mind? [TL 064B] Or do you assert that [the truth body]

---

280. In most editions of the *Supercommentary*, Gyaltsap's scribe does not reproduce the
Buddha Garland Sutra quotes in full. Other citations from this sutra below are paraphrases
with interpolations.

exists in an entirely different way? Or in an inseparable way? Because you accept [the ultimate truth] as a knowable phenomenon, do you think of it as a permanent entity? Or impermanent?

"In the case of the first position, any sentient being would be inevitably a buddha, yet he or she never recognizes that he or she is a buddha! If you insist that there is no fault in such an assertion, then you would be forced to make such a speech, repudiating the Buddha as a foolish, idiotic, and ignorant person, not even knowing whether he himself was a buddha or a sentient being.

"In the case of the second position, by taking that truth body endowed with the twofold purity that exists within the continuum of a sentient being as the basis of differentiation, is it or is it not obscured by the incidental taints in the continuum of a sentient being? If the former were the case, then it would be in contradiction to the [notion] of the truth body endowed with the twofold purity. If the latter were the case, then the continuum of a sentient being and the twofold purity would be the same in nature. This would refute your own position that the continuum of a sentient being is thoroughly tainted by taints. Furthermore, if the truth body endowed with the twofold purity existed within the continuum of a sentient being as the [mind's] reality, what else would be more incorrect than saying that [the continuum of a sentient being] is both mingled with taints and free from incidental taints in its objective condition? There is no other way that would stand up to the above examination.

"In the case of the third position, it would be totally incorrect to assert that a sentient being and a buddha are mingled together, because two opposite simultaneous things are not able to have a relation of relativity.

"In the case of the fourth position, the assertion that the truth body endowed with the twofold purity primordially and intrinsically dwells within the continuum of a sentient being in an inseparable manner [TL 065A] would contradict all reasonings.

"Putting aside [the position of] being impermanent for a while, if [the ultimate truth] were a permanent phenomenon, then it would be a spatial, temporary thing with limited characters. You would admit inevitably that it is impermanent. If it were not a spatial, temporary thing with limited characters, you would admit inevitably that what exists in the continuum of a particular person, e.g., Devadatta, also exists in the continuums of all sentient beings, as this is a thing unsuitable to be spatial and temporary. Furthermore, the past things would still exist in the future and the future things would already exist in the past. And the one who falls asleep would also be awake and the one who stays awake would also be asleep; thus, no difference could be drawn between sleeping time and nonsleeping time. Viewing [the ultimate truth] as a permanent entity, like blue or yellow, not depending on the negation of the negatee, amounts to the [notion] of permanence [as conceived] only by the ones outside this tradition. Although the Vaibhāṣhikas accept a permanent entity as something having functionality, they consent that it depends on the negation of the negatee. No single Buddhist scholar would accept a permanent entity as an independent establishment.[281] Furthermore, is the ultimate truth—a permanent entity—at the time when it is seen directly, absolutely identical to the ultimate truth at the time out of equipoise? Or is it different? In the first case, someone named Devadatta, who directly [TL 065B] sees the ultimate truth in equipoise, would also directly see the ultimate truth out of equipoise, as the ultimate truth at different times is absolutely identical. In the second case, it would reject your own assertion that [the ultimate truth] is not suitable to be a spatial, temporary thing with limited characters."

The topic of the metaphor for the obscuring factor:

> The ultimate truth, which is the object of the path of producing all the intuitive wisdom of the Tathāgata, exists within the continuums of sentient beings. Bound by the grasping at the conception, which is the grasping at truth status about the person and aggregates, however, the childish are unaware of the Tathāgata's intuitive wisdom, in general. Neither do they know of it well by means of analogies and reasons, nor do they directly experience it by the perceptual validating cognition.

The topic of the metaphor for the removal of obscuration in the continuums of sentient beings:

> Hence, having seen the ultimate realm, which is the ultimate truth and the state of all the sentient beings, by his unobstructed intuitive wisdom, the Tathāgata resolves to be a teacher, for the sake of cleansing of all taints the tainted reality within sentient beings' continuums.

281. *bsgrub pa rang dbang pa.*

This expression clearly shows that the reality that exists within all sentient beings is designated as the intuitive wisdom of the Tathāgata, as reality is the object of the equipoise wisdom of the Tathāgata and the [TL 066A] Tathāgata's intuitive wisdom is produced by directly realizing the ultimate, and meditating on it to completion.

[So the Tathāgata declares:]

> Alas! These sentient beings are not properly aware of the intuitive wisdom of the Tathāgata, the ultimate truth, though the object of it penetrates them. I shall free these sentient beings, no matter how, from all the fetters such as attachment made by constructs of the grasping at truth status, by means of the teaching of the holy path. In this way, they will loosen the big knot of the grasping at the conception, which is the grasping at truth status and its instinct, by producing the antidote, the strength of the holy intuitive wisdom, themselves, and they will personally realize the intuitive wisdom of the Tathāgata, attaining sameness with the Tathāgata's intuitive wisdom.

[Accordingly], he teaches those sentient beings the path of the Tathāgata, thus removing all the bonds made by constructs. And when all the bonds made by constructs are eliminated, this immeasurable intuitive wisdom of the Tathāgata becomes useful to all sentient beings.

[This statement that the immeasurable intuitive wisdom of the Tathāgata, i.e., reality,] was not previously useful to all sentient beings and will become useful depending on the meditation of the path contradicts [your assertion that all sentient beings] are primordially buddhas endowed with the twofold purity. A sentient being attains buddhahood depending on the meditation of the path. If you claim that a buddha endowed with twofold purity primordially exists within the continuum of a sentient being, then, while the mind of a sentient being is mingled with taints, its natural state would be free from any taints. No other people would conceive of such an arrangement, except idiots! [TL 066B]

3.1.2.1.2.1.2.2.2.2.2.4. Difficulty of Understanding Enlightened Activities of the Victor . . . 4.1. The Main Meaning

«82» Here, the enlightened activities of the Victor simultaneously reach all [the disciples] at any time, spontaneously without effort, without motivational conceptual thought, [yet act] according to the intentions of the disciples, according to virtuous roots collected by the disciples, with none left out; this is an inconceivable place.

3.1.2.1.2.1.2.2.2.2.2.4.2. Sutra Reference

Thus, [the Buddha states in the *King Dhāraṇīshvara Sutra*:][282]

> In order to introduce the sentient beings to the enlightened activities of the Tathāgata, though the enlightened activities are immeasurable, they are taught briefly with a summarized number of the thirty-two excellences. However, worthy son, the true, profound, and magnificent enlightened activities of the Tathāgata are inconceivable; immeasurable; unknown directly to all the world; unrealized directly by depending on the words of others, so unexpressed by letters and difficult to be acquired by others; dwelling in all the buddha fields, so having magnificent abode; collectively engaged [by buddhas], thus equal to all buddhas; spontaneously accomplished, so beyond any effort and exertion; of no motivational conceptual thought as equal to space; engaged [by buddhas] while always remaining in the equipoise of the ultimate truth, where duality declines, thus, of no differentiation as the act of the ultimate element.

Then, after showing the simile of a pure sapphire (*vaiḍūrya*) jewel, [the Buddha] teaches in detail the conclusion:

> O son of good family, you should know the enlightened activities of the Tathāgata by means of alternate ramifications as follows: inconceivable, pervasive in all, no blemish whatsoever, as

282. For the next two quotes, see above, p. 77 ff.

they are engaged in the world yet not tainted with the worldly faults, incessant and pervasive in the three times, and keeping the lineage of the Three Jewels from being cut off by [constantly] producing all good things of transcendence. [TL 067A] The body of the Buddha, in which inconceivable enlightened activities of the Tathāgata dwell, never casts off its undifferentiated space-like defining characteristic and shows itself in all the buddha fields. The speech [of the Buddha] never casts off its inexpressible reality in the context of the decline of duality and teaches the sentient beings the Dharma with the proper language skill. And the mind secret [of the Buddha] is free from all objects of the mind, always remaining in the equipoise of the ultimate truth, where duality declines, yet is perfectly aware of the activities and intentions of the minds of all sentient beings.

3.1.2.1.2.1.3. Specific Arrangement of Cause and Conditions...
3.1. The Root Text

The "object to be realized" is the ultimate truth mingled with taints. If it is realized, all the excellences of the Buddha will be produced; if otherwise, even liberation from the life cycle would not be possible. This single base called "element" is the ultimate object to be determined and to be realized. It is the cause of the purification from taints. Although it is not the cause that produces the intuitive wisdom of the Buddha, it is designated as the cause in the sense that it is the object of the equipoise wisdom of the noble bodhisattvas, which is the chief cause for producing the intuitive wisdom of the Buddha. There would be no origination of the intuitive wisdom of the Buddha if there was a lack of it. The direct realization of the ultimate truth is the ultimate enlightenment, and its components are the excellences of the Buddha. By these excellences, the enlightened activities cause disciples— those with one of the three types of spiritual potential—to realize the ultimate truth. [Of these four] respectively, one basis is the cause and [the remaining] three are the conditions for purifying taints. Hence, we should know that the ultimate truth of the continuums of disciples, [TL 067B] for whose sake *The Sublime Continuum* is taught, is the substantial basis, and the other three [bases], the enlightenment, etc., as the causal refuge accomplished in other's continuums, are the conditions.

3.1.2.1.2.1.3.2. The Commentary . . . 2.1. Statement of Cause and
Conditions

«83» Of these four bases of import, the first basis, the ultimate truth
mingled with taints, should be regarded as the "object to be realized"
because the ultimate truth includes the ultimate objective condition of all
things knowable. The second basis is the ultimate realization of the ultimate
truth, the "enlightenment"; this is the realization in which all taints have
come to an end. The components of the enlightenment are the third basis;
the "altruistic components of the enlightenment" are these excellences of
the Buddha. The fourth basis is [comprised of] the "[enlightened activ-
ities] that cause realization" because those components of the enlightenment cause other people, i.e., disciples, to realize the ultimate truth. Hence,
in terms of this, we should know that these four bases being the factors of
cause and conditions, are presented as the spiritual potential of the Three
Jewels. The last three bases are the conditions for attaining the fruitional
Three Jewels and are designated as "spiritual potential." In no sense can
those be the twofold spiritual potential as expounded below.

3.1.2.1.2.1.3.2.2. How [the Four Bases] Become Cause and Conditions

«84» In regard to that, we should understand that the first of these four
bases is the cause for the origination of the Three Jewels, the ultimate objective, depending on the purification of that tainted ultimate truth, because
the ultimate truth is designated as the seed of the transcendent things. All
of these originate from the meditation that objectifies it, and it is the basis
of the real seed that is the wisdom of bodhisattvas in the form of an individual's proper mental engagement [TL 068A] on the topic of reality before and
after attaining the first stage. Thus, one basis [the fourth] is the cause. This
indicates that the tainted ultimate truth is designated as the cause instead
of being the producing cause.

How do the other three turn out to be conditions? These should be
understood to be the conditions for the production of the Three Jewels as
the objective to be attained in the way that the production of the Three Jewels depends on the purification of that tainted ultimate truth. This purification is done by the proper mental engagement based upon messages from
others, i.e., the universal vehicle instructions taught by the Buddha who

was already enlightened—the Tathāgata who has realized unsurpassed perfect enlightenment, performed the thirty-two enlightened activities of the Tathāgata with those excellences of the Buddha such as the ten powers, and so on. Thus, these three bases, the enlightenment, etc., are the conditions.

Although the messages from others and the proper mental engagement are indispensable for attaining enlightenment as the external condition and the internal condition, respectively, for the sake of understanding the expanded meaning, they are arranged as causes and conditions in connection with those four bases.

These explanations above have determined what the four vajra-like points are, whose objects they belong to, [TL 068B] the reason they are difficult to understand, and how, if understood, they become the cause and conditions for the unsurpassed enlightenment.

3.1.2.1.2.2. Specific Differentiations . . . 2.1. Exposition of the Element or Tathāgata Essence as a Causal Factor . . . 1.1. Prelude . . . 1.1. General Prelude

Henceforth, the remaining text should be known as a detailed teaching of the discriminations among these four bases in stages.

3.1.2.1.2.2.1.1.2. Specific Prelude

«85» In terms of reality mingled with taints, [the Buddha] states in the sutra that all sentient beings are endowed with the tathāgata essence. For what reason and for what purpose does [the Buddha state thus]? This is a prelude with questions. In this prelude, it is extremely clear that the tathāgata essence, which is said to be possessed by all sentient beings, is treated as a causal factor alone. We should thus know that taking the tathāgata essence as the truth body is not the meaning of this treatise and its commentary. Later in the text no extra question on the purpose of teaching the element is made; this prelude therefore asks for the meaning of the term "tathāgata essence" and the necessity of the proclamation that sentient beings are endowed with it.

3.1.2.1.2.2.1.2. The Main Meaning ... 2.1. Brief Statement on the Element, the Tathāgata Essence, by Indicating a Threefold Import [TL 069A] ... 1.1. General Meaning ... 1.1. Identifying the Tathāgata Essence

«86» The tathāgata essence is expounded with reference to the fruition of the Tathāgata, the nature of the Tathāgata, and the causal factor of the Tathāgata. Hence, the mere reality and the truth body of the perfect enlightenment cannot serve as the exemplification of the essence, since in this treatise and its commentary it is explained to be something at a sentient being's stage, and as a causal factor alone.

To describe the three exemplifications: the truth body activities of the perfectly enlightened Buddha—who himself has attained his fruition by realizing the path that purifies the element—radiate and pervade all sentient beings. Thus, all sentient beings are proclaimed as having the tathāgata essence since they have that very susceptibility to permeation by the truth body activities, as that is the distinctive quality of the consciousness continuum of each sentient being.

A similar meaning is found in the *Ornament of Clear Realization*:[283]

> The Buddha is said to be pervasive because of his vast activities;
> [he is also said to be eternal because his enlightened activities are inexhaustible.]

[TL 069B] The Buddha proclaims that all sentient beings are endowed with tathāgata essence, thinking that they all have reality that is naturally isolated from taints in their continuums. Although it is true that the nature of a sentient being and the nature of a buddha is the same reality that is naturally isolated from taints, being the nature of a buddha, it is [called] tathāgata essence while yet mingled with taints in the continuums of sentient beings.

Intending [to say] that all sentient beings are endowed with the spiritual potential for buddhahood[284] as a causal factor, which causes the attainment of the three bodies, the Buddha proclaims that they are all endowed

---

283. D3786, f. 11b.6
284. *buddha-gotra, sangs rgyas kyi rigs.*

with the essence. The naturally existing potential[285] is one of the [twofold] potential. In view of possession of the potential, it is said to be the essence with regard to the causal aspect of the Tathāgata. In view of possession of the ultimate truth, it is said to be the essence with regard to the nature of the Tathāgata.

Hence, we shall know that the sutras, such as the *Tathāgata Essence Sutra*, along with this treatise and its commentary, determine precisely that the so-called tathāgata essence has three points: the receptive ability in the continuums of sentient beings for the enlightened activities of the truth body, the ultimate truth mingled with taints in the continuums of sentient beings, and the spiritual potential for buddhahood that can be transformed into the three bodies, existing in the continuums of sentient beings. The particular pattern of uniting the necessity of such determination and the stages of the path will be expounded in the "benefits" section. [TL 070A]

Lacking the understanding of these points, someone asserts that the truth body is also the essence expounded here with reference to the three categories of the essence: fruitional, natural, and causal. This is an arrangement that produces wonder for the deluded, but it is not the meaning of this treatise and its commentary. So read with your eyes wide open!

[In addition,] as to the enlightened activities that cause the higher rebirths,[286] we shall know that these enlightened activities have already entered into all sentient beings, and therefore, not one of them has not experienced the status of god or human. As to the enlightened activities that cause the ultimate good,[287] all sentient beings must have the susceptibility to them as well.

3.1.2.1.2.2.1.2.1.1.2. How It Is Taught in the *Tathāgata Essence Sutra*

The *Tathāgata Essence Sutra* first uses a simile of the Tathāgata's emanation:

O noble child, just as images of the Tathāgata are sitting cross-legged inside the ugly lotuses created by the Tathāgata, emit-

285. *svabhāvavasthita-gotra, rang bzhin du gnas pa'i rigs.*
286. *abhyudaya, mngon mtho.*
287. *niḥśreyasa, nges par legs pa.*

ting hundreds of thousands of rays of light. . . . So the Tathāgata sees the tathāgata reality within those totally addicted sentient beings, [a reality] unshakable and untainted by all states of existence. . . .

The tathāgata essence is then explicated in detail by nine similes. In this *Sublime Continuum*, the essence is determined thoroughly by the nine similes of the obscured factor and their corresponding points and the nine similes of the obscuring factors and their corresponding points. Another important arrangement is also determined in this treatise with reference to the ten points, which is not found literally as elucidated in the *Tathāgata Essence Sutra* [TL 070B] but in the *Shrīmālādevī Lion's Roar Sutra*. What is determined in this treatise shall be held as the real meaning of the essence.

[The Buddha] explicated extensively with emphasis in the extensive, middling, and brief *Transcendent Wisdom Sutras* that all things, from matter up to omniscience, are devoid of intrinsic reality and are therefore free from all the extremes of reification. Similarly, in this *Tathāgata Essence Sutra*, which belongs to the final [Dharma] wheel, [the Buddha] explicated emphatically that the minds of sentient beings are naturally pure, as they are void of intrinsic existence and the obscuring taints are incidental in this regard. In this treatise, which is an accurate commentary on the intention of the *Tathāgata Essence Sutra*, the way of proving that taints are incidental is explicated with reference to the fact that addictions and conceptuality are isolated from intrinsic existence, as Asaṅga states that "addictions are terminated primordially." Just as this establishment of taints as incidental is declared in the *Transcendent Wisdom Sutra*, the reason proving that the mind is truthless[288] is also similar in meaning to what is taught in that sutra. Hence, we can understand that the *Tathāgata Essence Sutra* is an ultimate definitive meaning sutra, just like the *Transcendent Wisdom Sutra*.

Someone says that the *Tathāgata Essence Sutra* is an exemplar of a sutra that is of interpretable meaning, because it declares there to be an actual permanent entity as described in the *Visit to Laṅka Sutra*. This idea is mistaken. If the *Tathāgata Essence Sutra* were not literally intended [TL 071A] but was interpretable in meaning, there would be not the slightest need for this

288. *bden stong.*

treatise to have the section below, which consists of questions and answers that show the necessity of the teaching on the element.

There is someone else, as well, who asserts that the *Tathāgata Essence Sutra* is a sutra that is definitive in meaning, teaching a permanent real entity. This would just change the name of the personal self constructed by the outsiders to the "sugata essence" and would contradict the *Visit to Laṅka Sutra*, in which the so-taught essence theory proves to be interpretable.

Yet another person asserts the fundamental consciousness—which is different from the collection of the six consciousnesses determined in Master Asaṅga's *Universal Vehicle Compendium*—as the essence, and that that is what this treatise and its commentary mean. This idea completely lacks examination, as there is not even the smallest fragment of this treatise and its commentary that explicates such a fundamental consciousness and it is not accepted in the Master's own system that accepts external things. I will explain. If it were accepted in the Master's own system, then the ultimate three vehicles must also be accepted. This would be in direct contradiction to the text's establishment of the ultimate single vehicle above and the verse below [including] "the *White Lotus of the Holy Dharma* [*Sutra*] and so on, teaching the thatness of things. . . ."

[The Buddha] states in the *Dense Array Sutra*:[289]

> The various realms are the fundamental,
> And also the virtuous sugata essence,
> And the Tathāgata teaches [TL 071B] that essence
> Using the word "the fundamental."
> That the essence is renowned as the fundamental
> Is not understood by the feeble-minded.

This statement does not indicate that the essence as a permanent entity and the fundamental consciousness as an entity different from the collection of the six consciousnesses are the meanings mutually intended for one another, in spite of the fact that this statement seems to show that the essence is the intended meaning for the fundamental consciousness. In addition, these two are not synonyms in terms of designation. What, then, is the meaning of this passage? [The Buddha] expounded in the *Visit to Laṅka Sutra*

---

289. H113, f. 85a.6–7. See Thurman, *The Central Philosophy of Tibet*, 350.

that the sutra teaching such an essence cannot be taken literally but has a deeper intention, intending emptiness free from any reifications of a basis, including emptiness, signlessness, and wishlessness. Likewise, intending the very same emptiness, [the Buddha] teaches the fundamental consciousness as an entity different from the collection of the six consciousnesses. Being unaware of this, the feeble-minded literally take the sutras teaching the fundamental consciousness and the essence as intending just such, hence [taking] these two as synonyms in terms of their intended meaning. We shall therefore not regard "essence" and "fundamental consciousness" as literally equivalent just because they are synonyms. So intending, the *Visit to Lanka Sutra* states:[290]

> Mahāmati, this deep understanding of the sutras of all buddhas has the nature of emptiness, nonproduction, nonduality, and lack of intrinsic reality status. . . .

3.1.2.1.2.2.1.2.1.1.3. Explaining the Purpose of Other Sutras

If the *Tathāgata Essence Sutra* [TL 072A] is indicated to be a definitive meaning sutra literally intended, then how do you present as interpretable the following statement as found in the *Visit to Lanka Sutra*?[291]

> [Mahāmati asks:] The Bhagavān promulgates the tathāgata essence in his discourses, saying it is naturally clear-light, primordially pure, endowed with the thirty-two marks, and existing within the bodies of all sentient beings. You say it is like a precious gem, wrapped in a filthy rag, being permanent, stable, and eternal, but wrapped with the [rag] of the aggregates, elements, and sense media, [overpowered by attachment, hatred, and ignorance, and tainted with conceptual thoughts.] How is this tathāgata essence theory different from the [soul-] self theory of the outsiders? For the outsiders also espouse a self as permanent, inactive, qualityless, all-pervading, and indestructible.

---

290. H110, f. 135a.5–6.

291. H110, f. 135b.4–136b.7. See Thurman, *The Central Philosophy of Tibet*, 347.

In reply, the Bhagavān states: O Mahāmati, my teaching of tathāgata essence is not the same as the outsiders' self theories. O Mahāmati, the tathāgatas, saints, and buddhas teach the essence intending the meaning of words such as "emptiness," "reality-limit," "nirvana," "birthlessness," "signlessness," and "wishless-ness," in order to avoid the fear of selflessness on the part of the childish. [TL 072B] Their discourse with reference to the tathāgata essence teaches the state of nonconceptuality, the noumenal object.

O Mahāmati, present and future bodhisattvas should not become attached to it as a self. O Mahāmati, for example, potters manufacture a variety of vessels out of one mass of clay particles with their hands, manual skill, a rod, water, thread, and effort. O Mahāmati, likewise, the tathāgatas also teach objective selfless-ness, which is freedom from all conceptual thoughts. Endowed with the wisdom of that [selflessness] and with liberative arts, they, like a potter, teach it with various expressions in words and letters either as tathāgata essence or as selflessness.

Thus, O Mahāmati, the teaching of the tathāgata essence is not the same as the outsiders' self theories. O Mahāmati, in order to educate the outsiders who are attached to self theories, the tathāgatas teach the tathāgata essence, thinking that those beings whose thoughts have been dominated by soul-self ideologies will come more quickly to unsurpassed perfect enlightenment if their thoughts dwell in the sphere of the three doors of liberation. . . .

These statements [TL 073A] prove the interpretability of other interpre-table sutras that cannot be taken literally, as mentioned before. In order to help disciples of future generations, pretending some doubts, Mahāmati questions if [the statement] could be taken literally that within the bodies of all sentient beings there exists a permanent and substantial tathāgata essence that, like a precious gem wrapped in a filthy rag, is decorated with the thirty-two marks but wrapped with the rags of contaminated aggre-gates, elements, and sense media, overpowered by three poisons, and mixed with the taint of conceptual thoughts, it would be no different from advocacy of a personal self. If it has a deeper intention, then what is the intended basis? What is its purpose? What is the refutation of the literalness [of this teaching]? The Bhagavān proves the interpretability [of that statement] in answer: the intended basis is "emptiness" and so on; this [kind] of sutra was taught for the purpose of educating in stages the childish disciples of the disciple vehicle and the hermit buddha vehicle who are afraid of selflessness, and the outsiders who are attached and previously habituated to self theories as the ultimate truth; if taken literally, then [this teaching] would be no different from the soul theories advocated by the outsiders, and we should know that the refutation of the literalness [of this teaching] consists of the reasoning refuting a personal self as well.

In the *Stainless Light*, the great commentary on the *Glorious Kālachakra Tantra*, [TL 073B] the reasoning for refuting the permanent entity is used extensively. We shall therefore know that there is a serious flaw in a theory accepting the ultimate truth that is a permanent entity as the final intention of the *Stainless Light* and this treatise. In regard to the statement of [Dharmakīrti's] *Commentary on Validating Cognition*, "validating cognition is not permanent," it would be catastrophic to say that the text [merely] refutes [the position that] conventional validating cognition is permanent, for the outsider Shaivist accepts Shiva as the validating cognition of a permanent entity. Furthermore, dependent on this treatise we shall have a full realization that the *Elucidation of the Intention Sutra* is interpretable in meaning because, as aforementioned, it indicates the ultimate three vehicles, the fundamental consciousness that is different in actuality from the collection of the six consciousnesses, and the relative and the perfect [of the three realities] as established with intrinsic identity. We can therefore understand that there would be a great obstacle to proclaiming the Buddha's teaching and its proper explanation if we were to accept that there is no difference between the *Elucidation of the Intention* and the *Tathāgata Essence Sutra* in being definitive.

3.1.2.1.2.2.1.2.1.2. Detailed Meaning . . . 2.1. The Root Text

The *Tathāgata Essence Sutra* states that "all sentient beings are ever endowed with tathāgata essence." This statement is made by intending the facts: that the truth body of the Tathāgata suffuses all sentient beings, that is, all beings are receptive to the Tathāgata's liberative activities, and that reality as the nature of both the Tathāgata and a sentient being is undifferentiated, [TL 074A] that is, reality mingled with taints exists within all sentient beings. It is made also by thinking about the fact that the naturally existing potential, which is fit for transforming into the truth body, and the specific potential that has come from one's attainments, which is fit for transforming into the material body, exist within all sentient beings. Therefore, it is made in terms of three factors: susceptibility to the Tathāgata's liberative activities, nature, and the causal aspect [of the Tathāgata].

Question: What is the difference between the naturally existing potential and the reality mingled with taints that exists within a sentient being?

Reply: Although there is not the slightest distinction [in meaning] between these two, their applications are different: the former is explained separately to indicate [the tathāgata essence as the factor] fit for transforming into the truth body at the causal stage; the latter to indicate the undifferentiated nature between the Tathāgata and a sentient being.

3.1.2.1.2.2.1.2.1.2.2. The Commentary

«87» In short, by three kinds of factors with regard to connotation and purpose, [the Bhagavān] states in the *Tathāgata Essence Sutra* that all sentient beings are ever endowed with tathāgata essence. This means that (1) sentient beings are receptive to the liberative activities of the Tathāgata's truth body; (2) reality mingled with taints is undifferentiated from the ultimate truth of the Tathāgata in terms of its nature; and (3) the spiritual potential exists [in every sentient being].

«88» These three factors will be taught [in detail] below according to [TL 074B] the *Tathāgata Essence Sutra* in the section of the nine similes, starting with the verse, "Because the element consists of the threefold nature, it has a resemblance to the Buddha, etc. . . ."

The [following] determination of the element by the arrangement[292] of ten points is not intended literally in the *Tathāgata Essence Sutra*, but is implicit in the sutra if we examine the definitions closely. This is well explained by oral instructions. As to the literalness, the sutra clearly shows the proof with the nine similes.

292. *vyavasthāpana, rnam gzhag.*

3.1.2.1.2.2.1.2.2. Detailed Exposition of the Proof . . . 2.1. The Proof of the Element Being Naturally Pure with Ten Arrangements . . . 1.1. Indicating Summary . . . 1.1. Prelude

Thus, to summarize:

3.1.2.1.2.2.1.2.2.1.1.2. The Root Text

Nature is the tripartite tathāgata essence just explained. These three [factors] with reference to the tathāgata essence are also included within the category of nature.

The causes refer to faith, etc., which cause the tripartite meaning [tathāgata essence] to be purified. These are the purifying causes applicable to being the causes with reference to the tripartite meaning. Thus, these should not be held as the ones that produce the tripartite meaning, seeing that these are the causes that purify reality from taints and purify the spiritual potential, thereby [TL 075A] attaining the truth body by means of the purifications.

The fruitions are the attainment of the transcendence of purity and so on, by means of the purification of the element by faith, etc.

Question: Are the fruitions of the element not supposed to be shown here? Why are the fruitions of faith, etc., explained?

Reply: The four fruitions of faith, etc., are likewise the fruitions of the element, owing to the fact that the attainment of the four fruitions by means of the purification of the element surely depends upon the purifying forces such as faith.

The cultivation of the renunciation of the life cycle that comes from ascertaining its vices, and the aspiration for nirvana from ascertaining its virtues, should be known as the actions of the spiritual potential that exists [within all sentient beings].

"Possession" refers to the possession of the four causal excellences such as faith, etc., as well as the possession of the seven fruitional excellences such as superknowledge,[293] etc.

The categories of engagement are determined to be the following two: the one regarding the nature existing in the state of impurity, etc.; the other

293. *abhijñā, mngon shes.*

one regarding the engagement [itself], which consists of [the arrangements] of the states, all-pervasiveness, immutable eternity, and undifferentiated excellences. These are not distinct from one another in terms of their realities. The distinction is merely concerned with their contexts. Therefore, the same nature pervades all states. Someone may wonder whether there would be a contradiction in asserting the same pervasive nature, if the three different states are intrinsically established. There is no such contradiction, since the emptiness of intrinsic reality is immutable in the three states. Because of the unchangeability in the extremely pure state, at the time of ultimate fruition, [TL 075B] the three excellences of the three liberations associated with the disciples, and so on, are undifferentiated in terms of their natures. This is the meaning of the undifferentiated [excellences]. In other words, in actuality, there are no ultimate liberations associated with the disciples and hermit buddhas different from the excellences of the Buddha.

These ten [points] should be known as the ones that cause the intended meaning of the ultimate element,[294] the element designated as the "tathāgata essence" in the sutras, to be determined. A proper understanding of the element is contingent upon that.

3.1.2.1.2.2.1.2.2.1.1.3. Categories

«89» In summary, concerning the ten points, they should be known as the arrangements of the tathāgata essence, which is the perceptual object of the ultimate wisdom that is the subject perceiving reality. What are the ten points? They are: (1) nature [of the element]; (2) causes [of its purification]; (3) fruition [of its purification]; (4) actions [of the element]; (5) endowment [of the element]; (6) function [of the element in general]; (7) distinct states [of its function]; (8) omnipresence; (9) unchangeability [of the element by means of states]; and (10) indivisible excellences.

3.1.2.1.2.2.1.2.2.1.2. Exposition of Each Meaning . . . 2.1. Nature and Causes . . . 1.1 Prelude

«90» Here [is the first verse concerning the points of "nature" and "causes."]

294. *don dam pa'i dbyings.*

3.1.2.1.2.2.1.2.2.1.2.1.2. Brief Statement . . . 2.1. Nature . . . 1.1. Similes and
Their Implications

The three [aspects of the tathāgata essence], with reference to their characteristics, are analogous to a wish-fulfilling jewel, space, and water, respectively.
Their common characteristic is purity. More specifically, the truth body of the
Tathāgata is analogous to a wish-fulfilling jewel. Their reality is analogous
to space. The spiritual potential is analogous to pure water. [The treatise]
explains the truth body with respect to its diffusion of liberative activities.
In order to make it easy to understand that [sentient beings are] receptive to
its activities, [TL 076A] the truth body is explained to be analogous to a wish-
fulfilling jewel. If the truth body itself were taught as the element, there would
be no point mentioning the word "diffusion" unnecessarily in the verse (I.28),
which states, "by virtue of the diffusion of the Buddha's body." Their common
characteristic is ever naturally pure and untainted by addictions in actuality.

3.1.2.1.2.2.1.2.2.1.2.1.2.1.2. Causes

The truth body is the reality purified of all taints and the transformation
of the spiritual potential by purification; [it] emerges by means of faith in
the universal vehicle teaching, higher wisdom including the category of
the transcendence of wisdom in the mental continuums of bodhisattvas,
infinite concentrations of bodhisattvas, and great compassion, which are
analogous to the seed, mother, womb, and nurse, respectively.

3.1.2.1.2.2.1.2.2.1.2.1.3. Detailed Exposition . . . 3.1. Nature . . . 1.1. Question

«91» Here, [what is shown by the former half of this verse?]

3.1.2.1.2.2.1.2.2.1.2.1.3.1.2. Answer . . . 2.1. The Root Text

All sentient beings that are receptive to the liberative activities of the
truth body of the Tathāgata have the power to attain that truth body because
these activities are endowed with the power to fulfill all wishes. Reality mingled with taints is in the immutable form of being empty of intrinsic reality
because reality is immutable. And the characteristic of the developmental
potential is by nature moistened with compassion toward sentient beings

when the seeds have been planted. Because of that, these three [factors] [TL 076B] are analogous to the excellences of a wish-fulfilling jewel, space, and water, respectively, with reference to their particular characteristics, and to natural purity with reference to their common characteristic.

3.1.2.1.2.2.1.2.2.1.2.1.3.1.2.2. The Commentary

«92» Concerning these aforementioned three [factors] in verse 28, the similarity of the tathāgata essence's excellences to those of the pure wish-fulfilling jewel, space, and water, respectively, should be recognized with reference to its particular and general characteristics: this is the brief statement. Now, in a more detailed exposition, the truth body of the Tathāgata should be known to be analogous to a wish-fulfilling jewel, with reference to its particular characteristic in terms of its nature being powerful enough to fulfill wishes for all good things, worldly and transcendent, etc. Although reality is unchanged by causes and conditions, it should be known to be analogous to uncreated space, which cannot be posited as something other than the mere exclusion of resistant tangible objects, and with reference to its particular characteristic in terms of its nature being immutable as the mere exclusion of truth status. The potential of the Tathāgata, which refers to the developmental potential besides the naturally existing potential, should be known as being analogous to water, which is moist in nature, with reference to its particular characteristic in terms of its nature being moist with compassion toward sentient beings.

Among all sentient beings, there is no one who has not developed [in some of their beginningless infinite lives] compassion toward each and every sentient being, wishing them to be free from suffering. All sentient beings are already included as part of the object toward which compassion is developed. And all of them are already the ones who have developed compassion. If the compassion, which was developed toward each and every sentient being during the time when he or she used to be our object of compassion, was not destroyed by adverse conditions such as hatred, etc., [TL 077A] and was not separated from favorable conditions including a habitual affinity for compassion, that compassion would be the great compassion that is the mind in the form of wishing all sentient beings to be free from suffering. However, if such a mind remains a mediocre one, because it can be destroyed by adverse conditions and lack of favorable conditions, it cannot be called the "universal compassion." Still, that compassion is considered to be one of the causes of the great compassion, and here we should know that the developmental potential is the uncontaminated seed produced by hearing the holy Dharma, as well as the great compassion of bodhisattvas, etc.

And here, with reference to the general character, all [three,] the truth body, intuitive wisdom, and compassion, are naturally ever untainted by addictions—which [latter] are devoid of real status and have never infiltrated the [three former's] objective conditions due to a disparate habit pattern—and are naturally pure; those [three things] should be known to be analogous to a wish-fulfilling jewel, space, and water [respectively].

3.1.2.1.2.2.1.2.2.1.2.1.3.2. Causes ... 2.1. Question

«93» Here, [what is shown by the latter half of this verse?]

3.1.2.1.2.2.1.2.2.1.2.1.3.2.2. Answer ... 2.1. General Explanation ... 1.1. The Root Text ... 1.1. Explaining Obscured Persons and Their Obscurations

There are four kinds of obscurations to the attainment of omniscience: (1) enmity toward the universal vehicle teaching by desire-doomed ones; (2) belief in a personal self [-soul] by the outsiders; (3) inclination of disciples to desert sentient beings, resulting from the fear of suffering in the life cycle; and (4) indifference of hermit buddhas to the welfare of sentient beings, not thinking, [TL 077B] "I'm going to free sentient beings from suffering." Although the obscurations are differentiated in terms of people, these should be eliminated by everyone who embarks on the universal vehicle path.

The division of the multitude of sentient beings into three groups, i.e., (1) those who desire worldly existence; (2) those who aspire for liberation from worldly existence; and (3) those who wish for neither of them, should be known as a factor in the determination of the path to obtain the unlocated nirvana.

3.1.2.1.2.2.1.2.2.1.2.1.3.2.2.1.1.2. Explaining Characteristics of Causes Being Antidotes

Strong faith in the universal vehicle teaching, etc., should be known as the four causes of purifying the element from taints.

3.1.2.1.2.2.1.2.2.1.2.1.3.2.2.1.2. The Commentary . . . 2.1. Brief Statement

≪94≫ In brief, there are three kinds of sentient beings among them: (1) those who desire worldly existence and have no desire for liberation, thereby falling to the extreme of the life cycle; (2) those who aspire for liberation from the life cycle, thereby falling to the extreme of nirvana; and (3) those who wish neither of them, thereby not falling to either extreme.

3.1.2.1.2.2.1.2.2.1.2.1.3.2.2.1.2.2. Detailed Exposition . . . 2.1. Explaining Obscured Persons . . . 1.1. Explaining Respectively . . . 1.1. Those Who Have Fallen to the Extreme of the Life Cycle

≪95≫ In regard to those who have desire for cyclic life, they are of two kinds. One consists of (a) those who feel animosity for the path to liberation and repudiate its possibility; or the wrong-desiring ones,[295] who know it is possible but remain indifferent about it. Therefore they do not have the spiritual potential for nirvana, [TL 078A] and are called "those whose spiritual potential has been severed," being people who only desire the life cycle and do not aspire to nirvana. Though their inability to feel repulsed by everything in the life cycle and aspire to liberation [is only] temporary, there is an intention behind labeling them "those whose spiritual potential has been utterly severed," as will be proven later. The other consists of (b) those who are Buddhists, but have certainly fallen into such a pattern. Some of these are only somewhat receptive to the education of monastic discipline, but temporarily are not [receptive] even to [the teaching on] the coarse[296] emptiness of a personal self. Adhering to the individual vehicle canon, they are hostile to the universal vehicle teaching, repudiating it as not being the word of the Buddha. With reference to them, the Bhagavān declared:

295. *log sred can.* See above, p. 92 note 98.
296. *rags pa.*

I am not their teacher; they are not my disciples. O Shāriputra, I speak of them as dark ones, covered in the thick darkness of ignorance, constantly afflicted by the inexhaustible misery of its consequence, migrating from darkness to greater darkness, and kept in deep darkness.

3.1.2.1.2.2.1.2.2.1.2.1.3.2.2.1.2.2.1.1.2. Those Who Have Fallen to the Extreme of Nirvana . . . 2.1. General Teaching

«96» Here, [as to the kind who aspire to liberation from the life cycle, they are also of two types: (a) those who have engaged, but lack liberative art; and (b) those who have engaged with liberative art.]

3.1.2.1.2.2.1.2.2.1.2.1.3.2.2.1.2.2.1.1.2.2. Explaining Them in Order Respectively . . . 2.1. Those Who Have Engaged but Lack Liberative Art

[Those who have engaged but lack liberative art are further divided into three types:] the first type of person is [from the] various fundamentalist groups, an outsider to this Dharma in terms of both philosophic view and religious praxis, such as the Chārvāka materialists, the Parivrājaka, and the Jain ascetics, etc. Their theories are either eternalistic or nihilistic, e.g., some of them even repudiate the [possibility of] higher rebirths in the framework of reincarnation, and some, though accepting the higher rebirths, repudiate the possibility of liberation. [TL 078B]

[The latter] two types of people are faithful to this teaching, but their conduct is similar to the fundamentalists, erroneously taking a negative view [of the Buddha's teaching] on the topic of emptiness. Who are those people? The second type of person lacks faith in the ultimate truth and believes in a substantial personal self that is not [merely] designated upon the spatial collection and temporal continuity of the [five] aggregates and is akin to [the kind of self] imagined by the fundamentalists. The Vātsīputrīya school, for example, holds such a theory. This type of Buddhist is similar to the aforementioned [type of Buddhist who has the desire for worldly existence] in accepting a personal self. But while the former [type] does not aspire to liberation and is hostile to the universal vehicle teaching, the latter aspires to liberation alone, and some of them are not hostile to the universal vehicle teaching. It should be known that there are two kinds of people in the Vātsīputrīya school: one who repudiates [the authenticity of] the universal vehicle sutras, and the other who does not. Such is also true in other schools, such as the Vaibhāṣhika, etc. As to the sutra reference about these persons, they are temporarily unable even to listen to [the teaching on] the coarse emptiness of a personal self. The Bhagavān has declared:

> One who lacks faith in emptiness is not different from a fundamentalist.

Someone asserts that impermanence is concomitant[297] with anything that exists and takes this as the intention of the seven treatises on validating cognition. Activating a latent predisposition for such perverse views causes severe deterioration. That is, one who talks like this would not properly understand [TL 079A] and believe the arrangement proved by validating cognition, that the permanence proposed by theorists is the exclusion[298] of disintegration. Consequently, he or she would repudiate the arrangement proved by validating cognition that the topic of selflessness is an absolute negation;[299] it is the mere exclusion of a personal or objective self, realized by the wisdom that has recognized selflessness. Thus, it should be known that [this kind of assertion] indicates a strong latent predisposition for a conceptual insistence on a self of persons.

The third type of person feels excessive pride, thinking, "I have comprehended the ultimate meaning of reality," but actually has not, and holds a wrong view of emptiness by grasping at emptiness as possessing truth status. Here, the door of liberation [asserted by these people] also leads to holding an unrealistic view of emptiness. Although the wisdom that realizes emptiness is the door or means of liberation, if the habit of grasping at truth status with respect to emptiness is formed, it is said to be a temporarily untreatable view. Apparently, this view refers to [one kind of] Experientialist theory that accepts the emptiness of subject-object duality as an ultimate truth that has truth status due to its [supposed] intrinsic identifiability. This has been well explicated by Jey Rinpoche (Tsong Khapa), the omniscient one.

---

297. *khyab pa.*
298. *vyavacchinna, rnam par bcad pa.*
299. *prasajyapratiṣedha, med dgag.*

Otherwise, this view would not fit into any of the three groups, including the one discussed below.

Knowing how to posit the arrangement that the grasping at truth status is negated by validating cognition, keeping in mind that intrinsic identifiability is involved, we will not make the mistake of seeing the object of negation as something having truth status. As mentioned in [Shāntideva's] *Guide to the Bodhisattva Way of Life*: "when the object of negation is negated, no basis for analysis is left."[300] {TL 079B} For someone who understands subtle emptiness, there is no basis for the truth conviction about the intrinsic identifiability of the object of negation, when under the scrutiny of the wisdom that realizes emptiness. Thus, when accepting an emptiness that merely negates a coarse negatee, one is doomed to make the mistake of forming a theory with respect to its true establishment. As long as there is a strong grasping at truth status with respect to a coarse emptiness, [the unrealistic view] is untreatable. On the other hand, this [way of holding the] viewpoint of the Experientialist school should be known as the means of maturing to the realization of the subtle emptiness propounded by the Centrists.

Here "those who have engaged but lack liberative art" denotes the type of people who, while incorporating a full range of the universal vehicle praxis into their experience, have formed a theory in disharmony with the ultimate view of emptiness by truth conviction about emptiness. But we should know it would be a great erroneous view uninformed by the knowledge of the stages and paths if we accept the viewpoint of the idealist school, which is an obstacle to obtaining liberation. As to the sutra reference, with reference to these, [the Buddha] states in the *Questions of Kāshyapa Sutra*:[301]

> O Kāshyapa, the belief in a personal self as great as Mount Sumeru is considered superior to the belief in an [erroneous] emptiness by those who have excessive pride.

This passage indicates that [some idealists], while driven by the unconscious personal self-habit, do not accept [such a personal self-habit] as the fundamental [mistaken] view, and do not consider the emptiness of the

300. Chapter IX, v. 110.
301. H 87, f. 231a.4–5.

personal self-habit as the ultimate, asserting instead that the emptiness of the subject-object duality is the ultimate truth. Thus, in dependence upon an unconscious personal self-habit, they also engage in the conceptual imagination of such a personal self, and this makes it even more difficult [for them] to dispel [the obscurations].

It is not valid to set forth this treatise *Commentary* as a teaching on the information-only system [TL 080A] in light of the following fact: the holy Master Asaṅga, out of his concern to educate a certain type of person who has the potential for the idealist view, pioneered the way as a champion of the information-only [idealist] system and gave extensive teachings on it. In [Asaṅga's] *Bodhisattva Stages*, he interprets this sutra reference to be refuting the realitylessness philosophy that asserts that there is no such thing, even as small as an atom, that has intrinsic identifiability, but here he interprets the same sutra reference to be refuting [the idealist system] which accepts emptiness as having truth status. It is true that this sutra reference is sometimes taken as a reference to the disciple schools, but is by no means exclusive. Otherwise, there would be no attention to the Experientialist theory in the context of this text.

3.1.2.1.2.2.1.2.2.1.2.1.3.2.2.1.2.2.1.1.2.2.2. Those Who Have Engaged with Liberative Art

«97» Those who have engaged with liberative art are further divided into two types: (1) those who are engaged in ultimacy determination,[302] which refers to the understanding of the subtle emptiness with respect to personal selflessness and objective selflessness, and the experiential realization upon attaining the path of insight, conforming to the disciple vehicle; and (2) those conforming to the hermit buddha vehicle, which is in accord with the disciple vehicle with respect to the pattern of realizing emptiness. This statement indicates that [some people associated with] the disciple vehicle or the hermit buddha vehicle do understand the two subtle selflessnesses, by virtue of the aforementioned fact that those who do not realize the meaning of reality, who accept both things and emptiness as having truth status, are the type of people who have engaged with but lack liberative art in terms of philosophical viewpoint. If the term "liberative art" denotes the praxis for obtaining buddhahood and the basis for such praxis,

---

302. *samyaktva-niyāma, yang dag pa nges pa nyid.*

i.e., cultivation of the [enlightnment] spirit with respect to the universal vehicle, it would be rational to include disciples and hermit buddhas in the type of people who have engaged with but lack liberative art. Therefore, the ultimate liberative art for obtaining liberation or omniscience [TL 080B] in terms of philosophical viewpoint is nothing but the understanding of the subtle emptiness. Although the noble disciples and hermit buddhas have that understanding, it is not necessarily true for everyone in the disciple vehicle or the hermit buddha vehicle. This has been mentioned before and will be explicated again later.

3.1.2.1.2.2.1.2.2.1.2.1.3.2.2.1.2.2.1.1.3. Those Who Have Not Fallen to Either Extreme

«98» As for the kind who wishes neither of them—rebirth in the life cycle by the force of addictions and karmic evolution, and nirvana, which is obtained by cutting off rebirth in the life cycle—these are the people who are extremely sharp in intelligence and stand firmly on the universal vehicle. The disciples of the universal vehicle sutras are of two types: principal and mediocre. The latter refers to the Experientialists, and the former to the people "who are extremely sharp in intelligence," incorporating the full range of views and practices of the universal vehicle into their experience. They do not desire the life cycle as the desire-doomed do, nor are they those who have engaged with but lack liberative art like the fundamentalists, nor are they those who have realization with liberative art, like disciples and hermit buddhas; rather, they have entered the path to attain the [realization of the] equality of the life cycle with nirvana. They are intent with pure thought on the unlocated nirvana and act with pure conduct in an addiction-free life cycle, where they take rebirths out of compassion and prayer. The basis for, or root of, their conception of the spirit [of enlightenment] with respect to the universal vehicle, is absolutely pure and grounded in firm compassion, and they think, "May all sentient beings be free from suffering," and, with high resolve, they think, "I shall be responsible for liberating them from suffering!" This is the great Centrist way of incorporating the complete path of the universal vehicle, which eliminates both extremes of the life cycle and of nirvana, in [actual] experience.

3.1.2.1.2.2.1.2.2.1.2.1.3.2.2.1.2.2.1.2. All of Them Subsumed Under Three Groups

«99» Here, those [desire-doomed ones who have desire for worldly existence and those Buddhists who have certainly fallen into the same way are called the group of people who are definitely mistaken. Those people who aspire for liberation from worldly existence but lack liberative art are called the group of people who are undetermined. Those people who aspire for liberation from worldly existence with liberative art and those who wish for neither and have entered the path to obtain the equality are called the group of people who have become determined on reality.] These statements are easy to understand.

3.1.2.1.2.2.1.2.2.1.2.1.3.2.2.1.2.2.2. Their Obscuration ... 2.1. Statement

«100» [TL 081A] Aside from those people who stand firmly in the universal vehicle and have realized that there are no intrinsically real obscurations, [there are four other kinds of people, namely: the desire-doomed, the fundamentalists, the disciples, and the hermit buddhas.] These four stand fully obscured and cannot come to realize very well the tathāgata element and do not understand it with the full share of the method of the voidness of intrinsic reality. Therefore, as for [the treatise] not teaching in general the way in which the disciples and hermit buddhas do not realize voidness, one can still understand [that intention] by its teaching later—picking out specifically the space-treasury samādhi—that they do not meditate [such voidness].

3.1.2.1.2.2.1.2.2.1.2.1.3.2.2.1.2.2.2. Explanation

«101» What, then, are the four obscurations? These are: (1) enmity toward the universal vehicle teaching—this is the obscuration of the doomed ones, and its antidote is the meditation on faith in the bodhisattvas' teachings of the universal vehicle; (2) the belief in a [substantial personal] self—this is the obscuration of the outsider fundamentalists, and its antidote is the meditation on the bodhisattvas' transcendent wisdom; (3) the knowing of the life cycle as dire and the fear of its sufferings, thereby abandoning sentient beings without paying attention—this is the obscuration of those who are associated with the disciple vehicle, its antidote being the bodhisattvas' space-treasury concentration, etc.; and (4) the aversion to the welfare of sentient beings and indifference to the welfare of sentient beings, not taking responsibility by thinking, "I shall be responsible to liberate them from suffering"—[TL 081B] this is the obscuration of those who are associated with the hermit buddha vehicle, and its antidote is the bodhisattvas' meditation on the great compassion. Each obscuration is explained in conjunction with each antidote.

3.1.2.1.2.2.1.2.2.1.2.1.3.2.2.1.2.2.2.3. Précis

≪102≫ [These are the four types of obscuration of the four kinds of sentient being. By meditating on the] four kinds of antidote [to these obscurations, such as faith, etc., bodhisattvas will obtain the ultimate pure truth body, the unsurpassed aim.] In sum, the whole body of antidotes consists of, initially, enormous faith in both the causal aspect and the fruitional aspect of the universal vehicle teaching; then, cultivation of the spirit of supreme enlightenment by means of the meditation on great compassion; and [finally] meditation on the distinctive concentration of the universal vehicle, which integrates mental quiescence with transcendent insight.

3.1.2.1.2.2.1.2.2.1.2.1.3.2.2.2. Explaining in Detail Characteristics of Causes Being Antidotes to Obscurations . . . 2.1. Prelude

≪103≫ Accompanied by these four causes of achieving the four purities such as the transcendence of purity, etc., one becomes the child of the Dharma King in the tathāgata family. How so?

3.1.2.1.2.2.1.2.2.1.2.1.3.2.2.2.2. The Root Text

≪104≫ Faith in the causes and effects of the supreme vehicle is like a seed that produces the child of a universal emperor. The wisdom that realizes emptiness—adorned by the magnificent factor of liberative art—is similar to a mother producing the buddha qualities. As explained in the statement, "the mother is wisdom; the father is liberative art,"[303] the wisdom realizing

303. Although similar statements are found in a number of texts, the only verbatim

emptiness is likened to a mother since it is a common cause of the enlightenment of all three vehicles, while liberative art is presented as being like a father since it is the uncommon cause.[304] Abiding in the blissful womb of meditative concentration (samādhi), such as those of "the sky treasury"[305] and others, with the wet nurse of compassion, whosoever is a child that is nourished by great compassion—so important throughout the beginning, middle, and end—[TL 082A] they should be known as a child born as a follower of the Sage. There are three types of faith: pure faith in the causes and fruits of the universal vehicle Dharma, faith that is the wish to attain [realizations], and the faith of belief, and the faith that is taught here is the latter. That faith is [taught] for the purpose of knowing it as the root of all Dharma.

≪105≫ Here is a verse that refers to the meanings of "fruition" and "actions."

3.1.2.1.2.2.1.2.2.1.2.2.2. Brief Statement . . . 2.1. Statement on the Fruition

The ultimate transcendences of purity, supreme self, bliss, and eternity are the fruition. These will be explicated below in more detail.

3.1.2.1.2.2.1.2.2.1.2.2.2.2. Statement on the Actions

Renunciation of the life cycle's sufferings, on the understanding that they are like unbearable pus, aspiration for obtaining peace, i.e., nirvana, and the prayer "May I attain!"—are actions and significance of the spiritual potential. [TL 082B]

---

occurrence is in the *Questions of Druma, the King of Kinnaras Sutra* (*Ārya-druma-kiṁnararāja-paripṛcchā-nāma-mahāyāna-sutra*; *'phags pa mi 'am ci'i rgyal po sdong pos zhus pa zhes bya ba theg pa chen po'i mdo*), H158, fol. 437a.7.

304. This statement expects the reader to be aware of Tibetan polyandry, a cultural form in that culture where one woman can take several brothers as husbands. The idea here is that the wisdom that enables enlightenment is the mother, who unites with three fathers, one who produces a follower of the disciple vehicle, another a bodhisattva, and a third the Vajrayāna adept practitioner—all three coming from the same mother.

305. D'Amato (2012, 174n2) notes that this refers to "a particular form of concentration (*samādhi*), namely the *gagana-gañja-samādhi*," and cites Anacker (1984, 283n57), that "the 'power' [of this concentration] comes from the realization of limitlessness, which can be gained by meditating on the sky."

3.1.2.1.2.2.1.2.2.1.2.2.3. Detailed Exposition of Fruition . . . 3.1. Fruition . . .
1.1. Question

«106» Here, [what is shown by the former half of this verse?]

3.1.2.1.2.2.1.2.2.1.2.2.3.1.2. Answer . . . 2.1. General Explanation about the
Defining Characteristics of the Fruition Obtained by the Four Antidotes
. . . 1.1. The Root Text

The fourfold fruition of these [causes], such as faith in the universal vehicle teaching, etc., is, in brief, distinguished by eliminating the fourfold delusion about the truth body of the Tathāgata by the four antidotes that are the
opposites of these delusions.

3.1.2.1.2.2.1.2.2.1.2.2.3.1.2.1.2. The Commentary . . . 2.1. Brief Statement

«107» [The fruition of these four excellences,] faith, etc., [explained as
the causes of the purification of the tathāgata element, is, in sum, the fourfold transcendence of excellences in the truth body; these antidotes are the
opposites of the four delusions, respectively.]

3.1.2.1.2.2.1.2.2.1.2.2.3.1.2.1.2.2. Detailed Exposition . . . 2.1. Explaining the
Delusions and the Abandonment-Fruition Obtained by Antidotes . . .
1.1. The Main Meaning . . . 1.1. Delusions about the Conventional Reality

[In general,] there are notions of eternality, bliss, self, and purity regarding the impermanence, suffering, selflessness, and impurity, respectively, of
things such as matter, etc. Such notions are called the "fourfold delusion."
Ordinary people who are not under the influence of any philosophical
viewpoint have this sort of delusion, [TL 083A] which is mistaken about the
conventional reality of the noble truth of suffering.

3.1.2.1.2.2.1.2.2.1.2.2.3.1.2.1.2.2.1.1.2. Delusions about the Ultimate Reality

The opposite of these notions should be known as the fourfold nondelu-
sion. Which four? They are the notions of impermanence, suffering, selflessness, and impurity regarding impermanence, etc., of things such as matter,

etc. Such notions are called the "four nondelusions." Furthermore, these very [nondelusions] are accepted here as delusions with reference to the truth body of the Tathāgata, whose defining characteristics are eternal, etc.

The wisdom that realizes the aggregates' impermanence, etc., and the mind asserting the aggregates as permanent, etc., share the same object of apprehension but are opposites with respect to their habit patterns. The former habit patterns are in accordance with conventional reality. Therefore, they are the perfect antidotes to the permanence-habit, etc. They are posited as erroneous with reference to the truth body as long as the truth-status-habit regarding the aggregates' impermanence, etc. is involved. Nevertheless, it would be an unrealistic view to accept the mind asserting the aggregates to be impermanent, etc., to be erroneous with respect to its object; [that is, it would be] a nihilism that repudiates relativity. The assertion that it is not even tenable to accept the aggregates as impermanent is an obstacle to liberation and should be known as the system of Hva-shang, the Chinese abbot who asserted that nothing exists whatsoever and that nothing should be accepted. If this were valid, then we would not be able to differentiate error and nonerror in any way. Furthermore, the selflessness that is involved with the truth-status-habit is a coarse one because the subtle selflessness, when realized by validating cognition and not forgotten, would never give way to a theory confirming the truth-status-habit applied to the negation that negates such a self. But supposing that the mind of the truth-status-habit regarding selflessness, which is the negation of the subtle negatee, [TL 083B] actually arises, this mind should be understood to be an unconscious [truth-status-habit].

[Objection:] This is unacceptable because since beginningless time in the life cycle, people have not been familiar with the emptiness of intrinsic identifiability, which is the basis of such a truth-status-habit.

[Reply:] There is no such fault. Although we have not been familiar with the paths and the fruition of the universal vehicle since beginningless time in the life cycle, the truth-status-habit that is produced by apprehension of them, unrelated to analysis by means of reasoning, should be understood to be an unconscious [truth-status-habit]. Otherwise, it would be impossible for the *Ornament of Clear Realization* to list many suppositions[306] regarding

---

306. *vikalpa, rnam par rtog pa.*

subjects and objects that are the factors to be removed on the path of meditation of the universal vehicle.

3.1.2.1.2.2.1.2.2.1.2.2.3.1.2.1.2.2.1.1.3. Fruition Obtained by Eliminating the Delusions

The antidote to these [delusions is the arrangement of the four transcendent excellences of the truth body of the Tathāgata: transcendent permanence, transcendent bliss, transcendent self, and transcendent purity]. Those meanings will be explicated below.

3.1.2.1.2.2.1.2.2.1.2.2.3.1.2.1.2.2.1.2.1. Sutra Reference ... 2.1. Reference to the Four Delusions of Permanence, etc.

«108» Furthermore, this passage of the treatise should be understood in detail according to the sutra—this is the prelude to the sutra reference. [In the *Shrīmālādevī Lion's Roar Sutra*, Shrīmālādevī declares]:

> O Bhagavān, [sentient beings have a delusion regarding the five compulsive aggregates; they have a notion of their permanence, bliss, self, and purity regarding the impermanence, suffering, selflessness, and impurity (of things), respectively.]

This fourfold delusion can be understood to be erroneous with respect to its conceived objects,[307] even by conventional validating cognition. No understanding of emptiness is required.

3.1.2.1.2.2.1.2.2.1.2.2.3.1.2.1.2.2.1.2.2. Reference to the Truth-Habit Regarding Permanence, etc.

> O Bhagavān, even all the disciples and hermit buddhas, owing to their grasping at truth status, have a delusion about the truth body of the Tathāgata, which is free from all truth reifications and is the object of the omniscient intuitive wisdom, and have

307. *zhen yul.*

never seen it before by their independent intuitive wisdom of emptiness.

People who have potential for the disciple vehicle or the hermit buddha vehicle and do not understand the subtle emptiness [TL 084A] have delusions about the truth body because of their habit of clinging to the truth status of their realizations of impermanence, coarse selflessness, etc. As for noble disciples and hermit buddhas who have experiential realization of the subtle emptiness, they still have a delusion about the truth body because of their inability to realize emptiness by their own power, as do people who have potential for the universal vehicle and have sharp intelligence, as well as [still being gripped by] the manifestation of their unconscious truth-status-habit regarding impermanence, etc. Even the saints of the disciple vehicle and the hermit buddha vehicle lack the antidote required for obtaining the fruitional transcendence of the supreme self, because they do not meditate on the transcendence of wisdom.

3.1.2.1.2.2.1.2.2.1.2.2.3.1.2.1.2.2.1.2.3. Reference to Antidotes

O Bhagavān, if sentient beings have the notion of permanent eternity—then, by means of the attainment of the antidote that is [the realization] of the bodhisattvas' [realization of the] equality between the life cycle and peace; by means of the meditation on the antidotes to the twelve links of relativistic origination, which are subsumed under the category of objective obscuration and are perceived as the factors to be eliminated, of self; by means of the understanding of the mere exclusion of the reifications of personal self and objective self as the natural condition and the ultimate truth of things, and of purity; by means of the realization of [the mind] being naturally pure and of the evil evolutionary instincts of the three doors being the factors to be eliminated—they would be children born of the heart of the Buddha.

Objection: Did the text not state that the notion of eternity, etc., is erroneous? Why does the Buddha call people who have such understanding "heart children?"

Reply: They are similar in names but not similar in connotations. [As the sutra states:]

O Bhagavān, those sentient beings [would not be people of delusions. O Bhagavān, those sentient beings would truly perceive. For what reason? O Bhagavān, this is because the truth body of the Tathāgata is transcendent eternity, transcendent bliss, the transcendent self, and transcendent purity. O Bhagavān, those people who perceive the truth body of the Tathāgata in this way perceive truly. Those who perceive truly] are the heart children of the Buddha.

3.1.2.1.2.2.1.2.2.1.2.2.3.1.2.1.2.2.2. Explaining the Correlation of Fruition and Causes ... 2.1. Explaining Respectively ... 1.1. Brief Statement
[TL 084B]

«109» The order of the four transcendent excellences of the truth body of the Tathāgata should be known as the reverse of the order of causes just mentioned, i.e., faith, wisdom, concentration, and great compassion. It will be explicated below that the reverse of the order as stated in the sutra, "the truth body of the Tathāgata is transcendent eternity, transcendent bliss, transcendent self, and transcendent purity" is in accordance with the order of causes.

3.1.2.1.2.2.1.2.2.1.2.2.3.1.2.1.2.2.2.1.2. Detailed Exposition ... 2.1. Explaining the Correlation of the Transcendence of Purity and Cause, Which Is Faith in the Universal Vehicle Teaching

Here, (1) being opposite to taking delight in the impure life cycle by the desire-doomed ones who are fully occupied with it and feel enmity toward the universal vehicle teaching, the transcendent purity should be understood to be the fruition obtained by the meditation on faith in the bodhisattvas' universal vehicle teaching. We should understand that there are four factors mentioned in this explanation: obscuration, the type of person who has it, the antidote to it, and the fruition obtained by the meditation on the antidote.

3.1.2.1.2.2.1.2.2.1.2.2.3.1.2.1.2.2.2.1.2.2. Explaining the Transcendence of Supreme Self as the Fruition of Meditation on the Transcendence of Wisdom . . . 2.1. The Main Meaning

(2) Being opposite to taking delight in the self-habit of outsider fundamentalists concerning the compulsive aggregates, which are devoid of [both] personal self and objective self, the transcendent self [TL 085A]—the truth body isolated from all reifications of personal self and objective self—should be understood to be the fruition obtained by meditation on the transcendence of wisdom, which is the experiential realization that persons and aggregates are devoid of any intrinsic reality even as small as an atom.

3.1.2.1.2.2.1.2.2.1.2.2.3.1.2.1.2.2.2.1.2.2.2. Specific Explanation of the Import of Supreme Person

Indeed, all the outsider fundamentalist groups assert that persons and things, such as matter, etc.—which do not have as their nature a self of truth status or independence status[308]—have a truly established self [as their nature]. Persons and things in this way are asserted to have such a self by the fundamentalists, and are deceptive with respect to such a [false] characteristic of having a self. [Such a self] does not exist in the object of knowledge, hence it is always selfless. [On the contrary,] the Tathāgata has obtained the transcendence of supreme selflessness by the intuitive wisdom that knows things just as they are and truly realizes reality. Selflessness truly perceived by an intuitive wisdom that knows things just as they are is not deceptive with respect to its characteristic of being selfless as established by the nature of things, and is the reality that is truly perceived in total mental equanimity by the Buddha; hence it is always accepted as the reality, nature, and self of things. Here, personal selflessness and objective selflessness are meant by "self," and this is based on the understanding that a positive, independent self as a permanent entity does not exist among the objects of knowledge—as [a sutra states:][309] [TL 085B] "He stays in the way of truth-void, elaboration-free emptiness of truth by means of not abiding in any truth-status [of things] that would be apprehendable if the things had truth-status."

308. *rang dbang du grub pa.*
309. Source unidentified.

Here, the exemplification of the supreme self is clearly explicated as self-lessness, which is perceived by the Buddha's intuitive wisdom that knows things just as they are. Thus, the assertion that the exemplification of the supreme self is not the mere exclusion of a personal self and objective self but is a positive, independent self, a permanent entity, should be known as coming from a great habitual affinity for the outsider fundamentalists' view. And this assertion, which accepts such an obsession with an erroneous self as the realization of the meaning of reality, should be known as the chief negandum of this treatise and its explanation commentary. If you do not believe this when you read them, then open your eyes and read them carefully! Think about whether "self" means a positive, independent, permanent entity and you will come to the understanding that only selflessness is explicable.

3.1.2.1.2.2.1.2.2.1.2.2.3.1.2.1.2.2.2.1.2.3. Explaining the Transcendence of Supreme Bliss as the Fruition of Meditation on the Transcendence of Meditation

(3) [Being opposite to taking delight in the cessation of the sufferings of] the life cycle [by those associated with the disciple vehicle who have fear of the sufferings of the life cycle, the transcendence of supreme bliss concerned with all matters, mundane and transcendent, should be understood to be the fruition obtained by the meditation on the space-treasury concentration, etc.] The transcendence of supreme bliss is the uncontaminated bliss that is obtained by means of the complete elimination of the mind-made bodies [conditioned by] instinctual ignorance-driven evolutionary action. It is also explicated by the aforementioned four factors.

3.1.2.1.2.2.1.2.2.1.2.2.3.1.2.1.2.2.2.1.2.4. Explaining the Transcendence of Eternity as the Fruition of Meditation on Great Compassion

(4) [Being opposite to taking delight in the tranquil abode by those associated with the hermit buddha vehicle who are indifferent to the welfare of sentient beings, the transcendence of eternity with respect to absolute pure mastery works as long as the life cycle exists, without interruption,] for the welfare of sentient beings. [This] should be understood to be the fruition [obtained by meditation on the bodhisattvas' great compassion.] This is easy to understand.

3.1.2.1.2.2.1.2.2.1.2.2.3.1.2.1.2.2.2.1.3. Précis

«110» [Thus, the attainment of the four kinds of transcendent excellences regarding purity, self, bliss, and eternity in the truth body of the Tathāgata are, respectively, the fruition of the bodhisattvas' meditations on faith, wisdom, concentration, and great compassion.] This explains that the four kinds of transcendence are obtained, respectively, by the four kinds of causes.

3.1.2.1.2.2.1.2.2.1.2.2.3.1.2.1.2.2.2.2. Summary

Because of these four kinds of causes, the Tathāgata is acclaimed as the ultimate element, pervading infinite space, [TL 086A] and reaching to the end of time—these are three distinctive features of the truth body with reference to nature, pervasiveness, and time as stated in the sutra. Alternatively, this [statement] can be divided into four meanings and will be, respectively, explicated by the following four [statements]. Indeed, the Tathāgata is the one who has become the ultimate element endowed with twofold purity because he has obtained the utterly pure ultimate element by means of the elimination of addictive obscurations and objective obscurations by the meditation on faith in the universal vehicle teaching, which is the realization of the twenty-one types of uncontaminated intuitive wisdom in causal and fruitional aspects. He is the one who has become infinite space because he has realized the space-like ultimate selflessness, the emptiness of intrinsic reality that is free from all reifications of sentient beings and their environments, by the meditation on the transcendence of wisdom, and because he has become the supreme Lord of the Dharma, pervading all disciples in all worlds and teaching all, by the meditation on the space-treasury concentration, etc. "Pervading all disciples" denotes the liberative activities of the Tathāgata's body, which simultaneously teaches all disciples who are suitably receptive to the Dharma. [This position is unlike] outsiders' systems, such as the Vaisheṣhika school, which accept that the part that pervades disciples in the east also pervades disciples in the west. He is the one who will reach to the end of time because he is endowed with the [TL 086B] inexhaustible compassion toward all sentient beings [developed] from the meditation on the great compassion.

3.1.2.1.2.2.1.2.2.1.2.2.3.1.2.1.2.2.3. Detailed Exposition of the Obstacles for Three Types of People to Obtain the Truth Body . . . 3.1. The Main Meaning . . . 1.1. Categories of Obstacles to the Attainment of the Truth Body

«111» For the attainment of the four kinds of transcendent excellences of the truth body of the Tathāgata, there are four impediments even in the case of the saints of the disciple vehicle and the hermit buddha vehicle, who are staying in the uncontaminated element and have eased the life cycle sufferings by the power of their experiential realization of ultimates, as well as for bodhisattvas who are dwelling in the pure stages, have completely eliminated addictive obscuration, and have obtained the ten powers. [These four impediments] have the defining characteristics of (1) conditions, such as craving and grasping, which are included in the category of the addictive obscurations; (2) causes, such as karmic evolution; (3) originations, such as name-and-form, and (4) destructions, such as old age and death.

3.1.2.1.2.2.1.2.2.1.2.2.3.1.2.1.2.2.3.1.2. Explaining the Nature of Obstacles

There are four aspects in this regard. First, "condition" is defined as the ignorance instinct-driven evolutionary action ground,[310] which is in the nature of uninterrupted homogeneous nonaddictive ignorance included in the category of objective obscurations and is like a "foundation" inasmuch as it has created an opportunity for homogeneous addictions to be continually produced in the past, just as addictive ignorance of the grasping at truth status regarding persons and aggregates is the cause of creational activities, [TL 087A] consisting of virtuous, nonvirtuous, and immutable karmic evolutionary actions.

Second, "cause" is defined as karmic evolutionary action that is uncontaminated by addictions but is [still] conditioned by instinctual ignorance-driven evolutionary action. This is the substantial cause of the mind-made body,[311] i.e., the motivation with subtle effort, included in the category of

---

310. *ma rig pa'i bag chags kyis las [kyi sa].*

311. *manomayātmabhāva-kāya, yid kyi rang bzhin gyi lus.*

thought,[312] producing cognitions[313] of body and speech. As mentioned before, it is just creational activities.

Third, "origination" is defined as the accomplishment of the threefold mind-made body, having the foundational instinctual ignorance-driven evolutionary action as the cooperative condition and uncontaminated karmic evolutionary action as the substantial cause, just as the accomplishment of the threefold worldly existence—the desire realm, the [pure] material realm, and the immaterial realm—is conditioned by the four kinds of mental creations, i.e., desire, conviction, discipline-sanctity self-righteousness, and soul-theory obsession, and [is] caused by contaminated karmic evolution. The mind-made body is the body that is mind-like and travels without any impediment. It cannot be perceived by those whose realization is inferior to that of the three types of people.

Fourth, "destruction" is defined as the death of the inconceivable transformation, like the one experienced by someone going through the "in between"[314] period who, supposing he will stay for two weeks, is going to die at the end of the first week, which is conditioned by the accomplishment of the threefold mind-made body, just as old age and death are conditioned by birth, under the control of karmic evolution and addictions.

3.1.2.1.2.2.1.2.2.1.2.2.3.1.2.1.2.2.3.1.3. How Obstacles Function

≪112≫ [TL 087B] Saints, hermit buddhas, and bodhisattvas who have obtained the powers will not obtain the transcendence of supreme ultimate purity, depleted of all obscurations, as long as they have not extirpated the instinctual ignorance-driven evolutionary action, which is the foundation of all addictions. Therefore, they are not utterly free from the fetid trace of addictions that is included in the category of objective obscurations.

They will not obtain the transcendence of self uncreated by the addictive and objective obscurations, which is not only the perceptive realization of the twofold emptiness but also the opposite of all truth-[status] perception, insofar as they follow a habitual pattern[315] of subtle identity reifica-

---

312. *abhiprāya, bsam pa.*

313. *rnam rig.*

314. *antarābhava, bar do.*

315. *kun spyod.*

tion[316] depending on the foundational instinctual ignorance-driven evolutionary action, [since for them] the perception of intrinsic identifiability is still intact despite the fact that they no longer have the habitual conviction about intrinsic identifiability, and they are still driven by the aforementioned uncontaminated karmic evolution.

They will not obtain the transcendence of supreme bliss as the extinction of suffering, which is the fruition of addictions and the mind-made bodies insofar as these bodies have originated depending on the foundational instinctual ignorance-driven evolutionary action and uncontaminated karmic evolution that are motivated by the habit of subtle identity reification conditioned by the foundational instinctual ignorance-driven evolutionary action.

And they will not obtain the transcendence of permanent eternity unchanged by birth and death, insofar as they have not overcome the death of inconceivable transformation, and as long as they have not actualized the tathāgata essence, the reality-limit,[317] by the way of constant equipoise by stopping all defilements[318] with respect to addiction, karmic evolution, and birth.

Such an explanation of the topic of eternity is intended to thwart the formation of the notion that it is a permanent entity as accepted by the outsider fundamentalists!

Those [bodhisattvas] on the path of learning [TL 088A] are able to simultaneously manifest emanated bodies in three thousand world systems of the universe multiplied by a thousand million, etc., and to develop innumerable disciples to the extent that they are eligible for the fruition of sainthood, just as fruit ripens. Nevertheless, during this time, these activities are done by means of motivation for teaching with subtle effort, yet these activities depend upon the realization of the reality-limit. When we can stay forever in the equipoise regarding reality without ending it as long as the life cycle exists, having stopped not only the stages of operation with respect to the twelve links of relativistic origination included in the category of addictions, but also all the stages of operation included in the category of objective obscurations, we have obtained the fourfold transcendence that is

---

316. *sūkṣma-nimitta-prapañca, mtshan ma'i spros pa spyod pa phra mo.*

317. *bhūtakoṭi, yang dag pa'i mtha'.*

318. *saṁkleśa, kun nas nyon mongs.*

called "transcendent eternity" in particular. Thus, the assertion that accepts a positive, independent, permanent entity should be known as a system outside this [Buddhist] Dharma. If bodhisattvas did not develop sentient beings in such numbers as aforementioned, they would fall into the nihilistic extreme despite the realization of the reality-limit! And we should know that the extent of the development of sentient beings as explicated in [Maitreya's] *Ornament of the Universal Vehicle Sutras* and [Haribhadra's] *Clear Meaning* commentary on the *Ornament of Clear Realization* [TL o88B] is also based on that [number].

Just as the twelve links of relativistic origination with respect to the category of addiction are included in the three points regarding addiction: the addiction of addiction, the addiction of karmic evolution, and the addiction of birth, these [obstacles] also consist of the three meanings regarding addiction: the foundational instinctual ignorance-driven evolutionary action similar to the addiction of addiction, the creational uncontaminated karmic evolution similar to the addiction of karmic evolution, and the accomplishment of the threefold mind-made body and death of inconceivable transformation similar to the addiction of birth.

3.1.2.1.2.2.1.2.2.1.2.2.3.1.2.1.2.2.3.2. Sutra Reference

≪113≫ Again, this passage of the treatise is to be understood in detail according to the *Shrīmālādevī Lion's Roar Sutra*:

> O Bhagavān, conditioned by creations and caused by contaminated karmic evolution, there is the production of the threefold worldly states such as the desire realm, etc. [Likewise, O Bhagavān, conditioned by the foundational instinctual ignorance-driven evolutionary action and caused by uncontaminated karmic evolution, there is the production of the threefold mind-made body of saints, hermit buddhas, and bodhisattvas who have attained powers. O Bhagavān, for the production of the threefold mind-made body in these three stages and for the accomplishment of contaminated karmic evolution, the foundational instinctual ignorance-driven evolutionary action is the condition.]

It is suitable to explain "these three stages" as the stage of disciple, etc., in accordance with the statements below in the sense that temporary fruitions of the three vehicles before the attainment of the truth body are endowed with a chance for attaining the three [mind-made] bodies.

3.1.2.1.2.2.1.2.2.1.2.2.3.1.2.1.2.2.3.3. Indicating That Only the Tathāgata's Truth Body Is Endowed with Fourfold Transcendence

≪114≫ Thus, in these three mind-made bodies of saints, [hermit buddhas, and bodhisattvas,] etc., there are no transcendences of purity, self, bliss, and eternity despite the fact that all suffering has been eliminated. Seeing this, [the *Shrīmālādevī Lion's Roar Sutra*] states:

> Only the truth body of the Tathāgata [is the transcendence of purity, the transcendence of self, the transcendence of bliss, and the transcendence of eternality.]

3.1.2.1.2.2.1.2.2.1.2.2.3.1.2.2. Explaining, Respectively, the Defining Characteristics of the Four Fruitions . . . 2.1. The Root Text

The truth body of the tathāgatas is transcendent purity because it is naturally pure and because the evolutionary instincts for addiction are completely removed. It is the transcendent supreme self because it is concomitant with the permanent pacification of reification of dualistic perception regarding selflessness, directly realizing that there are neither reifications of personal self as imagined by the outsiders [TL 089A] nor does selflessness [itself] have truth status. It is transcendent bliss because the mind-made aggregate, which is produced by nonaddictive ignorance and karmic evolution, and its causes, the foundational instinctual ignorance-driven evolutionary action and karmic evolutionary action [itself], have been reversed and completely eliminated. In addition, it is transcendent eternality by virtue of the realization of the sameness of the life cycle and nirvana in terms of their emptiness of intrinsic reality, the ultimate freedom from both extremes.

3.1.2.1.2.2.1.2.2.1.2.2.3.1.2.2.2. The Commentary

«115» In brief, [the transcendent purity in the truth body of the tathā-gatas should be understood] for two reasons: (1) by the general characteristic of natural purity; and (2) by the special characteristic of the removal of taints by means of powerful antidotes.

[The transcendent supreme self, too, should be understood] for two reasons: (1) because it is free from self-reification and so free from falling to the extreme [self] of the outsiders, which is the extreme of the life cycle resulting from the habitual conviction about a personal self; and (2) because it is free from selflessness-reification, having eliminated the falling to the extreme [selflessness] of the disciples, which is the extreme of nirvana, despite their direct realization of selflessness. This demonstrates the way of being free from the two extremes in terms of fruition. As for the way in terms of apprehended object, freedom from self-reification is the realization of the twofold selflessness, and freedom from selflessness-reification is the realization of the twofold selflessness as lacking intrinsic reality status. And freedom from elaborations regarding the way of the realization [of selflessness] occurs with the decline of [TL 089B] the dualistic experience of selflessness.

The [transcendent] bliss is likewise to be understood for two reasons: (1) because of the destruction of taking rebirth [driven] by karmic instincts that ensures continuity of homogeneous ignorance, on account of the elimination of all kinds of origin of suffering regarding the twofold obscuration; and (2) because of the actualized cessation of the mind-made bodies on account of the actualization of all kinds of cessation of suffering.

As for the transcendent eternality, it is explicated under three subcategories: (a) the main meaning; (b) the sutra reference; and (c) [unlocated] nirvana as liberation from two kinds of extreme.

First, there are two kinds of falling to the extremes of the life cycle and of nirvana: one regarding the conventional reality, the other regarding the ultimate reality. In conventional terms, falling to the extreme of the life cycle is taking rebirth in the life cycle driven by karmic evolution and the addictions. Falling to the extreme of nirvana is seeking a nirvanic peace that is the attainment of stopping any rebirth, even that driven by compassion and vows, with the view that any kind of rebirth in the life cycle is an object of negation. In ultimate terms, these two are the habitual convictions about truth status in [both] the life cycle and nirvana as eliminated and attained. Regarding the truth body of the Tathāgata, in ultimate terms, (1) he does not fall to the nihilistic extreme by minimizing the life cycle to the extent of its being impermanent, as something with intrinsic reality that is realized as newly eliminated; (2) nor does he fall to the eternalistic extreme by exaggerating nirvana to the extent of being permanent, as something that has recently acquired intrinsic reality. [TL 090A] In conventional terms, (1) the truth body of the Tathāgata does not fall to the nihilistic extreme, as the Tathāgata does not minimize the life cycle as being impermanent, taking rebirth instead by the force of compassion and vows, despite having ceased being driven to do so by karmic evolution and addiction; (2) nor does the truth body of the Tathāgata fall to the eternalistic extreme of exaggerating nirvana as being permanent, not showing the way of establishing its attainment by depending on the mere discontinuation of rebirth in the life cycle as the objective to be attained. [As stated next] in the *Shrīmālādevī Lion's Roar Sutra*:

≪116≫ Second, it states:

[If someone perceives the created as impermanent,] O Bhagavān, [that would be a nihilistic view. And it would not be correct. If someone perceives nirvana as eternal, O Bhagavān, that would be an eternalistic view. And it would not be correct.]

Viewing the created life cycle as previously having intrinsic reality and then later vanishing is a nihilistic view. Viewing mere rebirth in the life cycle as an object of negation is also a nihilistic view, as taught in this text. In light of this, we should know that it would be a mistake to repudiate the conventional [reality] by accepting the view that the created is impermanent, for that is a nihilistic view. Likewise, viewing nirvana as having intrinsic reality is an eternalistic view. Viewing nirvana as an attainment dependent on discontinuing mere rebirth in the life cycle as an ultimate objective is also an eternalistic view, as taught in this text. Thus, we should know that it would be an erroneous view to repudiate [the actual] nirvana by accepting the view that nirvana is permanent and eternalistic, for it is inappropriate to hold that nirvana is either permanent or impermanent.

Third, it is said, by the demonstration that the truth body is free from two kinds of extremes—that the means by which the mode of the ultimate element that causes nirvana is actualized—that ultimately the life cycle itself lacks intrinsic reality status, i.e., [TL 090B] the natural nirvana;[319] and the nonabiding nirvana is the ultimate extinction of incidental taints on the basis of direct realization of that. [This is true] because [the Tathāgata] has actualized the nonabiding nirvana without constructing such a duality of the life cycle and nirvana after he had developed a habitual affinity for intuitive wisdom, which realizes the sameness of the two.

3.1.2.1.2.2.1.2.2.1.2.2.3.1.2.3. Demonstrating That the Wisdom Realizing Emptiness and the Great Compassion within the Bodhisattva's Continuum Are the Root of the Truth Body

«117» Although it is appropriate to consider this [following] passage of the commentary as the continuation of the previous passage, it seems that this is the exposition of the verse below; [I.39] thus it comes before [the treatise]. This passage shows that the unlocated place, which is neither close nor far from all sentient beings, is obtained by two causes that cause the extremes of the life cycle and nirvana to be excluded. Which two? The noble bodhisattvas do not get close to all sentient beings, because all evolutionary instincts for attachment have been eliminated by their wisdom, which is the direct realization of emptiness, impermanence, suffering, etc. Stopping the fall to the extreme of the life cycle—ceasing the type in terms of the ultimate—is done by the wisdom that realizes emptiness; stopping the type with respect to [the conventional,] the mere rebirth in the life cycle, is done by the force of compassion and vows. Likewise, bodhisattvas do not feel remote from sentient beings, because those beings will never be abandoned due to the bodhisattvas' great compassion. [TL 091A] This superb wisdom and liberative art are the methods for the attainment of the perfect enlightenment that is not situated in the extremes of either the life cycle or nirvana. Indeed, the noble bodhisattvas have eliminated all evolutionary instincts for attachment by the intuitive wisdom that is the realization of emptiness, impermanence, etc., for the sake of their own perfection, thereby being deeply intent upon nirvana but having no desire to attain it; and not staying in the extreme of the life cycle, as do those wrong-desiring ones who do not have the spiritual potential for nirvana. This statement means that

---

319. *prakṛtiparinirvaṇa, rang bzhin gyis myang 'das.*

[the noble bodhisattvas] have acquired antidotes that cause all the evolutionary instincts to be eliminated, and succeed as much as circumstances allow, but have not yet completely eliminated them. Owing to their motivation of great compassion, they never abandon suffering sentient beings. They take rebirth in the life cycle for the sake of others, thereby acting in the life cycle and not staying in the extreme of nirvana, as do those who aspire only for peace.

3.1.2.1.2.2.1.2.2.1.2.2.3.1.2.3.2. Prelude

«118» Thus these two excellences, wisdom and compassion, are the root of the unsurpassed enlightenment.

3.1.2.1.2.2.1.2.2.1.2.2.3.1.2.3.3. The Root Text

[Though] having completely severed self-cherishing by the wisdom that is the realization of emptiness, impermanence, etc., and not staying in the extreme of the life cycle, compassionate noble bodhisattvas do not attain the extreme of nirvana owing to their other-cherishing, which wishes for all beings to be free from suffering. Thus, [TL 091B] depending on a habitual affinity for techniques—which is comprised of the aforementioned wisdom and compassion—for actualizing unsurpassed enlightenment, the noble bodhisattvas have not fallen either into the extreme of the life cycle or of nirvana.

The *Ornament of Clear Realization* states: "[They] stay neither in the life cycle because of wisdom, nor in nirvana because of compassion." A former scholar explicates this statement as an exclusive reference to wisdom realizing emptiness, which stops the extreme of the life cycle. It clearly shows that that person does not understand at all, because both noble Vimuktasena and Haribhadra explain "wisdom" to be what perceives the disadvantages of the life cycle. The validating cognition that realizes the disadvantages of the life cycle is that of the conventional reality, not the one that fathoms the ultimate. In addition, the aforementioned disciples who aspire only for peace are the ones who are so determined, but temporary in that lineage. Do not hold some Experientialists' literal explanation of this point to be true of the *Elucidation of the Intention Sutra*.

3.1.2.1.2.2.1.2.2.1.2.2.3.2. Actions . . . 2.1. Question

« 119 » Now, [with reference to the aforementioned meaning of "actions," what is demonstrated by the latter half of that verse (I.35)?]

3.1.2.1.2.2.1.2.2.1.2.2.3.2.2. Answer . . . 2.1. Proving Inference . . . 1.1. The Root Text

If the naturally pure tathāgata element and the uncontaminated seeds did not exist, aversion to suffering would not arise by [beings] perceiving its faults. Desire, aspiration, and prayer for nirvana would also not arise by perceiving its bliss. The proof induced by this statement is as follows: [TL 092A] the spiritual potential for buddhahood exists in sentient beings, because it is apparent that they have desire for the abandonment of the life cycle due to their aversion to it and their desire to attain nirvana.

3.1.2.1.2.2.1.2.2.1.2.2.3.2.2.1.2. The Commentary . . . 2.1. Sutra Source

« 120 » So the *[Shrīmālādevī Lion's Roar] Sutra* states:

O Bhagavān, if there were no tathāgata essence, then there would arise neither aversion to suffering nor desire for nirvana, nor the wish, aspiration, or prayer for it.

3.1.2.1.2.2.1.2.2.1.2.2.3.2.2.1.2.2. Explication

Here, in brief, the tathāgata element, the pure spiritual potential, even of those people who are definitely deluded, causes two kinds of action. It develops aversion to the life cycle on the basis of perceiving the faults of suffering, and it calls forth desire, wish, aspiration, and prayer for nirvana on the basis of perceiving the virtues of bliss. Here, "wish" means manifested desire, regarding nirvana as the aim with excellences. "Desire" means longing for the attainment of the desired aim, having desire for the attainment of that aim with excellences. "Aspiration" means searching for the means to obtain the desired aim. This is easy to understand. "Prayer" means causing the wish by thinking of the desired aim and feeling joy by perceiving that nirvana can be achieved by liberative arts.

3.1.2.1.2.2.1.2.2.1.2.2.3.2.2.2. Establishment by Means of Circularity . . .
2.1. The Root Text

«121» Perceiving the life cycle as having the faults of suffering and nirvana as having the excellences of bliss is due to the existence of the [spiri-
tual] potential. Why? Those who lack the spiritual potential do not have
such perceptions. The former part of this statement demonstrates positive
concomitance[320] and the latter part demonstrates negative concomitance.[321]

3.1.2.1.2.2.1.2.2.1.2.2.3.2.2.2.2. The Commentary . . . 2.1. Establishment of
Spiritual Potential by Means of Circularity [TL 092B]

Because of the existence of the spiritual potential for liberation within
their continuums, the people who are endowed with positive excellences
perceive the life cycle as having the faults of suffering by pondering the
general and specific disadvantages of the life cycle, and nirvana as having
the excellences of bliss. It would not be logical for [these thoughts] to arise
without cause and conditions. When hearing of the faults of the life cycle
and the benefits of nirvana, and when the mere sound of [the teachings on]
emptiness causes the hairs of the body to stand on end, etc., it is an indication of the existence of the virtuous roots associated with liberation. This
association is not identical to the one with reference to the five paths, for
it is not required to meditate on the paths. It would be difficult to produce
genuine vows for individual liberation without these thoughts; we therefore make an effort to deposit evolutionary instincts for aversion to the life
cycle by perceiving its faults. It should be known that we are endowed with
the virtuous roots associated with liberation when we have developed such
thoughts by hearing just once the teaching properly given by a virtuous
friend.

3.1.2.1.2.2.1.2.2.1.2.2.3.2.2.2.2.2. Proving Consequence

Why is this so? If these perceptions would arise without cause and conditions in terms of the situation where sins such as killing, etc., have not

320. *rjes 'gro.*
321. *ldog pa.*

been depleted, then the wrong-desiring ones would have such perceptions despite their lack of potential for nirvana. The authentic reasoning induced by this consequence is as follows: [TL 093A] the proper acquisitions with the four kinds of wheel, i.e., the conditions for the attainment of liberation, such as reliance upon sages, previous merit collection, staying in conducive locations, and proper prayer and mentation, are the awakening conditions of the potential free from incidental taints existing from beginningless time. The existence of the spiritual potential can be realized on the basis of such awakening. Indeed, the mind that perceives the faults of the life cycle and the benefits of nirvana will not arise as long as faith in the Dharma of one of the three vehicles has not been developed. This demonstrates the opposite of the thesis of the consequence.

3.1.2.1.2.2.1.2.2.1.2.2.3.2.2.2.2.3. Establishing the Sutra Statement Concerning the Person Who Will Not Attain Liberation as Having a Deeper Intention . . . 3.1. Sutra Reference

«122» The spiritual potential exists even within those people whose spiritual potential has been temporarily severed. For what reason? The *Ornament of the Light of Wisdom Sutra* states:

> After this, due to hearing the holy Dharma, the intuitive wisdom light rays of the tathāgata sun fall upon the bodies of even those people who are confirmed in error; [certain] bodhisattvas with pure high resolve, some who have the potential for the hermit buddha vehicle, some who have the potential for the disciple vehicle, and [even some] sentient beings who are endowed with virtuous high resolve and correct belief, respectively, thus it will benefit them and produce the proper cause of future [liberation]. The [light will] cause their virtuous qualities to increase.

3.1.2.1.2.2.1.2.2.1.2.2.3.2.2.2.2.3.2. Establishing the Sutra Statement as Having a Deeper Intention . . . 2.1. Its Purpose and Intended Basis [TL 093B]

«123» As to the statement that "wrong-desiring ones have the quality of no nirvana forever," as found in many sutras such as the *Great Total Nirvana Sutra*, it is so declared because feeling enmity toward the universal vehicle teaching and dislike of liberation is the cause of being doomed; they increasingly strengthen the attachment to the erroneous life cycle. They will not attain liberation when roaming in the life cycle for a time long beyond countless eons; it is thus stated for the purpose of freeing them from their enmity.

3.1.2.1.2.2.1.2.2.1.2.2.3.2.2.2.2.3.2.2. Indicating How to Fault the Literal Meaning

No sentient being could be impure forever with [merely] incidental taints; thus, due to the existence of the naturally pure potential and developmental potential within all beings, it is impossible to never attain buddhahood.

Objection: We shall analyze this position. If it is possible for all sentient beings to attain buddhahood, then for the last few buddhas, his altruistic enlightened activities would be very limited and his merit store would be incomplete since he can only benefit very few sentient beings. When all beings have become buddhas, their altruistic enlightened activities would have also come to an end; thus they would fall into the extreme of peace, for there would be no single sentient being left who needs help. [TL 094A] On the other hand, if it is not possible for all sentient beings to obtain buddhahood, then it would be futile for buddhas to take the responsibility of placing all beings in a buddhahood similar to their own and to turn the wheel of Dharma in the form of the twelve enlightened activities until the end of the life cycle. If all beings [are instructed] to seek the mere cessation of suffering in the life cycle, then [the Buddha] would not have the complete characteristic of the great compassion of the universal vehicle; that is to say, if he does not place all beings on the level of buddhahood similar to his own, he would be stingy with the Dharma! These five refutations are in contradiction to your position. If all beings are capable of attaining the cessation of suffering in the life cycle, then the ultimate single vehicle can be well established. It would be effortless to establish that all beings will attain buddhahood. If it is not possible for some sentient beings to attain even liberation, this would contradict the fact that the holy Master [Asaṅga] proves with sutra sources and reasoning that [such a statement] cannot be taken literally, for it has a deeper intention. Therefore, you must explain it. In addition, if it is possible for all sentient beings to attain buddhahood, then it would be invalid to explain that the life cycle is endless.

Reply: Here, I shall first refute the views held by opponents, and then present my own.

First, someone asserts that setting aside consideration of the certainty that all beings will become buddhas makes even its possibility questionable. In order to establish the possibility of producing a result, the collection of causes must be complete [TL 094B] and be posited as the reason. If all beings have already completed the collection of causes of buddhahood, then there would be no sentient being who has not entered the path to liberation. And for this reason, the life cycle would never come to an end, as sentient beings are caught up in the life cycle until that point. As to the establishment of the ultimate single vehicle, it means that all sentient beings who have entered the path will become buddhas. This assertion does not seem to be logical. It is the logicians' intention that the completion of the collection of causes is concomitant with the possibility of producing the result; it is not their intention, however, that the possibility of producing the result is concomitant with the completion of the collection of causes, since it contradicts logic. For example, although it is possible for barley seeds to produce sprouts, this does not require the completion of all causes.

Furthermore, can noble disciples possibly attain buddhahood or not? If they can, it would be valid to state that they have completed the collection of causes of buddhahood. If that is acceptable, then it would be valid to state that they have entered the path of the universal vehicle, and that you accept reasons and concomitances in both theses as well as the attribute in the later thesis. [This would lead to the conclusion that] your assertion is deficient [in reasoning,] since all beings have not merely entered the path. If they cannot, this would be in direct contradiction to your position and to the concept of the ultimate single vehicle.

Moreover, it is quite clear that if all beings will become enlightened, we must accept that it is possible for them to become buddhas. Other people assert that the mode of the life cycle being endless is like that [mentioned above], that it is not possible for all beings [TL 095A] to become buddhas despite the fact that [theoretically] they will become enlightened; and if it were acceptable that the fact that all beings will become enlightened is concomitant with the possibility of all beings becoming buddhas, then it would demonstrate the thesis that does not show any validating cognition and accepted reason, as in the following case. It follows that it is possible for all things to disintegrate because all things do disintegrate. What fault can be found in our assertion? It is highly acceptable to state that it would be possible for all phenomena to disappear if it is possible for all phenomena to disintegrate. If it is not possible for all phenomena to disappear, then we must accept that it is not possible for all phenomena to disappear. A phenomenon exists until this point and will disappear after that, since it is possible for all phenomena to disintegrate. This means that it would be impossible for a phenomenon to exist after that point. [For example,] it can be established that blue exists until this point and will disappear after that, since it is possible for blue to disintegrate. If the reason were not established, blue would be a permanent entity, for it is impossible for blue to disintegrate after it has been produced by its own causes. It also follows that it is impossible for all phenomena to disintegrate. Someone faults our position by the following thesis: it follows that all beings are invariably dead because all beings will invariably die. This clearly reveals the coarse intelligence of this person. Understand my previous thesis properly! [TL 095B] Do I say that "all beings have invariably become buddhas?" or that "it is possible for all beings to become buddhas?"

As to the statement that "all beings will become enlightened, but it is by no means certain," it is a clear sign indicating that this person does not know reasoning. Is your ascertainment that "all beings will become enlightened" gained by the force of validating cognition in your continuum or not? If the former were the case, then it follows that it is certain for all beings to become enlightened because it is ascertained by the force of validating cognition. If you argue that this association cannot be established since in reality it is uncertain, despite the certainty ascertained by the force of validating cognition, then it follows that this ascertainment is an erroneous cognition with respect to the conceptual object because its certainty only exists in your mind and has nothing to do with reality. If you assert that it is not certain that fire will produce smoke despite the fact that it is established by validating cognition, it would be impossible for unfavorable conditions to exist, as stated in [Dharmakīrti's] *Commentary on [Dignāga's] Validating Cognition Compendium* that "it is uncertain because of possible obstacles." Likewise, if enlightenment is certain, then it would be impossible for unfavorable conditions to exist. Both your example and your meaning cannot be established. In regard to that example, if it is ascertained by the force of validating cognition, then this contradicts your statement that it is uncertain that fire produces smoke. If it is not ascertained by validating cognition, then the meaning of the thesis is not established by validating cognition. But you claim that "there is no proof whatsoever for the subject of my thesis." This reveals your sheer stupidity. [TL 096A]

Moreover, it follows that noble disciples and hermit buddhas would certainly [not] become enlightened because the obstacles of unfavorable conditions of enlightenment possibly exist. You have accepted this concomitance. If so, it contradicts your assertion of the certainty of the ultimate single vehicle. The meaning of that statement in [Dharmakīrti's] *Commentary on [Dignāga's] Validating Cognition* is not as you have construed. I have given a detailed exposition in the commentary on this text. On the contrary, if it were the position you accept, then it would follow that it is uncertain for the vase to exist since there are possible obstacles of unfavorable conditions for the existence of the vase. Therefore, why must there be a contradiction between possible obstacles of unfavorable conditions for production and the lack of power to stop production?

If the latter were the case, to say your ascertainment that "all beings will become enlightened" is not gained by the force of validating cognition, then it follows that your thesis would be unacceptable and that your investigating cognition does not agree with the truth, since your thesis is not established by validating cognition. If there were no concomitance in this case, then there would be a refutation that "there is no authentic reason for nonobservation of the nonappearing."[322] And you have to accept that there is no proof whatsoever for all hidden phenomena, since there would be no other authentic reasons as well. Thus, the difference between a realized scholar and an ignorant person is the one between knowing and not knowing how to truly establish the meaning of accepted theses by validating cognition.

If validating cognition established that all beings will become enlightened [TL 096B] but there were no certainty, then validating cognition would not be able to establish anything with certainty. After you have ascertained the certainty, there would be no greater ignorance than to proclaim that there is no certainty that all beings will become enlightened. Can you decide whether all beings will become enlightened according to their own objective conditions? If not, it would contradict your assertion. If you could

322. *mi snang ma dmigs pa.*

decide that they will not become enlightened, it would also contradict your assertion. If you could decide that they will become enlightened, it would contradict the opposite, that it is uncertain that they will become enlightened. If you claim that there is nothing to be decided on according to sentient beings' own objective conditions, your decision that all beings will become enlightened would be irrelevant.

> Having neither the ability to explicate flawless reasoning
> Nor the instruction revealing the sutras as personal advice,
> We should wisely maintain equanimity toward the Buddha's teaching,
> Instead of proclaiming, "I shall explain the Buddha's intention."

Second, I have explained above that it would contradict reasoning if we accept that all beings will become enlightened, but not with certainty. It would also be hard to sustain reasoned analysis if we claim that all beings will not become enlightened. If all beings' minds were not naturally pure, then we must accept that there would be knowable things that have truth status, and that it would be impossible to posit the ultimate truth since all things' emptiness of truth status cannot be established by validating cognition. [On the other hand,] if it is provable by validating cognition that the mind is naturally pure, then it can be established by the same reasoning that taints along with the evolutionary instincts of the grasping at truth status [TL 097A] are incidental, and possibly to be removed. Otherwise, we must accept that taints enter into the nature of the mind as the outsider Mīmāṁsā tradition asserts. If you claim that taints established by validating cognition are removable but the antidotes for eliminating them are not possibly developed in the continuum, is it due to the lack of the technique that eliminates taints in the continuums of all beings that an antidote is not developed? Is it because no one knows, despite the existence of the technique? Is it because no one would possibly seek that technique despite the existence of such people who know it? Is it because the people who know the technique could not possibly teach it out of compassionate motivation? Is it because it is impossible to meditate on that technique and implement it despite the fact that the teaching is available?

The first position is not correct since taints will come to an end by meditating on the wisdom that realizes selflessness. The second is not correct since it is established by reasoning that there are teachers who have perfected their meditation on the wisdom that realizes selflessness, the technique used for the benefit of sentient beings. The third is not correct since there is no sentient being who would not seek higher rebirths when exhorted by buddhas, since all beings are endowed with the twofold spiritual potential for buddhahood. Despite the fact that [some people] temporarily do not seek the ultimate good, since [these people] would have renounced the life cycle and would be seeking nirvana, and owing to the unwavering compassion [of the Buddha] in the form of taking responsibility to place all beings in buddhahood, these people would eventually seek the ultimate good. [TL 097B] This can also be established on the basis of correct reasoning of the authentic sutras proved by the three kinds of analysis. The fourth is not correct since the Buddha Bhagavān would never cease the activity of teaching the Dharma because of his unwavering compassion toward all beings that is like caring for his only child, when they voluntarily seek [liberation]. The fifth is not correct since this treatise and the commentary thereon, etc., prove that the spiritual potential will awaken in the right conditions at a certain time. Therefore, we shall not accept that all beings cannot become enlightened and that it is uncertain for them to do so, if we accept that there is no person who would not possibly beome enlightened. Indeed, we shall accept that all beings will become buddhas, because they will all become enlightened.

Implying that all beings are already buddhas has been explained to be incorrect. If you claim that it follows that sentient beings would never exist because they will become buddhas, there is no concomitance between not existing and becoming a buddha. You have no choice but to accept that it would be impossible for all beings to exist, because of utter nonexistence of things. You have also to accept, as mentioned above, that there would be no sentient beings, the object that buddhas aim to benefit. It follows that sentient beings would cease to exist because they would become buddhas. If so, bodhisattvas on the eighth stage would cease to exist because they would become buddhas. It is concomitant by the same force. Thus you have to accept all three consequences. [TL 098A] The proof of this concomitance is that if someone were a buddha, he would necessarily not be a sentient being. Analyze it carefully and you will realize that you failed to differentiate the position that all beings will become buddhas from the one that all beings are already buddhas. You may ask, if all beings would become buddhas, then where and when would these buddhas exist?[323] In that case, [I shall ask,] when you think "I shall attain buddhahood for the benefit of sentient beings," within which continuum would that perfect buddhahood to be attained exist? And when? If you reply that it exists within the continuum of the Buddha, when we have attained perfect buddhahood, since the buddhahood to be attained does not exist within the continuums of bodhisattvas on the path of accumulation and since cause and fruition are not simultaneously arising, then likewise, my answer would be the same. Why do you find it to be unacceptable?

If the life cycle had a beginning, it would come into existence without causes; thus there is no starting point. Nevertheless, is there an end point? Someone claims that the life cycle in general does not have an end, but a specific life cycle does. This is a contradiction since it is similar to the claim that something does not exist in things but exists in a vase. Therefore, both the general and specific life cycle have an endpoint. As to the sutra statement that "the end of the life cycle is not found," we shall understand that it means that the childish should not assume the certainty of the time for liberation despite the fact that there is no sentient being who would not possibly obtain liberation as explained above. [TL 098B] Someone claims that "the life cycle does not have an end but all beings will be enlightened." This is a totally contradictory burden. This is enough for elaborations.

3.1.2.1.2.2.1.2.2.1.2.2.3.2.2.2.2.3.2.3. Sutra Reference ... 3.1. Prelude

≪124≫ It is unacceptable to maintain that it is impossible for sentient beings to be purified from incidental taints. Intending the existence of natural purity and possible purity from incidental taints in all beings without discrimination, the Bhagavān therefore declares:[324]

3.1.2.1.2.2.1.2.2.1.2.2.3.2.2.2.2.3.2.3.2. Sutra Passage

The minds of sentient beings and their taints are beginningless, but incidental taints will come to an end. The mind is naturally

---

323. "All beings would have become buddhas" (*sems can thams cad sangs rgyas pa yod*). This literally means "all beings have obtained buddhahood." In order to clarify what the term means, Gyaltsap puts this question to himself.

324. Source unidentified.

pure and endowed with unending engagement in [altruistic activities] until the end of the life cycle after it has been purified of all incidental taints; the naturally pure reality [of the mind] is not to be directly seen because outside it is covered by a beginningless sheath of taints, just like a gold image concealed in mud, etc.

3.1.2.1.2.2.1.2.2.1.2.3. Possession . . . 3.1. Prelude

«125» Here, [is one verse with reference to the meaning of "possession."]

3.1.2.1.2.2.1.2.2.1.2.3.2. Brief Statement . . . 2.1. Possession of the Causal Excellences

The spiritual potential existing within sentient beings should be understood to be like a great ocean, an inexhaustible store of immeasurable jewels of excellent qualities. Just like a great ocean that is the container of jewels, and so on, containing jewels and water, the element in the continuums of sentient beings is the abode of the [TL 099A] four excellences [of faith, wisdom, concentration, and compassion]. Faith is like the container, wisdom and concentration are like jewels, and compassion is like the water.

3.1.2.1.2.2.1.2.2.1.2.3.2.2. Possession of the Fruitional Excellences

[The element] is like a lamp, because its nature possesses seven inseparable fruitional excellences: [knowledge of] magical operations, divine hearing, telepathy, knowledge of former lives, knowledge of death migrations and future lives, knowledge of the cessation of taints, and the cessation of taints.

3.1.2.1.2.2.1.2.2.1.2.3.3. Detailed Exposition . . . 3.1. Possession of the Causal Excellences . . . 1.1. Question

«126» Here, [what is shown by the former half of the verse?]

3.1.2.1.2.2.1.2.2.1.2.3.3.1.2. Answer . . . 2.1. The Root Text

Because it consists of the four causal excellences—that is to say, (1) faith in the universal vehicle, which is the cause for purifying the truth body; (2)

the unique mental quiescence; and (3) transcendent analysis of the universal vehicle, the cause of obtaining a buddha's intuitive wisdom; and (4) compassion, the cause for receiving the Tathāgata's great compassion—the element is demonstrated to be like an ocean, by means of three similes of faith being the ocean bed, mental quiescence and transcendent analysis the jewels, and compassion the water.

3.1.2.1.2.2.1.2.2.1.2.3.3.1.2.2. The Commentary . . . 2.1. Statement

«127» On account of the three points, namely, faith, meditation and wisdom, and great compassion, [which are analogous to the three aspects of a great ocean, respectively, the meaning of "possession" should be understood in terms of the tathāgata element being endowed with (the excellences of) the cause.]

3.1.2.1.2.2.1.2.2.1.2.3.3.1.2.2.2. Exposition . . . 2.1. Categories of Excellence

Then, which are the three points? [They are (1) the cause of purifying the truth body; (2) the cause of obtaining a buddha's intuitive wisdom; and (3) the cause of receiving a tathāgata's great compassion.]

3.1.2.1.2.2.1.2.2.1.2.3.3.1.2.2.2.2. Exposition of Each Category

[TL 099B] Here, (1) the cause of purifying the truth body is to be known as the meditation on faith in the universal vehicle. This cause is of paramount importance since, if they lacked it as foundation, there would be no meditation on the concentration of integrated mental quiescence and transcendent analysis and meditation on the great compassion; (2) the cause of obtaining a buddha's intuitive wisdom, the meditation on wisdom and concentration as the path of preventing the extremes of the life cycle and nirvana, which is the technique for attaining the unlocated nirvana; and (3) the cause of receiving a tathāgata's great compassion in order to purify the elements of all beings, the meditation on the great compassion of bodhisattvas.

3.1.2.1.2.2.1.2.2.1.2.3.3.1.2.2.2.3. Similes and Their Implications

The meditation on faith in the universal vehicle is analogous to an ocean bed since it holds immeasurable and inexhaustible jewels of wisdom and concentration as well as the water of compassion, causing all the excellences of the Buddha to be accomplished. The meditation on wisdom and concentration is analogous to a jewel because it is free from any conceptual thought, such as that "this result should be given," and is endowed with inconceivable powerful excellences that are by nature capable of producing fruition. The meditation on the great compassion of bodhisattvas is analogous to the water, never going beyond [its nature of being] moist and nurturing, because it has the sole taste of a supreme moistness [permeating] all beings with the wish for them to be free from suffering.

This conjunction of [the element] with the four causal excellences in terms of these three causes—the cause for purifying, the cause for obtaining, and the cause for receiving—of the three things—the truth body, a buddha's intuitive wisdom, and compassion—is called "possession."

3.1.2.1.2.2.1.2.2.1.2.3.3.2. Possession of the Fruitional Excellences . . . 2.1. Question

«128» Here, [what is shown by the latter half of the verse?]

3.1.2.1.2.2.1.2.2.1.2.3.3.2.2. Answer . . . 2.1. The Root Text [TL 100A]

In the stainless state called "the element," or the stainless uncontaminated ultimate element state, the fruitional excellences of the five superknowledges, the intuitive wisdom of the cessation of contaminations, and that stainless cessation [itself] are inseparable in terms of nature, thereby being analogous to a lamp's light, heat, and color. Intuitive wisdom of the cessation of contaminations is the [experiential] knowledge of the cessation of contaminations, the perceptive intuitive wisdom of that stainless cessation. That cessation is also called "liberation."

3.1.2.1.2.2.1.2.2.1.2.3.3.2.2.2. The Commentary . . . 2.1. The Main Meaning . . . 1.1. Brief Statement

[On account of the three points that are analogous to three aspects of a lamp] respectively, [the meaning of "possession" should be understood in terms of the tathāgata element being endowed with (the excellences of) the fruition.]

3.1.2.1.2.2.1.2.2.1.2.3.3.2.2.2.1.2. Detailed Exposition ... 2.1. Categories of Excellence

Then, which are the three points? [They are (1) the superknowledges; (2) the intuitive wisdom of the cessation of contaminations; and (3) the cessation of contamination.]

3.1.2.1.2.2.1.2.2.1.2.3.3.2.2.2.1.2.2. Similes and Their Implications

In regard to the fruitional excellences, the five superknowledges are analogous to light because they have a characteristic of engaging in the elimination of darkness, which is discordant with the experiential knowledge of the perceptual object. The whereabouts of teachers, friends, and disciples are perceived directly. The presence or absence of attachment, and so on, in the minds of others is perceived directly. Having directly seen immeasurable previous lives of self and others, the connections between disciple and teacher, etc., are perceived directly. Intuitive wisdom [TL 100B] of the cessation of contaminations is analogous to heat because of its characteristic of consuming the fuel of karmic evolution and addictions without remainder. The transformed cessation of contamination is analogous to color because of its characteristic of being stainless, pure, and clear-light transparency. Here it is stainless because it has eliminated the addictive obscuration of the grasping at truth status regarding persons and aggregates. It is pure because it has eliminated the objective obscuration that includes evolutionary instincts for addictions and erroneous truth-[status] perception. It is clear-light transparency because it is not in the mind's nature to be [subject to] these two incidental obscurations.

3.1.2.1.2.2.1.2.2.1.2.3.3.2.2.2.1.3. Précis

Thus, these seven things, which consist of the five superknowledges, the intuitive wisdom of the cessation of contaminations, and the cessation [itself] in the continuums of those people who have nothing further to learn, are inseparable from each other in terms of nature in the stainless ultimate element. [These seven things] are [the object of] eternal meditative equipoise on reality free from all taints, being not differentiated but identical to the ultimate element. This is called "possession."

3.1.2.1.2.2.1.2.2.1.2.3.3.2.2.2.2. Sutra Reference

«129» With reference to its meaning, [the simile of a lamp is to be understood in detail] according to the *Sutra [Teaching the Absence of Increase and Decrease (in the Realm of Beings)]*:

> Shāriputra, just as [a lamp is undifferentiated by and inseparable from its light, heat, and color, the precious stone is also undifferentiated by and inseparable from its light, color, and shape. Likewise, Shāriputra, the truth body taught by the Tathāgata is undifferentiated by the excellences of the Tathāgata, which are far beyond the sands of the Ganges in number, and is inseparable from the excellences of the intuitive wisdom.]

This sutra teaches that these excellences are possessed at the time of the ultimate fruition, not existing within the continuums of ordinary individuals.

3.1.2.1.2.2.1.2.2.1.2.4. Categories of Engagement . . . 4.1. The Main Meaning . . . 1.1. Prelude

«130» There is one verse with reference to the meaning of "engagement." There are two kinds of engagement: engagement with respect to persons and engagement with respect to category, according to the sites and the different time periods, respectively, in which reality appears.

3.1.2.1.2.2.1.2.2.1.2.4.1.2. Statement

Engagement with respect to persons refers to the presence of reality in three kinds of person: ordinary people, nobles, and completely perfect buddhas. [TL 101A] Engagement with respect to category refers to the presence of reality in three categories of impurity: with taints, of partial separation [from taints], and cessation of all obscurations. Owing to this engagement, the perceiver of reality has taught that this tathāgata essence, reality mingled with taints, is in sentient beings. The element that is the natural purity of the minds of sentient beings serves as the foundation for sentient beings to attain buddhahood because it produces a buddha's excellences when meditated upon; this is the mine of excellences. Reality mingled with taints is called the "tathāgata essence" because it includes the essential methods for the attainment of perfect buddhahood.

3.1.2.1.2.2.1.2.2.1.2.4.1.3. Exposition ... 3.1. Question

≪131≫ What is shown by this [verse]?

3.1.2.1.2.2.1.2.2.1.2.4.1.3.2. Answer ... 2.1. The Root Text

The reality of the continuums of ordinary people is erroneous since it is mingled with the seeds of taints and the seeds of obscurations to reality that have not been eliminated in the slightest. The reality of the continuums of buddhas-to-be, direct perceivers of the truth, is the opposite, and is correct since the seeds of taints have been eliminated to various degrees, although not totally terminated. The reality of the continuums of the tathāgatas, who ultimately realize it as it is, is absolutely correct without reification. Although the second stage mainly refers to those noble bodhisattvas, other noble beings should also be included.

3.1.2.1.2.2.1.2.2.1.2.4.1.3.2.2. The Commentary

≪132≫ [TL 101B] It should be understood that there are three different categories of engagement with the tathāgata element. In which [sutras] have these been taught? These have been taught in the *Transcendent Wisdom Sutras*, etc., with reference to the nonconceptual intuitive wisdom that is the direct realization of reality. Thus, you should not repudiate the *Transcendent Wisdom Sutras* along with this treatise and its commentary by claiming "this sutra teaches the self-emptiness of the conventional [reality] only, but not the other-emptiness of the ultimate reality, since it has been proved that this sutra does state the categories of the ultimate."

To whom have these been taught? To bodhisattvas. On what basis have they been taught? And how? There are three different kinds of engagement with the general characteristic of the pure reality of all things being the emptiness of intrinsic reality, as taught [in the sutra] of ordinary people who do not perceive reality, of nobles who perceive reality, and of the tathāgatas who have obtained the ultimate purity in perceiving reality. What are these three? They are erroneous, correct, and absolutely correct without reification, respectively. Here, to be more specific, "erroneous" refers to the reality of the childish on account of being mingled with erroneous notions of permanence, etc., for something that is actually impermanent, etc.; having addictive thoughts of attachment, etc., and views that insist upon tolerance and acceptance of what is held by erroneous notions. "Correct" refers to noble beings because they, being opposite from ordinary people, have eliminated error to various degrees. And "absolutely correct without reification" refers to completely perfect buddhas, because they have destroyed addictive obscurations and their evolutionary instincts, as well as objective obscurations.

3.1.2.1.2.2.1.2.2.1.2.4.2. Its Ramifications . . . 2.1. General Prelude

≪133≫ The other [four points taught hereafter should be understood to be the ramifications of the meaning of engagement: categories different in state, but not in nature, establishing the same nature pervading all states, establishing the nature as being immutable, and establishing possession of indivisible excellences of liberation at the time of being absolutely pure.]

3.1.2.1.2.2.1.2.2.1.2.4.2.2. Expositions of Each Meaning . . . 2.1. Categories Different in State but Not in Terms of Nature . . . 1.1. Prelude

Here, [there is one verse with reference to the point of "states."]

3.1.2.1.2.2.1.2.2.1.2.4.2.2.1.2. Statement

The reality of being impure, [both] pure and impure, and absolutely pure are, respectively, called the element of an ordinary being who has not eliminated the seeds of obscurations in the slightest; the element of the continuum of a noble bodhisattva who has eliminated the seeds of mental constructs to various degrees but has not completely eliminated obscurations; and the Tathāgata. This is a statement of the categories of reality. Although it is acceptable to establish the reality of being extremely pure as the tathāgatas without contradiction, it is not acceptable to establish the reality of the former two as ordinary beings and bodhisattvas, since it is the outsiders' way that posits the ultimate truth as a person. The word "called" indicates that the reality of the three kinds of people is the basis of their designations, just as none of the collections, continuums, components, etc., can be accepted as an exemplification of "person," since "person" is designated as being dependent on the collection and continuums of the aggregates. To explain in more detail, as stated in the *Transcendent Wisdom Heart Sutra*, [TL 102B] "matter is emptiness; emptiness is matter." When investigating the mode of existence with regard to the nature of matter, we will know that there is no intrinsic reality of matter even as small as an atom; and when investigating under the sway of the previous understanding of the basis on which matter is designated, we will know that something devoid of intrinsically identifiable reality is designated as matter. Likewise, something devoid of intrinsically identifiable reality is designated as the three kinds of people. The meaning of tathāgata essence is to be understood in light of this.

3.1.2.1.2.2.1.2.2.1.2.4.2.2.1.3. Detailed Exposition . . . 3.1. Question

«134» What is shown by this [verse]?

3.1.2.1.2.2.1.2.2.1.2.4.2.2.1.3.2. Answer . . . 2.1. The Root Text

The element, reality mingled with taints, is demonstrated by the designations of three names in accordance with its three sequential states, which are not exemplifications of the element, as aforementioned. What is the element? It is subsumed under the six points of nature, etc., as explained above. The meaning determined by those six is further summarized and is demonstrated by the designations of three names in accordance with three states.

3.1.2.1.2.2.1.2.2.1.2.4.2.2.1.3.2.2. The Commentary . . . 2.1. The Meaning of the Words

Any teaching on the stainless element—which is the basis of the differentiation of the element into states by the Bhagavān, [made] in detail in many profound Dharma discourses, [with terms] such as "nonproduction," "noncessation," etc.—[has hitherto been subsumed under six points, namely: nature, causes, fruition, actions, possession, and engagement.] This element is also to be known as taught by the teaching of three names in accordance with the three states, respectively. That is to say, [TL 103A] (1) it is called the "element of sentient beings" in the impure state. A general term notwithstanding, this name is for ordinary beings alone since it is distinguished by the state when the seeds of taints have not been eliminated in the slightest; (2) it is called "bodhisattva" in the [mixed] pure and impure state. A general term notwithstanding, this refers to the noble beings as clarified in the sutra as proof. Moreover, it should be known that the bodhisattva is the chief type in this state, and noble disciples and hermit buddhas are also included because they are not considered ordinary people—this statement is also true for "categories of engagement"; [and (3) it is called "the Tathāgata" in the absolutely pure state.]

3.1.2.1.2.2.1.2.2.1.2.4.2.2.1.3.2.2.2. Sutra Reference

«135» As the Bhagavān states [in the *Sutra Teaching the Absence of Increase and Decrease (in the Realm of Beings)*]:

> O Shāriputra, this reality mingled with taints will be designated as the "truth body" if it has been purified. When it is covered with the sheath of limitless addictions, carried by the current of the life cycle, staying in the continuum of an ordinary being in the life cycle by the forces of karmic evolution and addictions, and going in circles between death and birth in the course of the life cycle without beginning and end, it is called the "element of sentient beings."

> This same truth body, O Shāriputra, when it has felt aversion to the sufferings in the current of the life cycle and has become free from attachment to all the objects of desire, venturing forth into the enlightened activities for the sake of enlightenment by means of the ten transcendences after the mastery of all of the eighty-four thousand aggregates of Dharma, it is called "bodhisattva." Because it is unacceptable to maintain that the truth body circles in the life cycle, reality, which will be designated as the truth body if it has been purified, is called "bodhisattva" when it is qualified by those [features]. Those features are demonstrated

by the enlightened activities of a noble bodhisattva who has realized the disadvantages of the life cycle, perceiving them as the opposite [to liberation], and who has ventured forth into the enlightened activities by means of the ten transcendences after the mastery of all of the eighty-four thousand aggregates of Dharma, [TL 103B] which are the antidotes to the eighty-four thousand [erroneous] conducts of a sentient being.

Furthermore, O Shāriputra, as for this very truth body, it has the elimination of the perfection of one's own benefit, having become pure by the process, respectively, of the elimination of active addictions, the elimination of the truth of suffering as fruition, and the elimination of objective obscurations. As for the perfection of other-benefit, [it is the attainment of the power of a person who is unsurpassed in all knowable objects and, unobscured in nature, obtains the unimpeded power of mastery over all things. Then this (truth body) is called "the Tathāgata, the Saint, the Perfectly Accomplished Buddha."]³²⁵

The objective obscurations [are eliminated] by the processes of the twofold realization of the reality and relativity of those objective things.

3.1.2.1.2.2.1.2.2.1.2.4.2.2.2. Establishing the Same Nature Pervading All States . . . 2.1. Prelude

«136» [Here is one verse referring to the meaning of the "all-pervasiveness" of] the tathāgata [element in these three occasions: (1) having elimination of manifest addictions; (2) having fruition of cessation of the truth of suffering; (3) having freedom from objective obscurations]. The distinction [of the element] can be made just on the basis of these occasions, since emptiness of intrinsic identifiability is all-pervading in the three occasions. If the distinction were made in terms of nature, it would contradict this fact that [emptiness of intrinsic identifiability] is undifferentiated and is all-pervading in three states.

---

325. This last part of the quote is actually mostly paraphrase, and the final comment is commentary, which we specified with the brackets in this case.

3.1.2.1.2.2.1.2.2.1.2.4.2.2.2.2. Statement

Just as space naturally pervades all places that are free from tangible objects, without thinking, "I shall pervade all empty vessels," so the nature of the mind—the stainless element[326] that is empty of intrinsic identifiability—should be known likewise as all-pervasive in all things. The term "stainless element" does not exclusively mean that the nature of the mind is free from incidental taints; instead, it means that the nature of the tainted mind is [already] engaged in the path. Uncompounded space is a mere exclusion of tangible objects and would not arise as a positive, independent entity. Although it pervades all different vessels, it does not arise [TL 104A] in different forms in terms of its nature; [rather, it is only that] different names are placed on vessels that hold space. The pure nature [of the mind] is a mere exclusion of intrinsic identifiability. Although it is all-pervasive in all things, it likewise does not arise as different forms in terms of its nature. Thus, one nature is all-pervading the [various] states, and its distinctions are made merely by the states.

3.1.2.1.2.2.1.2.2.1.2.4.2.2.2.3. Detailed Exposition . . . 3.1. Question

≪137≫ What is shown by this [verse]?

3.1.2.1.2.2.1.2.2.1.2.4.2.2.2.3.2. Answer . . . 2.1. The Root Text

The general characteristic of that element, reality, pervades people who have all sorts of faults, people who have excellences of the elimination of the seeds to various degrees, and people who have the ultimate excellences, as space is all-pervading in the vessels of clay, copper, and gold, which are the inferior, medium, and supreme aspects of forms, respectively.

3.1.2.1.2.2.1.2.2.1.2.4.2.2.2.3.2.2. The Commentary . . . 2.1. The Meaning of the Words

≪138≫ [The nature of the mind of] an ordinary being, [a noble, and a perfect buddha, being free from conceptual thought, is the general charac-

---

326. *dri ma med pa'i dbyings.*

teristic (of the element). Therefore, it is all-pervading, all-engaging, equal, and of no difference in these three states of having faults, excellences, and the ultimate pure excellences, just as space pervades all the vessels of clay, copper, and gold.] This is easy to understand.

3.1.2.1.2.2.1.2.2.1.2.4.2.2.2.3.2.2.2. Sutra Reference

≪139≫ For this reason, [the Buddha states in the *Sutra Teaching the Absence of Increase and Decrease (in the Realm of Beings)*—immediately after the teaching:]

> Therefore, O Shāriputra, the element of sentient beings and the truth body are not different from each other. The element of sentient beings, reality mingled with taints, is nothing but the truth body when it has been purified from all taints, and the truth body is nothing but the element of sentient beings when emptiness of intrinsic identifiability is mingled with taints. In fact these two are nondual—while they appear to be dissimilar in terms of their nature, [TL 104B] the difference is only semantic.

It would contradict reasoning if we maintained that the element of sentient beings is a synonym for the truth body. Although the path in space flown by a crow would not appear different from the one flown by a vulture, and space [itself] does not appear in different forms in different vessels, there is a distinction in mere expressions. Aside from the mere fact that emptiness of intrinsic identifiability is called the "element of sentient beings" when mingled with taints and is called the "truth body" when free from them, it does not arise as different forms in terms of nature. This is the meaning of the sutra.

3.1.2.1.2.2.1.2.2.1.2.4.2.2.3. Establishing the Nature Being Immutable . . .
3.1. Prelude

≪140≫ The tathāgata element, [being all-pervading in these above-mentioned three occasions is, moreover, immutable either by addictions or by means of purification.] There are fourteen verses with reference to this subject. These fourteen verses are rootlike, consisting of twelve verses that demonstrate the immutability in the impure state, one verse on the immutability in both the impure and pure state, and one verse on the immutability in the absolute pure state. [If verses of explanation are included,] there would be thirty-five verses in total: one verse of summary, twelve rootlike verses with reference to the first state, one rootlike verse and twelve verses of explanation with reference to the second state, one rootlike verse and six verses of explanation with reference to the third state.[327] [TL 105A]

3.1.2.1.2.2.1.2.2.1.2.4.2.2.3.2. Exposition of Meaning . . . 2.1. General Statement . . . 1.1. The Root Text

[The verse on the unchangeability of the all-pervading element can be summarized as follows:]

The mind's emptiness of intrinsic identity is the immutable reality, the same reality, the mere exclusion of intrinsic identity, in the absolute pure state, the same as it was before in the state of an ordinary being as well as in the state of a noble disciple, noble hermit buddha, or noble bodhisattva.

Objection: "The same reality after . . . what it was before" cannot be established since the former two states are tainted and the last state is free from taints and is endowed with excellences.

Reply: There is no fault. Though possessing incidental faults, the mind may possibly be separated from those faults. This can be established because it is possible for all the buddha excellences to be produced, and the mind naturally has the nature for producing excellences. The mere exclusion of intrinsic identifiability cannot be changed into something else by the faults or by the excellences. All kinds of water become of one taste; so do all things in the essence of emptiness of intrinsic identifiability. The ultimate truth cannot be changed into something else, except being the mere exclusion of intrinsic identifiability, and does not arise in different forms when it is experienced by any noble one in concentration. Thus, it is called "immutable." [TL 105B] The claim that [ultimate reality] is a positive, independent, permanent entity should not be understood as the viewpoint of those who follow our teaching.

---

327. There are actually only four verses of explanation with reference to the last state. So there are thirty-three verses in total about the meaning of immutability.

3.1.2.1.2.2.1.2.2.1.2.4.2.2.3.2 1.2. Explanations of Each Point

≪141≫ There are fourteen verses in the root text. The fourteenth verse does not differentiate the various excellences of the extremely pure occasion in terms of that of which it is free and its actuality, just stating that its freedom is unknown. [In the impure state, as well as in (both) the pure and impure states that are shown by the verses, (the tathāgata element) is endowed with incidental (faults) of fundamental and subsidiary addictions. (On the other hand), it is endowed by nature with the excellences of the Buddha in the perfectly pure state, which are indivisible, inseparable (from the truth body), inconceivable, and far greater in number than the sands of the Ganges, as demonstrated by the fourteenth verse. Therefore, it is demonstrated that the tathāgata element is eternally immutable like space throughout the different times.]

3.1.2.1.2.2.1.2.2.1.2.4.2.2.3.2 2. Explanation of Each State . . .
2.1. Unchangeability in the Impure State . . . 1.1. Question

≪142≫ Here, [what are the twelve verses with reference to the immutable characteristic in the impure state?]

3.1.2.1.2.2.1.2.2.1.2.4.2.2.3.2 2.1.2. Answer . . . 2.1. [The Tathāgata Element] Is Unchanged by Karmic Evolution and Addictions That Cause the Aggregates, etc., to Arise . . . 1.1. The Root Text . . . 1.1. Brief Statement . . . 1.1. Being Unaffected by Tainted Things

Space is all-pervading in world environments, and because it is subtle in the sense that it is uncompounded, it is the mere exclusion of resistant tangible objects and is not the directly apprehended object of the sense faculties. The element is completely unaffected by the faults of the world environment such as dust, etc., so the naturally pure element, the uncontaminated place that universally exists in all sentient beings, [TL 106A] is completely unaffected or unchanged by karmic evolution and addictions.

3.1.2.1.2.2.1.2.2.1.2.4.2.2.3.2 2.1.2.1.1.1.2. Being Unaffected by Their Arising and Disintegrating

Just as all world environments such as the wind sphere, etc., arise and disintegrate because of the [supernova] fire at the end of the world, etc., and on the basis of space, so in the uncompounded naturally pure element, all the sense faculties arise and disintegrate, but the element itself cannot be changed by those things that arise and disintegrate.

3.1.2.1.2.2.1.2.2.1.2.4.2.2.3.2 2.1.2.1.1.2. Detailed Explanations . . . 2.1. Being Unaffected by Things Disintegrating

Just as space has never before been burned by fires, so this reality mingled with taints is not burned by the fires of death, sickness, and aging, and cannot be destroyed. The plural "fires" refers to three kinds of [supernova] fire [occurring at the end of the world]. Since it is conventionally simple in content, being unaffected by things disintegrating is explicated first.

3.1.2.1.2.2.1.2.2.1.2.4.2.2.3.2 2.1.2.1.1.2.2. Being Unaffected by Things Arising . . . 2.1. Similes

The earth sphere is sustained by the water sphere, the water by the wind, and the wind by space; uncompounded space is, however, known to be sustained by neither wind nor water nor earth.

3.1.2.1.2.2.1.2.2.1.2.4.2.2.3.2 2.1.2.1.1.2.2.2. Implications

Similar to this simile, the aggregates, elements, and media of senses such as eyes, etc., which are included in the consequence, are based upon their own causes, including karmic evolution and addictions. Karmic evolution and addictions, such as attachment, etc., are always based upon irrational thought, the grasping at truth status in persons and things. [TL 106B] This irrational thought is based upon purity, the mind's own objective condition, yet the mind's nature, the ultimate truth, is not based upon any of these things, including karmic evolution and addictions, in terms of its ultimate objective condition.

When investigating whether or not karmic evolution and addictions, etc., are established by intrinsic reality, only their emptiness of intrinsic reality will be realized, since these things have no intrinsic reality status even as small as an atom. When investigating how this objective condition of being empty of intrinsic identity exists, it is known as nothing other than the emptiness of intrinsic reality. That is what is meant by the statement "being unchanged by karmic evolution and addictions, etc." Therefore, this statement means that the emptiness of intrinsic reality cannot be changed, even in the impure state, into something else by karmic evolution and addictions, etc., and does not mean that it cannot become free from taints caused by antidotes. These [statements] emphasize the naturally pure ultimate truth of the mind, that is, its emptiness of intrinsic reality, emptiness of intrinsic identity, or emptiness of any kind of truth status; implicitly, [the statements] establish that the taints are incidental. Also, the nine similes taught in the *Tathāgata Essence Sutra* explain by giving an explicit emphasis on the incidentality of the taints, implicitly also establishing that the mind is empty of truth status and free from reification, as we shall see below.

3.1.2.1.2.2.1.2.2.1.2.4.2.2.3.2 2.1.2.1.1.2.2.3. Connections between Each Simile and Import . . . 3.1. The Main Meaning

The aggregates, elements, and sense media, which are included in the consequence, [TL 107A] should be known as being akin to the earth sphere, since they are the results of karmic evolution and addictions and serve as the basis for future consequences, just as earth serves as the support of four continents, Mount Meru, etc. The karmic evolution and the addictions of sentient beings are to be known as akin to water, which is the support of earth and is based upon unstable wind, since these serve as the basis for the contaminated aggregates and are based upon irrational thought. The irrational thought by which nothing is established as conceived is known to resemble the wind sphere, which is the support of water and is based upon space. The nature of mind, the ultimate reality, is baseless, corresponding to the habit pattern of irrational thought, and its locationlessness, as regards irrational thought, etc., is like space.

3.1.2.1.2.2.1.2.2.1.2.4.2.2.3.2 2.1.2.1.1.3.2. Specific Explanation of Analogies between the Similes and Their Implications . . . 2.1. The Distinctive Feature of Irrational Thought

Irrational thought abides within the nature of the mind, which is devoid of truth and free from reifications. By means of irrational thought, karmic evolution and addictions are produced. The former part [of this verse] demonstrates that irrational thought abides within the emptiness of truth status and the latter part demonstrates that it is the support of karmic evolution and addictions. [Taken together,] this verse establishes that karmic evolution and addictions are baseless and rootless.

3.1.2.1.2.2.1.2.2.1.2.4.2.2.3.2 2.1.2.1.1.3.2.2. Distinctive Feature of Karmic Evolution and Addictions

From the water sphere of karmic evolution and addictions, which are respectively the substantial causes and cooperative conditions [of the life cycle], [TL 107B] the evolved aggregates, elements, and sense media occur, arising and disintegrating by the forces of karmic evolution and addictions just as the water sphere arises and subsides.

3.1.2.1.2.2.1.2.2.1.2.4.2.2.3.2 2.1.2.1.1.3.2.3. Distinctive Feature of Their Basis

The nature of the mind, the ultimate truth, is like the space element free from arising and disintegrating: it has neither substantial causes nor cooperative conditions, nor these causes and conditions in collection, nor arising, enduring by the force of causes, or final destruction. This treatise does not explain in detail, but briefly demonstrates in summary that [the tathāgata element] is never changed by addictive things into something else, with the intention that if it did so, it would be apprehended as doing so, [which it is not,] and if people understand that [the nature of the mind] cannot be changed by arising and disintegrating into something else, they will easily understand that it also cannot be changed by karmic evolution and addictions.

3.1.2.1.2.2.1.2.2.1.2.4.2.2.3.2 2.1.2.1.1.3. Précis . . . 3.1. Being Immutable by Karmic Evolutionary Actions and Addictions

The nature of the mind, the ultimate truth, is clear-light and as immutable as space, which does not change into something else by [being occupied by and occupying] diverse vessels. The nature of the mind has never become afflicted by attachment, etc., the incidental taints that arise from irrational thought, the habitual grasping at truth status.

If you claim that the mind will not be changed by addictions because it is void of intrinsic reality, then this is an argument that does not differentiate between the categorical differential[328] and the ground differential.[329] Addictions do not abide differently from the mind [TL 108A] in terms of sharing the same object with it. Although the nature of the mind is to apprehend an object and reality is the ultimate of an object, the mind contaminated by obscuring addictions cannot perceive it. However, addictions cannot always cause contamination since they are incapable of remaining once pervaded by the wisdom that realizes emptiness, they themselves being incapable of perceiving reality in the slightest. If you then claim that reality would also not be obscured by addictions, [you should know that] addictions cause obstacles for the mind of one's own continuum, [obstructing the mind's ability] to perceive [objects' reality] and to realize its own continuum's reality; hence, [reality] is mingled with taints.

Although [taints] also obscure the perception of reality of a buddha's continuum, which has the same characteristic as our reality, a buddha's reality does not become mingled with taints, because obscuring addictions do not belong to a buddha's continuum, as well as because the reality to be obscured is located within our own continuums. Suppose there is a person with bad vision who cannot perceive a thing far away; this problem exclusively belongs to this person, but not to that thing. Otherwise, a person who has clear vision and is in front of a thing would also not perceive it. In light

---

328. *rang ldog.*

329. *gzhi ldog.* These terms refer to the way objects are conceptualized, according to Buddhist epistemology developed by Dignāga and Dharmakīrti, and further refined and developed in Tibet. The former describes the interface between mental concept and object as conceptually differentiated from its background field, while the latter focuses on the interface between the conceptualized object and its ground in the transconceptual, inconceivable object itself.

of this, we should understand as well the meaning of the *Ornament of Clear Realization* [passage], starting with "pure fruition including matter, etc."

3.1.2.1.2.2.1.2.2.1.2.4.2.2.3.2 2.1.2.1.1.3.2. Being Immutable by Creation and Destruction . . . 2.1. Prelude

≪143≫ [TL 108B] How is this tathāgata essence in the impure state immutable in its nature, [and how is this] illustrated by this simile of space, which is unaffected by the creative and destructive forces in world environments?

Although the nature of reality does not change because it is permanent and uncompounded, the mode of unchangeability should be known here, as explained above, for the purpose of educating those people who wish to eliminate addictions and to realize the meaning of the ultimate truth of all things' ultimate objective condition, which does not go beyond the emptiness of intrinsic reality and cannot be changed by anyone into something else. Although nirvana is also permanent, we do not have to resort to outsider traditions that accept [liberation] as a positive, independent, permanent entity without understanding the status of permanence known to the insider scholars.

3.1.2.1.2.2.1.2.2.1.2.4.2.2.3.2 2.1.2.1.1.3.2.2. The Root Text

This reality mingled with taints cannot be produced by karmic evolution and addictions that are akin to the collection of the water sphere, etc., for it is unaffected by things that are produced. Even the fierce fires of death, sickness, and aging that cause severe sufferings cannot consume it, for it is unaffected by things that disintegrate. The former part and the latter part of this verse demonstrate that [reality] is free from production and disintegration, respectively.

3.1.2.1.2.2.1.2.2.1.2.4.2.2.3.2 2.1.2.1.2. The Commentary . . .
2.1. Brief Statement . . . 1.1. Being Unaffected by Creation

≪144≫ [TL 109A] The creation of the consequence that consists of the aggregates, [elements, and sense media is based upon the water of karmic evolution and addictions, which is, in turn,] produced by the wind sphere of irrational thought. [This evolutionary action, however, does not cause any creation and formation] of the nature of the mind that is akin to space.

3.1.2.1.2.2.1.2.2.1.2.4.2.2.3.2 2.1.2.1.2.1.2. Being Unaffected by Disintegration

[In the same way, in order to destroy the world that consists of the aggregates, elements, and sense media founded on the wind-like improper mentation and water-like evolution and addictions, a group of fires arise that are death, sickness, and aging.] It should be known, however, that even by these arising fires of death, etc., this nature of the mind cannot be destroyed.

3.1.2.1.2.2.1.2.2.1.2.4.2.2.3.2 2.1.2.1.2.1.3. Conclusion

Thus, in the impure state, [though all the taints of karmic evolution, addictions, and birth arise and disintegrate like world environments, the uncreated tathāgata essence is, like space, without creation and cessation. Therefore, it is shown to be an absolutely immutable reality.]

3.1.2.1.2.2.1.2.2.1.2.4.2.2.3.2 2.1.2.1.2.2. Sutra Reference

«145» [This space simile] refers to the means of [entering] the door of the distinctive reality of clear-light luminosity with regard to natural purity; its teaching is natural purity, and its door is the method of realizing it. Starting from there, the details of this space simile should be understood in detail according to the *Questions of Gaganagañja Sutra*; and there are two parts to this: its not being corrupted by addictions and its not being disrupted by birth and death.

3.1.2.1.2.2.1.2.2.1.2.4.2.2.3.2 2.1.2.1.2.2.1. [The Element] Not Being Corrupted by Addictions

In some translations [of the following quote] it begins with "O friends, addictions. . . ." Our version rather indicates that this is a question to the Teacher.

O Great Seer,[330] addictions are darkness, since they obscure the perception of reality. Purity is luminosity, since the perception of reality illuminates all things. Addictions are weak because they are not sustainable when antidotes are present; transcendent analysis is powerful. Addictions are incidental; natural purity is the root of all things. Addictions are made of imaginative constructs, for there is nowhere for them to adhere; [TL 109B] nature is free from imagination, for it is the natural objective condition of all things.

3.1.2.1.2.2.1.2.2.1.2.4.2.2.3.2 2.1.2.1.2.2.2. [The Element] Not Being Corrupted by Birth and Death . . . 2.1. Detailed Exposition . . . 1.1. Similes

O Great Seer, it is like this: [this great earth is supported by water. Water is supported by wind, and wind is supported by space. But space, in turn, is not supported by anything.] Thus, [among these four elements, space is more powerful than any of the three elements of earth, water, and wind. It is also firm and immovable. It has no decrease and no increase. It is not created and does not cease. It is supported by its own nature.] The three elements are endowed with creation and disintegration, are unstable, and are perceived as changeable. But space is their opposite.

3.1.2.1.2.2.1.2.2.1.2.4.2.2.3.2 2.1.2.1.2.2.2.1.2. Implications

Likewise, the aggregates, elements, and sense media have their support in karmic evolution and the addictions. Karmic evolution and addiction have their support in irrational thought, and the latter, in turn, has its support in the natural purity. Therefore, it is said: the mind is naturally clear-light, but it is tainted by incidental addictions. Here, all these things of irrational thought, karmic evolution, addiction, aggregates, elements, and sense media are produced by the conglomeration of causes and conditions. When these causes and conditions are separate, they will cease. [On the contrary],

330. A title of the Buddha addressed by his disciples. According to another version, it is replaced with "friends" addressed by the Buddha.

the nature of the mind has no cause and no conditions. Consequently, it has no conglomeration of causes and conditions or conglomeration by nature. It is thus not created and does not cease.

3.1.2.1.2.2.1.2.2.1.2.4.2.2.3.2 2.1.2.1.2.2.2.1.3. The Conjunction between Similes and Implications

«146» Here, [nature is akin to] space, [irrational thought to wind, karmic evolution and addiction to water, and the aggregates, elements, and sense media to earth.]

3.1.2.1.2.2.1.2.2.1.2.4.2.2.3.2 2.1.2.1.2.2.2.2. Conclusion

Therefore, it is said that all things are completely devoid of any intrinsically real root. They have an essence-free root; there is not the slightest essence that is sustained when under investigation by reason that analyzes the ultimate. They have a root of nonabiding with intrinsic reality when they still exist. They have a root of purity of intrinsic reality in past, present, or future. And for this reason they have a root that is free from the root of intrinsic reality. The first statement indicates that [all things] [TL 110A] do not have a root that is established in ultimate terms, and the last four indicate that they do have roots in conventional terms.

3.1.2.1.2.2.1.2.2.1.2.4.2.2.3.2 2.1.2.1.2.3. Review

«147» The nature of the mind in the impure state has been explained to be analogous to space on account of its immutable characteristic; irrational thought, karmic evolution, and addictions, as analogous to wind and water, respectively, on account of their characteristic of cause; and the aggregates, elements, and sense media, which are produced from the former two, as analogous to the earth element on account of their characteristic of being the consequence of karmic evolution.

3.1.2.1.2.2.1.2.2.1.2.4.2.2.3.2 2.1.2.2. Being Unchanged by Aging, etc., Akin to Fires, etc., Which Cause the Aggregates, etc., to Disintegrate

3.1.2.1.2.2.1.2.2.1.2.4.2.2.3.2 2.1.2.2.1. Prelude

«148» The fires of death, sickness, and aging, which cause the disintegration of the consequence of karmic evolution, have not yet been explained as being analogous to the fire element on account of their characteristic of [causing] headaches for sentient beings who stay in the life cycle. So I shall explain.

It will also be acceptable if the former statement starting with "the nature of the mind in the impure state" is included in the prelude here in order to remind us of what has been already explained.

3.1.2.1.2.2.1.2.2.1.2.4.2.2.3.2 2.1.2.2.2. The Root Text

The three fires of death, sickness, and aging are to be known, respectively, as being analogous to the fire at the end of the world, by which all world environments are incinerated; to the fire of hell, by which the bodies in the hells are incinerated; and to ordinary fire, by which firewood is incinerated. These three fires [of death, etc.,] always destroy the body, health, and youth, respectively.

3.1.2.1.2.2.1.2.2.1.2.4.2.2.3.2 2.1.2.2.3. The Commentary . . . 3.1. The Reasons [Aging, etc.,] Are Analogous to the Similes [of the Three Fires]

«149» Death, sickness, and aging, [TL 110B] as analogous to the fires, should be understood for three reasons, respectively: (1) because [death] permanently causes the six senses to be no longer possessed by a person; (2) [sickness] causes various kinds of suffering to be experienced; and (3) [aging] causes the compounded consequences of karmic evolutionary actions and addictions to develop. Even by these fires, the tathāgata element in the impure state cannot be changed at all. These statements should be known as the demonstration of the techniques for cultivating the will to liberation by contemplating the faults of the life cycle and feeling it to be repulsive.

3.1.2.1.2.2.1.2.2.1.2.4.2.2.3.2 2.1.2.2.3.2. Sutra Reference

«150» Here, "death, etc." is stated in the *Shrīmālādevī Lion's Roar Sutra*:[331]

> O Bhagavān, this so-called death and this so-called birth are merely mundane, conventional terms. Bhagavān, this so-called death causes the continuums of senses that are produced by karmic evolution and addictions to cease, and this so-called birth causes other senses of the same type to be obtained. O Bhagavān, the tathāgata essence, the ultimate truth, however, is never born, never ages, never dies, and is never born [again]. Why? Because, O Bhagavān, the tathāgata essence is beyond the sphere marked as created, is eternal, stable, peaceful, and everlasting, as explicated above.

3.1.2.1.2.2.1.2.2.1.2.4.2.2.3.2 2.2. Unchangeability in the Pure and Impure State . . . 2.1. Prelude

«151» [Now there is a verse with respect to unchangeability in the [both] pure and impure state.] The "pure and impure state" does not mean that a demarcation between pure and impure can be clearly drawn. Rather, it demonstrates that the pure and impure aspects of the state of the noble bodhisattvas are decided with respect to different points of view. Their state is pure because [the noble bodhisattvas] are free from birth, etc., by the force of karmic evolution and addiction, and it is impure because of their manifestations of birth, etc., by the force of compassion. Or else, in terms of the extinction of birth under the influence of karmic evolution and addictions, it is pure when compared with ordinary people and impure when compared with the Buddha. [TL 111A]

3.1.2.1.2.2.1.2.2.1.2.4.2.2.3.2 2.2.2. Brief Statement

Free from birth, death, sickness, and aging under the influence of karmic evolution and the addictions, the intelligent noble bodhisattvas have

---

331. Gyaltsap here adds pertinent qualifiers to the quote, as usual, and the scribe includes them in the quote.

directly realized the nature of the element as it is, and this realization has a distinctive quality of extensive activities. By means of this cause of the direct realization of the nature of the element, and by cultivating compassion for beings, though freed from the poverty of birth, etc., under the influence of karmic evolution and the addictions, the intelligent ones do take rebirth in the life cycle. Alternatively, though they are free from birth in the life cycle under the influence of karmic evolution and the addictions, nevertheless, due to the cause of perceiving other beings' suffering of birth, the intelligent ones depend on birth in the life cycle owing to their compassion. Thus, the first three lines [of this verse] show its distinctive quality of purity and the last line shows its distinctive quality of impurity.

3.1.2.1.2.2.1.2.2.1.2.4.2.2.3.2 2.2.3. Detailed Exposition . . . 3.1. Question

≪152≫ What is shown by this [verse]?

3.1.2.1.2.2.1.2.2.1.2.4.2.2.3.2 2.2.3.2. Answer . . . 2.1. The Unchangeability in the Pure and Impure State Explained with Respect to the Distinction of Birth . . . 1.1. The Distinction of Being Pure . . . 1.1. The Root Text

The noble bodhisattvas have completely eliminated from the root itself the suffering of death, sickness, and aging under the influence of karmic evolution and addictions. The suffering of the life cycle does not apply to them [TL 111B] because their birth is not under the influence of karmic evolution and addictions. While having realized the meaning of emptiness, the noble disciples of the individual vehicle still take rebirth under the influence of karmic evolution and addictions owing to their lack of the distinctive power of liberative art. But this does not hold true for the noble bodhisattvas.

Objection: The explanation above that [the noble bodhisattvas] take rebirth in the life cycle of their own volition contradicts the explanation found in the commentary on the *Ornament of Clear Realization*, stating that "they are eliminating the karmic instinct for ignorance and [unrealistic] views but not the taint of desire[332] and the taint of existence,[333] for they

---

332. *'dod pa'i zag pa.*
333. *srid pa'i zag pa.*

still take rebirth of their own volition."[334] The commentary makes it clear that the taints of desire and existence are the causes of their taking rebirth [in the life cycle].

Answer: The connotation of this commentary is as follows: There is absolutely no need for addictive ignorance and the futile views, extreme views, etc., [no need] for involvement with the accomplishment of self-aims and other-aims. So these should be specifically eliminated by [the holy] bodhisattvas. The taints of desire and existence are not necessarily the causes for them to take rebirth because the noble bodhisattvas are born by the force of compassion and vows and, when dying, they do not crave the contaminated aggregates owing to the fear of losing [their sense of] "I." Born as a world emperor, etc., by the force of compassion and vows, when begetting a royal child they have the active taint of desire. Born in the material realm and so on, by the force of prayerful vows, they have the active taint of existence. [TL 112A] However, the taints [in these cases] are harmless, just as the effect of poison is lessened by special mantra and medicine. [Moreover,] addiction is defined as something that causes the mental continuum to be agitated. Absolute peace of the mental continuum is declared to be nirvana. Agitation, being the opposite of nirvana, is the truth of suffering, and addiction is its cause. Nevertheless, the addiction that exists in the mental continuums of the noble bodhisattvas is a [mere] verbal expression, not fitting the definition of addiction.

3.1.2.1.2.2.1.2.2.1.2.4.2.2.3.2 2.2.3.2.1.1.2. The Commentary

«153» In the impure state, as explained above, the substantial cause of the fires of death, etc., [sickness and aging] is the fuel-like birth included in [the link of] name-and-form, bridging the gap between lives based upon irrational thought—the truth-habit—karmic evolution, and addictions, such as attachment, etc. The commentary then demonstrates that [for bodhisattvas] there is no death, etc., because there are no causes for these things. In the [both] pure and impure state, however, for bodhisattvas who have obtained the mind-made body, there are no fruitional three fires of suffering that we know of because there is no trace of birth whatsoever. [This] bridges the gap between lives based upon karmic evolution and addictions,

334. Source unidentified.

owing to the direct realization of emptiness distinguished by extensive liberative art.

3.1.2.1.2.2.1.2.2.1.2.4.2.2.3.2 2.2.3.2.1.2. The Nature of Impurities [and] the Distinction of the Cause of Connecting Purity with Impurities . . .
2.1. The Root Text

≪154≫ Because of directly realizing stainless reality distinguished by extensive liberative art, they have passed beyond birth, and so on, based upon karmic evolution and the addictions. Still, the compassionate ones display birth, [TL 112B] death, aging, and sickness by [the force of] vows. The former part of this verse demonstrates the cause of connecting purity with impurities. The latter part demonstrates the nature of impurities.

3.1.2.1.2.2.1.2.2.1.2.4.2.2.3.2 2.2.3.2.1.2.2. Explanation . . . 2.1. Brief Statement

Indeed, because of their total engagement in the three realms by the force of compassion and vows by means of their virtuous roots, bodhisattvas properly engage with the three realms out of compassion on the basis of their power of voluntary control of their births. They display the appearance of birth, of aging, of sickness, and of death. These statements demonstrate the nature of impurity. The commentary then demonstrates the cause of connecting [purity] with these impurities as follows: But for them, there are, in reality, no such things [as] birth, etc., by the force of karmic evolution and addictions. Because, of course, they have truly realized that the element, included in [the category of] the ultimate truth, has no birth and no arising, as it is.

3.1.2.1.2.2.1.2.2.1.2.4.2.2.3.2 2.2.3.2.1.2.2.2. Detailed Exposition . . .
2.1. The Way of Taking Rebirth by the Force of Compassion and Vows . . .
1.1. The Sutra Reference . . . 1.1. Identifying the Causes for Taking Rebirth in the Life Cycle

≪155≫ This state of bodhisattvas should be understood in detail according to the *[Questions of Sāgaramati] Sutra* as follows:

[What are the addictions associated with the virtuous roots that serve as the cause of the life cycle for those] bodhisattvas?

There are eight meanings explained: (1) taking voluntary rebirth in order to complete the stores [of merit and wisdom]; (2) [taking rebirth in worldly existence out of their own volition] for the purpose of bringing other beings under their care; (3) meeting with the buddhas in other bodies motivated by faith in the victors; (4) not being exhausted when engaging in looking after disciples; (5 and 6) developing energy in upholding the teachings of holy victors [TL 113A] and accomplishing the aims of beings; (7) motivating ambition for the spiritual conception that is the [bodhisattva] conduct and its basis; (8) undertaking the practice of the transcendences motivated by that ambition. Mainly these are the causes of [a bodhisattva's] taking rebirth.

3.1.2.1.2.2.1.2.2.1.2.4.2.2.3.2 2.2.3.2.1.2.2.2.1.1.2. Refuting Virtuous Roots Being Addictions as Defined . . . 2.1. The Reason for Designating Virtuous Roots as Addictions

«156» [The sutra continues:]

[Then, Sāgaramati asked:] Why then, O Bhagavān, are the virtuous roots called "addictions"?

[The Bhagavān answered:] O Sāgaramati, it is in the sense that bodhisattvas join themselves to the three realms by these addictions of such a nature; for the three realms are originated from addictions.

Here, the bodhisattvas join themselves to the three realms out of their own volition, by their skill in liberative art, and by their cultivation of the power of virtuous roots. Thus, these are called "addictions associated with virtuous roots," inasmuch as their functions are similar.

Here, a certain someone quotes the *Questions of Sāgaramati Sutra*, and equates [the "addictions"] with the addictions that are not to be eliminated by the path wisdom,[335] as identified in the *Ornament of Clear Realization* when defining the nature of the path wisdom. This is incorrect. The virtuous roots associated with compassion and vows as defined in the *Ornament of Clear Realization* are explicated in terms of liberative art as part of the path wisdom, because [in that context] it has nothing to do with the question of whether or not they are to be eliminated by the path wisdom. The *Ornament of Clear Realization*, at this point, demonstrates [that the path wisdom of] bodhisattvas actually transcends [the wisdom of] the disciples, which takes the addictions as the chief [obscuration] to be eliminated.

3.1.2.1.2.2.1.2.2.1.2.4.2.2.3.2 2.2.3.2.1.2.2.2.1.1.2.2. Refuting Those [Virtuous Roots] Being Addictions as Defined

Here, bodhisattvas join themselves to the three realms out of their own volition by their liberative art and their cultivation of the power of virtuous roots. Therefore, these are called "the addictions associated with virtuous roots," inasmuch as they cause bodhisattvas to join themselves to the three realms, but not under the influence of [actual] addictions in the mind.

[The noble bodhisattvas] have mastery over taking embodiments in accordance with their wishes instead of taking rebirth by the force of addictions against their wishes. Thus, for them, how can the addictions be the cause of taking rebirth? [TL 113B]

3.1.2.1.2.2.1.2.2.1.2.4.2.2.3.2 2.2.3.2.1.2.2.2.1.1.2.3. The Necessity of Displaying Birth, etc., in the Three Realms . . . 3.1. Simile

O Sāgaramati, suppose there was an only son of some merchant or householder. Suppose he was beloved, handsome, cherished, and attractive. Suppose this boy, being a child, fell into a filthy pit while playing. The mother and relatives of this boy saw him fall into the filthy pit. Upon seeing this they cried, were distressed, and screamed. They could not, however, take the boy out by entering the pit. Then the boy's father came to that place and saw his only son fallen into the filthy pit. Upon seeing this and

335. *lam shes.*

moved by the fervent wish to pull out his only son, he jumped quickly into the filthy pit without any feeling of disgust, and took out his only son.

3.1.2.1.2.2.1.2.2.1.2.4.2.2.3.2 2.2.3.2.1.2.2.2.1.1.2.3.2. Import

O Sāgaramati, this analogy is made in order to make clear a special meaning. What meaning is suggested by this analogy? O Sāgaramati, "filthy pit" is a synonym for the three realms. "Only son" is a synonym for sentient beings, for bodhisattvas have a notion of the only child toward all sentient beings. "Mother and relatives" is a synonym for those people who belong to the disciple vehicle and hermit buddha vehicle since they, having seen sentient beings fallen into cyclic life, are distressed and cry out, but have no ability to rescue them. "Great merchant or householder" is a synonym for bodhisattvas, who are pure, untainted, of untainted mind, [and who] have directly realized the uncreated Dharma, but still take rebirth in the three realms of their own volition for the sake of sentient beings' development.

Although noble disciples and hermit buddhas frequently have great compassion toward all beings in cyclic life, thinking, "May all beings be free from suffering!" just as a compassionate mother, having seen her only son fall into a filthy pit, would do, they would not actually take responsibility by thinking, "I shall make this happen." Therefore, they are inferior to universal vehicle [bodhisattvas].

In order to demonstrate that great compassion is distinguished in terms of its function of realizing sentient beings' aims, the sutra states as follows:

O Sāgaramati, such is the great compassion of bodhisattvas that, being thoroughly free from all rebirths driven by karmic evolution and addictions, they still take rebirths in worldly existence. Empowered by wisdom and skill in liberative arts, they are never harmed by taints; and, in order to liberate sentient beings from all the bondage of addictions, they teach the Dharma. [TL 114A]

3.1.2.1.2.2.1.2.2.1.2.4.2.2.3.2 2.2.3.2.1.2.2.2.1.2. Summarized Meaning of the Sutra

«157» By this sutra passage, the [both] pure and impure state is illustrated in the sense that powerful bodhisattvas engage with rebirth out of their own volition for the sake of others, by the power of their virtuous roots and compassion, but at the same time, owing to the power of their wisdom and liberative art, they are not tainted.

3.1.2.1.2.2.1.2.2.1.2.4.2.2.3.2.2.2.3.2.1.2.2.2.2. Detailed Exposition of the Reason for Not Taking Rebirth by the Force of Karmic Evolution and Addictions ... 2.1. Prelude

«158» Here, when bodhisattvas have obtained the accurate direct realization of this naturally pure tathāgata element as uncreated and unoriginated, they automatically become bodhisattvas who do not take rebirth driven by karmic evolution and addictions. This point should be understood in detail according to the sutra as follows:

3.1.2.1.2.2.1.2.2.1.2.4.2.2.3.2 2.2.3.2.1.2.2.2.2.2. Sutra Reference ...
2.1. Quoting Sutra ... 1.1. The Way of Perceiving the Actuality

> O Sāgaramati, realize that things have no real intrinsically identifiable essence—being free of objective self—and that there is no creator of any consequence that has intrinsic identifiability—no owner, no sentient being, no life, no person, and no self—being free of subjective self. Indeed, such things are [only] established according to [the bodhisattvas'] wish, for they, having directly realized selflessness, have the power to transform objects. Thus, do not think or imagine, ...

3.1.2.1.2.2.1.2.2.1.2.4.2.2.3.2 2.2.3.2.1.2.2.2.2.2.1.2. The Cause of Taking Rebirth While Perceiving the Actuality

> ... O Sāgaramati, know that bodhisattvas who believe this immutable reality would never cultivate the feeling of resistance toward anything. They are endowed with the pure intuitive per-

ception that there is nothing that causes benefit or harm. Thus, they know correctly the reality of things and will never cast off the armor of great compassion.

3.1.2.1.2.2.1.2.2.1.2.4.2.2.3.2 2.2.3.2.1.2.2.2.2.2.1.3. Proof . . . 3.1. Simile

O Sāgaramati, suppose there were an invaluable sapphire gem, well purified, well cleaned, and stainless. Suppose it were left in mud and remained there for a thousand years. Then, this stone was taken from the mud and cleaned by washing and purification. Even being cleaned well, however, it never abandoned its nature of a jewel, pure and stainless.

Purification and cleansing, etc., have been explicated as above [in the section of the *King Dhāraṇīshvara Sutra*].

3.1.2.1.2.2.1.2.2.1.2.4.2.2.3.2 2.2.3.2.1.2.2.2.2.2.1.3.2. Import

In the same way, O Sāgaramati, bodhisattvas know the mind of sentient beings as being naturally clear-light. But they also perceive that the same mind is tainted by incidental addictions.

3.1.2.1.2.2.1.2.2.1.2.4.2.2.3.2 2.2.3.2.1.2.2.2.2.2.1.3.3. Summarized Meanings of Purity and Impurity . . . 3.1. Summarized Meaning of Purity. [TL 114B]

Thus, the bodhisattvas think as follows: "These addictions would never penetrate the naturally clear-light mind of sentient beings. Being incidental, these addictions are the production of incorrect imaginations. We can teach these sentient beings the Dharma in order to purify their addictions." Thus, they will never let their minds become discouraged. Instead, they will cultivate the spirit of engaging with sentient beings many times. Again they will think as follows: "These addictions have no power and strength. They are powerless, weak, and have no real support at all. These addictions are [produced] by incorrect imaginations. We will never feel angry with addictions if we investigate them with correct and proper mentation. We will never connect ourselves with addictions, so we will investigate them in detail. We would do better not to connect with addictions. It is not good to connect with addictions. If we connected ourselves with addictions, how could we teach the Dharma to sentient beings who are bound by the bondages of addictions in order to eliminate these addictions? In any case, we will never connect ourselves with addictions, and then we will teach the Dharma to sentient beings in order to eliminate their bondage by addictions."

[This passage demonstrates the bodhisattvas'] distinguished wisdom that discerns addictions. Having realized that the minds of sentient beings are naturally clear-light and addictions are incidental, bodhisattvas commit themselves to destroying sentient beings' addictions, and endeavor to act based upon this commitment. They have also realized that if they themselves were under the control of addictions, they would be unable to perfect the welfare of sentient beings. And they teach the Dharma to sentient beings in order to eliminate their addictions.

3.1.2.1.2.2.1.2.2.1.2.4.2.2.3.2 2.2.3.2.1.2.2.2.2.2.1.3.3.2. Summarized Meaning of Impurity

On the other hand, we shall connect ourselves with those addictions associated with virtuous roots that cause the life cycle to be connected, in order to develop sentient beings.

The causes of creating the mind-made bodies are the foundational instinctual ignorance-driven evolutionary actions and the uncontaminated karmic evolutionary actions, as explicated above. Although those bodies are created out of compassion and vows in the same manner, the bodies discussed here are the ones that can be directly perceived by the validating cognition of other ordinary people, such as an embodied world emperor, an embodied Shakra god, etc.

3.1.2.1.2.2.1.2.2.1.2.4.2.2.3.2 2.2.3.2.1.2.2.2.2.2.2. Exposition of the Meaning . . . 2.1. Actual Exposition

«159» Here, the expression "the life cycle" is accepted as the threefold mind-made body that is the reflection of the three realms within the uncontaminated element. It is the life cycle because it is created by uncontaminated virtuous roots. At the same time, it is nirvana because it is uncreated by contaminated karmic evolution and addictions.

3.1.2.1.2.2.1.2.2.1.2.4.2.2.3.2 2.2.3.2.1.2.2.2.2.2.2. Sutra Reference

With regard to this meaning, the *[Shrīmālādevī Lion's Roar] Sutra* states: [TL 115A]

> Therefore, O Bhagavān, as for the life cycle, it is created as well as uncreated. And as for nirvana, it [also] is created as well as uncreated.

Nirvana means "transcending the sorrow of addictions." Thus, [those bodhisattvas] transmigrate in the life cycle by the force of the class of objective obscurations. The meaning of the sutra is given as follows: being endowed with the ubiquitous functioning of the subtle reifications of signs[336] [arisen from the mind,] there is a mixture of created and uncreated, and that state is called the "[both] pure and impure state."

3.1.2.1.2.2.1.2.2.1.2.4.2.2.3.2 2.2.3.2.1.2.2.2.2.2.3. Exposition of Knowledge of the Termination of Contaminations in Particular . . . 3.1. General Statement

«160» This state is chiefly established for the confrontation[337] [sixth] bodhisattva stage, because [in this stage], bodhisattvas, proceeding to the attainment of the intuition of the cessation of contaminations,[338] directly realize the elimination of addictions by means of their meditations on unobstructed transcendent wisdom and great compassion, yet still do not actualize that attainment in order to protect all sentient beings. That is to say, although bodhisattvas have attained the cessation of contaminations by the power of wisdom, they do not actualize that attainment, due to [their] great compassion. [This thought,] to not actualize that attainment, is not posited as the chief attainment [for the noble bodhisattvas,] until they have obtained the sixth stage, despite the fact that, by means of wisdom, they

336. *mtshan ma.*
337. *abhimukhī, mngon par gyur pa.*
338. *āsravakṣayajñāna, zag pa zad pa'i mngon par shes pa.*

have obtained liberation from the life cycle under the influence of karmic evolution and addictions since the first stage. This indicates that the perfection of the wisdom transcendence depends upon the perfection of the meditation transcendence in the fifth stage. The meaning of the sameness between the life cycle and nirvana is directly realized by the power of the wisdom transcendence in the sixth stage; however, it is not actualized, due to the power of compassion.[339] This thought [of not actualizing] is [posited as] the chief attainment of the sixth stage. [TL 115B]

3.1.2.1.2.2.1.2.2.1.2.4.2.2.3.2 2.2.3.2.1.2.2.2.2.2.3.2. Sutra Reference

«161» Concerning this knowledge of the cessation of contaminations, there is a simile of a man [who has just arrived in a city] in the *[Questions of Ratnachūḍā] Sutra*:

Suppose there were a huge city millions of leagues away and difficult to reach, full of dangers, and no food on the way. However, all kinds of suffering would cease to exist as soon as one had arrived there. Having heard of the excellences of this city, a man who had an attractive, beautiful, charming child ignored all difficulties with strength and endeavor and traveled a long distance to the city. While one foot stepped on the doorstep and the other remained outside the door, he remembered his child and thought, "Ah! I shall see the city in the future, after my child is brought here." Therefore, he did not enter, but returned home to bring his child back to the city.[340]

Thus, noble child, bodhisattvas cause the five superknowledges to be cultivated by means of transcendent meditation and [transcendent] wisdom on the basis of great effort, great exertion, and high resolve. Having the mind purified by concentration and the superknowledges, they confront [the reality of] the cessation of contamination. Having the mind purified by the intuitive wis-

---

339. The difference here is expressed by *thob pa* or *mngon sum du rtogs pa* and *mngon du byed pa*.

340. This passage seems to be a paraphrase of the *Ratnacūḍa-sutra* made by Gyaltsap.

dom of the cessation of contamination, to protect all sentient beings by means of the cultivation of the spirit of great compassion, again, they [merely] confront the cessation of contamination when they have produced the unobstructed wisdom in the sixth stage. Thus, bodhisattvas who are in the confrontation bodhisattva stage obtain the power to actualize the cessation of contamination, so their state is explained as "pure."

The "cessation of contamination" refers to the attainment of the cessation equipoise[341] by which an adept is able to remain in the direct equipoise of the actuality, [TL 116A] the limit of reality, as long as he wishes. A person who is definitely [endowed with] the spiritual potential of the universal vehicle does not obtain the cessation equipoise until the sixth stage, where the transcendences of meditation and wisdom are perfected. In its post-attainment [meditation], while the truth-status-habit occasionally manifests infrequently, most appearances of objects of knowledge in their multiplicity arise like reflections in a mirror. [Only] in the eighth stage, all appearances of objects of knowledge in their multiplicity invariably arise as mirror reflections upon the attainment of the realization of the sameness of the life cycle and nirvana, in which the [habitual] perception of truth-appearance arises simultaneously with the [conviction] of its emptiness of truth status, not in the slightest like our [novice's more dualistic] situation.

The meaning of this sutra is explicated as follows: bodhisattvas at the sixth stage, having such a nature, wish to protect sentient beings who go astray and remain in the life cycle by the force of the two kinds of self-habit. With their great compassion, bodhisattvas proclaim: "I shall lead the others to this correct realization." While familiarizing themselves with the techniques for the bliss of peace after the attainment of the pacification of all-pervasive compounded suffering, bodhisattvas do not taste it. When looking at sentient beings who are confronting the life cycle, bodhisattvas, by contrast, are confronting nirvana. In order to perfect the accessories of unsurpassed enlightenment, they return from the places of meditation where they have obtained the cessation equipoise and voluntarily take rebirths in the desire realm. [TL 116B] Wishing to work for the sake of sentient beings as quickly as possible, they have obtained the power to manifest all

341. 'gog pa'i snyoms 'jug.

kinds of embodiments of ordinary people by taking various rebirths, [even] in the form of animals. From this point, their state is explained as "impure." The purity that is demonstrated from the viewpoint that bodhisattvas are unaffected by the faults of ordinary beings in the life cycle is explained as "impurity" in comparison with the Buddha. [At the same time,] the impurity that is considered from the viewpoint that bodhisattvas take rebirth in the life cycle is explained as "purity" in comparison with ordinary beings.

3.1.2.1.2.2.1.2.2.1.2.4.2.2.3.2 2.2.3.2.2. The Unchangeability in the Pure and Impure State, Which Is Explained in Comparison with the Buddha and Ordinary Beings . . . 2.1. Prelude

«162» There is another meaning of the verse [I.66], which is like the root [verse] of what is explained above, as follows:

3.1.2.1.2.2.1.2.2.1.2.4.2.2.3.2 2.2.3.2.2.2. The Root Text . . . 2.1. Explanation of the Excellences of Purity and Impurity of Four Types of Bodhisattva . . . 1.1. Bodhisattva Who Has Cultivated the Ultimate Spirit at the First Time . . . 1.1. The Excellences of Self-Benefit

The first nine verses are the exposition of the excellences of purity and the tenth is the exposition of the excellences of that impurity in comparison with the Buddha. [TL 117A]

The addicted, who are blinded by ignorance, perceive the buddha children—who have [already] directly realized this immutable reality for the first time by cultivating the transcendent spirit, and have thereby been liberated from birth and death by the force of karmic evolution and addictions—as experiencing the disadvantages of the life cycle, as though they [still] were born, sick, dying, etc., in the same way as they themselves experience [them]. But in reality, the bodhisattvas are doing so out of compassion and vows—this is really wonderful! Moreover, this verse demonstrates the distinctive excellences of great compassion and explicates [this state] to be impure in comparison with [the state of] the Buddha.

3.1.2.1.2.2.1.2.2.1.2.4.2.2.3.2 2.2.3.2.2.2.1.1.2. The Excellences of Other-Benefit

Having obtained the experiential sphere of noble beings, the absolute elimination of sufferings including birth, death, etc., those on the first [bodhisattva] stage are moved by compassion and show themselves taking rebirth, etc., within the experiential sphere of the naive; thus, the artfulnesss and compassion of these [true] friends of sentient beings are truly excellent.

3.1.2.1.2.2.1.2.2.1.2.4.2.2.3.2 2.2.3.2.2.2.1.2. The Bodhisattva Who Has Entered the Enlightened Activities . . . 2.1. Remaining in the World Yet Unaffected by Its Faults

Though those bodhisattvas at the second stage up to the seventh stage have transcended all worlds of alienated beings, disciples, and hermit buddhas, they do not hold themselves apart from the way of the world, such as taking rebirth, etc. They remain and act within the world for the world, without being affected by worldly taints. Otherwise, they would be unable to benefit others because they would have fallen under addiction's sway and would be oppressed by all kinds of suffering. [TL 117b]

3.1.2.1.2.2.1.2.2.1.2.4.2.2.3.2 2.2.3.2.2.2.1.2.2. Application of Import to Simile

Just as a lotus born in water is not spoiled by the water, similarly, those [bodhisattvas] who have been born in the world and have engaged in the enlightened activities are never spoiled by worldly things. Therefore, they are liberated from birth and death by the force of karmic evolution and addictions, and take rebirth according to their wishes.

3.1.2.1.2.2.1.2.2.1.2.4.2.2.3.2 2.2.3.2.2.2.1.3. The Bodhisattva Who Has Obtained Nonregression

In order to accomplish their enlightened activities of benefiting sentient beings, the intelligence of the bodhisattvas at the eighth stage, who have obtained nonregression[342] in all ways, is like a perpetually burning fire [that

---

342. *avaivartika, phyir mi ldog pa.*

symbolizes] the perfection of benefit for others. At the same time, they are always immersed in the meditation on peace that is free from suffering by the elimination of addictions and stressful exertion because they have obtained power by means of nonconceptual intuitive wisdom. Although they are able to actualize nirvana that pacifies all-pervasive suffering, they [do not make it happen but] have obtained the stage of irreversibility in all ways. They have effectively destroyed any chance of producing the thought that seeks liberation out of exclusive self-benefit. The mode of appearance of objects in their multiplicity after the attainment of the yoga of sameness between the life cycle and nirvana is explicated, as above. As to the constant meditation on peace, it does not refer to uninterrupted homogeneous equipoise, because no one other than a buddha can directly perceive all things and teach the Dharma to sentient beings while remaining equipoised in ultimate reality. [TL 118A] Therefore, it indicates that [bodhisattvas at this stage] enter equipoise in actuality without stressful effort, due to the pacification of laborious endeavors. All activities in the post-attainment [concentration] are established with the essence of the equipoise that directly realizes actuality. It is intended by implication that [bodhisattvas at this stage] are endowed with the excellences such as the immediate attainment of the ninth stage, the tenth stage, etc.

3.1.2.1.2.2.1.2.2.1.2.4.2.2.3.2 2.2.3.2.2.2.1.4. The Bodhisattva Who Is One Birth Away from Enlightenment . . . 4.1. The Cause of the Perfect Enlightened Activities . . . 4.1.1. The Cause of Engaging in the Enlightened Activities without Effort

Due to the power of [their previous vows], such as the vow "May I benefit sentient beings!" and being free from stressful endeavors and all conceptual thoughts that habitually insist on the truth status of things, bodhisattvas who are one birth away from enlightenment do not make any great effort to motivate themselves to teach, etc. Instead, they engage in spontaneous enlightened activities in order to develop sentient beings. Although addictive obscurations, the grasping at truth status in things, has been eliminated from the eighth stage onward, strenuous endeavors such as the motivation for teaching the Dharma have been pacified in this stage. [Bodhisattvas at this stage] engage in other-benefit with effortless grace.

3.1.2.1.2.2.1.2.2.1.2.4.2.2.3.2 2.2.3.2.2.2.1.4.1.2. Knowing Various Enlightened Activities Appropriate for Disciples

Those bodhisattvas know precisely whatever art educates disciples and whatever content of teaching, physical form, conduct, and behavior of coming, going, etc., would be most appropriate for disciples. [As to conduct,] for example, they show the way of taking pleasure in desires in order to educate people who have attachment. [TL 118B]

3.1.2.1.2.2.1.2.2.1.2.4.2.2.3.2 2.2.3.2.2.2.1.4.2. Engaging in the Enlightened Activities without Effort

In this way, those bodhisattvas of intelligence who are unobstructed by adverse conditions properly engage themselves, depending upon those causes, in benefiting beings as limitless as the sky, continually and spontaneously, with effortless grace.

3.1.2.1.2.2.1.2.2.1.2.4.2.2.3.2 2.2.3.2.2.2.2. Explanation of Excellences of Purity and Impurity of a Bodhisattva in the Last Worldly Existence . . . 2.1. The Distinction of Purity

During the post-attainment concentration, bodhisattvas in their last worldly existence become equal to a tathāgata on account of the way they benefit sentient beings. By means of their enlightened activities of teaching the Dharma, etc., they properly and nondeceptively take action in the world to liberate sentient beings. The word "post-attainment" indicates that [bodhisattvas at this stage] become equal to a buddha in terms of the number of sentient beings to whom they teach the Dharma in the post-attainment [concentration], in their performance of enlightened activities that permeates all beings, etc. However, they are not equal to a buddha in all aspects, because they, unlike a perfectly enlightened buddha, cannot teach the Dharma to sentient beings, etc., while remaining in the actual experience of direct equipoise. Furthermore, they must eliminate the taint that habitually insists on the actual dichotomous presence of the two realities. No one other than a buddha directly perceives knowable objects in their multiplicity by the same mind that directly realizes knowable objects as they are. The equipoised and post-attainment [concentrations] are thus different in actuality for anyone who has not yet become perfectly enlightened. [TL 119A]

3.1.2.1.2.2.1.2.2.1.2.4.2.2.3.2 2.2.3.2.2.2.2.2. The Distinction of Impurity

Despite the fact that the number of disciples to whom the Dharma is taught by the ultimate bodhisattvas and the perfectly enlightened buddha is the same, etc., it should be known that [the ultimate bodhisattvas and the perfectly enlightened buddha] are not the same in all aspects, for there is as great a difference between these two, as there is between the atom and the earth, or between [water] in a bull's hoofprint and in the ocean. Thus, the former verse (v. 77) demonstrates the sameness of the number of beings to be helped, etc., in the post-attainment [concentration], and the latter demonstrates the difference in general terms such as the way of performing activities, etc. There are differences in the conditions: whether or not all motivated efforts of the three doors [of body, speech, and mind] are pacified, and whether or not they are able to perform enlightened activities of teaching the Dharma, etc., while remaining in the actuality of equipoise. It is unacceptable to make the distinction that these two are equal in terms of benefiting ordinary people, but are not in terms of helping nobles. It should be known that there is a difference between these two, like there is between [water] in a bull's hoofprint and [water] in the ocean, even in the case of placing an ordinary being in the liberation of nirvana.

3.1.2.1.2.2.1.2.2.1.2.4.2.2.3.2 2.2.3.2.2.3. The Commentary ... 3.1. General Statement

«163» Of these ten verses, taken respectively, [the first] nine verses refer to the "purity" [of the noble bodhisattvas] in comparison to the absolute taint of alienated people below the joyous[343] [first] stage of the bodhisattva; the tenth verse refers to the "impurity" [of the noble bodhisattvas] in comparison to the supreme purity of the Buddha above the Dharma cloud[344] [tenth] stage. In brief, the purity and impurity of the four kinds of bodhisattva in the ten bodhisattva stages are explained therein. The four kinds of bodhisattva are as follows: (1) bodhisattvas who have conceived the spirit

343. *pramuditā, rab tu dga' ba.*
344. *dharmameghā, chos kyi sprin.*

[of enlightenment] for the first time; (2) bodhisattvas who have engaged
with activities; (3) bodhisattvas who have reached the stage of irreversibility; and (4) bodhisattvas who are one birth away from enlightenment.
[TL 119B]

3.1.2.1.2.2.1.2.2.1.2.4.2.2.3.2 2.2.3.2.2.3.2. Specific Expositions

«164» There are five [expositions] in number:

(1) On the excellences of bodhisattvas who have cultivated the ultimate
spirit for the first time: the first and second verses demonstrate the characteristics of pure excellences of bodhisattvas in the first stage, the joyous.
These bodhisattvas have perceived the transcendent reality that has never
been perceived before since beginningless time. These two verses explicitly
demonstrate the excellences of purity by [stating] the realization of the
"all-pervasiveness" of the ultimate element in the first stage. The aspect of
impurity is thus implicit in the verses.

(2) On the excellences of bodhisattvas who have engaged in activities:
the third and fourth verses demonstrate the characteristics of the pure
excellences of bodhisattvas in the immaculate [second] stage up to the far-
reaching [seventh] stage, because these bodhisattvas perform unblemished
enlightened activities and have obtained the power that eliminates the
resistance of the six transcendences, such as the entanglement of stinginess,
immorality, etc., respectively.

(3) On the excellences of bodhisattvas who have reached the stage of
nonregression: the fifth verse demonstrates the characteristics of pure excellences of bodhisattvas in the immovable [eighth] stage because these bodhisattvas constantly remain in the meditation pertaining to the attainment of
great enlightenment, which is the practice of the sameness between the life
cycle and nirvana, the cause of the truth body.

(4) On the excellences of bodhisattvas who are separated from enlightenment by one birth: the sixth, seventh, and eighth verses demonstrate the
characteristics of the pure excellences of bodhisattvas in the Dharma cloud
stage, because these bodhisattvas have perfected all the techniques for benefiting themselves and others and have obtained the power to develop sentient beings, and because this is their last birth prior to the attainment of the
stage of a buddha, the supreme unsurpassed perfect enlightenment.

(5) On the excellences of ultimate bodhisattvas: the ninth and tenth verses
demonstrate the sameness as well as the difference between bodhisattvas

who have achieved perfection and a buddha in terms of the excellences of benefiting themselves and others, as explicated above.

3.1.2.1.2.2.1.2.2.1.2.4.2.2.3.2 2.3. Immutability in the Absolute Pure State . . . 3.1. Prelude

«165» Now, here is one verse with respect to the immutability in the absolute pure state. [TL 120A]

3.1.2.1.2.2.1.2.2.1.2.4.2.2.3.2 2.3.2. Exposition . . . 2.1. Statement

This is a rootlike verse, as explained above. Thus, the truth body of a buddha in the absolute pure state is eternal because this state of the ultimate attainment is uncreated and its nature is immutable, unlike the mind-made body, which is produced by the foundational instinctual ignorance-driven evolutionary action and uncontaminated karmic evolutionary action, because the previous one has to be abandoned in order to obtain a new one. This is because the truth body is naturally endowed with inexhaustible ultimate excellences. It is the nondeceptive ultimate refuge of beings because the truth body is limitless into the future, not only naturally pure but also purified from all incidental taints. This statement shows the meaning of eternality, for [the truth body] would not be the ultimate refuge if it were previously purified from incidental taints but later not purified. Its nature is always free from the two extremes of reification and repudiation because the truth body is nonconceptual regarding reality, due to the cessation of all errors. This statement shows the meaning of natural peace and the peace of [the purification from] all incidental taints. It also has an indestructible character because its nature is not created by either contaminated or uncontaminated [karmic evolutionary actions]. This statement shows the meaning of immutability.

3.1.2.1.2.2.1.2.2.1.2.4.2.2.3.2 2.3.2.2. Exposition . . . 2.1. Question

«166» What is demonstrated by this verse?

3.1.2.1.2.2.1.2.2.1.2.4.2.2.3.2 2.3.2.2.2. Answer . . . 2.1. The Root Text . . . 1.1. The Implicit Statement on the Meaning of Negation

[TL 120B] [The truth body] has no birth, including not only rebirth by the force of addictions but also by [the voluntary] taking of the mind-made body. It has no death, including not only the addictive one but also the one of inconceivable transformation. [It is] unharmed not only by the forces of karmic evolution and addictions but also by the nonaddictive evolutionary ignorance instincts. It has no aging, including not only that caused by the forces of addictions and contaminated karmic evolution but also that caused by uncontaminated karmic evolution that causes transmutation. Eternity, etc., is by implication a negation excluding its resistance. . . .

3.1.2.1.2.2.1.2.2.1.2.4.2.2.3.2 2.3.2.2.2.1.2. On the Meaning of Noncessation

. . . because this truth body of the Buddha is eternal, enduring, peaceful, and immutable.

3.1.2.1.2.2.1.2.2.1.2.4.2.2.3.2 2.3.2.2.2.1.3. Detailed Exposition of the Meaning of Negation

This truth body of the Buddha does not have birth even with a mind-made body, because it is eternal. Here, the meaning of eternality is explicated in connection with its negatee, birth by mind-made body. This truth body does not have an inconceivable death of transformation, because it is enduring. This truth body is unharmed by the diseases of the subtle evolutionary instincts for ignorance, because it is peace. [TL 121A]

The meanings of enduringness and peace are explicated in connection with the recognition of their negatees as well. They have no aging conditioned by uncontaminated karmic evolution because they are unchanged by karmic evolution. The meaning of eternality, etc., is explicated in this way. [The truth body] is not explained as a permanent entity that is positively established and independent.

3.1.2.1.2.2.1.2.2.1.2.4.2.2.3.2 2.3.2.2.2.2. The Commentary

≪167≫ While abiding on the stage of the Buddha, which is absolutely stainless, naturally pure, clear-light, the tathāgata element has been purified from all incidental taints and thus has no birth even in the form of the mind-made body, because it is eternal. [The element] has no repeated death even in the manner of inconceivable transformation, because it is enduring. The body and mind [of the buddhas] are unharmed by the sickness of producing the foundational instinctual ignorance-driven evolutionary action, with regard to both its beginning and end, and with regard to its continuum, because it is peace. Thus, because of the development of the fruition of uncontaminated karmic evolution and because of the absence of the factors for birth and death that are included in both categories of addictive obscurations and objective obscurations, the truth body has no aging. Thus, [the element] is unaffected because it is immutable.

3.1.2.1.2.2.1.2.2.1.2.4.2.2.3.2 2.3.2.3. Application of Exposition to Statement . . . 3.1. Sutra Reference to the Meaning of Eternality, etc. . . . 1.1. The Root Text.

≪168≫ [TL 121B] The meanings of eternality, enduringness, peace, and immutability are to be known with reference to the uncreated element and a tathāgata's truth body by each pair of terms. How? As for the meaning of eternality, "untransformable," is a term, and "endowed with inexhaustible excellences" is an explanation. Likewise, "refuge of beings" and "limitless into the future" are, respectively, the term and explanation for the meaning of enduringness. "Always free from the two [extremes]" and "nonconceptual" are, respectively, the term and explanation for the meaning of peace. "Indestructible character" and "uncreated nature" are, respectively, the term and explanation for the meaning of immutability. The meaning of eternality, and so on, should be understood according to the *Sutra [Teaching the Absence of Increase and Decrease (in the Realm of Beings)]* that will be explicated below.

3.1.2.1.2.2.1.2.2.1.2.4.2.2.3.2 2.3.2.3.1.2. The Commentary

≪169≫ The distinction of each pair, term, and explanation of the meaning of each term—eternality, enduringness, peace, and unchangeability, respectively—with respect to the uncompounded element should be understood according to the sutra. [TL 121B]

3.1.2.1.2.2.1.2.2.1.2.4.2.2.3.2 2.3.2.3.2. Application of Exposition to Statement . . . 2.1. The Root Text

The untransformable nature of the truth body is the meaning of eternality because the truth body is endowed with the inexhaustible, infinite excellences of a buddha. The former part [of this statement] is the term and the latter part is the explanation for the meaning of eternality. Its nature of being a nondeceptive refuge at any time is the meaning of enduringness, because it exists as far as the farthest limit into the future. The former part [of this statement] is the term and the latter part is the explanation for the meaning of enduringness. Being free from two extremes and from all incidental evolutionary instincts is the meaning of peace, because it is nonconceptual in nature. The former part is the term and the latter part is the explanation for the meaning of peace. [TL 122A] Being free from disintegration by death is the meaning of immutability, because it has the quality of being unaltered by either contaminated karmic evolution or uncontaminated karmic evolution. The former part is the term and the latter part is the explanation for the meaning of immutability.

3.1.2.1.2.2.1.2.2.1.2.4.2.2.3.2 2.3.2.3.2.2. Connection with Sutra

[The *Sutra [Teaching the Absence of Increase and Decrease (in the Realm of Beings)]* states:]

> This untransformable truth body, Shāriputra, is eternal because of its inexhaustible characteristic. This refuge truth body, Shāriputra, is enduring because it exists as far as the farthest limit. This nondual truth body, Shāriputra, is peace because of its nonconceptual nature. This indestructible truth body, Shāriputra, is immutable because it has the characteristic of being unaltered.

The meaning of this passage is summarized as follows: this immutable truth body is eternal because it is free from the twelve links of relativistic origination that are included in addictive obscurations, or the twelve links that are included in objective obscurations; that is to say in brief, it has no birth of a mind-made body in actuality. It is enduring because it is free from the death of the inconceivable transformation. It is peace because it has eliminated the evolutionary instincts for ignorance. It is immutable because it is unaltered by uncontaminated karmic evolution.

3.1.2.1.2.2.1.2.2.1.2.4.2.2.4. Establishing Possession of the Indivisible Excellences of Liberation at the Time of Being Absolutely Pure . . .
4.1. Prelude

≪170≫ Here is one verse with reference to this meaning of "the indivisible excellences of intuitive wisdom and elimination" in connection with this pure state of tathāgata essence that has reached the ultimate point of being absolutely pure and free from incidental taints without exception.

3.1.2.1.2.2.1.2.2.1.2.4.2.2.4.2. Exposition . . . 2.1. Brief Statement [TL 122B]

Buddhahood possesses all kinds of excellences, including wisdom, intuitive wisdom, and the liberation of the disciple vehicle, hermit buddha vehicle, and universal vehicle, in an indivisible manner.

[Buddhahood] is the truth body that is primordially pure at the ultimate point. It is the tathāgata endowed with the excellences of the ultimate realization of reality. It is the noble truth of cessation included in ultimate truth; it is the ultimate elimination of all incidental taints in addition to natural purity. It is unlocated nirvana. Like the sun and its rays, its excellences are indivisible. Therefore, it should be known that there is no unlocated nirvana apart from buddhahood.

These four excellences indicate that they are possessed by the truth body in an indivisible manner, being its natural purity, the intuitive wisdom that is the direct realization of that [purity], the elimination of all incidental taints, and the attainment by means of antidotes to those [taints], respectively. This statement does not indicate that saints and hermit buddhas lack authentic nirvana. Instead, it is thus taught in order to establish the ultimate single vehicle because no one other than the Buddha has the ultimate excellences of liberation, intuitive wisdom, and wisdom that do not require further improvement. [TL 123A]

3.1.2.1.2.2.1.2.2.1.2.4.2.2.4.2.2.2. Detailed Exposition . . . 2.1. The Reasoning about the Indivisibility of the Ultimate Excellences . . . 1.1. Question

«171» Here [what is demonstrated by the former half of this verse?]

3.1.2.1.2.2.1.2.2.1.2.4.2.2.4.2.2.1.2. Answer . . . 2.1. Brief Statement . . . 1.1. The Root Text

It should be known, in brief, that there are four synonyms for the truth body, the tathāgata, etc., because the meaning of this is the stainless element that is the natural purity free from all incidental taints and is classified into four aspects, to be explained below. This classification does not make a division of the excellences between ultimate and nonultimate.

3.1.2.1.2.2.1.2.2.1.2.4.2.2.4.2.2.1.2.1.2. The Commentary

In short, the tathāgata essence as the stainless element has four synonyms in accordance with these four meanings.

3.1.2.1.2.2.1.2.2.1.2.4.2.2.4.2.2.1.2.2. Detailed Exposition . . . 2.1. Question

«172» Which, then, are the four meanings indicated by those four synonyms above?

3.1.2.1.2.2.1.2.2.1.2.4.2.2.4.2.2.1.2.2.2. Answer . . . 2.1. The Root Text

The ultimate purity [of the tathāgata essence] is called "the truth body" because the element, which is distinguished by its natural purity within the continuums of sentient beings, makes it possible that all the excellences of a buddha can be developed, thereby being indivisible from them. It is called "tathāgata" because of the attainment of the ultimate realization of its potential reality. It is called "noble truth" because the ultimate truth, which is neither false nor deceptive, has been purified from all taints. [TL 123B] And it is called "unlocated nirvana" because it is natural peace from primordial time [in the form of] the ultimate, the elimination obtained by antidotes.

3.1.2.1.2.2.1.2.2.1.2.4.2.2.4.2.2.1.2.2.2.2. The Commentary . . . 2.1.
Application to Each Sutra

«173» [With reference to (the first meaning that is the tathāgata essence, it is) indivisible from the buddha qualities. The following statement from the *[Shrīmālādevī Lion's Roar] Sutra* states:

> O Bhagavān, the tathāgata essence is not devoid of the buddha excellences that are indivisible, inseparable, and inconceivable, far greater in number than the sands of the Ganges.]

[This statement demonstrates that] the tathāgata essence primordially has inseparable [excellences, where] all antidotes can be produced [on the basis of the tathāgata essence] and all incidental taints can be separated from [the tathāgata essence]. As for the distinctiveness of the six sense media, it bears on the fact that those inner sense media such as eye are devoid of truth.

3.1.2.1.2.2.1.2.2.1.2.4.2.2.4.2.2.1.2.2.2.2. Application of the Statement to the Exposition

«174» For these four meanings, there are four synonyms, namely: (1) the truth body; (2) the tathāgata; (3) the ultimate truth; and (4) nirvana, respectively. For what reason? The sutras state as follows:

> [O Shāriputra, the so-called tathāgata essence is a synonym for the truth body.
>
> O Bhagavān, the tathāgata and the truth body are not different from each other. Bhagavān, the truth body is nothing but the tathāgata.
>
> The so-called cessation of sufferings, O Bhagavān, indicates the truth body of the tathāgata, who is endowed with such excellences.

The so-called ultimate element of nirvana, O Bhagavān, is a synonym of the truth body of the tathāgata.]

3.1.2.1.2.2.1.2.2.1.2.4.2.2.4.2.2.2. The Established Meaning and the Nature
of Indivisibility ... 2.1. Question

«175» Here, [what is demonstrated by the latter half of the verse?]

3.1.2.1.2.2.1.2.2.1.2.4.2.2.4.2.2.2.2. Answer ... 2.1. The Root Text

The truth body of the tathāgatas itself should be understood as possessing indivisibly the excellences of the perfect enlightenment regarding all
kinds of things and the excellences of eliminating taints along with their
evolutionary instincts, and thus it is the ultimate nonduality of perfect
buddhahood and unlocated nirvana. Further, to explain specifically, [this
is the equality of] manifestly perfect enlightenment in regard to all forms,
elimination of any instinctual taint, and ultimate nonduality of nirvana.

3.1.2.1.2.2.1.2.2.1.2.4.2.2.4.2.2.2.2.2. The Commentary

What is the reason? These four synonyms of the uncontaminated element [TL 124A] converge into a single meaning, the tathāgata element. Therefore, these four are identical in meaning. Hence, in terms of the Dharma of
nonduality, the "buddha" and "nirvana" should be viewed as "indivisible" or
"inseparable"; that is to say, they are "nondual." The former is thus named
because of its perfect enlightenment regarding all kinds of things, and
the latter because of the elimination of taints along with the evolutionary
instincts. These take place simultaneously with the perfect enlightenment
in the stainless element.

3.1.2.1.2.2.1.2.2.1.2.4.2.2.4.2.2.3. The Simile ... 3.1. The Nature of
Indivisibility of Excellences ... 1.1. The Main Meaning ... 1.1. The Root
Text

«176» The ultimate liberation has the characteristic of being indivisible from the excellences. They are of all kinds, excluding none, and of
immeasurable varieties: [they are called] extensive excellent qualities with

inconceivable numbers and powers; profound excellent qualities with stainless elimination free from taints and their evolutionary instincts. The tathāgata is such a nirvanic liberation. In light of this, the explanation of ultimate liberation in the continuums of disciple saints and hermit buddha saints should be known as of intentional [meaning].

3.1.2.1.2.2.1.2.2.1.2.4.2.2.4.2.2.3.1.1.2. The Commentary . . .
2.1. The Explanation of Three Different Kinds of Ultimate Liberation Being Intentional

«177» This point is made clear in the [*Shrīmālādevī*] *Lion's Roar Sutra* in connection to the nirvana of saints and hermit buddhas:

> O Bhagavān, this so-called "nirvana" is a technique used by the buddhas.

This sutra passage demonstrates that this nirvana, which is the mere pacification of sufferings in the life cycle and is stated as the ultimate objective for some disciples who are temporarily determined in having the spiritual potential for the disciple vehicle or the hermit buddha vehicle, is a technique used by the perfectly enlightened ones. [These perfectly enlightened ones] are the supreme lords of the Dharma who prevent their [disciples'] regression from perfect enlightenment, just as an illusory city in the forest is created by a skillful captain for exhausted travelers headed for the ocean [in the middle of] their long journey. [TL 124B]

3.1.2.1.2.2.1.2.2.1.2.4.2.2.4.2.2.3.1.1.2.2. The Liberation Indivisible from Four Excellences Being Exclusively Buddhahood

«178» [On the other hand,] the [*Shrīmālādevī Lion's Roar*] *Sutra* states as follows:

> O Bhagavān, the Tathāgata, the Saint, the Perfectly Enlightened Buddha is endowed with the immeasurable, inconceivable, and ultimate pure excellences because of his attainment of nirvana.

≪179≫ This sutra passage demonstrates that, having obtained nirvana, which is characterized as indivisible from the accomplishment of the four kinds of excellent qualities, the perfectly enlightened ones are identified as being this nirvana. Therefore, as both the Buddha and nirvana are endowed with an inseparable quality, no one can obtain nirvana without becoming a buddha. This statement demonstrates that the ultimate nirvana must be identical to the one indivisible from the four excellences. Thus, it indicates that disciples and hermit buddhas do not possess the ultimate nirvana. It does not indicate that they do not have the mediocre one.

Objection: It is unnecessary to clear the doubts about whether or not disciples and hermit buddhas have the ultimate nirvana.

Answer: Although it is unnecessary to establish such a point for those who are certain of the ultimate single vehicle or those who are definite in having the spiritual potential for the universal vehicle, such a point is established for the purpose of introducing the universal vehicle to some people who are not determined in having the spiritual potential for the disciple vehicle or the hermit buddha vehicle, and for the purpose of guiding disciple saints and hermit buddha saints who remain in equipoise in the element of peace of the universal vehicle by the exhortation of the buddhas in the form of emissions of light. Moreover, it should be known that it is uncertain what will happen when they hear the mere words "ultimate single vehicle."

3.1.2.1.2.2.1.2.2.1.2.4.2.2.4.2.2.3.1.2. The Simile of Painters ... 2.1. Prelude

[TL 125A] ≪180≫ The buddhas are endowed with all excellences because the "emptiness endowed with every supreme aspect"[345] has been established within the stainless element.

This statement demonstrates that the emptiness endowed with every supreme aspect is the reality free from all taints, and is the intuitive wisdom that directly realizes the emptiness of all kinds of elimination and realization without exception. It does not indicate that ultimate truth is empty of everything conventional, because if that were true, there would be no excellences at all.

---

345. *sarvākāravaropetaśūnyatā, rnam pa thams cad kyi mchog dang ldan pa'i stong pa nyid.*

3.1.2.1.2.2.1.2.2.1.2.4.2.2.4.2.2.3.1.2.2. The Root Text . . . 2.2.1. The Simile

Since its ultimate perfection accomplishes the buddha excellences, the techniques for the accomplishment of a buddha's four kinds of excellence is the wisdom included in the path of learning that realizes emptiness replete with all its excellences, such as generosity, etc. How is this so? Compare this to a group of painters who are specialized in drawing different parts [of the body] such as the head, etc. As an example, whichever part one [painter] knows, such as the head, the others who are specialized in drawing hands, etc., cannot understand.

The reigning king gives them a canvas, with the following order: "You all must paint my full-length portrait on this!" Having received the command, these painters start their own work of painting. However, one of them engaged in this work leaves for a foreign land. [TL 125B]

Because of his absence, having gone to another land, this full-length portrait with its all parts would remain unfinished. This is the simile.

3.1.2.1.2.2.1.2.2.1.2.4.2.2.4.2.2.3.1.2.2.2. The Implications

The emptiness endowed with every supreme aspect is the reality of perfect buddhahood obtained from practices based on the stores of merit and wisdom, free from all incidental taints. In addition, it refers to the Buddha's intuitive wisdom that always remains in equipoise on ultimate truth, yet is adorned with the complete set of liberative arts such as generosity, etc. When in the path phase, it refers to the meditation that is the integration of mental quiescence and transcendent analysis directly realizing emptiness and is adorned with liberative arts such as generosity, etc.

The stores of merit and wisdom illustrated by their likeness to these painters are: generosity, including the motivation to give one's body, enjoyments, and roots of virtue for the welfare of all sentient beings; ethics, which includes the common thought that restrains [one] from resistance to ethics and the distinctive thought that eliminates the mentation for seeking self-liberation only; tolerance, which includes the difficult work of understanding each teaching, accepting sufferings, and minimizing occasions of anger, etc.; creativity, meditation, and wisdom, etc. These are the stages of the path on the basis of conventional reality and the stages of the path on the basis of the ultimate reality, [respectively]. [TL 126A] The intuitive wisdom in the mental continuums of the perfectly enlightened ones is the accomplishment of these complete stages; [intuitive wisdom] realizes emptiness endowed with every supreme aspect of liberative arts. It is illustrated as the portrait of the king in the sutra. Furthermore, the *[Questions of Ratnachūḍā] Sutra* states that the so-called emptiness endowed with every supreme aspect is emptiness endowed with [every kind of] generosity without exception, with [every kind of] ethics without exception, and so on.

Therefore, to accept that the ultimate truth adorned with all excellences such as the [ten] powers, etc., exists from beginningless time within the continuums of all beings would be no different in the slightest from the position of the outsiders' Shaivism that accepts an eternal, self-originated omniscience. A certain someone accepts the ultimate reality as an eternal entity and the conventional as its transformation. This position cannot be differentiated from the Sāṃkhya philosophy, which accepts the principal (*pradhāna*), an eternal entity, as the nature of the transformations such as matter, sound, etc., and as the ultimate reality. So please do not injure the impeccable teaching of the Buddha by proclaiming that these misapprehensions, which reify what does not exist, are the intended meaning of the *Glorious Kālachakra Tantra*, the ultimate teaching of the Buddha. The arrangement of the two realities according to the great commentary *Stainless Light*, [TL 126B] that all functions are viable despite the fact that all things—even those as small as an atom—are not established by intrinsic reality, is in agreement with what the Protector Nāgārjuna elucidated, by giving examples of vase and space. [This point] should be known from other texts.

3.1.2.1.2.2.1.2.2.1.2.4.2.2.4.2.2.3.1.2.3. The Commentary...
2.3.1. The Magnificent and Profound Excellences... 1.1. The Excellences of Realization

«181» In regard to the magnificent excellences, even each of these six transcendences, such as generosity, etc., should be known as "immeasurable" in the emptiness endowed with every supreme form [of art], since it is differentiated into limitless varieties in the sphere of the Buddha. The profound excellences are "inconceivable" and difficult to realize on account of their number and power.

3.1.2.1.2.2.1.2.2.1.2.4.2.2.4.2.2.3.1.2.3.1.2. The Excellences of Elimination

It [elimination] is "supremely pure" because of the removal without exception of the karmic instincts for resistances, such as stinginess, etc.

3.1.2.1.2.2.1.2.2.1.2.4.2.2.4.2.2.3.1.2.3.2. The Reasoning . . . 2.1. The Mode of Accomplishment of Excellences in the Three Pure Stages . . . 1.1. The Attainment of the Excellence of the Spontaneous Path at the Eighth Stage

«182» [TL 127A] Below the seventh stage, the [tolerance of] the uncreated reality is obtained by means of concentration on emptiness endowed with every supreme aspect; [this] is the intuitive wisdom of the direct realization of the emptiness adorned with infinite liberative arts such as generosity, etc. Because of this attainment, [bodhisattvas] at the eighth stage, immovable, accomplish all the excellences of the buddhas in the stainless element on the basis of their nonconceptual, faultless, uninterrupted, and spontaneously engaging path wisdom that directly knows the three paths of disciples, etc.

Here, [the text indicates that] the attainment during practice of the sameness of the life cycle and nirvana spontaneously engages with the causes that conform with the truth body. The great Lama-translator [Ngog] Loden Sherab states on this basis that bodhisattvas will not actualize the path of the disciple until the eighth stage, in which the path wisdom is produced in the manner [that all appearances of objects of knowledge in their multiplicity invariably arise as] reflected images. However, as to the position [held by Ngog-lo] that knowledge and the elimination possessed by the "stream enterer"[346] up to the hermit buddha are identical to the bodhisattva's tolerance of the uncreated reality, as is stated in the *Sunlight*:[347]

How is this tolerance explained as the tolerance of the reality intuition[348] concerning sufferings? This is the tolerance recog-

---

346. *srotāpanna, rgyun zhugs.*

347. *nyi snang* (*sūryāloka*). This may be a Tibetan scholar's nickname for Vimuktasena's *Commentary on [Haribhadra's] Ornament of Clear Realization, Quintessential Instructions on the Transcendent Wisdom in Twenty-Five Thousand Lines* (Tōh. 3787), though we were unable to locate the specific language of this passage in any source.

348. *dharmajñānakṣānti, chos shes pa'i bzod pa.*

nized as included in the path of the disciples, but not the one recognized as the path wisdom [of bodhisattvas].

[TL 127B] It is explained [in detail] in the section called, "Means of Determining Stages of Path" of the *Ornament of Clear Realization.*

3.1.2.1.2.2.1.2.2.1.2.4.2.2.4.2.2.3.1.2.3.2.1.2. The Attainment of Excellence of Upholding All Holy Teachings of the Buddha on the Ninth Stage

By means of innumerable ocean-like means of concentration, such as the "space treasury," etc., and recitation of secret mantra, etc., [bodhisattvas] at the ninth stage, positive intelligence, accomplish immeasurable excellences on the basis of their wisdom upholding the immeasurable buddha excellences without exception.

3.1.2.1.2.2.1.2.2.1.2.4.2.2.4.2.2.3.1.2.3.2.1.3. The Attainment of Excellence of Realizing All Subtle Secrets at the Tenth Stage

[Bodhisattvas] at the tenth stage, Dharma cloud, accomplish inconceivable excellences on the basis of their intuitive wisdom that discovers the subtle secret of all buddhas.

3.1.2.1.2.2.1.2.2.1.2.4.2.2.4.2.2.3.1.2.3.2.2. The Mode of Accomplishment of Ultimate Excellences

Immediately after [this stage], the supreme pure excellences are accomplished on the basis of knowledge that liberates from the addictive obscurations along with their evolutionary instincts and the objective obscurations because of the attainment of buddhahood. [In other words,] the elimination that extinguishes the two obscurations and their evolutionary instincts causes the attainment of the perfect, ultimate emptiness endowed with every supreme aspect.

3.1.2.1.2.2.1.2.2.1.2.4.2.2.4.2.2.3.1.2.3.3. Disciples and Hermit Buddhas
Lacking Those Excellences

«183» As disciple saints and hermit buddhas cannot perceive these four
foundations of the intuitive wisdoms in these stages, which are the foundations of the [aforementioned] four kinds of excellent qualities,[349] they are
said to be far from the element of nirvana that is characterized as indivisible from the accomplishment of the four kinds of excellent qualities. This
statement demonstrates that disciples and hermit buddhas cannot obtain
the ultimate nirvana.

3.1.2.1.2.2.1.2.2.1.2.4.2.2.4.2.2.3.2. The Explanation of the Simile . . .
2.1. The Similarity between Simile and Import . . . 1.1. The Root Text

«184» Wisdom is the ultimate realization of the knowable as it is,
[TL 128A] intuition directly realizes the knowable in its multiplicity, and liberation is included in the elimination that extinguishes all taints. These are
clear in ultimate reality, clear-light in their multiplicity of the knowable
without exception, and pure in terms of being free from all taints, respectively. These three factors are undifferentiable in reality; therefore they are
similar to the indivisibility of the actualities of light, rays, and the sun itself.

3.1.2.1.2.2.1.2.2.1.2.4.2.2.4.2.2.3.2.1.2. The Commentary . . .
2.1. General Statement of the Similarity between Simile and Import

[TL 128B] «185» Wisdom, intuition, and liberation are the illustrations of
the element of nirvana that is characterized as indivisible from the accomplishment of the four kinds of excellences. They are shown to be analogous
to the sun in four aspects, namely, by three [individual] aspects, and by one
[in general]. The light, the rays, and the sun itself are not identical but are
the same reality.[350]

---

349. It seems that Gyaltsap does not agree with Ngog-lo's idea here.
350. *ngo bo tha dad med pa rnam pa gcig.*

3.1.2.1.2.2.1.2.2.1.2.4.2.2.4.2.2.3.2.1.2.2. Specific Explanation

Here: (1) the transcendent nonconceptual wisdom in the continuum of a buddha is analogous to light because it dispels the darkness [that hides] the ultimate truth of the knowable object; (2) the omniscient intuition that is obtained subsequently is analogous to the luminosity of the net of rays because it engages with all kinds of objects of knowledge in their entirety; (3) the natural liberation that is the basis of the above two is analogous to the purity of the sun because it is absolutely free from taints, being [ultimate] clear-light. Meditative equipoise and post-attainment meditation are the same actuality in the continuums of perfectly enlightened ones. Thus, it should be known that [the buddha intuition] perceiving things as they are, perceives things in their multiplicity; and [the buddha wisdom] perceiving things in their multiplicity perceives things as they are. . . .

3.1.2.1.2.2.1.2.2.1.2.4.2.2.4.2.2.3.2.1.2.3. Conclusion

. . . and (4) as these three are indivisible from the ultimate element in terms of their actualities, they are analogous to the three distinctive factors of the sun, i.e., light, etc., which are indivisible [from the sun]. Wisdom, etc., represents the nirvana indivisible from the four excellences in terms of these things being analogous to the sun.

3.1.2.1.2.2.1.2.2.1.2.4.2.2.4.2.2.3.2.2. Establishing That Disciples and Hermit Buddhas Lack Ultimate Liberation and Nirvana . . . 2.1. The Root Text

«186» The ultimate nirvana must be the collection of excellences in all forms: as innumerable excellences, inconceivability, and purification from all taints. Therefore, until perfect buddhahood is attained, there is no attainment of the ultimate nirvana, just as the sun cannot be seen without its light and rays. Thus, it should be known that lacking proper understanding of this detailed establishment of the indivisibility of excellences causes the mistake of accepting that disciples and hermit buddhas do not reach an authentic nirvana.

3.1.2.1.2.2.1.2.2.1.2.4.2.2.4.2.2.3.2.2.2. The Commentary . . .
2.1. The Literal Meaning

«187» This element that is endowed with the possibility of origination of pure virtuous excellences as its own nature since beginningless time is the reality that is indivisible from the possibility of origination of all excellences of the buddhas. It would be in direct contradiction to the following statements if [the element were deemed as] endowed with all excellences in the indivisible manner from the beginning [of time]. Therefore, until the attainment of the tathāgata who possesses unobstructed intuitive perception, it is unfeasible to actualize the realization of nirvana that is characterized as the liberation from all obscurations, just as the sun cannot be seen without perceiving its light and rays.

3.1.2.1.2.2.1.2.2.1.2.4.2.2.4.2.2.3.2.2.2.2. Sutra Reference

Therefore, the *[Shrīmālādevī Lion's Roar] Sutra* states as follows:

> O Bhagavān, the ultimate realization of nirvana does not exist in the inferior life cycle and superior nirvana in terms of taking as an object of negation the mere rebirth in the life cycle. O Bhagavān, the realization of nirvana is equal to wisdom. O Bhagavān, nirvana is equal to intuition, equal to liberation, and equal to the intuitive experience of liberation. Therefore, O Bhagavān, it is said that the element of nirvana is of one taste, of equal taste, that is to say, [it is of one] taste with knowledge and liberation.

This passage demonstrates that the ultimate nirvana must be the collection of the four kinds of excellent qualities in the indivisible manner. [TL 129A]

3.1.2.1.2.2.1.2.2.1.3. Précis . . . 3.1. The Root Text

«188» Above, the tathāgata essence has been explained by means of the arrangement of ten kinds of meanings, such as nature, etc. Likewise, the element is explicated by this arrangement with an emphasis on its natural purity and by implication, by the taints as incidental. The following text explains [the element and taints] in the reverse manner. In our opinion, this [verse] can be regarded as the précis without contradiction, despite the fact that it is also suitable that this explanation is a prelude to the next part.

3.1.2.1.2.2.1.2.2.1.3.2. The Commentary

Thus, with reference to the existence of reality as being eternal in the way it is analogous to the ultimate limit into the future, the arrangement of this tathāgata essence has been explained by ten meanings.

3.1.2.1.2.2.1.2.2.2. Proof of the Element Being Obscured by Incidental Taints with Nine Similes . . . 2.1. Prelude

« 189 » The minds of sentient beings are naturally pure. Nevertheless, [this purity] exists under the covering of addictions. The fact that the addictions are incidental and are unable to penetrate the nature of the mind should be known by the nine similes. Furthermore, there is no contradiction in taking this section as a brief statement rather than a prelude.

The covering of addictions is essentially unconnected because it is unable to penetrate the nature of the mind, although it has coexisted [with the mind] since beginningless time. The naturally pure reality, likewise existing since beginningless time, is essentially connected because it penetrates the nature of the mind. It should be understood by the nine similes in the *[Tathāgata Essence] Sutra* that the tathāgata essence is concealed by the limitless coverings of addictions.[351]

3.1.2.1.2.2.1.2.2.2.2. Explanation . . . 2.1. General Meaning . . . 1.1. A Definitive Number of Eighteen Similes

« 190 » Question: Why are there exactly two sets of nine similes each for representing the category of addiction and the category of purity?

[TL 129B] Answer: There are exactly nine similes used to represent the category of obscuring addictions because there are exactly nine meanings for the nine obscurations, represented by the similes. There are exactly nine

---

351. This paragraph is listed as a separate section in currently available Tibetan editions. A proper subtitle might be missing.

obscurations, including (1–3) the seeds of the three poisons and (4) the active, strong forms of these three as one. Or else (1) all three poisons are counted as one in their active forms, and then are differentiated in terms of being the causal addictions that bring about either (2–3) the two higher realms or (4) the desire realm. [The remaining five] obscurations are those that are (5) based upon the foundational instinctual ignorance-driven evolutionary action; (6) eliminated by the path of insight; (7) eliminated by the path of meditation; (8) based upon the impure stages; and (9) based upon the pure stages.

There is also a reason that there are exactly nine similes used to represent the category of purity, and this is again that there are exactly nine meanings represented by the similes. These are three [aspects with respect to the tathāgata essence, namely] the truth body, reality, and the spiritual potential. The truth body is divided into three parts: (1) the realizational Dharma[352] and, among the textual Dharma teachings,[353] (2) those sutras that expound the ultimate truth or (3) those that expound the conventional truth. There are no divisions to (4) reality. The spiritual potential is further divided into two: (5) naturally existing and (6) developmental. As to these two, the first has the ability to be transformed into (7) the truth body, and the second has the ability to be transformed into (8–9) the two kinds of material body, [beatific body and emanation body]. The number of meanings would be exactly nine by means of detailed counting. Thus, because there are eighteen different meanings to be represented, the similes used to represent them are then exactly eighteen in number.

3.1.2.1.2.2.1.2.2.2.2.1.2. Explaining the Similarity between Similes and Implications

(1) Attachment and the lotus have similar features because they make us happy immediately after they become active, but later on can cause us to be unhappy.

Question: Did you say before that the lotus represents attachment in its latent form? Why are you now saying that attachment and a lotus are comparable in terms of their causing us happiness when they are active?

352. *rtogs pa'i chos.*
353. *bstan pa'i chos.*

Answer: No problem. Since attachment makes us happy when it is [TL 130A] active, its latent form can still be represented by the simile given. In addition, this explanation of similarity should be understood in a broad sense.

(2) Hatred and bees that make us feel ill at ease are comparable. (3) Misknowledge and the husk that acts to obscure us from perceiving the essence within are comparable. These three are established separately because they each have a different ability to produce themselves in a homogeneous outcome over a period of time. (4) These three in their active states and filth are similar. Both are unbearable. When active in a strong form, [the three poisons] motivate us to commit bad actions; and since bad actions make our lives miserable, they are unbearable just like filth. These three in their active forms are established as one group of obscurations because they are no different in their ability to produce bad actions. (5) Karmic instincts for ignorance and earth are comparable because ignorance is an obscuration to the attainment of self-original [intuitive wisdom] just as earth is [an obscuration] to a treasure. (6) Those [obscurations] eliminated by the path of insight are comparable to a fruit, for they are destroyed immediately after the path of insight has originated and the sprout has originated, respectively. (7) Those [obscurations] eliminated by the path of meditation are similar to tattered rags because their essence has worn out. (8) Obscurations based upon the impure stages are similar to women in that they both are obscurations to self-realization. (9) Obscurations based upon the pure stages and being smeared slightly with mud are similar in that they are both slightly obscured by something subtle. This is the similarity between similes and meanings with respect to obscuration.

Now regarding the explanation of the similarity between similes and points with respect to what is obscured: (1) The truth body and a buddha [statue] are similar in that there is nothing in the world comparable with them. (2) The sutras that expound ultimate reality are similar to honey in [TL 130B] that they give us the single taste of bliss when experienced. (3) The sutras that expound conventional reality are similar to the essential grain within a husk, for they are specifically designed to suit individual needs. (4) Reality is likened to gold because its nature will never turn bad. (5) The naturally existing potential is likened to a treasure because it exists in itself and is not established with effort. (6) The developmental potential is likened to a cultivated tree because it is established through effort. (7) The truth body is likened to a self-arisen image made of precious jewels because it is not a new acquisition bestowed by others and because it is the basis for perfect excellences. (8) The beatific body is likened to a world emperor because it enjoys sovereignty over the great Dharma. (9) The emanation body is likened to an image fashioned in gold because it is no more than a mere reflection.

3.1.2.1.2.2.1.2.2.2.1.3. Dispelling Doubts

Objection: Since the latent form of attachment is an obscuration to expounding teachings and the two kinds of spiritual potential as well, it is incorrect to present it as an obscuration only to the teachings in the form of realization. Likewise, since the remaining eight kinds of obscuration also obscure the teachings in the form of realization, it is incorrect to present them only as an obscuring attachment in its latent form. Furthermore, since the attachment in its latent form also acts as an obscuration to the remaining eight obscured objects, then it is uncertain that each individual simile and its topic among the nine similes such as the lotus, etc., represent the obscurations; and [it is uncertain] that the nine similes such as the buddha [statue], etc., represent the obscured.

Answer: Yet there is no contradiction here, because we assert that the points [of these two sets] are not definitive in having a connection between what is obscuring and what is obscured, unlike similes that are definitive in having such a connection. Conformities exist between the nine obscurations and the nine similes representing them as well as between the nine obscured objects and the nine similes representing them, respectively. Furthermore, the nine obscurations possessed by the four kinds of individual are distinguished by different definitions, not by different substances. [TL 131A]

3.1.2.1.2.2.1.2.2.2.2.2. The Ramifications . . . 2.1. The Similes Representing the Fact That the Tathāgata Essence Is Made Manifest When the Nine Obscurations Have Been Removed . . . 1.1. Brief Statement . . . 1.1. The Similes of Obscurations and Their Obscured Objects

Question: Which are the nine similes?
Reply: [They are]: (1) the statue of a buddha existing within an ugly lotus; (2) the honey amid bees; (3) the kernels within fruit husks; (4) gold inside

filth; (5) a treasure of jewels beneath the floor of a poor man's house; (6) the sprout of a fruit tree, etc., grown from a small fruit, its seed; (7) a buddha image in tattered rags; (8) a world emperor in a poor woman's womb; and (9) a statue made of precious gold existing within a clay [mold]. It should be known that this naturally pure element exists in all sentient beings, obscured by the taints of incidental addictions, just in the way described by these similes. This verse demonstrates the plain fact that, although obscured by incidental taints, the element exists by using a buddha within a lotus, etc., as examples.

3.1.2.1.2.2.1.2.2.2.2.1.1.2. Each Individual Simile

As to analogies, the taints should be known as analogous to the lotus, the bees, the husks, filth, the floor, the fruit, the tattered rags, the woman severely afflicted by burning misery, and clay. The supreme element, which is stainless by nature, should be known as analogous to the statue of a buddha, the honey, the kernel, gold, a treasure, a nyagrodha tree, a precious image, a supreme ruler of the world, and a precious statue.

3.1.2.1.2.2.1.2.2.2.2.1.2. Detailed Exposition . . . 2.1. The Four Taints Including Attachment in Its Dormant Form and so on, Proved to Be Incidental by Using Similes . . . 1.1. The Three Poisons in Their Dormant Forms . . . 1.1. Attachment in Its Dormant Form . . . 1.1. Prelude

«191» The addictions are like the petal sheath of the faded lotus, and the tathāgata element is akin to a buddha.

3.1.2.1.2.2.1.2.2.2.2.1.2.1.1.1.2. The Root Text . . . 2.1. Brief Statement . . . 1.1. Simile

Suppose the statue of a buddha, shining and adorned with a thousand excellent marks, were abiding within a fetid and faded lotus with petals closed. When perceived by a man with the pure divine eye, it would be extracted from the petal sheath of the lotus.

3.1.2.1.2.2.1.2.2.2.2.2.1.2.1.1.1.2.1.2. Import

Similarly, the Tathāgata sees with his buddha eye his own reality even in those who are in the Avīchi hell. [TL 132A]

3.1.2.1.2.2.1.2.2.2.2.2.1.2.1.1.1.2.1.3. Means of Purifying the Element from the Taints

Who purifies these taints? The lord buddhas, who are unobstructed owing to their complete elimination of taints, and who are the masters of compassion, remain till the limit of the future to liberate the childish from the obscuration of attachment in its dormant form. Alternatively, there would be no contradiction in explaining . . .

3.1.2.1.2.2.1.2.2.2.2.2.1.2.1.1.1.2.2. Detailed Exposition

. . . just as a person with the divine eye perceives a tathāgata within the closed faded lotus flower and cuts away the petals in order to reveal him, the Tathāgata perceives the nature of the tathāgata essence within all beings, covered with the sheath of taints, attachment, hatred, etc., and destroys such obscurations by means of compassion.

3.1.2.1.2.2.1.2.2.2.2.2.1.2.1.1.2. Hatred in Its Dormant Form . . . 2.1. Prelude

«192» The addictions are like honeybees, and the tathāgata essence is akin to the honey.

3.1.2.1.2.2.1.2.2.2.2.2.1.2.1.1.2.2. The Root Text . . . 2.1. Statement . . .
1.1. Simile

Suppose a clever person, having seen honey surrounded by a swarm of bees and endeavoring to get it, with technical skill, would completely separate the swarm of bees from it.

3.1.2.1.2.2.1.2.2.2.2.2.1.2.1.1.2.2.1.2. Import

Similarly, the Great Sage, with his omniscient eye, perceives this honey-like essence of the mind,[354] the reality of sentient beings' minds, which is all of a single taste of sweetness . . .

3.1.2.1.2.2.1.2.2.2.2.1.2.1.1.2.2.1.3. Means of Purifying the Element from the Taints

. . . and brings about the complete and perfect elimination of the bee-like obscurations of the naturally pure element of sentient beings, turning them into something unproduced, by means of the turning of the wheel of Dharma. [TL 132B]

3.1.2.1.2.2.1.2.2.2.2.1.2.1.1.2.2.2. Exposition

Just as a man who endeavors to get honey surrounded by myriad bees disperses them all and makes use of the honey in making food, etc., as he planned, the reality of the uncontaminated wisdom within sentient beings is like the honey. The taints that cause obscurations to this [reality] are like bees, and the perfectly enlightened buddha, skillful victor over bee-like obscurations, is like that man who is skilled at dispersing bees.

3.1.2.1.2.2.1.2.2.2.2.1.2.1.1.3. Ignorance in Its Dormant Form . . .
3.1. Prelude

«193» The addictions are like an outer husk, and the tathāgata element is akin to the inner kernel.

3.1.2.1.2.2.1.2.2.2.2.1.2.1.1.3.2. The Root Text . . . 2.1. Statement . . .
1.1. Simile

The kernel of grain is covered by an outer husk, and, if [the husk is] not removed, cannot be consumed by any person. It would never be delicious food for them; those people seeking food, and so on, must take it out from the husk.

---

354. *viditaṁ dhātuṁ, rig khams.*

3.1.2.1.2.2.1.2.2.2.2.1.2.1.1.3.2.1.2. Import

Similarly, the naturally pure tathāgata essence, the element, in sentient beings is mixed with the taints of addictions.

3.1.2.1.2.2.1.2.2.2.2.1.2.1.1.3.2.1.3. Means of Purifying the Element from the Taints

As long as it is not freed from them, it cannot perform the enlightened activities of a buddha in the three realms. Hence, the buddhas cleanse sentient beings of their taints in order to help them obtain buddhahood. This statement directly shows the fault of obscurations caused by the taints and implicitly indicates the means of cleansing them. [TL 133A]

3.1.2.1.2.2.1.2.2.2.2.1.2.1.1.3.2.2. Exposition

Just as kernels of grain like rice, wheat, barley, etc., have not been fully threshed by using necessary means and still have beards and cannot be enjoyed as delicious food for humans; [likewise], the king of Dharma, being reality mingled with taints, is the potential present in sentient beings for, having the body or nature unreleased from the husk of addictions, will not grant the taste of Dharma joy to beings afflicted by the hunger of addictions. Thus, the buddhas work to cleanse sentient beings from addictions and help them experience the taste of holy Dharma. That is to say, the buddhas are the masters of Dharma teaching; the taints can be cleansed only by the disciples themselves.

3.1.2.1.2.2.1.2.2.2.2.1.2.1.2. The Three Poisons in Their Active Forms . . . 2.1. Prelude

≪194≫ The addictions are like a place rotting with filth, and the tathāgata element is akin to gold.

3.1.2.1.2.2.1.2.2.2.2.1.2.1.2.2. The Root Text . . . 2.1. Statement . . . 1.1. Simile

Suppose, while a person was walking hurriedly along a road, their gold fell into a place rotting with filth. This gold, being of indestructible nature without deterioration, would remain there as it was in the filth for many centuries. Then a god with a pure divine eye, seeing it there, would tell a man: "Here is a piece of gold. Cleanse this supreme precious thing, and fashion it into something valuable such as an image of the Tathāgata." Likewise, having taught the Dharma, the Tathāgata would cleanse sentient beings from taints.

3.1.2.1.2.2.1.2.2.2.2.1.2.1.2.2.1.2. Import

Similarly, the Muni perceives the excellences of sentient beings, the naturally pure element, drowned in filth-like addictions . . .

3.1.2.1.2.2.1.2.2.2.2.1.2.1.2.2.1.3. Means of Purifying the Element from the Taints

. . . and pours the rain of holy Dharma over all beings, according to their psychological makeups and thoughts, in order to purify that mire of addictions, to cleanse their obscurations.

3.1.2.1.2.2.1.2.2.2.2.1.2.1.2.2.2. Exposition

Just as a god, perceiving gold fallen into a place rotting with filth, tells people with great insistence about that gold being the most beautiful of things, so that it might be completely cleansed, so, perceiving that the tathāgata essence designated as such—the essence of the precious perfect buddhahood within all beings—has fallen into addiction's great mire, the Victor teaches them Dharma in order to purify it. [TL 133B]

3.1.2.1.2.2.1.2.2.2.2.1.2.2. Karmic Instincts for Misknowledge Proved to Be Incidental by Using Simile

3.1.2.1.2.2.1.2.2.2.2.1.2.2.1. Prelude

«195» The addictions are like [being] underground, and the tathāgata element is akin to a treasure of jewels.

3.1.2.1.2.2.1.2.2.2.2.1.2.2.2. The Root Text . . . 2.1. Statement . . . 1.1. Simile

Suppose there were an inexhaustible treasure beneath the floor in a poor man's house. This man does not know of it. Also, the treasure cannot say to him, "Here I am!"

3.1.2.1.2.2.1.2.2.2.2.1.2.2.2.1.2. Import

Similarly, in the minds of sentient beings, there is a treasure of jewels capable of producing all excellences, the naturally stainless reality that is the two kinds of selflessness, neither newly established nor negated. Without recognizing this reality mingled with taints in their continuums, these sentient beings constantly experience the sufferings of being deprived of liberation's happiness in various ways. A buddha would appear in the world in order to eliminate these sufferings. [TL 134A]

3.1.2.1.2.2.1.2.2.2.2.1.2.2.2.2. Exposition

Just as a jewel treasure in the house of a poor man would not say to him, "I, the jewel treasure, am here!" nor would the man know it to be there, all beings, who have the treasure of Dharma capable of producing all the buddha excellences in the house of their mind, are like the poor man due to ignorance of its existence. To enable those beings to obtain this treasure— the truth body endowed with two kinds of purity—the Sage has taken rebirth perfectly, and has turned the wheel of Dharma for his disciples who have three different kinds of spiritual potential.

3.1.2.1.2.2.1.2.2.2.2.1.2.3. The Proof That the Addictions to Be Eliminated by the Path of Insight and the Path of Meditation Are Incidental by Using Similes . . . 3.1. The Proof That the Addictions to Be Eliminated by the Path of Insight Are Incidental by Using Similes . . . 1.1. Prelude

«196» The addictions are like the skin of fruit, and the tathāgata element is akin to [the quality of] a sprout contained within a seed.

3.1.2.1.2.2.1.2.2.2.2.2.1.2.3.1.2. Exposition of Meaning . . . 2.1. Statement . . .
1.1. Simile

The imperishable quality capable of producing a sprout is contained within a seed of the fruit of a mango tree or an orange tree and the like. When in the presence of cooperative conditions, such as plowed soil, water, manure, and so on, the sprout will gradually grow into the nature of a kingly tree.

3.1.2.1.2.2.1.2.2.2.2.2.1.2.3.1.2.1.2. Import

Likewise, enclosed within the skin or sheath of the fruit-like ignorance, etc., in sentient beings, the virtuous ultimate element is pure by nature. [TL 134B] And so, by depending on this, and by that virtue leading to the universal vehicle path, the conditions of awakening spiritual potential gradually transform into the nature of a king of sages.

3.1.2.1.2.2.1.2.2.2.2.2.1.2.3.1.2.2. Exposition

Just as a tree grows from a seed within the skin of a banana or mango fruit and is conditioned by water, sunshine, air, soil, time, and space that accommodates the growing plants, it is the seed of perfect buddhahood, the natural purity, from which the sprout of buddhahood is produced. Contained within the skin of sentient beings' fruit-like addictions, and conditioned by these, by the virtue of study, meditation, and realization, the Dharma of the universal vehicle will first emerge and then increase more and more, thereby giving rise to buddhahood.

3.1.2.1.2.2.1.2.2.2.2.2.1.2.3.2. The Proof That the Addictions to Be
Eliminated by the Path of Meditation Are Incidental by Using Simile . . .
2.1. Prelude

«197» The addictions are like tattered rags, and the tathāgata element is akin to a precious image.

3.1.2.1.2.2.1.2.2.2.2.1.2.3.2.2. Exposition of Meaning . . . 2.1. Statement . . . 1.1. Simile

Suppose a buddha statue made of precious materials, such as gold, wrapped in tattered, smelly rags, fallen on a desolate road and trampled by travelers, were seen by a god. In order to retrieve it from obscuring rags and trampled dust, he would point it out to travelers.

3.1.2.1.2.2.1.2.2.2.2.1.2.3.2.2.1.2. Import

Likewise, the Buddha who has the unobstructed eye perceives, even in animals, the nature of the Tathāgata wrapped in the various forms of addiction, which is reality mingled with taints . . .

3.1.2.1.2.2.1.2.2.2.2.1.2.3.2.2.1.3. Means of Purifying the Element from the Taints

. . . and, for the purpose of liberating sentient beings, demonstrates the techniques included in the paths of three kinds of spiritual potential. [TL 135A]

3.1.2.1.2.2.1.2.2.2.2.1.2.3.2.2.2. Exposition

Just as if a god were to see a precious buddha statue wrapped in smelly rags and fallen on a road, he would point it out to people in order to retrieve it from the obscuring rags, the Victor, perceiving even in animals the naturally pure element fallen on the road of the life cycle, wrapped in tattered rags of addictions, teaches the Dharma in order that sentient beings be liberated from the life cycle.

3.1.2.1.2.2.1.2.2.2.2.2.1.2.4. Taints Related to the Impure Stages and the Pure Stages Proved to Be Incidental by Using Similes . . . 4.1. Taints Related to the Impure Stages Proved to Be Incidental by Using Simile . . . 1.1. Prelude

«198» The addictions are like a pregnant woman, and the tathāgata element is akin to a chakravartin contained in the embryonic elements.

3.1.2.1.2.2.1.2.2.2.2.2.1.2.4.1.2. Exposition of Meaning . . . 2.1. Statement . . . 1.1. Simile

Suppose an ugly and poor woman, staying in a shelter for the homeless, bore a glorious world emperor inside her, yet did not realize that a ruler existed within her womb.

3.1.2.1.2.2.1.2.2.2.2.2.1.2.4.1.2.1.2. Import

Birth in the life cycle of the three realms is like a shelter for the homeless. Impure sentient beings with incidental taints are like the pregnant woman bearing a world emperor. The naturally stainless element is like that within the womb; because one has it, one is ultimately protected in stages.

3.1.2.1.2.2.1.2.2.2.2.2.1.2.4.1.2.2. Exposition

[TL 135B] Just as an ugly woman dressed in dirty clothing experiences the greatest suffering in a shelter for the homeless [while] the ruler is inside her womb without her knowledge, even though the protector resides within, sentient beings believe themselves unprotected and, by the power of the addictions, never find peace of mind, and thus remain in the place of suffering of the life cycle. The Buddha expounds the Dharma to sentient beings in order to eliminate their addictions. Although this cleansing is not mentioned directly, it should be known within the textual context.

3.1.2.1.2.2.1.2.2.2.2.2.1.2.4.2. Taints Related to the Pure Stages Proved to Be Incidental by Using Simile . . . 2.1. Prelude

«199» The addictions are like a clay mold, and the tathāgata element is akin to a golden image.

3.1.2.1.2.2.1.2.2.2.2.2.1.2.4.2.2. Exposition of Meaning . . . 2.1. Statement . . . 1.1. Simile

Suppose that inside the clay [mold] there were a buddha statue of melted gold, complete in all parts and free from defects of gold. But outside it is covered with the clay in the nature of earth. Seeing it and knowing about it, a person would remove the outer covering to expose the gold inside.

3.1.2.1.2.2.1.2.2.2.2.1.2.4.2.2.1.2. Import

Likewise, the one who has attained supreme enlightenment thoroughly sees the nature [of the mind] as luminosity, and the obscuring taints as incidental . . .

3.1.2.1.2.2.1.2.2.2.2.1.2.4.2.2.1.3. Means of Purifying the Element from the Taints

. . . purifies sentient beings resembling jewel mines capable of producing limitless buddha excellences from obscurations. Therefore, the supreme enlightenment endowed with two kinds of purity is obtained.

3.1.2.1.2.2.1.2.2.2.2.1.2.4.2.2.2. Exposition

Just as an expert removes clay, knowing that enclosed within is a [TL 136A] beautiful and peaceful statue made of pure shining gold, the omniscient one knows of the peaceful mind, pure by nature like pure gold. [This omniscient one] removes obscurations by means of expounding the Dharma that demonstrates the paths and fruition of three vehicles, cleansing incidental taints, like chipping away the clay covering the precious statue. The entire section above is a detailed exposition of the similes for what is obscured and what obscures. [These similes] demonstrate that taints are incidental and can be cleaned away. And they also describe the means of purification and the way to remove obscurations, etc.

3.1.2.1.2.2.1.2.2.2.2.1.3. Précis . . . 3.1. Prelude

«200» The summarized meaning of the similes is as follows:

3.1.2.1.2.2.1.2.2.2.2.2.1.3.2. The Root Text . . . 2.1. The Similes for What Obscures

Within a lotus, amid bees, inside the husk, filth, and ground, within the fruit skin, within tattered rags, in the womb of a woman, and inside clay . . .

3.1.2.1.2.2.1.2.2.2.2.2.1.3.2.2. The Similes for What Is Obscured

. . . that is like a buddha, the honey, the grain, gold, a treasure, a tree, a precious statue, a chakravartin, and a golden image. [This] explanation is done in pairs; that is, "within a lotus" is connected with "a buddha," up to "inside clay" is connected with "a golden statue."

3.1.2.1.2.2.1.2.2.2.2.2.1.3.2.3. Taints Related to the Natural Purity of the Mind Proved to Be Incidental

Similarly, it is said that the tathāgata essence, the truthlessness nature of the mind free from the taints with intrinsic unreality, is beginningless, and is not bound by the covering of sentient beings' addictions, though they are beginningless as well. [This is] because they lack intrinsic reality status and cannot penetrate the nature of the mind, and because the mind has lacked intrinsic reality status from the very beginning.

3.1.2.1.2.2.1.2.2.2.2.2.1.3.3. The Commentary

«201» [TL 136B] In brief, these similes given in the *Tathāgata Essence Sutra* demonstrate that, for all sentient beings, the defiling factors over their minds without beginning are incidental, for the mind is empty of intrinsic reality; the pure excellences are simultaneous with and inseparable from the mind without beginning for [the same reason that] the mind is lacking intrinsic reality status. Therefore, the sutra states as follows:

Living beings are tainted because of the taints on the mind; they are pure because their mind is pure by nature.

3.1.2.1.2.2.1.2.2.2.2.2.2. The Represented Implications . . .
2.1. Divisions of What Obscures the Element . . . 1.1. Prelude

«202» Here, what has been demonstrated by the nine similes, the lotus sheath, etc.? Which ones are the taints on the mind?

3.1.2.1.2.2.1.2.2.2.2.2.1.2. Detailed Exposition . . . 2.1. The Root Text . . .
1.1. The Division of the Taints into Nine Groups of Identity

There are nine groups of taints: (1–3) attachment, hatred, and ignorance in their latent states existing within the continuums of those who are free from attachment to the desires of childish ordinary people. [These] are the objects destroyed by transcendent intuitive wisdom and are also the motivation behind karmic evolution that causes beings to be reborn in the two higher realms; (4) [the] intense outbursts [from attachment, hatred, and ignorance] are the motivation behind both virtuous and nonvirtuous karmic evolution that cause beings to be reborn in the desire realm alone; (5) the evolutionary instincts for ignorance existing within the continuums of saints that cause uncontaminated karmic evolutionary actions; (6–7) the eliminations of the paths of insight and meditation existing within the continuums of both ordinary people and noble beings; (8–9) and those related to the impure and pure stages. [TL 137A] These nine groups are not divided in terms of different actualities. Instead, these divisions are made from the point of view of different identities. [Moreover,] the latent states of the three poisons should not be taken as their seeds alone because the active addictions that cause establishment of the two higher realms are also included herein. However, the hatred that causes the establishment of the two higher realms is not active, for it is not in any way the addiction that would cause beings to be reborn in one of the two higher realms.

3.1.2.1.2.2.1.2.2.2.2.2.1.2.1.2. Demonstrated by the Similes

These nine taints that obscure the element are demonstrated well by the similes of the lotus sheath, etc., in order to explain that taints are incidental.

3.1.2.1.2.2.1.2.2.2.2.2.1.2.1.3. Elaborate Divisions Being Limitless

It should be understood that the coverings of secondary taints, if elaborately divided, have limitless millions of divisions.

3.1.2.1.2.2.1.2.2.2.2.2.1.2.2. The Commentary . . . 2.1. Brief Statement on Taints as Incidental

≪203≫ In brief, these nine kinds of addictions cannot penetrate the nature of the mind, and hence can be separated [from the mind], being incidental, in connection to the tathāgata element that is pure by nature just as a lotus sheath, etc., up to a buddha statue, etc.

3.1.2.1.2.2.1.2.2.2.2.2.1.2.2.2. Detailed Exposition of Each Nature . . . 2.1. Name Divisions

What are the nine addictions? They are: (1) the addiction characterized as the latent state of attachment; (2) the addiction characterized as the latent state of hatred; (3) the addiction characterized as the latent state of ignorance; (4) the addiction characterized as the intense outburst of attachment, hatred, and ignorance. The term "intense" indicates that this group of taints also includes the addictions that are the motivation behind killing, etc., causing sentient beings to be reborn in the miserable realms; [TL 137B] (5) the addiction included in the foundational instinctual ignorance-driven evolutionary action; (6) the addiction to be eliminated by [the path of] insight; (7) the addiction to be eliminated by [the path of] meditation; (8) the addiction related to the impure stages; and (9) the addiction related to the pure stages.

3.1.2.1.2.2.1.2.2.2.2.2.1.2.2.2.2. Each Definition . . . 2.1. Explaining the Latent and Active Three Poisons

≪204≫ Although all taints can be included in the addiction to be eliminated by [the path of] insight and the addiction to be eliminated by [the path of] meditation, this division is made in order to explain that the active addictions and their seeds should be eliminated in stages, however much the taints to be eliminated still remain when one has obtained sainthood

of the individual vehicle, etc. Here, (1–3) the addictions that exist in the continuums of those worldly people who are freed from attachment and, being the cause of creational activity that accumulates immovable karmic evolution of which the place of evolutionary development is definite, give rise to the material and the immaterial realms. [These addictions] can only be destroyed by transcendent intuitive wisdom, because the addictions included in the ground of the "pinnacle of the life cycle"[355] cannot be eliminated by the worldly path, despite the fact that the subtle and coarse active addictions in the realms below the medium of absolute nothingness[356] can be eliminated by such a path. They are called the addictions characterized as the latent state of attachment, hatred, and ignorance. Their seeds can only be eliminated by the transcendent path. (4) Those that exist in the continuums of the sentient beings who indulge in attachment, etc., and that, being the cause of creational activity that accumulates meritorious karmic evolutionary action—which causes one to be reborn as a celestial being or a human—and demeritorious karmic evolutionary action—which causes one to be reborn in one of the miserable realms—give rise to the desire realm alone, and are to be destroyed by the wisdom of the meditation on impurity, etc., which is the yoga of the pure conduct. That is the active attachment overpowered by the concentration of the meditation on impurity, and the active hatred [overpowered] by the meditation on love, etc. They are called the addictions characterized as the intense outbursts of attachment, hatred, and ignorance. For the system that accepts a fundamental consciousness different in nature from the aggregate of the six consciousnesses, the active intellect endowed with the addictions that are included in the ground of the desire realm[357] cannot be eliminated despite the fact that the people in the desire realm have obtained the first contemplation state,[358] as indicated in [Vasubandhu's] *Thirty Verses*, by the statement "connected to the realm where one takes rebirth." But here we should not think in this way. [TL 138A]

---

355. *srid rtse'i sa.*
356. *ci yang med pa['i skye mched].*
357. *'dod pa'i sa.*
358. *dhyāna, bsam gtan.*

3.1.2.1.2.2.1.2.2.2.2.2.2.1.2.2.2.2.2. Explaining the Karmic Ignorance Instincts

(5) Those [ignorance instincts] that exist in the continuums of bodhisattvas endowed with powers, disciple and hermit buddha saints are the cause that produces the uncontaminated karmic evolution, being the subtle energy of the motivation behind karmic evolution of the three doors, and give rise to the three kinds of mind-made body free from the taints of addictions, are [only] to be destroyed by the Tathāgata's intuitive wisdom of enlightenment. These are called the addictions included in the foundational ignorance instinct-driven evolutionary action. Although these saints work for sentient beings' welfare by assuming the mind-made bodies that are established by means of the foundational ignorance instinct-driven evolutionary action and the uncontaminated karmic evolutionary actions, the ability to spontaneously, effortlessly accomplish sentient beings' welfare without the need to rely [on even subtle motivation] is one of the distinctive features of perfect buddhahood alone. Therefore, the explanation states that "[such instinct-driven addictions] are to be destroyed by the Tathāgata's intuitive wisdom of enlightenment." However, it does not indicate that the first moment of omniscience on the uninterrupted path[359] is the direct eliminator of the foundational instinctual ignorance-driven evolutionary action. If that were so, one would not obtain the ultimate elimination because [even the Buddha's omniscience] would still be working on the elimination of what is to be eliminated in one's continuum. There is no need to mention that the first moment of omniscience would not be the uninterrupted path, if there were not [full elimination of even] the slightest taint during the time of the uninterrupted path of the last continuum[360] in the tenth stage. [TL 138B]

Question: Since the taints related to the three pure stages are explained below as the objects destroyed by the vajra-like concentration, why is this kind [of taint] said to be the object destroyed by the Tathāgata's intuitive wisdom?

Reply: As explained before, although the subtlest ground of the evolutionary instincts for ignorance is directly eliminated by the uninterrupted

359. *ānantaryamārga, bar chad med lam.*
360. *rgyun gyi tha ma.*

path of the last continuum in the tenth stage, [bodhisattvas who have] the last continuum in the tenth stage are still in need of motivation with subtle effort to teach the Dharma to sentient beings, etc., by taking the mind-made bodies, etc. Thus, this statement is made in order to explain that teaching the Dharma to sentient beings by means of the elimination of such bodies and karmic evolutionary action is one of the distinguishing features of the ultimate realization of the reality-limit alone. On the other hand, when remaining in the trance of the uninterrupted path of the last continuum, [bodhisattvas] do not directly perceive knowable objects in their multiplicity, not to mention that they could directly benefit sentient beings by teaching the Dharma, etc. There are many related points, but I shall leave them for the time being.

3.1.2.1.2.2.1.2.2.2.2.2.1.2.2.2.2.3. Explaining What Is to Be Eliminated by the Paths of Insight and Meditation . . . 3.1. General Meaning . . . 1.1. Definitions of the Two Obscurations

An addictive obscuration, by definition, is the kind of obscuration to the attainment of liberation that is paired with omniscience. Objective obscuration, by definition, is the kind of obscuration to the attainment of omniscience that is paired with liberation. Furthermore, it is so called because it is an obscuration to the attainment of permanent trance focused on the knowable objects; for it lasts until the end of the life cycle and is also an obscuration to the attainment of the direct perception of all knowable objects in their multiplicity. An addictive obscuration is explained as mental turbulence. [TL 139A] Mental peacefulness, the opposite of addictive obscuration, is the nirvana from mere liberation that eases the suffering of the life cycle. Mental turbulence is the suffering of the life cycle. The addictions or addictive obscuration is the producer. It should be understood that the truth of the path causes the attainment of nirvana.

3.1.2.1.2.2.1.2.2.2.2.2.1.2.2.2.2.3.1.2. Recognizing Exemplifications

An addictive obscuration is an addictive ignorance, the mind that grasps at truth status in persons and aggregates, as well as active attachment, etc., which is produced by addictive ignorance, along with its seeds. Objective obscuration is an erroneous truth-habit concerning objects as well as the addictive instinct that produces that habit. Here, the liberation that is the complete elimination of the addictive obscurations has been obtained by the disciple and hermit buddha saints, as well as by bodhisattvas in the eighth stage and above. The liberation that is the complete elimination of the objective obscurations has been obtained only by the buddhas.

3.1.2.1.2.2.1.2.2.2.2.2.1.2.2.2.2.3.1.3. Distinction between What Is to Be Eliminated by the Path of Insight and What Is to Be Eliminated by the Path of Meditation

The conscious theoretical kind of addictive obscuration, which is destroyed by the path of insight, includes the thought that "the truth status of persons or aggregates is acceptable," along with its seeds, as well as the assertion of truth status, derived from an analysis of truth status, along with its seeds. [TL 139B] It should be understood that attachment, etc., is also derived from such conscious addictive obscurations. The unconscious instinctual type of addictive obscuration, which is destroyed by the path of meditation, includes the unconscious truth-status-habit, independent of any analysis upon attachment, etc., along with its seeds. The unconscious instinctual type of objective obscuration is understood to be obscuration itself. Its conscious theoretical variety is the thought that "this truth-habit is not erroneous," with the accompanying perceptual consciousnesses apprehending visual objects, etc., which maintain the truth-status perception in objects, along with its seeds.

3.1.2.1.2.2.1.2.2.2.2.2.1.2.2.2.2.3.1.4. Rough Explanation of the Mode of Eliminating the Seeds

The mode of counteracting what is to be eliminated by the path of insight, etc., is explained as follows: at the time when the uninterrupted path of the universal vehicle path of insight associated with the tolerance of the quality of suffering[361] has been produced, its direct target, the seeds of that which is to be eliminated by the path of insight, started to cease. Therefore, the future production of [the antidote] is simultaneous with the future cessation of [the taints]. These seeds produced by a homogeneous previous cause

361. *sdug bsngal chos bzod.*

become something no longer to be produced [that is] conditioned by the force of this uninterrupted path. Produced by the uninterrupted path, the initial path that has obtained the truth of cessation, where these seeds are incapable of being produced because of the impression left as the antidote, is called the "path of liberation."

Although the corresponding taints become something that no longer exist and are no longer produced at the time of the uninterrupted path, since this happens because of the lack of favorable conditions, the cessation by means of discernment[362] is not obtained. In this light, the uninterrupted path of the last continuum in the tenth stage still cannot be termed the "complete elimination" despite the fact that at that time there are no taints of negative tendencies,[363] even as small as a single atom. This is so because the path, by which the [taints] are incapable of being produced due to an impression left as the antidote, has not been obtained. If this reason were not established, the fruition would be simultaneous with the cause.

Someone asserts that while there is no direct object to counteract at the time of the uninterrupted path of the path of insight, there are subtle taints of negative tendencies at the time of the uninterrupted path of the last continuum. This is a mixture of the theory "the elimination by means of what is to be produced" with [the theory] "the elimination by means of what is to be eliminated." The assertion that the first moment of omniscience directly counteracts these [subtle taints of negative tendencies] should be known as being ignorant of the system of the elimination and antidote. [TL 140A] Furthermore, that person failed to ascertain the meaning of the statement in [Asaṅga's] *Abhidharma Compendium* that "[the elimination] is not the past because it ceases," thus not fully understanding why the seeds to be eliminated and their direct antidote, the uninterrupted path, are accepted as simultaneous despite the fact that the three modes of the elimination of the active [addictions mentioned in Asaṅga's *Abhidharma Compendium*] are unacceptable.

If so, [according to this person], one then must accept that the light of the counteracting force and the darkness of the direct object to be counteracted are also simultaneous, as illustrated [in the text] by such an example. Thus, this uninterrupted path neither eliminates the seeds—its direct

362. *so sor brtags 'gog.*
363. *duṣṭhula, gnas ngan len.*

object to be counteracted or eliminated—after its own time, like destroying a vase with a hammer; nor [does it eliminate them] before its own time, like pushing away something in the front; nor [does it do so] in its own time by way of ceasing together with [the seeds to be counteracted], like yoked yaks falling from a cliff. But then, what does this "counteraction" mean? It means that the future production of this antidote dependent upon the preceding familiarization is simultaneous with the future cessation of the homogeneous type of seeds to be eliminated, and that the seeds to be eliminated are becoming something no longer to be produced by means of this simultaneous production of antidote and cessation of the seeds.

3.1.2.1.2.2.1.2.2.2.2.2.1.2.2.2.2.3.1.5. Specific Explanation of Tolerance and Knowledge in Connection with the Path of Insight

When the reality of the four noble truths has been realized directly by way of water pouring into water, [TL 140B] one is no longer frightened of this profound Dharma, previously formidable and unfamiliar [for those] in the life cycle. Thus, [this realization] is called "the tolerance of the Dharma." There are four kinds of tolerance from the point of view of specific aspects with respect to determining the reality of the four noble truths. Like water pouring into water, the realization of the situation that the mind realizing reality does not feel any fear is called "subsequent tolerance."[364] Moreover, there are four kinds of subsequent tolerance in terms of realization [that are] divided from the point of view of specific aspects with respect to the subject [observing] reality of the four noble truths. These eight tolerances are of the same nature but not identical. At this time, the truth of cessation free from incidental taints has not been obtained. [Subsequent tolerance] is posited on the realization of the [observing] subject, instead of on the realization of the reality of the four noble truths. However, [this system] does not accept direct, apperceptive, self-reflexive consciousness.[365] The path of liberation that obtains the path of cessation free from incidental taints will be produced without arising from this meditative equipoise. At this time, there are four kinds of "knowledge of the Dharma"[366] that realize the reality

364. *rjes bzod.*
365. *rang rig mngon sum.*
366. *dharmajñāna, chos shes.*

of the four noble truths, as well as four kinds of "subsequent knowledge"[367] realizing the [observing] subject. These eight knowledges are of the same nature but not identical. Thus, a single instant of the direct realization of truth in a single session's meditative equipoise is produced as having the nature of the sixteen instants of tolerance and knowledge. This system does not accept such theories as [those that posit that] subsequent tolerance is produced after the production of tolerance of the Dharma, etc.

3.1.2.1.2.2.1.2.2.2.2.2.2.1.2.2.2.3.2. Its Ramifications

There are two kinds of people who enter higher education [on the path]: alienated individuals who have entered the path and nobles. Here, (6) those addictions existing in the continuums of alienated individuals being educated on the path are destroyed by the wisdom obtained by means of the first insight into transcendent reality. [These] are called the addictions to be eliminated by [the path of] insight. And (7) those [addictions] existing in the continuums of nobles being educated on the path are destroyed by the wisdom of the meditation on transcendent reality, perceiving it as it is; they are called the addictions to be eliminated by [the path of] meditation.

3.1.2.1.2.2.1.2.2.2.2.2.2.1.2.2.2.2.4. Explaining the Taints Related to the Impure and Pure Stages

(8) Those [addictions] that exist in the continuums of bodhisattvas who have not reached the ultimate perfection of the stages above the seventh, and are discordant with the wisdom obtained on the [first] seven stages, and will be destroyed by the wisdom of meditation of the [last] three stages beginning with the eighth stage, are called the addictions related to the impure stages. (9) Those that exist in the continuums of bodhisattvas who have reached the ultimate extinction of addictions and are discordant with the wisdom obtained by means of the meditation of the [last] three stages beginning with the eighth [TL 141A] are destroyed by the wisdom of the "vajra-like" concentration, and are called the addictions related to the pure stages. Each description of these nine taints explains the respective posses-

---

367. *anujñāna, rjes shes.*

sor,[368] nature, and antidote. [For example,] the description of "those that are discordant with the [first] seven stages" indicates that these addictions exist within the continuums of bodhisattvas below the eighth stage, that these are obscurations to the attainment of the stages above the seventh, and that their homogeneous continuums are eliminated by the wisdom of the pure stages. The description "those that exist in the continuums of bodhisattvas who have reached the ultimate extinction of addictions" indicates that the elimination [of all taints] without remainder depends on the uninterrupted path of the "vajra-like" concentration.[369]

3.1.2.1.2.2.1.2.2.2.2.2.1.3. Précis . . . 3.1. The Root Text

«205» In short, as explained above, it should be known that these nine addictions, attachment, etc., are, respectively, well demonstrated by the nine similes of the lotus sheath, and so on. Someone in the past asserted that this verse is not appropriate as part of the treatise, that instead it is a commentary on the line "by the similes of the lotus sheath, etc." (v. 131). Nevertheless, according to available books of the Great Lotsawa's translation, I think this must be a summary verse of the treatise.

3.1.2.1.2.2.1.2.2.2.2.2.1.3.2. Statement on Elaborate Divisions Being Limitless

And, if taken in detail, these addictions can be differentiated into 84,000 types, and hence, are as infinite as the Tathāgata's intuitive wisdom. On this point, the *Tathāgata Essence Sutra* states that the tathāgata essence is covered by the sheath of addictions with limitless divisions.

3.1.2.1.2.2.1.2.2.2.2.2.2. Whom Do They Obscure . . . 2.1. The Root Text

«206» It should be understood that by these taints, the childish, the individual vehicle saints, persons being educated—including ordinary peo-

368. *rten.*

369. Apparently Gyaltsap here takes "the ultimate extinction of addictions" as the extinction of addictive obscurations in the eighth stage and "the elimination [of all taints] without remaining" as the elimination of objective obscurations just before the attainment of buddhahood.

ple who have entered the paths, noble beings of the individual vehicle, and the wise ones who are the noble bodhisattvas—are, respectively, contaminated by four kinds of taint, including the three poisons in the latent states and their outbursts. [There is] one kind of taint that is the ground of evolutionary instincts for ignorance; two kinds of taints including those to be eliminated by the path of insight and those to be eliminated by the path of meditation; and two kinds of taints including those related to the impure stages and those related to the pure stages. [TL 141B]

3.1.2.1.2.2.1.2.2.2.2.2.2.2.2. The Commentary

«207» The Bhagavān states in the *Tathāgata Essence Sutra* that all sentient beings are endowed with the tathāgata essence. In brief, "all sentient beings" here refers to the four types of beings. They are: (1) ordinary people; (2) saints; (3) persons being educated [on the path]; and (4) bodhisattvas. These are tainted by four, one, two, and again by two kinds [of addictions] respectively, in connection with [obscurations to] the uncontaminated element. It should be known that [these beings] have the obstacles to permanently remaining in the equipoised trance focused on the uncontaminated element.

3.1.2.1.2.2.1.2.2.2.2.2.2.3. Explaining the Similarity between the Similes and the Implications of What Obscures the Element . . . 3.1. General Prelude

«208» Furthermore, how should the respective similarities between nine addictions obscuring the element, attachment, etc., and the lotus sheath, etc., obscuring a buddha statue, etc., be understood? Does similarity between these similes and meanings exist? The text also questions the reason for the similarity between similes and meanings of the element: how should the buddha essence be understood to be analogous to a buddha statue, etc?

3.1.2.1.2.2.1.2.2.2.2.2.3.2. . . . 2.1. Detailed Exposition . . .
1.1. The Three Poisons in Instinctual Latency and Their Outbursts

Just as a lotus grown from mud delights the mind when it first appears, but later that delight disappears when the lotus has perished, as in this simile, so is attachment's joy. Just as a swarm of bees sting and cause uneasiness when irritated, likewise, when hatred arises, it brings suffering to the heart, thereby causing uneasiness. Just as the kernel of rice, etc., is obscured by the external husk, likewise, the direct perception of the meaning of the essence is obscured by the covering of ignorance. [TL 142A] Therefore, these two are analogous in terms of obscuring.

Just as filth is something unbearable and unpleasant, those having attachment engage in passion; in this way, the intense outbursts that motivate unwholesome behaviors are similar to filth, for they lead to a pitiable life, thus being unbearable.

3.1.2.1.2.2.1.2.2.2.2.2.3.2.1.2. The Ground of Ignorance-Instinct-Driven Evolutionary Actions

Suppose that a treasure of jewels is obscured by the earth. Being unknown, that treasure cannot be obtained; likewise, that self-originating [intuitive wisdom] in sentient beings, the attainment of the tathāgata essence free from all taints, is obscured by the earth of evolutionary instinctual ignorance and cannot be perceived. Therefore, these two are analogous.

3.1.2.1.2.2.1.2.2.2.2.2.3.2.1.3. Taints to Be Eliminated by the Paths of Insight and Meditation

Just as the sprout and such gradually grow and split and damage the skin of the seed, likewise, the direct and fresh perception of reality immediately and quickly overcomes those [addictions] to be eliminated by [the path of] insight. Therefore, these two are analogous. Having cultivated [this perception] repeatedly with connection to the noble path, the essence of the futile views is destroyed. Their residues, those to be eliminated by the wisdom of the path of meditation, are demonstrated to be similar to the tattered rags, for they both become depleted of the essence.

3.1.2.1.2.2.1.2.2.2.2.2.3.2.1.4. Taints Related to the Impure and Pure Stages

The taints related to the seven stages are similar to the impurities of the womb because they both obscure self-awareness. The nonconceptual intuitive wisdom obtained in the eighth stage is like release [TL 142B] from that womb without the exertion of force, simply as a consequence that effortlessly came from the previous karmic evolution. The taints related to the three stages are known to be like slight stains of mud, the objects to be destroyed by the Bhagavān's vajra-like concentration.

3.1.2.1.2.2.1.2.2.2.2.2.3.2.2. Précis

«209» It should be understood that, as explained above, the nine taints, attachment, and so on, are analogous to the lotus and the other. Although these [two lines] are suitable as the prelude of the next section, it is explained as the précis of the section above.

3.1.2.1.2.2.1.2.2.2.2.2.2.4. Explaining the Similarity between Similes and Implications of the Element That Is Obscured ... 4.1. General Statement ... 1.1. The Root Text

Because the element is included within the threefold nature, i.e., the truth body of the Tathāgata that permeates all sentient beings, etc., it is similar to the similes of the buddha statue, and so on.

3.1.2.1.2.2.1.2.2.2.2.2.4.1.2. The Commentary

«210» The analogy between the tathāgata essence, being the cause for purifying the mind, and a buddha statue, etc., should be understood with reference to the threefold nature [of the tathāgata essence].

3.1.2.1.2.2.1.2.2.2.2.2.4.2. Specific Explanations ... 2.1. General Connection between Similes and Implications ... 1.1. Question

«211» What is the threefold nature of the element that is said to be the tathāgata essence possessed by all sentient beings?

3.1.2.1.2.2.1.2.2.2.2.2.4.2.1.2. Answer ... 2.1. The Root Text

The natures of this element are the truth body, reality, and also spiritual potentials.
They are respectively known by three, one, and five similes in order to demonstrate that this element pervades all sentient beings.

3.1.2.1.2.2.1.2.2.2.2.2.2.4.2.1.2.2. The Commentary

«212» This element, as the nature of [sentient beings'] receptivity to the enlightened activities of the truth body in light of the pervasiveness of the activities, is understood by the [first] three similes: the buddha statue, honey, and the kernel [of the grain]. Its being the nature of reality, which is the tathāgata essence identical to the natural [TL 143A] purity of the truth body without distinctions, is understood by one simile: gold. The tathāgata essence, the nature of the spiritual potentials from which a buddha's three bodies are produced, is understood by [the remaining] five similes: the treasure, the tree, the precious statue, the emperor, and the golden statue.

3.1.2.1.2.2.1.2.2.2.2.2.2.4.2.2. Detailed Exposition of Similarities . . . 2.1. The Truth Body . . . 1.1. Divisions . . . 1.1. Question

«213» Here, how is the truth body understood?

3.1.2.1.2.2.1.2.2.2.2.2.2.4.2.2.1.1.2. Answer . . . 2.1. The Root Text

The tathāgata essence is said to be pervasive in all sentient beings because the truth body is known as having two aspects: the realizational truth body, which is the direct realization of the ultimate element, naturally pure and free from all incidental taints, and thus perfectly stainless; and the instructional truth body, which is the fruition of the natural outflow from the manifest realization of reality in the Buddha's mental continuum, consisting of sutra discourses that are definitive in meaning, teaching the profound ultimate truth, and sutra discourses that are interpretable in meaning, teaching a variety of conventional things including person, aggregates, etc., by means of various words and letters.

3.1.2.1.2.2.1.2.2.2.2.2.2.4.2.2.1.1.2.2. The Commentary

«214» The Buddha's truth body should be understood as having two aspects: the realizational truth body and the instructional truth body.

[TL 143B] The first [aspect] is the perfect stainless ultimate element that is the object experienced directly by the nonconceptual intuitive wisdom in meditative equipoise. Two different expressions, "experienced object" and "object," are [used] in order to demonstrate the distinction between the permanent meditative equipoise [of the buddhas] and [impermanent] meditative equipoise. Moreover, it is known as the Dharma realized by the Tathāgata's individual introspective wisdom in meditative equipoise—it is what is to be realized, and the realizational truth body realizes it.

The second [aspect] consists of the sutra discourses, the fruition of the natural outflow[370] of realization in the perfectly stainless ultimate element, and the cause of the attainment of the truth body. This comes from learning the sutra discourses and meditation on their meanings. [Then] teachings come forth for other ordinary people who are endowed with the three different kinds of spiritual potential, or are not determined to be of a specific type of potential according to their motivations. Moreover, this is known as the Dharma to be taught. The teaching is further divided into two, according to the means of arranging either subtle or extensive Dharma: (a) the teaching expounding ultimate truth—the way of the profound Dharma— in the sutra collection for bodhisattvas; and (b) the aphorisms, the sutras in prose and verse mingled with prophecies, verses, special utterances, narration, etc., expounding the variety of things of the conventional reality. As for the twelve sutra types, some sutras state that there are nine types. This is merely a difference in classification.

3.1.2.1.2.2.1.2.2.2.2.2.4.2.2.1.2. The Actual Explanation of the Similarities ... 2.1. The Root Text

«215» Because it is ultimately transcendent, there is no conceivable analogy for the truth body with respect to realization in the world. Thus, the tathāgata statue and the element are shown to be similar, of the nature of the truth body that is naturally pure, free from all incidental taints, and all-pervasive in sentient beings. When the teaching on the subtle profound ultimate truth is experienced by means of the sutra dicourses that are definitive in meaning, one experiences the nature of all [TL 144A] things in one taste that grants unlimited joy, like the one sweet taste of honey; while the sutra discourses that are interpretable in meaning, which teach the various aspects of conventional reality, are known to be like the kernel within the covering husks of various grains. This explanation of the two types of

---

370. *niṣyanda, rgyu mthun pa.*

sutra discourses, definitive in meaning and interpretable in meaning, and the corresponding similes are an elaborated explanation of the meaning of "diffusion" as mentioned in [verse 1.28 stating that] "all sentient beings are always endowed with the tathāgata essence, by virtue of the diffusion of the buddhas' bodies." The diffusion of the truth body means the pervasiveness of the buddhas' activities. The buddhas' enlightened activities enter into all sentient beings by means of teaching the Dharma to a variety of disciples by means of speech. Since [sentient beings] are always susceptible to the buddhas' activities, it is said that "the truth body is all-pervasive in them."

3.1.2.1.2.2.1.2.2.2.2.2.4.2.2.1.2.2. The Commentary . . . 2.1. Explaining the Literal Meaning Demonstrated by the Three Similes

«216» Thus, the statement that "sentient beings are endowed with the tathāgata essence" is made with these three similes: the buddha statue, honey, and a kernel, with reference to the meaning that without exception, the Tathāgata's truth body is all-pervasive in sentient beings. Indeed, there is no one among sentient beings who remains outside of the possibility of the attainment of the Tathāgata's truth body, just as there is no matter that can exist outside of space, such as the inside of a vase.

3.1.2.1.2.2.1.2.2.2.2.2.4.2.2.1.2.2.2. Sutra Reference about the Pervasion of the Truth Body

«217» As [Maitreya's] *Ornament of the Universal Vehicle Sutras* states:

Just as space free from any obstructive tangible objects is always all-pervasive in vessels, similarly, this natural pure truth body is accepted as the nature all-pervasive in sentient beings.

[TL 144B] Just as space is always pervasive in matter, similarly, this natural pure truth body is pervasive in all sentient beings.

The former half of this verse is a summary of the meaning of [Maitreya's] *Ornament of the Universal Vehicle Sutras* and the latter half is a quotation. However, these sutra references are the same in connotation. Regarding natural purity, there is an enormous distinction [between buddhas and sentient beings] as to coarseness and subtlety.

3.1.2.1.2.2.1.2.2.2.2.2.2.4.2.2.2. Reality . . . 2.1. The Root Text

«218» Being immutable by nature from excellent to inferior, perfectly granting desired fruitions, and being virtuous and excellent owing to being free from sin and not penetrated by taints, this reality pure by nature, the mind's emptiness of intrinsic reality, is therefore said to be like objects of gold that are stuck in filth. The nature of the Tathāgata, which is ultimate truth, the emptiness of intrinsic reality, penetrates the nature of the mind in all sentient beings without the slightest deviation in its way of presenting.[371] Intending this, [the Buddha] declared that "all sentient beings are endowed with the tathāgata essence."

3.1.2.1.2.2.1.2.2.2.2.2.2.4.2.2.2.2. The Commentary . . . 2.1. The Literal Meaning

«219» Notwithstanding their being associated with limitless addictions and sufferings, because of their natural luminosity, that is, being empty of intrinsic reality, the minds of sentient beings do not show any change. Therefore, they are called "reality" in the sense that they are immutable like excellent gold. Furthermore, without difference in nature, all sentient beings will join the rank of "tathāgata" whenever they have purified all incidental addictive and objective obscurations, even those [sentient beings] who are affected by the causes of definite wrongdoing—so-called "ones who will not obtain nirvana." [TL 145A] This statement should be thought of as a demonstration that the reality of all sentient beings is the Tathāgata, or

---

371. *rnam par 'char tshul.*

that reality purified from all taints is the Tathāgata. Thus, the statement that "sentient beings are endowed with the tathāgata essence" is made with this simile of gold and refers to the meaning that reality is indivisible and undifferentiated in terms of the appearance made by its nature. This passage well explains the second topic of the tripartite tathāgata essence found in the statement that "all sentient beings are endowed with the tathāgata essence." Furthermore, it would reveal a great deficiency in analysis if you accepted [the statement that] all sentient beings are endowed with tathāgata essence with the intention of demonstrating that the natural purity of the mental continuum of an authentic tathāgata and that of a sentient being are indivisible, unlike blue and yellow as two [separate] things.

3.1.2.1.2.2.1.2.2.2.2.2.4.2.2.2.2.2. Sutra References . . . 2.1. Of the Sutra

«220» Having in view the nature of the mind, the pure and nondual reality, the Bhagavān declared in the *Ornament of the Light of Wisdom Sutra*:

> O Mañjushrī, the Tathāgata knows full well that not the slightest thing can be found as a basis of the grasping at truth status, the cause of production of his own substantial aggregates, and hence, he protects sentient [TL 145B] beings from their self-habits. By means of his own purity, he has understood the natural purity of sentient beings. His own purity and the natural purity of the sentient beings are nondual; they cannot be divided into two.

3.1.2.1.2.2.1.2.2.2.2.2.4.2.2.2.2.2. Of the Root Text

«221» It is also stated in [Maitreya's] *Ornament of the Universal Vehicle Sutras*:

> Though the natural purity is undifferentiated among all the buddhas and the sentient beings, reality, after purification from all taints, is buddhahood; therefore, all sentient beings are endowed with the tathāgata essence based on the intended meaning that the reality that exists within sentient beings is not different from the reality of the buddhas.

3.1.2.1.2.2.1.2.2.2.2.2.2.4.2.2.3. The Spiritual Potentials . . . 3.1. The Root
Text . . . 1.1. Similarity between Simile and Import Concerning the Nature
of the Spiritual Potentials

«222» Like a treasure remaining from the very outset and a fruit tree
grown by means of effort, the spiritual potential is known to be twofold: the
naturally existing potential that remains as the nature of the mind without
beginning, and the developmental potential that has been newly produced
from study and contemplation. The latter is called "supreme," for it has more
important functions.

3.1.2.1.2.2.1.2.2.2.2.2.2.4.2.2.3.1.2. The Similarity between Simile and
Import of Functions of the Spiritual Potentials . . . 2.1. Types of Function

By this twofold potential, the naturally existing potential and the developmental potential, a buddha's three bodies are considered to be [TL 146A]
obtained by means of, first, the awakening of the potential under appropriate conditions, and next, the cultivation of the spirit of supreme enlightenment and the activities: attainment of the first body, the truth body, by the
former [natural] potential; attainment of the two material bodies by the latter [developmental] potential. The accomplishment of cultivating the store
of wisdom brings about the truth body endowed with two kinds of purity,
including purification of taints and the intuitive wisdom of knowing things
just as they are. The accomplishment of cultivating the store of merit brings
about two material bodies and the intuitive wisdom of knowing things in
their multiplicity. It should be understood that the Buddha's material body
adorned with marks and signs is the apparent manifestation of intuitive
wisdom in his mental continuum, thus devoid of the slightest inert substances, the accumulation of atoms, and the like. If you assert that the Buddha's material body is the mere perceptions his disciples would have, and
that there is absolutely nothing included within the Buddha's continuum,
it will make your position not different in the slightest from the outsider
Mīmāṁsaka assertion that it is impossible for a person who has eliminated
all taints to exist. Similarly, it should be understood that it would be a mis-

take, as well, to assert that there is no perception of objects of knowledge in all their varieties within the natural vision[372] of the Buddha, etc.

3.1.2.1.2.2.1.2.2.2.2.2.4.2.2.3.1.2.2. Explanation of Similarity between Simile and Import

As to the similarity between simile and import of the beautiful natural body,[373] it is known to be like a precious statue, not created by nature because of other causes and conditions, as well as the precious treasure of excellences such as the powers, fearlessnesses, etc. As to the perfect beatific body, owing to the enjoyment or possession of the kingdom of the great universal vehicle Dharma, it is analogous to a world emperor. Because it has the nature of an image when compared to marks and signs of the beatific body, the emanation body is like a golden image. [TL 146B]

3.1.2.1.2.2.1.2.2.2.2.2.4.2.2.3.2. The Commentary . . . 2.1. Possession of Tathāgata Essence Because of the Existence of the Buddha Potential

«223» Thus, the tathāgata element is demonstrated to be the essence of all sentient beings with these five similes: a treasure, a tree, a precious statue, an emperor, and a golden image, with reference to the fact that there exists within all sentient beings the buddha potential that produces a buddha's three bodies. Indeed, buddhahood is distinguished by a buddha's three bodies. Therefore, since the tathāgata element, the twofold potential, is the cause of attainment of the three bodies, the word "element" is here used in the sense of "cause," despite the fact that the word *dhātu* can be translated as "cause,"[374] "ultimate element,"[375] "realm,"[376] etc.

3.1.2.1.2.2.1.2.2.2.2.2.4.2.2.3.2.2. Sutra Reference . . . 2.1. Prelude

The twofold potential is the cause of obtaining the three bodies, so it

---

372. *rang snang.*
373. *svabhāvakāya, ngo bo nyid kyi sku.*
374. *hetu, rgyu.*
375. *dhātu, dbyings.*
376. *dhātu, khams.*

is said that there exists in each sentient being the essence, the tathāgata element, established within their continuum. But these sentient beings do not know about it. If realized, it will bring great benefit to sentient beings, as will be explained later.

3.1.2.1.2.2.1.2.2.2.2.2.2.4.2.2.3.2.2.2. Sutra Citation

«224» The Buddha declared in the *Abhidharma Universal Vehicle Sutra*:

> The element, the [twofold] potential, that exists without beginning is the foundation, basis, and support of all things of [both] the life cycle and nirvana. Because of its existence, there are the life cycle and the attainment of nirvana. [TL 147A]

If the nature of the mind were impure, it would be impossible for the taints to be purified; if the production of the excellences were not feasible, their production would be unacceptable; if the spiritual potential did not exist, the life cycle and the attainment of nirvana would be absurd, because all is established on the basis of the naturally pure potential. A fundamental consciousness different in nature from the collection of six consciousnesses is not accepted in this commentary. However, in other treatises, the noble bodhisattva, master Asaṅga, pioneered the way as a champion of the Experientialist system, which establishes such a consciousness by citing the same sutra. Thus it would not cause any fault if you [disagree with me] by saying that, if it were the statement on the existence of the twofold potential and a sutra reference to the existence of the spiritual potential, this verse would no longer prove the existence of fundamental consciousness, as it is the statement of the Bhagavān on proving the existence of the potential.[377]

3.1.2.1.2.2.1.2.2.2.2.2.2.4.2.2.3.2.2.3. Explanation of Its Meaning Relying on Other Sutras . . . 3.1. "Without Beginning"

«225» Question: How is it here that "it exists without beginning"?

Answer: It has been taught and ascertained by the Buddha in the *Shrīmālādevī Lion's Roar Sutra*, with reference to the tathāgata essence,

---

377. Because such an objection would only prove the point.

that "the beginning limit is not to be found." It is unacceptable to speculate that [the tathāgata essence] came into being at a certain point, and hence did not exist before that point.

3.1.2.1.2.2.1.2.2.2.2.2.2.4.2.2.3.2.2.3.2. "The Element"

«226» As to the "element," it is declared in the *Shrīmālādevī Lion's Roar Sutra*:

O Bhagavān, this tathāgata essence is the essence of transcendent qualities because all transcendent qualities will arise by means of meditation that apprehends this tathāgata essence and the essence of naturally pure excellences, because it is the ultimate objective condition of these excellences. [TL 147B]

3.1.2.1.2.2.1.2.2.2.2.2.2.4.2.2.3.2.2.3.3. "The Foundation of All Things"

«227» As to the statement "the foundation of all things," this sutra declares:

Therefore, O Bhagavān, the tathāgata essence is the foundation, the basis, and the support of the uncompounded things, which are connected with the possibility of being separated from all taints, not dissociated from the possibility of cultivating all antidotes, and hence, impossible to be separated from the excellences. [At the same time], O Bhagavān, this tathāgata essence is also the foundation, the basis, and the support of the compounded things, which are unconnected, dissociated, and thus possible to be separated because [all taints] cannot penetrate the nature [of the mind].

3.1.2.1.2.2.1.2.2.2.2.2.2.4.2.2.3.2.2.3.4. "There Is the Life Cycle"

«228» As to the statement "because of its existence, there [is] the life cycle," the *Shrīmālādevī Lion's Roar Sutra* declares as follows:

Owing to the existence of tathāgata essence, O Bhagavān, this [essence] is designated as "the life cycle."

It is logical for sentient beings to transmigrate in the life cycle because of the existence of the potential. Otherwise, it would be illogical.

3.1.2.1.2.2.1.2.2.2.2.2.2.4.2.2.3.2.2.3.5. "There Is Nirvana"

《229》 As to the statement "and the attainment of nirvana," the *Shrīmālādevī Lion's Roar Sutra* states as follows:

O Bhagavān, if there were no tathāgata essence, there would be neither aversion to suffering nor desire, longing, and prayer for nirvana.

The renunciation of the life cycle and the aspiration for liberation would not arise if the spiritual potential did not exist. These are the actions of the spiritual potential as explained above. To sum up what has been explained so far, the single reality can be divided into three in terms of the means of explanation; that is, it is the spiritual potential from the viewpoint of being the pure object in the causal state, it is reality from the viewpoint of being pervasive and the nature, and it is the truth body's diffusion from the viewpoint of being the fruition.

3.1.2.1.2.2.1.2.2.3. The Subjects That Realize the Element . . .
3.1. Demonstrating That Disciples and Hermit Buddhas Realize the Element by means of Faith . . . 1.1. Connection with the Previous Section . . .
1.1. Demonstrating That All Beings Are Endowed with Tathāgata Essence

《230》 [TL 148A] Furthermore, by what kind of valid evidence should this tathāgata essence, which exists the whole time among all [sentient beings] without distinction, be perceived? It should be perceived by the valid evidence of reality that proves that things would reasonably become such and not otherwise. What is this essence like? It is as vast as the truth body, for it is pervasive in all sentient beings, as demonstrated in the line "by virtue of the diffusion of the buddhas' bodies." It has the characteristic of being indivisible from the Tathāgata in terms of nature and actuality, as demonstrated in the line "in virtue of the indivisible ultimate truth." And it is of the nature of the definitive potential beyond doubt, as demonstrated in the line "by virtue of the existence of the spiritual potential."

3.1.2.1.2.2.1.2.2.3.1.1.2. The Sutra Reference

«231» The Buddha declared [in the *Tathāgata Essence Sutra*]:

O noble child, this is the reality of things. Whether the Tathāgata appears in the world or not, these sentient beings are always endowed with the tathāgata essence.

The emptiness of intrinsic reality of sentient beings' minds was not established newly by the Tathāgata, nor will it be eliminated after he is gone—it remains at all times.

3.1.2.1.2.2.1.2.2.3.1.1.3. Explanation of the Meaning

«232» The reasoning of the reality here refers to the proving reasoning, syllogism, or the method of realizing that the nature of sentient beings' mind would reasonably be empty by intrinsic reality alone and not otherwise. To summarize, one should not conceive of the ascertainment or the proper understanding itself, which is the reasoning that ascertains and examines reality. [TL 148B] The realization, or the reality reasoning, does not occur because it is the mode of realization [arrived at] by means of mere intellectual speculation. Neither is this [reality] accessible to conceptual thought [that is] dependent upon the word of others. It is accessible only by means of faith. [The reality] realized by permanent meditative equipoise is the object experienced by the Buddha alone.

Here, someone asserts that the reality, ultimate truth, can only be realized dependent upon the Tathāgata's sutras. This reveals that this person did not master the Buddha's teaching thoroughly and does not understand the sequence of the realizations of obscure objects of comprehension and of extremely obscure objects of comprehension.

3.1.2.1.2.2.1.2.2.3.1.2. The Root Text

«233» On the occasion of the last life cycle of existence, bodhisattvas will become buddhas independent of others, thus being self-arisen ones. For disciples, hermit buddhas, alienated individuals, and those who have just entered the universal vehicle, the Buddha's ultimate truth is the emptiness of intrinsic reality and can be understood only by faith, but not by the means of following the Dharma . . .

3.1.2.1.2.2.1.2.2.3.2. Demonstrating That There Is No Other Mode of Realization for Four Kinds of People . . . 2.1. The Root Text

. . . just as the blazing sun cannot be perceived [by the blind]; they cannot realize ultimate truth by their power, just as one can barely see the sun by means of narrowed eyes. According to someone's explanation, the former half of this verse teaches that ultimate truth can only be realized by means of following sutras even for those who are endowed with the spiritual potential for the universal vehicle, and the latter half teaches that there is absolutely no realization for these four kinds of people. This explanation is incorrect, as should be explained later. [TL 149A]

3.1.2.1.2.2.1.2.2.3.2.2. The Commentary . . . 2.1. Brief Statement . . . 1.1. The Literal Meaning

«234» In brief, there are four kinds of individuals who are classified as blind to the tathāgata essence. Who are these four? They are: (1) alienated individuals; (2) disciples; (3) hermit buddhas; and (4) bodhisattvas who have just entered the vehicle.

3.1.2.1.2.2.1.2.2.3.2.2.1.2. Sutra Reference

«235» As is declared in the *Shrīmālādevī Lion's Roar Sutra*:

O Bhagavān, for those who are stuck in the futile view, for those who are attached to misconceptions, for those whose minds have deviated from emptiness, the tathāgata essence is not their object of experience.

This passage means that alienated individuals do not understand the meaning of the subtle emptiness due to their habitual insistence on a personal self and their possessiveness, and do not actually enter into the respective paths for [those who have] the three kinds of spiritual potential. Likewise, disciples and hermit buddhas understand merely coarse emptiness in the form of the sixteen aspects [of the four noble truths], such as impermanence, etc., but not subtle selflessness. It is also clearly evident, as will be explained later, that bodhisattvas who have newly entered the vehicle cannot understand the meaning of subtle emptiness either.

Someone asserts that such people who are endowed with the spiritual potential for the disciple vehicle or the hermit buddha vehicle are childish because [the treatise] has taught that alienated individuals cannot perceive the tathāgata essence, and hence it demonstrates that even noble disciples and hermit buddhas do not directly realize its reality. If so, it would be pointless to mention separately that it also holds true for bodhisattvas who have just entered the vehicle because they, too, are alienated individuals. Furthermore, it is a general statement that these four kinds of people do not realize the tathāgata essence, which is reality free from reifications. Since a few alienated individuals have fully realized the meaning of emptiness, it would be incorrect to take this statement as showing that no alienated individuals can understand [emptiness]. If it is thus mentioned because the text teaches [that those bodhisattvas] do not directly realize emptiness, it would again be pointless to make a [TL 149B] distinction by stating, "[those] who have just entered the vehicle," because ordinary bodhisattvas at the "tolerance" and "supreme phenomenon" levels of the path of application after many great eons' cultivation still do not directly realize emptiness because they have entered the universal vehicle path. Therefore, it should be understood that when the text states that there are people who do not realize reality mingled with taints, i.e., the tathāgata essence, it refers to the three distinct types of people who have different spiritual potentials as well as to alienated individuals. It would be a contradiction of the statement of the treatise that "it is accessible to faith" if we take the text as showing that noble disciples and hermit buddhas do not realize the reality even in the slightest.

3.1.2.1.2.2.1.2.2.3.2.2.2. Detailed Exposition . . . 2.1. Those Who Lack Understanding by Having Fallen into the Futile View

«236» Here, "those who are stuck in the futile view" refers to (1) alienated individuals. Indeed, they cannot believe in the uncontaminated element or the ultimate truth that naturally stops the futile view because of their habitual adherence to egoism and possessiveness; that is the nonunderstanding of selflessness by accepting a personal self and property in connection with contaminated things such as the aggregates, etc. That being so, how could they be expected to recognize the tathāgata essence that is the object of the omniscient [buddha]? This is impossible. [Realizing] the tathāgata essence in permanent meditative equipoise is one of the distinguishing features of the omniscient [buddha] alone.

3.1.2.1.2.2.1.2.2.3.2.2.2.2. Those Who Lack Understanding Because of Attachment to Misconceptions . . . 2.1. Explanation of Misconceptions

«237» [Next,] "those who have an affinity for misconceptions" refers to people who are endowed with the spiritual potential to be (2) disciples or (3) hermit buddhas. They temporarily do not believe or understand the meaning of emptiness. Why? This is because, although the tathāgata essence should be meditated upon as eternal, they indulge in the meditation on the notion of impermanence instead of meditating upon the notion of eternity. Likewise, although the tathāgata essence should be meditated upon as blissful, they indulge in the meditation on the notion of suffering instead of meditating upon the notion of bliss. Although the tathāgata essence should be meditated upon as being regarded as self, they nevertheless indulge in the meditation on the notion of selflessness instead of meditating upon the notion of self. And [TL 150A] though the tathāgata essence should be meditated upon as pure, they indulge in the meditation on the notion of impurity instead of meditating upon the notion of purity. The tathāgata essence should be meditated upon as eternity, bliss, self, and purity with the understanding of its distinctive basis that is reality free from reifications. It would be pointless to meditate on it in the opposite way as [impermanence,] suffering, selflessness, and impurity. Although the tathāgata essence is the ultimate truth of things such as aggregates, etc., [disciples and hermit buddhas] indulge in the meditation on impermanence, suffering, selflessness in its coarse forms, and impurity as the ultimate truth of phenomena such as contaminated aggregates, etc., instead of having the notions of eternality, bliss, self, and purity and meditating on them. Because of their nonbelief, they are not interested in seeking and meditating on the techniques for the attainment of the transcendent eternality, which is the ultimate realization of the sameness between the life cycle and nirvana without deterioration; the transcendent bliss, which is the elimination of even the mind-made body and its cause, uncontaminated karmic evolution; the transcendent self, which is absolute pacification of all reifications of self-habit and grasping at truth status regarding selflessness; and the transcendent purity, which is the complete elimination of the foundational ignorance-instinct-driven evolutionary action.

If you become attached to mere literalness and do not even care for a detailed explanation of the literal meaning like someone did, should you contemplate which disciple or hermit buddha would meditate on the tathāgata essence as impermanent, suffering, and impure?

3.1.2.1.2.2.1.2.2.3.2.2.2.2.2. Being Misunderstanding of Reality

Thus, this enumeration explains that this element, which is characterized as the supreme eternality, the supreme bliss, the supreme self, and the supreme purity, is also not the object experienced by any disciple or hermit buddha because they focus on the path that is [TL 150B] involved with the mental habit of holding to the truth status of impermanence, etc., in direct contradiction to the attainment of the truth body.

3.1.2.1.2.2.1.2.2.3.2.2.2.2.3. Proof . . . 3.1. Prelude

«238» As for this fact that [the element] is not the object experienced by those who indulge in misconceptions with the notions of impermanence, suffering, selflessness, and impurity, the Bhagavān has explicated it in detail in the *Great Total Nirvana Sutra* with the example of a jewel in the pond. It runs as follows.

3.1.2.1.2.2.1.2.2.3.2.2.2.2.3.2. Sutra Reference

3.1.2.1.2.2.1.2.2.3.2.2.2.2.3.2.1. The Simile

> Mendicants, suppose that in the hot season, people put on their
> swimsuits and were playing in the water with various ornaments
> and enjoyments. Suppose then, someone would lose a valuable
> sapphire jewel in the water. Thus, in order to retrieve this sap-
> phire jewel, all the people, leaving aside their ornaments, would
> dive into the water. They would mistake pebbles or gravel in the
> pond for the real jewel and take them out, thinking: "I have got
> the jewel!" Looking at them from the bank of the pond, they
> would notice: "It is not the jewel at all!" Meantime, the water of
> that pond would seem to shine by the power of that jewel. Such
> perception would make them realize its quality and proclaim:
> "How wonderful!" Then a skillful and intelligent person would
> get the real jewel out.

The statement "in order to retrieve this sapphire jewel, all the people,
leaving aside their ornaments, would dive into the water" is used as an analogy for [disciples and hermit buddhas'] turning away from worldly distrac-
tions and their engagement in pursuit of the meaning of the ultimate truth.
"They would mistake pebbles or gravel in the pond for the real jewel" stands
for their misconceptions about the ultimate truth of all things as impermanence and the refutation of the subjective self in coarse forms. "Looking at
them from the bank of the pond, they would notice: 'It is not the jewel at
all'" stands for an awareness of their own previous mistakes after realizing
the meaning of emptiness. "The water of that pond would seem to shine by
the power of that jewel" stands for their misconceptions about the ultimate
truth of all things as the refutation of the subjective self in coarse forms.
"A skillful and intelligent person would get the real jewel out" stands for
people who have understood the meaning of emptiness.

3.1.2.1.2.2.1.2.2.3.2.2.2.2.3.2.2. The Implications

> Likewise, O mendicants, you who are ignorant of the ultimate
> truth of things meditate with all perceptual habits, maintaining

that all things are impermanent, that all things are suffering, that all things are selfless, and all things are impure, and meditate repeatedly and increasingly. But all these attempts are useless. Therefore, mendicants, you should become skillful, not taking those like the pebbles or gravel in the pond. O mendicants, these things upon which you meditate with all perceptual habits, maintaining that all things are impermanent, that all things are suffering, that all things are selfless, and all things are impure, and meditate repeatedly and increasingly, are [actually] eternal, blissful, pure, and endowed with self.

These [perceptual habits] should be understood in detail, according to the sutra, as misconceptions with regard to the arrangement of the ultimate truth of things.

These statements mean the same thing as taught in [Āryadeva's] *Experientialist Four Hundred* and [TL 151A] [Nāgārjuna's] *Sixty Stanzas on Reasoning*: that the path to the realization of the sixteen [aspects of the four noble truths], including impermanence, etc., is the path that brings [disciples and hermit buddhas] to maturity in attaining their respective enlightenment. Here, in order to establish the single vehicle, this path is demonstrated clearly by the commentary to be the one that brings [disciples and hermit buddhas] to maturity in attaining the four kinds of transcendence.

3.1.2.1.2.2.1.2.2.3.2.2.2.3. Those Who Lack Understanding Because of Deviation from Emptiness

3.1.2.1.2.2.1.2.2.3.2.2.2.3.1. General Statement

«239» [Lastly,] "those whose minds have deviated from emptiness" refers to (4) bodhisattvas who have just entered the vehicle and are deprived of the understanding of the tathāgata essence with regard to emptiness of intrinsic reality.

3.1.2.1.2.2.1.2.2.3.2.2.2.3.2. Specific Explanation

Although these bodhisattvas have cultivated the spirit of supreme enlightenment, they do not understand the meaning of emptiness. They are the universal vehicle people who think the emptiness of the subjective self in the coarse form is the door to liberation, since [they assume] it newly destroys previous truly established things, thinking that nirvana means annihilation and disintegration of the real existence of the addictions, attachment, etc., by the force of meditating on antidotes. This statement indicates that there are certain bodhisattvas who do not really understand the meaning of emptiness except in the view accepted by Sautrāntika disciples as explained in [Vasubandhu's] *Treasury of Abhidharma* and its commentary, as well as in [Dharmakīrti's] *Seven Logical Treatises*.

Furthermore, there are great heroic bodhisattvas who are Experientialist idealists, who use ultimacy-analytic rational cognition[378] to understand and realize the ultimate reality of the way things are as an emptiness with truth status, being devoid of substantial subject-object dichotomy, by negating the external objectivity of material things, etc., [TL 151B] thus relying on emptiness as truth status itself.

By this [statement], one should understand the sound refutation of their assertion that [Maitreya's] *The Sublime Continuum of the Universal Vehicle Treatise* does not go beyond the information-only system. And if someone asserts that the former position amounts to nihilism and the latter amounts to eternalism, then one should understand that both positions fall to the extremes of [both] nihilism and eternalism.

3.1.2.1.2.2.1.2.2.4. Recognizing the Nature of the Element . . . 4.1. Question

«240» How then, is this tathāgata essence proclaimed as the pattern of emptiness, which is not the object for those with the [above] deviant mentalities?

3.1.2.1.2.2.1.2.2.4.2. Answer . . . 2.1. The Root Text . . . 1.1. The Main Meaning . . . 1.1. The Basis: The Ultimate Reality of Things

From this naturally pure element, there have never been any intrinsically real, previously existing, then newly eliminated addictions and conceptual objects of subjective and objective self-habits. This statement teaches that adherence to the truth status of anything is a reification deviating from the

378. *mtha' thug dpyod pa'i rigs shes.*

meaning of the ultimate truth, and the conceptual objects of such adherence could never be established from the beginning. Although the habit of grasping at the truth status of the addictions is included in the grasping at the truth status of objects, it is explained separately on purpose. The twofold selflessness is absolutely nothing original to be newly added upon the element, since emptiness of the subjective and objective selves is the nature of the element. [TL 152A] This statement teaches that the assertion of the nonexistence of the twofold selflessness is a repudiation mistakenly applied to the meaning of ultimate truth, and that the negation of the conceptual objects [of the self-habits] is not newly presented. If the statement that "there is no taint to be removed; there is no antidote to be produced" were explained in a general sense without qualification, it would be a repudiation of both what is to be eliminated and its antidote.[379]

Moreover, these first two lines can again be explained in a positive way: if the addictions with truth status could be established as not being previously existent and newly removable, then the emptiness of truth status of the addictions would be established as not being previously nonexistent and newly posited. This is an explanation in terms of being the elucidation of the categorical differential.[380] If explained in terms of exemplification: ultimate truth is established on the basis of the fact that there is no recent removal in the slightest of a previously truly established person and aggregates. And conventional reality, in which all enlightened activities and agents are possible by virtue of their emptiness of intrinsic identifiability, is also established on the basis of the fact that there is no recent establishment in the slightest of a previously nonexistent, magical relativity that is empty of truth status. In summary, this verse teaches the integration between ultimate truth, which is the emptiness of truth status, devoid of anything involved as the object of the grasping at truth status, and conventional reality, in which all arrangements of deeds and agent are accepted [as viable] by the same [philosophical] system [that accepts emptiness], and thus, are possible.

3.1.2.1.2.2.1.2.2.4.2.1.1.2. The View That Realizes Reality

Reality that is emptiness of intrinsic identifiability of person and aggre-

---

379. *spang gnyen.*
380. *rang ldog dngos bstan.*

gates should be perceived truly by the intuitive wisdom that realizes freedom from intrinsic reality status. This is the view that realizes the meaning of ultimate reality . . . [TL 152B]

3.1.2.1.2.2.1.2.2.4.2.1.1.3. Fruition Coming from Habitual Affinity for This View

. . . and is conjoined with extensive arts, the activities, correct perception that reaches liberation, and the attainment of perfect buddhahood, from habitual affinity for this view.

3.1.2.1.2.2.1.2.2.4.2.1.2. Proof

From this element, intrinsically real addictions are absolutely nothing previously present to be newly removed. The element is primordially empty of grasping at the truth status of incidental [taints], which have a character of being separable from it by the cultivated affinity for antidotes. This teaches the objective condition of the twofold truth; that is, it is possible to separate the addictions by the habitual affinity for antidotes, while the addictions have never partaken of intrinsic reality from the beginning.

The emptiness of grasping at the truth status of the addictions is absolutely nothing original to be newly added upon this element. The element is not empty from the beginning of the emptiness of grasping at the truth status of the addictions, the object [of the wisdom of emptiness] that makes possible the production of the unsurpassed buddha excellences such as the powers, etc., of character indivisible from it. This teaches that the ultimate truth, the object of the wisdom that directly realizes selflessness, which is the cause of producing the buddha excellences such as the powers, etc., exists from the very beginning. These expositions teach the basis, which is both conventional and ultimate truths, and the path, which is the wisdom that directly realizes selflessness and its capacity to obtain fruition, perfect buddhahood, etc. The assertion that these [expositions] teach self-emptiness of the conventional—e.g., that the vase is empty of the vase itself, and other-emptiness of the ultimate that is the truth status of the ultimate truth—should be understood to be the ultimate reification and repudiation, far from what is accepted [by master Asaṅga].

3.1.2.1.2.2.1.2.2.4.2.2. Explaining That Emptiness Is Not the Object
for Those Whose Minds Have Deviated from Its Recognition ... 2.1.
Explanation of the Ultimate Reality ... 1.1. The Main Meaning

≪241≫ [TL 153A] What is demonstrated by this statement? There are certainly not two kinds of self, the objects of the subjective and objective grasping at truth status. In turn, the causes of the taints are newly removed from
this naturally pure element of the Tathāgata, since this element is by nature
devoid of intrinsically identifiable incidental taints. This teaches ultimate
reality to be empty of intrinsic reality status, empty of intrinsically identifiable status, and empty of intrinsic objectivity status. In light of this, the
arrangement of the two realities [of this treatise] should be understood to
be equivalent to the position of the savior Nāgārjuna. Also, there are not
even the slightest previously existent newly eliminated two selflessnesses,
serving as the objects of the wisdom that directly realizes selflessness and is
the cause of purification by antidotes of this element, since its nature is the
emptiness of intrinsic reality, the reality indivisible from the excellences, etc.

3.1.2.1.2.2.1.2.2.4.2.2.1.2. Sutra Reference ... 2.1. Regarding the Proof

≪242≫ Therefore, the Buddha states in the *Shrīmālādevī Lion's Roar
Sutra* as follows:

> The tathāgata essence is empty of the truth status of the sheath
> of all addictions that can be definitely [TL 153B] differentiated and
> separated from the nature of the mind by the force of antidotes.
> The tathāgata essence is not empty of the buddha excellences
> that are inconceivable, far beyond the sand grains of the Ganges
> in number, and cannot be differentiated, as inseparable [from
> the essence].

3.1.2.1.2.2.1.2.2.4.2.2.1.2.2. Regarding the Way of Realization of the Truth
of the Path

Thus, the [fact] that anything that has intrinsic reality does not exist is
truly observed as the "emptiness of that [intrinsic reality]" by the wisdom
that directly realizes selflessness. The [fact] that what remains in the post-

observation context—namely that emptiness of intrinsic reality—is truly correctly understood with the thought, "that is permanently how it is."[381]

3.1.2.1.2.2.1.2.2.4.2.2.1.3. Précis

These two verses demonstrate the exact definition of "emptiness" because they teach about emptiness as free from the two extremes of reification of truth status and repudiation of conventional [things].

3.1.2.1.2.2.1.2.2.4.2.2.2. Teaching That It Is Not the Object for Those Whose Minds Have Deviated and Who Attach to Errors . . . 2.1. Emptiness Being Not the Object for Those Whose Minds Have Deviated and the Others . . . 1.1. The Main Meaning

«243» Those whose minds have deviated from emptiness because of falling into the extremes of reification and repudiation and are distracted in those speculations, neither practicing meditation nor concentration upon it, are thus called "those whose minds have deviated from emptiness." Indeed, lacking intuitive wisdom of ultimate emptiness, no one would be able to realize and obtain the pure reality, the ultimate element, which is free from conceptual thought. This demonstrates that the naturally pure element is ultimate truth.

3.1.2.1.2.2.1.2.2.4.2.2.2.1.2. Sutra Reference

Intending this point, the Buddha declared [in the *Shrīmālādevī Lion's Roar Sutra*]:

> [The intuitive wisdom of the tathāgata essence is nothing but the Buddha's intuitive wisdom of emptiness. This tathāgata essence has never been perceived and has never been realized by disciples and hermit buddhas.]

This teaches that the intuitive wisdom of the tathāgata essence is the

---

381. Gyaltsap interestingly takes note of the quality of the space-like equipoised samādhi attained in the realization of selflessness, which, upon being remembered, is experienced as a permanent, absolute, space-like state.

Tathāgata's intuitive wisdom, intending [their] permanent meditative equipoise. The statement that it is not the sphere of disciples and hermit buddhas indicates—as previously explained—that they [TL 154A] cannot realize it by their own power.

3.1.2.1.2.2.1.2.2.4.2.2.2.2. Logical Proof

«244» This section is divided into three parts.

First, this tathāgata essence, shown to be the essence of the truth body, is said to be an object not experienced by those who have fallen into the futile view, since the intuitive wisdom of the ultimate element is the antidote to extremist views.

Second, the tathāgata essence is the transcendent essence, and is said to be an object not experienced by those who indulge in misconceptions, since the truth body is demonstrated as an antidote to the truth conviction of the worldly things, such as impermanence, etc.

Third, the tathāgata essence, as the truth body, the essence of the perfectly pure excellences, is said to be an object not experienced by those whose minds have deviated from emptiness, since the transcendent truth body, from which the pure excellences are indivisible, is by nature empty of incidental taints, which are separable. The element is naturally pure because it is emptiness free from the extremes of reification and repudiation. The statement "the pure excellences are indivisible from it" teaches that the element is devoid of being an object of repudiation, and the statement "it is empty of incidental taints" teaches that the element is devoid of being an object of reification.

3.1.2.1.2.2.1.2.2.4.2.2.3. Teaching That It Is the Object Experienced by Bodhisattvas in the Ten Stages . . . 3.1. The Main Meaning

«245» If the direct realization of [the element] with reference to the unique intuitive wisdom that is undifferentiated from the ultimate element is the ultimate, then it will render the [supposed] variety of vehicles in three different systems nonultimate. While the natural purity of the transcendent truth body, i.e., the ultimate truth, is realized by intended disciples of *The Sublime Continuum* with respect to objective universals[382] during

382. *don spyi.*

the paths of accumulation and application, its direct perception [TL 154B] is here accepted as the "slight" observation of the tathāgata essence in a short period of meditative equipoise by bodhisattvas abiding on the ten stages, unlike the Buddha's experience in permanent meditative equipoise, since the [bodhisattvas] have to alternate between meditative equipoise and post-attainment [conventional] awareness . . .

3.1.2.1.2.2.1.2.2.4.2.2.3.2. Sutra Reference

. . . [to paraphrase what] is said:

> Just as the sun in the sky [is seen only intermittently] through a
> gap in clouds, even noble bodhisattvas in the great stages with
> pure vision of wisdom cannot perceive Thee, O Ultimate Truth,
> at all times because their perception of ultimate truth is [slight,]
> in meditative equipoise alone; thus their intelligences are still
> partial. O Bhagavān, your truth body can only be perceived by
> those with infinite intelligence that pervade the space of ultimate
> truth of infinite objects of knowledge by means of permanent
> meditative equipoise.

Someone asserts that the "slight" observation refers to the scope of the direct realization of reality instead of being a short period of perception owing to alternate meditative equipoise and subsequent attainment experienced by the noble bodhisattvas. This should be known as the story told by someone unable to formulate the arrangement.

3.1.2.1.2.2.1.2.3. Demonstrating the Need to Proclaim That Living Beings Are Endowed with the Tathāgata Essence

«246» This includes the arrangement of disputes and the [TL 155A] disputation and refutation about the uselessness [of this teaching on the tathāgata essence]. Although it is also correct to explain this following section as the exposition of the prior section starting with "being the realization of [the element] with reference to the unique intuitive wisdom" along with the verses as proof, this would not contradict the explanation just mentioned above.

3.1.2.1.2.2.1.2.3.1. Disputes and Summary as Prelude ... 3.1.1. Disputes

Question: If this tathāgata essence is thus so difficult to recognize inasmuch as it is not always the object even for supreme noble ones who are abiding on the pure stages characterized as ultimately free from attachment, then what is the use of this teaching to the childish? It is useless to teach them because they would not be able to understand.

Although the disputes about uselessness and contradiction are both presented in the treatise, while the latter dispute is extremely clear, the former is a bit unclear and is palpable only in the reply that rebuts the dispute. Therefore, the commentary adds a supplement to the treatise.

3.1.2.1.2.2.1.2.3.1.2. Summary

≪247≫ Reply: There are two verses summarizing the purpose of this teaching on the element: the first is a doubt, and the second is the response.

3.1.2.1.2.2.1.2.3.2. Brief Statement on Disputes and Replies ... 2.1. General Meaning ... 1.1. Disproving the Improper Perspective ... 1.1. The Explanation of the Treatise as Teaching the Need to Proclaim the Element as a Permanent Entity Being Nonsense

Assertion: In the second wheel [of the Dharma] all things are said to be similar to clouds, dreams, and illusions. In this final wheel it is said that there exists a tathāgata essence, a permanent entity. As to the refutation of the arguments of contradiction between these two wheels and the uselessness of the teaching on [tathāgata essence]: [TL 155B] the *Transcendent Wisdom Sutra* teaches that all conventional things are empty of intrinsic objectivity,[383] inert emptiness,[384] nihilistic emptiness,[385] and partial emptiness;[386] that is, they are self-empty, e.g., the vase is empty of the vase itself. Yet the final Dharma wheel teaches that within the continuums of all sentient beings there exists a tathāgata essence, a permanent entity, endowed

383. *rang gi ngo bos stong pa.*
384. *bem stong.*
385. *chad stong.*
386. *nyi tshe'i stong pa.*

with all excellences such as the powers, etc. [This] is to say that ultimate reality is the profound other-emptiness devoid of all conventional things. This is the necessity [of the teaching on the element]. The verses starting with "it has been said that the reality-limit is forever empty of a created thing" are the refutation of the argument about contradiction. Moreover, it shows that ultimate reality is empty of all conventional things.

Reply: There is no need to explain this in this manner, since an understanding of a permanent entity existing within one's continuum would not be conducive in the slightest to the conception of the spirit of enlightenment. According to your explanation, since an 'ultimate' sentient being is a permanent entity, he or she would not have an aspiration to become a buddha. In addition, there would be no need for this being to become a buddha again because he or she has been a buddha from the beginning. As to a 'conventional' sentient being, if it were empty of itself just like a child of a barren woman, not existent among objects of knowledge, which discouraged sentient being would be inspired by such a teaching of the existence of a tathāgata essence as a permanent entity? [TL 156A] There is not a single [insider] who would not be an opponent of this outsiders' view that falls to the extremes of both eternalism and nihilism![387] Furthermore, listen! Since you claim that the reality-limit is empty of suffering and its origination is comprised of karmic evolution, addictions, and the evolved aggregates, is it devoid of the conventional truth of the path as well? If you are still not convinced, then wipe your eyes and read carefully! Although this system should be refuted in detail, since it is an obviously an erroneous speculative idea, I think that this much refutation is enough to serve the purpose, and it is therefore not in need of further elaboration.

3.1.2.1.2.2.1.2.3.2.1.1.2. The Explanation of the Treatise Teaching the Reason the *Tathāgata Essence Sutra* Is Said to Be Interpretable in Meaning Being Irrelevant

Someone claims that the meaning of self-emptiness is similar to the assertion above. [According to this philosophical position,] no identification of anything can be made in the slightest, and hence, no distinction

---

387. *rtag chad kyi lta ba'i mthar ltung ba 'di las pha rol tu chos 'di las phyi rol tu gyur pa su la yang med do.*

between being correct and incorrect can be drawn in the slightest. This position renders earnest determinations of ethical choice [undertaking-and-abandoning][388] quite useless. In such a system, the arrangement of all conventional things cannot be established by validating cognition. The refutation that depends on the mistaken perspective alone is a completely contradictory act, since even the perspective on which the conventional things are based cannot be proved to be mistaken in this system. In addition, it is a repudiation of ultimate truth to accept it as not existent and not nonexistent. Therefore, no distinction can be made between the *Tathāgata Essence Sutra* that is interpretable in meaning [according to this person] and the other sutras that are definitive in meaning. If the topic of the *Tathāgata Essence Sutra* were accepted according to the assertion above, to explain that this sutra is not literally intended indicates [TL 156B] that this person does not clearly understand what is taught in the sutra and how the holy [Maitreya] explains it in this treatise.

Question: But then, what is the point of the passage from the *Tathāgata Essence Sutra* in which the Buddha states the following?

> This poor householder thinks of himself as poor and wanders above [a treasure] without hearing of, knowing, and perceiving it. Likewise, noble child, underneath all sentient beings' insistently reifying minds there exists a tathāgata essence, a great treasure of all the buddha excellences such as the ten powers, the confidences, and the distinctive excellences. However, these beings have grown attached to matter, sound, smell, taste, and texture, hence they transmigrate within the life cycle. Not hearing of this great Dharma treasure, they will not obtain it and will not make an effort to cleanse it [from taints].

This passage does not demonstrate that a buddha endowed with the two-fold purity exists within the continuums of sentient beings, since it states literally that the tathāgata essence is a treasure from which the powers, etc., will come about. It does not state that the tathāgata essence is the excellences such as the powers, etc., in and of themselves, since earlier the sutra states:

---

388. *heyopādeya, blang dor.*

Within afflicted beings possessing all addictions there exists the reality of the Tathāgata that is immovable and is not affected by any state of existence. Perceiving this, the Buddha proclaims: "They are all like me!"

Intending sentient beings' possession of reality as the mind's nature, [TL 157A] which is not different from the reality of the Tathāgata and is never penetrated by the taints, the Buddha proclaims: "They are all like me!" This is the point of this sutra statement, just as [it is the point of] the explanation offered in this treatise. The sutra does not advocate even literally that a buddha exists within a sentient being, because this [second] statement clearly explains the intention of the [first] statement. If this meaning of the word as stated in the sutra were unacceptable, since in this sutra the Buddha also states "perceiving all living beings' tathāgata essence," you have to accept sentient beings themselves as tathāgata essence. In order to avoid the misunderstanding that there exists within the continuum of a sentient being a buddha's truth body endowed with the twofold purity, the sutra clearly states the existence of the reality, not the truth body endowed with the twofold purity as fabricated in someone's system. The intelligent ones should thus understand this matter by means of careful analysis. Even explained according to the assertion of certain Centrists who treat grasping at truth status as part of objective obscuration, it would be hard for this person to think that the statement on clouds, etc., means that the nature of the mind is simply empty of suffering and its origin. Since the establishment of the *Tathāgata Essence Sutra* as interpretable in meaning does not correspond with what is explicated in this treatise, this sutra must be accepted as definitive in meaning. If it had to be considered interpretable because it cannot be taken literally but only by means of the explanation of the meaning of the word, then the statement from the *Transcendent Wisdom Sutra* that "there is no matter, no sound . . ." must also be accepted as intentional and unsuitable to be taken literally, because they are both in the same situation. [TL 157B]

3.1.2.1.2.2.1.2.3.2.1.1.3. Explanation That It Is Not the Intention of This
Treatise That It Belongs to the Information[-only] System, in Which the
Second Wheel Is Established as Interpretable in Meaning

The explanation for [this section of] disputations and refutations accepting the assertion of Experientialism as one's own system is not the topic of
this treatise. The *Transcendent Wisdom Sutra* is established by Experientialists as interpretable in meaning by means of a process of showing the inti-
mated basis, the need, and the refutation of literalness, and the *Elucidation
of the Intention Sutra* is considered definitive in meaning. [However,] in this
treatise, the *Transcendent Wisdom Sutra* is considered definitive in meaning. Moreover, it would be insufficient [for supposed Experientialists] to
explain the topic of the message from the *Transcendent Wisdom Sutra* that
all things are empty—for example, the taints are empty of suffering and its
origin—because [Experientialists] accept the grasping at the truth status of
things as the misapprehension of substantial subject-object dichotomy. But
such emptiness is not taught in this treatise.

3.1.2.1.2.2.1.2.3.2.1.2. Adopting a Proper Perspective

Dispute about a contradiction: it has been taught in the *Transcendent
Wisdom Sutra* of the second Dharma wheel that all things are incidental,
like clouds, dreams, and illusions. This teaching contradicts the statement
in the *Tathāgata Essence Sutra* that the nature of the mind is immutable for
eternity.

Reply: There is no difference in terms of definitiveness in meaning
between the *Transcendent Wisdom Sutra* of the second wheel and the
Tathāgata Essence Sutra of the final wheel. [TL 158A] Since the grasping at
truth status is established as incidental, included in the addictions, and
unable to penetrate the nature of the mind, this effortlessly proves all things
to be empty in truth, free from reifications. I shall explain this point in the
section on the meaning of the word.

Dispute about uselessness: Being difficult to understand, it is useless to
teach the childish about the element.

Reply: It is thus taught in order to dispel the five faults.

3.1.2.1.2.2.1.2.3.2.1.3. Refutation of Disputes

Question: If the grasping at truth status is accepted as an addictive obscuration, then why is the imagination about truth status regarding the three focal points explained below an objective obscuration?

Answer: There are evolutionary instincts for the conviction about truth status in three focal points, not in the grasping at truth status itself. [Furthermore,] there is no contradiction in taking grasping at truth status as an objective obscuration, since such an arrangement of what is to be eliminated and its antidote is explicated for disciples to whom it is temporarily inappropriate to teach subtle selflessness.

3.1.2.1.2.2.1.2.3.2.2. Its Ramifications . . . 2.1. Challenges

Challenge about the contradiction: It has been taught in this and that *Transcendent Wisdom Sutra,* such as the *Transcendent Wisdom Sutra in Eighteen Thousand Lines* and the *Transcendent Wisdom in One Hundred Thousand Lines,* that all objects of knowledge—like clouds, dreams, and illusions—are forever empty of intrinsic identifiability. Why has the Buddha declared here in the *Tathāgata Essence Sutra,* and also in the *Shrīmālādevī Lion's Roar Sutra,* etc., in the final wheel of Dharma, that the tathāgata essence, which penetrates the nature of the mind, exists in sentient beings? Being incidental is in direct contradiction to penetration into the nature [of mind].

Challenge about the uselessness: Since the childish would not be able to know [the tathāgata essence], what is the use of this teaching to them?

There are respectively two replies to the challenges of contradiction and uselessness. It is stated in the prelude to this section that "there are two verses summarizing the purpose of this teaching: the first is the doubt, and the second is the response."

Objection: Although the second verse is a reply to the dispute of uselessness, there is no reply to the disputes of contradiction. [TL 158B]

Answer: There is no problem. The explanation of the necessity of proclaiming the existence of the naturally pure element also serves as a reply to the disputes of contradiction, since its meaning is summarized in this verse and will be clearly stated below.

3.1.2.1.2.2.1.2.3.2.2.2. Replies

There is a need [for the Buddha] to state that there exists within all sentient beings the naturally pure element, which is the foundation for possible production of all the buddha excellences. It has been taught for the purpose of dispelling five faults as follows: (1) the fault of being disheartened, which is an obscuration to cultivation of the spirit of supreme enlightenment, thinking, "I will not be able to attain unsurpassed enlightenment because I do not have the spiritual potential for buddhahood," hence obscuring the cultivation of the spirit; (2) the fault of contempt for inferior beings when one has cultivated the spirit but has not realized that all beings have the spiritual potential for buddhahood, which is an obscuration to performance of the bodhisattva activities, thinking, "I can attain enlightenment, but not the others," hence obscuring the performance of enlightened activities with the wish to direct all sentient beings to perfect enlightenment; (3) the fault of reification, apprehending things established in unreality as in reality, which obscures the realization of the meaning of the ultimate reality; (4) the fault of repudiation, denying reality, the naturally pure element, which makes all buddha excellences possible, hence misunderstanding the two realities; and (5) the fault of excessive attachment to oneself, of self-cherishing, which obscures the realization of equal exchange between self and other that is the cause of producing the spirit of supreme enlightenment, hence obscuring the conception of the spirit on the basis of the equal exchange. [TL 159A]

This teaching on the existence of the element has been taught for the purpose of dispelling these five faults, thereby cultivating the spirit of supreme enlightenment and learning the enlightened activities in general, and the last transcendences in particular, in order to realize the element. Having realized that the naturally pure element taught in the final wheel is equivalent to the emptiness explicated in the middle wheel, we shall come to understand that the former and later teachings are not mutually contradictory.

3.1.2.1.2.2.1.2.3.3. Detailed Exposition . . . 3.1. Prelude

«248» The meaning of these two verses should be known briefly by the following ten verses:

3.1.2.1.2.2.1.2.3.3.2. The Root Text . . . 2.1. Explaining No Contradiction between the Former and Later Teachings

In the *Transcendent Wisdom Sutra*, all things are said to be incidental and empty of intrinsic reality; in this final wheel, reality that penetrates the nature of the mind has been taught. These two statements are not mutually contradictory, since the teaching of this [final wheel] that the reality-limit—the tathāgata essence as the natural purity of sentient beings' minds—is forever empty of compounded things including suffering and its origin, which are incidental things that cannot penetrate the nature of the mind, is also the topic of the *Transcendent Wisdom Sutra*.

We shall understand this topic in the following way: the mere emptiness of suffering and its origin stated in this [final wheel] is taught within the context of the teaching on the emptiness of the reality of all things. The foremost addiction is the truth-habit, the conviction of the truth of things. This [truth-habit] is [merely] incidental, unable to penetrate the nature of the mind. This refers to the fact that nothing can be established in the mind as that which is apprehended by this [truth-habit], since no other techniques [TL 159B] than the negation of the supposed object of the truth-habit can be used to establish the emptiness of the intrinsic reality of all things. If the addictions are proved to be incidental, then karmic evolution and development, which are produced by the addictions, are incidental as well. Since the addictions, karmic evolution, and development, which are produced by the addictions, are said in the *Transcendent Wisdom Sutra* to be incidental, [the position that] all things are empty of intrinsic reality should be established as the topic of the sutra.

[Furthermore,] since this emptiness of intrinsic reality of sentient beings' mind is stated in the *Tathāgata Essence Sutra* to be the existence of the element, these two teaching procedures of the middle and final wheels are proved to be not only compatible but also equivalent. If explained according to the Centrist system that accepts the grasping at truth status as an objective obscuration, this reply would also appear to be a bit inappropriate. Thus, this treatise and its commentary should be explained according to the savior Nāgārjuna's assertion as explicated by master Chandrakīrti. Through many lines of reasoning that block any possible deficiency, this way of explanation has been proven to perfectly fit [the treatise's] meaning of the word. Therefore, the Omniscient Jey Rinpoche [Tsong Khapa] Losang Drakpa's eloquent elucidation of this treatise and its commentary should be known as a complete explanation of the intention of these treatises, and as truly outstanding.

Since the occurrence of addictions is incidental to the mind, they are like clouds. Karmic evolution and evolutionary development are like a dream, an illusion, etc. These should be understood in the following way: the addictions are likened to the clouds because the occurrence of addictions is incidental to the mind; karmic evolution, motivated and produced by the addictions, is like the experience in dreams because it is produced by delusion and is not established by what is experienced; and the contaminated aggregates, the development of addictions and karmic evolution, are likened to illusions made by magic because they are not established in reality, despite appearing in such a way. [TL 160A] However, if these statements were the proof of the teaching on emptiness of all things, it would be irrelevant to the teaching on emptiness of suffering and its origin alone. The assertion that ultimate truth is empty of all conventional things reveals this person's poor understanding, for this treatise never teaches emptiness of the conventional truth of the path directly or indirectly!

3.1.2.1.2.2.1.2.3.3.2.2. Explaining the Need for Proclaiming the Existence of the Element . . . 2.1. Brief Statement

Thus, the emptiness of intrinsic identity of all things, arranged previously in the second wheel and again in this *Sublime Continuum* of the final wheel, in order to dispel these five faults and cultivate the five excellences, the existence of the tathāgata essence within all sentient beings, along with the need for this teaching, has been taught.

3.1.2.1.2.2.1.2.3.3.2.2.2. Detailed Expositions . . . 2.1. Specific Expositions . . . 1.1. Obscuration to the Cultivation of the Spirit of Supreme Enlightenment

The need for sentient beings to realize the existence of the spiritual potential for buddhahood within each of them is described as follows: first, not learning about this naturally pure element, which makes all the buddha excellences possible to achieve, some of them feel disheartened. [They] think, "I will not be able to attain buddhahood," [TL 160B] because of the fault of self-contempt, [and they think they] will never cultivate the spirit of enlightenment. Thus, this teaching has been taught for the purpose of cultivating the spirit by means of the elimination of such faults.

3.1.2.1.2.2.1.2.3.3.2.2.2.1.2. Obscuration to Performance of the Enlightened Activities

Second, some disciples have cultivated this spirit but have not realized the existence of the spiritual potential for buddhahood within all sentient beings. Due to pride, they think: "I can attain buddhahood, so I am superior!" They insistently accept the notion that those who have not cultivated this spirit are inferior. Thus, this teaching has been taught to motivate [such persons] to perform the enlightened activities for sentient beings' welfare with the understanding that all beings are capable of attaining buddhahood.

3.1.2.1.2.2.1.2.3.3.2.2.2.1.3. Obscuration to the Distinctive Deed— Realization of the Import of the Ultimate Reality . . . 3.1. Coming under the Sway of Faults If Not Realized

Correct understanding of the ultimate truth for sentient beings' welfare will never arise in those who think in this way. Thus, since they are apprehending the intrinsic reality of the unreal by means of the faults, they will not cognize reality, the emptiness of the intrinsic identifiability of the faults.

3.1.2.1.2.2.1.2.3.3.2.2.2.1.3.2. Means of Realizing It

These faults of sentient beings, attachment, etc., are not real, as they are newly fabricated by conditions, and are incidental, that is, relativistically originated. In reality, these faults do not have an intrinsically identifiable self-substance, while the excellences are pure by nature.

3.1.2.1.2.2.1.2.3.3.2.2.2.1.4. Obscuration to Cultivation of Love and Compassion That Are Causes for Cultivating the Spirit

3.1.2.1.2.2.1.2.3.3.2.2.2.1.4.1. Explaining from the Reversed Perspective

If one apprehends the unreal faults as if established in intrinsic reality and repudiates the emptiness of intrinsic reality that makes the real excellences, the buddha excellences, possible to attain, one will not develop love, the wish for all beings to be filled with happiness, and compassion, the wish for all beings to be free from suffering, by means of the practice of other-cherishing, by which the wise see the equality between oneself and other sentient beings in terms of [everyone's] possession of the spiritual potential for buddhahood and the capacity for obtaining buddhahood. [TL 161A]

3.1.2.1.2.2.1.2.3.3.2.2.2.1.4.2. Explaining from the Positive Perspective

On the contrary, by learning this teaching on the existence of the spiritual potential for buddhahood within all sentient beings, there arises in the mind of these disciples enthusiasm for the attainment of buddhahood, respect for other sentient beings as for the Teacher, wisdom that realizes that the faults are not established by means of any intrinsic reality, intuitive wisdom that realizes that all buddha excellences are possible to reach, as well as great love, as explicated above.

3.1.2.1.2.2.1.2.3.3.2.2.2.2. Brief Statement on the Benefits of Being Free from the Five Faults

Because of production in the continuums of these disciples of these five excellences, in which the stages of the universal vehicle path are included, the fault of self-contempt will be absent and the equality between oneself and others in terms of the capacity for obtaining buddhahood will be recognized. Realizing that the faults are not established by means of any intrinsic reality, that possession of the excellences is possible, [and realizing] the equality between oneself and sentient beings in terms of the capacity for attaining buddhahood, one will swiftly attain perfect buddhahood by meditating on the stages of the universal vehicle path.

3.1.2.1.2.2.1.3. Title of the Chapter

This concludes a clear exposition of tathāgata essence encapsulated in the first summary verse, starting from the line, "Buddhas' wisdom enters into the hosts of sentient beings," in *The Sublime Continuum of the Universal Vehicle, Analysis of the Precious Spiritual Potential*. Although it seems appropriate to take the "first verse" as the verse on the arrangement of the whole treatise, I think the explanation just mentioned is correct. This concludes the exposition of reality, [the tathāgata essence], which is mingled with taints, as well.

> Based on my venerable teacher's personal instructions,
> I have clearly elucidated with simple words
> The topic of the sutras such as the *Shrīmālādevī* and the
>   *Tathāgata Essence*,
> As explicated by the Father and Son Bodhisattvas.[389]

Thus, the exposition of the first chapter of the commentary of the treatise elucidating the intention of the universal vehicle sutras definitive in meaning is completed.

---

389. Maitreya and Asaṅga.

CHAPTER II
Enlightenment

3.1.2.1.2.2.2. Exposition of Enlightenment, and so on . . . 2.1. Exposition of Enlightenment Endowed with Twofold Purity . . . 1.1. Prelude

«249» Now the reality free from taints shall be explained.

Although there is no contradiction in connecting this [sentence] to the ending statement above, this [sentence] should be regarded as the prelude for what will be explained. [TL 161B] Why, here, is it called the reality free from taints? Because the taintless element of buddhas, ultimate reality with a pure nature, is free from all characteristics of incidental taints. The arrangement of transformation is based on the total removal of taints from the mental consciousness that has been previously tainted. In brief, it should be understood in terms of eight factors.

3.1.2.1.2.2.2.1.2. Explanation of the Meaning . . . 2.1. Brief Statement . . . 1.1. Division of Eight Factors . . . 1.1. Question

«250» What are the eight factors?

3.1.2.1.2.2.2.1.2.1.1.2. Answer . . . 2.1. The Root Text

(1) Purity refers to the actuality of enlightenment, [TL 162A] since it has the nature of collecting the twofold purity. (2) The intuitive wisdom of meditative equipoise and the intuitive wisdom of post-attainment, [aftermath] equipoise, which are the causes for the attainment of this enlightenment, are the means. (3) Cessation refers to the cessation of all taints by means of a habitual affinity for these two causes. It is both enlightenment and fruition. So it has the feature of fruition. (4) [The enlightenment also] has the function that brings about perfect self-benefit and benefit for others

owing to its directly perceiving all objects of knowledge and being free from all taints. (5) Relying on it, the two benefits are accomplished—this refers to its possessing the excellences of ultimate transformation. (6) The profound truth body, the magnificent beatific body, and also the great being supreme emanation body, the last perceivable even by ordinary beings in performing its altruistic enlightened activities—this refers to its feature of dividing into different types of excellences. (7) This feature of division [into appropriate types] will remain until the end of the life cycle—this is its feature of permanence. (8) [The enlightened activities] engaged in according to disciples' faculties, thoughts, timing, etc.—this is its feature of being unmistaken.

Here, unlike what is explained in the section that analyzes the element, the feature of fruition does not refer to the one accomplished in the future, and also the feature of function does not refer to the one produced later on, the basis of [enlightenment] itself. Instead, it should be understood that [fruition] refers to enlightenment itself and [function] refers to the simultaneous accomplishment of the two benefits at that time.

3.1.2.1.2.2.2.1.2.1.1.2.2. [Asaṅga's] Commentary . . . 2.1. Nominal Divisions

This verse talks about the following eight factors: nature, fruition, function, possession, divisions, permanence, and inconceivability.

3.1.2.1.2.2.2.1.2.1.1.2.2.2. Explaining Each Factor

«251» There is a sutra reference regarding the nature of enlightenment endowed with the twofold purity. Here it should be known that the element, [TL 162B] which is the natural purity, is designated as the tathāgata essence when it has not yet been released from the sheath of addictions, and as the nature of transformation when purified of incidental taints. Why? The *[Shrīmālādevī Lion's Roar] Sutra* states:

> O Bhagavān, if one has no doubt about the tathāgata essence trapped within the sheath of a hundred trillion addictions, he will have no doubt about the Tathāgata's truth body that is free from the sheath of addictions.

The "two intuitive wisdoms that are the causes of attaining such enlightenment" refers to the transcendent intuitive wisdom of nonconceptual meditative equipoise and the common intuitive wisdom of post-attainment equipoise, which [again] has dualistic perception. The causes for transformation, which are the transcendent intuitive wisdom and the common intuitive wisdom included in the paths of insight and meditation, are expressed under the name "attainment" since they are possible to attain.

The fruition of these two intuitive wisdoms is the two kinds of freedom, those from addictive obscuration and from objective obscuration.

The transcendent intuitive wisdom brings about self-benefit, and the common intuitive wisdom brings about benefit for others, in terms of the corresponding results that these two bring about.

The possession refers to the excellences as the basis for bringing about the twofold benefit.

The division refers to the three bodies as distinguished by the features of being profound, magnificent, and great of being, their engagement continuing as long as there is one sentient being, and [by] their feature of inconceivability.

3.1.2.1.2.2.2.1.2.1.2. Summary

«252» The summary verse states that the stage of buddhahood is analyzed and settled by these eight factors: the nature of enlightenment, its attaining cause, the fruition attained by that cause, the function of bringing about the twofold benefit, the possession of the excellences as the basis for bringing about [the twofold benefit], the division of the three bodies, [TL 163A] the perpetuity of engagement, and inconceivability as the distinguishing features of that division.

3.1.2.1.2.2.2.1.2.2. Detailed Explanation . . . 2.1. Explanation of Nature and Cause . . . 1.1. Prelude

«253» Here, buddhahood, with its nature of enlightenment endowed with the twofold purity, and the means to attain that, are in turn taught by the verse with respect to the factor of nature and the factor of cause.

3.1.2.1.2.2.2.1.2.2.1.2.2.1.2. Statement . . . 1.2.1. The Nature of Enlightenment . . .
1.1. Explaining Natural Purity

The so-called natural luminosity of the mind was previously obscured by
the incidental dense clouds of addictive obscurations and objective obscurations. It is called buddhahood later, when purified.

3.1.2.1.2.2.2.1.2.2.1.2.1.2. Explaining Purity of Incidental Taints . . . 2.1.
Intuitive Wisdom

Buddhahood is the experiential realization of the ultimate reality, and is
like the sun with its clear-light.

3.1.2.1.2.2.2.1.2.2.1.2.1.2.2. Abandonment

Buddhahood is taintless, naturally pure, just like space.

3.1.2.1.2.2.2.1.2.2.1.2.1.2.1. The Relying Excellences

The Buddha is endowed with all excellences, as aforementioned, its perpetuity being freedom from aging, its stability being freedom from sickness,
and its immutability being freedom from death.

3.1.2.1.2.2.2.1.2.2.1.2.1.2.2. The Cause of Attaining It

The nature of enlightenment [TL 163B] is attained by relying on the nonconceptual intuitive wisdom of reality and the distinguishing intuitive
wisdom of all objects of knowledge. Furthermore, "that which is called
natural luminosity like the sun" refers to the buddhahood with perfect
realization, which is the experiential realization of objects of knowledge
just as they are and in all their varieties. "And space" refers to the buddhahood with perfect abandonment, which is free from the taints of those
incidental obscuring dense clouds of addictive obscurations and objective
obscurations. "Endowed with buddha excellences and perpetual, stable, and
without change" refers to the relying excellences. "Its attainment" refers to
the cause of the attainment of enlightenment.

3.1.2.1.2.2.2.1.2.2.1.3. Explanation . . . 3.1. Prelude

«254» The meaning of this verse, in brief, should be understood by the following four verses.

3.1.2.1.2.2.2.1.2.2.1.3.2. The Root Text . . . 2.1. The Factor of Nature . . . 1.1. General Statement

The Buddha's enlightenment endowed with the twofold purity is distinguished from others by the intuitive wisdom of all buddha excellences being undifferentiated in nature, natural purity, and purity of incidental taints, i.e., by elimination, realization, and the excellences depending on them.

3.1.2.1.2.2.2.1.2.2.1.3.2.1.2. Detailed Explanation . . . 2.1. Excellences of Abandonment and Realization

The characteristic of the clear-light intuitive wisdom that sees all objects of knowledge just as they are and in all their varieties, like the sun, refers to the excellent qualities of intuitive wisdom. The characteristic of elimination that, like space, is free of incidental taints, refers to the excellent qualities of elimination. [TL 164A] The natural luminosity is not newly created by causes and conditions. This naturally pure reality pervades without any differentiation in terms of nature, possessing countless kinds of buddha excellences, in number beyond the sand grains in the river Ganges.

3.1.2.1.2.2.2.1.2.2.1.3.2.1.2.2. Recognizing What Is to Be Abandoned

The taints cannot penetrate the nature of the mind just like the clouds cannot penetrate the nature of space, since their intrinsic reality does not exist. The taints pervade the mental continuums of sentient beings just as the clouds pervade space. The taints are incidental just like the incidental emergence of the clouds.

3.1.2.1.2.2.2.1.2.2.1.3.2.2. Its Cause

The nonconceptual intuitive wisdom in meditation and its postattainment intuitive wisdom realizing all phenomenal objects of knowledge are accepted as the two intuitive wisdoms that are the causes of the attainment of enlightenment, free from the two kinds of obscurations.

3.1.2.1.2.2.2.1.2.2.1.3.3. [Asaṅga's] Commentary

The twofold purity is said to be in the nature of transformation. Here, the purity, in brief, is of two kinds: natural purity and purity without taints. The natural purity is [primordially] released from being endowed with reality status but has not yet been separated from incidental taints, since the natural luminosity of the mind has not been separated from incidental taints. The natural luminosity of the mind is the purity without taints when it has separated from all incidental taints, just like water, etc., is [primordially] released and separated from taints, etc.

This passage can be regarded as the prelude to the fruition factor. However, it is more appropriate to take it as the conclusion of the previous section.

3.1.2.1.2.2.2.1.2.2.2. Explanation of Fruition . . . 2.1. Prelude

«255» Here, the verse regarding the purity without taints states as follows:

3.1.2.1.2.2.2.1.2.2.2.2. Statement . . . 2.1. Explaining the Freedom from Addictive Obscuration as the Fruition of the Habitual Affinity for Meditative Equipoise's Intuitive Wisdom That Realizes Reality

[TL 164B] [Enlightenment] is like a lake full of lotus blossoms in clean water, since it is endowed with the excellences of non-taints owing to its abandonment of attachment; like the full moon released from the mouth of Rāhu, since it is endowed with the light of compassion owing to its abandonment of hatred; like the sun released from the mass of clouds, since it is endowed with untainted luminosity owing to its abandonment of tainted ignorance.

3.1.2.1.2.2.2.1.2.2.2.2.2. Explaining the Excellence of the Material Body That Is Endowed with Three Features and Has Abandoned Objective Obscurations as the Fruition of the Habitual Affinity for the Aftermath Store of Merit

A buddha should be understood as the one endowed with the excellences of the abandonment of all objective obscurations, etc., akin to the Sage, honey, essence, precious gold, underground treasure, tree, a buddha image made of stainless jewels, an emperor, and a golden statue, as mentioned in the section on analysis of the element, when completely released from individual obscurations. The similes of essence and gold demonstrate the purity of incidental taints and natural purity. The simile of the Sage demonstrates transcendence. The similes of precious gold, emperor, and golden statue demonstrate in turn the possession of all the excellences of the material body, surpassing the disciples, etc., and the perfection of matter. The similes of honey, [TL 165A] treasure, and tree demonstrate in turn making [beings] satisfied with the Dharma joy, the elimination of [beings'] poverty with excellences, and the enlightened activities that cause the bliss of liberation. Specifically, the former two similes represent the truth body, the middle four the material body, and the latter three the activities.

3.1.2.1.2.2.2.1.2.2.2.3. Explanation . . . 3.1. Prelude

«256» The meaning of this verse, in brief, should be understood by the following eight verses.

3.1.2.1.2.2.2.1.2.2.2.3.2. [Asaṅga's] Commentary . . . 2.1. General Statement of the Objects Engaged by the Two Exalted Wisdoms

In brief, the purification of incidental addictions of the three poisons including attachment, etc.—just like the clear lake of the lotus, the moon released from Rāhu, and the sun released from clouds—is said to be the result of nonconceptual intuitive wisdom. The definite attainment of the Buddha's three bodies endowed with all kinds of excellences, which is accomplished by immeasurable merit including generosity, etc., is said to be the result of post-attainment intuitive wisdom. Despite the fact that there is no difference between the nature of meditative equipoise and the nature of subsequent attainment as well as no difference between the nature of the truth body and the nature of the material body, this explanation is given in terms of the different results [attained by the two intuitive wisdoms].

3.1.2.1.2.2.2.1.2.2.2.3.2.2. Explaining the Similarity between Simile and Meaning Regarding the Fruition of Meditative Equipoise

As to the abandonment of attachment, this [kind of] buddhahood should be understood as the clear water pond full of lotuses since it has abandoned the taint of attachment and pours the water of meditation, which is unshakable and benefits beings with the three kinds of miracles,[390] upon the lotuses of disciples. [TL 165B] As to the abandonment of hatred, this [kind of] buddhahood is akin to the clear full moon since it has been released from the Rāhu of hatred toward sentient beings and its light of great love and compassion pervades all beings. As to the abandonment of ignorance, this [kind of] buddhahood is akin to the untainted sun since it has been released from the mass of clouds of ignorance and eliminates beings' darkness of ignorance with light of the intuitive wisdom that knows things just as they are and the intuitive wisdom that knows the varieties of things.

3.1.2.1.2.2.2.1.2.2.2.3.2.3. Explaining the Similarity between Simile and Meaning Regarding the Fruition of Aftermath

This buddhahood should be understood as being akin to the buddha form, honey, and kernel since it is endowed with unsurpassed excellences equal to the Buddha, and bestows the rare taste of the Dharma without the husk of the two obscurations. This buddhahood should be understood as being akin to gold, treasure, and tree since its nature is pure, it eliminates poverty with excellent substances, and it causes the fruition of liberation to ripen. It is the same in meaning to explain [the tree] as "bestowing the fruition." This buddhahood should be understood as being akin to the statue made of jewels, the emperor, and the golden statue since it is endowed with

390. *cho 'phrul.*

the jewel of the realizational intuitive truth body, its beatific body is the supreme lord among beings with two feet, and its supreme emanation body has precious forms.

3.1.2.1.2.2.2.1.2.2.3. Explanation of Function ... 3.1. Explaining the Function as Being Able to Perfect the Twofold Benefit

[TL 166A] «257» The transcendent nonconceptual intuitive wisdom and its post-attainment intuitive wisdom are the causes of the transformation with the designation of "fruition of freedom." Their functions are said to be the perfection of the two benefits of self and others. The perfection of the two benefits is the function of the two intuitive wisdoms with respect to their being the two intuitive wisdoms, and is the cause of that function with respect to the disciples.

Here, how is the perfection of the two benefits achieved? The perfection of self-benefit refers to the attainment of the truth body without obscurations, owing to the liberation from addictive obscuration along with its evolutionary instincts as well as objective obscuration. The perfection of benefit for others refers to the effortless engagement of the display of the two bodies and the power over the teaching in the life cycle until its end, based on the self-benefit. The display of the two bodies refers to different bodily forms in correspondence with different disciples. The power over the teaching refers to a buddha's single verbal voice understood by different disciples according to their own languages.

3.1.2.1.2.2.2.1.2.2.3.2. The Nature of Function ... 2.1. Prelude

«258» There are three verses regarding the function factor:

3.1.2.1.2.2.2.1.2.2.3.2.2. Statement ... 2.1. Explaining Benefit for One's Truth Body

The freedom from the taints of the two obscurations is the elimination. The intuitive wisdoms that pervade all objects of knowledge just as they are and in their varieties are the realization. The reliant supreme excellences have the feature of indestructibility. This means that buddhahood is endowed with the body that is firm, peaceful, permanent, and immutable since the aforementioned causality included in the category of objective obscuration has been completely broken.

3.1.2.1.2.2.2.1.2.2.3.2.2.1. Explaining the Other-Benefit Material Body

The material body is the site of accomplishing the benefit for others. The detailed explanation is as follows: it should be understood that the perfection of the enlightened activities of the buddhas' material body makes it possible for it to become the cause of the fortunate disciples' enjoyment of the objects of the superior six sense media, [TL 166B] included in the category of the excellences of realization, just like space, which makes it possible that beings' six consciousnesses can experience corresponding objects. The further explanation is as follows: the superior six sense media in the conventional sense refers to the eye consciousness that sees the object of the form of Buddha Amitābha, and so on, which are not created by the four elements; the ear consciousness that hears the wonderful speech of the holy Dharma, such as the paths and fruitions of the three kinds of spiritual lineage, which is pure without any faults; the nose consciousness that smells the suddhas' fragrance caused by pure ethics; the tongue consciousness that tastes the ambrosia of great noble beings' Dharma; the body consciousness that experiences the tactile bliss of meditative equipoise caused by bodily fluency; and the mental consciousness that realizes the meaning of the intrinsically profound emptiness.

When they have reached the higher level, the conventional six consciousnesses can experience the objects just mentioned. And, [for instance], one single mental consciousness can experience all objects. As to the fact that ultimately there is nothing producing and nothing to be produced, if thinking of subtle reasoning of analyzing the ultimate, the meaning of reality will be realized and the ultimate uncontaminated bliss will be given. The Tathāgata is like space, being the absence of the cause of producing and of being produced in the ultimate sense, since the Tathāgata is free from the reification of the four extremes. [TL 167A] Although a buddha's material bodies lack any intrinsic reality even as small as an atom, they can bestow all goodness, worldly and transcendent.

3.1.2.1.2.2.2.1.2.2.3.2.3. Explanation . . . 3.1. Prelude

«259» The meanings of these three verses should be understood, in brief, by the eight verses that follow.

3.1.2.1.2.2.2.1.2.2.3.2.3. The Root Text . . . 3.1. Recognizing the Objects Engaged by the Power of the Two Intuitive Wisdoms

In short, the function of the meditative intuitive wisdom that experientially realizes the ultimate truth, included in the universal vehicle paths of insight and meditation, should be known as the truth body that has been freed from all obscurations in its own continuum, and the post-attainment intuitive wisdom that realizes all phenomenal objects of knowledge as the material bodies that purify the truth body [present] in others' continuums.

3.1.2.1.2.2.2.1.2.2.3.2.3.1.2. Explaining the Truth Body . . . 2.1. General Statement

The liberation and the truth body should be known as having the two aspects of the truth body and the material body, included in elimination and realization, as well as the one aspect of the excellences relying on them, since the first two are uncontaminated, the intuitive wisdoms pervade all objects of knowledge, and the latter consists of the excellences of stability, etc.

3.1.2.1.2.2.2.1.2.2.3.2.3.1.2.2. Detailed Explanation . . . 2.1. Explaining Elimination and Realization

[The truth body] is uncontaminated since all addictions and evolutionary instincts have been eliminated. [TL 167B] The intuitive wisdoms are accepted as being pervasive since these are free of the hindrance of grasping at truth status in all objects of knowledge, and free of the obstacles of knowing just a little.

3.1.2.1.2.2.2.1.2.2.3.2.3.1.2.2.2. Explaining the Excellences Relying on Them

[The truth body] is uncreated since its nature is ultimately indestructible by karmic evolution and addictions. Its indestructibility is explained, in short, by being stable, etc. This is a combination of statement and

explanation. The four kinds of destruction should be known as the opposite of stability, etc. How? [The truth body] should be known as being stable, peaceful, eternal, and immutable, since it is free from decay, [from]
the aging process from youth to old age, [from] the change caused by sickness, [from] the interruption of a beginning, which is birth, and [from] the
inconceivable mutation of death.

3.1.2.1.2.2.2.1.2.2.3.2.3.1.2. Explaining the Material Bodies . . . 1.2.1.
Statement

This uncontaminated intuitive wisdom within a buddha's mental continuum should be known to be the ground, since it is the basis for the virtues
consisting of all goodness, accomplished by those disciples by means of its
appearance as material bodies in front of them.

3.1.2.1.2.2.2.1.2.2.3.2.3.1.2.2. Its Proof . . . 2.1. Simile

Just like space, while not being the cause producing senses, consciousnesses, etc., is the cause or basis that makes it possible for matter, sound,
scent, tastes, textures, and mental objects to be seen, heard, etc.

3.1.2.1.2.2.2.1.2.2.3.2.3.1.2.2.2. Meaning

Such two bodies are the cause of the cultivation of uncontaminated excellences. In whose continuum will these excellences be cultivated? Among the
objects of the stable bodhisattvas' sense faculties. How are such excellences
cultivated? [TL 168A] By the practice without effort. A certain version trans-
lates as "without obscuration." In that case it means there is no taint of
obscuration of the cultivation of excellences within others' continuums.

3.1.2.1.2.2.2.1.2.2.4. Explanation of Possession . . . 4.1. Refuting the
Possession of Superficial Excellences

«260» The *Ornament of the Light of Wisdom Sutra* states that "Buddha has the nature of space, and the nature of space is its non-nature." This
is stated in terms of a tathāgata's unique ultimate characteristic. For what
reason? If a tathāgata lacked any ultimate excellence and was seen merely as

[possessing] the thirty-two marks of a great person, then an emperor would be a tathāgata as well.

3.1.2.1.2.2.2.1.2.2.4.2. Establishing the Possession of Ultimate Excellences . . . 2.1. Prelude

Here [the verse with respect to the meaning of possession of ultimate excellent qualities states as follows:]

3.1.2.1.2.2.2.1.2.2.4.2.2. Statement

The Buddha's ultimate excellences should be known as inconceivable, permanent, stable, peaceful, and immutable, super peaceful, pervasive, thought-free, and like space, unattached, unobscured, beyond tangibility, invisible, ungraspable, virtuous, and taintless.

3.1.2.1.2.2.2.1.2.2.4.2.3. Explanation . . . 3.1. Prelude

«261» [The meaning of] this verse [is understood in brief by the following eight verses:] [TL 168B]

3.1.2.1.2.2.2.1.2.2.4.2.3.2. The Root Text . . . 2.1. Recognizing the Basis of Excellences

The perfection of the two benefits for self and others is demonstrated by the truth body, which belongs to one's own continuum and is the liberation from all kinds of taints, and the material bodies, which belong to one's own continuum and have the function of clearing away the obscurations of the attainment of the truth body [potential] in others' continuums. It should be known that the basis of the accomplishment of this twofold benefit is endowed with the fifteen excellences such as being inconceivable, etc.

3.1.2.1.2.2.2.1.2.2.4.2.3.2.2. Explaining the Excellences . . . 2.1. The
Excellences Divided by Abandonment . . . 1.1. The Uniqueness of
Profoundness . . . 1.1. Realization in All Times Being the Distinctive
Property of Only the Buddha

The eternal realization of buddhas' transcendent reality body and intuitive wisdom body is the object of the omniscient intuitive wisdom only.
Except for a buddha, these are not always the objects for others' three types
of wisdom, those made of study, contemplation, and meditation. Thus, even
those noble beings who have a wisdom body but are not buddhas must
realize that it is inconceivable.

3.1.2.1.2.2.2.1.2.2.4.2.3.2.2.1.1.2. Others Cannot Realize in This Way

The ultimate truth is subtle; thus it is not an object for wisdom made of
study to fully realize. Being ultimate, it cannot be fully realized by wisdom
born of contemplation. Transcendent reality is profound; hence it is not
an object for any worldly wisdom born of meditation, etc., [TL 169A] to fully
realize. Why? Like the blind with regard to visible forms, the childish have
never before seen such a reality; thus it is inconceivable. Even noble ones
perceive it [only] occasionally, not always, as babies occasionally [glimpse]
the sun from within the house where they are born.

3.1.2.1.2.2.2.1.2.2.4.2.3.2.2.1.2. The Uniqueness of Permanence

Since the truth body is free from being born by the power of karmic
evolution and addictions, it is eternal. Since it is without cessation of death
at the end, it is stable. Since the two factors of mental depression and agitation are not present, it is peaceful. It is immutable, for the reality ever exists,
never getting old from youth. This describes the uniqueness of eternality
that is free from birth, aging, sickness, and death, included in both categories of addictive obscuration and objective obscuration.

3.1.2.1.2.2.2.1.2.2.4.2.3.2.2.1.3. The Uniqueness of Bliss

It is absolutely peaceful, without any suffering, because it is the ultimate
nature of the truth of cessation. This describes its uniqueness of bliss.

3.1.2.1.2.2.2.1.2.2.4.2.3.2.2.1.4. The Uniqueness of Exalted Wisdom

Since all phenomenal objects of knowledge are realized, the intuitive wisdom that knows the varieties of things is all-pervasive. Since it does not dwell upon any mode of grasping at truth status, it is without conceptualization.

3.1.2.1.2.2.2.1.2.2.4.2.3.2.2.1.5. The Uniqueness of Abandonment

Since the addictions are completely eliminated, [such wisdom] has no attachment to truth status and has eliminated addictive obscurations. Since all objective obscurations are cleansed, it is in all ways unobstructed in regard to objects of knowledge and has eliminated all objective obscurations. [TL 169B] Being free from those two factors of mental depression and agitation, the meditative obscurations, and being suited for samādhi practice, it is free from rough contacts that cause mental and physical unfitness and result from mental depression and agitation, which are the obscurations of the production of the bliss of mental and physical fluency.

3.1.2.1.2.2.2.1.2.2.4.2.3.2.2.2. The Naturally Existing Excellence

Since reality is not material, it cannot be seen with the eyes. Since it is free from the signs of valid reason, it cannot be fully realized and apprehended by reasoning. It is virtuous, for being naturally pure, distinguished by the purity of incidental taints. It is free from incidental taints, since taints are completely abandoned.

3.1.2.1.2.2.2.1.2.2.5. Explanation of Division . . . 2.1. General Prelude

«262» This buddhahood is akin to space since it is endowed with special qualities. The transcendence of eternality is undifferentiated from uncreated excellences, as long as the life cycle remains, bringing about help and benefit to sentient beings by distinguished purification with inconceivable great liberative art to accomplish well-being, compassion, and wisdom that directly knows all objects of knowledge. It should be known that the causes of such [activities] are the reality [body], the beatific [body], and the emanation [body]. These three [bodies] without taint uninterruptedly, constantly, without wavering for even an instant, steadfastly, and spontaneously engage [in such activities] without any effort, for [buddhahood] is endowed with special qualities not in common with [those of] the last existence of the tenth stage and below.

3.1.2.1.2.2.2.1.2.2.2. Explaining Each Meaning . . . 2.1. Division of Three Bodies [TL 170A] . . . 1.1. Prelude

«263» Here, [there are four verses concerning the categories of the buddha body with respect to the meaning of divisions:]

3.1.2.1.2.2.2.1.2.2.2.1.2. Explanation . . . 2.1. Brief Statement . . . 1.1. General Meaning . . . 1.1. The Time When the Fruition Is Accomplished

The uninterrupted path of the last existence of the tenth stage [bodhisattva] meditates on ultimate reality in the manner of water pouring into water. At that time, the perception of all phenomenal objects of knowledge does not appear in the slightest in such meditation, since the taint that apprehends the two realities as separate natures has not [yet] been eliminated. However, this path is of the nature that has the potential to realize all twenty-one categories of uncontaminated intuitive wisdom. In the next instant, when the liberation path is produced, all dualistic perceptions subside with respect to transcendent knowables, like water pouring into water, and such meditation directly perceives all phenomenal objects of knowledge, like an apple in one's palm. At that time, objective obscurations are eliminated, reality is realized, and this is called the total enlightenment about all things and all aspects. The type of body corresponding with the ornaments of marks and signs at the time of the last existence of the tenth stage turns into the beatific body endowed with the five characteristics, the five excellences, and [TL 170B] the five determinations, when the truth body is realized. And a supreme emanation body, having the beatific body as a cooperative condition, educates disciples by means of the twelve activities [of a buddha life]. In this case, [the emanation body and the beatific body] do not have a common cause. However, there are certain emanation bodies that have a cause in common with the beatific body, thus having a connection of dependence[391] with the latter. The esoteric paths should be

391. *rag las kyi 'brel ba.*

added onto the transcendent paths after the three countless eons in order to accomplish the material body. One may refer to other literature for a detailed account.

3.1.2.1.2.2.2.1.2.2.2.1.2.1.1.2. Recognizing the Natures of the Three Bodies

The natural purity distinguished by the purity of taints, as well as the purity of taints itself of the material body and the intuitive wisdom truth body, is called the uncreated body or the reality body. Master Jñānagarbha's *Analysis of the Two Realities* states that "it is the natural reality in connection with the reasons." This means that the natural purity is what is understood by the ultimacy-analytic rational cognition.

[Here,] someone thinks that if there is not the body of the twofold purity within sentient beings' continuums since beginningless time and it is produced at the time of enlightenment, it would be impermanent. Our response is that this fault is the result of the fact that this person does not understand the difference between the meaning of eternality taught by the wise and that taught by the fool, as well as the difference between a temporary entity and a temporary eternality. Otherwise, one must accept that the destruction of a house in the morning exists since beginningless time or the destruction of a house in the afternoon exists since the morning of that day.

The intuitive wisdom truth body consisting of [TL 171A] the twenty-one categories of uncontaminated intuitive wisdom is said to be the fourth body in esoteric teachings. Bodhisattva Haribhadra takes the same position. This is just a matter of difference in grouping and does not mean it cannot be included in the three bodies. Why not? If you respond that it is neither the natural reality body, nor the other two, then I reply that it would be true that it cannot be included in the four bodies as well. If I say a copper-colored nail of the beatific body is not one of the four bodies that you would accept, then what do you reply? If you answer no, I reply that since it is a part of the beatific body, then no contradiction would be found in my assertion that the intuitive wisdom truth body is part of the natural reality body. If you respond that if so, then the intuitive wisdom truth body would be uncreated, I will say that you will then also have to accept that the nail is [the whole beatific body] with thirty-two marks and eighty signs. If your assertion can be accepted, so can mine, since both are the same in all respects. If you respond that the nail is just a part of the beatific body, not the beatific body itself, which is posited upon all marks and signs as a collection, I will say that the intuitive wisdom truth body is also a part of the natural reality body, not the natural reality body itself, which is posited upon the collection of the twofold purity. Therefore, the intuitive wisdom truth body is posited as a separate body for a special purpose.

As for the supreme emanation body, it is emanated for certain alienated individuals by the intuitive wisdom truth body [TL 171B] as a material body adorned with marks and signs. It migrates thorough death from the Tuṣhita heaven, and [then appears to live as a prince] up to appearing to become a buddha in front of the bodhi tree.

3.1.2.1.2.2.1.2.2.2.1.2.1.1.3. Refuting Wrong Ideas

Someone asserts that a buddha's natural reality body is not a buddha itself. No other sin is greater than this, since it repudiates the body with the twofold purity. Since it is neither an ultimate excellence nor a provisional excellence, it would not be an excellence at all. If you do not accept the former reason [it is an ultimate excellence], then you contradict yourself by saying it is not a buddha. If you agree, then since the ultimate abandonment is not an ultimate excellence, the same goes for the ultimate realization.

Someone asserts that the perception of the two kinds of material body exists only with respect to the disciples' vision but not to that of the buddhas, so it is not included within the buddhas' continuums. Saying this is a great sin. If so, then there would certainly not be any such thing as the two kinds of material body of a buddha, since it is not perceived by omniscient intuitive wisdom. If you do not accept the reason, then you contradict yourself by saying it does not appear to buddhas' own vision. If you say this means that buddhas are always in meditative equipoise in reality, therefore they do not have that appearance, my response is: this is incorrect for the reason I mentioned before. Do you accept that the two kinds of material body are not included in any person's continuum? Or that they are? If you accept the former, then a noble bodhisattva who practices generosity, ethics, etc., would not attain the ultimate fruition since the ultimate fruition of the cultivation of the store of merit [TL 172A] would not be included in any person's continuum.

If you say that when a last existence of the tenth stage [bodhisattva] becomes a buddha by practicing generosity, etc., in his own continuum, his mental continuum is broken and completely becomes the pure nature of reality, then we respond that, if so, you cannot refute the Lokāyata materialists' position that a person has a mind up to death but becomes absolute nothingness after death. I do not agree that the Lokāyata materialists' position is the Buddha's intention; thus it should be understood that the assertion that a holy being does not have a mind in his meditation is also refuted.

If you say that the two kinds of material body are included within sentient beings' continuums only, then, for example, when a person named Devadatta has perfected his practice in generosity, ethics, etc., the perfection of deathless longevity, extensive enjoyment, etc., is accepted as only the perception of a disciple named Yajñadatta. This should be known as the ultimate wrong idea about karmic evolution, accepting that a karmic evolutionary act is wasted and a karmic evolutionary action's result can be experienced even though it has not been performed.

Furthermore, someone asserts that there is no created excellence in the slightest within a buddha's continuum. We respond that it should be known that it is an outsider's mistaken idea to accept the termination of mind and the termination of things. This also refutes the assertion that the two kinds of buddhas' material body are not buddhas with sutra references [TL 172B] such as the statement of the Buddha that "those who see me in forms. . . ." The person who made such an assertion must be insane. How can one accept that [the two kinds of buddhas' material bodies] are not buddhas?

Further, it should be known that buddhas do not have coarse material bodies made of atoms. The material body is posited upon the basis of the intuitive wisdom of the buddhas. The detailed arrangement of a buddha's bodies should be understood on the basis of these discussions. I shall only say this much, afraid that more would be superfluous. However, it should be known that the two kinds of buddhas' material bodies depend on worldly thinking concerning correct conventions—as mentioned in [Haribhadra's] *Clear Meaning*: "[things] appear according to correct conventions."

3.1.2.1.2.2.2.1.2.2.2.1.2.1.2. Specific Meanings . . . 2.1. The Truth Body . . .
1.1. Stating the Possession of the Five Characteristics

[The truth body] is without production at the beginning, abiding in the middle, and disintegration at the end, thus being uncreated. It is indivisible from the nature of the ultimate element, thus being undifferentiated and free from the two extremes of reification and repudiation; rid of the three obscurations of addiction, cognition, and meditation, thus being pure; untainted by intrinsic reality; and not fully realized by conception. The realization of the nature of this ultimate element [TL 173A] is the perception of a yogi in introspective meditative equipoise, thus being radiant. The subject [mind] is distinguished by the twofold purity of nature and abandonment. "Untainted" and "not conceptualized" are grouped as the fifth excellent quality.

3.1.2.1.2.2.2.1.2.2.2.1.2.1.2.1.2. Stating the Possession of the Five Excellences

The untainted sphere of a tathāgata, which is the natural reality body, is endowed with [five] excellences. It cannot be fathomed, thus being extensive, and countless in number beyond the sand grains in the river Ganges. It is inconceivable for the conception of the four extremes, peerless, and is the abandonment of faults of addiction along with their evolutionary instincts.

3.1.2.1.2.2.2.1.2.2.2.1.2.1.2.2. The Beatific Body

"Bodies shot through with the various lights of holy Dharma" refers to the display of body and expression of speech. "Enthusiasm to accomplish the task of beings' liberation" refers to the deed of mind. These are distinguished by the manner in which all enlightened activities are spontaneously accomplished without any thought, like the enlightened activities of a king of wish-fulfilling jewels. It appears as a variety of bodies, yet it is not of any intrinsically real nature of those [bodies]. To certain disciples, it appears as a body made of accumulated atoms, but such is not its actual nature.

3.1.2.1.2.2.2.1.2.2.2.1.2.1.2.3. The Emanation Body

A supreme emanation body [of a buddha] initially enters the path to [bring about] the peace of the world. Fully maturing, it arises from the uncontaminated sphere, [TL 173B] and becomes the material body that was prophesied in the universal vehicle [taught by a previous buddha]. It then abides permanently in an uninterrupted way in this world, just as the material realm is uninterruptedly present in the realm of space. It should be understood that the single intuitive wisdom of a buddha can simultaneously display billions of material bodies [throughout the universe].

3.1.2.1.2.2.2.1.2.2.2.1.2.2. Extensive Explanation ... 2.1. Prelude

«264» [The meanings of these four] verses [should be understood by the following twenty verses:]

3.1.2.1.2.2.2.1.2.2.2.1.2.2.2. The Root Text ... 2.1. General Division ... 1.1. Explaining the Basis of Division

The omniscience of those self-arisen ones—who realized enlightenment by themselves, not depending upon other teachers, directly realizing all objects of knowledge, when as the bodhisattvas of the last existence, [they reach] the total abandonment of obscurations—this is called "buddha-hood." It is also called "supreme complete nirvana," "inconceivable for the lowly," "saint," and "the Bhagavān of individual introspective intuitive wisdom." This states the basis of the division of the three bodies.

3.1.2.1.2.2.2.1.2.2.2.1.2.2.2.1.2. The Reason This Division Is Made

When these are categorized, they can be divided into three: the profound natural reality body, the magnificent beatific body, and the great person emanation body, with the aforementioned and further to-be-told properties of the excellences as the reason.

3.1.2.1.2.2.2.1.2.2.2.1.2.2.2.1.3. The Divided Things

Here the three bodies, such as the natural reality of the truth body, etc., are divided.

3.1.2.1.2.2.2.1.2.2.2.1.2.2.2.2. Detailed Exposition of Each Nature ... 2.1. The Natural [TL 174A] Reality Body ... 1.1. The Number of Characteristics and Excellences

Of these, the natural reality body of a buddha is to be known as having five characteristics, such as "uncreated," etc., and, in brief, five excellences such as "unfathomable," etc.

3.1.2.1.2.2.2.1.2.2.2.1.2.2.2.2.1.2. Explaining Each of Them . . . 2.1. Explaining the Five Characteristics

The buddha reality body is uncreated, since it is far from production, abiding, and disintegration, and totally indivisible in terms of the nature of its excellences. The two extremes of reification and repudiation are completely abandoned. It is definitively freed from the three obscurations of addiction, objective cognition, and meditative equipoise. These four characteristics are distinguished by abandonment, etc. It is untainted by intrinsic-reality-habits, being the object of the yogi/nīs' introspective intuitive wisdom, and being the ultimate element with natural purity. For these four reasons it is declared to be clear-light.

3.1.2.1.2.2.2.1.2.2.2.1.2.2.2.2.1.2.2. Explaining the Five Excellences

The beatific body truly has five excellences of (1) being unfathomable in any limiting measure; (2) countless in number; (3) inconceivable in terms of thoughts at the four extremes; (4) unequaled by others; and (5) ultimately pure without taints. It is the ultimate of the twofold purity.

3.1.2.1.2.2.2.1.2.2.2.1.2.2.2.2.1.3. The Reason the Five Excellences Are Divided

Since it is (1) magnificent with respect to its excellences; [TL 174B] (2) not to be numbered; (3) not an object of thought; (4) unique to buddhas, not others; and since (5) the addictive and evolutionary instincts are eliminated, these are said to be the reasons for the five excellences, which are in the same order of unfathomable, and so on.

3.1.2.1.2.2.2.1.2.2.2.1.2.2.2.2.2. The Beatific Body . . . 2.1. Explaining Each Point . . . 1.1. The Body Adorned with Marks and Signs and the Continuation of the Corresponding Types of the Speech, Teaching Dharma without Interruption

It perfectly enjoys the Dharma of the universal vehicle, consisting of various declarations on definitive and interpretative meanings with respect to the ultimate and conventional truths.

As is its nature, [the beatific body] is adorned with marks and signs. The speech of Dharma and its corresponding type will continue forever without interruption until the end of the life cycle, appearing as teaching the same universal vehicle Dharma. This states that [the beatific body] is determined in its nature and its enjoyment in connection with the continuation of its physical display and uninterrupted communicative utterance.

3.1.2.1.2.2.1.2.2.1.2.2.2.2.1.2. The Continuation of the Enlightened Activities and the Effortlessness of These Three without Interruption

The fruit corresponding to the pure cause of great compassion is uninterrupted, benefiting the ultimate bodhisattvas in a direct way and the people with three different spiritual potentials in an indirect way, since [a buddha] has perfected the practice of compassion over the course of three uncountable eons. This states the continuation of enlightened activities without interruption.

Totally without any calculation in performance of those three [activities], and spontaneously, [a buddha] completely fulfills all wishes of disciples just as desired. This states the non-calculation and spontaneity.

3.1.2.1.2.2.1.2.2.1.2.2.2.1.3. Appearance in Various Aspects without Intrinsic Reality

[TL 175A] Like the nature and power of a wish-fulfilling jewel, appearing as various things but lacking any intrinsic reality as the appearance might suggest, [the beatific body] fully abides in the enjoyment of the universal vehicle Dharma with miraculous powers. The display of bodies, such as the supreme emanation body, conditioned by the beatific body, appears as different entities, but in reality they are not [different]. This states the uniqueness of the power of the beatific body. Furthermore, the beatific body itself appears to have intrinsic reality but in reality in does not.

3.1.2.1.2.2.1.2.2.1.2.2.2.2.2. Brief Statement . . . 2.1. The Actual Statement

Uninterrupted verbal expression, display of body, and action are performed without strenuous effort. And to show various different continuums that are not of such a nature, here are explained the varieties and the five [excellences].

3.1.2.1.2.2.2.1.2.2.2.1.2.2.2.2.2.2.2. Establishing the Various Appearances by a Simile

Just as, due to various colors, a jewel that does not have various colors appears as having those colors but in reality does not, so, due to the various conditions of sentient beings' spiritual lineages and inclinations, the all-pervading Bhagavān seems to appear in a way that he is not, as aforementioned.

3.1.2.1.2.2.2.1.2.2.2.1.2.2.2.2.3. The Emanation Body . . . 3.1. The Nature of the Supreme Emanation Body

By means of great compassion, [TL 175B] exactly knowing the world of the three kinds of spiritual lineage with different characters, dispositions, and instincts, by having this as the cause, having seen all worlds, not stirring from the truth body, [the Bhagavān displays] various actual emanations adapted for the benefit of disciples. This states that the beatific body emanates the emanation bodies.

3.1.2.1.2.2.2.1.2.2.2.1.2.2.2.2.3.2. The Way the Twelve Enlightened Activities Benefit

Here, let us take the example of the twelve enlightened activities performed by the Buddha. Where the Buddha performed these enlightened activities is the desire realm, and more specifically, the place of action in Jambudvīpa, since renunciation is more readily developed there. The Buddha was first born into the excellent birth in the desire realm, as a celestial being named Shvetaketu (White Banner) in the Tushita heaven, whence he would descend to [our world of] Jambudvīpa. This is the first deed of the twelve activities. His entering the womb [of his mother] is the second. Taking birth is the third.

Being skilled in the sixty-four types of arts, and the sciences and crafts, etc., is the fourth. Delighting in the company of royal consorts is the fifth. Leaving the court and renouncing [the layman's life] with self-arisen vows is the sixth. Practicing the mortifications by the river Nairañjana for six years is the seventh. Proceeding to the foot of the bodhi tree at the Vajra Seat is the eighth. Completely overcoming the hosts of devils is the ninth. Complete enlightenment in all things is the tenth. Turning the wheel of Dharma in its three cycles is the eleventh. [TL 176A] And the thorough passing beyond sorrow demonstrated in front of the twin sal trees in the city of Kuṣhinagara is the twelfth.

If being born in the Tuṣhita heaven is regarded as the first, then entering the womb and taking birth are counted together as one deed, where would one display [a twelfth deed]? All these enlightened activities are displayed in thoroughly impure worlds. As to the duration of the display, it will continue as long as the life cycle remains.

3.1.2.1.2.2.2.1.2.2.1.2.2.2.3.3. Showing the Procedure for Guiding Disciples

With the words "all created things are impermanent," "all contaminated things are suffering," "all things are selfless," and "nirvana is [the only] peace," the supreme emanation body who knows the art of liberation teaches the disadvantages of the life cycle, encouraging beings and disciples to develop weariness with the three realms of existence and to fully enter the state of peaceful nirvana. For those who have the spiritual potential for the universal vehicle, the Buddha also first guides them with the view that is the four insignia of the Dharma, as aforementioned. For those who are temporarily determined on the disciple and hermit buddha vehicle lineages, the Buddha guides them to the individual vehicle nirvana by giving such [dualistic] teachings. Then he causes those who have perfectly followed the path of peace far away from suffering and origination and who believe that they have attained the ultimate state of nirvana to arise from the sphere of peace. By the *White Lotus Sutra*, etc., he explains the reality of things, the purity of the three wheels, with the intention of establishing the one vehicle [for all], thus causing them to abandon their former view that merely seeks the cessation of suffering [TL 176B] in the life cycle and no more, educating them with the intuitive wisdom and art of the universal vehicle, and thus causing them to gain maturity in the universal vehicle. Then he grants them the prophecy of their [future] unsurpassed great enlightenment.

Question: This needs to be analyzed. When saints of the disciple and hermit buddha vehicles arise from the sphere of peace and enter upon the universal vehicle path, will they enter upon the path of accumulation, or upon the path of insight?

Answer: I shall refute others' positions first. Someone accepts that disciples have the realization of the selflessness of objective things, so he asserts that they will not enter into the universal vehicle path of insight or below it, since they have continuously realized emptiness. Therefore, there is no such need for them, and thus they will enter upon the seventh bodhisattva stage, and above. Someone [else] claims that the disciples do not have the realization of the objective selflessness. Thus he asserts that they will enter into the universal vehicle path of accumulation because they first need to study and contemplate emptiness, then enter into the path of application with the wisdom of meditation on the general meaning of emptiness in order to newly realize emptiness in a direct way on the path of insight.

Response: These views are incorrect. It follows that, even though they lack it, there would be no need for the disciples to cultivate the universal vehicle path [TL 177A] of insight, since they have continuously realized selflessness. Only those who have not realized selflessness need to cultivate the universal vehicle path of insight in order to newly realize it. If so, what is your answer? You may reply that the universal vehicle path of insight is distinguished by the realization at the first time of the subtle emptiness, not by the realization at the first time of the mere selflessness. Therefore, they still need to cultivate it.

Response: In this case, then the person who holds the former assertion should accept that disciples must cultivate the universal vehicle path of insight in their continuums since this path is distinguished by vast collections of merit and wisdom, and the cultivation of such a path needs the universal vehicle path of accumulation and application as its cause. If you reply that there is no problem here, as, according to the former assertion, the collection of merit included in the universal vehicle path will be completed on the seventh stage and above, my response is: if so, then one who desires the unsurpassed enlightenment should enter into the disciple vehicle path first because he can attain sainthood in three rebirths with great endeavor, and then he does not need to cultivate the sixth stage and below. Instead he enters into the seventh stage directly, and because it is the universal vehicle path of accumulation and application, he needs to collect merit for an incalculable eon. Therefore, [TL 177B] because of that it should be known that it is incorrect if you assert that saints of the disciple vehicle do not need to cultivate the universal vehicle path of accumulation and application, or that the eighth stage is the lowest universal vehicle path for saints to enter.

Second, [I will establish my own theory]. The saints of the disciple and hermit buddha vehicles, granted that they have realized directly both subtle selflessnesses, [still] must enter into the universal vehicle path of accumulation when they are converted to the universal vehicle. First, they need to analyze the infinite categories included in the collection of merit by study and contemplation, then put them into practice with the intuitive wisdom of meditation for countless eons. Finally they will achieve the first bodhisattva stage and the twelve excellences of "the hundred," etc. If you assert that saints on the universal vehicle path of accumulation and application are naive ordinary people, it should be recognized as a deprecation of holy persons. Moreover, it is a terrible wrong view if you think that the abandonment on the transcendent path can be reversed and that liberation is not reliable.

You might assert that they must have cultivated part of the universal vehicle path of insight, since they have already realized emptiness before and they do not need to realize it anew. I respond that you should think of my response to your position on how disciples who do not have the realization of objective emptiness enter into the universal vehicle path. Here the disciples who have become saints have realized the meaning of emptiness by reliance on a brief reasoning. Once entered into the universal vehicle path, [TL 178A] they analyze and ascertain the meaning of emptiness by means of countless lines of reasoning, as mentioned in the *Wisdom: Root Verses on Centrism*. The realization of the "pervasiveness of the ultimate element" is posited as the first bodhisattva stage, not that of the noble beings of the disciple and hermit buddha vehicles. Furthermore, although there is no difference in the realization of the ultimate element, there is a huge difference [between the universal vehicle and the other vehicles] in the power of destroying the opposing forces, akin to the difference between Mount Meru and a mustard seed. Therefore, whether disciples are accepted as having the realization of objective emptiness or not, they enter into the universal vehicle by means of the path of accumulation.

In addition to this, suppose there are two persons, one determined in the universal vehicle lineage and the other temporarily determined in the disciple vehicle lineage, and both enter into the path of accumulation: in terms of the attainment of the unsurpassed enlightenment, the universal vehicle person will achieve it very fast, while the other will go quite slowly—this is the difference. Although there are many lines of reasoning to prove this, I am afraid it will be too much, and so will not elaborate here.

Someone asserts that the statement in the *White Lotus Sutra* proclaiming that the disciples enter into the universal vehicle path, which you use as a proof, is intended for those disciples whose final enlightenment can be changed. Response: Your assertion does not have any valid reason in a direct or oblique way. Moreover, if you say this is a general expression used for a particular situation, this also cannot be trusted. Hence it should be known that this sutra is a sutra [TL 178B] that well establishes the ultimate one vehicle.

3.1.2.1.2.2.2.1.2.2.1.2.3. Conclusion

The buddha reality—and the truth body that is eternally absorbed in that—is difficult to understand; thus it is profound. The perfectly beatific body, with its multitude of abilities to discipline disciples, is magnificent. The supreme emanation body, which is perceived even by alienated individuals, strongly leads disciples according to their aims and thoughts. Thus, this set of three bodies should be known, respectively, as the profound [body], the beatific body, and the great lord.

Here, the first is the truth body and the latter are the material bodies. As matter abides in space, the latter two bodies abide in the first, the truth body, since the two kinds of material body can abide in transcendent reality when it is completely purified of taints.

3.1.2.1.2.2.2.1.2.2.2.2. Explaining the Uniqueness of Being Permanent . . . 2.1. Prelude

«265» Here [is one verse with respect to these three bodies' eternal performance of benefiting beings and bringing about happiness:]

3.1.2.1.2.2.2.1.2.2.2. 2.2. Explaining the Meaning . . . 2.1. Statement . . . 1.1. The Seven Reasons the Material Bodies Are Permanent

The material bodies remain in the life cycle until it ends, since they have the endless causes of the two kinds of inexhaustible stores as prerequisite, and the sentient beings who are the objects the buddhas aim to benefit are inexhaustible—the only purpose of becoming a buddha is to benefit beings. They have unbroken compassion, committing to benefit beings until the end of the life cycle, and superknowledges. They are endowed with the intuitive wisdom that knows the varieties of things [TL 179A] and the intuitive wisdom that knows things just as they are, as well as the perfect bliss of meditative equipoise that is never harmed by suffering. They are masters of the Dharma and are never driven by any faults.

3.1.2.1.2.2.2.1.2.2.2. 2.2.1.2. The Three Reasons the Truth Body Is Permanent

The demon of death has been vanquished. Being naturally abiding, not any sort of intrinsically real entity, it is the nondeceptive protector of all worldly beings, i.e., disciples. Therefore, it should be known that being permanent is unique to the three bodies.

3.1.2.1.2.2.2.1.2.2.2. 2.2.2. Explanation . . . 2.1. Prelude

«266» Its [condensed meaning should be known by the six verses (II.63–67)].

3.1.2.1.2.2.2.1.2.2.2. 2.2.2.2. The Root Text . . . 2.1. Explanation of Each Point . . . 1.1. The Seven Reasons the Material Bodies Are Permanent . . . 1.1. The Cause of Helping the World

As to having the inexhaustible stores as prerequisite, buddhas offered their bodies, lives, and enjoyments and upheld the holy Dharma in order to benefit sentient beings. As to their inexhaustible purpose, they made the commitment that they would place all beings in the state of unsurpassed enlightenment, and, in order to benefit all sentient beings, they fulfill their vow as initially taken. As for the fulfillment of that commitment, buddhahood is both cleansed from addictive obscurations and purified from objective obscurations, with full engagement of compassion until the end of the life cycle. [TL 179B] As for showing the bases of magical powers that enable the buddhas to stay until the end of the life cycle, they stay and act forever by means of these four bases of magical powers.

3.1.2.1.2.2.2.1.2.2.2. 2.2.2.2.1.1.1. The Cause of Nonforsaking

They stay forever from attachment and aversion in terms of what is undertaken and what is forsaken, since by intuitive wisdom they are freed from the habit fixed on the dualistic extremes of the life cycle and nirvana. They have the perfect bliss of meditative equipoise that is never harmed by suffering, since they always possess the perfect bliss of samādhi, beyond imagination. They are never under the control of any faults since, while acting in the world, they are untainted by worldly things.

3.1.2.1.2.2.2.1.2.2.2. 2.2.2.2.1.2. The Three Reasons the Truth Body Is Permanent

[The truth body] is the state where the devil of death has been completely destroyed, since it is free from dying and is the attainment of peace, and no devil of death roams therein. It is naturally abiding in lack of intrinsic reality status since the Sage is distinguished by always being in the meditation of reality that is of uncreated nature, and has been primordially in the peace of the emptiness of intrinsic reality. It is the eternal refuge for the world, since it has both the purpose and the power of a refuge, thus being fit to be a refuge, etc., for all those who are bereft of refuge.

3.1.2.1.2.2.2.1.2.2.2.2.2.2.2. Conclusion

The first seven reasons show the permanence of the material bodies, while the latter three clarify why the truth body is eternal. This statement illustrates permanence in terms of the inexhaustibility of the causes that bring about the benefit and happiness of sentient beings, not a "permanent entity" that is an established, independent thing.

3.1.2.1.2.2.2.1.2.2.2.3. Explaining the Uniqueness of Being Inconceivable [TL 180A] . . . 3.1. Prelude

«267» [It should be known that the mode of transformation attained] by tathāgatas [is inconceivable. The verse concerning the meaning of inconceivability is as follows:]

3.1.2.1.2.2.2.1.2.2.3.2. Statement

There are six reasons concerning the inconceivability of buddhas' three bodies, the first five concerning the truth body and the sixth concerning the material bodies.

Even the noble bodhisattvas cannot conceive the sphere of the Victor, [even knowing] the nature, divisions, and number regarding the three bodies, since [the truth body] cannot be fully understood by speech, not being its object. [The truth body is inconceivable,] since it is included in the ultimate, being the object of meditation, and since it is not a field or object for mistaken thought and is beyond any example. It cannot be fully comprehended by reason and example, since it is transcendent and unsurpassed. These are the reasons the truth body is inconceivable. [As for the inconceivability of the material bodies], if you assert that this inconceivability is in direct contradiction to a common acknowledgment that noble bodhisattvas can directly perceive the material bodies but the childish cannot, we respond that, although noble bodhisattvas can directly perceive them, the material bodies are inconceivable, since they are not included in either the extreme of existence or peace, being of the nature of the unlocated nirvana.

3.1.2.1.2.2.2.1.2.2.3.3. Explanation [TL 180B] . . . 3.1. Prelude

«268» Its condensed meaning is comprised of the individual explanations of the meanings of inconceivability and how they fit with the two bodies.

3.1.2.1.2.2.2.1.2.2.3.3.2. The Root Text . . . 2.1. Explaining Each Point of Inconceivability

It is inconceivable to the persons who are not fully enlightened, since it cannot be verbally expressed in such a way that it can be perfectly realized. It is inexpressible since it consists of the ultimate. It is the ultimate since it cannot be conceptually constructed in a perfect manner. It is not inferable since it is not fully inferable by thought in a comprehensive manner. It cannot be scrutinized since it is unsurpassed. It is unsurpassed since its excellent qualities are not included in existence and peace. It is freedom since it does not dwell on extremes of existence and peace. This is because there is no discrimination about the excellent qualities of peace and the faults of existence—[buddhas] realize the ultimate equality of these two.

3.1.2.1.2.2.2.1.2.2.2.3.3.2.2. Explaining It in Terms of Two Bodies

The [first] five reasons show that the truth body is beyond the reach of conceptual thought since it is difficult to understand and is subtle. The sixth reason shows that the material bodies are inconceivable since they show various continuums emanated from one body but in reality are not [really any one of] such entities.

3.1.2.1.2.2.2.1.2.2.2.3.3.2.3. Conclusion

Thus the last mode of the self-arisen ones, or buddhas, which are the three bodies, the ultimate transformation, is not even seen by those great sages, bodhisattvas on the pure stages who have attained power. The Victor's three bodies [TL 181A] are inconceivable to them, since all his excellences of unsurpassed intuitive wisdom, great compassion, and so on, are finally perfected.

3.1.2.1.2.2.2.1.3. Title of the Chapter

Thus, the exposition of the commentary of the second chapter "The Enlightenment Endowed with the Twofold Purity" of *The Sublime Continuum of the Universal Vehicle, Analysis of the Precious Spiritual Potential,* elucidating the intention of the universal vehicle sutras definitive in meaning, is completed.

> Based on my holy teacher's instructions, clearly
> I have explained great enlightenment with its two purities,
> Attained by the purification of the naturally pure
> Tathāgata element, by the teaching of sixty purifications.[392]

---

392. *sbyongs byed drug cu'i chos kyis sbyangs pa.* We need a super-super commentary to figure out the source of these "sixty."

CHAPTER III
Excellences

3.1.2.1.2.2.2.2. Exposition of the Excellences on the Basis of the Enlightenment . . . 2.1. Prelude . . . 1.1. Prelude of the Previous Statement

"The suchness free from taints has been explained." As mentioned previously, this statement can be regarded as the conclusion of the last chapter. Someone who asserts that enlightenment exists within a sentient being's continuum is completely unable to see this conclusion and the prelude of [Asaṅga's] *Commentary*, which states that the element is the "tainted suchness" and the enlightenment is the "suchness free from taint."

3.1.2.1.2.2.2.2.1.1. Prelude of the Next Statement

《269》 Now I shall discuss those untainted excellences on the basis of that enlightenment. The reason [they] are untainted [TL 181B] is that these excellences are not different in nature from the enlightenment endowed with the twofold purity, akin to the lights, colors, and shapes. Therefore, a verse after that regarding the buddhas' excellences is presented:

3.1.2.1.2.2.2.2.2. Explaining the Meaning . . . 2.1. Brief Statement . . . 1.1. Brief Statement Regarding Those on the Basis

Benefit for oneself, i.e., the truth body, and benefit for others, i.e., the material bodies on the basis of that truth body, are equivalent to the ultimate body and the conventional bodies. The first body is endowed with the thirty-two excellences of freedom, and the second body is endowed with the thirty-two marks as the fruit of evolutionary development. These should be known as the sixty-four kinds of excellences on the basis of the two bodies.

3.1.2.1.2.2.2.2.2.1.2. Brief Statement Regarding the Basis

«270» Question: What is stated by this? Answer: The place of self-perfection, which is included in the ultimate perfection of self-benefit, is the ultimate body, including the uncreated truth body and the intuitive truth body. The first body, i.e., the self-benefit truth body, is endowed with the excellences of freedom, which are the powers, etc. The symbolic body of sages, which teaches disciples by using conventional words, is the basis of others' marvelous qualities, bestowing upon disciples the higher rebirths and the ultimate goodness. The second body has the evolved excellences, which are the thirty-two marks of a great being.

3.1.2.1.2.2.2.2.2.2. Detailed Explanation by Means of Similes . . . 2.1. Prelude

«271» The following text passages discuss the powers, and so on, and how to understand these by the similes such as a vajra. [TL 182A]

3.1.2.1.2.2.2.2.2.2.2. Explaining the Meaning . . . 2.1. The Actual Meaning . . . 1.1. General Statement by Means of a Summary Stanza

The summary verse states: The [ten] powers are like a vajra that cleanses and destroys the obscuration of ignorance within disciples' continuums. The four fearlessnesses act like an intrepid lion amid the entourage. The eighteen distinctive qualities of a tathāgata are like space, because of his attainment of the uncommon excellences. The so-called teaching refers to the action of teaching. The Sage's teaching, i.e., the two kinds of material bodies, which give teaching by their natures, are like a water-moon since the beatific body appears like a reflection as the fruit of the collection of merit, and the supreme emanation body in turn appears like a reflection of that [beatific body].

3.1.2.1.2.2.2.2.2.2.2.1.2. Detailed Explanation of Each Point . . . 2.1. Explaining the Excellence of Freedom . . . 2.1. Explaining the Ten Powers . . . 1.1. Prelude

«272» The powers possessed [by the two bodies] refers to those that follow:

3.1.2.1.2.2.2.2.2.2.1.2.1.2. The Root Text . . . 2.1. Divisions

1. Experientially knowing the causality of the life cycle such as suffering, etc., respectively, without any mistake about the valid law of causality, is the power of knowing right from wrong. It is accomplished by the solid conviction of the certainty of the law of causality as well as of the two types of the spirit of enlightenment, and their accessories. [TL 182B]

2. Experientially knowing the certainty of karmic evolution, the way karmic evolution increases, the fact that any produced karmic evolutionary action will not be lost, and the fact that the consequence of a karmic evolutionary action that an individual did not commit cannot be experienced by this [same] person is the power of knowing the consequences of actions. It is accomplished by the conviction of [the certainty of the] law of causality.

3. The power of knowing the various inclinations of beings, superior and inferior, i.e., deluded ones and pure ones, such as having faith, etc., is accomplished by the previous actions of giving suitable teachings to disciples with different inclinations.

4. The power of knowing different types of disciples in terms of the spiritual lineages of their continuums is accomplished by the previous actions of giving suitable teachings to disciples of different types.

5. The power of knowing the various capacities [of disciples] for individual vehicle and universal vehicle [practices] is accomplished by the previous actions of giving suitable teachings to disciples with different capacities.

6. The power of knowing all paths that lead everywhere, including the paths of the six transmigrations in the life cycle and the paths to the three kinds of enlightenment, is accomplished by the previous practice of various vehicles and paths.

7. The power of knowing the tainted state and the pure state due to meditations, liberations, concentrations, trances, etc., is accomplished by the previous practice of concentrations.

8. Experientially knowing all previous births of self and others is the power of remembering former lives. [TL 183A] It is accomplished by not wasting virtuous roots while on the path of learning.

9. The power of knowing deaths and future lives, which is included in divine sight, is accomplished by the previous generosity of offering light to beings and faithfully teaching the transcendent path.

10. The power of knowing that taints are pacified is accomplished by previous actions of giving teaching for the sake of the termination of taints, and the self-actualization of this aim. These are the ten kinds of powers.

3.1.2.1.2.2.2.2.2.2.1.2.1.2.2. Explaining the Simile and the Similarity

«273» The statement that "the term 'vajra-like' means" is the prelude. The actual explanation is as follows: six intuitive wisdoms—including knowing right from wrong, knowing the consequences of karmic evolution, knowing the various types, knowing the various capacities of beings, knowing their inclinations both tainted and pure, and knowing all paths—pierce the armor of untainted ignorance, i.e., objective obscuration. Therefore, such power resembles a vajra. Three intuitive wisdoms—including knowing absorptions, etc., knowing former lives, knowing deaths and future lives revealed by divine sight—destroy the firm walls of meditative obscuration. Therefore such power resembles a vajra. Knowing the exhaustion of taints fells the trees of addictive obscuration. Therefore, such power resembles a vajra.

3.1.2.1.2.2.2.2.2.2.1.2.2. Explaining the Four Fearlessnesses . . . 2.1. Prelude

«274» The attainment of the four fearlessnesses refers to those that follow: [TL 183B]

3.1.2.1.2.2.2.2.2.1.2.2.2. Actual Meaning

1. [Buddhas] admit that "we are perfectly enlightened in all things." No valid accusation that "you do not know this" can stand against such a statement. The accomplishment of this fearlessness comes from previous non-stinginess in [teaching the] Dharma.

2. [Buddhas] state that addictive obscuration and objective obscuration are the obscurations to liberation and omniscient intuitive wisdom, and thus come to an end. No valid accusation that "attachment, etc., are not the obscurations to liberation" can stand against such a statement. The accomplishment of this fearlessness of stating the obscurations comes from previously not succumbing to obscurations.

3. [Buddhas] state that these paths are the ones leading to the attainment

of liberation. No valid accusation can stand against such a statement. The accomplishment of this fearlessness of stating the path of liberation comes from their previous habitual practice of the path of liberation.

4. [Buddhas] state and admit that "we have attained the cessation of addictions and evolutionary instincts without remainder." No valid accusation can stand against such a statement. The accomplishment of this fearlessness of admitting the exhaustion of impurities comes from previous abandonment of deluded pride.

The subjects and purposes of [buddhas'] teaching in connection with the four fearlessnesses are demonstrated as follows:

The first fearlessness [shows] that [buddhas] have omniscient intuitive wisdom about all objects of knowledge, and [also can] cause others to gain such wisdom. [TL 184A]

The second fearlessness [shows] that [buddhas] have abandoned all things to be abandoned within their own continuums, and cause others to abandon those within others' continuums.

The third fearlessness [shows] that [buddhas] have relied upon the paths, and cause others to rely upon them.

The fourth fearlessness [shows] that [buddhas] have the unsurpassed and stainless cessation to be attained, and cause others to attain [such cessation] in others' continuums.

It should be known that the attainment of such fruition comes from their previous habitual practice of recognizing the suffering coming from the disadvantages [of the life cycle], abandoning its origin, relying upon the paths, and realizing cessation, as well as giving teaching to others. Therefore, the great sages are fearless and unhindered anywhere among objects of knowledge, since they ultimately teach the truth, the unmistaken four noble truths, accomplishing the welfare of self and others.

3.1.2.1.2.2.2.2.2.2.1.2.2.3. Application of Simile to Meaning

«275» The statement "the term 'lion-like' means" is the prelude.

The application of the simile to the meaning goes like this: the lord of beasts is ever fearless of other animals to the far ends of the jungle, undauntedly roaming among all beasts. Likewise, in any societies, the Bhagavān of Sages is a Human Lion as well, remaining at ease without fear, independent, endowed with stable concentration, with the strength to overcome any hostile forces. [TL 184B]

3.1.2.1.2.2.2.2.2.2.1.2.3. Explaining the Eighteen Distinctive Excellences of the Buddha . . . 3.1. Prelude

«276» The possession of the eighteen distinctive excellences of the Buddha refers to the following:

3.1.2.1.2.2.2.2.2.2.1.2.3.2. Explaining the Meaning . . . 2.1. Statement . . . 1.1. Recognizing Natures

There are six [excellences] included in behavior: (1) there is no mistake with regard to the physical, such as wandering onto a stray path, etc.; (2) there is no mistake with regard to the verbal, such as boisterousness, etc.; (3) the Teacher never forgets; (4) his concentration never falters; (5) there is no thought of difference between the life cycle and nirvana; (6) there is no indifferent equanimity without analysis in each case.

There are six distinctive realizations: (7–12) his will, creative energy, mindfulness, and wisdom never fail, nor do his liberation or intuitive insight of liberation. The last two refer, [respectively,] to unfailing abandonment, and realization that directly experiences unfailing abandonment.

There are three distinctive activities: (13–15) all actions of body, speech, and mind are preceded and controlled by wisdom.

There are three distinctive wisdoms: (16–18) this wisdom is unobstructed with regard to all knowable things in all three times.

3.1.2.1.2.2.2.2.2.2.1.2.3.2.1.2. These Are Special Features of Buddhas

Thus these eighteen excellences are distinctive to the Teacher, unshared by others.

3.1.2.1.2.2.2.2.2.2.1.2.3.2.2. Explanation

[TL 185A] Mistakenness, boisterousness, forgetfulness, not concentrating due to mental agitation, thoughts of difference between the life cycle and nirvana, and indiscriminate equanimity—the Sage does not have any of these. His will to teach beings, his creative energy to benefit beings, and his mindfulness in accurately seeing all beings' continuums, his pure and unstained wisdom, his constant liberation, and his intuitive insight of liberation recognizing all knowable objects, do not fail. His three enlightened activities are preceded and controlled by wisdom. He manifests his vast knowing, always unhindered in its vision of the three times.

I will not describe the causes of these eighteen distinctive excellences since it would be too prolix. By such realization of distinctive excellences, the Buddha fearlessly turns the great wheel of holy Dharma for beings with the three different spiritual potentials. Only buddhas are endowed with such insight and such great compassion—this is what all buddhas attain. Moreover, the insight just mentioned is a distinctive feature of the [great] compassion that turns the wheel of Dharma.

3.1.2.1.2.2.2.2.2.2.1.2.3.2.3. Application of Similes

«277» The statement "the term 'space-like' means" is a prelude. Application of this simile to its meaning goes like this: the nature or characteristic of an entity, such as firmness, wetness, warmth, motion, and so on, is not the characteristic of space. Any of the characteristics of space, such as being non-obstructive, able to contain material [TL 185B] things, and so on, is not a feature of matter. However, it is still similar to many other things. Earth, water, fire, wind, and space, being equally objects of an ordinary person's consciousness, have something in common with the world. The eighteen distinctive excellences and worldly beings have nothing in common, not even as much as a single atom—thus they are "distinctive."

3.1.2.1.2.2.2.2.2.2.1.2.2. Explaining the Evolved Excellences . . . 2.1. Prelude

«278» The bodily possession of the thirty-two signs of the great being refers to the following:

3.1.2.1.2.2.2.2.2.2.1.2.2.2. Explaining Meaning . . . 2.1. Detailed Explanation

1. His feet are well set like the belly of a turtle. This is the consequence of his previous firm vows.

2. He has wheel signs on the palms of his hands and feet. This is the consequence of his previous service to his mentors.

3. His arches are broad and his ankle bones do not protrude. This is the consequence of his previous non-disparagement of others.

4. He has long fingers and toes. This is the consequence of his previous protection of beings.

5. His fingers and toes are webbed. This is the consequence of his previous causing of harmonious relations between others.

6. His skin is soft and smooth, and remains youthful. This is the consequence of his previous generosity of giving away soft clothes.

7. His body has seven round curves at the backs of the hands and feet, neck, and shoulders. This is the consequence of his previous generosity of giving away food. Although the description found in the *Questions of Ratnadārikā* differs from [that in] other sutras, these are not to be thought of as being contradictory.

8. His calves are like an antelope's. This is the consequence of his upholding the Dharma of previous buddhas in a complete way. [TL 186A]

9. His penis is retracted in a sheath like an elephant's. This is the consequence of his previous maintaining secrecy and [even] renunciation of sexual activity.

10. His torso is like a lion's. This is the consequence of his previous undertaking of vast, virtuous enlightened activities in [gradual] steps.

11. There is no hollow between his clavicles. This is the consequence of his previous undertaking of merit.

12. His shoulders are round and even. This is the consequence of his previous generosity of fearlessness and offering condolence.

13. His hands and arms are round, soft, and even, and his arms are long. This is the consequence of his previous enthusiastic assistance to others.

14. His stainless body is endowed with an aureole of light. This is the consequence of his previous undertaking of the ten skillful virtues without weariness.

15. His neck, unblemished, resembles a conch. This is the consequence of his previous generosity of giving medicines. This sign is not found in other sutras.

16. He has a lion's cheek. This is the consequence of his previous deed of causing others to perfect their virtues.

17. His forty teeth are equal in both jaws, with twenty in each. This is the consequence of his previous equanimity toward others.

18. His teeth are without gaps. This is the consequence of his previous deed of causing others to work out disharmonies.

19. His teeth are even and pure. This is the consequence of his previous generosity of giving beautiful jewels.

20. His teeth are very white. This is the consequence of his previous vigilance in his three enlightened activities by means of body, [speech, and mind], etc.

21. His tongue is long and slender. This is the consequence of his previous maintaining of truthful speech.

22. He has an infinitely keen sense of supreme taste. This is the consequence of his immeasurable previous merits as well as his generosity of giving delicious food. [TL 186B]

23. He has an effortless, original voice like the kalavinka bird's, and like the tone of [the god] Brahmā. This is the consequence of his previous gentle speech.

24. His beautiful eyes are like blue lotuses. This is the consequence of his previous meditation on loving [all beings].

25. His lashes are like a cow's. This is the consequence of his previous habitual practice of nondeception.

26. He has a white hair-tuft curling to the right between his eyebrows, embellishing his face. This is the consequence of his previous praising of those worthy of praise.

27. His head has a turban-shaped protrusion on the crown. This is the consequence of his previous respect to his mentors.

28. His clean, firm skin is golden-hued, like that of a supreme being. This is the consequence of his previous diligence in requesting teachings and his generosity of giving pleasant clothes and bedding.

29. His body hairs are fine and soft; each of them curls to the right and stands straight up. This is the consequence of his previous retreat in quiet places, upholding and promoting the holy Dharma, and following the instructions of his mentors.

30. His stainless hair resembles a blue gem in color. This is the consequence of his previous compassion toward all beings, and his renunciation of weapons.

31. His body has the symmetry of a banyan tree. This is the consequence of his previous concentration on the equality of self and others.

32. The Great Sage who is all good and without any [prior] example has a tall, straight body that is seven cubits high, with a thick trunk endowed with

the strength of [the god] Nārāyana. This is the consequence of his previous erection of buddha idols, reconstruction of damaged stupas, protection and consolation given to frightened people, and his peacemaking between offended parties. [TL 187A]

3.1.2.1.2.2.2.2.2.2.2.1.2.2.2.2. Conclusion

The Teacher is so described in the *Questions of Ratnadārikā* as possessing these thirty-two signs, which are inconceivable to people of lesser intelligence, and [superior to] those of human kings.

3.1.2.1.2.2.2.2.2.2.2.1.2.2.2.3. Application of Similes to Meaning

The statement that "the term 'like a reflection of moon in water' means" is a prelude. Application of the simile to meaning goes like this: Just as in autumn the form of the moon is seen by ordinary people in the cloudless sky and in the deep blue water of a clean lake, the form of the all-pervasive Bhagavān, i.e., his beatific body, is seen by the victor heirs in the circle of the Buddha's retinue. Holy disciples and hermit buddhas as well as certain types of ordinary people can see the supreme emanation body, which is like a reflection of the beatific body.

3.1.2.1.2.2.2.2.2.2.2.1.2.3. Conclusion Based on Numbering

Therefore, in total the Tathāgata has sixty-four kinds of [excellences]: the ten powers, the four fearlessnesses, the eighteen distinctive excellences, and the thirty-two signs of a superbeing.

3.1.2.1.2.2.2.2.2.2.2.2. Application to Sutra Reference . . . 2.1. Prelude

This is the conclusion of the previous section.

3.1.2.1.2.2.2.2.2.2.2.2.2. The Root Text

«279» These sixty-four excellences are included in the thirty-two excellences of freedom and the thirty-two evolved excellences. [TL 187B] Each excellence's nature along with its cause is taught in the *Questions of Rat-*

nadārikā in their order as mentioned here. The details should be known as following this particular sutra.

3.1.2.1.2.2.2.2.2.2.2.2.3. [Asaṅga's] Commentary

Therefore, the sixty-four excellences of a tathāgata described in such order should be understood according to the *Questions of Ratnadārikā*.

3.1.2.1.2.2.2.2.2.3. Summarized Meanings of Similes . . . 3.1. Prelude

«280» The similes of the vajra, the lion, space, and the water-moon are taught, respectively, for these excellences. Their summary should be understood by the following ten verses.

3.1.2.1.2.2.2.2.3.2. The Root Text . . . 2.1. Brief Statement

The powers are indestructible by opposing forces, as taught by the simile of the vajra. The fearlessnesses are never weakened, as taught by the simile of the lion. The distinctive excellences of a buddha are incomparable, as taught by the simile of pure space. The two kinds of material body are unmoving, as taught by the simile of the water-moon.

3.1.2.1.2.2.2.2.3.2.2. Explanation of Each Simile . . . 2.1. Explaining the Common Features Regarding the Excellence of Freedom . . . 1.1. Detailed Explanation . . . 1.1. The Common Features Regarding the Powers . . . 1.1. The Distinctions of the Powers

As for the powers, such as knowing the causality of the life cycle and knowing how virtuous and nonvirtuous karmic evolutionary action produces happiness and suffering, respectively, first the six powers, then the three, and then the one, [TL 188A] in this order, have totally dispelled the obscurations to intuitive wisdom and meditation, along with those [obscurations'] evolutionary instincts, which resemble armor, a firm wall, and a tree, as they were pierced, shattered, and felled.

3.1.2.1.2.2.2.2.2.3.2.2.1.1.1.2. Explaining the Meaning of "Indestructible" . . .
2.1. Statement

Being weighty, essential, steadfast, and unchangeable, the powers of the
Great Sage are similar to a vajra.

3.1.2.1.2.2.2.2.2.3.2.2.1.1.1.2.2. Explanation

Why do they have weight? Because they are the ultimate essence of all
Dharmas. Why the ultimate essence? Because they are the ultimate of the
steadfast excellences. Why steadfast? Because they are unchangeable by any
opposing forces. Being unchangeable, they are like a vajra.

3.1.2.1.2.2.2.2.2.3.2.2.1.1.2. The Common Features Regarding the
Fearlessnesses . . . 2.1. Statement

Since he is not intimidated, is independent of others, is stable in his
mind, and is endowed with power to destroy opposing forces, the Sage is
like a lion. The Human Lion does not have fear in any company.

3.1.2.1.2.2.2.2.2.3.2.2.1.1.2.2. Explanation

Directly knowing everything knowable, free from the cause of fear, he
always remains unafraid of anyone, no matter who. Seeing that even pure
beings who have completely purified their addictions are not his equal, he is
not dependent on others. [TL 188B] He is stable since his mind is one-pointed
as to all things. He is endowed with power, having completely transcended
any evolutionary action driven by the ignorance instinct.[393]

3.1.2.1.2.2.2.2.2.3.2.2.1.1.3. The Common Features Regarding the Special
Excellences

Concerning the minds of ordinary beings, disciples, highly self-interested
hermit buddhas, insightful bodhisattvas, and self-originated truly perfect
buddhas, there are five similes for these five progressive levels of fineness:
the first four qualities sustaining the life of all such worldly beings are lik-

---

393. *ma rig pa'i bag chags kyis las zad pa'i rgal ba'i phyir.*

ened to earth, water, fire, and wind. Since the distinctive excellences of a buddha transcend the features of the worldly and of those beings beyond the world other than a buddha, they are similar to space, which simile is also applicable to the Buddha.

3.1.2.1.2.2.2.2.3.2.2.1.2. Conclusion

So the truth body manifests as these thirty-two excellences, the nature of the truth body and these excellences being indivisible, like a precious gem with its luminosity, radiance, and shape.

3.1.2.1.2.2.2.2.3.2.2.1. Explaining the Common Features Regarding the Evolved Excellences . . . 1.1. Explaining Excellences and Their Bases

Granting satisfaction whenever they are seen by disciples, these excellences depend on the so-called thirty-two signs in connection with the two kinds of material body, i.e., the supreme emanation body and the beatific body, [TL 189A] with their perfect enjoyment of the universal vehicle Dharma.

3.1.2.1.2.2.2.2.3.2.2.1.2. Explaining the Common Feature of Simile and Meaning

Those far from the pure element, the childish people who do have the fortune to see the Buddha by purification of their negative karmic evolutionary actions—those disciples, and hermit buddhas—see the supreme emanation body in the world, like the form of the moon in water. Those close to the pure element, who are the ultimate bodhisattvas, see the beatific body in the mandala of the Buddha, like the form of the moon in the sky. Therefore, these are beheld in two ways.

3.1.2.1.2.2.2.2.3. Title of the Chapter

Thus the exposition of the commentary of the third chapter "The Excellences Depending on the Enlightenment, Endowed with the Twofold Purity" of *The Sublime Continuum of the Universal Vehicle, Analysis of the Precious Spiritual Potential*, elucidating the intention of the universal vehicle sutras definitive in meaning, is completed.

Based on my venerable teacher's personal instructions,
I have clearly elucidated the intention of the Father and Son,
The thirty-two fruitions of the profound realization of freedom
As well as the thirty-two fruitions of the magnificent path.

CHAPTER IV
Enlightened Activities

3.1.2.1.2.2.2.3. Exposition of Enlightened Activities on the Basis of
Excellences . . . 3.1. Prelude . . . 1.1. The Prelude of the Previous Section

The untainted excellences [of the Buddha have been discussed].

3.1.2.1.2.2.2.3.1.2. The Prelude of the Next Section

«281» Now [I will discuss the enlightened] activities [of the Victor,
which are the activities of those excellences].

3.1.2.1.2.2.2.3.2. Exposition of the Meaning . . . 2.1. [TL 189B] Brief Statement
. . . 1.1. The Meaning of Effortlessness

In brief, [buddhas] engage in these [activities] in two ways: effortlessly
and continuously. Thus, there is a verse regarding the effortlessness and
continuousness of the buddhas' enlightened activities:
The pervasive Bhagavān, the Enlightened One, always effortlessly, spontaneously engages in the activities, such as intuitively knowing the various
temperaments, spiritual potentials, and faith of the disciples who desire a
higher rebirth or one of the three kinds of enlightenment; the [best] arts
of education, including the two kinds of material body, the emanated boat,
bridge, etc., as well as the peaceful and terrifying liberative arts. Such education suits [the disciples'] temperaments and will bring them the fruits of
higher rebirth or ultimate goodness, [so the Bhagavān] goes wherever they
are, at the right time, in order to teach them those arts.

3.1.2.1.2.2.2.3.2.1.2. The Meaning of Continuation . . . 2.1. Summary . . . 1.1. Detailed Explanation . . . 1.1. The Six Similes.

The six similes are an ocean, the sun, space, a treasure, clouds, and the wind.

3.1.2.1.2.2.2.3.2.1.2.1.1.2. The Six Implications

The six referents are the ten [bodhisattva] stages that originate [the excellences], the two kinds of stores that are the basis [of the ten stages], the great enlightenment as the fruition, the sentient beings that make enlightenment possible, the two obscurations that obscure beings' attainment of enlightenment, and the great compassion of the Buddha that eliminates obscurations. [TL 190A]

3.1.2.1.2.2.2.3.2.1.2.1.1.3. The Common Features of the Six Similes and Implications

The ten stages are like an ocean, since the water of intuitive wisdom ever increases [during these stages], thereby serving as the source of jewels of excellences. The two kinds of stores are like the sun, since they nourish all beings. The great enlightenment is like space, since it has limitless profound and magnificent excellences. The sentient beings are like a treasure, since they are the source of the jewels of the buddha excellences. The two obscurations are like clouds, since they are incidental, have no intrinsic reality, and do not [really] differ from what is obscured. The great compassion is like the wind, since it can dispel these obscurations.

3.1.2.1.2.2.2.3.2.1.2.1.2. Summary of This Section

The continuousness of the enlightened activities originates from its causes. This is demonstrated by "stage" and "store" since they definitely will bring about the great enlightenment and be the basis of that enlightenment. The enlightened activities have the nature of continuousness. This is demonstrated by "enlightenment" and "sentient being." The enlightened activities benefit disciples in this way. This is demonstrated by "addiction" and "great compassion."

3.1.2.1.2.2.2.3.2.1.2.2. The Meaning of the Text

The ten stages are likened to an ocean, since they are the source of multitudes of supremely precious excellences of the buddhas and because of the definite accomplishment of the causal and fruitional vehicles without exception, due to the increase of the water of intuitive wisdom. The two kinds of store are likened to the sun, since the sunlight of merit and wisdom enables the definite accomplishment of all vehicles without exception, [TL 190B] nourishing all beings. The great enlightenment is likened to space, since its excellences are vast, without middle or end, thus all-pervasive like space. Sentient beings are likened to a treasure, since [the buddhas] see that all beings without any distinction are the treasure that is able to elicit the untainted excellences of the buddhas, thereby being the source [of excellences]. The addictive and objective obscurations are likened to the clouds since they are like the incidental nets of clouds. The buddhas' compassion is likened to the wind, since it dispels those [cloud-like] obscurations in disciples' continuums. These should be understood in this way.

3.1.2.1.2.2.2.3.2.2. Detailed Explanation . . . 2.1. Prelude

«282» The summary of these two features should be understood by the following two and eight verses, respectively.

3.1.2.1.2.2.2.3.2.2.2. Explaining the Meaning . . . 2.1. Explaining the Spontaneity of the Enlightened Activities . . . 1.1. General Explanation

For whom is the disciples' continuum? How? By which education, such as by a peaceful way or a fierce way? Where? When? Since thought as such does not occur during these activities, the Sage's enlightened activities always function spontaneously.

3.1.2.1.2.2.2.3.2.2.2.1.2. Specific Explanations

[He] acts appropriately and spontaneously [according to] the temperaments of the disciples, such as [by considering their] various spiritual potentials and seeds, he employs the many means such as teaching on perfect generosity, and so on, [TL 191A] [as would be suitable] for each, providing education by different bodily displays and verbal utterances at whatever place and time [would be appropriate].

3.1.2.1.2.2.2.3.2.2.2.2. Explaining the Continuity of the Enlightened Activities . . . 2.1. Statement

Since, with regard to the definitive bringing about of great enlightenment, its basis of being brought about, its fruition, those sustaining the fruition, the obscurations to attaining such fruition, and the condition for cutting off these [obscurations], there is no conceptual thought, [a buddha's enlightened activities are continuous and uninterrupted].

3.1.2.1.2.2.3.2.2.2.2.2. Explanation . . . 2.1. Recognizing the Six Implications

The ten [bodhisattva] stages definitely bring about great enlightenment. The two stores of merit and wisdom provide the cause of their production, growing, and sustenance. Great enlightenment is the fruition of these two stores. The capability of the attainment of enlightenment is sustained in beings' continuums. These beings are obscured by endless addictions, the secondary addictions, and the evolutionary instincts included in objective obscuration.

A buddha's great compassion is the condition that at all times destroys these [obscurations]. To conclude: depending on a buddha's great compassion, the two obscurations in beings' continuums will be destroyed. By amassing the two stores and traveling on the ten stages in steps, [beings] will attain the fruition of great enlightenment. This is the meaning of the continuousness of activities. [TL 191B]

3.1.2.1.2.2.3.2.2.2.2.2.2. Presenting the Six Similes

These six referents regarding the continuous engagement in activities, being similar to an ocean, the sun, space, a treasure, clouds, and wind, are to be understood accordingly.

3.1.2.1.2.2.2.3.2.2.2.2.2.3. Explaining the Common Features of Similes and Implications

Holding intuitive wisdom's increasing water and excellences like gems, the ten stages are like an ocean. Nourishing all sentient beings, the two stores are like the sun. Being vast and without any middle or end in terms of its excellences, enlightenment is like the element of space. The element of beings is like a treasure since the reality of enlightened ones, the natural purity capable of producing all excellences, abides within them. Coincident, pervasive of what is obscured, and not existent in terms of their intrinsic reality, beings' addictions are like a host of clouds. Always ready to dispel these obscurations, the endless compassion is similar to wind. It is also suitable to state "endless wind."

3.1.2.1.2.2.2.3.2.2.2.2.3. General Summary

The release [is accomplished] by other conditions included in the ten stages and the two stores. The simile of release for the sake of others and the simile of its basis demonstrate the cause of the continuity of enlightened activities benefiting others. They see the equality of themselves and sentient beings in terms of the nature of reality. The simile of enlightenment and the simile of sentient beings demonstrate the nature of the continuity of enlightened activities benefiting others. The simile of addiction and the simile of endless compassion demonstrate the fact that their activity will not be completed [TL 192A] to its full extent; therefore, their enlightened activities will never cease until the end of the cyclic life.

3.1.2.1.2.2.2.3.2.3. The Way That the Enlightened Activities Engage Illuminated by the Simile . . . 3.1. Prelude

«283» After the previous chapter's statement regarding a buddha's uncreated excellences, the [same] sutra says:[394]

---

394. Here the Buddha addresses Mañjushrī in the vein of the sutra below, and Gyaltsap is remembering a passage closely connected to the passages quoted previously from the *Ornament of the Light of Wisdom Engaging the Sphere of All Buddhas Sutra* (D100).

O Mañjushrī, the Buddha is proclaimed "the one who manifests without any birth or death." . . . Why previously did one have doubt and worry about that?

Having cleared away the doubt that thinks, "Since the Buddha is uncreated and undestroyed, and without conceptual thought, how does he function ceaselessly and effortlessly to accomplish effectively the disciples' wishes according to their scope and their season, etc.?" Then, in order to create faith in the inconceivable scope of the Buddha, [the sutra teaches] in great detail using examples.

3.1.2.1.2.2.2.3.2.3.2. Explaining the Meaning . . . 2.1. Brief Statement . . .
1.1. The Root Text

«284» How are these meanings demonstrated by the similes? A tathāgata is similar to an indra god, to the drum in heaven, and to clouds. These three similes demonstrate the natures of a buddha's body, speech, and mind. The simile of a Brahmā god demonstrates the enlightened activities associated with body and speech. The simile of the sun demonstrates the enlightened activities associated with the mind. The three similes of a precious gem, an echo, and space [TL 192B] demonstrate the secret of body, the secret of speech, and the secret of the mind immersed in the ultimate. The simile of the earth demonstrates the ultimate transformation, the great compassion as the basis of the natures of body, speech, and mind, as well as of the activities and the secrets.

3.1.2.1.2.2.2.3.2.3.2.1.2. Showing Meanings Will Be Explained Later

A detailed explanation of this summary-like verse should be known in its sequence by the following paragraphs.

3.1.2.1.2.2.2.3.2.3.2.2. Detailed Explanation . . . 2.1. Detailed Analysis of the Similes and Implications . . . 2.1.1. The Natures of Body, Speech, and Mind Illustrated by the Similes . . . 1.1. Body Illustrated by the Simile of Indra's Form . . . 1.1. No-Thought Illustrated by the Simile . . . 1.1. The Simile

«285» The statement "the [simile] 'like Indra's form'" is a general prelude. The simile of Indra is explained in four subsections:

3.1.2.1.2.2.2.3.2.3.2.2.1.1.1.1.1. The Way That the Image Is Reflected on the Pure Ground

[TL 193A] If the surface of the ground of this world system or Jambud-vīpa changed into the nature of stainless sapphire, because of its purity one would see in it the form of the lord of all [desire realm] gods, Indra, with his following of many goddesses. One would see his beautiful palace, "the All-Victorious," the "Joyful" garden, and other divine abodes, the gods' various palaces, and manifold celestial items enjoyed by the gods.

3.1.2.1.2.2.2.3.2.3.2.2.1.1.1.1.2. This Condition Causes Others to Adopt Virtue

Once the assembly of men and women who inhabit the surface of the earth saw this vision, each would say: "Before a long time passes, may I too become like the lord of gods!" They would utter prayers like these—this refers to their intention—and to achieve this feat of becoming a lord of gods they would adopt virtue, such as a layperson's vow, and remain within it.

3.1.2.1.2.2.2.3.2.3.2.2.1.1.1.1.3. Reborn in Heaven without Knowing Reality

"This is just a vision." There would not be any such understanding in these people. Still their virtuous enlightened activities would lead them to be reborn in a celestial existence after they have departed from the surface of the earth.

3.1.2.1.2.2.2.3.2.3.2.2.1.1.1.1.4. There Is No Contradiction between the Fact That This Appearance Is the Cause of Benefit and That It Has No Conceptual Thought

This vision of Indra's image is free from thought and does not involve the slightest movement at all, and yet it is accompanied by great benefit on the earth, causing humans to achieve the state of a celestial being.

3.1.2.1.2.2.2.3.2.3.2.2.1.1.1.2. The Implications . . . 2.1. The Appearance of the Buddha's Body Is Due to the Purity of Mind

As demonstrated by this simile, [TL 193B] those endowed with untainted motivation such as faith in the Buddha, and so on, having cultivated the excellences of faith, etc., will perceive in their own minds the Buddha's appearance, which is endowed with signs and marks. They will see the Buddha while he is walking, while he is standing, sitting, or sleeping, and begging alms, etc. They will see him [engaging] in manifold forms of conduct. They will see him teaching the means leading to peace without suffering, as well as silently resting in meditative equipoise when not teaching, or displaying various forms of miracles in connection with body and speech. Endowed with great splendor and magnificence, [the Buddha] will be seen by all sentient beings who have pure karmic evolutionary momentum.

3.1.2.1.2.2.2.3.2.3.2.2.1.1.1.2.2. This Appearance Has Temporary and Ultimate Benefits

Once having seen this, they too will wish for buddhahood—this is the special intention after seeing the Buddha; therefore, to practice all transcendences, such as generosity and so on, in order to attain buddhahood, adopting its causes in a genuine way, and so they will attain the state they longed for—this is the special evolutionary action after seeing the Buddha.

3.1.2.1.2.2.2.3.2.3.2.2.1.1.1.2.3. This Appearance Has No Thought Yet It Can Benefit

These appearances of a buddha's material body are totally free from thought included in "mental articulation"[395] that [motivates one] to benefit beings. And the truth body does not involve the slightest movement. Nevertheless, they are accompanied by great temporary and ultimate benefits in the world. [TL 194A]

3.1.2.1.2.2.2.3.2.3.2.2.1.1.1.2.4. The Disciples Do Not Know Its Reality Yet Will Achieve Supreme Fruit . . . 4.1. In Terms of the Cause

Ordinary beings apprehend a buddha's material body as the one made of the collection of atoms. When a buddha's material body, which is in reality a buddha's intuitive wisdom, appears to the childish, they or the disciples do not have such insight: "This is the appearance of my own mind." Yet,

395. *yid kyi brjod pa.*

seeing this form causes [the purpose of the lives of] these beings to become meaningful.

Based on this statement, someone asserts that the two kinds of material body are not real buddhas but mere visions in disciples' minds. This position has been refuted before. Otherwise the two kinds of material body would be some erroneous conventional things. This statement does not show that the two kinds of material body are mere visions in disciples' minds. Instead it means that a perfectly enlightened one directly appears in the disciples' eye consciousness. [However,] one that directly appears to the disciples' eye consciousness is not a perfectly enlightened one himself. It is a mistake if you apprehend in this way. Furthermore, a buddhas' material bodies are not bodies made of the collection of atoms. It is also a mistake if you apprehend in this way. Therefore, it should be known that the basis of the appearance of a buddha's material body consists of a buddha's material body as well as of sentient beings' consciousness. The one that directly appears to sentient beings' consciousness is a reflection of a buddha but not a buddha himself. However, we shall not repudiate our Teacher by saying that the two kinds of a buddha's material body are reflections of a buddha but not that buddha himself. [TL 194B]

Furthermore, the supreme emanation body that directly appears to the childish is the reflection of the beatific body. This is the topic expressed by this simile.

3.1.2.1.2.2.3.2.3.2.2.1.1.1.2.4.2. In Terms of the Fruit

Then, relying on gradually beholding this form, i.e., accumulating two kinds of stores, all those who follow this universal vehicle will directly see their inner truth body included in their own continuums, by means of the eye of intuitive wisdom.

3.1.2.1.2.2.3.2.3.2.2.1.1.2. No Mistaken Creation and Extinction by the Simile . . . 2.1. Statement . . . 1.1. The Simile . . . 1.1. Although [the Buddha] Does Not Exist the Way He Appears as Having Creation and Extinction

If the earth of Jambudvīpa was rid of fearful places, such as valleys, ravines, etc., and turned into an even surface of blue sapphire that was flawless, radiant in color, and beautiful in shape—the distinguished basis; having a gem's multifold qualities and unstained luster—the distinguished adornment; various divine abodes and the forms of gods and their lord would shine forth within it because of its purity—the distinguished appearance of gods' forms. Then, as the earth gradually lost these properties and purity, these reflections would be invisible again and appear no more. [TL 195A]

3.1.2.1.2.2.2.3.2.3.2.2.1.1.2.1.1.2. This Appearance Is the Cause of the Desired Fruit

Yet, for their attainment of the state of Indra, the men and women would maintain vows and the pure conduct of disciplined behavior, practicing generosity, etc., scattering flowers, and so on, with wishes.

3.1.2.1.2.2.2.3.2.3.2.2.1.1.2.1.2. The Implications

Likewise, in order to make the Sage appear in the disciples' mind, which is similar to the ground of pure sapphire, the victor heir, with pure faith in the Buddha and sheer delight, would conceive the spirit of becoming a buddha. This shows that the appearance is the cause of benefit.

3.1.2.1.2.2.2.3.2.3.2.2.1.1.2.2. Explanation ... 2.1. The Simile and Import Regarding the Production of Appearance

Just as reflected by the pure sapphire ground, the physical appearance of the lord of gods is seen, likewise the form of the Sage is reflected in the purified ground of sentient beings' minds.

3.1.2.1.2.2.2.3.2.3.2.2.1.1.2.2.2. The Simile and Import Regarding the Extinction of Appearance

Whether these reflections of the Buddha will rise or set in beings' minds depends on their own minds' being polluted when faith is lost or unpolluted when faith is developed. Like the reflection of Indra, it appears in the worlds as being produced and extinguished, but the body of Indra itself is not produced or extinguished because of that. Similarly, the material bodies of the Buddha apprehended in the disciples' minds appear as being produced and extinguished, [TL 195B] but the material bodies are not viewed as "newly existent" or "extinguished." Although certain beings are unable to see the buddha body, it constantly benefits them without interruption.

3.1.2.1.2.2.2.3.2.3.2.2.1.1.2. Speech Illustrated by the Simile of the Drum in Heaven . . . 2.1. The Distinguished Feature of the Way of Benefiting Beings . . . 1.1. Protecting Gods from Being Careless . . . 1.1. Brief Statement . . . 1.1. The Simile

«286» The [simile] called "like the heavenly drum is as follows" is the prelude:[396] by the power of the former virtue of the gods in the Thirty-Three Heaven, a gigantic drum appears in the space above the Victorious Palace. This drum involves no effort of motivation, origin of sound such as tongue, palate, etc., or thought of "I"; no round form, etc., in shape, and no intention of making sound at all. The drum resounds again and again with "all created things are impermanent" and "all tainted things are suffering," "all things are selfless" and "nirvana is peace," admonishing all the carefree gods attached to worldly pleasure to develop renunciation of the life cycle and to seek their liberation. [TL 196A]

3.1.2.1.2.2.2.3.2.3.2.2.1.1.2.1.1.1.2. The Implications

Likewise, as demonstrated by this simile, though free from effort in motivation for teaching and so on, the buddha speech of the all-pervasive Bhagavān, the totally enlightened one, permeates sentient beings without exception, teaching the Dharma to those of good fortune who are about to be liberated.

3.1.2.1.2.2.2.3.2.3.2.2.1.1.2.1.1.1.2. Detailed Explanation . . . 2.1. The Simile and Import of the Distinguished Cause Regarding Sound

Just as the sound of the drum arises among the gods from their own previous good evolutionary actions, the Dharma spoken to the worldly beings by the Sage arises in the world from beings' own previous good actions.

---

396. In the next four paragraphs, Gyaltsap closely paraphrases the *Sublime Continuum* verses IV.31–35.

3.1.2.1.2.2.2.3.2.3.2.2.1.1.2.1.1.2.2. The Simile and Import of the
Distinguished Fruit

Just as the sound of the drum accomplishes peace free from suffering
without motivated effort, origination of sound, form such as round shape,
etc., or the intention of "making sound," likewise, the Dharma, the buddha
speech, causes the accomplishment of the peace of nirvana in the disciples'
continuums without effort or any other such thing.

3.1.2.1.2.2.2.3.2.3.2.2.1.1.2.1.2. Protecting the Gods from Being Hurt . . .
2.1. The Simile

The sound of the drum in the city of heaven acts as the cause, yielding
the gift of fearlessness to the gods and granting them victory over the hosts
of antigods, when these, driven by their addiction to jealousy, make war
upon them, and it dispels the gods' carefree play motivated by attachment.
Moreover, addiction here refers to the special feature of the gods. [TL 196B]

3.1.2.1.2.2.2.3.2.3.2.2.1.1.2.1.2.2. The Implications

Likewise, as happens in the worlds, the buddha speech expresses the
way of the path, overcoming the addiction of attachment and the feeling
of manifest suffering by teaching the Dharma of the contemplations and
the trances, and proceeding to [both] the mere [personal] liberation and
the unexcelled peace of unlocated nirvana, eradicating the addictions
and sufferings of beings by teaching [the Dharma] that leads to liberation
and omniscience.

3.1.2.1.2.2.2.3.2.3.2.2.1.1.2.2. The Distinctive Feature of the Buddha Speech
. . . 2.1. The Reason That Other Heavenly Instruments Cannot Be the
Simile . . . 1.1. Question

«287» Why is the simile of a drum in heaven used to demonstrate that
the buddha speech brings about benefits? Because, except for the drum,
other instruments in heaven do not serve the same purpose. Only these
attractive sounds arise in their ears due to [their] previous activities. Here
"attractive sounds" refers to the sounds coming from the Dharma drum.
Other music in heaven comes after this.

3.1.2.1.2.2.2.3.2.3.2.2.1.1.2.2.1.2. Answer

Those [other instruments] have four qualities that do not correspond to [the excellences] of the voice of a tathāgata. Therefore, they cannot be used as its similes. What four? They are [that they are] partial, which refers to [those instruments] not exceeding their [TL 197A] timing and not repeating themselves again and again; not being beneficial, as they connect their listeners to carefree [amusements]; not being blissful, as they cause excessive increase of lust for pleasures; and not causing transcendent renunciation [to escape] from the life cycle.

3.1.2.1.2.2.2.3.2.3.2.2.1.1.2.2.2. The Reason That the Drum in Heaven Is Used as the Simile

The Dharma drum in heaven illustrates "being impartial," since it exhorts careless gods and does so in [constant] time. It illustrates "being beneficial," since it protects the gods from the harm and fear caused by the titanic antigods, etc., and makes them maintain their mindfulness. It illustrates "being blissful," since it causes [disciples'] continuums to become free from lust for improper desires, and accomplishes the delight and bliss of the Dharma. It illustrates "renunciation for liberation," since it proclaims the sounds of "impermanence, suffering, emptiness, and selflessness," and eradicates all mishaps and harm.

3.1.2.1.2.2.2.3.2.3.2.2.1.1.2.2.3. The Reason That the Buddha Melody Excels Other Music . . . 3.1. Brief Statement . . . 1.1. Prelude

«288» In brief, the mandala of the buddha melody is by far superior, since it has the common feature of these four features of the Dharma drum. Thus the verse regarding the mandala of the buddha melody goes as follows:

3.1.2.1.2.2.2.3.2.3.2.2.1.1.2.2.3.1.2. The Root Text

Pervasive in all beings, of ultimate benefit, bestowing temporary delight, and endowed with the threefold miracle that will be explained below, the Sage's voice is by far superior to the instruments in heaven.

3.1.2.1.2.2.2.3.2.3.2.2.1.1.2.2.3.2. Detailed Explanation ... 2.1. Prelude

«289» These four features by which [the buddha speech] is explained in summary, to be understood by the following four verses:

3.1.2.1.2.2.2.3.2.3.2.2.1.1.2.2.3.2.2. The Root Text ... 2.1. Detailed Explanation

The mighty sound of the drum in heaven does not reach the ears of those dwelling on earth, such as humans, etc., whereas the drumming sound of the buddha speech is superior, since it even reaches the worlds beneath earth, i.e., the hells, which are the seeds of the life cycle. Millions of instruments resound in heaven to set the fire of passion ablaze and to increase it. [TL 197B] The single voice of the Lord of Compassion is superior, since it manifests to quench all the fires of suffering. The sweet and bewitching sound of the instruments in heaven among the gods causes the increase of their distraction, whereas the speech of the Lord of Compassion is superior, since it exhorts one to reflect and commit the mind to the meditation that eliminates mental depression and agitation.

3.1.2.1.2.2.2.3.2.3.2.2.1.1.2.2.3.2.2.2. Conclusion

Any cause of happiness for earthly beings, humans, gods, and the beings in the unfortunate realms, in all the worlds without exception, to speak briefly, fully depends upon this voice that pervades all the worlds, not forsaking one, by miracles.

3.1.2.1.2.2.2.3.2.3.2.2.1.1.2.2.3.2.3. [Asaṅga's] Commentary

«290» The bliss that comes from the elimination of sufferings and mistakes depends upon the buddha speech. Therefore, the buddha speech is said to have the power that definitely eliminates mistakes and sufferings. The miracle of the body refers to the single body or multitude of bodies that pervades all worlds in the ten directions by the power of the buddhas' miracles. The miracle of the mind refers to the mind that knows the different states of the beings' minds without exception, directly seeing beings' deep unconscious. The miracle of instructional speech refers to the speech that teaches the [TL 198A] path to liberation as well as the path to higher rebirth [as a prerequisite].

3.1.2.1.2.2.3.2.3.2.2.1.1.2.3. It Is Not the Fault of Buddha Speech That a Few Disciples Cannot Hear . . . 3.1. Prelude

«291» Such an unobstructed mandala of the buddha speech encompasses like space all objects without interruption. It cannot be perceived by the disciples in all times and in all its aspects. This is not the fault of the mandala of the buddha speech itself.

A verse regarding this fault is as follows.

3.1.2.1.2.2.3.2.3.2.2.1.1.2.3.2. The Root Text

Without hearing, one cannot experience subtle sound, and all sounds loud or subtle do not even reach the ears of the gods. The former beings do not have ears, and the latter beings do not pay attention to what they hear— it seems to them that the sounds do not exist. Likewise, as the object of apprehension of the very finest intuitive wisdom, the subtle and profound Dharma only reaches the ears of someone whose mind is free of addiction, when being given the teaching on higher rebirth and ultimate goodness. Certain people temporarily are unable to hear it. This is not the fault of the buddha speech itself.

3.1.2.1.2.2.3.2.3.2.2.1.1.3. [Buddha's] Mind Illustrated by the Simile of Clouds . . . 3.1. Prelude

«292» The [simile] called "cloud-like" goes as follows:

3.1.2.1.2.2.3.2.3.2.2.1.1.3.2. Explaining the Meaning . . . 2.1. Explaining by Simile the Cause of Maturing the Disciples . . . 1.1. Statement . . . 1.1. The Simile

The monsoon clouds in summertime continuously and without any effort pour down their torrents of water, causing, on earth, the best possible crops [to grow]. [TL 198B]

3.1.2.1.2.2.2.3.2.3.2.2.1.1.3.2.1.2. The Implications

Just so, from the cloud of the buddha compassion the raincloud of the Victor's holy Dharma pours down its waters without thought, causing a harvest of virtue for beings, including higher rebirth and ultimate goodness. Therefore, it has that feature in common with the clouds.

3.1.2.1.2.2.2.3.2.3.2.2.1.1.3.2.1.2. Explanation . . . 2.1. The Simile

Just as the wind-born clouds cause rain to fall when the worldly beings follow the path of virtue, such as abandonment of killing, etc., . . .

3.1.2.1.2.2.2.3.2.3.2.2.1.1.3.2.1.2.2. The Implications

. . . so the buddha clouds of compassion, driven by compassion's wind, pour down the holy Dharma rain to nurture the virtue of beings in their continuums.

3.1.2.1.2.2.2.3.2.3.2.2.1.1.3.2.1.2.3. Explaining Its Meaning

The cloud of the Lord of Sages is the cause of the harvest of virtue for beings in the life cycle. What kind of cloud? It holds the essence of the untainted waters of the memory commands of language, meaning, etc., and the samādhis such as "the heroic march."[397] This cloud is under the sway of intuitive wisdom and great compassion. It abides in the midst of space unaffected by any faults. [TL 199A] What kinds of faults? They are the change that is the extreme of existence and the nonchange that is the extreme of peace. This indicates that intuitive wisdom is unaffected by the extreme of existence, and compassion is unaffected by the extreme of peace.

3.1.2.1.2.2.2.3.2.3.2.2.1.1.3.2.2. Explaining the Difference of Taste as the Result of Different Recipients by the Simile . . . 2.1. Prelude

≪293≫ The difference caused by various vessels:

---

397. *dpa' bor 'gro ba.*

3.1.2.1.2.2.2.3.2.3.2.2.1.1.3.2.2.2. Explaining the Meaning . . . 2.1. The Simile

Water of the eight qualities—cool, sweetly delicious, soft, clean, harmless to the throat, harmless to the stomach, pure, and light when it falls from the clouds—on earth acquires a great many tastes by touching salty and other ground.

3.1.2.1.2.2.2.3.2.3.2.2.1.1.3.2.2.2.2. The Implications

When the waters of the Dharma of the holy eightfold path included in the threefold education rain from the heart of the vast cloud of love and intuitive wisdom, they will also acquire many kinds of tastes, such as individual vehicle, universal vehicle, etc., by the different grounds of beings' continuums in the three kinds of spiritual lineages who have not entered the path to liberation.

3.1.2.1.2.2.2.3.2.3.2.2.1.1.3.2.3. Explaining the Engagement of [Enlightened Activities] without the Thought of Benefit and Harm by the Simile . . . 3.1. Prelude

«294» The engagement without bias:

3.1.2.1.2.2.2.3.2.3.2.2.1.1.3.2.3.2. The Root Text . . . 2.1. The Simile Regarding Different Recipients

Those with devotion to the universal vehicle, those who are neutral, and those with animosity are three groups [of beings] similar to humans who desire rain in order to grow crops, peacocks that are unaffected by the rain and remain neutral, and hungry ghosts that are burned by their own flames but never die. [TL 199B]

3.1.2.1.2.2.2.3.2.3.2.2.1.1.3.2.3.2.2. Detailed Explanation of Common Features . . . 2.1. The Simile Regarding Happiness and Anger

At the end of spring, when there are no clouds in the sky, human beings are unhappy and peacocks that rarely fly remain neutral. But hungry ghosts are happy. When rain is falling in summertime, the hungry ghosts suffer, but human beings are happy, and peacocks remain neutral. Similar to this, the arising and nonarising of the Dharma rain from the host of clouds of compassion also [lead to opposite reactions] in worldly beings who long for the universal vehicle Dharma or are hostile to it, respectively.

3.1.2.1.2.2.3.2.3.2.2.1.1.3.2.3.2.2.2. The Simile Regarding Nonconsideration of Benefit and Harm

When releasing a deluge of heavy drops or hurling down hailstones and thunderbolts, as in the line "emanating shattering diamond stones," a cloud never heeds any tiny beings such as ants, etc., hungry ghosts, or those who have sought shelter in the hills, not [considering] benefit or harm. Likewise, the cloud of intuitive wisdom and love of the buddhas does not heed whether its vast and subtle drops, i.e., its vast arts and profound ultimate truth that is difficult to understand, will purify the addictions of those who seek the teaching of the universal vehicle. It also pours down the Dharma rain with no bias for those who are hostile to the universal vehicle, increasing the evolutionary instinct for holding the view of a self. [TL 200A]

3.1.2.1.2.2.3.2.3.2.2.1.1.3.2.4. Explaining That the Fire of Suffering Can Be Extinguished by the Simile ... 4.1. Prelude

«295» Extinguishment of the fire of suffering:

3.1.2.1.2.2.3.2.3.2.2.1.1.3.2.4.2. Explaining the Meaning ... 2.1. The Suffering That Is Observed by Compassion ... 1.1. The Basis of Cyclic Life

In this cycle of beginningless birth and death, five paths are open for sentient beings to tread. [Sentient beings] are wandering in the life cycle under the sway of karmic evolution and addictions without beginning. If no efforts are made to stop it, it will never naturally reach its end, thus it is beginningless and endless.

3.1.2.1.2.2.3.2.3.2.2.1.1.3.2.4.2.1.2. The Disadvantages of Cyclic Life

Just as no sweet scent is found in excrement, no genuine happiness will be found among the five kinds of beings. Beings mistakenly apprehend the suffering that diminishes in strength as happiness. But [pain] from weapons or from a wound touched by salt, and so on, never transcends the nature of suffering. [TL 200B]

3.1.2.1.2.2.2.3.2.3.2.2.1.1.3.2.4.2.2. Means of Eliminating Suffering . . . 2.1. Giving Teachings

The great rain of holy Dharma pours down in cascades from the cloud of compassion, soothing and appeasing this pain of the life cycle.

3.1.2.1.2.2.2.3.2.3.2.2.1.1.3.2.4.2.2.2. Realizing the Disadvantages of the Life Cycle on the Basis of Teaching

"Even the gods have the suffering of death and transmigration, and humans suffer from desperate striving for enjoyment!" Realizing this, those endowed with the critical intuitive wisdom of the path to liberation have no desire for even the highest [state] of a lord of humans and gods such as Indra, a world emperor, etc., cultivating the genuine ambition to seek liberation. [Those who possess] the intuitive wisdom that realizes the disadvantages of the life cycle and the advantages of liberation, i.e., the proper ideation as the inner condition, faithfully follow the holy words of the Tathāgata, i.e., the other's verbal teaching as the outer condition. So insight makes them see: "This contaminated aggregation is the truth of suffering! This karmic evolution and addiction is the truth of origination! This cessation of suffering is the truth of cessation! And this wisdom directly realizing selflessness is the truth of the path!"

3.1.2.1.2.2.2.3.2.3.2.2.1.1.3.2.4.2.2.3. Familiarizing Oneself with the Reality of the Four Noble Truths in Order to Attain Liberation

In the case of illness, if one does not know its danger, no desire will arise to cure it and one will not seek a means of cure, so one needs to diagnose it first. Then one will realize that if its cause is not removed the illness cannot be cured, so one removes its cause. As a result, one will attain the happy state of health, relying on suitable medicine that removes the cause [of illness]. [TL 201A] Similarly, one first needs to recognize suffering by the understanding of impermanence, suffering, etc., by direct experience or logical reasoning. Then one must remove its cause, the origin, since the elimination of suffering is not like removing a thorn, but rather cutting its cause. If one cuts down the origin, one will come in contact with its cessation in one's continuum, and then with practice, rely on the suitable path in order to attain liberation.

3.1.2.1.2.2.2.3.2.3.2.2.1.2. The Three Enlightened Activities Illustrated by the Similes ... 2.1. The Enlightened Activities of Body and Speech Illustrated by Emanations of Brahmā ... 1.1. Prelude

≪296≫ The [simile] of being "Brahmā-like" goes as follows:

3.1.2.1.2.2.2.3.2.3.2.2.1.2.1.2. Explaining the Meaning ... 2.1. The Simile and Import Regarding Effortless Engagement of the Enlightened Activities of Body and Speech ... 1.1. The Simile and Import Regarding Engagement of the Enlightened Activities in Disciples with Pure Continuums ... 1.1. The Simile

Just as Brahmā, without departing from his abode, effortlessly shows his appearance in all the desire realms of the gods in order to inspire them to cut down [sensuous] passion ... [TL 201B]

3.1.2.1.2.2.2.3.2.3.2.2.1.2.1.2.1.2. The Implications

... so, without moving from the truth body, ever in the meditation of suchness, the Sage effortlessly demonstrates illusory appearances in every world and teaches beings who have the karmic evolutionary fortune.

3.1.2.1.2.2.2.3.2.3.2.2.1.2.1.2.1.2. The Simile and Import Regarding Engagement of the Enlightened Activities in Inferior Disciples ... 2.1. The Simile

When Brahmā, never departing from his measureless palace, has manifested his images in the desire realm, he is seen by the gods. This vision inspires them to abandon their delight in sensuous objects by teaching the disadvantages of sensual desires.

3.1.2.1.2.2.3.2.3.2.2.1.2.1.2.1.2.2. The Implications

Similarly, without moving from the truth body, the Tathāgata's material bodies are seen in all worlds by beings who have the karmic evolutionary fortune. By teaching them the holy Dharma, this vision inspires them to practice the Dharma, dispel all their taints, and attain the state of liberation and omniscience.

3.1.2.1.2.2.3.2.3.2.2.1.2.1.2.1.3. The Cause of Engagement of the Enlightened Activities

By his own former vows and prayers and the power of the virtue of the gods in the desire realms, Brahmā appears and teaches without any deliberate effort. So does the self-arisen emanation body appear and give teaching to disciples. This is produced by the power of the Buddha's own former prayerful vows and the power of the purity of disciples' continuums.

3.1.2.1.2.2.3.2.3.2.2.1.2.1.2.2. Temporarily Not Appearing in Certain Disciples' Minds

«297» "Temporary nonappearance means . . ." is the prelude. The explanation of its meaning goes:

He moves from Tuṣhita and enters the womb, is born in Lumbinī, [TL 202A] and goes to his father's palace in Kapilavastu. He enjoys amusement among his concubines and then leaves home and seeks solitude, undergoes austerity, and defeats all the devils in front of the bodhi tree. He finds the great enlightenment at dawn and shows the path to the citadel of peace by turning the wheel of Dharma. The Sage, having shown these activities, becomes temporarily invisible to those without the karmic fortune by displaying his nirvana. Therefore, the enlightened activities of the Buddha's body and speech are limitless. It indicates that one should make an effort to meet the Buddha by the recollection of the Buddha, etc.

3.1.2.1.2.2.3.2.3.2.2.1.2.2. The Deed of Mind Illustrated by the Sun . . . 2.1. Prelude

«298» The [simile] of being "sun-like" goes as follows:

3.1.2.1.2.2.2.3.2.3.2.2.1.2.2.2. Explaining the Meaning . . . 2.1. Statement

When the sun blazes down, lotuses, etc., open, while, simultaneously, kumuda (night lily) flowers close. The sun does not at all consider the benefit and fault of the water-born flowers' opening and closing. The sun of the holy one acts likewise, not discriminating according to the benefit and fault of the disciples.

3.1.2.1.2.2.2.3.2.3.2.2.1.2.2.2.2. Explanation . . . 2.1. The Sun and the Application to Import . . . 1.1. The Simile and Import Regarding Engagement without Thought . . . 1.1. Prelude

«299» There are two kinds of sentient beings: disciples and nondisciples. Here the similes of "lotus-like" and "vessel of pure water" refer to disciples:

3.1.2.1.2.2.2.3.2.3.2.2.1.2.2.2.2.1.1.2. The Root Text . . . 2.1. The Simile

As the sun shining its own light simultaneously and without consideration makes lotus flowers open their petals and brings ripening to other crops, as well as makes kumuda flowers close . . .

3.1.2.1.2.2.2.3.2.3.2.2.1.2.2.2.2.1.1.2.2. The Implications

. . . so the sun of the Tathāgata's speech manifests, shining its rays of the holy Dharma on the lotus-like beings to be trained without any effort and without harboring any calculation or idea. [TL 202B]

3.1.2.1.2.2.2.3.2.3.2.2.1.2.2.2.2.1.2. Explaining the Way That the Illumination Eliminates Darkness . . . 2.1. Actual Meaning

By the truth body and the material bodies of the Buddha, the sun of the Omniscient One's speech rises in the sky, which is the very essence of enlightenment, in front of the bodhi tree, to shine light beams of wisdom on the disciples, ripening their continuums so they will be liberated.

3.1.2.1.2.2.3.2.3.2.2.1.2.2.2.2.1.2.2. Pervading All Vessels

Thus, as the moon is reflected in vessels of pure water, simultaneously the sun of the Tathāgata is mirrored in countless reflections in all disciples, as in water vessels, owing to the purity of these disciples' continuums.

3.1.2.1.2.2.3.2.3.2.2.1.2.2.2.2.1.3. The Simile and Referent Regarding the Vessels . . . 3.1. Prelude

«300» Although the buddhas do not have any thought, they reveal themselves and teach the three kinds of beings. [As for the simile of] being "sun-like," its meaning is like this: the three kinds of beings refer to those who are determined [for enlightenment], not determined, and determined on wrongdoing.

3.1.2.1.2.2.3.2.3.2.2.1.2.2.2.2.1.3.2. The Root Text . . . 2.1. Brief Statement

[From] within the space of the truth body, which continuously pervades every object, the buddha sun shines on the disciples of different levels of purity [like] on mountains, as merited by each. [TL 203A]

3.1.2.1.2.2.3.2.3.2.2.1.2.2.2.2.1.3.2.2. Detailed Explanation

Just as the rising sun with thousands of far-reaching light beams illuminates all the worlds and then gradually sheds its light on the highest mountains, then on the medium-sized and the small or lowest, the Buddha sun gradually shines on the assembly of beings with different levels of excellences.

3.1.2.1.2.2.3.2.3.2.2.1.2.2.2.2.2. [The Buddha's Activities] Are Superior to the Sun . . . 2.1. Prelude

«301» The mandala of light is superior:

3.1.2.1.2.2.3.2.3.2.2.1.2.2.2.2.2.2. The Root Text

The sunlight is superior in comparison with the lights of jewels, lamps, etc., since it covers a broader radiation radius and is more beneficial.

However, the sun does not radiate to the end of space in every field as the mandala of buddha light does, nor can it show the reality of all objects of knowledge just as they are and in their varieties [to those] confined to the darkness of ignorance. Appearing in the clarity of a pure land, or for disciples who have clear wisdom, by means of a mass of lights emitting various colors of activities, those of compassionate nature show the reality of all objects of knowledge just as they are and in their varieties to beings, and destroy their ignorance and suffering without remainder. When a buddha goes to the city, people without eyes become able to see things. [TL 203B] Being freed from all meaningless episodes of suffering in bad migrations, they see the meaningful and experience [the happiness] of higher rebirths and ultimate goodness. When, blinded by delusion, they fall into the sea of cyclic life and are wrapped in the darkness of the views of extremist habits, the sunlight of buddha compassion illumines their vision and they see the very realities they never saw before, i.e., the supreme higher rebirth, liberation, and omniscience.

3.1.2.1.2.2.2.3.2.3.2.2.1.3. The Three Secrecies Illustrated by the Similes . . .
3.1. Explaining the Secrecy of Mind by the Simile of a Wish-Fulfilling Jewel . . . 1.1. Prelude

«302» The [simile] of being "wish-fulfilling-jewel-like" is as follows:

3.1.2.1.2.2.2.3.2.3.2.2.1.3.1.2. Explaining the Meaning . . . 2.1. Accomplishing Everything without Any Thought . . . 1.1. Statement . . . 1.1. The Simile

A wish-fulfilling jewel, though free from notions, simultaneously and in the most perfect manner grants each of the desires (such as food and clothing) of all who dwell in its field of activity (such as placing it on top of a banner or making offerings and requests).

3.1.2.1.2.2.2.3.2.3.2.2.1.3.1.2.1.1.2. The Implications

Likewise, beings of different ways of thinking, when they rely on the wish-fulfilling compassion of a buddha, will hear various kinds of [TL 204A] teachings on the means of accomplishing higher rebirth and ultimate goodness, though he generates no notions of these and no effort.

3.1.2.1.2.2.3.2.3.2.2.1.3.1.2.1.2. Explanation

As a precious jewel, which is free from thought, fully bestows the desired riches on others, doing so without any effort, the Sage always remains for others' sake, as merited by their dispositions and preferences, and as long as existence lasts, doing so without any effort.

3.1.2.1.2.2.3.2.3.2.2.1.3.1.2.2. Explaining Rarity by the Simile . . . 2.1. Prelude

«303» It is rare for a buddha to appear:

3.1.2.1.2.2.3.2.3.2.2.1.3.1.2.2.2. The Root Text

The best jewels are very hard to find for beings who desire them. Why? Because they are lying underground or in the ocean. Likewise, one should understand that beings who are held in the grip of the addictions that obscure the vision of the Buddha, and whose karmic gifts are poor, will hardly see the Tathāgata in their minds.

3.1.2.1.2.2.3.2.3.2.2.1.3.2. Explaining the Secrecy of Speech by the Simile of Echo . . . 2.1. Prelude

«304» The [simile] of being "echo-like" is as follows:

3.1.2.1.2.2.3.2.3.2.2.1.3.2. The Root Text

Just as the sound of an echo arises due to the perception of others, without motivated thought or purposeful labor of the conjunction of the tongue and palate, and abiding neither outside like the sound of a conch nor inside like thoughts, [TL 204B] so the speech of the Tathāgata arises due to the respect, etc., arisen from the condition of the faith of others, without motivated thought or purposeful labor of the tongue and palate, and abiding neither outside like the sound of a conch nor inside like thoughts.

3.1.2.1.2.2.2.3.2.3.2.2.1.3.3. Explaining the Secrecy of the Body by the Simile of Space . . . 3.1. Prelude

«305» The [simile] of being "space-like" is as follows:

3.1.2.1.2.2.2.3.2.3.2.2.1.3.3.2. The Root Text

Space is nothing material at all and does not appear if obscuration is present. It is neither an object [of the senses] nor a basis that is distinctly discerned.[398] Furthermore, this refers to a noncharacteristic condition, a nonimmediate condition, a nonobjective condition, and a nonfundamental condition. It is totally beyond being a path for the eye. Its explanation goes: it has no form and is not to be displayed. Nevertheless it is seen as being high and low, but it is not at all like that. Likewise, all [enlightened activities] are seen as of the Buddha, such as his descending from the Tuṣhita heaven, his entering total nirvana, etc., but he is not at all like that. Although it seems that the Buddha newly goes into nirvana, etc., he is not at all like that.

3.1.2.1.2.2.2.3.2.3.2.2.1.4. The Basis of These All Illustrated by the Similes . . . 4.1. Prelude

«306» The [simile] of being "earth-like" is as follows:

3.1.2.1.2.2.2.3.2.3.2.2.1.4.2. The Root Text

Crops that grow from earth will increase and gradually become firm and voluminous with leaves, without thinking that "I am produced by the earth," on the support of the soil that has no idea such as "I shall grow these." [TL 205A] Likewise, relying on the compassion of the Buddha, who like the earth is free from ideas of benefiting beings, every root of virtue of sentient beings without exception will flourish and grow to its completion.

398. *yongs su gcod du.*

3.1.2.1.2.2.3.2.3.2.2.2. Explaining the Summary and Purposes of the Similes . . . 2.1. Prelude

«307» The summary of those similes:

3.1.2.1.2.2.3.2.3.2.2.2.2. Explaining the Meaning . . . 2.1. Actual Meaning

It is not obvious for any ordinary being that one could perform an act—such as stretching one's body or giving verbal teaching—without exerting deliberate effort. If the Buddha does not have any ideas, how could it be possible for him to constantly give teachings? Therefore, nine similes that illustrate the natures of body, speech, and mind as well as enlightened activities and secrecies are taught in the sutra to cut the doubts of the disciples.

3.1.2.1.2.2.3.2.3.2.2.2.2.2. Its Proof . . . 2.1. Statement

The place where these nine similes are explained in great detail is the *Ornament of the Light of Wisdom Sutra*, which by means of its very name teaches their necessity and purpose. [TL 205B]

3.1.2.1.2.2.3.2.3.2.2.2.2.2.2. Explanation

How does the name teach? This sutra teaches the buddha excellences with the nine similes. Adorned with the far-reaching light of wisdom arisen from hearing it, those bodhisattvas of insight will quickly develop faith and enter all the magnificent and profound fields of experience of a buddha.

3.1.2.1.2.2.3.2.3.2.3. Summarized Meaning of the Implications Illustrated by the Similes . . . 3.1. Actual Meaning . . . 1.1. Brief Statement of the Actual Meaning . . . 1.1. Statement

This point of the constant engagement of the buddha activities is made clear to understand by the nine examples of Indra's reflection in the sapphire ground, etc. The concise meaning of the nine similes and the nine facts, when apprehended precisely . . .

3.1.2.1.2.2.2.3.2.3.2.3.1.1.2. Explanation

... is to illustrate the display of a buddha's material body, the sound of his speech, and the all-pervasiveness of his mind; the illusory emanation of the enlightened activities of body and speech; the radiating of wisdom that is the activity of his mind; the three great secrecies of his body, speech, and mind; and the fact that compassion, which is the ultimate basis of all those, is attained. These nine facts are understood by the nine similes, illustrating that the buddha activities are constant, without interruption, and free of any effort.

3.1.2.1.2.2.2.3.2.3.2.3.1.2. Explaining the Intended Meaning...
2.1. Statement

[TL 206A] When a buddha engages in activities, all streams of effort result from observing things with a fully pacified conceptual thought, and with the mind being free from all notions, similar to Indra's reflection appearing within the stainless sapphire ground, etc., creating the cause of higher rebirth, etc., for beings.

3.1.2.1.2.2.2.3.2.3.2.3.1.2.2. Explanation

Pacification of effort resulting from observing things with conceptual thought [is the proposition]; the mind free from ideas, its reasoning. In order to establish the meaning of this reality, the similes of Indra's form, etc., are given. Using this as an example, the simile of Indra's reflection is given in order to prove that the nature of the Teacher is free from the life cycle.

3.1.2.1.2.2.2.3.2.3.2.3.1.2.3. The Teacher Has Gone Beyond Cyclic Life and Performs the Enlightened Activities without Effort

Here the meaning of the chapter, which is the buddha activities illustrated by the nine similes, is as follows: the nine aspects of physical display, etc., show that the Teacher or Fully Enlightened One has no birth and death by the power of addictions, no body made of mind or inconceivable birth and death of changing, and yet perfectly manifests without any effort, engaging in constant activities.

3.1.2.1.2.2.2.3.2.3.2.3.1.3. Detailed Explanation of the Actual Meaning . . .
3.1. Prelude

«308» There are four summary verses of similes regarding this fact:

3.1.2.1.2.2.2.3.2.3.2.3.1.3.2. The Root Text . . . 2.1. General Statement

[TL 206B] The nature of the body, speech, and mind of a buddha, the three activities, and the three secrecies that are similar to Indra's reflection, the drum in heaven, clouds, Brahmā's emanation, the sun, the precious king of wish-granting jewels, an echo, space, and the earth, fulfill others' benefit, effortlessly and as long as existence may last, and are only conceived of by yogis by means of sutras and inner realization.

3.1.2.1.2.2.2.3.2.3.2.3.1.3.2.2. Explanation

The buddha bodies are displayed like the lord of gods appearing in the sapphire jewel ground, helping worldly beings attain higher rebirth. The explanation of buddha speech being well bestowed resembles the drum of the gods. With cloud hosts of intuitive wisdom and great compassion, the all-embracing Buddha pervades the limitless number of beings down to the deepest hell and up to the peak of existence, pouring down the Dharma rain. These three give the conjunction of the similes and facts, concerning the three natures of body, speech, and mind.

Like Brahmā, not moving from the truth body, his sphere devoid of taint, he displays a manifold number of illusory appearances in connection with body and speech. Like a sun, his intuitive wisdom mind radiates its brilliance. These three give the conjunction of the similes and facts concerning the three enlightened activities of body, speech, and mind.

The secrecy of buddha mind resembles a pure and precious wishfulfilling jewel. The secrecy of buddha speech has no letters with motivation to speak, like an echo resounding from a rock. [TL 207A] Similar to space, his body is pervasive, formless, and permanent because it is constant. These three give the conjunction of the similes and facts concerning the three secrecies.

Like the earth that is the basis for humans, etc., [to live], a buddha is the ground holding without exception and in every way all medicinal herbs of beings' unstained excellences, which are the higher rebirth and ultimate goodness. The buddha ground is the ultimate transformation of the nature of great compassion.

3.1.2.1.2.2.3.2.3.2.3.2. Explaining the Common Features of Similes and Implications . . . 2.1. Question

«309» Furthermore, how do these similes illustrate that buddhas are permanent, and do not arise and cease yet appear to do so in the vision of disciples? And also, [how do they illustrate] that the Buddha's enlightened activities are effortlessly performed for all beings without interruption?

3.1.2.1.2.2.3.2.3.2.3.2.2. Answer . . . 2.1. Explaining the Common Feature Regarding Nonarising and Nonceasing

The cause for a buddha's material bodies to be seen in the mind similar to pure sapphire is the purity of this ground, including the faith in the Buddha, etc., within a disciple's continuum, achieved by the cause of a firm faculty of irreversible faith. Some disciples temporarily cannot see the Buddha because of their undeveloped faith, etc. Since the virtue of disciples' faith, etc., arises and ceases, the form of a buddha in their minds appears to be arising and ceasing. Like Indra, the Sage who is the truth body is free from arising and ceasing, never moving from the meditation on the nature of reality. Therefore, it should be known that a buddha's beatific body does not show his entering into nirvana, etc., even in the disciples' vision.

3.1.2.1.2.2.3.2.3.2.3.2.2.2. Explaining the Common Feature Regarding Nonthought

Effortlessly, like the simile of Indra's reflection free of thoughts, he constantly manifests his activities, displaying physical forms, etc., without interruption, his truth body being free from any birth of new increase and death of new decrease for as long as the life cycle may last. [TL 207B]

3.1.2.1.2.2.2.3.2.3.2.2.3. Explaining the Sequence of the Similes . . .
3.1. Brief Statement

The condensed meaning of these nine similes is explained herein as being in a definite order. Due to their common features of similarity, the order of these similes corresponds to [the order of] facts, while dissimilar properties of the excellent qualities of the former simile and the latter fact eliminate total similarity in all respects.

3.1.2.1.2.2.2.3.2.3.2.2.3.2. Detailed Explanation

A buddha's material body is like a reflection because it serves as the condition for beings to cultivate virtue upon seeing it, despite the fact that it is free from any thought, and yet dissimilar, since Indra's reflection is not endowed with his melody of teaching. [TL 208A]

The buddha speech is like the drum of the gods, teaching on the four insignia of the Dharma, and yet dissimilar, since the drum does not bring benefit to beings all the time. The Buddha's great compassion is similar to a vast cloud, causing the crops of disciples to ripen, and yet dissimilar, since the rain of a cloud does not eliminate worthless seeds of the suffering of bad migrations, etc. The enlightened activities of a buddha's body and speech are like the mighty Brahmā, benefiting beings with his emanations without moving from his seat, and yet dissimilar, since Brahmā does not cause the ultimate maturity of permanent bliss. The activity of a buddha's mind is like the orb of the sun, pervading all beings and causing them to ripen, and yet dissimilar, since the sun does not always overcome the darkness of ignorance. The secrecy of a buddha's mind is like a wish-fulfilling jewel, effortlessly bestowing all desired things, and yet dissimilar, since the jewel does not need eons to be formed and is not so rarely found. The secrecy of a buddha's speech is similar to an echo, appearing as the sound that exists outside, and yet dissimilar, since an echo arises from the cause and conditions of others' talk.

A buddha's body secrecy is similar to space, [TL 208B] and yet dissimilar, since space is not a ground of pure virtue. A buddha's ultimate transformaton of great compassion is similar to the earth mandala, providing the basis for sustaining infinite goodness, but it is not similar in all respects, since the earth mandala does not support all excellences, while a buddha's compassion serves as support for all perfections without exception of all mundane and transmundane beings.

3.1.2.1.2.2.2.3.2.3.2. 2.3.3. Establishing the Exalted Wisdom of the Ultimate Transformation as the Basis of All Excellences

Question: How does it become the basis of all perfections? Answer: Based upon all buddhas' enlightenment, which is the ultimate transformation, the path beyond the world will arise, as will the path of virtuous enlightened activities leading to the state of higher rebirth, the four kinds of mental stability, the four immeasurables, [love,] compassion, etc., and the four immaterial trances. Relying upon these two paths, one can travel to the city of higher rebirth and liberation. Therefore, the way of the engagement of a buddha's activities can be understood unmistakenly on the basis of these nine similes.

3.1.2.1.2.2.2.3.3. Title of the Chapter

This is an exposition of the fourth chapter, "The Tathāgata's Enlightened Activities on the Basis of the Buddha's Enlightenment," of *The Sublime Continuum of the Universal Vehicle, Analysis of the Precious Spiritual Potential,* a treatise that explains the intention of the universal vehicle sutras definitive in meaning. [TL 209A]

> Based on my venerable teacher's personal instructions,
> I have clearly elucidated the intention of Father and Son,
> The way of constant buddha activities without interruption
> By the power of attainment of the sixty-four excellences.

The exposition of the "activities" included in the verses belonging to the body of the treatise is completed.

CHAPTER V
Benefit

3.1.2.2. Explaining the Benefit of Having Faith in These . . . 2.1. Explaining the Meaning of This Chapter . . . 1.1. Actual Meaning

3.1.2.2.1.1.1. Prelude

«310» There are six verses regarding the benefit of having faith in these aforementioned four places, as follows. Although the fruitional Three Jewels are not included in the four facts to be realized, these verses should be understood as showing the benefit of having faith in the fruitional Three Jewels as well, since they are the cause of the four places.

3.1.2.2.1.1.2. Brief Statement . . . 2.1. General Statement of the Benefit of Having Faith in the Four Places . . . 1.1. Showing That These Four Places Are the Field of Experience of the Buddha Only

The four places are the buddha element, which is the reality mingled with taints, [TL 209B] the buddha enlightenment endowed with two kinds of purity, the buddha excellences included in freedom and evolutionary maturity, and the continuous, effortless buddha activity. These four places are the object of faith. It can be inferred that these places are the fruit of the Three Jewels, which are inconceivable even for those purified beings on the great [ten bodhisattva] stages. If so, of whom will they be the object? They are the field of experience of their teacher, the totally enlightened Buddha.

3.1.2.2.1.1.2.1.2. The Benefit of Having Faith

Those bodhisattvas of insight, who have devotion to and desire for this buddha domain by means of first having faith in the aforementioned fruition of the Three Jewels, and then in the four places included in the cause and conditions [of the fruit], become vessels for the multitude of the sixty-four kinds of buddha excellences, while those truly delighting in these inconceivable properties will excel in merit resulting from generosity, ethics, and concentration, being superior to all sentient beings who do not have such faith. [TL 210A]

3.1.2.2.1.1.2.2. Specific Explanation ... 2.1. Being Superior to the Virtue Resulting from Generosity

One person, who does not have such faith [yet who] is motivated to strive for unsurpassed enlightenment, may turn to the Dharma kings or [even] the fortunate one, the Buddha, as object, and offer fields of gold adorned with jewels as a gift, equal in number to the atoms in all buddha fields, and may continue doing so every day for a long time. Another person may hear just a word of the sutras or the treatise that teaches the seven vajra facts, and upon hearing it become filled with devotion. One who has such devotion will attain merit far greater and more manifold than the virtue sprung from the [above] practice of generosity.

3.1.2.2.1.1.2.2.2. Being Superior to the Virtue Resulting from Morality

An intelligent person who does not have such faith [yet] is motivated by the wish for enlightenment, may by body, speech, and mind maintain a flawless moral conduct and do so automatically, even over the course of many eons. Another person may hear just a word of the sutras or the treatise that teaches the seven vajra facts, and upon hearing it become filled with devotion. One who has such devotion will attain merit far greater and more manifold than the virtue sprung from the [above] practice of ethics.

3.1.2.2.1.1.2.2.3. Being Superior to the Virtue Resulting from Meditation

A person who has no such faith may finally achieve the four meditative trances and the Brahmā abode of the four immeasurables, thus quenching all addictions' fires such as attachment, etc., [TL 210B] within the three realms of existence, and may cultivate these as a means to reach the desired unchanging and perfect enlightenment. Another person may just hear a word of these sutras or the treatise, and upon hearing it become filled with devotion. One who has such devotion will attain merit far greater and more manifold than the virtue sprung from this [above] practice of meditation.

Here the faith or devotion refers to the faith in the seven vajra facts, not lack of faith in general. Furthermore, the virtue resulting from meditation here refers to the worldly meditations, not the ultimate holy abodes.

3.1.2.2.1.1.2.3. The Proof of Having Faith in the Four Places Being Superior to the Virtues Included in Three Things

The virtue of having faith in the seven vajra facts and their places [of realization] is far superior to the virtue included in three things mentioned here. Why so? Since generosity yields only wealth, and ethics leads [only] to the higher states of existence, the meditation taught here eliminates the manifest addictions as controlled by individual tendencies. Wisdom that realizes the reality mingled with taints as one of the four or seven places abandons all addictive obscurations and objective obscurations along with their instinctual seeds.

[TL 211A] This wisdom is therefore superior to those three kinds of virtue, and its cause is studying and having faith in these four facts as the first step.

3.1.2.2.1.1.3. Detailed Explanation . . . 3.1. Prelude

≪311≫ The meaning of these verses is further explained in the nine verses that follow.

3.1.2.2.1.1.3.2. The Root Text . . . 2.1. General Statement of Praise for Study and Having Faith in These Four Places . . . 1.1. Recognizing the Object of Faith

The presence of the suchness reality mingled with taints is able to produce the buddha excellences and to be purified with the sixty purifying factors. Its result is the enlightenment by means of the . . .

3.1.2.2.1.1.3.2.1.2. The Ultimate Three Jewels Will Be Attained Because of Faith

... purification of taints. Its sixty-four excellences and the achievement of benefit to beings through its activities are the objects of a buddha's direct understanding.

When the intelligent one with the spiritual potential for the universal vehicle is filled with devotion toward the presence of these four, as explained above, [and realizes] that he himself is endowed with the ultimate truth, the emptiness of intrinsic reality, which when meditated upon is the source of all the excellences such as power, etc., and is the basis capable of purifying all taints, thus finding the ability to attain the enlightenment endowed with two kinds of purity by means of [TL 211B] the purification of taints and the excellences such as power, etc., upon the attainment of such enlightenment—the person who has such faith will be endowed with the fortune to quickly attain the state of a tathāgata, the ultimate Three Jewels.

3.1.2.2.1.1.3.2.2. Specific Explanation ... 2.1. Praise for Being the Cause of Perfection of Thought—Conception of the Spirit [of Enlightenment]

Those who realize that "this object is inconceivable for other people and is present within myself as the element, the natural purity, and someone like me who practices the universal vehicle path can attain the enlightenment endowed with the two kinds of purity, the attainment which will hold such excellences and endowment," will aspire to it, filled with faith. Their conventional spirit of enlightenment will never degenerate and be ever present in them.

What is such a spirit of enlightenment? It is the vessel of all excellences. What kind of excellences? Excellences such as total enlightenment, longing for its causes such as the transcendence of generosity, etc., diligence and enthusiasm in achieving them, mindfulness of not forgetting them, and meditative stability and intuitive wisdom, which are the last two transcendences included in the unique mental quiescence and transcendent insight of the universal vehicle, and so on. [TL 212A] The first three, longing, etc., refer to the general practice of the universal vehicle. As discussed in the *Ornament of Clear Realization*, this is the gradual path in which one first practices love and compassion, then cultivates the unsurpassed spirit of enlightenment, and then practices the transcendences of generosity, etc. The point of the third chapter of that treatise is that for the person with middling capacity, the spirit [of enlightenment] must be cultivated. It is also the first stage of the three stages of purifying taints illustrated by the simile of the jewel as mentioned above in the *Questions of King Dhāraṇīshvara Sutra*. [Asaṅga's] *Commentary* explains this as the intention of the root text [of the treatise].

3.1.2.2.1.1.3.2.1.2.2. Praise for Being the Cause of the Perfection of Action

The conventional spirit of enlightenment being ever present in them without turning back, the victor heirs will not regress since they become firm in the perfection of action, i.e., the practice of the transcendences of generosity, etc. The transcendence of merit will be refined until it is transformed into the cause of total purity that is the transcendence of wisdom.

3.1.2.2.1.1.3.2.1.2.3. Recognizing the Nature of Two Collections . . .
3.1. Actual Meaning

Once these five transcendences included in the collection of merit [TL 212B] are not considered to have truth status in their threefold segmentation, which are the gifts to be given, the giving agent, [and the recipient,] they will become perfect. The cause of their purity is the transcendence of wisdom included in the store of wisdom since their opposite forces are completely abandoned. These are also the benefits of studying and having faith in these four places.

3.1.2.2.1.1.3.2.1.2.3.2. No Difficulty That the First Five Transcendences Cannot Be Included in the Three Things

Question: The merit is said to be the three things sprung from generosity, ethics, and meditation. Why are the five transcendences here said to constitute the store of merit?

Answer: No contradiction is involved. It should be known that the five transcendences are included in the three things, respectively, since the merit of generosity includes generosity, that of ethics includes moral conduct, and that of meditation includes the two aspects of tolerance and meditative stability, while the diligence [transcendence] accompanies all three.

3.1.2.2.1.1.3.2.3. Being Great Having Cultivated Faith after Study ... 3.1. Recognizing the Two Obscurations

The karmic instincts for the notions of the three segments, i.e., action, object, agent, as having truth status are viewed as objective obscurations. The impulses of avarice, etc., [toward objects] considered to have truth status are regarded as addictive obscurations. Here, the perception of the three segments [of an action] as having truth status is viewed as an objective obscuration. Although we can follow the two stages in the *Ornament of Clear Realization*, presenting an arrangement for the disciples who are temporarily unreceptive to hearing the teaching on the subtle selflessness, [TL 213A] I think it is reasonable to explain the grasping at truth status as an addictive obscuration and its subtle karmic instinct as an objective obscuration. The definitions of the two obscurations have been discussed above, and should be understood in that way.

3.1.2.2.1.1.3.2.3.2. The Unexcelled Cause for It Is the Cause of the Antidote

Since, apart from the wisdom that directly realizes the meaning of emptiness, there is no other cause or means to remove these two obscurations, this wisdom is superior to the other transcendences. Its first basis being the study of those sutras and treatises; such study is of supreme benefit.

3.1.2.2.1.2. Showing the Completion of the Exposition ... 2.1. Detailed Explanation ... 1.1. The Way of Teaching the Dharma ... 1.1. The Basis of This Composition ... 1.1. On What Basis

This is based on the trustworthy words of the Buddha, which are proven to be pure based on the three ways of analysis, such as the *Questions of King Dhāraṇīshvara Sutra*, the *Shrīmālādevī Lion's Roar Sutra*, the *Tathāgata Essence Sutra*, [TL 213B] the *Ornament of the Light of Wisdom Engaging the Sphere of All Buddhas Sutra*, etc., and on unflawed reasoning that analyzes the teachings.

3.1.2.2.1.2.1.1.1.2. For What Reason

The author of this treatise himself has actually taught it for the purpose of purifying himself from subtle taints of instinctual negative attitudes,[399] and in order to care for all those intelligent disciples endowed with faith in this profound teaching and its resultant perfect meritorious virtue. And as for this statement [of the Noble Asaṅga himself,] it is not definitive in meaning, just made to take care of some ordinary disciples, since the Bhagavān Maitreya actually had already realized the truth body [and had no need to further purify himself of any taints].

3.1.2.2.1.2.1.1.2. Explaining Natures . . . 2.1. Explaining the Nature of Elucidating the Treatise

«312» As a person with eyes sees forms by relying on the light of a lamp, lightning, a radiant jewel, or sun and moon, the great import can be seen by the intuitive wisdom eye that sees the ultimate nature and relative variety of all knowables by relying on the speech of the Sage, which illuminates his discourses, as endowed with the four specific perfect understandings— that which directly sees the unerring temporary and ultimate meaning, and those that understand etymology, teaching, and confident eloquence; and thus did [Asaṅga] elucidate this *Sublime Continuum of the Universal Vehicle Treatise.* [TL 214A]

3.1.2.2.1.2.1.1.2.2. Recognizing the Nature of the Buddha Word to Be Taught

Any speech that is meaningful to people, temporarily and ultimately, and well connected with the Dharma that is free of all flaws of scripture, which removes all addictions of the three realms when its meanings are put into practice, and shows the benefit of the total peace resulting from the eradication of addictions and sufferings [that] is the speech of the Sage, the totally enlightened Buddha, while any different speech that does not talk about the means to higher rebirth and ultimate goodness is other, not the speech of the Buddha.

399. *gnas ngan len.*

3.1.2.2.1.2.1.1.3. Admonition to Respect a Causally Concordant Effect

«313» Whatever someone has explained with undistracted mind not intent on worldly fame and gain in the life cycle, exclusively in the light of the Victor's teaching as the authority and conducive to the path of attaining mere [personal] liberation as well as the ultimate liberation of buddhahood, [this] one should place on one's head as [being] the words of the Sage, and enthusiastically engage in study, contemplation, and meditation on it, as it is a causally homogeneous effect of the words of the Buddha. [TL 214B]

3.1.2.2.1.2.1.1.2. Admonition to Beware of the Pitfall of Disparaging the Dharma . . . 2.1. Admonition to Be Diligent in the Method of Not Disparaging the Dharma . . . 1.1. Admonition to Respect the Dharma without Pretense of Authority[400] . . . 1.1. Abandoning Pretense of Authority

«314» One should not distort the sutras, discourses given by the Sage himself, taking interpretable meaning discourses to be definitive meaning discourses, taking definitive meaning ones as interpretable in meaning, or disparaging any of them as not being the Buddha's teaching. Why? Because there is no one in this world more skilled in teaching the Dharma than the Victor, the totally enlightened Buddha, and his intention is not so easy to understand with a careless, unprepared mind. [TL 215A] It is also because no other has such omniscient intuitive wisdom, knowing without exception the extensive phenomenal objects of knowledge and knowing the profound supreme reality just as it is.

3.1.2.2.1.2.1.2.1.1.2. The Disadvantages of Authority Pretense

Since such authority pretense can destroy those following the way of the Sage's holy Dharma and further damage it, it definitely results in hurling oneself into one of the bad transmigrations.

400. *dbang za ba.*

3.1.2.2.1.2.1.2.1.2. Admonition for Being Biased Due to Attachment and Hatred . . . 2.1. The Disadvantages of Being Biased

We should not be seduced by the polluted vision of bad theories and allow our minds to join with it. Those blinded by addictions and deluded ignorance revile the noble ones, say that the noble beings of the individual vehicle are not real nobles or that there is no saint in the world, and despise the teachings these noble beings have spoken—and all this stems from views fixated on bad theories.

3.1.2.2.1.2.1.2.1.2.1.2. Means to Stop It

If one is possessed by a view fixated on bad theories, one has the disadvantages of the difficulty of freeing oneself from [that view] and being temporarily unable to accept realistic views, just as a clean cloth can be totally transformed by dye, but never an oily cloth. Everyone who has self-esteem should be very cautious, and not be seduced by ill-founded theories.

3.1.2.2.1.2.1.2.2. Admonition to Stop the Cause of Disparaging the Dharma

«315» The cause of disparaging the teachings taught by the Tathāgata, bodhisattvas, and disciples can be any of these: a feeble intellect; inability to distinguish realistic from unrealistic; lack of striving for virtue; [TL 215B] reliance on false pride, proclaiming realization and attainment when in reality there is none; a nature obscured by deprivation of the pure Dharma resulting from one's previous karmic evolutionary actions; taking the interpretable in meaning literally for the definitive meaning; craving profit from wealth; being under the sway of one's own wrong views; relying on those fake teachers who disapprove of the Dharma; staying away from those real teachers who uphold the holy teachings; and, due to having attachment to this life and poor faith in supreme states such as higher rebirth, etc., abandoning the teachings of the Saint. Those who care for themselves should forsake bad influence, rely on authentic teachers, overcome their deluded pride, and practice the path to liberation and omniscience for the sake of their future, etc. Be cautious!

3.1.2.2.1.2.1.2.3. Explaining the Disadvantages of Disparaging the Dharma
… 3.1. Falling into Bad Migrations Because of Disparaging the Dharma

«316» Wise people must not be as deeply afraid of fire and vicious poisonous snakes, of murderers or lightning, as they should be of the danger of disparaging the profound Dharma. Fire, snakes, enemies, and thunderbolts only deprive us of this life, but cannot send us to the utterly fearful states of direst pain. Furthermore, the person who disparages the Dharma will experience many difficulties even in this life, and will go to the deepest hell in the next life.

3.1.2.2.1.2.1.2.3. Being Unable to Liberate Oneself from Cyclic Life

Even someone who has relied on evil friends again and again, and thus has heeded harmful intentions toward a buddha, causing blood to flow from a buddha's body, who has committed any of the other most heinous acts—killing father, mother, or a saint, or splitting up the Saṅgha—will be quickly liberated from these sins once genuinely realizing the ultimate reality, the ultimate truth that is the lack of intrinsic reality status. But where could liberation occur for someone whose mind is hostile to the Dharma? For the time being, such a one would lack such an opportunity. Therefore anyone who cares for himself should not create the karmic pitfall of destroying the Dharma, such as disparaging authentic teachers, getting fixated on bad theories, disparaging the meaning of reality, etc.

3.1.2.2.1.2.1.3. Dedication to Enlightenment with the Virtue from Composition

Having properly explained the seven vajra facts and the places of the fruitional Three Jewels, the intrinsically pure element that is the reality mingled with taints, the flawless enlightenment endowed with the two kinds of purity, the excellences on the basis of enlightenment such as the powers, and the activities on the basis of the excellences, may any virtue Maitreya himself has harvested from this lead all beings to see the Sage, Amitāyus Buddha who is endowed with infinite light. When [they] see him, may it open their stainless Dharma eye that perceives all things, attaining the tolerance of the birthlessness of things,[401] and may they reach unsurpassed great enlightenment. This teaches future generations of disciples that even a small or minor virtue should also be dedicated.

3.1.2.2.1.2.2. Conclusion ... 2.1. Prelude

«317» The summarized meaning of these ten verses should be understood by the following three verses:

3.1.2.2.1.2.2.2. The Root Text

On what basis and for what reason has this been composed? This is answered by the verse starting with "Based on the trustworthy words of the Buddha and on reasoning." What is the nature of the elucidating treatise, the nature of the buddha word to be taught, and the nature of what they explain? These are answered, respectively, by the next two verses starting with "As someone with eyes sees by relying on a lamp." What is the causally homogeneous [effect] of the buddha word, the untainted treatise explaining the Buddha's intention, about? This is answered by the verse starting with "Whatever someone has explained with undistracted mind."

[These subjects] have been taught by means of four verses. Two verses starting with "There is no one in this world" show the means to purify oneself from the sin of disparaging the Dharma, and one verse starting with "Due to a feeble intellect" shows the cause of degeneration and admonishes against doing so. Thereupon, by means of two further verses, starting with "Skillful beings must not be as deeply afraid of fire," the defect and the effect of disparaging the Dharma is explained. We are admonished for causing such a defect. [The virtue] is dedicated to all beings to be born in the mandala of Buddha Amitāyus's retinue, attaining the tolerance of birthlessness and [then] unsurpassed enlightenment. What is dedicated is the virtue of giving the teaching of the sutras on the seven vajra places and the treatise elucidating them. The two aspects of fruition, temporary and ultimate, are explained in a summarized way by the last verse starting with "Having properly explained the seven facts."

---

401. *mi skye ba'i chos la bzod pa.*

3.1.2.2.2. Title of the Chapter

This is an exposition of the fifth chapter, "Benefit," of *The Sublime Continuum of the Universal Vehicle, Analysis of the Precious Spiritual Potential*, a treatise that explains the intention of the universal vehicle sutras definitive in meaning.

> Based on my venerable teacher's personal instructions,
> I clearly elucidated the intention of the Father and the Son,
> The benefit that will bring about a person's wishes
> Coming from proper study on the seven facts and places.

The exposition of the verses belonging to the body of the treatise is completed.

4. Meaning of the Conclusion . . . 4.1. Dedication of Composing the Treatise

«318» I have attained inconceivable immeasurable merit by means of this exposition of the untainted holy Dharma Jewel of the universal vehicle, *The Sublime Continuum of the Universal Vehicle, Analysis of the Precious Spiritual Potential*, a treatise that distinguishes the sutras definitive in meaning from those interpretable in meaning. Due to this, may all beings become vessels for studying, contemplating, realizing, and actualizing the untainted meaning of the holy Dharma Jewel of the universal vehicle!

4.2. The Author of the Treatise

Master Asaṅga's *Commentary* of the holy savior Maitreya's *Sublime Continuum of the Universal Vehicle, Analysis of the Precious Spiritual Potential*—which distinguishes the sutras definitive in meaning from those interpretable in meaning—as a treatise that explains the intention of the universal vehicle sutras definitive in meaning, is completed.

4.3. The Manner in Which It Was Translated

It was translated from Sanskrit into Tibetan and edited based on careful study and analysis by the great Paṇḍita Sadjana, who was a grandson of the

Brahmin Ratnavajra, a great scholar of the Glorious Incomparable City in the land of Kashmir, and by the Tibetan translator and champion of Tibetan Buddhism, the Shākya monk [Ngog] Loden Sherab, in this Glorious Incomparable City (Shrīnagar).

> The essential meaning of all the sutras of the Victor,
> Relativity, and the path of the profound Middle Way
> [That] is free from all extremes—
> In accordance with the intention
> Of all the sutras of definitive meaning—
> Is [given] in the words of the holy Regent,
> Producing ever greater clarity.

> The supreme port of entry for many of the wise
> To the path of the universal vehicle,
> The seven vajra facts of causes and effects,
> The sutras of faith and the ornament of stainless reason—
> All are distinguished [in *The Sublime Continuum*],
> With great clarity in terms that are easy to understand.

> The one called Asaṅga—renowned in all three realms,
> Prophesied by the Victor as the analyst
> Of the definitive and the interpretable—
> Explained, just in accord with the wishes
> Of [Maitreya,] that most supreme of beings.
> And his explanation was well combined
> With sutra discourses of definitive meaning,
> Such as the *Questions of King Dhāraṇīshvara*,
> The *Shrīmālādevī*, the *Tathāgata Essence*, and others.

> The words of the Regent are very weighty,
> And the wishes of the Great Champion
> Are also difficult to understand.
> Yet, from the personal instructions
> Of the Foremost Lama's teachings
> These [points] are distinguished
> With great clarity, precisely, and without confusion.

All phenomena are relativistically arisen,
Like the moon reflected in the surface of water.
Having seen [all things] to be just like that,
With compassion, [he] gathered [the key points]
In one place, and composed a perfect
Complete commentary on the Sage's teachings—
Thus, I pay homage to my Lama.

Without the personal instructions
That dawn as advice on textual systems,
Without the force of reasoned analysis
Concerning the meaning of the sutras,
Even if one wished to gaze into the ocean
Of the mass of teachings of the Victor,
One would be like a blind man
Holding a torch aloft in his hand.

Although I have detailed the intention
Of the treatise of the Noble One
With analysis that reveals with reasons
The meaning of the sutra discourses,
If this [commentary] is found to have any errors,
May my teacher, together with all the gods, forgive [me]!

By whatever virtue I have amassed in this way,
May all transmigrants—wherever they might be
[In realms] extending throughout space—
Embarking on the great ship of the supreme vehicle way,
Be led across the ocean of the omniscient Victor!

May I, as well, in all my lifetimes,
Never be separated from this wonderful path, and
When Maitreya approaches the seat of enlightenment,
May I be satiated with the ambrosia
Of the holy Dharma of the universal vehicle!

This, *The Sublime Continuum of the Universal Vehicle Treatise*—which explains the intention of the universal vehicle sutras that are definitive in meaning—was first heard by me from the great teacher of Buddhism, the venerable Rendawa Kumāramati; and then, from the mouth of the foremost, precious, omniscient [Tsong Khapa] Losang Drakpa Palsangpo, peerless on this earth, I completely received the teaching. Thus, I, a Dharma teacher, Darma Rinchen, bowing down to the dust of [the feet of] that great mentor for a long period, wrote this commentary at the request of Gungru Gyaltsen Sangpo, a great virtuous friend who has perfectly crossed over the ocean of exoteric and esoteric sutras, among others. It was written at the magnificent glorious monastery of Nenying. The scribe was Taktsel Karpap Döndrup Kunga. May this make it possible for the precious exoteric and esoteric teachings to spread in all directions and to remain forever!

APPENDIX, BIBLIOGRAPHIES, AND INDEXES

APPENDIX
Tibetan Names (Phonetic-Transliterated Equivalents)

PHONETIC RENDITION	WYLIE TRANSLITERATION
Butön Rinchendrup	bu ston rin chen grub
Chenga Kunpangpa	spyan snga kun spangs pa
Chenga Sönam Drakpa	spyan snga bsod nams grags pa
Choney Drakpa Shedrup	co ne grags pa bshad grub
Darma Rinchen	dar ma rin chen
Deshin Shekpa (Fifth Karmapa)	de bzhin gshegs pa
Dolpopa Sherab Gyaltsen	dol po pa shes rab rgyal mtshan
Dragyap Losang Tenpa	brag g.yab blo bzang bstan pa
Draktokpa Shönnu Tsultrim	brag thog pa gzhon nu tshul khrims
Dulzin Drakpa Gyaltsen	'dul 'dzin grags pa rgyal mtshan
Gendundrup (First Dalai Lama)	dge 'dun grub
Gö Lotsawa Shönnu Pal	'gos lo tsā ba gzhon nu dpal
Gungru Gyaltsen Sangpo	gung ru rgyal mtshan bzang po
Gyaltsap Darma Rinchen	rgyal tshab dar ma rin chen
Gyalwang Trinlay Namgyal	rgyal dbang 'phrin las rnam rgyal
Hva-shang	hwa shang
Jamchen Chöjey Shākya Yeshe	byams chen cho rje śākya ye shes
Jangchup Gyaltsen (Tai Situ)	byang chub rgyal mtshan (ta'i si tu)

PHONETIC RENDITION	WYLIE TRANSLITERATION
Khedrup Gelek Palsangpo	mkhas grub dge legs dpal bzang po
Khenchen Rinchen Gyaltsen	mkhan chen rin chen rgyal mtshan
Khenchen Yakpa	mkhan chen g.yag pa
Kungapal	kun dga' dpal
Kyektön Kachupa Lodrö Denpa	skyegs ston bka' bcu ba blo gros brtan pa
Maja Jangchup Tsöndru	rma bya byang chub brtson 'grus
Mugey Samten Gyatso	dmu dge bsam gtan rgya mtsho
Ngog Loden Sherab	rngog blo ldan shes rab
Panchen Sönam Drakpa	paṇ chen bsod nams grags pa
Rendawa Shönnu Lodrö	red mda' ba gzhon nu blo gros
Rongtön Shakya Gyaltsen	rong ston śākya rgyal mtshan
Taktsel Karpap Döndrup Kunga	stag tshal mkhar phab don grub kun dga'
Tashi Palden	bkra shis dpal ldan
Trisong Detsen	khri srong lde'u btsan
Tsong Khapa Losang Drakpa	tsong kha pa blo bzang grags pa
Tsungmey Rinchen Shönnu	mtshungs med rin chen gzhon nu
Wang Drakpa Gyaltsen	dbang grags pa rgyal mtshan

Selected Bibliographies

CANONICAL SOURCES

Sūtras and Tantras

Abhidharma Universal Vehicle Sūtra (**Abhidharma-mahāyāna-sūtra*; *Chos mngon pa'i theg pa chen po'i mdo*). Not extant in Indo-Tibetan canon.

Buddha Garland Super-Magnificent Sūtra (*Buddha-avataṃsaka-nāma-mahāvaipūlya-sūtra*; *Sangs rgyas phal po che zhes bya ba shin tu rgyas pa chen po'i mdo*). Lhasa 94. phal chen, ka 1b.1–378a.4; kha 1b.1–359a.4; ga 1b.1–386a.3; nga 1b.1–370a.7; ca 1b.1–390a.7; cha 1b.1–341a.6 (vol. 41–46). Tōh. (D) 44.

Chapter on Firm High Resolve Sūtra (*Ārya-sthirādhyāśaya-parivarta-nāma-mahāyāna-sūtra*; *'Phags pa lhag pa'i bsam pa brtan pa'i le'u zhes bya ba theg pa chen po'i mdo*). Lhasa 225. mdo sde, tsa 267a.6–282a.5 (vol. 63). Tōh. (D) 224.

Dense Array Sūtra (*Gaṇḍavyūha-sūtra*; *Sdong po bkod pa'i mdo*). Chapter 45 of the *Buddha Garland Sūtra* (*Buddha-avataṃsaka-nāma-mahāvaipūlya-sūtra*; *Sangs rgyas phal po che zhes bya ba shin tu rgyas pa chen po'i mdo*). Lhasa 94. phal chen, ka 1b.1–378a.4; kha 1b.1–359a.4; ga 1b.1–386a.3; nga 1b.1–370a.7; ca 1b.1–390a.7; cha 1b.1–341a.6 (vol. 41–46). Tōh. (D) 44.

Elucidation of the Intention Sūtra (*Saṃdhinirmocana-sūtra*; *Dgongs pa nges par 'grel pa zhes bya ba theg pa chen po'i mdo*). Lhasa 109. mdo sde, ca 1b.1–87b.7 (vol. 51). Tōh. (D) 106.

Glorious Kālachakra Tantra (*Paramādibuddhoddhṛta-śrī-kālacakra-nāma-tantrarājā*; *Mchog gi dang po'i sangs rgyas las phyung ba rgyud kyi rgyal po dpal dus kyi 'khor lo zhes bya ba*). Lhasa 371. rgyud, ka 28b.5-186b.3 (vol. 79). Tōh. (D) 362.

Great Drum Sūtra (*Mahābherīhāraka-sūtra*; *Rnga bo che chen po'i mdo*). Lhasa 223. mdo sde, tsa 141a.3–208b.4 (vol. 63). Tōh. (D) 222.

Great Total Nirvana Sūtra (*Mahāparinirvāṇa-sūtra*; *Yongs su mya ngan las 'das pa chen po'i mdo*). Lhasa 122. mdo sde, nya 1b.1–222b.5 (vol. 54). Tōh. (D) 120.

King of Samādhis Sūtra (*Samādhirāja-nāma-mahāyāna-sūtra*; *Ting nge 'dzin gyi rgyal po zhes bya ba theg pa chen po'i mdo*). Lhasa 129. mdo sde, ta 1b.1–269b.4 (vol. 55). Tōh. (D) 127.

Ornament of the Light of Wisdom Engaging the Sphere of All Buddhas Sūtra (*Sarvabuddha-viṣayāvatāra-jñānālokālaṁkāra-nāma-mahāyāna-sūtra*; *Sangs rgyas thams cad kyi yul la 'jug pa'i ye shes snang ba'i rgyan ces bya ba theg pa chen po'i mdo*). Lhasa 103. mdo sde, ga 483a.4–535a.4 (vol. 49). Tōh. (D) 100.

Questions of Gaganagañja Sūtra (*Ārya-gaganagañja-paripṛcchā-nāma-mahāyāna-sūtra*; *'Phags pa nam mkha mdzod kyis zhus pa zhes bya ba theg pa chen po'i mdo*). Lhasa 149. mdo sde, da 319a.5–460b.7 (vol. 57). Tōh. (D) 148.

Questions of Kāshyapa Sūtra (*Ārya-kāśyapa-parivarta-nāma-mahāyāna-sūtra*; *'Phags pa 'od srung gi le'u zhes bya ba theg pa chen po'i mdo*). Lhasa 87. dkon brtsegs, cha 211a.6–260b.5 (vol. 40). Tōh. (D) 87.

Questions of King Dhāraṇīshvara Sūtra (*Dhāraṇīśvararājaparipṛcchā-sūtra*); a.k.a. *Teaching on the Great Compassion of the Tathāgatas Sūtra* (*Ārya-tathāgata-mahākaruṇā-nirdeśa-nāma-mahāyāna-sūtra*; *'Phags pa de bzhin gshegs pa'i snying rje chen po nges par bstan pa zhes bya ba theg pa chen po'i mdo*). Lhasa 148. mdo sde, da 153b.6–319a.5 (vol. 57). Tōh. (D) 147.

Questions of Ratnachūḍā Sūtra (*Ārya-ratnacūḍa-paripṛcchā-nāma-mahāyāna-sūtra*; *'Phags pa gtsug na rin po ches zhus pa zhes bya pa theg pa chen po'i mdo*). Lhasa 91. dkon brtsegs, cha 350a.5–418a.6 (vol. 40). Tōh. (D) 91.

Questions of Ratnadārikā (*Ratnadārikā-paripṛcchā*; *Bu mo rin chen gyis zhus pa*), a.k.a. *Instructions Regarding the Universal Vehicle Sūtras* (*Ārya-mahāyānopadeśa-nāma-mahāyāna-sūtra*; *'Phags pa theg pa chen po'i man ngag ces bya ba theg pa chen po'i mdo*). Lhasa 170. mdo sde, pa 412a.6–490a.3 (vol. 59). Tōh. (D) 169.

Questions of Sāgaramati Sūtra (*Ārya-sāgaramati-paripṛcchā-nāma-mahāyāna-sūtra*; *'Phags pa blo gros rgya mtshos zhus pa zhes bya ba theg pa chen po'i mdo*). Lhasa 153. mdo sde, na 1b.1–180a.3 (vol. 58). Tōh. (D) 152.

Questions of Ugra Sūtra (*Ārya-gṛhapati-ugra-paripṛcchā-nāma-mahāyāna-sūtra*; *'Phags pa khyim bdag drag shul can gyis zhus pa zhes bya ba theg pa chen po'i mdo*). Lhasa 63. dkon brtsegs, ca 1b.1–50b.6 (vol. 39). Tōh. (D) 63.

Shrīmālādevī Lion's Roar Sūtra (*Ārya-śrīmālādevī-siṁhanāda-nāma-mahāyāna-sūtra*; *'Phags pa lha mo dpal phreng gi seng ge'i sgra zhes bya ba theg pa chen po'i mdo*). Lhasa 92. dkon brtsegs, cha 418a.6–454a.4 (vol. 40). Tōh. (D) 92.

Sūtra on the Six Sense Media (**Ṣaḍāyatana-sūtra*; *Skye mched drug gi mdo*; 六根聚 經). Not extant in Indo-Tibetan canon.

Sūtra on the Ten Stages (*Daśabhūmika-sūtra*; *Sa bcu pa'i mdo*). Chapter 31 of the *Buddha Garland Sūtra* (*Buddha-avataṃsaka-nāma-mahāvaipūlya-sūtra*; *Sangs rgyas phal po che zhes bya ba shin tu rgyas pa chen po'i mdo*). Lhasa 94. phal chen, ka 1b.1–378a.4; kha 1b.1–359a.4; ga 1b.1–386a.3; nga 1b.1–370a.7; ca 1b.1–390a.7; cha 1b.1–341a.6 (vol. 41–46). Tōh. (D) 44.

Sūtra Showing the Entry into the Realm of the Inconceivable Excellences and Wisdom of the Tathāgatas (*Ārya-tathāgata-guṇa-jñāna-acintyaviṣaya-avatāra-nirdeśa-nāma-mahāyāna-sūtra*; *'Phags pa de bzhin gshegs pa'i yon tan dang ye shes bsam gyis mi khyab pa'i yul la 'jug pa bstan pa zhes bya ba theg pa chen po'i mdo*). Lhasa 186. mdo sde, ba 167a.3–226a.2 (vol. 61). Tōh. (D) 185.

Sūtra Teaching the Absence of Increase and Decrease [in the Realm of Beings] (*Anū-natvā-pūrṇatva-nirdeśa-parivarta [sūtra]*; *'Grib pa med pa dang 'phel ba med pa nyid bstan pa*; 佛說不增不減經), T.668, K.490, Nj. 524. Not extant in Indo-Tibetan canon.

Tathāgata Essence Sūtra (*Tathāgatagarbha-nāma-mahāyāna-sūtra*; *De bzhin gshegs pa'i snying po zhes bya ba theg pa chen po'i mdo*). Lhasa 260. mdo sde, zha 1b.1–24a.2 (vol. 67). Tōh. (D) 258.

Teaching of Akshayamati Sūtra (*Akṣayamati-nirdeśa-nāma-mahāyāna-sūtra*; *Blo gros mi zad pas bstan pa zhes bya ba theg pa chen po'i mdo*). Lhasa 176. mdo sde, pha 122b.5–270b.1 (vol. 60). Tōh. (D) 175.

Transcendent Wisdom Heart [Sūtra] (*Bhagavatī-prajñāpāramitā-hṛdaya*; *Bcom ldan 'das ma shes rab kyi pha rol tu phyin pa'i snying po*). Lhasa 26. sna tshogs, ka 259a.6–261a.3 (vol. 34). Tōh. (D) 21.

Transcendent Wisdom [Sūtra] in One Hundred Thousand Lines (*Śatasāhasrikā-prajñāpāramitā*; *Shes rab kyi pha rol tu phyin pa stong phrag brgya pa*). Lhasa 9. 'bum, ka 1b.1–544a.1; kha 1b.1–535a.7; ga 1b.1–564a.6; nga 1b.1–506a.5; ca 1b.1–544a.2; cha 1b.1–536a.6; ja 1b.1–535a.3; nya 1b.1–563a.7; ta 1b.1–521a.7; tha 1b.1–528a.3; da 1b.1–540a.3; na 1b.1–521a.7 (vol. 14–25). Tōh. (D) 8.

Transcendent Wisdom [Sūtra] in Twenty-Five Thousand Lines (*Pañcaviṁśati-sāhasrikā-prajñāpāramitā*; *Shes rab kyi pha rol tu phyin pa stong phrag nyi shu lnga pa*). Lhasa 10. nyi khri, ka 1b.1–558a.6; kha 1b.1–548a.6; ga 1b.1–537a.7 (vol. 26–28). Tōh. (D) 9.

Transcendent Wisdom Sūtra in Eight Thousand Lines (*Ārya-aṣṭasāhasrikā-prajñā-pāramitā-nāma-mahāyāna-sūtra*; *'Phags pa shes rab kyi pha rol tu phyin pa brgyad stong pa*). Lhasa 11. brgyad stong, ka 1b.1–450a.4/(ornamental ed.) 1b.1–523b.2 (vol. 29). Tōh. (D) 12.

Transcendent Wisdom Sūtra in Eighteen Thousand Lines (*Ārya-aṣṭādaśasāhasrikā-prajñāpāramitā-nāma-mahāyāna-sūtra*; *'Phags pa shes rab kyi pha rol tu phyin pa khri brgyad stong pa zhes bya ba theg pa chen po'i mdo*). Lhasa 12. khri brgyad, ka 1b.1–453a.5; kha 1b.1–449a.3; ga 1b.1–317a.5 (vol. 30–32). Tōh. (D) 10.

Visit to Laṅka Sūtra (*Ārya-laṅkāvatāra-mahāyāna-sūtra*; *'Phags pa lang kar gshegs pa'i theg pa chen po'i mdo*). Lhasa 110. mdo sde, ca 87b.7–307a.4 (vol. 51). Tōh. (D) 107.

White Lotus Sūtra (*Saddharmapuṇḍarīka-sūtra*; *Dam pa'i chos pad ma dkar po zhes bya ba theg pa chen po'i mdo*). Lhasa 116. mdo sde, ja 1b.1–285b.2 (vol. 53). Tōh. (D) 113.

Indian and Tibetan Texts

Āryadeva. *Experientialist Four Hundred* ([*Yogācāra-*]*catuḥśatakaśāstra-nāma-kārikā*; [*rnal 'byor spyod pa*] *bstan bcos bzhi brgya pa zhes bya ba'i tshig le'ur byas pa*). Tōh. (D) 3846. dbu ma, tsha 1b.1–18a.7.

Asaṅga. *Abhidharma Compendium* (*Abhidharmasamuccaya*; *chos mngon pa kun las btus pa*). Tōh. (D) 4049. sems tsam, ri 1b.1–77a.7.

———. *Bodhisattva Stages* (*Yogācārabhūmau-bodhisattvabhūmi*; *rnal 'byor spyod pa'i sa las byang chub sems dpa'i sa*). Tōh. (D) 4037. sems tsam, wi 1b.1–213a.7.

———. *Disciple Stages* (*Yogācārabhūmau-śrāvakabhūmi*; *rnal 'byor spyod pa'i sa las nyan thos kyi sa*). Tōh. (D) 4036. sems tsam, dzi 1b.1–195a.7.

———. *Sublime Continuum Commentary* (*Mahāyānottara-tantra-śāstra-vyākhyā*; *theg pa chen po rgyud bla ma'i bstan bcos rnam par bshad pa*). Tōh. (D) 4025. sems tsam, phi 74b.1–129a.7.

———. *Universal Vehicle Compendium* (*Mahāyānasaṃgraha*; *theg pa chen po bsdus pa*). Tōh. (D) 4048. sems tsam, ri 1b.1–43a.7.

Chandrakīrti. *Introduction to the Central Way* (*Madhyamakāvatāra-nāma*; *dbu ma la 'jug pa zhes bya ba*). Tōh. (D) 3861. dbu ma, 'a 201b.1–219a.7.

Dharmakīrti. *Commentary on [Dignāga's] Validating Cognition Compendium* (*Pramāṇavārttikakārikā*; *tshad ma rnam 'grel gyi tshig le'ur byas pa*). Tōh. (D) 4210. tshad ma, ce 94b.1–151a.7.

Dolpopa Sherab Gyaltsen. *Ocean of Definitive Meaning* (*Ri chos nges don rgya mtsho*).

Dragyap Losang Tenpa. *Reservoir of Excellences* (*Rgyal tshab kyi rnam thar yon tan chu gter*). Cited in Gyalwang Trinlay Namgyal, *'Jam mgon chos kyi rgyal po tsong kha pa chen po'i rnam thar thub bstan mdzes pa'i rgyan gcig ngo mtshar nor bu'i phreng ba*.

Guṇaprabha. *Discipline Sūtra* (*Vinayasūtra*; *'dul ba'i mdo*). Tōh. (D) 4117. 'dul ba, wu 1b.1–100a.7.

Gyaltsap Darma Rinchen. *Sublime Continuum Supercommentary* (*theg pa chen po rgyud bla ma'i ṭīkka*). In *Collected Works of Rgyal-tsab dar-ma rin-chen*, vol. 3 (GA). Bkra-shis-lhun-po: n.d.

———. *Illuminator of the Path to Liberation* (*rnam 'grel thar lam gsal byed bsdus don*). In the *rJe yab sras gsung 'bum*.

Gyalwang Trinlay Namgyal. *'Jam mgon chos kyi rgyal po tsong kha pa chen po'i rnam thar thub bstan mdzes pa'i rgyan gcig ngo mtshar nor bu'i phreng ba*. Xining: Mtsho sngon mi rigs par khang, 1981.

Haribhadra. *Clear Meaning Explanation of the Transcendent Wisdom Sūtra in Eight Thousand Lines, the Illumination Ornament of Clear Realization* (*Ārya-aṣṭasāhasrikā-prajñāpāramitā-vyākhyāna-abhisamayālaṁkārāloka-nāma*; *'phags pa shes rab kyi pha rol tu phyin pa brgyad stong pa'i bshad pa, mngon par rtogs pa'i rgyan gyi snang ba zhes bya ba*). Tōh. (D) 3791. shes phyin, cha 1b.1–341a.7.

Jangchup Gyaltsen (Tai Situ). *Last Testament Annals* (*bka' chems deb ther*; a.k.a. *lha rigs rlangs kyi rnam thar*).

Maitreyanātha. *Analysis of Phenomena and Reality* (*Dharmadharmatā-vibhāga*; *chos dang chos nyid rnam par 'byed pa*). Tōh. (D) 4022. sems tsam, phi 46b.1–49a.6; Tōh. (D) 4023. sems tsam, phi 50b.1–53a.7.

———. *Analysis of the Middle and Extremes* (*Madhyāntavibhāga*; *dbus dang mtha' rnam par 'byed pa'i tshig le'ur byas pa*). Tōh. (D) 4021. sems tsam, phi 40b.1–45a.6.

————. *Ornament of Clear Realization (Abhisamayālaṃkāra; mngon par rtogs pa'i rgyan).* Tōh. (D) 3786. shes phyin, ka 1b.1–13a.7.

————. *Ornament of the Universal Vehicle Sūtras. (Mahāyānasūtrālaṃkāra; theg pa chen po mdo sde'i rgyan).* Tōh. (D) 4020. sems tsam, phi 1b.1–39a.4.

————. *The Sublime Continuum of the Universal Vehicle, Analysis of the Precious Spiritual Potential (Ratnagotra-vibhāga-mahāyānottaratantra-śāstra; theg pa chen po rgyud bla ma'i bstan bcos).* Tōh. (D) 4024. sems tsam, phi 54b.1–73a.7.

Nāgārjuna. *Letter to a Friend (Suhṛllekha; bshes pa'i spring yig).* Tōh. (D) 4182. spring yig, nge 40b.4–46b.3.

————. *Precious Garland of Advice to the King (Rājaparikathā-ratnāvali; rgyal po la gtam bya ba rin po che'i phreng ba).* Tōh. (D) 4158. skyes rab/spring yig, ge 107a.1–126a.4.

————. *Sixty Stanzas on Reasoning (Yuktiṣaṣṭikākārikā-nāma; rigs pa drug cu pa'i tshig le'ur byas pa zhes bya ba).* Tōh. (D) 3825. dbu ma, tsa 20b.1–22b.6.

————. *Wisdom: Root Verses on Centrism (Prajñā-nāma-mūlamadhyamaka-kārikā; dbu ma rtsa ba'i tshig le'ur byas pa shes rab ces bya ba).* Tōh. (D) 3824. dbu ma, tsa 1b.1–19a.6.

Puṇḍarīka. *Stainless Light (Vimalaprabhā-nāma-mūlatantrānusāriṇī-dvādaśa-sāhasrikā-laghukālacakra-tantra-rāja-ṭikā; bsdus pa'i rgyud kyi rgyal po dus kyi 'khor lo'i 'grel bshad, rtsa ba'i rgyud kyi rjes su 'jug pa stong phrag bcu gnyis pa dri ma med pa'i 'od ces bya ba).* Derge (sde dge) 845. dus 'khor, shrī 1b.1–469a.7 (vol. 100).

Shāntarakṣhita. *Central Way Ornament (Madhyamakālaṃkāra; dbu ma rgyan gyi tshig le'ur byas pa).* Tōh. (D) 3884. dbu ma, sa 53a.1–56b.3.

Shāntideva. *Guide to the Bodhisattva Way of Life (Bodhicaryāvatāra; byang chub sems dpa'i spyod pa la 'jug pa).* Tōh. (D) 3871. dbu ma, la 1b.1–40a.7.

Tsong Khapa Losang Drakpa. *Essence of True Eloquence Treatise on the Analysis of Interpretable and Definitive Meanings (gSung rab kyi drang ba dang nges pa'i don rnam par phye ba gsal bar byed pa legs par bshad pa'i snying po).* In the *rJe yab sras gsung 'bum* [Collected works of Tsong Khapa, Gyaltsap, and Khedrup].

————. *Golden Rosary of Eloquence (Legs bshad gser gyi phreng ba).* In the *rJe yab sras gsung 'bum.*

————. *Illumination of the Intent: Commentary on the Introduction to the Central Way* (*dbu ma la 'jug pa'i rnam bshad dgongs pa rab gsal*). In the *rJe yab sras gsung 'bum.*

————. *Ocean of Reason* (*dbu ma rtsa ba'i tshig le'ur byas pa shes rab ces bya ba'i rnam bshad rigs pa'i rgya mtsho*). In the *rJe yab sras gsung 'bum.*

————. *Stages of the Path to Enlightenment* (*Byang chub lam gyi rim pa chen mo*; and *byang chub lam gyi rim pa chung ba*). In the *rJe yab sras gsung 'bum.*

Vasubandhu. *Treasury of Abhidharma* (*Abhidharmakośakārikā*; *chos mngon pa'i mdzod kyi tshig le'ur byas pa*). Tōh. (D) 4089. mngon pa, ku 1b.1–25a.7.

Vimuktasena. *Commentary on [Haribhadra's] Ornament of Clear Realization, Quintessential Instructions on the Transcendent Wisdom in Twenty-Five Thousand Lines* (*Ārya-pañcaviṁśati-sāhasrikāprajñā-pāramitopadeśa-śāstrābhisamayā-laṁkāra-vṛtti*; *'phags pa shes rab kyi pha rol tu phyin pa stong phrag nyi shu lnga pa'i man ngag gi bstan bcos mngon par rtogs pa'i rgyan gyi 'grel pa*) Tōh. (D) 3787. shes phyin, ka 14b.1–212a.7.

MODERN SOURCES

Anacker, Stefan. 1984. *Seven Works of Vasubandhu, the Buddhist Psychological Doctor.* Delhi: Motilal Banarsidass.

Ary, Elijah. 2015. *Authorized Lives: Biography and the Early Formation of Geluk Identity.* Boston: Wisdom Publications.

Brunnhölzl, Karl. 2014. *When the Clouds Part: The Uttaratantra and Its Meditative Tradition as a Bridge between Sūtra and Tantra.* Boston: Snow Lion.

D'Amato, Mario. 2012. *Maitreya's Distinguishing the Middle from the Extremes.* New York, NY: American Institute of Buddhist Studies.

Johnston, E.H. 1991. *The Uttaratantra of Maitreya: Containing Introduction, E.H. Johnston's Sanskrit Text, and E. Obermiller's English Translation.* Introduction and edited by H.S. Prasad. Delhi: Sri Satguru Publications. Electronic edition available at: www.uwest. edu/sanskritcanon, or http://gretil.sub.uni-goettingen.de/gretil/ 1_sanskr/6_sastra/3_phil/buddh/bsa073_u.htm.

Mathes, Klaus Dieter. 2003. *'Gos Lo tsā ba gZhon nu dpal's Commentary on the Ratnagotravibhāgavyākhyā.* Stuttgart: Franz Steiner Verlag.

Pedurma (*dpe bsdur ma*) edition of the Tibetan Tengyur. 2006. 110 volumes. Beijing: China's Publishing House of Tibetan Cultural Texts.

Takasaki, Jikido. 1966. *A Study of the Ratnagotravibhāga* (*Uttaratantra*). Rome: Is.M.E.O.

Thurman, Robert A.F. 1984. *The Central Philosophy of Tibet: A Study and Translation of Tsong Khapa's Essence of True Eloquence.* Princeton, NJ: Princeton University Press.

Thurman, Robert A.F., L. Jamspal, R. Clark, J. Wilson, L. Zwilling, M. Sweet, trans. 2004. *The Universal Vehicle Discourse Literature (Mahāyānasūtrālaṁkāra).* New York: American Institute of Buddhist Studies.

Wylie, Turrell. 1959. "A Standard System of Tibetan Transcription." *Harvard Journal of Asiatic Studies* 22: 261–67.

Index of Canonical Texts Cited

589

Index of Canonical Authors Cited

General Index

A

accessories of enlightenment, 108, 395, 517

aggregate(s7), 26–28, 60, 85, 86, 99, 100–102, 136, 141, 197, 235, 251, 262, 266, 267, 270, 272, 301, 305, 315, 316, 325, 334, 335, 338, 341, 363, 367, 368, 373–76, 378, 380–82, 385, 436, 438, 439, 447, 451, 460, 465, 466, 472, 479
mind-made, 88, 89, 345

aging, 99, 100–103, 111, 112, 264, 374, 378, 379, 382–86, 403, 404, 486, 494, 496

alienated individual(s), xi, 8, 52, 95–97, 154, 500

analysis
critical, 23, 159, 302, 327, 334, 357, 381, 439, 509, 520, 574
of the ultimate, 381, 412, 464, 492, 499
textual/doctrinal, 4, 22, 41, 44, 79, 151, 152, 167, 195, 243, 257, 275, 283, 288, 353, 358, 451, 474, 484, 485, 489, 508, 509, 566, 572–74
transcendental, 101, 361, 380, 412.
See also transcendent insight
(vipaśyanā)

anger, 107, 391, 412, 545

antidote(s), 8, 34, 66, 83, 84, 140, 232, 234, 245, 251, 259, 260, 264, 265, 267, 268, 306, 324, 330, 331, 333–37, 349, 357, 369, 375, 380, 406–8, 439–41, 443, 455, 464–67, 469, 476, 566

attachment, 6, 14, 66, 69, 71, 72, 90, 96, 100, 120, 126–30, 136, 140, 141, 146, 172, 230, 240, 259, 260, 262, 266, 269, 270, 276, 277, 285, 293, 299, 306, 315–17, 348, 353, 363, 366, 368, 374, 377, 385, 399, 420–24, 434–36, 438, 439, 443–46, 458, 460, 461, 464, 471, 473, 477, 480, 488–90, 497, 512, 518, 539, 540, 542, 548, 562, 569

B

bliss, blissful(ness), xi, 24, 84–89, 91, 92, 108, 137, 138, 147, 153, 155, 171, 290, 291, 332, 333, 335, 337, 339, 340, 343, 345, 346, 350, 351, 395, 421, 460, 461, 463, 489, 492, 496, 497, 511, 512, 541, 542, 559

body
mind-made, 90, 103, 111, 127, 339, 341–43, 346, 385, 392, 402–4, 406, 438, 461

buddha body, 146, 151, 498
beatific body (sambhogakāya), xi, 4, 14, 133, 150, 152, 163, 420, 422, 453, 484, 491, 497–99, 502–6, 510, 516, 524, 527, 537, 558
emanation body (nirmāṇakāya), xi, 4, 150–53, 163, 176, 180, 222, 274, 288, 312, 343, 420, 422, 453, 497, 498, 502, 503, 506, 529, 549, 556, 559
supreme, 484, 491, 498, 500, 502, 505–7, 510, 516, 524, 527, 537
material body(ies) (rūpakāya), 4, 13, 14, 147, 151, 154–56, 177, 202, 203, 246, 247, 249, 254, 257, 276, 287,

enlightenment, xi, 4, 11, 13, 15, 42, 43,
51, 54, 56, 58, 61, 62, 78, 90, 96, 110,
114–16, 120, 127, 144, 156–58, 166,
177, 183, 185, 186, 190, 199, 203–5,
207, 215, 216, 218–22, 237, 241–43,
245, 253–55, 257, 268, 269, 279,
282, 290–92, 295, 308–11, 332, 348,
354–59, 368, 398–401, 409–12, 417,
425, 437, 463, 483–86, 488, 499, 503,
510, 515, 517, 518, 529, 533, 537, 550,
560–64, 570, 574
endowed with the twofold purity, 484,
485, 487, 514, 515, 527
full, 200, 513, 556
great, 110, 154, 166, 176, 190, 242, 279,
401, 507, 514, 530–32, 549, 571
perfect/complete, 12, 53, 72, 75, 79, 111,
153, 200, 204, 216, 230, 282, 283, 291,
292, 300, 310, 316, 401, 409, 507
supreme, 44, 54, 58, 111, 125, 244, 401,
432
total, 498, 539, 561, 564, 567, 568
unsurpassed, 12, 53, 72, 75, 79, 90, 111,
200, 216, 282, 283, 291, 292, 300,
310, 316, 349, 395, 401, 477, 507–9,
511, 562, 571
evolutionary action(s) (karma), xi, xii,
4, 22, 26, 28, 64, 66, 72, 87, 88, 94,
99, 100–103, 107, 111, 112, 127, 141,
163, 175, 176, 203, 247, 254, 259–62,
266, 267, 269, 329, 339, 341–46, 363,
368, 373–86, 389, 390, 392–94, 396,
397, 402–6, 420, 434–38, 446, 461,
472, 478, 479, 493, 496, 501, 517,
518, 525–27, 536, 539, 546–49, 553,
569, 570
instincts of, 346, 384, 409, 414, 421,
427, 437, 566
experientialism (yogāchāra), 3–6, 12, 15,
24, 25, 44, 231, 290, 292, 326–29,
349, 454, 464, 475. *See also* idealism
(cittamātra); information-only
(vijñaptimātra)

F

faith, x, 17, 52, 58, 74, 80–84, 86, 87, 92,
93, 136, 167, 168, 175, 182, 185, 186,
213, 214, 220, 244, 251, 286, 298, 319,
321, 324–26, 330–33, 337, 340, 352,
360, 361, 387, 457–59, 517, 534, 535,
538, 547, 553, 555, 558, 561–65, 567,
569, 573
fundamental consciousness (ālayavijñāna), 22, 31, 263, 314, 317, 436, 454

G

grasping, 88, 142, 341
at emptiness as having truth status, 326,
461
at truth status, 26, 33, 34, 212, 230, 237,
239, 250, 255, 260, 261, 264–68, 272,
276, 301, 305, 306, 326, 327, 335, 341,
357, 363, 374, 377, 398, 451, 465–67,
474–76, 478, 493, 497, 566. *See
also* truth-habit; truth-status-habit;
habit pattern

H

habit pattern, 7, 26, 34, 88, 136, 155, 241,
250, 259, 267, 272, 274, 299, 322, 323,
326, 334, 336, 339, 342, 343, 346, 348,
349, 375, 377, 395, 439, 459, 460, 461,
465, 466, 483, 488, 489, 512, 519, 523.
See also truth-habit; truth-status-
habit; grasping
hatred, 14, 66, 120, 126, 127, 129, 146, 241,
259, 266, 315, 322, 421, 424, 434–36,
445, 488, 490, 569
high resolve (adhyāśaya), 32, 33, 83, 108,
237, 279, 329, 352, 394

I

idealism (cittamātra), ix–xi, 25, 29, 31,
327, 328, 464. *See also* experientialism (yogāchāra); information-only
(vijñaptimātra)
ignorance/misknowledge, 26, 27, 39, 65,
66, 87, 88, 108, 112, 123, 126, 127, 129,
138, 146, 157, 158, 163, 188, 230, 250,
259, 264, 266, 267, 279, 291, 296,